THE POLICE
AND THE COMMUNITY

Sixth Edition

David L. Carter
MICHIGAN STATE UNIVERSITY

The Late Louis A. Radelet

Prentice Hall
Upper Saddle River, New Jersey   Columbus, Ohio

Library of Congress Cataloging-in-Publication Data

Carter, David L.

The police and the community / David L. Carter, Louis A. Radelet.

—6th ed.

p.   cm.

Radelet's name appears first on the earlier editions.

Includes bibliographical references (p.) and index.

ISBN 0-13-619677-2

1. Public relations—United States—Police. 2. Police—United States. 3. Police psychology. 4. Criminal justice, Administration of—United States. I. Radelet, Louis A. II. Title.

HV7936.P8C34 1999

363.2—dc21   98-14531

                                                                                                          CIP

Acquisitions Editor: *Neil Marquardt*
Editorial Assistant: *Jean Auman*
Production Editor: *Trish Finley, Clarinda Publication Services*
Production Liaison: *Glenn Johnston*
Managing Editor: *Mary Carnis*
Creative Director: *Marianne Frasco*
Director of Manufacturing & Production: *Bruce Johnson*
Manufacturing Buyer: *Ed O'Dougherty*
Marketing Manager: *Frank Mortimer, Jr.*
Cover Designer: *Joe Sengotta*
Cover Art: *Michael Plank*

Photo Credits: (1) Brown Brothers. (2) Phil Sears/Silver Image. (3) Anita Bartsch/Impact Visuals. (4) Charles Gatewood/Stock Boston. (5) T.L. Litt/Impact Visuals. (6) Brian Palmer/Impact Visuals. (7) Dale Stockton. (8) Tom Kelly. (9) Charles Wenzelberg/New York Post. (10) Robert Fox/Impact Visuals. (11) Ricky Flores/Impact Visuals. (12) Ricky Flores/Impact Visuals. (13) Thomas Lyles/Impact Visuals. (14) Michael Dwyer/Stock Boston. (16) T. Gerson/Los Angeles Daily News: Gamma-Liaison. (17) Janet Century.

©1999 by Prentice-Hall, Inc.
Simon & Schuster/A Viacom Company
Upper Saddle River, New Jersey 07458

Earlier editions copyright © 1973 and 1977 by Louis A. Radelet (published by Glencoe Publishing Co., Inc.); copyright © 1980 and 1986 by Louis A. Radelet (published by Macmillan Publishing Co., Inc.); copyright © 1994 by Macmillan College Publishing Co., Inc.

Printed in the United States of America

10 9 8 7 6 5 4 3 2

ISBN 0-13-619677-2

Prentice-Hall International (UK) Limited, *London*
Prentice-Hall of Australia Pty. Limited, *Sydney*
Prentice-Hall Canada Inc., *Toronto*
Prentice-Hall Hispanoamericana, S.A., *Mexico*
Prentice-Hall of India Private Limited, *New Delhi*
Prentice-Hall of Japan, Inc., *Tokyo*
Simon & Schuster Asia Pte. Ltd., *Singapore*
Editora Prentice-Hall do Brasil, Ltda., *Rio de Janeiro*

*To Karen, Hilary,
Jeremy, and Lauren*

CONTENTS

Preface

Dramatic and rapid changes in the police-community relationship have occurred since the last edition of this text. Prompted largely by the creation of the Office of Community Oriented Policing Services (COPS) and its substantial funding to assist state and local law enforcement agencies, a dramatic increase has been seen in the number of police agencies adopting community policing. While most police departments are making a sincere effort to provide the best possible service for their communities, many of the agencies adopted community policing for the funding support and others hopped on the band wagon because it was the contemporary "thing to do." Even in these cases, however, benefits to the police community relationship will likely occur. Many of the changes in this book reflect the evolving nature of community policing, including issues and practices that the profession is currently exploring.

Above all else, policing is a behavioral phenomenon. The way leaders administer their organizations, the way officers perform their work, and the way the community responds to and interacts with the police are all fundamental to the goal of policing: Providing a safe, secure community. Because of this behavioral dynamic, this text emphasizes organizational and human principles, which guide the way the police and community interact with each other. Understanding this reciprocal relationship and its effect on the police function strikes at the essence of how a contemporary, community-based police department should operate. Moreover, it provides insight for officers and administrators alike for operations, decision-making, and planning.

Among the changes in this edition of the text, beyond the overall updating of research, are expansions of discussions on contemporary issues. A broadened discussion of the community policing concept is included in chapter 3 and the concept is integrated throughout all discussions of the issues in the text. There are also significantly expanded discussions on school-based programs by the police, technology, and political issues, particularly as they have emerged with greater inculcation of the community policing philosophy. Also included in this edition are more illustrations and anecdotes of police department programs and experiences as well as expanded discussions of international issues in the police-community relationship.

The preface to the fifth edition of this book provided insights on the significant transition that occurred from the traditional police-community relations model to the community-based philosophy of policing. That transition included debate between the late Lou Radelet and myself on the direction and character of the police-community relationship. Beyond that, the preface to the fifth edition acknowledged a number of people who, although they did not contribute directly to this edition, should nonetheless be recognized for their contributions and assistance to me over the years. Because of these factors, I have included the preface to the fifth edition in this text as well.

I would particularly like to thank again my friend Rick Holden at Central Missouri State University for his insights, thoughtful ideas, and friendship. Similarly, thanks also go to Merle Manzi of S,M,&C Sciences, Inc. of Tallahassee, Florida, for his friendship, humor, and ideas, whether we were sitting in a stoic British pub or a less-than-stoic bar in Thailand. And a special thanks to my dear friend Andra Katz of Wichita State University for her help, candid feedback, humor, and collusion on various projects and explorations covering four continents and Italian restaurants from Casablanca to Bangkok. Andi, you know I can always count on you.

Beyond the professional evolution that has occurred since the last edition of this text, important personal milestones have also passed. The unexpected death of my colleague and friend, Robert "Bob" Trojanowicz, who was a critical force in the development of the community policing philosophy, was a significant loss to our field. Beyond his professional leadership, Bob was a true friend who is missed. As a small tribute to Bob, I have included the foreword he wrote for the fifth edition of this text.

More personal was the passing of my mother, Alta Carter, who provided more support, encouragement, guidance and praise than a person could ask for. I was blessed with extraordinary loving parents who afforded me the opportunity to grow up in a "Leave It to Beaver" household. I miss them both dearly. For my children, I strive to give as much guidance and to be as good a role model as my parents were to me. Finally, thanks go to my wife, Karen, and my children Hilary, Jeremy, and Lauren, to whom I dedicate this book. You all know how special you are to me and how I depend on you. My thanks and love to you all.

David L. Carter
Mason, Michigan

Foreword to the Fifth Edition

The police understand that they alone cannot hope to reverse the escalating cycle of violence, drugs, and property crime that particularly threatens to engulf many of our most vulnerable citizens, who are trapped in decaying neighborhoods that look and sound more and more like war zones every day. Where once there were three police officers for each felony, there are now three felonies for each officer. For the police to help bring order from the chaos in this era of straitened resources, they must enlist those who need the help most as partners in the process of making troubled neighborhoods better and safer places in which to live and work. The police can play an important collaborative role in protecting, organizing, and thereby empowering the community, recognizing that it is the people who are ultimately responsible for the safety and well-being of their communities.

To tap into this potential, the majority of police departments in major jurisdictions have said they have already embraced community policing or plan to do so soon. Yet despite this new emphasis on enhancing their relationship with the community, the police today also find themselves battling a firestorm of negative publicity that erupted from the videotape of the Rodney King incident in Los Angeles and the beating death of Malice Green in Detroit. Even the far from conservative *Rolling Stone* magazine recently ran an article berating the media for unfairly transforming the image of police from "hero" to "thug" virtually overnight. By allowing people to hold officers accountable for their actions, community policing also holds the promise of restoring the tarnished luster of the police that these infamous cases unfortunately fostered.

Professor David Carter, a former police officer in Kansas City, Missouri, knows firsthand the challenges inherent in reinventing the relationship between people and their police. Through his succeeding academic career at Michigan State University's School of Criminal Justice, Professor Carter can also bring his years of teaching and research to this issue. Many of you may already be familiar with his efforts for the Police Executive Research Forum, his work with various police organizations, and his participation in training and technical assistance offered through MSU's National Center for Community Policing.

In revising this book, Professor Carter has updated the material with a special eye toward explaining why and how the police must become more proactive in dealing with the myriad of problems that they are asked to help solve. The book presents current research on a wide range of topics that impinge on the police-community relationship—police education, labor relations, corruption, drug use by officers, use of force, police patrol, accreditation, and, of course, community policing.

In a new chapter, entitled "Community Alliance," the discussion centers on creating a bridge between traditional police-community relations and community policing. This book also includes the revised Code of Ethics for the International

Association of Chiefs of Police as well as information on the growing commitment to "managing by values" and what to expect of the police-community relationship in the future.

Readers will appreciate Professor Carter's efforts to assemble and organize a broad array of perspectives on the topic. The insights he brings to this complex issue offer everyone, from beginning students to veteran officers, a fresh way of looking at this most critical and often difficult relationship. He also deserves applause for a "user-friendly" approach, identifying how line officers can forge a new community alliance, supported by policies and procedures from police management. I would personally like to thank him for making this valuable contribution to the field, one which can help police make the transition from being "apart" from the community to becoming "a part" of the community, as the late Professor Louis Radelet, a pioneer in the field, often said.

Robert Trojanowicz, Director
Former The National Center for Community Policing
Michigan State University and
Former Research Fellow, Kennedy School of Government
Harvard University

Preface to the Fifth Edition

The fifth edition of this stalwart text has been written with honor to the father of the police-community relations movement, the late Louis Radelet. His vision, innovation, and dedication to this important concern was a catalyst for progress, particularly during the turbulent 1960s when the police-community relationship was at a low ebb. Lou's humanitarianism always persevered when conflicts arose about how the police should resolve community-based conflict. He would warmly engage the people involved in the conflict with his calm, respected demeanor, and subtly begin the communications process. His approach was not to force reciprocity, but to have people embrace it. Lou was not only a leader, but also the epitome of "a gentleman and a scholar." His contributions to this field, and particularly his yeoman efforts in the beginning, will be long remembered.

I was honored when Lou asked me to work with him on this new edition of the text. As we discussed issues related to this revision prior to his untimely death, a clear philosophical shift in the police-community relationship (PCR) was occurring. On some points we agreed, on others we did not. It became apparent that our agreement and debate about the nature of the police-community relationship reflected changes the field was actually experiencing. When you ask police officials or academicians today to distinguish between community relations and community policing, you will receive a *wide* array of responses (as evidenced by a lively debate one night over "refreshments" in the FBI Academy's boardroom during a community policing workshop).

The growth of community policing has been dramatic in just the past five years. The change has been building like a wave, growing geometrically, yet with uneven distribution, and in a constant state of fluctuation. It has been seeking to reach a steady state which balances utility, resources, and the ability to instill organizational change. Though this revision of *The Police and the Community* is rather substantial, I have endeavored to keep intact Lou's philosophical concerns while reflecting the current significant trends in policing, in research, and in society.

Just as police management practices, investigative procedures, patrol operations, and juvenile justice responsibilities have changed, the concept of PCR has evolved a great deal since the first edition of this text. A wide body of research and experimentation in policing has taken the basic premises of PCR and molded them into both the operational persona of the street officer and the managerial visage of the police executive.

It is my belief that the principle of PCR "programs" has to be expanded into a broader perspective. That is, any activity must embody all police employees and the "customers" (a term I borrow from former Madison, Wisconsin Chief David Couper) of the police agency. From this view, we are not attempting to create PCR from the traditional "programmatic" perspective, but instead we are seeking a *community alliance*. This alliance has both theoretical and operational implications, which are presented throughout the text. These underpinnings are supported by discussion of established and current research on a range of policing issues. Police-community relations, it is argued, is the embodiment of everything a police officer says and does. The social, behavioral, and operational issues addressed throughout the text are fundamental to an effective PCR.

For example, the reader will find a significantly broader discussion of community-oriented/problem-oriented policing; current issues in excessive force; corruption, and other forms of police deviance; current perspectives on higher education of police officers; minority issues; the role of law enforcement accreditation; violence in the community; fear of crime; issues related to the homeless; and even police officer drug abuse. Thus, the intent is to establish a contemporary standard of PCR as it integrates organizational, operational, and individual issues within the framework of current research.

The police in a free society must perform their function only through *policing by consent*. This means that in order to use force, search and seize property, make arrests, and solve problems, their actions must have consent in two forms:

- Consent by legislation wherein laws are passed that authorize the creation and operation of police forces.
- Consent by the public that permits the exercise of extended authority by the police beyond specifically legislated mandates—such as in responding to noncriminal calls for service and performing problem-solving activities.

Community policing and, consequently, contemporary PCR must embody these principles in order to maximize their effectiveness and respond to the needs of citizens. These factors underlie every issue discussed in the text. The ideas expressed throughout this endeavor were formed from many sources with debate and advice from many colleagues and friends. While I cannot possibly acknowledge everyone, there are some people to whom I would like to give a "tip of the hat."

My colleague and friend Robert Trojanowicz of Michigan State and Harvard University has given me great support and advice over the years. His international leadership in community policing is particularly well known and I thank him for his contributions, friendship, and willingness to write the foreword for the fifth edition. I also thank my friend Darrel Stephens, Chief of Police at St. Petersburg, Florida, and former Executive Director of the Police Executive Research Forum, who wrote one of the "Perspectives" for the text. Darrel's contributions to policing are substantial and his support for my research is sincerely appreciated (as are all the meals he has bought for me over the years!). I sincerely want to thank Rolando del Carmen of Sam Houston State University, not only as the author of one of the "Perspectives," but also for his role as my mentor. Rolando has made significant contributions to the criminal justice discipline through his rigorous standards, leadership by example, and friendship.

I sincerely appreciate the work of Merry Morash, Director of the School of Criminal Justice at Michigan State, for writing the "Perspective" on women in policing, particularly given her schedule and my compulsive badgering of her on this and other matters. Merry has always graciously responded to my inquiries and been supportive of my work. And to a real trail blazer, Betsy Watson, Chief of Police in Austin, Texas, and former Chief in Houston, I give both my appreciation and respect. Her "Perspective" in the text provides articulate insight and vision. Betsy has the ability to "cut to the chase" by making critical observations on philosophical issues and placing them in a perspective which can be translated to policy. Her contributions to the text and the field of policing are substantial.

To Rick Holden, Central Missouri State University, my colleague in travel and doctoral studies, I thank for his candid observations in reviewing my work and his thoughts on the revisions. His contributions have significantly added to the quality of this revision. Similarly, I give thanks to my longtime friend, co-researcher, and travel partner (to who knows how many locations) Allen Sapp, also of Central Missouri State. Our shared research experiences as well as his always insightful comments have been of significant benefit. I would like to also thank the following for their assistance, insights, and suggestions in writing this book: Peter C. Kratcoski, Kent State University; William G. Doerner, Florida State University; Frank Schmalleger, Pembroke State University; Tom Barker, Jacksonville State University; and W. Fred Wegener, Indiana University.

I must give a special thanks to Fran and Kent Krieger for the hours I occupied a table at *Bert and Ernie's* in Plattsburg, Missouri, and for the gallons of coffee they kept pouring down me while I worked on this book. My appreciation also goes to my editor at Macmillan, Chris Cardone, who has been most helpful in facilitating my work on this book through her support, her flexibility, and her assistance in resolving problems—thank you, Chris.

I dedicate this edition to my family. To my mother, Alta Carter, for her consistent encouragement and pride in everything I have done (well, almost everything). And to my late father, Donald Carter, who was always enthusiastic and supportive about my endeavors, even to his final days while I worked on this text sitting next to his bed. Finally, to my wife, Karen, and children, Hilary, Jeremy, and Lauren, who have always been at my side, tolerating travel, awkward hours, and offering loving encouragement—you are always with me.

David L. Carter

Part One

FUNDAMENTALS

The Impact of the 1967 "President's Commission" on Policing Today

DARREL W. STEPHENS

City Administrator, St. Petersburg, Florida
Former Chief of Police, St. Petersburg, Florida Police Department and Former
Executive Director, Police Executive Research Forum

Policing in America has seen significant change over the past two and one-half decades. It was reported in the President's Commission *Task Force Report: The Police* (1967:138) that 85 percent of the officers in America in 1965 were assigned to the field without training. Today, most states have established minimum training standards that require officers to complete at least 400 hours of training before they are certified. Although many states allow up to one year after appointment to complete the training, most police agencies do not allow officers to work on the street without meeting the minimum training standard and completing an extensive Field Officer Training (FTO) program. Moreover, many of the urban police departments require as much as six months in basic police training before officers begin their field training phase.

Policing has changed in many other ways as well. At the time the President's Commission report was published in 1967, police departments throughout the nation were staffed almost exclusively by white males. There were no women in patrol assignments and one found relatively few blacks and Hispanics serving in the urban areas. Although the commission set a goal of a baccalaureate degree at the time, the average educational level of a police officer was 12.4 years of education, and in 1970 only 3.7 percent of the officers possessed a college degree. By 1988, in agencies serving populations greater than 50,000 persons, 22.6 percent of police officers had a degree and the average educational level had increased to 13.6 years. In municipal police agencies with more than 100 officers, the percentage of minorities has increased to 16 percent (blacks, 10 percent: Hispanics 6 percent) and women now account for 7 percent of the sworn officers (BJS, 1990). Although the majority of officers continue to be white males, policing is a much more diverse profession than it was just 25 years ago, with women and minorities having a significant impact.

No single document has had more impact on policing in America than the President's Commission on Law Enforcement and Administration of Justice. The *Task Force Report: The Police* alone contained thirty-five major recommendations on a wide area of policing issues. The recommendations included five on community relations, sixteen on personnel, ten on organization and operations, and four on the pooling of resources and services. Many of these recommendations have been followed by state and local government with the assistance of the federal government through the creation of the Law Enforcement Assistance Administration (LEAA). LEAA, which was established by the Omnibus Crime Control and Safe Streets Act of 1968, survived until 1978 when it was abolished by President Jimmy Carter. A similar agency, called the Office of Justice Programs, was established under the Crime Control Act of 1986; however, the level of funding is much less than the $850 million that LEAA administered in its final years.

The recommendations of the President's Commission served as the primary guide for LEAA programs. The LEAA established and supported state criminal justice planning agencies and, in the larger urban areas, criminal justice planning councils as well. These agencies not only administered LEAA funds, they established plans to improve and coordinate criminal justice activities.

One of the most significant programs of the LEAA was the Law Enforcement Education Program (LEEP). There are few senior level police officials in America today who did not benefit from the LEEP program. LEEP provided grants and scholarships to both in-service and pre-service people to attend college. The program played a significant role in increasing the overall educational level of policing. Moreover, the program was the primary stimulus for the development of wide-scale college and university degree programs for law enforcement and criminal justice students.

The President's Commission also raised some fundamental questions about the role and the impact of the police that have provided the impetus for much of the research and improvements that have taken place since 1967. In many ways, these questions set the first agenda for research in policing. In the questions raised by the commission, there was recognition and acknowledgment that the police role was much broader than dealing with crime. They suggested:

1. There is need to recognize the variety of functions that police perform today, particularly in the large urban community. The demands upon police are likely to increase in number and complexity rather than decrease.
2. Important and complex social, behavioral, and political problems can adequately be dealt with by American government only if there is room for administrative variation, innovation, and experimentation of a kind presently lacking in the police field.
3. To deal adequately with current law enforcement needs, an explicit acknowledgment that police are one of the most important governmental administrative agencies in existence today is required. Major changes must be made to equip police to develop appropriate administrative policies and a willingness and capacity to conform with these policies (President's Commission, 1967:38.)

Even though one could make an argument today that some of these same issues currently exist in policing, the change has been dramatic. A major source of the change emanating from the President's Commission can be traced to these important recommendations.

Since the President's Commission reports, research has become an important aspect of change and improvement in policing. In the early to mid-1970s major research efforts examined the efficacy of the primary strategies the police used to deal with crime: preventive patrol, rapid response to calls for service, and follow-up investigations. This research revealed that the levels of preventive patrol had no significant impact on crime, that rapid response was not a major factor in making arrests or citizen satisfaction with the police, and that crimes were generally solved by information that citizens provided to the uniformed officer who initially responded—not the detective. As one might expect, this series of research findings shook the police world. Nevertheless, they also served as the foundation for significant change in policing because they provided valuable information on which to create new approaches while strengthening the old.

The President's Commission also made significant recommendations on police–community relations and crime prevention. They suggested that police agencies serving large communities should establish these special units to address relationships in the community as well as to establish programs aimed at educating the community in crime prevention. Both of these types of functions in police departments have flourished over the past 25 years. Many of the community relations units have evolved into department-wide community policing efforts or have been subsumed in the crime prevention function.

The President's Commission on Law Enforcement and Administration of Justice has had a far-reaching impact on policing in America. The beginning of many of the concepts and ideas that exist in the most progressive police departments today can be traced to the work of the President's Commission even though many in policing today have never seen the actual reports. Nevertheless, the problem-oriented community policing philosophy that many experts believe is the future of policing has its roots in the work of the President's Commission.

Bureau of Justice Statistics. (1990). *Law Enforcement Manpower Allocation Survey.* Washington: U.S. Department of Justice, Office of Justice Programs.

President's Commission on Law Enforcement and Administration of Justice. (1967). *Task Force Report: The Police.* Washington: U.S. Government Printing Office.

Chapter 1

FOUNDATION

A 19-year-old black college student in a criminal justice class observed:

> 'Why do the police always stop a black man when they see him alone late at night? They think if you are a black male out late at night, you're a criminal. Cops are prejudiced!'

That same week, a 26-year-old police officer in a graduate class states:

> 'I stop and check out people who are suspicious in light of my experience and the circumstances I observe at the time. I am accused of being prejudiced, but I am only trying to do my job.'

Observations as polar as these are not unique. They are common illustrations of problems to which this book is addressed. Different perspectives, poor communications, and concern about the nature of social control in a free society lie at the foundation of problems in the police-community relationship. These are the issues that must be explored, studied, and discussed.

Whereas most people seem to have a favorable view of the police most of the time, many people frankly prefer to avoid contact with them if at all possible. The outright hostility of some groups toward the police is a well-established reality. There seems to be something peculiar about the police relationship with the community that makes it the object of special study by scholars interested in such social processes as human and intergroup relations, governmental operations, bureaucratic organizations, and the administration and management of public service agencies.

Police and community relations is a subject that has come to the forefront of social concern in the United States and elsewhere. The problematic side of the relationship has been dramatized by the civil rights movement, by frequent and often volatile testing of the principle of equal protection of the law, and in a broader yet more basic sense by widely publicized confrontations of the *powerful* and the *powerless*. Police-community relations is thereby fundamentally a political phenomenon, and a good bit more. It is also a sociological phenomenon, since it invokes complex organizations, roles and goals, and a community context. It is psychological since it considers attitudes and community mental health. It is anthropological, and even theological and ethical, because it treats the nature of authority and the mainsprings of law. It is social work to the extent that community organization and community action are components. Finally, it is inevitably economic since one of its essential requirements is cost-effective service to taxpayers.

In a democratic society, the police exercise power with those from whom they derive their authority. Police authority is delegated, leased, so to speak, by the community served by the police. Consent of the governed is what gives policing its moral quality. But the ultimate responsibility for ordered liberty with justice remains with the community. Community understanding, commitment, and involvement in social control is one way of describing what police and community relations is all about. Crime and disorder, which are major concerns of the police, are community malignancies which imperil the quality of living. Law, community, justice, and morality: these cornerstones of Western democracy are inextricably linked. Police responsiveness and accountability to the community flow from this theoretical matrix. The clear message is that the police–community concept is more of a union than a relationship; that the centrality of the community role and responsibility in criminal justice is incontestable; and that what we are dealing with in these pages is far more timeless and crucially important than is suggested by allusions to urban street encounters of yesterday or today, or by efforts to evaluate the public image of the police.

SOME HISTORY

Since we will be focusing on American policing, some historical briefing is appropriate—brief because all this has been ably and much more adequately developed in other works familiar to students of criminal justice. The origin of the modern municipal police department in the British-American tradition can be traced back to 1829, the year in which Sir Robert Peel managed to secure approval by an apprehensive English Parliament of his bill for a metropolitan police.[1] There was considerable opposition to Peel's idea, as some members of Parliament were concerned that such a force might become a mechanism of political tyranny. A parliamentary committee had reported on an earlier Peel proposal "that forfeiture or curtailment of individual liberty which the creation of an effective police system would bring with it would be too great a sacrifice on behalf of improvements in police or facilities in detection of crime."[2] However, Sir Robert's bill finally became law, and the "Peelers," or "Bobbies," set the stage for our city police of today.

Peel's principles of law enforcement (Table 1-1) are well known but invite special attention by community-minded analysts. Each principle has a community dimension (e.g., "the police are the public and the public are the police"). These principles constitute a credo for proactive, as distinct from reactive, policing.

Peel's ideas, though, were not new; they were firmly rooted in the English tradition of justice. In the Anglo-Saxon England of a thousand years ago, every able-bodied freeman was a police officer. Every male from fifteen to sixty maintained such arms as he could afford. When the hue and cry was raised, every man within earshot dropped whatever he was doing and joined in the pursuit of the transgressor. Not to do so was serious neglect of duty.

Later, the constable became the chief peace officer, but the job was still unpaid and was rotated among many. Then came the justice of the peace, who was both judge and police officer, discharging certain police duties even in modern times, especially in the suppression of riots.[3] This was the beginning of judicial surveillance over the police. As towns developed, watchmen were employed for full-time work, but ordinary citizens retained a solemn duty to perform police functions.

By the seventeenth century, many abuses had appeared in this medieval police system. Unpaid constables sought to avoid duty. Some persons maneuvered their policy responsibilities to serve their private interests. As towns grew into cities, this

TABLE 1-1	Peel's Principles of Law Enforcement

1. The basic mission for which the police exist is to prevent crime and disorder as an alternative to the repression of crime and disorder by military force and severity of legal punishment.

2. The ability of the police to perform their duties is dependent upon public approval of police existence, actions, behavior, and the ability of the police to secure and maintain public respect.

3. The police must secure the willing cooperation of the public in voluntary observance of the law to be able to secure and maintain public respect.

4. The degree of cooperation of the public that can be secured diminishes, proportionately, the necessity for the use of physical force and compulsion in achieving police objectives.

5. The police seek and preserve public favor, not by catering to public opinion, but by constantly demonstrating absolutely impartial service to the law, in complete independence of policy, and without regard to the justice or injustice of the substance of individual laws; by ready offering of individual service and friendship to all members of the society without regard to their race or social standing; by ready exercise of courtesy and friendly good humor; and by ready offering of individual sacrifice in protecting and preserving life.

6. The police should use physical force to the extent necessary to secure observance of the law or to restore order only when the exercise of persuasion, advice, and warning is found to be insufficient to achieve police objectives; and police should use only the minimum degree of physical force that is necessary on any particular occasion for achieving a police objective.

7. The police at all times should maintain a relationship with the public that gives reality to the historic tradition that the police are the public and that the public are the police; the police are the only members of the public who are paid to give full-time attention to duties that are incumbent on every citizen in the interest of the community welfare.

8. The police should always direct their actions toward their functions and never appear to usurp the powers of the judiciary by avenging individuals or the state, or authoritatively judging guilt or punishing the guilty.

9. The test of police efficiency is the absence of crime and disorder, not the visible evidence of police action in dealing with them.[4]

watch-and-ward system was severely strained. Thugs became the terror of the community. Finally, in the early eighteenth century, Sir Henry Fielding organized the Bow Street Runners, a small corps of paid police officers whose rapidly acquired reputation for success in apprehending hoodlums undoubtedly helped to persuade Parliament of the wisdom of Peel's proposals. Anxiety regarding the possible abuse of treasured English civil liberties by overzealous, paid police officers gradually dissolved in the face of accumulating evidence to the contrary.

So it is that the English declare to this day that a police officer is someone who is paid to do what it is a citizen's duty to do without pay. Consider, for example, the law of arrest. In a seventeenth-century treatise, *The Country Justice* by Michael Dalton, there appears this sentence: "The Sherife, Bailifes, Constables and other of the King's Officers may arrest and imprison offenders in all cases where a private person may." This use of every citizen's right to arrest as the standard by which the right of officers to arrest is measured is significant when compared with modern treatises.[5]

It was not until 1827 that the rule differentiating the legal powers of lay persons from those of peace officers was established in England. It is also interesting that numerous private police agencies existed in England and Europe as far back as the eleventh century—for example, associations of merchants such as the Hanseatic League, and of property owners banding together as self-appointed "thief catchers," anxious to protect their special interests. The Peel reforms incorporated into the new Metropolitan Police many private police agencies that had been organized for what we today would refer to as security purposes.

T. A. Critchley, the eminent British police historian, has stated that a central point in British police philosophy is this: *what matters is not so much what a police officer does as what people think of him or her.*[6] This tone comes through in Peel's principles. Good relations with the public has always been a priority of the British police. Unarmed and with few powers not available to the ordinary citizen, they are utterly dependent upon public approval.

The parliamentary dilemma in the debate over Peel's ideas, which went on for some years, is interesting to review. The essential issue was the age-old governmental one of security versus liberty. If the state had no instrument of force to impose its will, growing civil disorder was predictable. Without order, liberty would be imperiled. On the other hand, force might prove to be the greater evil, a vehicle of tyranny. Dr. Samuel Johnson said it well:

> The danger of unbounded liberty and the danger of bounding it have produced a problem in the science of government which human understanding seems hitherto unable to solve.[7]

There were French and Prussian examples lending substance to the argument that a police force would endanger English liberties. An English police force would have to be singularly mild and controlled by safeguards against arbitrary power. During the period 1800–1820, one parliamentary committee after another rejected the proposal. But the Industrial Revolution was making many members of Parliament rich and propertied, and therefore concerned about robberies. The upshot was the passage, in 1829, of the Metropolitan Police Act, with scarcely any opposition or debate. It remains the governing statute of the London Metropolitan Police to this day.

Peel's principles, a wooden baton, top hat, and swallow coat: these were the signs of reconciliation of a dilemma that had generated years of bitterness, hostility, and suspicion. The result was a *service* rather than a *force*, with the police held answerable at all times to the public and to the law. No organizational plan was prescribed; wide discretion was left to the Commissioners of Police. The Metropolitan Police (Scotland Yard) was placed under the Home Secretary (Peel) and was in turn accountable to Parliament. Thus, the connection of the police with government was indirect, although centrally controlled and under the restraints of law.

Moreover, by paying police officers (constables) only a guinea a week, Peel made sure they would "stay close to the bedrock of the community" they policed. Their manner was ordinary. They headed off far more problems than they handled after the fact. And they were not called upon to enforce laws that did not command the general support of the law-abiding population.

In the United States, Peel's plan of police organization was substantially copied in New York City by 1844; during the ensuring ten years, similar organizational patterns appeared in Chicago, Philadelphia, and Boston. By 1870, the main features of the London Metropolitan Police were firmly established in this country.[8] The idea of lay people participating in police work was certainly evident in the early history of the western states. Public tribunals, councils, and vigilante activities were common, just as many private protective and security organizations exist today in business and industry.[9] Yet the system of political control of the police that developed in America differed from the English model. The decentralized pattern of early American police tended to place considerable power in the hand of ward and precinct politicians. This was subsequently to have both positive and negative implications for the police-community relationship.

IMPLICATIONS

Every society recognizes that the police function is essential to its survival. The question is one of the means necessary to maintain that function. In democratic societies, order is not an end in itself; rather, it is a means to the end of justice and the sanctity of individual liberty. Three additional points are notable:

1. In their attitudes and values, not surprisingly, police officers tend to mirror the socioeconomic, cultural, ethnic, occupational, and educational characteristics of the strata of society in which they are reared. Thus, if a high proportion of officers come from lower-middle- or upper-lower-class backgrounds, having had blue-collar working parents, Indo-European ethnic traits, and the like, it follows that what they say and do as officers will reflect the attitudes and values of that background.[10] (We will examine this point more thoroughly in a later chapter.)

2. In a democratic society, unlike totalitarian systems, the police function depends on a considerable amount of self-policing by every citizen. The system is rooted in personal responsibility. Law observance is the most vital part of law enforcement. Paid police officers, even under conditions of intensive specialization and extensive training, cannot possibly do the job for which they are constituted without the major part of that job being done by the self-policing of ordinary citizens. Traffic management is a case in point. The police spend a great deal of time and resources doing it, yet most of the task is done by drivers who "play by the rules."

3. Police are *part of*, not *apart from*, the communities they serve. In a democratic society, they are (ideally) a living expression, an embodiment, an implementing arm of democratic law. If such a principle as due process, for example, is to have practical meaning, the nature of police behavior is important. What the police officer does and how he or she does it is one weighty measure of the integrity of the entire legal system for each person with whom he or she comes in contact. For many people, police are the only contact that they may ever have with the legal system. If democratic law is to be credible and ethical for ordinary citizens, with standards of fairness, reasonableness, and human decency, it will be so to the extent that police behavior reflects such qualities.

The importance of the police officer in our system of democratic legal process and institutions is stressed in this line of reasoning, and the overall importance of police-community relations is evident. To view the police as "pigs" or as "dirty workers" carries with it an implied indictment of the system far more fundamental and far more serious than the momentary titillation of a serious indictment of the system.

This does not mean that the system should be spared from criticism. But criticism should be grounded in an understanding of the meaning of police service in a democratic society. Only through genuine police-community partnership can a police force strengthen the democratic way of life and maintain the stability of the community.

Certainly antisocial conduct must be controlled. But order must be maintained in ways that preserve and extend the values of democratic society—in short, by police methods that preserve human dignity, not by uncontrolled force. Former Associate Supreme Court Justice Louis Brandeis once said:

> Those who won our independence . . . recognized the risks to which all human institutions are subject. But they knew that order cannot be secured merely through fear of punishment for its infraction; that it is hazardous to discourage thought, hope, imagination; that fear breeds repression; that repression breeds hate; that hate menaces stable government; that the path of safety lies in the opportunity to discuss freely supposed grievances and proposed remedies; and that the fitting remedy for evil counsels is good ones. Believing in the power of reason as applied through public discussion, they eschewed silence coerced by law—the argument of force in its worst form.[11]

AUTHORITY

The noteworthy English social anthropologist, Michael Banton, refers to the difference between a police *force* and a police *service*.[12] He makes much of the point that police officers function most effectively (professionally?) when what they do and how they do it are supported by a moral consensus of the community. Officers possess both authority and power. Authority is *rightful* power; it has a moral quality. Banton argues that public resentment against police is usually directed against their exercise of power, under circumstances in which community support is questionable, ambiguous, or clearly divided. When officers function on the basis of assured community support (authority), their behavior is more predictable. Police officers whose conduct is uncertain, Banton suggests, rely on their power, unconcerned with whether their clients feel they are exercising it rightfully. What they do is then unpredictable.[13]

With Banton's help, let us further analyze the idea of authority. Authority is the basis of social control in a society. It means the right to command, to take action, to make decisions. Authority comes about, Banton writes, "from the free agreement of individuals to observe certain mutually convenient rules."[14] This sounds like the mainsprings of law in society, and properly so, for this is exactly what authority is. The necessity for law flows from human relations that make rules rationally prudent: to serve the interests of social order, justice, rights, and duties. It is what makes *community* possible. Politics? Politics is the process of making authoritative decisions that command assent. So it is in democratic societies.

To what end or purpose? Whence does authority, vested in the people, originate? The answer to these questions is in theology. The crux of the ancient argument about authority revolves less around the question of the origin and purpose of humanity than it does around the idea of "vested in the people." Divine right of kings and totalitarianism hold that authority resides in those who possess power. The people have little to say about it. "L'état, c'est moi!" The law, that's me. So proclaimed Louis XIV. It could as well have been any modern dictator or tyrant.

The decisive point for our purpose, as Banton explains, is this: If A can coerce or force decisions on B, this is power. If B willingly agrees (informed consent), this is authority. If one is recognized as an "authority" on a subject, his or her judgments, decisions, or opinions will be respected—that is to say, trusted. Again in this observation, the essence of community is suggested. These days we often hear references to "declining authority," sometimes called "the authority crises." But what seems really to be amiss are the abuses of power, authority arbitrarily imposed. Taxation without representation, in a manner of speaking.

Police officers are greatly concerned about what they see as declining respect for authority. Perhaps they have in mind such happenings as mass demonstrations for animal rights, the environment, against abortion, and the like. Actually, however, such demonstrations call into question certain public policy decisions and/or the process of arriving at such decisions. The decision-makers didn't ask us! There was insufficient consultation with those who dissent. Bureaucrats misused their power. Now this may or may not be the case. But the point is that it is so perceived by some people, and they publicly protest. This causes inconvenience and annoyance for the police. Yet what may be called "the authority system" is working just as it should. Some folks are "talking back," and in our time, we are seeing much more of this kind of questioning, appealing, and pursuing of grievances. As Banton says, the whole structure of power in social relations has changed in mass societies.[15]

Clearly, the media have had much to do with changing attitudes toward authority. Television, for example, has put a bright spotlight on public officials, including the police, and public policies. Through the media, policies can be immediately questioned and officials held accountable in public view. Authority is forced to justify itself.

To a social anthropologist or a political scientist, these things are elemental. It is important that this understanding of fundamentals also permeates the world of the police officer and other agents of criminal justice processes. An abundant literature on the role of authority is available, dating back to Plato and Aristotle.[16]

AUTHORITY AND THE POLICE

With all of these philosophical and sociological abstractions, what about the police?

As Banton muses, the police are conservative and have carried on their tasks without much systematic review of their role in society for what it is and what it ought to be.[17] There are two contrasting philosophies of society bearing upon coercion in criminal justice. One theory stresses individual responsibility for crime. Punishment and retribution for criminal infractions are emphasized in this view. The main purpose of the police is repressive: "to contain disruptive tendencies." The second theory stresses the social environmental causes of crime. Logically, those who subscribe to this view favor rehabilitation/reintegration in the correctional process. They are apt to see the main purpose of the police in a broader, "social work" perspective, with crime prevention a high priority. Of course, as we shall see later, this community policing movement is again reshaping our view of police authority, which merges these theories.

What we have here is a clash in social philosophy basic to understanding the fundamental role of the police and of criminal justice. We will explore this further in chapter 5. The difficulty is that proponents of each theory tend to insist that their side is altogether correct and the other side is altogether wrong. The truth, in general terms, proclaims a mix of both theories, varying in proportion to individual and social circumstances. In practical language, this means that the police, for instance, must at times be repressive and at times compassionate—and be wise enough to know when to act one way or the other. More than this, police organizations, in all their functions, must be designed to deal competently and professionally with each of these conflicting requirements. A formidable challenge indeed.

So it is that Banton speaks of the "law officer" and the "peace officer." One deals with the public largely in an adversarial way. The other deals with the public largely in a helping way. But bear in mind that we are speaking here of a single officer who must work both sides of the functional street. As for his or her authority and/or power, recall Banton's distinction. As law officer, there will be consensual community support for most felonies, less support for many misdemeanors. The latter will be the area where most police and community disagreements and tensions will occur. Authority is questioned. As peace officer, there will be consensual community support for most helping activities. Disagreements and tensions in police and community relations will arise when one faction of the community contends that the police are discriminatory in favoring another faction in their helping efforts. The argument pertains to fairness and justice. Again, authority is questioned.

Yet there is still some oversimplification in this analysis. What the police officer does as law officer is clearly repressive and punitive. The protection of society is paramount. But not everyone agrees that certain laws should be laws, and often the quarrel with police is not so much about *what* they do but about *how* they do it. The quarrel is more concerned with power and its exercise than with authority. To wit, "I don't question your right to do this, but I don't like how you do it." Now compare with Melville Lee, writing about the British view:

> The basis upon which our theory of police ultimately rests is the assumption that every lawful act performed by a police officer in the execution of his duties has the sanction and approval of the great majority of his fellow citizens.[18]

For those who join hands with Banton and other anthropologists in rejecting the idea that society is founded on force, everything falls into place. Prevention will be seen as the main task of the police, just as Peel saw it, and the peacekeeping mandate will loom large. The case for police professionalism, as we shall see shortly, also rests heavily on the police officer as peace officer. For the moment, however, a bit more rumination about authority is tempting, still relying considerably on Banton.[19]

AUTHORITY AND COMPLIANCE

Max Weber, the German sociologist and political economist, saw authority as one form of compliance. He dealt with three variations. *Macht* (might) means that A enforces his wishes on B despite resistance. *Herrschaft* (power) means that the commands of A will be obeyed by B and others. *Legitime Herrschaft* (authority) is a claim to obedience grounded in a belief that the claim is legitimate. See Figure 1-1.[20]

Bantson adds that in a democratic society, the circle of authority will be large, relative to that of might. In a dictatorship, just the opposite will prevail. He argues that primitive societies are far more democratic than the modern industrial, technological state. He writes:

> Bureaucratic administration may in the long run bring greater advantages to everyone, but in the short run it can sustain injustices, and people have become less ready to tolerate them. That someone is acting in virtue of powers conferred upon his office is not a sufficient justification if his decisions are called into question. . . . Citizens want to know more about the hidden reasoning behind the claims of authority.[21]

A society utilizes all three of Weber's forms of compliance. Balance should be the optimum objective. Banton asks how do we get the balance right. Part of the an-

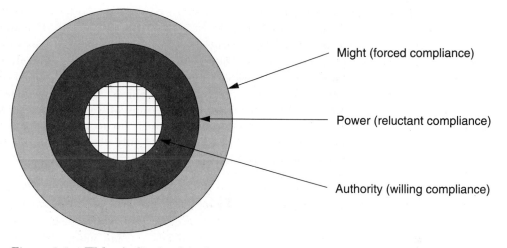

Figure 1-1. Weber's Circle of Authority

swer is that all claims to authority must be brought under scrutiny and criticism. If the claims do not command assent, modification is appropriate. Sometimes claims based on power may be brought "within the dominion of authority." But challenge in itself must be subject to rules. As Banton cautions, as he speaks of a school situation:

> There must be an understanding about who constitutes the jury, so that a teacher's claims to authority are weighed not only by the pupils but by their parents and by those who are responsible for running the school system. There must also be guidelines whereby the participants can evaluate the outcome.[22]

The State, as a political entity, is a larger or extended family, a collective person—a citadel of authority, which is its bond of unity (common-unity, i.e., community). This is the essential meaning of *sovereign* state. The State is a natural and necessary institution, according to generally accepted theory, with its purposes in the development of the moral, intellectual, physical, and material capacities of persons. There are three central ideas involved, in the democratic tradition:

1. The State exists for the good of individuals.
2. Individuals have rights which the State must not usurp.
3. Authority is vested in designated persons by compliance of the populace.

Every person by right is entitled to the means necessary to fulfill his or her human purpose, assuming it is socially acceptable. Justice should guide or regulate persons in their relationships with each other. To monitor this is one of the chief functions—indeed, duties—of the State. Law is a principal, formal means of doing this. Rights and duties are grounded in law. The general term for the behavior management implied in all this is *social control*.

So much for a brief review of some of the more vital philosophical principles undergirding democratic political institutions that are of special significance for the police function. These principles are often forgotten or overlooked in the tendency to see the police-community relationship as a recently coined "gimmick." Without a reminder of these fundamental principles at the beginning of this text, our perspective is disastrously handicapped.

A CONTEMPORARY FRAMEWORK

Kelling and more[23] provide a concise framework in the evolution of American policing philosophy by looking at three primary eras: political, reform, and community-based. Any historical typology cannot precisely define specific boundaries of time between the eras; rather, the temporal boundaries reflect points in transition. While Kelling and Moore's discussion addresses policing philosophy, I will expand on this, borrowing elements of their structure as a framework to discuss critical milestones, which helped shape not only police philosophy but also operational, organizational, and social events that have had an impact on police–community relations (PCR).

Pre-Political Era

The earliest developments of law and law enforcement are reflected in this broad era, which can be said to have started with the birth of the nation. There were diverse, uncoordinated attempts to develop a policing system to meet the unique needs of the day. The creation of the U.S. Marshals, for example, was a response to the needs of the U.S. District and Territorial courts. The Texas Rangers were initially created to deal with cattle rustling. Sheriffs and town marshals emerged as peace keepers in growing towns and settlements.

Innovation in policing began to emerge with the adaptation of principles from Peelian Reform in Britain being applied to New York, Philadelphia, and Boston. As structured law enforcement organizations, the inherent power of the police as an institution was increasingly recognized by politicians. (For detailed discussion on policing development during this time, see Holden, 1992.[24])

Political Era

In the mid-nineteenth century, the police began having a more prominent organizational presence in the cities. With the legitimate authority of arrest, search, and seizure also came the potential illegitimate authority of intimidation, intrusion, and political influence.

> . . . American police derived both their authorization and resources from local political leaders, often ward politicians. They were, of course, guided by the law as to what tasks to undertake and what powers to utilize. But their link to neighborhoods and local politicians was so tight that . . . early police [were viewed] as adjuncts to local political machines. The relationship was often reciprocal: political machines recruited and maintained police in office and on the beat, while police helped ward political leaders maintain their political efforts by encouraging citizens to vote for certain candidates, discouraging them from voting for others, and, at times, by assisting in rigging elections.[25]

The "spoils era" of politicization had begun. Competence to do a job—whether it was a police officer or any other position—was not the primary criteria. Rather, reciprocal political favoritism was of primary importance.

The concept of political patronage permeated big-city organizations. Higher echelon officials were appointed by "bosses," and these officials, in turn, gave promotions and "choice" assignments to subordinate officers on the basis of similar criteria. Thus, police organizations were predominantly "driven" by political issues.

"The earliest developments of law and law enforcement . . . can be said to have started with the birth of the nation."

In the 1920s political spoils were pervasive, and corruption in government—including the police—was commonplace. Fueled by organized crime during Prohibition and the rewards of political success through the patronage system, abuses of political authority were becoming increasingly obvious. In the policing arena, the increases in crime and corruption stood as symbols that reform had to occur or democratic values would become dangerously threatened.

The community was clearly aware of the patronage system and held no illusions that the police (or other government officials for that matter) were selected exclusively for their professional skills. Citizens recognized that the police would help them in cases of emergencies, but also understood that the primary allegiance of law enforcement was to the political machine, not to the community.

Despite the problems ingrained in the spoils system, some important people and events were emerging in the latter part of the political era that would lead law enforcement toward philosophical and operational reforms.

Reform Era

In 1931 the voluminous report of the National Commission on Law Observance and Enforcement—known as the Wickersham Commission, after the commission's chairman, Attorney General George Wickersham—was presented to President Herbert Hoover. It recommended many reforms in dealing with crime and order problems—for example, putting the police in civil service and focusing on scientific support for evidentiary analysis in criminal cases. The slogan, "Take the police out of politics," was bandied about widely and the idea of training for the police began to assume respectability. The 1920s had witnessed crime in dramatic headlines. The assumption was that properly trained police could do something about it. The thought that the police alone, no matter how well-trained, could do little to prevent or control crime had not yet developed. The new doctrine held that the police had to "professionalize," to become more effective in dealing with crime and to curb their own widespread involvement in it.

In 1933, Berkeley, California Police Chief August Vollmer, known as the father of American policing, started the first college-level police education and training program at the University of California at Berkeley. This was followed in 1935 by the creation of the School of Police Administration at Michigan State University (then called Michigan Agricultural College) in conjunction with the Michigan State Police.

Beyond the need for training, Vollmer emphasized the need for police reforms to:

- Enhance accountability for actions and behaviors to the public
- Ensure impartiality in law enforcement activities by not favoring (or disfavoring) any group regardless of their social or political position, and
- Increase the honesty of all police officers by attempting to rid the police service of corruption and political influence

As the reform movement grew, police management principles increasingly adopted the bureaucratic model (Max Weber) and premises related to scientific management (Frederick Winslow Taylor). These developments are personally reflected in the books written by former Chicago Police Department Superintendent O. W. Wilson (and former Chief of Police in Wichita, Kansas). Wilson's theories heightened reform efforts and increased the movement's visibility throughout law enforcement. His national leadership was changing the face of American policing, raising the reform movement of policing to a higher plateau, in pursuit of August Vollmer's—Wilson's mentor—vision.

While professional growth was occurring, the police were becoming more segregated from the community. This resulted from the desire to get the police away from the "corruptive influences lingering in the community." It was also an outgrowth of putting police services on a faster basis through the use of patrol cars, radios, and differing strategic approaches to unique police problems.

The reform era was important in the evolution of law enforcement. The police needed to gain control of their destiny, develop policy, and think about the nature of their work. They needed to look at how they were organized and examine the types of diverse responsibilities they had. However, times were changing in American culture more rapidly than the police were able to respond to this change. Perhaps the first hints that the reform era may have run its course emerged in the 1960s. In this decade several important factors began to reshape the police (as well as the rest of our society):

- U.S. Supreme Court decisions, under the leadership of Chief Justice Earl Warren, which significantly changed criminal procedure and, though resisted, police policy.
- The emergence of the youth "counterculture"—particularly visible because of the vast numbers of post–World War II "baby boomers"—whose lifestyle was characterized by widespread recreational drug use, sexual promiscuity (the "free love" movement), "hippies," and other factors.
- The Civil Rights movement, characterized by civil disobedience and heightened racial conflicts coinciding with vigilant attempts at social (and institutional) changes through peaceful protests and demonstrations.

- Protests against the Vietnam War, which also included civil disobedience and unprecedented, overt opposition to U.S. government policy.
- Violent, destructive riots in many of the nation's cities and on college campuses as manifestations of the collective effects of the Civil Rights movement, Vietnam War protests, and "counterculture."
- Technological advances and changes in reporting methods by the news media, wherein many of these events—including harsh reactions by the police—were recorded on film and broadcast to the nation on news programs.
- Provisions of the Civil Rights Act brought out of dormancy and used in lawsuits against the police for behaviors and policies alleged to have violated the civil rights of persons coming into contact with the police.

Collectively, these factors illustrated several things. First, it was increasingly clear that a chasm was growing between the police and the public. Not only did the public not know their local police officers, they began to distrust the police in general. Conversely, the police felt they were not supported, they distrusted citizens, and many times acted like an "occupation force" in the inner cities (typically minority communities). A second factor was that police organizations and practices had not "kept up with the times." That is, police institutional responses had not been tempered by the social change that was occurring. The police had made positive strides during the reform era, but they were nonetheless playing "catch-up" and were not prepared to handle further societal change.

Finally, training was still new and lacked sufficient depth and breadth to address the contemporary issues which it faced in the 1960s. These factors were also compounded by a paradox: The rigid organizational controls that were necessary to overcome the corruption and political influence characteristic of the spoils era became problematic during the 1960s because they institutionalized police responses and attitudes. Facing new demands, the police were inflexible, cloistered, and resistant to external influences of change.

The culmination of these events at the local governmental level led to action on the national level. In 1967, reports of the President's Commission on Law Enforcement and Administration of Justice were released. This landmark commission's multi-volume report addressed a continuum of issues facing the criminal justice system. With respect to the police the report recommended many changes. Some of those notably relevant to PCR include:

- Seeking increased communications between the police and community
- Increasing the responsiveness of the police to community concerns
- Fairly and objectively dealing with complaints against police officers
- Ensuring that police officers pursue their responsibilities with objectivity and impartiality
- Development of a more highly educated police force
- Increasing the number of minorities in the police ranks
- Creating mechanisms to facilitate increased citizen input to the police
- Facilitating community involvement on issues related to crime deterrence and apprehension

In 1968, there were two additional reports issued by the federal government: The National Advisory Commission on Civil Disorders and the National Commission on the Causes and Prevention of Violence. Although the inherent focus of these two reports was somewhat different, the findings and recommendations were very

THE LAW ENFORCEMENT STEERING COMMITTEE

The *Law Enforcement Steering Committee* (LESC) is a nonpartisan coalition of law enforcement associations that represents some 400,000 police practitioners. The LESC is the product of an unprecedented cooperative effort between law enforcement research organizations, police management, and labor. It is dedicated to the advancement of legislation and policy that will ensure the safety of citizens and the officers that protect them.

The LESC first emerged in 1985 as an ad hoc coalition of several police associations that united to combat the gun lobby's efforts to eliminate provisions of the 1968 Gun Control Act. The law enforcement community joined together to ensure that their views were accurately represented to policymakers during the debate on the legislation. The LESC achieved early success in retaining key provisions of the 1968 Act. By 1986 the LESC was composed of the leading national organizations that continue to make up the core of the committee. Subsequent activities of the committee have been effective in influencing legislation.

The LESC is a nonpartisan public interest group committed to the broad goal of protecting the nation's citizens. This commitment dictates that the coalition pursue a wide variety of public safety issues. Over the past several years the LESC has provided technical assistance and support for these initiatives as legislation:

similar with respect to the police. Once again, the need to have open communication with the community was paramount. Similarly, the need for the police to develop greater empathy with the community was important, as was the need for the police to better assess conditions within the community which might lead to civil disorder and violence. It was suggested that with this understanding the police might be able to prevent some of the disorder or, at the least, would be in a better position to manage the disorder, thereby minimizing the injury and property loss associated with such events.

Based on the President's Commission reports, and against the backdrop of the sociopolitical experiences of the 1960s, Congress passed the Omnibus Crime Control and Safe Streets Act of 1968. This legislation, for the first time, provided comprehensive federal funding for state and local criminal justice program development and research. The Law Enforcement Assistance Administration (LEAA) was created to administer the grant programs. Research, another aspect of its work, was conducted by the National Institute of Law Enforcement and Criminal Justice, an arm of LEAA. It bore responsibility for planning and experimenting with different criminal justice strategies to reduce crime. The Law Enforcement Education Program (LEEP) was designed as a grant and loan program to offset college education expenses for people working or planning on working in criminal justice.

- To impose stricter penalties for criminal activity
- To increase the resources of law enforcement organizations
- To keep guns out of the hands of criminals
- To more effectively address drug-related violence and crime
- To ensure that police officers are properly educated and trained
- To protect those who put their lives on the line to defend the nation's citizens.

The LESC sees its future role as providing lawmakers perspective on law enforcement issues as well as technical assistance on police-related matters. Management and labor have come together in one coalition to ensure that public safety issues are addressed without regard for partisan politics or special interests. The LESC'S greatest challenge will be communicating those views to those who can promote change in law and public policy.

Current members of the LESC include:

- Federal Law Enforcement Officers Associations
- Fraternal Order of Police
- International Association of Chiefs of Police
- International Brotherhood of Police Officers
- Major Cities Chief Administrators
- National Association of Police Organizations
- National Organization of Black Law Enforcement Executives
- National Sheriffs' Association
- National Troopers Coalition
- Police Executive Research Forum
- Police Foundation

Emergence of Police-Community Relations

The need to improve the quality of the police and community relationship had been recognized for some time. However, the intensity of the events during a relatively short time period in the 1960s set the stage for transition toward the community-based era. An important stimulus for this change came through the police-community relations movement. Attention was focused on cultural relations and community concerns beyond crime control.

Overt efforts at police-community relations initially emerged in training programs. Attempts to frame officers' thinking and change their behavior by providing them with a foundation of human relations training were begun in this period.

Community-Based Era. We are currently in the transition toward community-based policing. In truth, the fulcrum is still balanced on the side of reform/traditional policing strategies. Yet, a significant amount of research and experimentation appears to be rapidly moving us toward this new dawn. Importantly, the policing efforts currently being explored are not merely new police tactics. Instead, they represent a *philosophical change* on how we define and think about policing responsibilities. Moreover, this means a change in the way police service is delivered.

FOCUS 1.2

LAW ENFORCEMENT ACCREDITATION

A development to help professionalize law enforcement is accreditation by the Commission on Accreditation of Law Enforcement Agencies (CALEA). A voluntary, nonprofit corporation, CALEA is governed by a twenty-one–member commission administered by an executive director with a professional staff. The commission members are appointed by a joint action of CALEA's founding organizations: the Police Executive Research Forum, International Association of Chiefs of Police, National Organization of Black Law Enforcement Executives, and National Sheriffs' Association. The governing body gives philosophical direction and is responsible for final review of documentation and the awarding of accreditation to an agency.

The standards on which accreditation is based were developed to help law enforcement agencies achieve the following:

- Increase agency capabilities to prevent and control crime
- Enhance agency effectiveness and efficiency in the delivery of law enforcement services
- Improve cooperation and coordination with other law enforcement agencies and with other components of the criminal justice system
- Increase citizen and staff confidence in the goals, objectives, policies, and practices of the agency

The community-based philosophy builds on the body of research we have developed in police management, police-community relations, and police operations. It addresses internal factors such as officer attitudes and behaviors as well as external issues such as minority relations and community expectations. The remainder of this book will address a wide range of these issues as we prepare to enter the twenty-first century of policing.

PCR PROGRAM DEVELOPMENT IN AMERICA

1946–1955. Following World War II, interest in police training programs in human relations waned for a time. A few publications with relevant content appeared,[26] along with many general books dealing with race relations, prejudice, and the like. Milwaukee Chief of Police Joseph T. Kluchesky made news when he addressed the 1945 annual meeting of the International Association of Chiefs of Police on the topic, "Police Action on Minority Problems"[27] It was a speech that would be as appropriate today as it was then. President Truman's Committee on Civil Rights (1947), in its report *To Secure These Rights*, called attention to difficulties encountered by minorities in the areas of law enforcement and judicial processes, as well as in other institutional facets of the society.

Summer workshops in human relations for teachers and other community leaders were pioneered by the National Conference of Christians and Jews and other organizations dedicated to reducing tensions between elements of the community. A few

The standards address virtually every aspect of police operations and management, and include specific responsibilities in the area of community relations. Agencies are expected to adopt a policy that establishes a community relations plan, which includes, at a minimum:

- Establishing liaison with formal community organizations and other community groups
- Developing community relations policies for the agency (as a whole)
- Publicizing agency objectives, problems, and successes
- Conveying information transmitted from citizens' organizations to the agency
- Improving agency practices bearing on police-community relations
- Identifying training needs through interviews with citizen representatives, consultations with those involved in internal investigations, and conferences with supervisors, and
- Establishing community groups where such groups do not exist (CALEA, 1988:54–3.)

Commission on Accreditation of Law Enforcement Agencies. (1988). *Standards for Law Enforcement Agencies*. Alexandria, VA: CALEA.

police officers enrolled in these workshops as early as 1947, seeking help in understanding human relations problems or in setting up departmental training programs on the subject.[28]

The Southern Police Institute, established at the University of Louisville in 1950, scheduled twenty-six hours of instruction in human behavior and human relations in its thirteen-week curriculum. This instruction followed immediately upon the initiation of a Lohman-designed training program, *Principles of Police Work with Minority Relations*, in the Louisville Division of Police. In 1952, the Los Angeles County Conference on Community Relations reported on police departments in more than thirty major cities that had some sort of specialized training in human relations, race relations, the police and minority groups, and similar problems.[29] In the summer of 1952 at the University of Chicago, Lohman conducted the first national seminar on the subject, "The Police and Racial Tensions." This three-week-long seminar was attended by twenty-nine police officers from approximately twenty municipalities.

Philadelphia was the site in February, 1954, of a two-day conference jointly sponsored by the International Association of Chiefs of Police and the National Association of Intergroup Relations Officials and attended by police executives and intergroup relations professionals from approximately thirty cities. The agenda anticipated the decision of the Supreme Court in the school desegregation case, which came a few months later, in that the conference participants discussed gaining local cooperation to achieve orderly and just communities.

1955–1969. The Philadelphia conference set in motion a process of thought and a series of steps by the National Conference of Christians and Jews (NCCJ) that led to the establishment in 1955 of the National Institute on Police and Community Relations at Michigan State University as a cooperative venture of NCCJ and the MSU School of Police Administration and Public Safety. Only a few highlights from a more detailed source need be noted here.[30]

The institute, a five-day conference, proved so popular that it was repeated each May until 1970. It brought together teams of police officers and other community leaders to discuss common problems and to develop leadership for similar programs at the local or state levels. In peak years, more than 600 participants came from as many as 165 communities in thirty states and several foreign countries, and only seven states were never represented. As a result of the institute, such programs proliferated rapidly across the nation.

The stated purposes of the many programs initiated during this period tended to follow those of the national institute, expressed as follows:

1. To encourage police-citizen partnership in the cause of crime prevention.
2. To foster and improve communication and mutual understanding between the police and the total community.
3. To promote interprofessional approaches to the solution of community problems and to stress the principle that the administration of justice is a total community responsibility.
4. To enhance cooperation among the police, prosecution, the courts, and corrections.
5. To assist police and other community leaders to achieve an understanding of the nature and causes of complex problems in people-to-people relations and especially to improve police-minority group relationships.
6. To strengthen implementation of equal protection under the law for all persons.

In addition, certain basic assumptions supported these principles:

That the law enforcement officer occupies a crucially important position in the maintenance of order in the community. Yet is is vital that the police recognize that order in itself is not the ultimate end of government in the free society.

That, therefore, the principle of equal protection of the law for ALL citizens, and respect for their rights *as persons*, are absolutely fundamental under our system of government.

That police interested in police-community relations are committed to their own professional development. At a minimum, this means fair and impartial law enforcement regardless of personal opinions or prejudices.

That today's community, which the police officer is endeavoring to serve, is vastly different in community relations from the community of yesteryear. This implies a need for new concepts in police education and police training, especially as to social and behavioral science.

That police-community relations programs should involve a genuine educational process, the cultivation of dialogue across lines of diversity, and real effort to make communication more effective and mutual understanding a practical objective.

That each of us has something to learn from others regarding complex community problems, in their definition, diagnosis, and remedies. The police officer has something to learn from people who are not police officers, and the converse.

That police education in community relations does not add *new* burdens for law enforcement officers. That because police are in a unique position for dealing with social problems, they need help so that they may do so more effectively, particularly since conflict management has become the *main* task of the police in today's urban localities.

That current problems in race relations and civil rights represent extremely important subject matter in any police-community relations institute. Yet basic issues affect the police-community relationship that have little or nothing to do with race.

That there is also much more to the field of police-community relations than the traditional (and important!) matter of public relations.

That the improvement of the police-community relationship should not be an end in itself. The relationship is improved as the dialogue matures, in the process of working together in interprofessional approaches to the solution of community problems. Thus, a good police-community relations program may very well be, chiefly, a program in crime prevention . . . or one focusing on the attitudes of youth toward law and authority . . . or an action project in traffic safety. Any of the great issues in the administration of justice today may conceivably be the focus or pivot for police-community relations programs or projects.[31]

The National Conference of Christians and Jews—the mainspring of so many programs in this field since 1955—was founded in 1928 against the background of the religious bigotry that characterized the presidential election campaign of that year. It was conceived as a civic organization of religiously motivated individuals seeking, through education, to promote cooperation and mutual understanding among individuals of diverse religious, racial, and ethnic backgrounds without the compromise of any particular creed or faith. Through the years, this organization has fostered a great variety of programs by means of its regional offices across the country. These programs have been directed mainly toward leaders in the social institutional "trunklines" of society, which strongly influence the formation of attitudes: religious, educational, familial, political, and community organizations; the mass media; and labor and management groups. The organization became interested in police-community relations because of its commitment to orderly and just interaction among all citizens.

Generally, the programs developed during the 1955–1969 period accomplished the following objectives:

1. They developed what has come to be called a concept of police-community relations. Scholarly interest in the "sociology of the police" was stimulated.
2. They widely encouraged a teamwork or interprofessional approach to problems of police-community relations, by using a kind of laboratory method that brought together citizens of widely diversified community interests and the police and other criminal justice people to discuss problems of common interest. The essential question was, how can we work together to build a better community for all citizens?
3. They promoted the idea of police-community relations program development on a national scale.

In 1961, on a grant of funds from the Field Foundation, the School of Police Administration and Public Safety at Michigan State University conducted a national survey of 168 law enforcement agencies. The results of this survey strongly supported a case for the establishment of a National Center on Police and Community Relations. This center, with year-round services available, was activated August 1, 1965, at Michigan State, with the further help of a substantial enabling grant from the Field Foundation. The center's functions included:

1. Undertaking action-related research projects
2. Preparing, publishing, and circulating literature
3. Developing, and sometimes conducting, educational and training programs
4. Providing direct consultative service to interested police and community organizations
5. Training young professionals for work in the field of police and community relations

The center was the recipient of several federal grants, including one with which it conducted a national survey of police-community relations for the 1966 President's Commission on Law Enforcement and Administration of Justice. As of August 1, 1973, this center was merged into the more comprehensive Criminal Justice Systems Center under a substantial federal grant, the purposes of which were primarily geared to research and manpower development, as an arm of MSU's School of Criminal Justice (renamed such in 1970).

Another study, jointly undertaken in 1964 by the International Association of Chiefs of Police and the U.S. Conference of Mayors, surveyed police-community relations in cities with a population of 30,000 plus, with these findings:

1. Less than a third of the police departments studied had continuing, formalized community relations programs.
2. Two-thirds of the departments studied had, or were developing, plans to cope with racial demonstrations and disturbances.
3. In cities with more than a 5 percent nonwhite population, 70 percent of the departments reported that they were experiencing difficulties in recruiting nonwhite officers.
4. While more than 60 percent of the reporting departments indicated that they offered some training in police-minority group relations, there was wide diversity in the type and quality of training involved.
5. In only two regions did the responding departments report that they restricted the power of arrest of nonwhite officers—10 percent of those in the South Atlantic states and 14 percent of those in the West South Central states. Assignment of officers either on a nonracial basis or to racially mixed teams was becoming increasingly general.
6. More than half of the departments studied were being charged by racial groups with police brutality or differential treatment, or both. Roughly two out of ten departments reported that such complaints were increasing; about the same number reported them to be decreasing.[32]

Several federal agencies substantially encouraged programs in police-community relations in the 1960s. One was the United States Commission on Civil Rights, whose 1961 report devoted one of five volumes to the subject of *justice*. It was a thorough job of laying bare existing deficiencies in achieving equal justice for all in criminal justice processes.

The Community Relations Service, initially in the Department of Commerce and later shifted to the Department of Justice, still provides consultant and programmatic services for many police departments and community organizations concerned about problems of police-community relations. Numerous state and local public agencies for intergroup relations also help in this cause, as do several of the better-known private organizations, such as the Anti-Defamation League of B'nai B'rith, the National Association for the Advancement of Colored People, the Urban League, the American Jewish Committee, the Southern Regional Council, and Jewish Community Relations Councils in many cities. Many private educational consultant agencies have also become interested in police-community relations projects.

Beginning in 1965, the Office of law Enforcement Assistance of the U.S. Department of Justice took a special interest in police-community relations programs at the local level and funded many projects. One of its most significant contributions was the work of President Lyndon Johnson's Commission on Law Enforcement and Administration of Justice (1966–1967), whose studies were financed entirely by the Office of Law Enforcement Assistance. Many of these studies dealt with police-community relations. Consider this passage from *Task Force Report: The Police*, the commission report, for example:

> The need for strengthening police relationships with the communities they serve is critical today in the Nation's large cities and in many small cities and towns as well. The Negro, Puerto Rican, Mexican-American, and other minority groups are taking action to acquire rights and services which have been historically denied them. As the most visible representative of the society from which these groups are demanding fair treatment and equal opportunity, law enforcement agencies are faced with unprecedented situations on the street which require that they develop policies and practices governing their actions when dealing with minority groups and other citizens.
>
> Even if fairer treatment of minority groups were the sole consideration, police departments would have an obligation to attempt to achieve and maintain good police-community relations. In fact, however, much more is at stake. Police-community relationships have a direct bearing on the character of life in our cities, and the community's ability to maintain stability and to solve its problems. At the same time, the police department's capacity to deal with crime depends to a large extent upon its relationship with the citizenry. Indeed, no lasting improvement in law enforcement is likely in this country unless police-community relations are substantially improved.[33]

1969–1998. The riots and violent upheavals that occurred in various cities during the summer of 1967, and thereafter, marked a turning point in police-community relations programs. Suddenly, the nation was jolted into a realization of intense and profound divisions among its people, both racial and social. The assumptions of goodwill and commitment to the brotherhood of man that had more or less motivated programs in police-community relations during the 1955–1969 period were abruptly called into question. The possibilities of developing dialogue to build communication bridges across the chasms of intergroup differences were brought into instant doubt. Traditional patterns of community organization (block committees, precinct councils, and so on) were evidently not doing the job; many police officers and others began to express skepticism about whether it was "worth the effort" and to ask, "What have we done wrong?" There was widespread bewilderment. Some simply withdrew from further efforts; many adopted a "get tough" philosophy. The National Advisory Commission on Civil Disorders (popularly known as the Kerner Commission, after its chairman), proclaimed in its report that "our Nation is moving toward two societies, one black, one white—separate and unequal." As for police-community relations:

> The police are not merely a "spark" factor. To some Negroes police have come to symbolize white power, white racism, and white repression. And the fact is that many police do reflect and express these white attitudes. The atmosphere of hostility and cynicism is reinforced by a widespread belief among Negroes in the existence of police brutality and in a "double standard" of justice and protection—one for Negroes and one for whites.[34]

For those across the country who had been active in police-community relations programs of one kind or another during the 1955–1969 period, there may have been some tendency to overreact to the catastrophes in the cities. Perhaps it should not have been so great a shock to discover that police-community relations programs were indeed not doing the job. There were legitimate questions to be raised about the quality of these programs, without suggesting that the programs had no merit at all. Actually, there had been little effort to evaluate these programs carefully and scientifically. In fact, there was even some resistance to such research by eager program developers who preferred not to be reminded that the attitudes of many people were not being changed and that many people were not being reached. It was also true that there had been little or no progress in solving basic societal problems that vitally affect police-community relations.

In the period 1969–1973, more police-community relations programs than ever were initiated, often grandly portrayed as guaranteed riot insurance. Many such programs amounted to pure public relations, but a few government-funded programs had truly innovative features.

The Urban Coalition, a private action-research organization headquartered in Washington, D.C., issued a report in 1969 indicating that the nation had made little progress in coping with the problems identified a year earlier by the Kerner Commission. Another presidential commission was activated in the wake of the assassinations of Dr. Martin Luther King, Jr., and Senator Robert F. Kennedy—the National Commission on the Cause and Prevention of Violence, headed by Dr. Milton Eisenhower. This commission also made recommendations relative to violent crime—

STATE, COUNTY, AND LOCAL POLICE IN AMERICA

FOCUS 1.3

According to a study by the U.S. Bureau of Justice Statistics, during 1990 nearly 17,000 publicly funded state, county, and local law enforcement agencies were operating in the United States. This included forty-nine general-purpose state police departments, approximately 3,100 sheriffs' departments, and an estimated 12,288 general purpose local police departments. The remaining agencies in the 17,000 total consisted of "special" law enforcement agencies, such as transit police, conservation departments, campus police, and so forth.

Most sheriffs' offices and local police departments were small. Nearly two-thirds of the sheriffs employed fewer than twenty-five sworn officers and a third fewer than ten. About half of the local police departments employed fewer than ten sworn officers and about 91 percent of the local departments employed fewer than fifty sworn officers. Local police departments serving a population of one million or more employed one-fifth of all local officers in the United States Sheriffs' departments in the same population category similarly employed about a fifth of all deputies.

About 24 percent of all local police departments, 21 percent of the sheriffs' departments, and 12 percent of the state police departments required all regular for example, that cities should undertake "increased police-community relations activity in slum/ghetto areas in order to secure greater understanding of ghetto residents by police, and of police by ghetto residents." This commission also made recommendations pertaining to group violence, firearms, television programs, and campus disorders.

The National Institute on Police and Community Relations at Michigan State University was discontinued at the end of 1969. Its demise was a commentary on the evolution of issues and social forces pertinent to the field. The purposes, assumptions, and institute design of past years may have been relevant in their time. But it became imperative now to think about police-community relations programs in different terms, with more precise purposes that could be better measured as to results, and with somewhat fewer overgeneralized assumptions. The institute was revived in 1980 for a one-time twenty-fifth anniversary observance, with such enthusiastic Canadian participation that a 1981 Canadian-American Institute was held in Toronto. This, in turn, stimulated such interest that a 1982 Canadian-American Institute was held at the Renaissance Center in Detroit.

In early 1973, the six reports of the National Advisory Commission on Criminal Justice Standards and Goals appeared. The main interest of this commission was in crime reduction and prevention at the state and local levels. It was headed by former Delaware governor, Russell W. Peterson. Many of the recommendations of this commission echoed those made earlier by the 1967 President's Crime Commission, but some recommendations were more sharply drawn, some reflected clear advances in earlier thinking, and some went beyond what the preceding commission

field and patrol officers to wear protective body armor while on duty. The survey also found that some 90 percent of the state agencies, 74 percent of the sheriffs and 73 percent of the local police departments authorized their officers to carry semiautomatic sidearms.

Local police departments serving under 2,500 residents required an average of around 400 hours of training for new officers. Local police departments serving a population of 100,000 or more as well as state police departments required an average of more than 1,000 hours of training. About nine in ten sheriffs' departments had formal classroom and field training requirements for new recruits. The average length of required training ranged from 400 hours in departments serving under 2,500 residents to over 800 hours in departments serving a population of 500,000 or more.

The average annual operating expenditure for local police departments was around $1.7 million, ranging from over $334 million in departments serving a population of one million or more to $115,000 in those serving under 2,500 residents. By contrast, the annual sheriffs' departments budget was $3 million annually, ranging from about $92 million in departments serving 1 million or more to about $300,000 in those departments serving under 10,000 residents.

Reaves, Brian A. (1991). *State and Local Police Departments, 1990*. Washington, D.C.: U.S. Department of Justice, Bureau of Justice Statistics.
Reaves, Brian A. (1991). *Sheriffs' Departments, 1990*. Washington, D.C.: U.S. Department of Justice, Bureau of Justice Statistics.

had advocated. Two theses of the more recent commission stand out vividly: its stress on developing cooperation among all elements of the criminal justice system and its stress on the need for citizen participation in criminal justice decision-making processes.[35]

Partly as a result of the work of this commission, police-community relations programs and projects since the mid-1970s have been more apt to be identified as community-based crime prevention efforts. The Law Enforcement Assistance Administration (LEAA) strongly supported this trend, thereby stressing a primary goal of earlier police-community relations endeavors that had been subordinated in the 1963–1973 period of by the challenge of preserving urban order. In the 1970s, the tide of public concern shifted to predatory crime, with acknowledgment of the necessity for police-community cooperation to achieve anything significant in preventing crime. In the 1960s, the emphasis was an preventing civil disorder, which also required acknowledging the necessity for police-community cooperation to achieve anything significant.

That there has been an improvement in police-community relations in the United States during the past four decades can hardly be questioned. In the perspective of the late 1950s, as compared with the 1990s, progress is notable, and even more marked if one compares the years 1965–1968 with the 1980s and 1990s (despite the public outrage and violence following acquittal of four Los Angeles police officers on assault charges related to motorist Rodney King). Measured solely by the quantity of police-community programs and activities across the country, the comparison is truly impressive. LEAA funding provided a gigantic impetus. But closer, more probing study suggests a number of significant qualifications.

For one thing, many programs have amounted to pure public relations—not without some value, but still quite superficial. The labels of many programs have changed as "police-community relations" is seen as yesterday's story, and one that carries unpleasant memories. So today, we have "community service," "community affairs," and the like. The London Metropolitan Police, for instance, are now involved in a new "corporate strategy" (see Appendix A) focusing on strong police-community interaction. And of course, there is a great deal of activity in this country involving citizen-based crime prevention and detection (Neighborhood Watch, Crime Stoppers), sometimes curiously without acknowledging that such programs have anything to do with police-community relations. Nonetheless, the important consideration is that all this is going on for a good cause, no matter the labels and acknowledgments.

It is worth reflecting that two generations have passed since 1955. The police and civilian participants in the institutes of the 1950s and even of the 1960s are today's "golden agers," replaced by community-oriented police executives and Citizen's Police Academy graduates of the 1990s. The programmers have changed, as have the programs, but the apparent problems in the localities that are in the headlines as a result of flareups and tensions in police and community relations seem to be very similar to what they were in the publicized places of thirty years ago, albeit with less intensity. Racism, urban decay, rampant violent crime, citizen anxiety and fear, and the sharp increase in apparently permanent unemployment are all evidences of community deterioration. The link between these problems and police-community relations has long since been established and was clearly demonstrated in Los Angeles and other cities in 1992 following the Rodney King trial and as recently as 1997 in St. Petersburg, Florida.

THE EXERCISE IN POLICE-COMMUNITY RELATIONS

The American experience with police-community programs in the past forty years has generated considerable attention to defining what this is all about. It has been discovered that this is not an easy task. Just as with the riddle of defining crime, there appear to be as many interpretations as there are individuals disposed to offer their views. Police officers themselves have different conceptions of it, not to mention the often conflicting views held by various factions of the community. To some, police-community relations simply means public relations—that is, activities directed at creating and maintaining favorable impressions of a product, a firm, or an institution—in Madison Avenue terms, building an image. The emphasis is on *looking good*, not necessarily on *being* good, although public relations experts themselves insist that the best public relations is a quality product. For a police department, this means good community service.[36]

The fact is that what a police department views as good for the department may not necessarily be good for the community; or it may be good only for that part of the community to whom the police are particularly responsive and not for other parts. Frequently, some parts of the community are not adequately consulted in matters that ultimately affect all members of the community. Public relations communications have a tendency to be one-way.

Good public relations are, of course, important for any police agency. This area has been neglected in the past, apparently on the grounds that it is something of a luxury for a tax-supported service. Also, some police agencies may have preferred privacy. Some apparently still do. In any event, public relations and community relations, though often used interchangeable, are not identical. The President's 1966 Crime Commission, in *The Challenge of Crime in a Free Society*, made the distinction:

> A community relations program is not a public relations program "to sell the police image" to the people. It is not a set of expedients whose purpose is to tranquilize for a time an angry neighborhood by, for example, suddenly promoting a few Negro officers in the wake of a racial disturbance. It is a long-range, full-scale effort to acquaint the police and the community with each other's problems and to stimulate action aimed at solving those problems.[37]

Another way of viewing police-community relations, popular in the 1960s, was that PCR pertained to racial and ethnic minorities, to civil rights and civic disorder, to charges of "police brutality" and clamor for establishing citizen review boards. PCR was associated with such slogans as "Law and order must be preserved," and with the exchange in urban streets of obscene gestures and namecalling. In a word, it was confrontational and, often enough, violent. Small wonder that, today, the term "police-community relations" prompts sober resistance in many places.

There is no question that the police relationship with minorities of every description constitutes a special challenge. (This is addressed later in greater detail.) Yet there are problematic aspects of the police relationship with the community that have little or nothing to do with racial or ethnic considerations.

The Difficulty of Definition. Perhaps the first hurdle in trying to define police-community relations is agreeing on a concept of "community." By and large, intergroup relationship problems are most acute in metropolitan areas. It is there that what Maurice Stein called "the eclipse of community" (in his book of the same title) has occurred most dramatically. In fact, it may be argued that it is precisely because "community" in the functional sense has ceased to exist—or, more accurately, because the community is less *functional* than it once was—that relationship problems begin. A definition of the functional community has interpersonal and intergroup relations as its essence. Closely knit social relations are its heartbeat. When a community becomes dysfunctional, the chief aim of remedial programs is the restoration of social cohesiveness—to build unity where there is fragmentation.[38]

In the same vein, when we refer to "police-community" relations, we are associating entities that are quite dissimilar sociologically, and at the same time suggesting a false split. If in fact the police are part of the community, then why the hyphen? Moreover, "police" suggests a fairly unitary, encompassed, intellectually manageable occupational grouping. The "community" on the other hand is an amorphous, elusive, quicksilverish concept, especially when it is applied to the modern metropolis. To speak of the police relationship with the community is therefore misleading. Which community? A metropolis has many communities—clusters of people congregated by social class and education, by ethnicity and race, by religion, by age, by sex, by occupation or profession, and by other variables. So the police and other criminal justice agencies must relate to many communities, just as all public service institutions must.

To complicate the matter further, we will be saying, for instance, that the police function as a part of several social systems—the criminal justice system, for one. On the one hand, community relations for the *police* must be seen more comprehensively than in most discussions. On the other hand, *society's* attitude toward the police is, in some measure, society's attitude toward the entire criminal justice system, and toward government as a whole.

GENERAL AND PARTICULAR PERCEPTIONS

A general definition of crime would be that it is a violation of law. A general definition of police and community relations might say simply that it refers to the reciprocal attitudes of police and civilians. We are interested in the sum total of activities by which it may be emphasized that police are an important part of—not apart from—the communities they serve. We are also interested in the factors that contradict this positive principle. Properly understood, the principle is one for *total orientation* of a police organization. It is an attitude an an emphasis for all phases of police work, not merely for a specialized unit in the department. It is a way for a police officer to view his or her work in dealing with citizens. For citizens, it is a way of viewing the police officer: what the officer does and how it is done. Ideally, it is a matter of striving to achieve mutual understanding and trust, as with any human relationship. Every problem in police work today is in some sense a problem of police-community relations. Its solution depends, to some extent, upon police and community cooperation.

As the President's Crime Commission put it:

> Improving community relations involves not only instituting programs and changing procedures and practices, but re-examining fundamental attitudes. The police will have to learn to listen patiently and understandingly to people who are openly critical of them or hostile to them, since those people are precisely the ones with whom relations needs to be improved . . . police-citizen relationships on the street [must] become person-to-person encounters rather than the black-versus-white, oppressed-versus-oppressor confrontations they too often are.[39]

Thus conceived, the police-community relation has a *preventive* character. Its thrust is in working together in the community to anticipate and to prevent problems, to do something constructive about problems before a crisis occurs. It entails planning to avert crises. Police-community relations programs should operate on the premise that the best way to control a riot is to prevent it; the best way to control a crime is to prevent it. When the police are in the streets armed with shotguns, volleying tear gas, and crouched behind protective shields, it is too late for police—community relations. In a word, police-community relations, properly understood, is *proactive* policing, as contrasted with *reactive*.

Returning now to the definition of crime, there are particular as well as general perceptions of it. Each particular view tends to emphasize an experience and a conviction as to its causes. Why do individuals commit crime? The reasons may be medical, psychological, political, economic, sociological, etc. Crime is behavioral. How many possibilities are there in explaining why a particular individual behaves in a particular way in particular circumstances? Different schools of thought regarding crime causation emphasize different views.

So, too, with police and community relations. Sociologists stress role conflict, or organizational-environmental causes for police-citizen hostility. Psychologists stress attitudinal phenomena. Political scientists are preoccupied with police use of delegated power. Psychiatrists see it as a problem in community mental health. Public administration people focus on accountability and responsiveness, which are certainly key bywords in police and community relations.

Do all of these perceptions have merit? Clearly yes. Just as with crime, we are talking about human behavior. If the explanation turns out to be complex, so too are the problems. No single theory can be rejected.

THE TRADITIONAL TRIPOD APPROACH

Traditionally, community relations was viewed as a kind of tripod,[40] based on three equal components: public relations, community service, and community participation. One leg of the tripod, *public relations*, has already been defined. For a police department, an example of *community service* would be a youth program providing a variety of activities for children—recreation, sports, skill games, camping, music, and so forth. Community service is good public relations, but with the plus factor of providing some beneficial service to the community.

The third leg of the tripod, *community participation*, stresses interprofessional or teamwork approaches to solving community problems. It is the widely used social work concept of community organization, with particular attention to the pivotal responsibility of the police and other criminal justice agencies.

The idea of community participation may be clarified by an illustration. Take the crime problem. Clearly, the police are concerned about it. So are the courts and other criminal justice institutions. So are the schools, religious bodies, social-work agencies, various community organizations, labor unions and business management, and the mass media. The crime problem is extremely complicated. No single community force, not even the police, has the total answer. Police officers have a certain experience with the problem. It is not the same experience that, say, school principals have. Thus, the police have something to contribute, out of their experience, to the definition, diagnosis, and solution of the crime problem. So do school people. And so on, with other community entities.

The art of devising programs, therefore, is that of bringing together all these forces in some sort of cooperative, coordinated venture, to cope with problems too complex for any single force to solve alone. It is in this sense that police–community relations activity assumes a problem-solving character, with crime and quality-of-life issues as the problems. The program that emerges might be, primarily, one of comprehensive crime prevention. Or it might focus on some other problem—any problem involving a sense of common social consequence and shared responsibility. A focus on crime would probably be specific to certain types of crime, such as burglary or assault, since there is, in reality, no single "crime problem."

As experience and research evolve, however, a fourth leg is being added: active problem-solving strategies.

SOME IMPLICATIONS

Prior editions of this text have at this point listed some typical examples of public relations, community service and community participation activities of the police. The difficulty with such listings is that they quickly become dated.

The approach to police and community relations stressing problem solving through community participation has some implications that should be noted. It suggests, for instance, that it is not the goal of programs to persuade everyone to fall in love with the police. If, as a by-product of programs, some people learn to appreciate police officers more—even to the point of seeing them as "human," as neighbors and fellow citizens, and possibly even as friendly and personable "good guys"—this may be credited as a nice dividend. But the *primary* purpose in the community participation approach should be to solve hard problems, to improve the quality of police services, and to elevate the level of public respect for the police officer and for the system of government by law that he or she represents. Of course, respect must be earned, and the attitude and behavior of the police officer are the most important factors in this process. But citizens, also, should recognize their responsibilities in what a police officer may expect from them.

Full police participation in community problem-solving efforts assumes that police will be encouraged and motivated to rise to the highest level of their professional potential. In effect, this means the emergence of the police as authentic *community leaders*. Banton refers to the police officer as "a professional citizen."[41] The idea of the police as community leaders was even more strongly stated by sociologist David Bordua:

> We are, in short, asking the police to lead the community in race relations. For them merely to reflect the community would be a disaster. . . . It is . . . no help to have the police closely linked to the local community if that community's main concern is the suppression of Negroes. . . . The modern police cannot function simply as representatives of community culture—assuming it is coherent enough to be represented. They must stand aside from the culture to a large degree and function as community managers.[42]

This view of the police poses some difficulty. It would be rejected outright by those who claim that the police have no business acting as agents of social change. Moreover, there is a practical political consideration in the question of how far apart or ahead of their community the police can take a position on a controversial social issue. Bordua would allow for this while countering with the argument that, if the police are serious in their claims for professionalism, there are leadership responsibilities that go with it.

Bordua's target is the traditional *status quo* posture of the police. To some extent, the dysfunctionality of police service—and other aspects of criminal justice process—is deliberate, calculated, self-serving, and extremely difficult to eliminate because it is protected by organizations with some political clout, and by a phantom system of reciprocal favors and mutual back-scratching. Often in such circumstances, the public is led to believe that changes in established ways are dangerous, too expensive, unrealistic, or otherwise undesirable. Reformers should keep in mind that whenever innovative changes are contemplated, a certain amount of resistance is almost always encountered. The good faith and goodwill of all the actors in police-community relations dramas cannot be taken for granted. Reform in police processes is not a wild dream. The radical changes in policing policy and operations reflected in community policing since the mid–1980s reflects this reform.

QUESTIONS FOR DISCUSSION

1. Distinguish between police power and police authority.
2. Study Peel's principles and identify the *community* factor in each.
3. What are some of the critical factors that characterize each of the evolutionary eras of policing?
4. Define authority. Explain its linkage with law, social control, and the rights and duties of citizens.
5. What are some reasons why the police today seem to be more in the public eye than in the past?
6. When and under what circumstances did police training programs originate? How did this influence police-community relations?
7. Is the difficulty of a consensus definition of police-community relations in itself a part of the problem? Explain.
8. How did the President's Commission on Law Enforcement and Administration of Justice influence police-community relations?
9. Explain the traditional "tripod approach" approach to police-community relations and how that is changing during the community-based era.
10. Distinguish between *reactive* and *proactive* policing.

NOTES

1. W. L. Melville Lee, *A History of Police In England* (London: Methuen, 1901), chap. 12.
2. Charles Reith, *British Police and the Democratic Ideal* (London: Oxford University Press, 1943), p. 28.
3. Lee, *History of Police in England*, chap. 12.
4. Ibid.
5. This discussion relies heavily upon a series of three papers by Professor Jerome Hall of the Indiana University Law School, "Police and Law in Democratic Society," *Indiana Law Journal* 28, no. 2 (1953): 133 ff.
6. T. A. Critchley, *A History of Police in England and Wales*, 2nd ed., Patterson Smith Series in Criminology, Law Enforcement and Social Problems, no. 201 (Montclair, N.J.: Patterson Smith Publishing Corp.), pp. 38–50. Copyright © 1967, 1972 by T. A. Critchley.
7. Ibid.
8. Raymond Fosdick, *American Police Systems* (New York: Century, 1920), chap. 2. Peel also figured prominently in the development of the British colonial-military policing model, in Ireland as of about 1815, and then in India, Egypt, and other countries—quite a different model than that of the London Metropolitan Police. The Royal Canadian Mounted Police in Western Canada were also patterned to some extent on this model, although RCMP today has mellowed considerably.
9. For a further discussion of lay participation in law enforcement, see Jerome Hall, *Theft, Law and Society*, 2nd ed. (Indianapolis, Ind.: Bobbs-Merril, 1952).
10. For an elaboration of this point, see Geoffrey Gorer, "Modification of National Character: The Role of the Police in England," *Journal of Social Issues* 11, no. 2 (1955).
11. In a concurring opinion in *Whitney* v. *California*, 274 U.S. 357, 375 (1927).
12. Michael Banton, *The Policeman in the Community* (New York: Basic Books, 1964), pp. 6–7.
13. Michael Banton, "Social Integration and Police," *Police Chief* (April 1963): 8–20.
14. Michael Banton, "Authority in the Simpler Societies," *The Police Journal* (June 1970): 2.
15. Michael Banton, "Authority in the Mass Society," *The Police Journal* (July 1980): 10.
16. For example, C. J. Friedrich, "Authority," in *A Dictionary of Social Sciences*, Julius Gould and William L. Kolb, eds. (London: Tavistock, 1964), pp. 42–44; and Edward Shils, "The Theory of Mass Society," *Diogenes* (1962): 45–66.
17. Michael Banton, "Authority and Police Science," *The Police Journal* (August 1970): 13.
18. W. L. Melville Lee, op. cit., pp. 327–329.

19. Michael Banton, "Authority," *New Society* (12 October 1972).

20. A. P. d'Entreves, *The Notion of the State* (London: Clarendon Press, 1967). Sociologists will recognize that Talcott Parsons has also dealt with this in his translations of Max Weber.

21. Michael Banton, *New Society.*

22. Ibid.

23. George L. Kelling, and Mark H. Moore, "The Evolving Strategy of Policing," *Perspectives on Policing Series* (Washington: National Institute of Justice, 1988).

24. Richard Holden, *Law Enforcement: An Introduction* (New York: Prentice-Hall, 1992).

25. Kelling and Moore, 1988: 3.

26. For example, Alfred McClung Lee and Norman D. Humphrey, *Race Riot: Detroit, 1943* (New York: Octagon, 1968), a study of the 1943 Detroit riot. See also Davis McEntire and Robert B. Powers, *Guide to Community Relations for Peace Officers* (Sacramento, Calif.: Office of the Attorney General, State of California, 1958).

27. Joseph T. Kluchesky, *Police Action on Minority Problems* (New York: Freedom House, 1946).

28. As an example, see the description of Detroit Officer Irwin Lawler's training syllabus in Louis A. Radelet and Hoyt Coe Reed, *The Police and the Community: Studies* (Beverly Hills, Calif.: Glencoe, 1973), pp. 3–9.

29. Milton Senn, *A Study of Police Training Programs in Minority Relations* (Los Angeles: Law Enforcement Committee of the Los Angeles County Conference on Community Relations, 1952).

30. See the Introduction to Brandstatter and Radelet, eds. *Police and Community Relations* (Beverly Hills, Calif.: Glencoe, 1968).

31. Ibid. Reprinted by permission.

32. *Police–Community Relations Policies and Practices* (Washington, D.C.: International Association of Chiefs of Police and U.S. Conference of Mayors, 1964). Reprinted by permission.

33. U.S., President's Commission on Law Enforcement and Administration of Justice, *Task Force Report: The Police* (Washington, D.C.: U.S. Government Printing Office, 1967), chap. 6, p. 144.

34. U.S. National Advisory Commission on Civil Disorders, *Report of the National Advisory Commission on Civil Disorders* (Kerner Report) (Washington, D.C.: U.S. Government Printing Office, 1968), pp. 1, 5.

35. U.S. National Advisory commission on Criminal Justice Standards and Goals, *A National Strategy to Reduce Crime* (Washington, D.C.: U.S. Government Printing Office, 1973).

36. A broad overview of the field of police-community relations at the time was provided in Louis A. Radelet, "Public Information and Community Relations," a chapter of *Municipal Police Administration* (Washington, D.C.: International City Management Association, 1969).

37. U.S. President's Commission on Law Enforcement and Administration of Justice, *The Challenge of Crime in a Free Society* (Washington, D.C.: U.S. Government Printing Office, 1967), p. 100.

38. Maurice Stein, *The Eclipse of Community: An Interpretation of American Studies* (Princeton, N.J.: Princeton University Press, 1960). Also see Louis A. Radelet, "The Idea of Community," in A. F. Brandstatter and Louis A. Radelet, eds., *Police and Community Relations* (Beverly Hills, Calif.: Glencoe, 1968), pp. 80–84.

39. President's Commission on Law Enforcement, *Challenge of Crime*, p. 100.

40. This three-way analysis of community relations relies on Murray G. Ross, *Community Organization: Theory and Principle*, rev. ed. (New York: Harper & Brothers, 1955), pp. 23–26.

41. Michael Banton, "Social Integration and Police," *Police Chief* (April 1963): 9–10.

42. David Bordua, "Comments on Police-Community Relations," *Law Enforcement Science and Technology II* (Chicago: Illinois Institute of Technology Research Center, 1968), pp. 115–125.

Chapter 2

THE CONCEPT OF COMMUNITY ALLIANCE

As has been seen thus far, the evolution of policing has been rocky, long periods of plodding punctuated by moments of inquiry and reform. Generally speaking, these periods were motivated by either notable crime trends or scandals in police organizations. Nonetheless, the occurrences helped push policing out of a prolonged adolescence and into the throes of maturity.

Many factors have a strong influence on what the police do: the economy, changes in management philosophy, political ideology of elected officials, and social consciousness, to name a few. Regardless of the effects posed by social factors, the common denominator, which must be addressed, is the interaction between the police and community. This is the end to which this book is addressed.

There are some important themes which run throughout the book that cannot be neatly separated. These themes are the foundation for establishing the elusive goal of a firm, meaningful alliance between the police and community. This chapter is intended to present these issues from an integrated context, which briefly explains their meaning and relationship. These discussions will serve as the foundation of principles that will be developed throughout the remainder of the book.

Making the police and community allies in the "war against crime" is a primary goal, as is increasing the quality of life in a community. Yet obstacles appear to continually present themselves when initiatives are made to strengthen the relationship. These obstacles—endemic issues—have been the constant Achilles heel that both the police and community have attempted to resolve through a variety of programs and dialogue. Although a wide array of research is discussed in this chapter, there has been no attempt to address the minutiae of *caveats* and subtleties involved in each of the studies. Rather, the intent is simply to provide an overview of the issues, responses, and trends that permeate the realm of community alliance.

THE THEORETICAL CONTEXT

A fundamental theoretical issue in the police-community alliance is the *social contract*. Our constitutional form of government mandates that the ultimate authority for law lies with the people. As such, the citizens empower the government to create police forces which, acting in concert with the community, will maintain order in society. Thus, *social contract* essentially means that the police derive their authority from the community (much like the British concept described in Chapter 1). In accepting that authority, the police agree to perform their function in a manner consistent with community social and moral standards as well as within the standards of law. The community, in exchange, agrees to support the police (fiscal, legal, and emotional support) as an institution responsible for maintaining the sanctity of community standards. Moreover, while the police have the authority to restrict behavior and exercise *reasonably* intrusive practices with just cause, they remain accountable to the public. Police behavior should reflect both the *letter* of the law and the *spirit* of the law (i.e., a recognition of applied police discretion). An inherent recognition of the social contract is that authority and responsibility rest with the community, and the police are accountable to the community.

The evolution of our society has drawn us away from these basic principles. Populations have grown, policing has become both more complex and more "professionalized," and technological advances have touched virtually every aspect of our society. These, among many other dynamics of social development, have led the police (as well as other elements of government) to become *institutionalized*—that is, they tend to act as social entities in and for themselves, regardless of the obligations to their "roots." This phenomenon has resulted in increased isolation and alienation between the police and community. Certainly, the nature of the police-community alliance must be different today than it was over two centuries ago when the country was founded, but that alliance—an alliance with constitutional and social origins— must be fulfilled.

Community alliance is a broad conceptualization of efforts to enhance the relationship, communications, and exchange of ideas between police authority and responsibility and the needs of the public. This chapter explores issues, obstacles, and remedies which have encircled the goal of a stable community alliance.

CRITICAL OBSTACLES IN AN EFFECTIVE COMMUNITY ALLIANCE

Why has there been such difficulty in developing and maintaining a stable alliance between the police and the community? The answer, in a nutshell, is that it is the "nature of the beast." This dissonant relationship is a function of the nature of the policing responsibility in a free society. There are a number of endemic issues— problems that do not appear to be "resolvable"—that have permeated the police-community relationship. This section will explore some of the more prevalent issues that have placed a strain on this alliance.

Excessive Force

There is, perhaps, no single issue which stirs emotion in the police-citizen relationship so fervently as the use of excessive force[1] (Carter, 1985; Carter, 1984). The 1992 riot in Los Angeles demonstrates how quickly the tide can turn. The Los Angeles Police Department (LAPD) has enjoyed a reputation as a professional law enforcement agency that is well-trained and proactive in dealing with crime problems—a reputation that, perhaps, was much stronger in the public's mind than in that of the law enforcement community in general.

LAPD, and former Chief Darryl Gates in particular, have been credited for beginning Drug Abuse Resistance Education (DARE), a school-based, anti-drug education program that has become a fixture in schools nationwide. In addition, because of the gang and violence problems Los Angeles has experienced, the department initiated a number of programs, such as "street sweeps" in the Rampart and Newton Divisions of LAPD, as a proactive means of dealing with these problems. These activities received widespread support from citizens and even gained notice from the White House in both the Reagan and Bush administrations.

Within this framework of a professional image and wide public support for both the LAPD and Chief Gates, the Rodney King incident occurred. Across the country the videotaped images of LAPD officers beating and kicking a black man enraged the public. Even former President Bush publicly commented on the incident. The fire heated up when transcripts of officers' messages on the Mobile Digital Terminals (MDTs), containing racial slurs and comments about how routinely excessive force was used as a tool of the officers, were publicized. Immediate calls were made for Chief Gates' resignation and "The Christopher Commission" was created to investigate this and related incidents. Following the acquittal of the officers accused of assaulting Mr. King, civil disobedience and violence broke out not only in Los Angeles but also in Atlanta, Las Vegas, Minneapolis, and even Toronto.

The salient point to note was that while the public had shown strong support for the LAPD and its programs, the support was tenuous. Following the telecast of the King videotape, there were virtually no comments that this was a anomalous incident; rather the public focus was on the horror of officers using excessive force. While there are many issues involved in this illustration, for the current discussion one should note the fragility of the alliance between the police and community. The community, as illustrated in this case, wants the police to be proactive in dealing with such things as drugs and violence. Yet, that proactivity *must* be tempered by constitutional controls.

Moreover, an undercurrent of the Rodney King incident is the alliance (or lack thereof) the police have established with the *different* communities it serves (cf., Manning[2]). Although critical of the police in this case, the middle- and upper-class white communities in Los Angeles tended to view the incident as being the exception to the rule. However, the poor and minority communities charged that this behavior was commonplace. It was argued that this was a discriminatory action by the police that had become institutionalized as a means of dealing with crime in Los Angeles. Perhaps there is some truth to this. As an illustration, one LAPD officer told me during a research site visit that "we use a simple policing philosophy—compliance through pain."

Important lessons in community alliance learned from this incident first focus on the fragility of the police-community relationship. Furthermore, different types of alliances must be established with different communities. While law enforcement provides a great deal of lip service to this need, action is not always forthcoming.

Corruption

Law enforcement has experienced a notorious legacy of corruption, from informal individual graft to institutionalized cases of bribery and manipulation.[3] The "professionalism movement" in policing—particularly in the 1970s—addressed the issue of corruption by aggressive internal investigations, more careful hiring practices, upgrading of standards, better supervision, and generally increasing the quality of management. However, in recent years, law enforcement has experienced a "new generation" of corruption largely as a result of the vast amount of money in the illicit drug trade.[4]

Certainly, when corruption occurs, there is a loss of public confidence in the police because officers have abrogated their oath of office. In essence, they have intentionally violated critical responsibilities mandated through the codification of the social contract. Efforts to enhance the police-community alliance are met with cynicism and skepticism because the public has already been betrayed through the abrogation of duty.

Fortunately, serious cases of corruption are not widespread. However, there are corruption-related problems on a less visible scale that offer significant obstacles to community alliance. One such example is the issue of *gratuities*. There is a pragmatic debate of whether the acceptance of gratuities is corrupt behavior. From the common definitions of corruption, the acceptance of a gratuity—free meal, clothing discounts, and the like—is not corruption, unless there is actual or expected favorable behavior by the officer extended to the person providing the gratuity *as a result of the gratuitous act*.[5]

From a philosophical perspective the situation is somewhat different. Many citizens perceive the acceptance of gratuities as corrupt behavior. Public comments such as, "He'll never get a ticket; he gives cops free meals all the time," are all too common. This perception can be as damaging to community alliance as the serious cases of corruption. The same dynamics of mistrust and perceived negligence of duty are involved.

Ironically, citizens themselves also contribute to "the gratuity problem." They frequently provide the opportunity for a gratuity through the offer (regardless of their motives). In many ways this is a "chicken and egg" issue: Whose expectation for a gratuity comes first, the citizen's or the officer's? This is one reason corruption remains an endemic issue in policing.

Rudeness

One of the most common complaints—"beefs," as they are sometimes known—against officers is that an officer was rude. These accusations rarely come from persons arrested for serious crimes; instead they come from citizens receiving traffic citations, people reporting crimes to the police, or from persons simply asking directions. As in any case, there are two perspectives related to the rudeness of officers. From one perspective, officers must understand their obligation to answer, even tolerate, inquiries from citizens, particularly when some type of official action is being taken against the citizen. From another perspective, citizens should try and empathize with the types of questions and demands placed on officers, which become trying with repetition.

As one illustration, when I was a police officer I was repeatedly interrupted at dinner by citizens asking questions—directions, information about vehicle registration, and so forth. It seemed that every meal was peppered with these interruptions. A quiet meal was impossible to obtain unless I stayed in my patrol car. I rationalized that meal time was "my time" and that the citizen interruptions were rude transgressions. I then started "evasive action" to deal with these interruptions. As citizens approached, they would be ignored while I wrote reports or "listened" to the two-way radio. When a conversation could not be avoided during meal time, I was usually terse, clearly communicating my displeasure with the interruption. Despite receiving a citizen complaint about this rudeness, I rationalized the behavior because my personal meal time was being interrupted by the citizens (Internal Affairs agreed!).

My experience was repeated recently while I was in a major Midwestern city. Unable to locate a street, I saw a police officer eating a hamburger. Not thinking about my own meals as a policeman, I approached the officer to ask directions and was immediately—*rudely*—rebuffed. A comment to the effect of, "Can't you people leave me alone long enough to eat a hamburger?" followed. *Deja vú!* My immediate reaction was hostility toward the officer's rude behavior; then I recalled my own experiences and realized the damage I had done to community relations in Kansas City.

Rudeness is an endemic problem in policing because, being an inherent problem in human nature, it is one that is magnified by the nature of the police-citizen relationship. Small, seemingly inconsequential, moments of rude interactions can maintain a fabric of conflict that will continue to serve as an obstacle in the police-community alliance.

Authoritarianism

The literature is replete with research documenting the authoritarian personality characteristic of police officers (see Barker and Carter[6]). Some research indicates that policing attracts persons with an authoritarian personality. Other research suggests that authoritarianism is produced by occupational socialization (the latter appears to bear the weight of evidence). Regardless of its source, authoritarianism is clearly present in the police persona. Realistically, this has some beneficial effects. The interrogation of a suspect, handling a crime scene, conducting an investigation, maintaining control at a traffic accident, and resolving a domestic dispute are all situations in which police officers will be involved, and all require a degree of authoritarianism. However, this characteristic can become a problem if it emerges too strongly in situations requiring cooperation, compromise, or capitulation.

Dealing with the community, particularly in departments adopting the community policing philosophy, requires "tempered authoritarianism." On the one hand, officers will need to maintain the authoritative personality structure yet be able to replenish this characteristic in the appropriate situation.

Many officers are able to accomplish this quite easily; many others have greater difficulty. The authoritativeness of officers, particularly when it is *not* tempered in the appropriate circumstances, is a pervasive obstacle to community alliance. Authoritative behavior directed toward citizens is interpreted as a manifestation of the ability of the police to restrict the public's freedoms. Since such restriction is counter to the "freedom philosophy" embraced by Americans, authoritarianism represents a critical obstacle to a stable community alliance. Moreover, extreme authoritarianism—being "badge heavy" or having the "Wyatt Earp Syndrome"—can lead to conflict and produce an infectious, debilitating effect on community relationships.

Politics

Traditionally, politics has had a negative connotation. Perhaps it relates to the "spoils era" when political patronage was commonplace and incompetent and/or corrupt persons were appointed as police officials. Similarly, traditional views of "glad handing" (or "schmoozing"—a term I particularly like) with influential citizens and elected officials as a means to convert them to one's views, or in hopes of developing "favors" or obligations, was viewed as distasteful. This type of political maneuvering in the spoils era certainly had negative elements and imparted undue favoritism, in all realms of government, not just the police.

The political process has evolved, and so has the police executive's role in that process. Attitudes towards politics have not evolved at the same rate. It must be recognized that the police exist in a political environment, one with several different dimensions. At the executive level, police chiefs must be able to present budgets and negotiate policy changes within the political process. In some cases, chiefs—such as former chief Neil Behan (Baltimore County, Maryland), former chief Joe MacNamara (San Jose, California), former chief Gerry Williams (Aurora, Colorado), and the late Keith Berstrom (Tarpon Springs, Florida)—became more aggressively political to influence legislation at the state and national level on gun sale laws.

As a legislator from Missouri told me, ". . . politics are part of a legitimate and respectable process that is inherent in a democratic form of government." It is not a process of corruption, but one of education and information for legislators and decision-makers. I am not so naive as to suggest that the process is pure, but this is a practical view.

As police departments adopt the community policing philosophy, the role of politics becomes even more significant for the line-level officer. The need to interact with different units within the police department, different departments within the governmental structure, and different community constituencies requires the educational and persuasive skills characteristic of good politics. Unfortunately, this can be a two-edged sword for which the officer must make careful judgments.

In Flint, Michigan, for example, one officer's activism reached such a degree that he led a protest march (in uniform) in front of city hall. Needless to say, the city leaders were less than pleased with this officer's political activities. In another case (also in Flint), an officer had become such a strong advocate for a neighborhood that citizen groups protested when the department attempted to transfer the officer to another assignment. In the latter case, the political process interfered with the department's administrative prerogative to assign personnel.

At the other end of the spectrum, if a chief or line officer becomes too enmeshed in the political process, his or her action may be viewed as being too aggressive. In these cases, there may be a perception that the police department is going beyond its assigned role, a factor that can upset the delicate equilibrium of politicization and, at the extreme, lead to charges of an attempted "police state." In some respects, this has occurred in England and Wales.

When the provincial English constabularies were reorganized into forty-three regional police forces, British citizens expressed concern that they would lose a voice in the police role. This concern was countered with a control and funding structure that gave the policing regions input by having both citizen advisers to represent the public and some controls on police funding. Currently, there is a move by some chief constables and staff members in the British Home Office to explore the feasibility of creating a single national police force to replace the forty-three regional forces. The primary purpose would be to increase efficiency, although it is argued that effectiveness would also increase. The community has generally opposed this move, even if it would save money in the financially strapped United Kingdom. The Queen's subjects simply feel that a national police force would make the police too powerful with too much political influence.

In the United States, the autonomy enjoyed by local governments would most likely not be relinquished to any notable extent to increase efficiency or effectiveness. Concern for a police state reflects, among other things, the boundaries of community tolerance for politics by police officers.

Responding to Public Needs

A common perspective by the police is that analysis of reported crime and calls for service dictate the activities the police must perform. As professional law enforcement officers, the police are aware of community needs. The traditional view is that the public does not understand what it needs. While there is a ring of truth to this, there is also an element of elitism (and institutional authoritarianism). As observed by Madison, Wisconsin former Police Chief David Couper,[7] "How can we possibly know what the public wants unless we ask them?" The public, it appears, wants to have input on what the police do, yet the police feel they "know best."

When the police, in good faith, pursue activities that do not necessarily fulfill community desires, a chasm in the alliance occurs. If the community calls remain unanswered, the chasm will widen. Many of the activities the community wants the police to handle are typically viewed as "minor problems" by law enforcement—problems which consume scarce resources yet "don't put bad guys in jail."

For example, research through the National Center for Community Policing at Michigan State University has consistently shown that among the priorities the public wants the police to handle are barking dogs, abandoned cars, and trespassing juveniles. These types of incidents certainly do not have the same *machismo* influence as assaults and robberies nor the headline appeal of drug busts and serial murderers. Yet, while these minor incidents can touch many more citizens on a *daily* basis, more serious crimes will affect only a limited number of citizens for a limited time. As a result, the minor cases—which the police usually disdain—may have a greater overall effect on the quality of life in a community.

Given the broader reach of these quality-of-life problems and citizens' demands to address them, the police should respond to these issues with the same resolve they devote to more serious crimes. When the police do *not* respond and, even worse, tell the public that their problems are "minor" or "not important," the police-community relationship will become even more taxed.

Public Paradox

A theme which has underscored each of the issues discussed above is the public paradox related to the police function. This paradox is an inherent element which makes the endemic issues unsolvable. The paradox is that our system of government guarantees freedom and cherishes individual independence, free from government interference. The police represent a force which may lawfully deprive a person of those freedoms as well as lawfully invade the sanctity of one's privacy (within the realm of due process of law). Although citizens recognize the need for police power (the social contract) these powers nonetheless run counter to the basic freedom ethic of Americans. As a result, a conflict in the alliance, albeit frequently subtle, typically remains between the police and the public.

Perhaps this paradox is most overtly demonstrated in traffic enforcement. A traffic stop by a police officer is a temporary deprivation of freedom. It also symbolizes a formal institutional action to penalize a person for not following prescribed rules of behavior and movement. While citizens recognize the need for traffic regulations and their consequent enforcement, the action nonetheless represents a point of frequent conflict between the police and community. Moreover, this is aggravated when compounded by rudeness of the officer and/or clear exhibition of an authoritarian attitude.

This paradox, inherited from the essence of the social contract, stands clearly as the most pervasive endemic issue in the police-community relationship. It also contributes to robust checks and balances, which are necessary in our governmental system.

BALANCING THE ISSUES

Just as there are clearly identifiable endemic issues in the police-community alliance, there have been significant investments of energy and resources to resolve these problems at the same time efforts have been made to comprehensively fulfill the policing mandate. Though in concept consistent with the social contract, these initiatives—or responses—require efforts by both the police and community.

Civilian Review Boards

Primarily (but not exclusively) because of concerns about excessive force by officers, the movement toward civilian review boards began. The intent of civilian review was to maintain overt citizen involvement in the social contract *with police* by having citizens review complaints made against officers. The idea for this approach was that the general attitudes of citizens about the propriety of police actions would be incorporated in the deliberations of complaints against officers.

The structure of civilian review has varied widely, generally in an attempt to meet the specific needs of a city. Among the well-documented attempts at civilian review are the Philadelphia Police Advisory Board; the New York City Civilian Complaint Review Board; the Kansas City, Missouri Office of Civilian Complaints; San Jose, California's Ombudsman; Berkeley, California's Police Review Commission; Chicago's Office of Professional Standards; the Dade County, Florida Independent Review Panel; Portland's Police Internal Investigations Audit Committee; and the McAllen, Texas Police Human Relations Committee. Each of these bodies attempted to provide some type of citizen input, either directly into the complaint review process, as an audit process, or as an appeal process. Even in the most cooperatively formalized cases, civilian review has had mixed results. As observed by West:

> There is obviously not "one best model". . . . Rather, factors such as community attitude and support of the police, the presence of police malpractice problems, allegations of police department cover-ups, and the sociopolitical environment of the community must all be considered in a complaint review program.[8]

Although police departments have been generally resistant to civilian review, evaluations of these programs have found the citizens to be highly supportive of the police. In many cases, civilian review has been *more lenient* toward officer misconduct than have police managers in their review of misconduct cases.[9] One reason for this is the selection of persons who provide civilian review; they are people who typically support the police and are not truly representative of the entire community, particularly the poor and minority communities. This lack of real representation and the supportive attitude toward the police may be misleading if interpreted to be the sentiments of the total community.

Neighborhood Watch

Certainly the intent of Neighborhood Watch was not to establish a strong police-community alliance. It was viewed as a means to help prevent burglaries and increase the probability of apprehension of criminals. The concept evolved to also include safe havens for children and to address other crime-related problems (such as vandalism) that may be present in the neighborhood.

THE CITIZEN POLICE ACADEMY

The concept of the Citizen Police Academy (CPA) emerged in the late 1980s out of the perceived need to draw the police and community closer together as well as to make the public's view of the law enforcement working environment more empathic. Previous efforts by the police had provided information and public service programs and afforded citizens the opportunity to "ride along" with officers on patrol. The CPA provides a more structured, goal-driven mechanism to teach the public and the police. This primary purpose of a CPA is to develop a core of well-informed, responsible citizens who have the potential to offer service to the police and influence public opinion.

As one example, the Lakewood, Colorado CPA meets Wednesday night for eight consecutive weeks, with the ninth week being a graduation ceremony. Each CPA class meeting lasts three hours and generally covers three functional aspects of the police department's operations. All aspects of the department are discussed, from public relations to traffic enforcement to officer safety. (Traffic law enforcement tends to be of particular interest because of many citizens' first-hand "experience.") In addition to the classwork, the CPA class members are given the opportunity to complete an eight-hour tour of duty with a police officer as well as a short firearms course (both voluntary). One of the most important aspects of the CPA is to expose citizens to the duties, responsibilities, and issues facing patrol officers.

Before beginning a CPA, it is important that the police department set goals for the program. Some departments may want to use the CPA graduates to staff a "storefront" police station or neighborhood center. Others may want the citizens to volunteer their time to work with officers in the police station. Still others may want the CPA graduates to help "spread the reputation" of the department through presentations to civic groups and informal conversations with other citizens. Regardless of the intended purpose, the CPA curriculum must provide the citizen with the knowledge and tools to accomplish those goals.

A number of cities, besides Lakewood, have established Citizen Police Academies. Norfolk, Virginia; Tempe, Arizona; the Las Vegas Metropolitan Police Department; Prince George's County, Maryland; and Plano, Texas are all examples of the diverse agencies that have used the CPA. The benefits for police-community relations, enhanced communications, and functional assistance for the police department are well worth the time for a police agency to explore whether the CPA would be a project worthy of examination.

Tafoya, Sharon S. (1991). *The Citizen's "Police Academy": The Lakewood Model.* A paper presented at the Annual Meeting of the Academy of Criminal Justice Sciences. Nashville, Tennessee.

An obvious inherent element in Neighborhood Watch is to involve the community in crime deterrence and apprehension strategies. The organization of structured groups on a neighborhood basis not only increases acquaintances among those within the neighborhood but also provides a forum for the police to address the community on crime prevention techniques or other issues that may arise. As such, it increases the quality of the relationship between the police and community, and this ultimately helps address conflicts that are a by-product of the endemic issues. By its nature, Neighborhood Watch programs are proactive and long-term. Although this is desirable because it requires an extended, positive police-community interaction, it also has a limitation. Specifically, the police must be innovative and vigilant in keeping Neighborhood Watch programs active in order for them to be most effective. As an example, at a recent public forum sponsored by the Charleston, West Virginia police, block captains complained that it was difficult to keep citizens interested in the program. They appealed to the police to "do something." Overall, the beneficial consequences of Neighborhood Watch exceed the initial goal of the program by providing an additional avenue to strengthen the police-community alliance.

Crime Stoppers

Like Neighborhood Watch, Crime Stoppers was designed as a crime suppression and apprehension program. The difference, however, is that it had no explicit intent to ally the police and community. Crime Stoppers is a joint venture among citizens, the media, and police to locate and identify persons responsible for committing serious crimes (typically when there is a limited amount of evidence for investigators). Selected crimes are a weekly "focus" that is highlighted through descriptions and reenactments on television (or radio narrations) depicting the crime. Citizens may make anonymous calls to report information on the "focus crime" or any other crime. Selected crimes or information may also have a cash reward.

Does Crime Stoppers work? It is difficult to say without a comprehensive evaluation. The limitation of the program lies in the fact that Crime Stoppers is very probabilistic:

- A person must have observed some aspect of a crime,
- That crime must be selected to be aired on a Crime Stoppers program,
- That person must also see the program,
- The viewer must recognize it as the crime he/she observed,
- Finally the person report that crime to the "hotline."

Despite these delimiting probabilities, Crime Stoppers has been surprisingly successful nationwide. This suggests that citizens are aware of criminal occurrences and are sufficiently concerned about crime to both watch the program and make the report to the police.

An inference one may make as a result of Crime Stoppers is that the program has served as an electronic means to develop community alliance. Although it lacks the traditional elements of face-to-face contact and individual "bonding" between officers and members of the community, it nonetheless provides an avenue of understanding and involvement, which can support other community alliance efforts.

Volunteers

For a variety of reasons related to constrained resources, community relations, and community activism, police departments began using volunteers to assist in a wide range of organizational functions. At one end of the spectrum, volunteers were used as "reserve" or "auxiliary" officers to assist in law enforcement activities. Even these programs vary widely. Some reserve officers are used simply for traffic control; others, such as in Kansas City, Missouri, and San Bernardino County, California, provide reserve officers with full police powers and responsibilities. At the other end of the continuum of volunteers, departments use citizens who will do odd jobs at the department on an irregular or unscheduled basis.

Volunteers can be a valuable resource for a police department both because of the money saved in salaries and because of the expertise that can be gained from the volunteer. For example, the American Association of Retired Persons (AARP) has a structured process for soliciting, screening, and training volunteers to work with a police department. Relying on retired accountants, psychologists, teachers, lawyers, linguists, and other skilled persons can provide the department with expertise that might not otherwise be available.

An obvious additional advantage to volunteers is the community alliance role. They can provide a "citizen's perspective" on issues and serve as a sounding board for policies and practices. Hopefully, the volunteers will also serve as a community resource on matters relating to the police department.

The operational and community alliance roles for volunteers have great potential to increase the favorable profile of the police department. Unfortunately, most police organizations do not take complete advantage of the opportunities afforded through volunteers. Instead there is a tendency to treat them as interlopers in the sanctum of policing. This attitude, directed toward those who want help the police through volunteerism, will likely have a negative effect on the police-community relationship.

Crime Prevention

Crime prevention, based on a sociological concept, was generally a long-term approach aimed at youthful offenders. The underlying hypothesis was that potential criminal behavior would initially manifest itself in youthful behavior. As such, juvenile delinquency was a precursor—an early warning system perhaps—to adult criminality. Thus, in order to prevent future crime, one needed to identify youthful offenders and change their behavior. There are both theoretical and pragmatic limitations to this hypothesis; however, the basic premise appears to ring true. Unfortunately, because of legal, financial, and practical restrictions, the fruits of this hypothesis cannot be fully tested. Certainly, however, research in this vein contributed to greater thought about ways to *prevent* crime, not just apprehend criminals after the fact.

The 1970s saw a tremendous growth in the "physical crime prevention" movement. A very pragmatic approach, sometimes simply known as "locks and bolts," physical crime prevention initially relied on the premise that if it was more difficult for a burglar or thief to get access to property and, steal it, the less likely the intended crime would be committed. The concept grew to include programs such as Operation Identification, based on the premise that a thief was less likely to steal property if it was known that the property was clearly marked and recorded,

THE HOUSTON CITIZEN PATROL PROGRAM

The Houston, Texas Police Department created a program to aid the police in dealing with crime. The *Citizen Patrol* was designed to provide a means for citizens to organize into patrol groups for the purpose of reducing crime in the community. Citizen Patrol can best be described as a proactive Neighborhood Watch. The police department provides citizen band radios and magnetic signs for citizens' vehicles as well as providing a training program for all participants. The citizen volunteers work in teams to patrol their neighborhoods looking for crimes, serving as additional "eyes for the police," and providing service assistance for the police and community.

Citizens who want to participate in the program volunteer in conjunction with a neighborhood group. The neighborhood group attends a comprehensive training program that addresses group responsibilities, the "do's and don'ts of the program," scheduling, and assorted matters. Each citizen group has three "organizational" positions. The *coordinator* serves as the liaison between the neighborhood group and the police department. This person recruits volunteers and is responsible for signing for the communication equipment loaned by the police department. He or she is also responsible for gathering all data from the other Citizen Patrol participants and putting it into report form, which is submitted to the police department each month.

Each citizen patrol group has a *base station operator*. This is a participant who acts as a dispatcher (via the citizens' band radio) to the patrolling units and as an information relay point to the police, fire, or ambulance service. The Base Station Operators receive information on crime and other problems from citizen patrollers and, by telephone, relay this to the appropriate response agency. Finally, the key participants in each group are the *patrollers*. These are the volunteers who use their own vehicles to patrol their neighborhoods.

The Houston program has been deemed a success both because of the assistance provided to the police and the closer bond that has been developed between the police and community. Currently there are 80 citizen patrol groups in Houston with nearly 3,100 volunteers who patrolled in excess of 82,000 person-hours in 1991. The program includes detailed scheduling plans, report accountability of all activities, a training manual/handbook for all participants, and a monthly newsletter, which is sent to all volunteers describing issues, problems, and other news related to the program.

Houston Police Department. (not dated.) *Citizen Patrol Training Manual*. Mimeographed training document of the Houston, Texas Police Department.

thereby making it more difficult to "fence" the goods. Other variations of the crime prevention theme grew with popularity among police departments. (For a comprehensive discussion of crime prevention, see Rosenbaum[10].)

From a theoretical perspective this movement relied on a probably fallacious assumption: That a crime would be *prevented*. In fact, the likelihood is that a crime would still be committed, just not at the initially intended location. Thus, the phenomenon of *displacement*. Despite this theoretical concern, police departments embraced the concept because as long as the community had been comprehensively canvassed with crime prevention surveys and "protections," displacement to another jurisdiction was fine.

Just as police departments embraced the concept, so did the public. The program seemed logical. It provided physical evidence of some behavior designed to reduce the probability of crime and, consequently, it reduced the fear of crime. As in the case of Neighborhood Watch, these crime prevention programs provided an avenue for the police to open doors to the "law-abiding" community and perform a service the citizens wanted. This, too, helped relieve some of the pressures associated with the endemic issues of community alliance. While there are many positive aspects of physical crime prevention, it lacks depth in dealing with problems to any substantive degree. Instead, it provides a cushion on which concerns about victimization and fear of crime may rest.

Police Community Relations

With its roots at the National Center for Police Community Relations at Michigan State University in the 1950s, led by Louis Radelet, the police community relations (PCR) movement attempted to resolve the tension between law enforcement and citizens by opening lines of communications. Although the initial ideas of PCR were to develop a means to exchange information, PCR evolved into a programmatic emphasis on teaching officers about communications with the public; teaching the public about the challenges and enigmas of police work; and developing reciprocal empathy about the plight of each group in their daily relationship.

The PCR movement was the first initiative that truly attempted to reach the community. The initial focus was to identify community leaders as a focal point for establishing liaison with the citizens. Positive relations between the community leadership and the police, it was theorized, would "trickle down" to community members. At the outset, PCR was largely one-sided. Its focus was predominantly on changing the community view of the police and making citizens more supportive and understanding of police actions.[11] By the 1970s virtually every police department of any size had a Police-Community Relations unit (or officer) and courses on PCR had become a staple in law enforcement/criminal justice college curricula.

As the movement matured, the focus on PCR become somewhat more reciprocal. It was felt that police officers needed to learn more about the social and psychological dynamics involved in their relationship with the community. Moreover, PCR needed to be practiced by *all* officers, not just those assigned to a PCR unit. As a result, emphasis also came to be placed on police training as a means of getting all officers to have a more communicative—sometimes civil—attitude toward the public. Particularly in the late 1970s, police departments also regularly incorporated crime prevention programs and Neighborhood Watch with the PCR unit. It was felt that this was an additional step to help the police and community communicate, as well as to make an effort to reduce crime.

PCR was the first comprehensive effort that attempted to resolve the endemic issues inherent in the community alliance. The movement recognized that disequilib-

". . . the police community relations movement attempted to resolve the anathema between law enforcement and citizens by opening lines of communications."

rium existed between the police and community, and it developed programmatic strategies to address this dissonance. The goal of PCR was to establish an effective dialogue between citizens and law enforcement and, consequently, develop better support for the police. It also sought to enhance police accountability to the public as conceptually proffered in the social contract.

Without question, the greatest focus of PCR efforts was on minority communities, for this is where the greatest disequilibrium existed between the police and the citizens. The need for better relations with minorities became evident in the 1960s. With the force of the Civil Rights movement, punctuated by civil disturbances and protest marches, it became evident that changes had to be made in police practices. The National Advisory Commission on Civil Disorders, the National Commission on the Causes and Prevention of Violence, and the President's Commission on Law Enforcement and Administration of Justice, all cited problems in police-community relations, particularly: excessive force, deprivation of constitutional rights, rudeness, insensitivity to minorities, and discriminatory practices. As a remedy to these and other strains in the police-community relationship, each of these commissions recommended that police departments develop aggressive PCR programs.

The PCR concept is currently being rethought. Concerns emerged from police executives that PCR did not delve deep enough. Despite the intent, PCR appeared to have become a veneer for police inadequacies—predominantly a *reactive* method to deal with problems. The proactive elements of PCR were limited and generally shallow.

Based on the evolving body of research on police practices and the increasingly apparent limitation of PCR programs, practitioners and theoreticians alike felt that the endemic issues of policing in general—not simply those related to community alliance—were not being effectively addressed. This is the framework from which the embryo of community policing was conceived.

Community Policing

Community policing emerged most evidently as a result of the experiments of Neighborhood Foot Patrol in Flint, Michigan; the Citizen Oriented Police Experiment in Baltimore County, Maryland; and Problem-Oriented Policing in Newport News, Virginia.[12] It must be recognized that community policing is a philosophy, not a tactic. It is a proactive, decentralized approach to policing, designed to reduce crime, disorder, and fear of crime while also responding to explicit needs and demands of the community. Community policing views police responsibilities in the aggregate, examining consistent problems, determining underlying causes of the problems, and developing solutions to those problems.[13]

Because community policing is a philosophy, it (ideally) permeates each unit of the organization. It strives for the *depth* that PCR never achieved through involving a wide range of community members in the policing responsibility as well as designing operational policies that seek to *solve problems*. In many ways, community policing represents a formalization of the social contract by the police through the development of shared responsibility for community problems and attempts to address the issues that most directly concern the community.

Reviews of community policing experiments in Flint, Michigan; Newport News, Virginia; Baltimore County, Maryland; McAllen, Texas; Ft. Pierce, Florida; Aurora, Colorado; Houston, Texas; and other cities appear very favorable. Law enforcement appears to be more effective, officers more satisfied, and the community alliance strengthened. It has been suggested by some that community policing has become "the accepted" way of policing in America. However, the concept is still new, too many variables are untested, and the long-term effects of community policing policies are not known: simply stated, more research is needed (see Klockars and Mastrofski[14].) Despite the unknowns, the potential for community policing appears bright. Based on the brief legacy of research in policing and what we have learned through other initiatives with community alliance, the *zeitgeist* for a more responsive and holistic philosophy appears to be embodied in community policing.

STABILITY ON THE HORIZON

While the endemic issues of policing cannot, by their nature, be completely resolved, they can be managed. Conflict will always exist, but good faith efforts will reduce the negative effects of the problem. In fact, it may be argued that the conflict inherent in the endemic issues is good. As noted previously, it is a form of checks and balances.

One element of emerging stability, as discussed above, is community policing. The impact it has had on the field thus far is the most significant *philosophical* change to occur in American law enforcement. Despite the spread of community policing and the spectacular growth of literature on the philosophy, it is by no means the norm of policing in this country. Moreover, there are no definitive evaluations to pass judgment on the operational soundness of the philosophy or the operational policies emerging from the philosophy's implementation. Despite these *caveats* there can be no doubt that at this early point in community policing's development, it seeks not only to provide more efficient and effective police service, it also *directly* addresses the endemic issues that plague the community alliance.

Other developments are occurring in law enforcement that also contribute to a more robust alliance. Coincidentally, these same factors support both the philosophical and operational precepts of community policing.

Values

Values are designed as *beliefs* and *principles* by which the police department fulfills its responsibilities. They represent the department's commitment, its "social contract," to the community. In the past few years an increasing number of police departments of various sizes and in different locales have articulated formal value statements (e.g., Alexandria, Virginia; Houston, Texas; Madison, Wisconsin; McAllen, Texas; Newport News, Virginia; Sandy, Utah; among others). These values serve as the standards against which all police behaviors are held.

Included in virtually all of the police department value statements are factors such as:

- Adherence to the Constitution and democratic values
- Commitment to rigorous law enforcement using a wide variety of policing resources to deal with crime
- Pursuit of crime prevention
- Understanding the nature of crime problems in neighborhoods as well as responding to the needs and concerns of citizens
- Commitment to an open and honest relationship with the community
- A pledge that police employees will perform their tasks with integrity and professionalism
- Solicitation of citizen participation in policing tasks
- Commitment to participating in programs that incorporate shared responsibility with the community

Formalized values serve as an institutional pledge to the community. If these standards can be incorporated not only into policy but also into the working persona of every police officer, then a stronger alliance will be established and the effect of the endemic problems will be minimized.

Higher Educational Levels

Since the 1967 recommendations of the President's Commission on Law Enforcement and Administration of Justice called for police officers to have a college education, a great deal of research has been conducted on the effects of higher education on police behavior. In sum, it has been found that the college experience provided people with decision-making, communications, and analytic skills that permitted a more effective and ethical performance of police responsibilities.[15]

The proportion of police officers who have received higher education has progressively increased since 1960. Whereas the average educational level of officers in 1967 was 12.3 years—barely more than a high school diploma—the current average level is 13.6 years, or well into the sophomore year of college.[16] Not only is the level of education increasing among police officers, it is also steadily rising for the public.

It may be inferred from the research on higher education that a better educated police force would address the tasks of policing with greater professionalism, civility, and humanity. If these factors alone could be accomplished, movement toward the goal of a strong community alliance would make a geometric leap forward.

Increased Workforce Diversity

As noted previously, the greatest (and most serious) conflict between the police and community has centered on relations with racial and ethnic minorities. There is no doubt that discrimination has occurred both during the exercise of police power and during the police employment process. As a result of the Civil Rights movement, court decisions, and greater awareness of past discrimination by police leaders, contemporary police executives have made great strides in increasing the racial, ethnic, and gender diversity of America's police forces. Although complete parity has not yet been accomplished, law enforcement has made notable accomplishments.

The findings of a Police Executive Research Forum study showed that minority representation in American law enforcement agencies approximates the general population. Moreover, educational levels of minorities in law enforcement are virtually the same as those of white officers.[17] On a related note, the same study found that 12.8 percent of all sworn police officers are women. Even though no empirical evidence was found on a national level, there are indicators that in 1970 women composed less then 2 percent of all sworn officers. Obviously, this amount of change in two decades is substantial. Further, it was interesting to note that women officers average a full year more of college study than men.

As the workforce approaches a true representation of a community's racial/ethnic composition, it also becomes more representative of mores and values. This, in turn, will both decrease levels of conflict and increase the strength of the alliance.

Changing Police Management Styles

As noted in chapter 1, Kelling and More[18] provide a concise discussion on how the management of law enforcement has evolved through three eras: political, reform, and community-based. The *political* era reflected patronage and general incompetence. During the *reform* era, efficiency, rigid controls, and autocracy were central themes in police management. The *community-based* era, the new direction of law enforcement, reflects the philosophy and values of community policing as described previously in this chapter. Clearly, as has been noted, this style of management is more conducive to a strong community alliance.

Within this era—and even more recent—another management movement is emerging: Deming's Quality Management. (For greater detail on this topic see Couper.[19]). The focus of Quality Management is to serve the needs of the organization's *customers*. In the case of law enforcement, customers are the citizens. Fundamental to the Quality Management philosophy is answering these questions:

- Does the police service meet the customers' desires?
- Can police service be presented more efficiently?

The premises of Quality Management argue that an organization must address the needs of both internal and external customers. Further, it is argued that most individual performance measures are counter-productive because they inspire individually centered conflict and competition rather than a quality customer-oriented service.

From the limited perspective of community alliance, suffice it to note that if citizens are viewed as *customers* of police service and efforts are expended accordingly, it is likely that a strong bond will develop between the police and community.

Media Merger

There has traditionally been a love-hate relationship between the police and the media. Law enforcement personnel would argue that the news media want information they do not have a right to, that the media are too critical of the police and fail to show the "police side" of controversies, and that media exposure complicates serious investigations. The media, on the other hand, argue that the police are too secretive and tread on the freedom of the press. Despite these conflicts, the police and media representatives interact on a daily basis, frequently quite congenially.

Since many public opinions about the police are strongly influenced by the media—both the news and entertainment media—the severity of the endemic issues as well as the strength (or weakness) of community alliance are related to media portrayals of the police. Because of concerns on both sides of the issue, the police-media relationship is stabilizing.

Police executives are establishing policies to work more cooperatively with the media and are opening doors, where possible, to media inquiries and interviews. As a result, a more trusting bond, based on give and take, is developing to enable both sides to meet needs unique to their own responsibilities.

This closer relationship is occurring not only with the news media, but with the police and entertainment media as well. Such programs as *COPS*, *Top Cops*, and *America's Most Wanted* reflect this trend. While the media's focus will always address the more sensational and intriguing issues (that is how an audience is drawn), a cooperative relationship will permit this portrayal in a more realistic light.

TAKING THE NEXT STEP

Community alliance is like fishing. You have to start with commitment, go to the right place, use the correct bait, have patience, be willing to change your strategy, and seize the opportunity at the right moment. Your efforts may not always result in "a keeper," but when the "big one" bites, it is enjoyable and rewarding. It is also an ongoing effort—you're never quite finished and must always strive for a better catch.

Assumptions and conjecture are plentiful on this issue, but there is one statement that can be made with granite-like resolve: Regardless of innovation, energy, and effort on behalf of the police, there will never be a completely harmonious community alliance. When the community stops questioning the police, the police should begin questioning themselves.[20]

QUESTIONS FOR DISCUSSION

1. What is the relationship between the *social contract* and police-community relations?
2. Explain the concept of *community alliance*.
3. Describe the critical obstacles to community alliance and discuss how they may exist within your community.
4. Why have politics and policing always appeared at odds when law enforcement is an artifact of a political environment?
5. Discuss the meaning of the *public paradox* and its impact on police-community relations.
6. What is your opinion of the Citizen Policy Academy and the Houston Citizen Patrol Program? Do you feel either would benefit your community? Describe why or why not.
7. Why did early police-community relations programs focus on minority communities?
8. Discuss how a change in police *management* styles can influence the police-community relationship.
9. Establishing an alliance with the community requires a balancing act between two ends of the social pendulum. Explain what is meant by this.
10. Distinguish between the concept of *community alliance* and the early concepts of *police community relations*.

NOTES

1. David L. Carter, "Theoretical Dimensions in the Abuse of Authority by Police Officers," *Police Studies*. vol. 7, no. 4 (Winter 1984): 224–36. David L. Carter, "Police Brutality: A Model for Definition, Perspective, and Control," in *The Ambivalent Force*, (3d ed.), A. Blumberg and E. Niederhoffer eds. (New York: Holt, Rinehart, and Winston, 1985), pp. 321–30.

2. Peter K. Manning, "The Police: Mandate, Strategies, and Appearance." In *Policing: A View From The Street*. Peter K. Manning and John Van Maanen, eds. (Santa Monica, CA: Goodyear Publishing Co., 1978).

3. John Dombrink, "The Touchables: Vice and Police Corruption in the 1980s" in *Police Deviance*. 2d ed., Thomas Barker and David L. Carter, eds. (Cincinnati: Anderson Publishing Co., 199).

4. David L. Carter, "An Overview of Drug-Related Misconduct of Police Officers: Drug Abuse and Narcotic Corruption," chapter in *Drugs and the Criminal Justice System*, R. Weisheit (Cincinnati: Anderson Publishing Company, 1990a). David L. Carter "Drug Related Corruption of Police Officers: A Contemporary Typology," *Journal of Criminal Justice* 1990b vol. 18, no. 2.

5. Thomas Barker and David L. Carter, eds., *Police Deviance*, 2d ed. (Cincinnati: Anderson Publishing Co., 1991).

6. Ibid.

7. David C. Couper, *What is Quality Policing?*, METAPOL Computer Bulletin Board Network. Staff Item 3. (Washington, D.C.: Police Executive Research Forum, 1988).

8. Paul West. "Investigation and Review of Complaints Against Police Officers." In *Police Deviance*, 2d ed. Thomas Barker and David L. Carter, eds. (Cincinnati: Anderson Publishing Co., 1991).

9. Ibid.

10. Dennis P. Rosenbaum, ed., *Community Crime Prevention: Does It Work?* (Beverly Hills, CA: Sage Publishing Co., 1986).

11. President's Commission on Law Enforcement and Administration of Justice, *Task Force Report: The Police* (Washington, D.C.: U.S. Government Printing Office *and* National Commission on the Causes and Prevention of Violence, 1967). *Law and Order Reconsidered* (Washington, D.C.: U.S. Government Printing Office, 1969).

12. Robert Trojanowicz (Undated), *The Neighborhood Foot Patrol Program in Flint, Michigan* (East Lansing, MI: National Neighborhood Foot Patrol Center). John Eck and William Spelman, *Problem-Solving*. (Washington, D.C.: Police Executive Research Forum, 1987).

13. Robert Trojanowicz and David L. Carter, *The Philosophy and Role of Community Policing* (East Lansing, MI: National Center for Community Policing, 1988). John Eck and William Spelman, *Problem-Solving* (Washington, D.C.: Police Executive Research Forum, 1987).

14. Carl B. Klockars and Stephen D. Mastrofski, eds., *Thinking About Police: Contemporary Readings*, 2d ed. (New York: McGraw-Hill, 1991).

15. David L. Carter and Allen Sapp, "The Evolution of Higher Education in Law Enforcement Organizations: Preliminary Findings from a National Study," *Journal of Criminal Justice Education* 1990 vol. 1, no. 1 (Spring)

16. David L. Carter, Allen D. Sapp, and Darrel W. Stephens, *The State of Police Education: Policy Direction for the 21st Century* (Washington, D.C.: Police Executive Research Forum, 1988).

17. Ibid., Carter and Sapp, 1990; Carter, Sapp and Stephens, 1988.

18. George L. Kelling and Mark H. Moore, "The Evolving Strategy of Policing," *National Institute of Justice/Harvard University Perspectives on Policing*. (Washington, D.C.: National Institute of Justice, 1988).

19. David C. Couper, *Quality Policing: The Madison Experience*. (Washington, D.C.: Police Executive Research Forum, 1991).

20. The idea of "community alliance" was first discussed by Larry Hoover in developing the theoretical foundation for the Texas Law Enforcement Management Institute. At Dr. Hoover's urging I developed the concept more broadly. My first work on this concept appears in Larry Hoover, ed., *Police Management: Issues and Perspectives* (Washington, D.C.: Police Executive Research Forum, 1992).

Chapter 3

COMMUNITY POLICING: MILESTONES AND FUNDAMENTALS

It was previously observed that the emerging philosophy of law enforcement is community-based. A significantly different perspective of police work, it is an effort to embody new responsibilities and stabilize them in an environment of change. While a range of definitions (or descriptions) of community policing exists, I will define it as

> . . . a philosophy, not a tactic. It is a proactive, decentralized approach to policing, designed to reduce crime, disorder, and fear of crime while also responding to explicit needs and demands of the community. Community policing views police responsibilities in the aggregate, examining consistent problems, determining underlying causes of the problems, and developing solutions to those problems.[1]

Community policing (CoP) is known by a wide range of labels, such as Problem-Oriented Policing (POP), Community Problem-Oriented Policing (CPOP), Neighborhood-Oriented Policing (NOP), Target-Oriented Policing (TOP), Police Area Representatives (PAR), Citizen-Oriented Patrol Experiment (COPE), Experimental Policing (EP), Neighborhood Foot Patrol, Community Foot Patrol, and many other labels which describe a police department's own unique philosophy. Although there are variations in the specific application of these concepts, for the purpose of this book all of these labels are synonymous.

Upon reading much of the literature on CoP, one might erroneously assume that the philosophy was an idea that was purely theoretical at the outset and eventually merged into practice. It was not a concept that suddenly appeared because "it seemed like a good idea." Rather, it grew out of the expanding body of research being conducted on police patrol, police management, and the range of endemic issues in policing discussed in chapter 2. CoP was not "discovered." It emerged out of the interactive effects of research and social evolution and, following a meandering path, eventually led to the articulation of the concept in police literature and field testing in police agencies across the country.

This chapter will examine critical milestones and research that led to the development of CoP as well as illustrate some applications of the concept.

Milestones of Development

In the late 1960s, police leaders, government officials, the academic community, and society began to question whether the police were performing their job in the most effective ways possible. The public wanted to know if the police were accomplishing their goals. Corruption scandals, accusations of political impropriety, excessive use of force, and clashes with Vietnam War protesters and civil rights demonstrators prompted closer scrutiny of police practices. The 1967 President's Commission on Law Enforcement and Administration of Justice examined various aspects of policing, noting the need for important changes in

- The quality of police personnel
- The quality of officer preparation and training
- The management structure of law enforcement agencies
- How the police relate to the community
- How the police deliver services to the community, and
- How the police define their responsibilities

As noted in chapter 1, in 1968 both the National Advisory Commission on Civil Disorders and the National Commission on the Causes and Prevention of Violence examined the riots of the 1960s and the circumstances that contributed to civil disorder. Among the findings, it was observed that the police had

- Paid too little attention to effective organization
- Not effectively examined deployment strategies
- Given inadequate attention to community issues and concerns
- Not adequately explored their internal biases
- Not seriously considered preventive or less coercive strategies to deal with civil disorder, and
- Not explored alternate strategies to deal with violence

It was also noted that there

> . . . is an evident inability of the police, as presently organized, manned [sic], financed, equipped, and led, to meet effectively any of the demands and expectations placed on them by the public. These inadequacies are evidenced in their inability to prevent a crime; their declining record in solving crimes known to them; their sluggish response to and indifferent investigation of all but major crimes or those involving important persons, businesses, or institutions. Particularly evident is the inability to deal effectively with crime in minority-populated ghettos for reasons which involve [considering] minority group attitudes and non-cooperation as important as police attitudes, facilities, and efficiency.[2]

The implication was clear: law enforcement must establish an open dialogue with the community, deliver comprehensive services, and reexamine the traditional police organizational structure and processes. The civil unrest of that era suggested that the process was not keeping pace with social change. Policing had to adopt an approach that empathized with the community, took advantage of emerging technologies, *and* balanced these with traditional responsibilities. Integrating

"Law enforcement must establish an open dialogue with the community, deliver comprehensive services, and re-examine the traditional police organizational structure and processes."

police tradition with a "high-tech, high-touch" philosophy would not be an easy task.

While the Commission reports of 1967 and 1968 drew attention to many policing issues, there was really no mechanism (or resources) for change until Congress passed the Omnibus Crime Control and Safe Streets Act of 1968. For the first time, the federal government provided financial assistance for local criminal justice programming. Among the many facets of the Act that proved particularly important in the eventual development of CoP was the Law Enforcement Education Program (LEEP) and the National Institute for Law Enforcement and Criminal Justice (NILECJ).

LEEP was intended to stimulate higher education among criminal justice personnel. In the case of the police, the belief was that better-educated law enforcement officers would provide more responsive and more comprehensive police service. It was felt that as college-educated officers moved into police leadership positions, they would explore more creative approaches and institute better planning. The current evidence suggests that these early educational policies have produced progress toward these crucial goals.[3] In addition, with the growth of criminal justice programs in higher education, research on criminal justice issues expanded among scholars, graduate students, and practitioners who had been exposed to the research process in college.

Though "basic research" is desirable, there was also a need to stimulate research that could influence social policy. The NILECJ, through grants and contracts, provided the first major research incentives which allowed police researchers to learn more about what works, what does not work, and what might work. Previously, such research had been sporadic and, consequently, our new knowledge about policing was incomplete. NILECJ was a cornerstone in the criminal justice research movement that was significantly expanded by private organizations such as the Ford and Mott foundations, who sponsored policy-directed research projects in law enforcement. Furthermore, research in policing sponsored by the National Science Foundation set important standards for methodological controls in law enforcement research.

With significant grant support from the Ford Foundation, the Police Foundation was created explicitly to conduct research on policing issues. Shortly afterward, the Police Executive Research Forum (PERF) was created. Consisting of college-educated police executives from major jurisdictions, PERF adopted a charter that defines its role as an organization to explore police policy research issues, with the findings debated among the nation's police leaders. Growth of the Police Foundation and PERF set the stage for an atmosphere of scientific research that would challenge traditional policing assumptions, evaluate policing strategies, and test net police-service alternatives. These approaches made up the essential ingredients for new law enforcement programs. CoP is based on the collective findings of this research. As such, the following discussions will look at some of the important research projects which contributed to the birth of community policing.

Another "leap" forward was made in 1994 when Congress created the Office of Community Oriented Policing Services (COPS) in the Department of Justice. COPS was intended to provide money for officer hiring incentives to increase state and local police agencies by 100,000 officers, nationwide. In addition, in 1997 COPS created thirty-five Regional Community Policing Training Institutes across the country and provided funding for experimentation and evaluation of community policing innovations.

RESEARCH ON WHICH COMMUNITY POLICING WAS DEVELOPED

Since police patrol represents the largest and most visible portion of law enforcement officers, a significant amount of research has been done to help us better understand the issues and effects of the patrol function.

Preventive Patrol

Perhaps one of the most important—and controversial—police research projects occurred in 1972, early in law enforcement's contemporary research history. The Kansas City, Missouri Police Department's (KCPD) Preventive Patrol Study was designed to question a sacred police strategy: Do marked police cars on random patrol actually prevent crime? The concept of preventive patrol postulated the "self-evident truth" that the mere presence of the police (or reasonable potential for their presence) would deter criminals from committing offenses in the immediate geographic area of the patrol.

The study used three controlled levels of routine preventive patrol in the KCPD South Patrol Division where the experiment took place. One "beat," termed *reactive*, received no preventive patrol: officers entered the beat only in response to a citizen's call for assistance. The intent of this strategy was to substantially reduce police visibility in that patrol beat. In the second type of beat, called *proactive*, police visibility was increased two to three times its usual level. The premise was that if preventive patrol actually deterred crime, there would be substantially less crime in the proactive beats. In the third area, termed *control*, the normal level of patrol—one marked car with a single officer—was maintained. After one year an analysis of the data found that the three types of beats had no significant differences in the level of crime, citizens' attitudes toward police services, citizens' fear of crime, police response time, or citizens' satisfaction with police response time.[4]

The results are not surprising when compared to an analogy with which many of us are familiar. If you are speeding down an expressway and see a marked police car along the side of the road, you will probably do the same thing as most people, slow down to the speed limit. Also, if you are like most drivers, once you have passed the police car and it is out of your sight, you resume speeding. The marked patrol car did not *prevent* speeding, but merely *interrupted* it.

The Kansas City study found that preventive patrol was not only uncommitted time but it was also non-productive time. The findings are *not* an argument that patrol officers are unnecessary; rather, the inference is that traditional assumptions about the effect of random police patrol on crime and citizens' attitudes may have been false. As such, the findings suggest that police agencies are wasting time and money by continuing or expanding traditional patrol procedures. The results suggested that police executives needed to

- Explore how police resources could better be used, and
- Examine what police processes may be more effective in dealing with crime problems and citizen concerns

Preventive patrol is a well-intentioned strategy that requires reconsideration. Based on what was learned in Kansas City, community policing has attempted to put uncommitted patrol time to better use. Further, it has sought to bring the police and community closer together, thereby narrowing the distance created when a patrol car was interposed between them. In addition, CoP attempts to reduce citizens' fear of crime and increase satisfaction with the police—two factors preventive patrol apparently did not improve.

Response Time

Another element initially examined in the KCPD Preventive Patrol Study addressed the issues associated with officer response time. Typically, response time was broadly defined as the amount of time it takes a police officer to respond to a citizen's call for assistance. Basically, it was assumed that the lower the response time, the greater the chance of apprehending the criminal. It was further assumed that a faster response would indicate the police are more efficient and that this would also add to citizen satisfaction with police service. Of course, "speed of response" is a matter of perception that is interpreted differently by citizens and the police.

Using some general measures, the Preventive Patrol Study found that response time and citizen attitudes did not vary among the three experimental districts. In fact, the findings stimulated more questions when it was learned that response time is a complex factor determined by distance, speed, geography, attitude of the officer, and behavior of the citizen who called the police. Further research was clearly warranted.

This rudimentary response-time finding continued to be debated because of the uncertain nature of its relevance and what it meant in terms of police operations. One argument for maintaining traditional patrol was the need to have police officers available for rapid response to calls. Thus, any new alternate patrol plans based on the preventive patrol finding had to be tempered by the need to make sure officers could respond rapidly to calls. These issues collectively led to a Law Enforcement Assistance Administration (LEAA) research grant for another project—the Kansas City Response-Time Study.

Two of the fundamental questions addressed by this study were:

- What effect does response time have on "producing favorable crime outcomes"?
- What is the effect of response time on citizen satisfaction with police?

On the "crime effects" issue the Kansas City Response-Time Study found

> First, although some patrol strategies affect police response time, a proportion of Part I crimes are not susceptible to the impact of rapid police response. Secondly for that proportion of crimes that can be influenced by response time, the time taken (by citizens) to report the incident largely predetermines the effect of police response time. Thirdly, the factors which produce reporting delays are primarily citizens' attitudes and voluntary actions rather than uncontrollable problems they encounter. Fourthly, if reporting time is not so long as to hamper police efforts, prompt field officer response has significant impact on certain types of crime (notably robbery) but limited impact on crime outcomes in general. Explicit in the arguments for increasing or altering resources to reduce response time is the assumption that rapid response time is essential in producing favorable crime outcomes in a substantial proportion of serious crimes. However, this assumption is dubious, given the results of this study.[5]

On the issue of citizen satisfaction, the study found the main determinant of citizen satisfaction was a citizen's *perception* of the police and *expectation* of response time. The amount of elapsed time was not, in itself, an important determinant. Rather, *it was whether the response time met the citizen's expectation for the response.* As one might assume, if the response took longer than the caller expected, the citizen was less satisfied. Conversely, if the police response time was faster than a citizen's expectation, the citizen tended to rate the performance and competence of the police higher.

Overall, the research has shown that the difference between experienced and anticipated response time is a major determinant of citizen satisfaction. Once again, these findings flew in the face of the traditional wisdom and the results were hotly debated. As a result, PERF conducted a follow-up study in crime-reporting patterns of citizens in San Diego, Peoria, Rochester, and Jacksonville (Duval County, Florida). While the PERF study measured additional factors, the Kansas City findings were confirmed: sophisticated technology and deployment strategies to shorten response time were well-intentioned, but misguided. The PERF report concluded

> . . . police departments' resources, long focused toward rapid response to all crime calls, would have to be reallocated to other, attainable objectives. . . . One answer [is] to adopt a strategy of community policing in which the police spend more time cementing relationships with residents of neighborhoods.[6]

Since fast response time neither effectively dealt with serious crime nor directly increased citizen satisfaction, this research paved the way for an exploration of different police strategies. Another important element was now in place for the development of community policing.

Differential Police Response

The preventive patrol and response-time findings provided the impetus for police managers and researchers to explore alternate patrol management strategies. Among these was a concept known as Differential Police Response (DPR). Traditionally, police calls have been dispatched in the order in which they were received with the exception of life-threatening situations. They, of course, received immediate attention. DPR recognizes that different calls should be assigned different priorities based on the "immediacy of need" for a police officer's presence. Recognizing—from the preventive patrol and response-time studies—that greater flexibility can be used in call management, DPR also developed alternative methods for handling calls.

The National Institute of Justice conducted DPR field tests in Garden Grove (California), Greensboro (North Carolina), and Toledo (Ohio). The objectives were to

- Reduce the number of nonemergency calls for service handled by immediate mobile response
- Increase the number of nonemergency calls for service handled by a telephone report unit, by delayed mobile response, or by other alternative responses
- Decrease the amount of time patrol units spent answering calls for service and increase the amount of time available for crime prevention or other activities
- Increase the availability of patrol units to respond rapidly to emergency calls
- Provide satisfactory explanations to citizens when they called for service about how their call would be handled
- Provide satisfactory responses to citizens for resolving their calls for service[7]

DPR is a resource time-management plan that matches operational needs to available police resources and expertise. It permits flexibility in handling calls while contributing to both increased responsiveness to community needs and efficiency in police operations. Furthermore, the research indicates that DPR allows patrol officers more time for crime-focused activities, such as investigation and prevention, as well as community service and administration.

In the NIJ filed test of DPR, several key findings have important implications for community policing

- Police departments can achieve a sizable reduction in the number of nonemergency calls for service handled by immediate mobile dispatch, without sacrificing citizen satisfaction.
- The results of the baseline citizen surveys showed an overall high public willingness to accept alternatives to immediate dispatch of a patrol unit for nonemergency calls.
- Three of four callers were willing to accept delays of up to an hour for nonemergency calls.
- As expected, there was a greater willingness to accept delays for calls that did not involve potential danger or threats.
- Citizen satisfaction with alternate services provided was high.
- Alternate responses are less costly than traditional mobile responses, and productivity levels are much higher for personnel using alternatives.[8]

The results imply that citizens want their problems handled when they call the police, but the response does not always have to come from a patrol officer arriving at the scene as soon as possible after the call is made. For example, the Houston Police Department uses a system called "tele-serve." Whenever a citizen is a victim of a crime, he or she can file a report by telephone to a tele-serve operator. Although an officer does not necessarily arrive at the scene, the citizen receives an immediate response to the call to the police department. The key element is the *response*, not the *method*. The results also indicate that educating the community about police capabilities and operations will help the public cooperate with the police on alternate problem-solving methods. Like the response-time research, the DPR evaluation found that informing the public about what the police would do and how much time it would take are important keys to success. Since DPR is also a time-management strategy, it provides patrol officers more time for other community policing and problem-solving activities. Thus, DPR provides better responsiveness to citizen needs and demands, more efficient use of police resources, and greater levels of citizen satisfaction, all of which are important in a community policing effort.

One- Versus Two-Officer Patrols

An emotional issue for many patrol officers (and police labor organizations) is whether there should be one or two officers assigned to each patrol car. The most common issue in this debate is *officer safety*. It is assumed that cars with two officers will provide greater safety in hazardous situations. The counter argument is inefficiency: Two-officer cars are more expensive because many calls require only one officer to perform the job. Thus, the presence of the unneeded second officer is wasteful of resources.

Many departments regularly use two-officer patrol cars; others use only one-officer cars, and still others use a combination. There is no precise formula to aid in this decision. Instead, police administrators rely on their philosophy, experience, nature of the community, labor agreements, and other relevant factors to make their decisions.

The most comprehensive research on this issue was conducted in San Diego, California. The study found that, based on factors such as cost, number of calls handled, arrests, response time, and handling of administrative duties, one-officer units are far more efficient and clearly as effective as two-officer patrols. On the emotionally laden issue of officer safety, the San Diego study found

> . . . both single and multiple . . . units had approximately equal involvement in assaults on officers. However, two-officer units were shown to have been involved in resisting arrest situations (and consequently, in total critical incidents) more frequently than were one-officer units, despite the fact that the units had equivalent exposure to potentially hazardous situations overall, and to arrest situations in particular. The groups had equivalent involvement in police vehicle accidents and had experienced equivalent exposure in terms of miles driven. . . . Two-officer units were found to be more frequently involved in assaults on officers, in resisting arrest situations, and in total critical incidents than were one-officer units. . . . *The weight of evidence from this analysis supports the conclusion that one-officer patrol unit staffing was safer for officers* (emphasis added).[9]

Community policing is a labor-intensive endeavor. It requires an officer to have extensive contact with citizens as well as a feeling of "ownership" for the area the officer patrols. Essentially, in any given area, CoP is a process which requires one officer, not a pair. As a result of the San Diego research, there is strong evidence to support the notion that one officer working alone is both safe and efficient.

Team Policing

The "buzz words" of patrol management in the 1970s and early 1980s were *team policing*. Rather than being a philosophy of policing (as is CoP,) team policing was a patrol management strategy which attempted to group officers by geographic location with the purpose of having them work cooperatively toward a common end. Much like a football team, the police team would have various officers with different expertise and responsibilities working together.

> The common feature linking most team policing programs is their reliance on the notions of decentralization and generalization. Thus, the hypothesis underlying team policing is that effective patrol and other services can be provided in an efficient manner via a decentralized (sometimes neighborhood-based) police department consisting of officers who are generalists in the law enforcement field.[10]

The actual structure, assignment, and operating philosophies varied significantly in the different cities which experimented with team policing. The effects of team policing projects are mixed. In many programs, the concept was well developed, but lacked clear policy direction. Furthermore, many evaluations were methodologically weak. In other cases, the concept simply was not given sufficient time to mature. One of the weaknesses of team policing may have been that it was a concept ahead of its time. With better-educated officers and more enlightened management throughout the chain of command, team policing may have been more successful. Despite its limitations, team policing established a conceptual foundation that was ultimately strengthened and redefined in community policing.

Patrol Deployment

The deployment of patrol officers has received constant attention from police administrators. Deployment refers to the assignment of officers based on geography, time, and the duties the officers must perform. Data from the U.S. Bureau of Justice Statistics show the tremendous variability in deployment. Throughout the United States there can be anywhere from no officers (in Alaska) to 8,667 officers (in New York City) for each 100 square miles.[11] Between these extremes are officer distributions that vary so much that no meaningful conclusions can be drawn. *There is no single factor or ratio that determines what the ideal police strength for a given geographic area should be.* The two most important deployment criteria are: (1) the *resources available* to the police agency, and (2) the *tasks officers must perform.* In other words, how many officers are available for performing what functions?

Deployment decisions vary, depending on

- Policing philosophy of the chief
- The geographic area
- Time of day
- Character of the community
- Types of calls received, and
- Demands for police service

In light of these factors, the patrol manager must answer a fundamental question: Given the number of personnel available, how can the department most effectively perform the functions the community expects? (The British refer to this as providing "value for money.") The answer lies largely in realizing that deploying officers based on numerical demands makes no sense unless we look first at *what we are trying to achieve* and then determine how to match the officers available to those needs. The goal is to balance quantity and quality—to answer calls for service, but in ways that address the community's true needs most effectively. Research on alternate patrol deployment has explored issues such as mathematical modeling, split-force patrol, directed patrol, and one- versus two-officer patrol cars. The results substantiate several findings

- No universal deployment tactic can be effectively applied to all law enforcement agencies, even agencies within defined size ranges.
- Different approaches can be used by multiple agencies as long as the approach is modified to meet the unique characteristics, demands, and resources of each.
- New deployment strategies should not be developed without evaluating the department's needs in terms of goals and objectives.
- Any new deployment plan should have an evaluation component and periodic assessments so it can be tailored to meet these results.
- Traditional deployment strategies, though effective in answering calls received, are inefficient when measured against citizen demands—they intervene in incidents without solving broader problems.[12]

Though deployment research does not directly address community policing, the findings provide support for the concept in that the research suggests there is no consistent deployment model which can be unilaterally applied. Rather, a patrol deployment plan must be tailored to each community.

Specialized Patrol

In an effort to make police patrol officers more effective, a variety of patrol configurations has been tried. The underlying theme of the different models was to efficiently handle calls for service, control crime, and make productive use of officers' "uncommitted" patrol time. Collectively, these experiments have been referred to as "specialized patrol." Different models of specialized patrol include split-force patrol (Wilmington, Delaware), directed patrol (Kansas City), low visibility patrol (New York, Boston, Nashville, Memphis, San Francisco, Miami), high visibility patrol (Alexandria, Cleveland, San Jose), and management of demand (Wilmington).

The evaluations of specialized patrol consistently showed that effectiveness (goal attainment) did not change, but efficiency (use of resources) generally improved with the different experiments. These successes spurred attempts to refine specialized patrol so that it would also be more effective. The Wilmington Management of Demand Project adopted alternate "response strategies" to address the unique demands placed on the police department by citizens. The result was that the police were better able to assess the demand for police services (both crime and noncrime) and respond more effectively to those demands.[13] The concept is dynamic because the police response changes when demand changes. Both the process of experimentation and the lessons learned from the evaluations provide insight and helped frame different operational strategies which could be used in CoP.

Summary of Research

The combined effect of police patrol research was to encourage a reassessment of police approaches to patrol administration and to consider new alternatives. The research highlighted the fact that the police have both crime and service responsibilities which many times require only one officer instead of two. Team policing emerged as a potentially important concept in putting the officer in closer contact

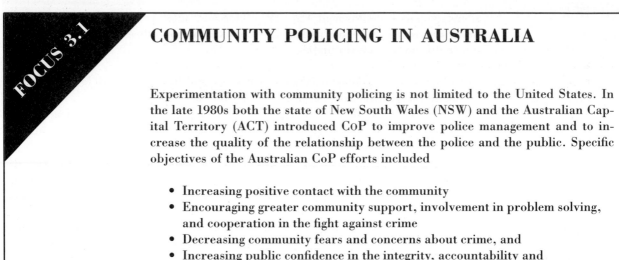

COMMUNITY POLICING IN AUSTRALIA

Experimentation with community policing is not limited to the United States. In the late 1980s both the state of New South Wales (NSW) and the Australian Capital Territory (ACT) introduced CoP to improve police management and to increase the quality of the relationship between the police and the public. Specific objectives of the Australian CoP efforts included

- Increasing positive contact with the community
- Encouraging greater community support, involvement in problem solving, and cooperation in the fight against crime
- Decreasing community fears and concerns about crime, and
- Increasing public confidence in the integrity, accountability and professionalism of police (Frank Small and Associates, 1992:1)

with neighborhood problems, but one that needed stronger direction and better evaluation. At the same time, other departments focused on using specialized patrol to improve overall efficiency. The Wilmington Management by Demand Project refined the concept further by adding an analytic element so that police could be more responsive to citizen demands. Each patrol strategy added to the research foundation that led to the conceptualization and experimentation with the next logical step: community policing.

NONPATROL RESEARCH AND INITATIVES LENDING SUPPORT
TO THE COMMUNITY POLICING CONCEPT

Research on factors other than patrol has also had an impact on thinking related to CoP. Most of these studies have not specifically focused on community policing efforts, but their findings are nonetheless important for understanding the concept.

Patrol Officer Time Commitment

A commonly cited statistic is that only 10 percent of a patrol officer's on-duty time is spent on crime-related activities. These include answering calls, investigating crimes, writing reports, processing arrestees, and testifying in court. The remaining 90 percent of an officer's time is spent handling noncriminal calls, traffic enforcement and control, gathering information, and simply doing nothing.[14] Certainly these statistics are, at best, an average which will vary by jurisdiction, beat, time, and season. Despite the variance, my own experience shows that even in the nation's largest cities and busiest patrol districts there is a surprising amount of uncommitted patrol time. Moreover, the vast majority of calls handled by patrol officers are noncriminal or, at the most, calls only peripherally related to crime. Collectively, this implies that traditional patrol operations are inefficient and perhaps misdirected. As a result, we can assume that officers have sufficient amounts of time to devote to other duties (provided officers are given direction on what to do and how to do it).

Evaluations of the CoP initiatives in both NSW and the ACT show that the residents are feeling safer with less fear of crime since the implementation of CoP. Dialogue between the police and public is increasing and the community is giving greater support to the police. Cooperation between the police and public is also increasing in the form of Neighborhood Watch and other joint crime-control ventures.

Plans include a greater integration of community policing initiatives throughout both police organizations. In addition, more emphasis will be placed on problem-solving strategies and broader application of CoP principles.

Frank Small & Associates, *Survey of Community Policing Initiative in New South Wales* (East Sydney, Australia: Frank Small & Associates Pty Ltd., 1991).
Frank Small & Associates, *Community Policing Initiatives in the Australian Capital Territory* (East Sydney, Australia: Frank Small & Associates Pty Ltd., 1992).

To neglect this implication risks decreasing the efficiency and effectiveness of the police force. Interestingly, research by the National Center for Community Policing (notably in Flint, Michigan; Aurora, Colorado; Alexandria, Virginia; and McAllen, Texas) suggests that while the public wants the police to respond to crimes, they have *equally strong demands* for order maintenance and service tasks, such as barking dogs, abandoned cars, and other quality-of-life issues. This conclusion is reinforced by citizen surveys performed by the police departments in Madison, Wisconsin; Fort Pierce, Florida; and Fort Collins, Colorado. Thus, the public demand for a police response to service calls will contribute to the proportionately lower numbers of crime calls.

Job Enrichment/Job Enlargement

Although these concepts have been studied for years, they have received renewed attention as a result of the "quality management" movement (see Couper[15] for a discussion), which sought

- To make employees more productive
- To provide better service, and
- To increase the quality of life at work

Job enrichment means that the employee's work experience is more rewarding. Job enlargement means that an employee is given broader occupational responsibilities. Together they improve morale and job satisfaction, increase individual decision-making, promote innovation and power sharing, and involve all members of the department in policy development and organizational plans. Though the literature shows that job satisfaction may not improve individual performance, it does show that job satisfaction contributes to lower turnover, less absenteeism and tardiness, and fewer grievances. Other research has shown that high job satisfaction—a factor produced by job enrichment—is a good predictor of longer life. Conversely, lower satisfaction is correlated with various mental and physical illness. There are also indications that occupational morale and job satisfaction are positively related to overall organizational productivity.

The paramilitary structure and bureaucratic organization of police departments have traditionally meant that they are rigid organizational environments. Officers have not been urged to be creative or to deviate from standard procedure. Rather, they have been told to adhere strictly to custom and practice. This rigidity contributes to complacency and to occupational lethargy, if not lower job satisfaction. In comparison, community policing can be professionally stimulating by providing the officers with challenges, opportunities for innovation, and rewards for creative solutions. By providing both job enrichment and job enlargement, CoP may contribute to lower attrition and a higher quality of life "on the job."

Performance Measures

An issue of constant controversy in policing is how to measure police performance. In other words, on what factors do we evaluate personnel to determine if their work behavior is consistent with departmental expectations. Traditional quantitative measures, such as the numbers of arrests, reports written, calls answered, miles driven, tickets issued, and so forth, do not really measure the breadth or substance of a police officer's responsibilities. The notable advantage of quantitative measures is that they are relatively easy to collect, document, and compare. Ideally, *qualitative* measures of an individual officer's performance should be collected. These include communication skills, how the officer relates to the public, how the officer manages different situations, and the quality of decisions made. These factors tell us what we really want to know about the officer's effectiveness. Unfortunately, not only is this information difficult to collect, it represents subjective assessments which could be challenged for accuracy if made part of an officer's personnel record.[16]

Police agencies should strive for a balance between quantitative measures and qualitative measures. To do this, a police administrator must first clearly establish the goals he or she is trying to accomplish. Once this is done, programs must be implemented to achieve these goals, with specific officer responsibilities spelled out. Officers would then be evaluated on the criteria detailed in the program. In some cases, evaluation methods would need to be nontraditional. For example, input might be sought from persons who have had contact with the officer, or the officer might be asked to write a self-assessment describing what he or she has accomplished that contributes to the department's goals. The officer might also be asked to define areas where more training or direction is needed to improve his or her performance.

The performance of the individual officer (and the police organization as a whole) requires specific, comprehensive plans for meaningful evaluation measures. Community policing affords a wider range of variables that can be measured. It requires that officers use initiative and creativity, factors which also need to be addressed in the evaluation process. Qualitative measures are particularly suitable for evaluating CoP responsibilities. Moreover, they can provide an important barometer of officer activity and success as well as a measure of organizational goals.

Citizen Demands for Police Service

As policing has matured, law enforcement leaders have increasingly accepted the fact that the public expects the police to handle more than crime deterrence, criminal investigation, and criminal apprehension. Through the type of calls the police receive from citizens, it is obvious that the public expects the police to deal with a wide variety of problems. As a result, the police have become more aggressive in assessing the service demands of the public.

While citizens agree that having the police respond to serious crimes is important, they also want the police to help with minor, but annoying problems, such as abandoned cars and juvenile trespassing. The police have learned that they must find ways to listen to people and establish a dialogue to determine the types of services they want. Preliminary research indicates that responding to community needs on these minor calls may significantly increase citizen satisfaction and confidence in their police. Madison, Wisconsin; Fort Pierce, Florida; Aurora and Fort Collins, Colorado; McAllen, Texas; and Lansing, Michigan are among the cities that have surveyed citizens to define the kinds of problems the police should address and to identify the public's perceptions about the strengths and weaknesses of police programs.

Integrated Criminal Apprehension Program

In 1975, the Law Enforcement Assistance Administration (LEAA) began funding the Integrated Criminal Apprehension Program (ICAP) that eventually was implemented in many cities nationwide. ICAP, originally developed as the Patrol Emphasis Program, was based on a synthesis of patrol-related research. It was intended to direct patrol resources toward crime problems that were identified through intensive crime analysis. It was envisioned as an operations support concept that touched on all aspects of patrol operations.

Based on previous research, ICAP programming relied on projects such as patrol work load, management-directed patrol, managing criminal investigations, and managing patrol operations. The focal point of ICAP was *crime analysis*. Relying on detailed analysis of crime trends, suspects' methods of operation (MOs), characteristics of trends, demographic, seasonal, and time characteristics, as well as other relevant variables, ICAP would identify problems to be addressed by the patrol force. ICAP would then analyze potential police responses to address the problem, select the most reasonable alternative—based on resources, potential effect, and nature of the strategy—and implement the response.[17] Ideally, this process would utilize the best empirical knowledge related to criminal apprehension, following a scientific approach to problem solving.

The effectiveness of ICAP was mixed. In part this was because of the complexity of the concept. It first required skilled crime analysts with expertise and knowledge about variable patrol and crime apprehension strategies. Moreover, ICAP was a fluid concept that required different organizational responses to various problems. The inherent nature of the police organization—even in enlightened departments— is to resist change. These organizational facets made the needed flexibility essential to ICAP more difficult to achieve.

Another problem was that ICAP was a *concept*, not a program. Although it relied on a solid foundation of research, the concept was not concrete. It was a conceptual application of the research to variable situations. As such, it was simply difficult for many to grasp how this information could be applied to "real world" problems. Although there are scientific components of ICAP, it can best be viewed as a systematic planning and program development process.

ICAP had a direct influence on the development of problem-oriented policing because of the emphasis on problem identification and police operational responses through crime analysis. Many of the problems identified through ICAP initiatives were found to be of a noncrime or peripheral crime nature, requiring the police to respond in nontraditional ways. Emerging from this desire to find nontraditional responses to deal with these problems was a re-thinking of police responsibilities and a broader interpretation of the police mandate.

A SYNTHESIS OF IMPLICATIONS FROM THE RESEARCH

The research shows a number of important findings. Among them are

- Random, marked patrol does not prevent crime.
- Patrol officers have a notable amount of "uncommitted" time.
- A fast response to a citizen's call does not increase the probability of apprehending criminals.
- It is not the speed of the response which shapes the citizen's satisfaction with the police, but whether the police fulfilled the citizen's *expectations* of a response time.
- Call management plans—for example, differential police response—can increase the efficiency and effectiveness of policing without sacrificing citizen safety.
- Meaningful deployment of patrol officers requires careful analysis of environmental factors and calls for service which will likely differ by time of day, season of the year, and geographic location.
- One-officer patrol cars are significantly more efficient than two-officer units.
- One-officer patrol cars do not pose undue threats to officer safety.
- Teams of police officers working toward commonly defined goals in a cooperative effort can provide more comprehensive police service.
- Unique patrol deployment schemes—specialized patrol—can be useful for meeting special circumstances or problems.
- Assigning patrol officers to geographic locations based upon population ratios is an inadequate method to meet the variability of demands for police service.
- Meaningful police performance measures must be developed in order for the measures to have a useful purpose in personnel assessment and direction.
- Job enlargement and enrichment for the patrol officer will help increase job satisfaction and provide an environment whereby officers will become more productive.
- Citizen demands for police assistance and problem solving related to noncriminal matters are a reality and must be addressed.

Although it is not a panacea, community policing addresses all these needs. By reallocating the patrol officers' time, CoP makes better use of personnel. Furthermore, by getting close to the community and establishing a dialogue with citizens, the public develops a different—and more accurate—measure by which to gauge an officer's competence and by which to determine their satisfaction with police service. Establishing a dialogue with the community also allows citizens to have a voice in defining and setting priorities for their needs. This targeted response, in turn, contributes to greater satisfaction on the part of minorities and helps establish better police-community relations. By the same token, when an officer is given the mandate to diagnose community problems and be creative in developing solutions, the officer serves in many new roles—community organizer, facilitator, educator, referral resource, and law enforcement officer—and this both enriches and enlarges the job.

No one argues that CoP is the answer to all problems the police face. Moreover, CoP will not work in every community. The concept *does* provide a logical, comprehensive approach to police service delivery that relies on a solid foundation of research.

THE SCOPE OF COMMUNITY POLICING INITIATIVES

While the amount of information about community policing is growing constantly, some nagging questions remain: Should it first be tested on a small scale? What types of new responsibilities should the police embrace? Where do the police "draw the line" in responding to community needs? How are traditional responsibilities and practices reconciled with changes required of community policing? How does the relationship between the police and other government departments change with a broadened police role? How will management and labor relations change within the police department? How can a resistant community be motivated? How do the police reconcile 911 call demands with community policing deployment? These and other questions need to be discussed—although admittedly not always answered—to further examine the breadth or scope community policing should have in a police organization.

The Issue of Community Policing Philosophy

If community policing is a philosophy of policing, can it be implemented on a partial basis within a police department? Can one philosophy (i.e., "reform" policing) apply to a certain assignment, shift, or geographical location while community policing applies to another assignment? Is community policing a philosophy of police management, police operations or both?

To answer these questions, a fundamental issue which must first be addressed deals with the inherent nature of the community policing movement. Many would argue that to even discuss it as a "program" is to miss its essence. Community policing, as defined by leaders in the field, is not a programmatic activity at all. Rather, it is a *philosophy* of police management and operations, as noted previously in the Trojanowicz and Bucqueroux definition.[18]

This perspective incorporates a new way of looking at the business of policing, which has ramifications for goals, operations, and management. Substantial shifts in what are defined as police responsibilities and how those are accomplished are inherently an element of a philosophical change of depth, not the superficiality of traditional programmatic shifts. In this vein, George Kelling and Mark Moore, in discussing the evolution of policing in America, observed that the movement toward community-based policing ". . . represent[s] a new organizational approach, properly called a community strategy," which ". . . operates from organizational assumptions different from those of reform policing."[19]

This new organizational approach embodies different methods of management; different operational responsibilities; and redefined relationships between officers and managers; between police and citizens; and between the police department and other departments of government. The actual structure of this movement remains static. For example, some discussions in both literature and practice argue that there are notable differences between community-based policing and problem-oriented policing. If so, is this a philosophical conflict that will limit program scope? On this point Moore and Trojanowicz observed that . . .

> If there is a difference between the strategy of problem solving and the strategy of
> community policing, . . . it lies in a different view of the status and role of the
> community institutions, and in the organization and arrangements constructed to
> enhance community involvement.[20]

Taken further, it may also be argued that differences similarly lie in program scope. Problem-oriented policing is somewhat more narrow, focusing more on readily defined—or discernible—problems, which can be addressed from a strategic approach. Community policing, however, views problems more broadly and includes a focus on "quality of life" issues as well as distinguishable problems which generate calls for service. Both, however, employ management styles which differ from tradition, both seek to establish a more efficient and effective police service, and both take a proactive approach to police operations.

Thus, the essential difference is in the way the concepts are operationalized, not the inherent philosophical goals. Even considering this debate, on the matter of philosophy Herman Goldstein has described problem-oriented policing by noting . . .

> In its broadest context, it is a whole new way of thinking about policing that has implications for every police organization, its personnel, and its operations. With an ever-present concern about the end product of policing as its central theme, it seeks to tie together the many elements involved in effecting change in the police so that these changes are coordinated and mutually supportive. It connects with the current move to redefine relationships between the police and the community. Fully implemented, it has the potential to reshape the way in which police services are delivered.[21]

Implicitly, Goldstein also appears to view this movement as a philosophical shift in policing. If it involves a "whole new way of thinking" about the police function and if it can "reshape the way police services are delivered," then the philosophical elements are in place. Interestingly, Goldstein infers that, despite its philosophical elements, it does not explicitly have to be "fully implemented."

Viewed practically, while community policing is a philosophical shift in the way police officers practice their profession, it is operationally difficult for most police departments to completely change their philosophical underpinnings in one comprehensive initiative. Incremental change is a much more manageable approach offering experimentation, a time for transition, and political safety as options.

Different attempts at community policing have brought different labels as a means to tailor the philosophy to the specific needs of communities. Whether it is Neighborhood Foot Patrol (Flint, Michigan); Problem-Oriented Policing (Newport News, Virginia); Quality Policing (Madison, Wisconsin); Neighborhood Oriented Policing (Houston, Texas); or Code Blue (Fort Worth, Texas), the essential idea is to bring a more responsive, scientific police presence into the community. Regardless of how it is labeled or explicitly implemented, each of these initiatives are attempting to deliver police service in a different manner, all of which subscribe to the consistent philosophical elements of proactive, service-driven policing.

In sum, if we accept that community policing is indeed a philosophy, can it be effectively introduced as the basis for a long-term organizational commitment on a piecemeal basis? This will largely depend on the commitment given to the change, the willingness to reallocate resources, and the amount of procedural flexibility management is willing to permit. If the department can permit—and absorb—these changes for a sufficient time to evaluate its effects, then an incremental approach will have value with the caveat that full implementation of the philosophy will likely be much slower in coming. Resocialization of personnel and restructuring of organizational processes are time-consuming changes which simply cannot be rushed.

The Management Orientation

There are, of course, many different theories of management applied to police organizations today. If one considers traditional or "reform" management, the questions to ask are: Can community policing work in a predominantly bureaucratic and scientific management environment? If so, what managerial reforms have to be made? If a more contemporary management philosophy is used by the police executive, we might ask, what are the implications of "total quality management" and "value-added management" for community policing initiatives? Related to this, relying on the concept of "reengineering the organization", the questions to consider are: If we blew this place up and started over, what would we do differently? What should we eliminate entirely? What can we do that would make things easier for our customers?

As noted in chapter 1, traditional police management is referred to as "reform" policing because of strides taken over the past fifty years to improve the quality of police service as well as efforts to gain greater organizational control and accountability, which had been lost through the spoils system of politics. The reform doctrine postulated that the police had to "professionalize", to become more accountable and more effective in dealing with crime while at the same time reducing corruption and malfeasance among police officers. Based on the work of former Berkeley, California Police Chief August Vollmer—"the father of American policing"—emphasis was given to (1) training needs of officers, (2) reforms that enhanced public accountability of the police for actions and misconduct, and (3) the ability to provide the most efficient and effective delivery of police service.

As the reform movement grew, police management principles increasingly adopted popular management philosophies of the day including the bureaucratic model (vis-à-vis Max Weber) and premises related to scientific management (vis-à-vis Frederick Winslow Taylor). These developments are exemplified in the books and management practices of former Chicago Police Superintendent O.W. Wilson, who heightened reform efforts and increased this "professional" vision throughout the law enforcement community. His national leadership was changing the face of American policing, raising the reform movement to a higher plateau in pursuit of the vision of August Vollmer—Wilson's mentor.

Reform policing is characterized by rigid organizational controls, limited discretion, personnel specialization, centralization of authority, organizational inflexibility, and clearly defined lines of authority, responsibility, and communications (i.e., chain of command). In addition, the authoritarianism and cynicism often found among line-level officers is also omnipresent among organizational relationships and processes. This is aggravated by the near obsessive-compulsive behavior found among police personnel and organizational procedures. These characteristics beg the question of whether community-based efforts and creative problem-solving can be effectively performed within this "reform" environment. The writer would argue that the answer is "no", which supports the need for inculcation of a revised philosophy of policing.

Given the responsibilities of a broadened mandate and the activities required of officers to fulfill those responsibilities, it appears that reform era police management is inconsistent with community-based organizational needs. As one illustration, a current concern increasingly expressed by police executives relates to the compatibility of law enforcement accreditation and community policing.[22] Accreditation was conceived and implemented within the parameters of reform era policing. As such, operational, management, and policy standards largely reflect the traditions of reform. Yet, as accreditation became a reality, the community-based era of policing was emerging. A number of chiefs, as well as the leadership of the International Association of Chiefs of Police (IACP), expressed concern that the reform-based accreditation standards and community policing were in conflict. While this does not appear to be inherently true, there are reasonable concerns that need to be addressed. Community policing, it appears, can be used in an accredited agency with some "tinkering" to policies and processes related to the accreditation standards. Going back to the issue of philosophy, this would seem to support the notion that community policing can be implemented on a limited basis within the department. However, this is an option that has limitations and may not be the most efficient methodology.

Community policing seems to be most compatible with contemporary management philosophies, such as total quality management (TQM), valued-added management, and re-engineering the corporation. Both community policing and contemporary management philosophies are driven by "customer" demands and are concerned about providing the best service possible. Both are concerned about resolving problems as comprehensively as possible, just as both are concerned with motivating employees and increasing employee job satisfaction. Indeed, we may consider viewing community policing simply as the application of quality management to police organizations.

Relying on contemporary management principles, several elements for improving a police department become apparent. Expanding on the work of David Couper and Sabine Lobitz, these elements may be summarized as follows:

1. A police executive should create and nurture a *vision* for the organization, which gives clear long-range direction for the department.
2. An executive's life and leadership style should be "in tune" with his or her personal beliefs and values as well as community expectations.
3. An executive must be able to listen to both employees and community members to understand desires, expectations, and problems. Listening should be an on-going process, which includes providing feedback on these concerns.
4. Personnel recruitment and selection should be done with an eye toward tomorrow in order to get the best possible employees to help meet the executive's vision. Avoid the attitude of hiring people simply to "fill positions."
5. It's "turf," not time in policing—that is, concern should be focused on neighborhoods' and citizens' problems, not time management and officer deployment schemes.
6. *Perceptions* by the community regarding crime, police performance, and quality-of-life problems are as important as actual problems and should not be ignored.
7. Executives should practice the quality improvement method in order to give the best possible service and value to the community in relation to the expenditure of police resources.[23]

The movement toward community policing requires significant organizational change—something which does not come easily for any organization. For police departments, which are paramilitary, bureaucratic structures with members who have been somewhat socially isolated from the community as a result of their occupation, attempts at change are particularly challenging. A common response in humans is to resist change; to say that a new approach will not work. Thus, most attempts to introduce change, regardless of the rationale, will be met with a natural defensiveness.

Our history of policing has shown, however, that many previously sacred beliefs about law enforcement have been forced to give way to new ideas after research suggested that there may be flaws in the traditional logic. Based on that knowledge, law enforcement leaders explored new police responsibilities and different operational tactics. Within this framework, community policing evolved and grew as research and experimentation pointed the way. Pundits have begun to look at the concept anew. They have witnessed how it flourishes in numerous departments and, though some still will not concede that it can work, at least they are willing to take a fresh look at the possibilities.

One contemporary line of management thought, which seems particularly compatible to community policing and the implementation of change, is "reengineering the corporation". An initial premise of this concept asks leaders to consider the question, "If we blew this place up and started over, what would we do differently?" It goes on to ask, "What should we eliminate entirely?" and "What can we do that would make things easier for our customers?"[24]

A fundamental element of the "reengineering" premise is to organize around *processes* rather than *departments*. Applying this to community policing has important ramifications for program scope. That is, to what extent can the structure of the police organization, deployment practices, and personnel assignments be altered to accommodate community policing initiatives where the scope of that initiative is limited? Using this approach, deployment practices would focus on facilitating officers' shift schedules to meet with citizens and community groups who can help solve problems, rather than organizing the department around traditional schedules for comprehensive twenty-four hour coverage. This, of course, has important implications for call management. Similarly, departments may consider disbanding or reducing criminal investigation divisions in order to have more uniformed officers with broader responsibilities—including investigations—to fully implement community policing. Needless to say, an effort to organize around processes will generate some negative reactions by many involved. It will be viewed as an inordinate expansion of program scope, but may be one that is required to fully (and effectively) see the benefits of this initiative.

The Scope of Police Operations

Many daily responsibilities of the police—such as answering calls for service, taking reports, traffic control—will continue under a community policing model, although in some cases, the method of handling the issue will differ. Beyond these activities, community police officers will perform additional duties to meet unique community demands or solve problems. By broadening the scope of officers' duties, are we making them more professional or more like "craftsmen"? How do we reconcile the differences between "community policing" and "problem-solving"? To what extent is it reasonable to respond to community demands that are on the periphery or outside the statutory mandate of the police (i.e., noncriminal problems)? At what point, if any, can we let go of traditional police activities (e.g., responding to nearly all calls, preventive patrol, or fast response times) to replace this with other work, such as problem-solving or being community organizers? These are important questions that have complex answers.

Inherent in any community policing endeavor is the *operational* impact of "program scope". Defining the actual activities for which officers are responsible and facilitating those activities poses significant problems the department must reconcile. For example, if community police officers are permitted to use "flex time" in their shifts this may pose both coverage problems for calls as well as animosity among other officers who do not have the flex time option. However, alternating shift times may be important for community police officers to accomplish their tasks. To resolve this operational paradox, police administrators tend to follow the easy path—forbidding the controversial activity, in this case, flex time. Yet, operational complexities must be addressed and resolved if community policing successes are to be realized.

There is no doubt that some abuses will occur. For example, in Houston during the 1980s, some officers were assigned to focus their efforts on "beat integrity." As implemented, officers used their own initiative to define problems, contact citizens, and perform whatever tasks the officer deemed necessary to reduce crime and manage public concerns in the beat. In many cases, officers were essentially "out of service" for the entire shift, and therefore unavailable to handle calls. Similarly, because officers were "out of touch," they frequently had no contact with supervisors throughout the shift, leading to some abuse of their discretionary "free time". One legend was that some officers would report to work and then attempt to drive to San Antonio, have their picture taken in front of the Alamo, and return to Houston before the end of their shift. These officers obviously were not professionally responsible and showed this through the abuse of their autonomy. (Regarding whether this legend is true, one police official said, "I've seen several pictures of HPD cars in front of the Alamo.") An important lesson from this experience is that flexibility and creativity can be implemented, but that does not absolve the need for accountability and supervision.

The operational scope of the police department is inextricably related to, first, the executive's interpretation of the community policing philosophy and, second, the management philosophy and values that the executive practices. These are put into practice via the corporate strategy of the department. "Defining a corporate strategy helps an organization, its employees, and its executives[understand the police department's mission]. An explicit corporate strategy tells outsiders who invest in the organization what the organization proposes to do and how it proposes to do it."[25]

Ideally the corporate strategy would be developed through a multi-stage approach, described as an:

> . . . iterative process that examines how the organization's capabilities fit the current and future environment. . . . A strategy is defined when the executive discovers the best way to use his[or her] organization to meet the challenges or exploit the opportunities in the environment.[26]

Unfortunately, this has all too frequently been done on an ad hoc basis as a reaction to changing trends in policing and changing demands of the community. This "catch-up" approach lacks vision, planning, and thoughtfulness, thereby limiting the efficiency and effectiveness of the police organization.

INGREDIENTS NECESSARY FOR COMMUNITY POLICING TO WORK

In a publication for the National Center for Community Policing, Harvard scholar Francis X. Hartmann, former New York City Police Commissioner Lee P. Brown, and St. Petersburg, Florida City Administrator Darrel W. Stephens discuss "what it takes" for community policing to work. The issues they present and questions they pose provide important insights to the understanding of community policing policies.[27]

Mission Statement

Does the department have an updated mission statement? Does it speak expressly of a partnership with the community? Is it actively promulgated among the officers and in the community? Has the department worked to develop and promulgate a set of values about what is important to the department? Do the values emphasize community involvement? Do the values include the importance of the officers? Are the values stressed as the guiding principles of the organization? Are they simple and straightforward? Is each officer familiar with them?

Decentralization

What problems do neighborhood police handle? Is responsibility for response to a problem likely to remain in the area and with the area officers and go to central as necessary, or vice versa?

Problem Solving

Is the patrol function exercised in a random fashion or is it directed toward problem solving? In the course of most ordinary working days, are the officers cruising the streets in cars waiting for a call from dispatch, or are they spending the bulk of their time addressing specific problems? Do the officers seek out problems? Do the officers attempt to determine the impact of their work?

Public Involvement

Are there mechanisms which allow the community to identify problems? Are these mechanisms generally known to the community? Or, must individual citizens and groups ask for special meetings?

How is the community involved in policymaking? Wide variations are possible, but meetings should be held with regularity and predictability. Meetings should involve police decision-makers, including the chief, rather than community-relations specialists. Community representatives should include not only safe, conservative persons with a stake in the area, but also those with whom the police are traditionally less comfortable.

Attitude Toward Citizens

If one sits in the communications room, what messages, both direct and indirect, are given to citizens who call the police? What is the role of response time? Is a policy on police response explained to callers in a nonabrasive fashion? Do officers disparage particular neighborhoods as being crime-ridden and not worth living in? Apart from ordinary daily cynicism, is there a sense of respect for the community being policed? Are most police waiting for "twenty and out," or are they dedicated to policing as a profession?

Management Systems

Does the department have management systems which support community policing? Given the fact that the officer on the street now has different responsibilities toward the community, does the management structure support those responsibilities? Have the roles of the first-line supervisors and managers, from lieutenant on up to the chief, changed? Have these roles been redefined to support the patrol and other functions interacting in partnership with the community around problem solving? Do mechanisms exist which promote communication between the patrol officers and the geographical area, or are the officers on their own to figure that out? Does the structure of the organization help them to get to know the community, or must the officers do this *despite* the organization? Do the officers feel that the organization encourages them to reach out for help with problems?

Performance Evaluation and Rewards

Is the department attempting to judge performance on measures related to quality of life rather than by the numbers of arrests and/or citations? Is there an attempt to develop processes of reward, recognition, and perhaps promotion which value permanence of assignment, knowledge of a community, and problem solving? If traditional rank structure is not helpful for community policing values, is the department attempting to address that issue?

Training

What is the focus of training, both in-service and for new recruits? Does information being imparted focus on problem solving, a sense of the way that the community experiences problems, how the city staffs various areas and functions, and to what agencies the community and the police look for assistance in problem solving?

Beat Boundaries

Does the department recognize, or is it in the process of working to recognize, existing *neighborhoods?* Are the departmental lines of responsibility consistent with areas of residence or commerce in the manner in which the citizens think about them? Or, does the department superimpose its own boundaries and precincts without regard for the citizenry's sense of boundaries? Are officers assigned to geographical areas with such regularity that there is a relationship of mutual knowledge between the officer and persons who live, work, or regularly use the area? Do many of these persons know the officer(s) by name, and would the officer be missed if he or she did not appear for a few days?

Elected Officials

Are the major elected officials familiar with what the police department is doing? Do they support it?

Program versus Philosophy

Is the community policing philosophy restricted to only part of the department, a unit or a program, or is it department- and community-wide? If it is not community-wide, is there movement in that direction? Does it include the lower ranks as well as the chief? Are the responsibilities of meeting with the community, problem solving, and the like perceived as the obligations of the whole department, or only of a special unit?

Media

How do the newspapers treat police issues? Is response time portrayed as a major criterion of police quality? Is Uniform Crime Report (UCR) data utilized as the major criterion of police performance? Is quality of life a criterion for which the police have some responsibility? Would a review of news clippings convey a sense that the police believe that they share responsibility with the community?

The Ideal Community Policing Department

No department is a paragon of the values represented by the concept of community policing, nor is there "one all-inclusive model" of CoP. Departments will differ in the ways they address the issues. There are, for example, many different ways of effectively including the community in policy discussions. Yet, these issues, if discussed at all levels of a department, can help steer the department in the direction in which good policing seems to be going.

APPLICATIONS OF THE COMMUNITY POLICING CONCEPT: SOME LANDMARK MODELS

A decade ago the term *community policing* was virtually unknown. Two scholars led the way in introducing the concept to law enforcement. Professor Robert Trojanowicz, Michigan State University, conducted the landmark research in Flint, Michigan under what was then known as Neighborhood Foot Patrol. Professor Herman Goldstein, University of Wisconsin, had his vision of Problem-Oriented Policing tested in Newport News, Virginia. The thoughts, publications, and research of these pioneers have been converted to practice by police departments across the United States as well as in other countries.

According to a study by PERF, nearly 41 percent of American police agencies serving populations of 50,000 or more were employing CoP. Another 19 percent indicated that they were developing CoP policies, and 11 percent planned on developing community policing policies within the next year.[28] A number of departments have played a leadership role in testing the concept. The following discussion provides a sample of the early experiments and illustrates how the concept has been applied.

Flint, Michigan: Neighborhood Foot Patrol

Professor Robert C. Trojanowicz reflected on the words of his father, a retired police officer, that the police had to be tough on crime but also help the citizens deal with crises they faced. The police officer was a public servant in the broadest sense, so he or she must be willing to do the job—albeit distasteful at times—and prepared to do it firmly and professionally, yet compassionately.

With funding support from the Charles Mott Foundation, Professor Trojanowicz worked cooperatively with the Flint Police Department to divide the city into "foot beats." In one important sense, Neighborhood Foot Patrol was *not* the same as foot patrol of the past. Officers were instructed, and given the flexibility, to be community organizers, community leaders, and problem solvers. The experiment emphasized that Neighborhood Foot Patrol was "tough on crime" and provided full-service law enforcement. The difference was the *method* of police service delivery and the increased responsibility of citizens to help themselves through such activities as volunteerism and Neighborhood Watch.

The Flint experiment emphasized the officers' "ownership" of their patrol beats. They had broad responsibilities for controlling crime and this included making the neighborhood they patrolled a better place in which to live. As was appropriate, officers were given wide flexibility in their working hours and in decisions related to the types of activities they used to accomplish their goals. They were urged to be creative and were evaluated based on their accomplishments within the neighborhood.[29]

Neighborhood Foot Patrol in Flint was a milestone in the CoP movement. It showed that alternate means of police management and operations were feasible and cost effective. It also showed that the community could be motivated to support the police and accept a new approach to policing. Just as important, the Flint experiment also directed attention toward additional research areas which need to be explored for the development of community policing.

Newport News, Virginia: Problem-Oriented Policing

Based on the concept of problem solving discussed by Professor Herman Goldstein,[30] a model to identify, analyze, and resolve specific community problems was developed. Following a pilot test of the concept, the National Institute of Justice funded the comprehensively evaluated Problem-Oriented Policing (POP) program in Newport News, Virginia. POP involves looking at police responsibilities from a different perspective. The police have traditionally viewed crimes and calls for service as *individual* incidents. The police response is therefore *reactive*, with the police viewing the incident as an individual occurrence rather than part of an aggregate problem. In POP, the

> police go beyond individual crimes and calls for service and take on the underlying problems that create them. To understand problems, police collect facts from a wide variety of sources, from outside as well as inside police agencies. To develop and implement solutions police enlist the support of other public and private agencies and individuals. *Problem-Oriented Policing is a department-wide strategy aimed at solving persistent community problems. Police identify, analyze, and respond to the underlying circumstances that create incidents* (emphasis in original).[31]

Thus, POP is a *proactive* strategy requiring a diagnosis of community problems and integration of the community in the response. Like Neighborhood Foot Patrol, POP required creativity and officer initiative. In addition, POP required that police management delegate more authority to officers and permit increased flexibility in decision-making.

The NIJ evaluation of the project tested two premises: (1) that police officers in any assignment could use these techniques as part of their daily routine, and (2) that problem-solving efforts would be effective. The evaluation found that both premises were true. It was recognized that officers would always have to respond to some incidents, but the POP approach made better use of departmental resources while increasing officer effectiveness.[32] The success of the Newport News experiment convinced NIJ to fund an extension of POP targeted specifically at drugs in San Diego, Tulsa, Atlanta, and Philadelphia. The project was evaluated by PERF with the results being consistent with the Newport News findings. The hope is that

POP will serve as a CoP tool applicable to both general and directed police responsibilities.

Baltimore County, Maryland: Community Foot Patrol Officer

The idea of the Community Foot Patrol Officer (CFPO) project can be found in Baltimore County's Citizen-Oriented Police Enforcement (COPE) program. COPE was designed to use the problem-oriented policing approach to identify and reduce fear of crime. COPE's success on this limited scale helped influence the department to organize a broader CoP approach. The mission of the CFPO is

> . . . to gain the trust and confidence of citizens within targeted communities to identify the true origins of their fears and concerns about crime and other forms of community disorder . . . and to seek appropriate solutions. While some of the identified problems may call for traditional police tactics, CFPOs must also consider nontraditional approaches and use their newly established partnerships to encourage citizen "self help" responses within the community.[33]

The department's findings reinforce the point that CFPOs are full-service law enforcement officers who not only walk foot beats but also

- Identify problems
- Interact with the community
- Diagnose potential problems, and
- Develop solutions that use resources from both inside and outside the department

Community foot patrol officers are evaluated on three types of information:

- *Input data*—describing the community and problems targeted
- *Activity data*—describing the tasks and activities performed by the CFPO
- *Results data*—describing the outcomes of CFPO actions (i.e., the officer's progress in solving community problems)

Note that these factors do not rely solely on traditional quantitative measures but include qualitative factors that reflect both effort and accomplishment. Another important element of CFPO is that, as a county department, the effects of CoP have been applied to rural areas.

Newark, New Jersey: Foot Patrol and Fear Reduction

CoP in Newark developed in stages, beginning with the Newark Foot Patrol Experiment. After passage of the Safe and Clean Neighborhood Act, Newark used its funding to implement foot patrol, with the goal of developing safe neighborhoods through the use of walking police officers. The officers were expected to maintain high visibility and communicate with both the residents and merchants in their assigned areas on matters related to crime and crime control. Although not as comprehensive as Neighborhood Foot Patrol in Flint, the Newark project was broader than "traditional" foot patrol.

The results of the project, which was evaluated by the Police Foundation, suggested that citizens were more aware of the police presence in foot patrol areas (as

PROBLEM-ORIENTED POLICING

The research on Problem-Oriented Policing (POP) placed the community policing (CoP) philosophy into a professional discussion of how to address a wide range of law enforcement responsibilities. Professor Herman Goldstein's work on this concept provides excellent insight into the policy application of the approach. Similarly, the work of John Eck and William Spelman presents a scientific framework that illustrates POP as well as empirically tests it. In their work, Eck and Spelman conceptualized the problem-solving process as a series of logical steps—scanning, analysis, response, assessment, and feedback—illustrated in the center of Figure 3-1. As further illustrated in this figure, an actual case application of POP/CoPs, the process inherently involves both the police and the community. CoP requires a commitment to change by both, working interactively, albeit in different roles.

This particular case study addresses a quality-of-life issue where Officer Cynthia Avery, of the Ann Arbor Police Department, applied POP to deal with a problem that had persisted for years.

The city of Ann Arbor, Michigan, is a generally "upscale" community a few miles west of Detroit. The city is a Metropolitan Statistical Area of some 200,000 people and home of the University of Michigan, a school of about 38,000 students. The Ann Arbor Police Department, an accredited law enforcement agency, serves the university as well as the city.

University cities often have some type of conflict between "town" and "gown." Citizens tend to view the transient students as disrespectful, too interested in partying, and generally disruptive. Similarly, college students tend to view the citizens as "them"; they feel that the citizens do not appreciate the revenue the students bring into the city; that the citizens are too cranky and make complaints against the students because of who they are, not what they may be doing. Ann Arbor is similar to many other university towns in this regard.

For several years residents from one neighborhood had been calling the police to complain about a fraternity. The complaints were typically related to noise, loud stereos, shouting, and "party noise," but also included such things as walking across citizens' yards and urinating in public. When officers responded to the calls they would drive down the streets listening for the noise, contacting the fraternity if they heard a disruption or contacting the complainants if further information was needed.

A number of approaches had been attempted to deal with the problem: asking the fraternity members to stop the noise, issuing formal warnings, developing "noise patrols," working with the prosecuting attorney to redefine how the city ordinances could be applied for entering fraternity houses and making arrests, issuing citations, working with the courts to increase the monetary damages assessed for noise violations to help offset the cost of the noise patrols, and even creation of a $10,000 peace bond. None of these efforts worked—at least for any length of time. It is important to note that while some of these strategies were innovative, they remained *reactive*.

POP is *proactive*, requiring a careful analysis of the problem and the development of solutions that are effective, preventive, and long-lasting. Officer Avery, receiving another noise complaint about the fraternity one evening, decided to attack the problem from a problem-solving approach. She looked beyond the symptoms characterized by the complaint, e.g., the noise, and began analyzing the broader dynamics involved, starting with a visit to the complainants.

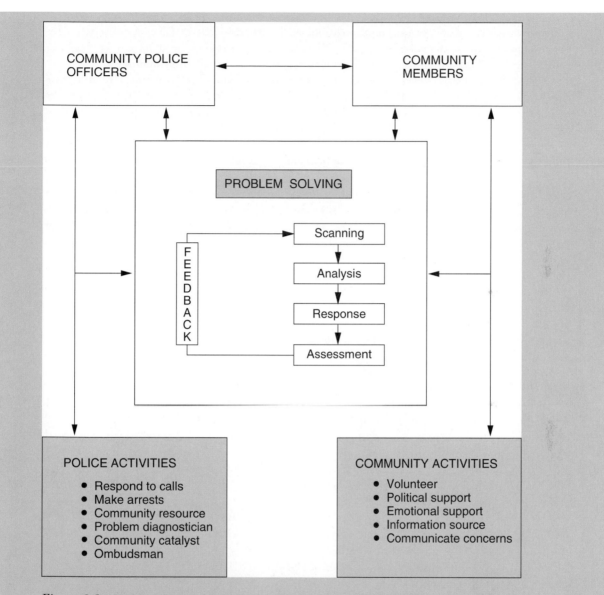

Figure 3-1 Problem-Oriented Policing and Its Constituent Relationships

As she drove down the street to the complainant's house she listened, but could hear no noise from the fraternity. The complainants were pleased when Officer Avery contacted them because this was rarely done. They were also taken aback when she explained that she could not hear any noise, either from the street or in front of the house. They asked her to come into the home, where she was surprised to her the music and noise from the party quite clearly. What she learned, after closer inspection, was that the unique geography of the area as well as the design of the fraternity house acoustically focused the noise toward the back of the homes in the neighborhood, yet was virtually inaudible on the street or in front of the house.

Officer Avery met with both the Neighborhood Association and the fraternity, finding both to be empathic with the other's concerns. Both groups seemed to want to resolve the problem

(continued)

and work with the other, yet a communications wall seemed to exist. Officer Avery recognized her next problem-solving role: open lines of communication between the groups and serve as a catalyst to help both parties solve the problem in a mutually satisfactory manner.

Officer Avery met with the fraternity president and explained the problem. He was enthusiastic about developing a solution that would go beyond the immediate year; he wanted to develop a long-lasting solution. The president asked Officer Avery to convey this to the Neighborhood Association while he prepared a document to serve as the fraternity's ground rules—a "contract for quiet." Following a presentation at the Neighborhood Association, Officer Avery found the citizens to be enthusiastic at the fraternity's intent, but somewhat skeptical.

She continued to lay the foundation for communications between the groups while at the same time explaining the police role and authority on matters related to noise problems. For example, the community members knew little about the law, how busy the police are, and enforcement options. Over three meetings, Officer Avery provided public education to the group, culminating with the Neighborhood Association's president going on a ride-along with her—an experience that proved to be *very* instructive. Similarly, she continued to explain police policy and law to the fraternity with respect to noise complaints.

Officer Avery's role as a catalyst served not only to educate the public, but also led to specific action by the fraternity. For example, after the fraternity president was shown the geographic problems contributing to the noise problem, he did two things. First, the plans for an intended renovation of the fraternity house were taken back to the architect for re-design to minimize the noise problem. Second, the fraternity built a "noise fence" at the back of their property, which not only muffled sound but also served to keep people from crossing neighbors' yards (and at least hid most of the public urination)!

A critical point was getting the fraternity and neighborhood group together in order to talk about their problems and formalize their solutions. At this point, Officer Avery "stepped back," taking a less active role in the communications so that the citizens and fraternity would work together directly. Her thought on this approach was that if the two became used to talking with each other directly, there would be less tendency to call the police when a problem arose.

The fraternity began feeling a sense of ownership in the neighborhood, contributing to a stronger relationship between "town and gown." The citizens similarly began to feel an ownership in the fraternity, often referring to them as "our fraternity." Both groups also felt ownership in Officer Avery. They feel comfortable talking with her about problems related to the police and their newly developed alliance.

Some important points in this experience show how POP works as well as the role of an officer. *First*, Officer Avery served as a line of communication between the groups and with the police. Exchanging thoughts, concerns, and ideas was an essential beginning point. *Second*, she served as an analyst to fully understand the problem at issue and look at its long-range dynamics. *Third*, she acted as a catalyst for action between the groups, encouraging their ongoing communications and development of ideas. *Fourth*, she consciously avoided "telling" either group what they should do. Although she facilitated and communicated their ideas, she wanted responses to the problem to be the product of those involved. *Fifth*, she was a public educator about law and police processes, a role she found to be important because both groups were making erroneous assumptions. *Sixth*, Officer Avery recognized the need for time and patience. The problem had been brewing for years and no "solution" had worked thus far. She recognized that time was necessary to get the groups talking, to develop ideas, to put them in place, and to see if they worked. It also required dedication of her personal time to work on the problem and, in particular, to meet with the Neighborhood Association. *Seventh*, she recognized that the relationship would remain fragile and that she was a critical link in the chain. As a result, she maintains contact with both groups and shepherds their initiatives. *Finally,* she recognizes that the solution to the problem is not absolute; it will require ongoing commitment and a method to maintain the relationship.

Police problem-solving requires innovation and creativity. It recognizes that quality-of-life issues must be addressed just as crime problems are and that proactive, future-oriented actions can contribute to more efficient policing as well as effective service delivery.

John Eck and William Spelman, *Problem-Solving* (Washington, D.C.: Police Executive Research Forum, 1987).
Herman Goldstein, *Problem-Oriented Policing* (New York: McGraw-Hill, 1990).

opposed to motor patrol). Residents also felt that serious crime had diminished in their neighborhoods and said they felt safer. These findings were particularly important because there was no statistical difference in either reported crime or victimization (determined by surveys) between the foot patrol and nonfoot patrol areas. Thus, reduction of fear of crime and improved perceptions of safety were achieved simply by using foot patrol.

Following the successes of the foot patrol project, the department implemented additional CoP strategies as part of the NIJ-sponsored Houston-Newark Fear Reduction Program. This project employed a wider range of activities, including community newsletters and efforts to reduce the signs of crime, neither of which had a significant effect in reducing fear or preventing crime. However, the Coordinated Community Policing program, designed to increase police-community information exchange and to manage both social disorder and physical deterioration, did have a significant positive impact. This points to the importance of citizen involvement in CoP. It provides strong evidence that one-way, proactive community-based police strategies alone are not sufficient.[34]

Houston, Texas: Neighborhood-Oriented Policing

The Houston Neighborhood-Oriented Policing plan was implemented hand-in-hand with a department-wide decentralization. With decentralization, the department attempted to bring all aspects of police service closer to each community it served. This approach would thereby make the police more responsive to the unique characteristics and needs of the diverse neighborhoods throughout the city. Each of four decentralized command stations in Houston had

> . . . a team of police officers and their supervisors [who were] responsible for planning and implementing policing strategies, with the cooperation of neighborhood residents, to address crime problems with specific neighborhood service areas.[35]

The Houston plan spells out the organizational values related to Neighborhood-Oriented Policing. Among them is the recognition that crime prevention is the top priority of the police department; that the police and community must work openly and cooperatively in dealing with crime problems; and that the department will use its resources in an attempt to increase the overall quality of life in Houston rather than simply focusing on individual crimes and crime trends. An assessment of the initial test of Houston's community policing approach found that the project

> . . . appears to have been successful in reducing citizens' levels of fear and in improving their perceptions of their neighborhood and their attitudes toward the

police. . . . The lack of positive program effects for blacks and renters may be a function of their lower levels of awareness of the program. The community station relied, in part, on established civic organizations to attract residents to station programs. To the extent that blacks and renters are less likely to be members of these organizations, the program needs to rely on other means of reaching these people.[36]

With the development of the combined command station and Neighborhood-Oriented Policing plan, these limitations have been addressed by alternate efforts that are more citizen-directed to increase their involvement. In the test phase, the problem of blacks and renters not becoming involved points out the importance of using broad-based, creative means to obtain the greatest participation possible.

NOP was started by former Houston chief Lee P. Brown, and after Brown was named police commissioner in New York City, was continued with a strong commitment from Chief Elizabeth Watson. Watson broadened the decentralization effort and reinforced her support for NOP. In 1992 Watson was relieved as chief after the election of a new mayor. The new chief pledged to continue the NOP project, but it would not be as high a priority.

Detroit, Michigan: Police Mini-Stations

In the Detroit model, defined areas of the city were targeted as neighborhoods where the quality of life could be enhanced by decentralized, community-based police mini-stations. Officers serving in the mini-station were assigned to a neighborhood with the specific responsibility of being community organizers and stimulators on matters related to crime control, fear reduction, and increased quality of life. Generally, the mini-station officer was to be proactive while the regular "beat cars" handled calls for service (reactive). To be included, neighborhoods had to meet certain criteria:

- Neighborhood with pervasive crime problems and fear of crime
- Predominantly residential
- High number of calls for service

The foundation of the program rested on two important concepts: (1) the officer had to become acquainted with the residents in the area and diagnose their unique crime and quality-of-life problems, and (2) the mini-station had to involve citizen volunteers in multiple capacities in order to develop programs that would address neighborhood problems. Mini-station officers were given complete responsibility for developing programs in their assigned areas. To fulfill this responsibility, they were given wide flexibility and permitted to explore nontraditional police responses to community conditions (whether they were of a criminal or noncriminal nature). Moreover, the mini-station supervisors evaluated officers on nontraditional qualitative factors of effort.

The Detroit program was not formally evaluated, but some internal assessments found positive results. For example, Neighborhood Watch and Vertical Watch (i.e., high-rise apartments and businesses) memberships increased and participation levels were sustained. Intelligence information and crime clearances increased and positive comments to the police department and city manager became commonplace. In addition, informal feedback from the officers involved in the project indicated that residents liked the program and that improvement in the appearance of some neighborhoods was obvious. These successes spurred the expansion of the program to other parts of the city.[37]

OTHER PROGRAMMING INITIATIVES

As a result of the growth of community policing—particularly as influenced by the COPS grant programs—many initiatives have evolved that are too extensive to individually document. Included are such diverse innovations as:

- Resident officer programs, wherein officers are given a housing supplement and live in the neighborhood they are responsible for policing
- Public housing units, where officers are permanently assigned to a public housing apartment complex with the purpose of getting to know the residents and responding to both reported crime and the specific problems that concern residents
- Sophisticated crime analysis, which assesses reported crime, calls for service, officer-initiated activity, time stratifications of officer activity, and uncommitted officer time balanced with geographic information systems that not only map the neighborhood but also contain demographic data
- Beat management plans on laptop computers to assist officers in problem solving and "self-deployment"
- Police department Internet home pages and listservs designed for enhanced communications and information exchange
- Expanded youth programs of all kinds, but particularly those based in the schools, which include Education Resource Officers, DARE officers, GREAT officers, and community-based officers whose "neighborhood" of assignment is a school
- Crime-specific suppression and enforcement programs as a problem-solving response to unique crime patterns and crime problems

The important point to note is that all of these are proactive, nontraditional, creative police initiatives specifically designed to meet the problems and needs of *individual* communities. This is the essence of community policing.

A CRITIQUE OF COMMUNITY POLICING

The early development and assessment of initiatives that ultimately led to community policing occurred with little consistency between the projects. In the early cases—for example, Flint, Newport News, Houston, Newark, and Baltimore County—there was little coordination between the programs largely because they were developed independently of each other. Conceptually the programs had similar ideas that researchers and administrators wanted tested to see if they would work. Moreover, the projects were evaluated by different organizations in relative isolation.

Most criticism of community policing programs can be viewed from two perspectives: (1) research/evaluation design, and (2) concept. In the case of the former, Greene and Taylor[38] identify several deficiencies in the tested programs. These include

- An inadequate operational definition of "community"
- Confusion about the appropriate level of analysis
- Design of the experiment to be able to adequately test the effects of CoP on specific variables (such as crime or fear of crime)
- Defining the "treatment" effect—that is, clearly and specifically defining what activities and factors constituted community policing
- Controls on how the "treatment" was implemented
- A lack of specification of the hypothesized outcomes of the experiments (hypotheses generally tested *a posteriori* instead of *a priori*)

To be sure, these methodological limitations have been present in a number of the studies. To a large extent, these limitations have been a function of two factors. First, the programs and evaluations were of an exploratory nature. Operation and control of variables were implemented to varying (and inconsistent) degrees; however, not all variables were clearly identified until the experiments were underway. Many of the specific policing activities were dependent on officer initiative and citizen responses. These factors were largely unknown and unanticipated until the research exploration was underway.

A second methodological problem was attempting to experiment with different policing tactics and activities in actual law enforcement agencies. Particularly in exploratory research, when the effects and outcomes of a concept are unknown, there is risk in the experimentation. Great care must be taken in order to protect the safety, security, and rights of the citizens. This is an ongoing issue in all aspects of research in policing. It is apparent that the actual policing responsibilities of the agency must take precedence over research design. These facets do not negate the threats to validity and reliability, but they do address the reasons for the limitations. Follow-up research currently being conducted by the National Center for Community Policing, the National Institute of Justice, and the Police Executive Research Forum are employing more rigorous methodologies in light of what was learned in the earlier research efforts.

The second area of criticism deals with the basic concept of community policing. There is concern by some critics about the propriety and viability inherent in the CoP philosophy. It may be argued that community policing is a solicitous attempt by the police to get into the good graces of the community. From another perspective, it may be argued that the police should take on no responsibilities beyond those of crime control and response to emergencies. It is also argued by critics that efforts to expand police responsibilities into quality-of-life issues are an improper broadening of police powers that may impinge on the democratic process. The responses to these criticisms are largely found in ideological differences. Police executives who support the CoP concept view the police as a social-service agency chartered by the community to address a wide range of social ills, ranging from major crime to barking dogs. It is a philosophical difference between administrative beliefs about policing that cannot be easily reconciled from either a legal or research perspective. I would argue that it is the prerogative of the police administrator to make a philosophical statement about the best manner to provide police service to the community and then follow that philosophy with a plan of action.

A Perspective

Community policing is not the exclusive province of the United States. It has emerged somewhat independently in other countries, because of their unique social, cultural, economic, and legal needs. Despite the differences, several fundamental elements remain the same. It was developed on a worldwide scale based on a recognition of the need to involve the community in policing processes. Australia, Canada, Germany, Thailand, Zambia, Sweden, Denmark, Finland, Great Britain, Japan, and Singapore have CoP models. While not definite, a general transition process appears to have emerged:

- First, the recognition is that traditional police approaches have not succeeded.
- Second, attitudes about the police function among administrators, line personnel, and citizens must change.

- Third, community assessments must be performed to identify new police responsibilities.
- Fourth, new organizational and operational approaches must be conceived to meet the newly defined police responsibilities.
- Fifth, the community must be enlisted to work cooperatively with the police to achieve the desired results.
- Finally, there must be a commitment both by law enforcement and the community to continue the program's growth.

Change is difficult for any organization. For police departments, which are paramilitary, bureaucratic structures with members who have been socially isolated from the community as a result of their occupation, attempts at change are particularly challenging. A common response in all people is to resist change—to say that a new approach will not work. This chapter has shown that many previously sacred beliefs about policing have been forced to give way to new ideas after research suggested that there may be flaws in the traditional logic. Based on that knowledge, law enforcement leaders explored new police responsibilities and different operational tactics. Within this framework, community policing evolved and grew as evaluations pointed the way. Naysayers have begun to look at the concept anew. They have witnessed how it flourishes in numerous departments, and though some still will not concede that it can work, at least they are willing to take a fresh look at the possibilities.

QUESTIONS FOR DISCUSSION

1. Explain in your own words the concept of *community policing*.
2. How does community policing differ from traditional police community relations?
3. Two national commission of the 1960s examined the riots and disorder of that decade. Discuss their significant findings as they relate to the contemporary concept of community policing.
4. The Kansas City Preventive Patrol Study was one of the most important research projects conducted in law enforcement. Discuss what made this study so important.
5. Discuss the factors that make police response time an important, and sometimes controversial, issue in policing.
6. The research clearly shows that one-officer police cars are both more efficient and safer than two-officer cars. Why is this an emotional issue with many police officers who prefer two-officer cars?

7. One of the most controversial police personnel issues of today is related to how a police officer's performance is evaluated. Discuss the issues related to traditional *quantitative* evaluation of performance as compared to the *qualitative* performance desired with community policing.
8. What is the purpose of having the police survey the community they police? How could this information be used?
9. The author states that "No department is a paragon of the values represented by the concept of community policing, nor is there one all-inclusive model of CoP." Why can there be no "singular model" of community policing?
10. Discuss the conceptual similarities and operational differences between the different community policing projects discussed in the chapter.

NOTES

1. Amended from Robert C. Trojanowicz and David L. Carter, *The Philosophy and Role of Community Policing* (East Lansing, MI: National Center for Community Policing, 1988). John Eck and William Spelman, *Problem-Solving* (Washington, DC: Police Executive Research Forum, 1987).
2. National Commission on the Causes and Prevention of Violence, *Law and Order Reconsidered*. (Washington, DC: U.S. Government Printing Office, 1969), p. 292.

3. David L. Carter, Allen D. Sapp, and Darrel W. Stephens, *The State of Police Education: Police Direction for the 21st Century* (Washington, DC: Police Executive Research Forum, 1988).
4. George L. Kelling, et al, *The Kansas City Preventive Patrol Experiment: Technical Report* (Washington, DC: Police Foundation, 1974).
5. Kansas City, Missouri Police Department, *Response Time Analysis: Executive Summary* (Kansas City, MO: Board of Police Commissioners, 1977), p. 23.

6. William Spelman and Dale Brown, *Calling the Police: Citizen Reporting of Serious Crime* (Washington, DC: National Institute of Justice, 1984), p. xi.

7. Michael Farmer, *Differential Police Response Strategies* (Washington, DC: Police Executive Research Forum, 1981).

8. Thomas McEwen, et al., *Evaluation of the Differential Police Response Field Test* (Washington, DC: National Institute of Justice, 1969), pp. 16–17.

9. John E. Boydston, et al, *Patrol Staffing in San Diego* (Washington, DC: Police Foundation, 1977), pp. 69–70.

10. Richard C. Larson and Michael Cahn, *Synthesizing and Extending the Results of Police Patrol Studies* (Washington, DC: National Institute of Justice, 1985), p. 95.

11. Bureau of Justice Statistics, *Report to the Nation on Crime and Justice* (Washington, DC: U.S. Department of Justice, 1988).

12. See Michael Levine and J. Thomas McEwen, *Patrol Development* (Washington, DC: National Institute of Justice, 1985).

13. Ibid., BJS, 1988; Michael Cahn and James M. Tien, *An Evaluation Report of an Alternative Approach in Police Response: The Wilmington Management of Demand Program* (Cambridge, MA: Public Systems Evaluation, Inc., 1980).

14. Ibid., BJS, 1988.

15. Ibid., BJS, 1988; David C. Couper, *Quality Policing: The Madison Experience* (Washington DC: Police Executive Research Forum, 1991).

16. See Robert C. Trojanowicz and Bonnie Bucqueroux, *Toward Development of Meaningful and Effective Performance Evaluations* (East Lansing, MI: National Center for Community Policing, 1991); Gerald Whitaker, et al, *Basic Issues in Police Performance* (Washington, DC: National Institute of Justice, 1982).

17. Darrel W. Stephens and Robert O Heck, "ICAP Is Many Things to Many Agencies," *Law Enforcement News* (December 17, 1981), p. 1.

18. Robert C. Trojanowicz and Bonnie Bucqueroux, *Community Policing*. (Cincinnati, OH: Anderson Publishing Company, 1990), p. 5.

19. George L. Kelling and Mark H. Moore, "The Evolving Strategy of Policing." *Perspectives on Policing #4*. (Washington, DC: Harvard University and National Institute of Justice, 1988), p. 11.

20. Mark H. Moore and Robert C. Trojanowicz, "Corporate Strategies for Policing." *Perspectives on Policing #6*. (Washington, DC: Harvard University and National Institute of Justice, 1988), p. 8.

21. Herman Goldstein, *Problem-Oriented Policing*. (New York, NY: McGraw-Hill Company, 1990), p. 3.

22. David L. Carter and Allen D. Sapp, "Issues and Perspective of Law Enforcement Accreditation: A National Study of Police Chiefs". *Journal of Criminal Justice* 1994 (21:5) pp. 187–210.

23. David Couper and Sabine Lobitz, "Leadership for Change: A National Agenda." *The Police Chief* 1993 (December), pp. 15–19.

24. Michael Hammer and James Champy, *Reengineering the Corporation*. (New York, NY: Harper Business, 1993).

25. Ibid., Moore and Trojanowicz, p. 2.

26. Ibid.

27. The concepts in this section are amended from Francis X. Hartmann, Lee P. Brown and Darrel W. Stephens, *Community Policing: Would You Know If If You Saw It?* (East Lansing, MI: National Center for Community Policing, 1989).

28. David L. Carter, Allen D. Sapp, and Darrel W. Stephens, *Survey of Contemporary Police Issues: Critical Findings* (Washington, DC: Police Executive Research Forum, 1991).

29. Robert C. Trojanowicz (undated), *The Neighborhood Foot Patrol Program in Flint, Michigan* (East Lansing, MI: National Neighborhood Foot Patrol Center).

30. Herman Goldstein, *Problem-Oriented Policing* (New York: McGraw-Hill, 1990).

31. Ibid., Eck and Spelman, 1987, p. xv.

32. Ibid., Eck and Spelman, 1987.

33. Baltimore County Police, Field Operations Bureau, *Community Foot Patrol Officer Guidelines and Procedures* (Towson, MD: Baltimore County Police Department, 1988).

34. George Kelling, *The Newark Foot Patrol Experiment* (Washington, DC: Police Foundation, 1981).

35. Kathryn Whitmire and Lee P. Brown (undated) *City of Houston Command Station/Neighborhood Oriented Policing Overview* (Houston: Houston Police Department) p. 2.

36. Ibid.

37. See Jerome Skolnick and David Bailey, *The New Blue Line* (New York: The Free Press, 1986).

38. Jack Greene and Ralph Taylor, "Community Based Policing and Foot Patrol: Issues of Theory and Evaluation," in *Community Policing: Rhetoric or Reality?*, J. Greene and S. Mastrofski, eds. (New York: Praeger Press, 1988).

Chapter 4

ETHICS AND THE POLICE

The police as well as other agents of criminal justice are basically concerned with human behavior. Therefore, criminal justice is saturated with questions of ethics. This means a concern for norms of conduct; for the rightness and wrongness of actions, and for the values that are the yardsticks for such judgments. Law is the formal codification of certain values of a society or culture. Since law is comprised of standards of proper or acceptable conduct, law and ethics are inextricably linked. Civil laws reflect governmental decisions rooted in civil authority. Ethics goes to conscience, frequently to a higher level of authority. Therefore, for some individuals, a conflict between specific laws and personal ethics may occur—a disharmony, as they may view it, between civil and divine mandates.

In recognizing how police officers develop their occupational ethics, the pragmatist must accept the fact that officer behavior is not always perfectly consistent with law and formally articulated policy. This does not mean that an officer's behavior is without moral implications. "Even a bent policeman has a conscience, as a British police official who resigned on principle once observed."[1] The questions we must ask are: What are the parameters of conscience? How are those parameters developed? Are the ethics of police officers skewed by the officers' occupational experiences? Is a formally articulated code of ethics merely symbolic or does the code help guide officer decision-making? What subcultural factors of the police environment influence police ethical development?

Law enforcement officers address these issues from a perspective of "applied ethics." That is, rather than contemplating a line of moral thought on a philosophical level, ethical questions are resolved through consideration of realistic outcomes of a decision. A fundamental element to this approach is the recognition that a *pragmatic* exploration of police ethics is necessary to effectively inculcate these values in the decision-making processes of police officers. This does not mean that philosophical issues should be ignored; it means that they are placed in a utilitarian perspective.

The importance of applied ethics is that they help officers develop a reasoned approach to decision-making instead of making decisions by habit. As such, ethics must be viewed as an admixture of attitudes, characteristics, moral upbringing, and occupational experiences that work together, guiding the working persona and thoughts of police officers. This admixture is important because of the demanding complexity of moral judgments police officers make about depriving people of their liberty and sometimes their lives. Given the largely unchecked discretion police officers exercise, it is incumbent that they be given an ethical foundation to ensure their decisions are *just* and *legal*. Both the letter of the law and spirit of the law must be

"Even a bent policeman has a conscience, as a British police official who resigned on principle once observed."

carefully balanced. As observed by Michael Brown, "Police discretion is above all a behavioral process in which the interpretation of events and the choice of alternatives are strongly influenced by the values and beliefs of the actor."[2] An officer's ethics significantly influences his or her discretion.

Being members of society themselves, police officers share many of the same values as other people. This means that the police will use their discretion in ways which may not fit the ideal of "perfect justice" but conform to a pattern of generally accepted social control. Taken a step further, the officer's decision-making criteria will be further influenced by the officer's experiences as accounted for by the subcultural ethics of policing.

There are two important implications of this phenomenon. First, institutionalized prejudices and values of law enforcement organizations will influence the way the law is enforced. Second, the police must perform their duties within the prevailing moral standards of society in general. Thus, the officer's sense of social morality and the need to attain "justice" may influence his or her behavior and lead the officer to seek this ideal in a manner that is not consistent with constitutional procedures and safeguards. To infuse organizational theory into the discussion, the officer's behavior may stem from the desire to meet *real* goals (e.g., get the offender off the street in any way possible) instead of *stated* goals (e.g., arrest and prosecute offenders according to rigidly defined constitutional standards).

The moral dilemma is further complicated by the occupational environment. A sense of frustration that "the courts will let criminals go" and a feeling of isolation from the community confirm the officer's view that "the public doesn't care about police problems." As a result, this may lead to a stronger sense of moral (vis-à-vis occupational) relief when a degree of justice can be achieved by the officer using his or her discretion on the street.

MORAL PHILOSOPHY IN COLLEGES

In the nineteenth century, moral philosophy—of which ethics is a branch—was the cornerstone of the typical college curriculum. Its origins traceable to medieval universities, moral philosophy was seen as the integrating subject, a force for common social and moral values shared by most people, the "anchor of stability."[3] What has happened to moral philosophy in the college curriculum in the twentieth century is a long and intricate story, the details of which need not delay us here. It is sufficient to recall that while the explosion and fragmentation of knowledge, particularly scientific and technological knowledge, have resulted in a college curriculum of similar character, the same developments have created an argument as to whether science and ethics are compatible. Science deals with quantities, particulars, chance, and probability. Ethics deals with qualities, wholes, purposes, principles, and ideals. Science is seen as "value free," as objective, probable, and always rational. Ethics is seen as subjective, emotive, unprovable, and sometimes even irrational.

In the present century, many educational giants have been involved in efforts to identify some common ground for fact and value in the curriculum, including Francis Greenwood Peabody, James Tufts, John Dewey, Charles L. Stevenson, Alexander Meikeljohn, James Conant, and Robert M. Hutchins. A spinoff of their efforts involved attempts to make a value-free sociology the new integrating force in the curriculum. When this effort failed, what remained was philosophy as a discipline, and its larger context of "liberal" or "general" education and the humanities.

The battle has not ended, nor is it likely to end soon. But today, there appears to be a rebirth of interest and concern for moral philosophy, for ethics, for "a return to basic values," with a renewed vision of the inseparable connection between the moral uses and the unity of knowledge. In large public universities, there are courses in legal ethics, business ethics, medical, and nursing ethics; and, in an increasing number of higher educational criminal justice programs, there are courses in the ethics of criminal justice.

A Charles F. Kettering Foundation-sponsored symposium put the case this way:

> . . . no genuine and enduring relationship can be established between education and values apart from our underlying conceptions of knowledge and ways of knowing. There has arisen in the modern world an increasingly dominant view that we can know only that which we can count, measure, and weigh. In this view—and it often dominates modern education in the schools and in the media—feeling, imagination, the will, intuitive insight are regarded as having little or nothing to do with knowledge and are frequently disparaged as sources of irrationality. In this view of knowledge and knowing, there is no place for purpose, mind, meaning, and values as constituents of reality. In consequence, our conceptions of knowledge often give rise to views of the world that provide little support for human values and for an education in which persons and the values of persons remain central.[4]

It should be noted that there is no quarrel with science and technology in higher education. Any such opposition would be clearly absurd. The plea is for balance—for wholeness—for more recognition that the "hard" and "soft" sides of education must be in symbiosis.

How can we explain the apparent surge to do this? Several reasons have been suggested:

1. In public affairs generally, there is increasing emphasis on *accountability*.
2. Hand in hand with this point, there is increasing attention to self-examination and analysis.
3. Social and political conservatism fuels the incentive to "return to old values."
4. Education in "soft" subject matter is seen as important in "broadening," for leadership and good citizenship.
5. In criminal justice, ethical dilemmas are routine. Many students seek courses that will help them make difficult judgments and decisions more wisely, more sensitively, more competently.

THE COMMUNITY DIMENSION

What is the community dimension in all this? The politics of it is, of course, a partial response to this question, but we must remain mindful that consensus and coalition suggest community as well as political dynamics. Regarding values in education, consensus and coalition are clearly pertinent considerations; indeed they underscore the heart of the problem. What values command sufficient consensus in a given community to make it politically feasible for schools to include them in the curriculum? And *how* is such matter to be taught? By whom?

The problems implied are not unlike the distinction we drew earlier between police authority and police power. Authority in the police context, you will recall, means a consensus of community support for what the officer does and how it is done. Power implies some doubt about such a consensus. Police and community friction arises from the exercise of power that is challenged as arbitrary by some factions of the community. It raises a question of consensus and it tests the boundaries of the social context.

Another point bearing repetition is that unethical behavior or practices in public affairs, often but not always illegal as well, require community complicity. Crooked cops depend upon crooked citizens! As a general rule, there is as much corruption among public officials as a particular community or society will tolerate and patronize.

ABOUT TEACHING ETHICS

Teaching ethics in schools and colleges has certain pedagogical angles meriting brief attention here. First, there is terminology to be clarified, as in any academic discipline. *Descriptive ethics* focuses on how people behave. *Metaethics* focuses on the concepts and terms that underlie reasoning about morals, for example, defining justice. *Normative ethics* focuses on the reasoning process leading to judgments about what is right or wrong and what ought to be done in particular situations. *Applied ethics* is an approach to normative ethics that focuses on making practical choices. By its nature, the function of ethics is practical. *Professional ethics* is a part of applied ethics. It focuses on moral decision-making in work settings.[5]

The study of ethics is partially inductive but mainly deductive. Therefore, its conclusions are not as rigid as mathematics. But sufficient certainty to satisfy the mind of a reasoning person is possible. The mind seeks the truth, the will seeks the good. To live is to act, and action is always for some purpose, to satisfy some need. What is life for? The answer reveals that duty is inseparable from destiny.

Why teach ethics? Daniel Callahan has answered this question as follows:

> Courses in ethics should be taught because morality is part of any reflective personal life, and because ethical perspective and specific moral rules are part of any cultural and civic life. That is only to say that ethical problems are inescapable.[6]

What are some reasonable goals in teaching ethics? Callahan identifies these[7]:

1. Stimulating moral imagination
2. Recognizing ethical issues
3. Eliciting a sense of moral obligation
4. Developing analytical skills
5. Tolerating—and reducing—disagreement and ambiguity

Callahan also lists some doubtful goals[8]:

1. To change student behavior. (It should influence how students *think* about moral issues, and perhaps how they *feel* about such issues.)
2. To present the teacher as a role model. No teacher "can have a full grasp of final moral truth."

These pedagogical observations have an obvious relationship to how a course in ethics is taught. The most important point is that indoctrination has no place in such a course. Great care must be taken to insure free expression and exchange of ideas to avoid turning the course into a propaganda forum for any particular view. Case analysis is an excellent technique, along with role playing and other hands-on exercises. Callahan puts it this way:

> A legitimate goal in the teaching of ethics is to help students develop a means and a process for achieving their own moral judgments. If "moral education" means something more than that—an education in specific moral rules, or specified traits of character—then it is illegitimate.[9]

None of this should be interpreted as meaning that teachers of ethics should be prohibited from espousing a particular moral viewpoint. The vital consideration is to keep open the flow and inevitable clash of views in the classroom. An ethics course should be an exercise in *logic:* rational evaluation of competing theories.

Teaching ethics is not easy, and it is likely to be attacked on such grounds as it:

• Violates the Constitution
• Jeopardizes pluralism
• Teaches religion
• Is "secular humanism"
• Is indoctrination
• Is biased
• Leaves students wishy-washy[10]

The answer to these objections is in sticking to carefully crafted course goals.

One final pedagogical consideration is in order. There is widespread skepticism about the possibilities in teaching ethics. Alasdair MacIntyre speaks to this:

> It is impossible in our culture now to find a systematic way of using such words as "ethical" and "moral" which does not already embody not merely a particular morality but a particular contentious morality which is at war with its rivals . . .[11]

However, it is imperative to recognize that there surely are many shared values and shared rules, even in a society as pluralistic as ours. Gert tells us that a moral rule must meet these tests: (1) it must be completely universal, without reference to person, group, place, or time; (2) it must be understandable by all rational persons; (3) it must be capable of being followed or broken by all rational persons; (4) it must be unchanging and unchangeable; and (5) it must be discovered, not invented.[12]

What are some moral rules that meet these criteria even in our pluralistic American culture? Examples:

- Do not kill
- Do not cause pain
- Do not deprive of freedom of opportunity
- Do not deceive
- Do not break promises
- Do not cheat

The moral rules are oriented to the avoidance of evil, to minimum requirements of morality. The ideals go beyond this, to be encouraged. A moral ideal may justify breaking a moral rule under some circumstances, but a utilitarian ideal does not.[13]

All of these perspectives are, perhaps, most succinctly summarized in the fundamental medical ethic: *Do no harm*. This is a similarly wise ethical principle for police officers.

PROFESSIONAL ETHICS

Before coming to grips with a few specific ethical issues in criminal justice, there is one more area for consideration. This is professional ethics, suggested by the organizational or institutional context of decision-making.

There are some fundamental marks recognized in professionalism: self-monitoring, development of a service ideal, financial gain not a primary goal, client-oriented, and presence of attitudinal factors. All these frequently intoned characteristics of a profession have clear ethical implications. But there are contemporary difficulties with the whole idea of professionalism so much so that the concept seems in danger of losing its significance.

An analysis of what's gone wrong is fair game in a college course, but inappropriate here. Besides, others have done it.[14] The wisdom in the matter points to the universities as having some responsibility for the troubles. Ditto the professional organizations. William May refers to "the institutionalization of professionals and the professionalization of institutions."[15] Professionals themselves share in the responsibility for the troubles, as they settle for minimum standards to protect mediocrity.

One fascinating aspect of professional ethics, of great interest in criminal and civil justice, is paternalism. Again, this is in itself a sizable subject. Consider a few specifics: for example, involuntary guardianship of the physically or mentally incapacitated; drunk driving; regulation of safety (e.g., seat belts, air bags, helmets for motorcyclists); brainwashing; and hypnosis.

The problem of paternalism is to strike a proper balance between needed protection or help and individual liberty or privacy. This is obviously an ethical issue, and as such calls for consensus criteria to guide judgments.

The point is that paternalism is sometimes justifiable, but it is generally thought that professionals are often excessively paternalistic. The case of the so-called "suicide doctor," Dr. Jack Kevorkian ("Dr. Death"), and numerous others dramatize the agonies of ethical choices in the professions as well as the need to draw an acceptable line in limiting paternalism.[16]

In the "real world," of course, ethical decisions always involve weighing options, choosing from among alternatives, each of which has some plus and some minus features. More often than not, one choice is not altogether right and another altogether wrong. It's the shades of gray that complicate the matter.

What are some of the variables to be weighed? These are illustrative:

- The relevance of the individual professional's knowledge to the decision
- The particular competence of the professional to make the decision
- The uniqueness of the professional's knowledge
- The credibility element
- An estimate of the probable efficacy of the decision in solving a problem
- The magnitude of the social cost or consequences of the decision, measured by moral rules
- The magnitude of the personal cost to the individual of the decision (e.g., risk to professional status)
- Legal, contractual, institutional obligations[17]

AN OPERATIONAL VIEW OF ETHICS FOR POLICE

Durkheim observed that "there's no form of social activity which can do without the appropriate moral discipline."[18] Law enforcement ethics are part of the police subculture and are determined by an integration of multiple factors that include individual morality, law, formal police policies, and an informal system of ethics derived from experiences in the occupational culture. This last factor—informal mores of the occupational culture—is the most pervasive determinant in the current status of police ethics.

The object of study in ethics is *morality*. This infers acceptance of certain factors as being right or wrong, based on the consensus of society. Morality is neither dichotomous nor absolute. Many factors shape one's belief system. For example, we all, as a society, agree that murder is immoral. This standard of morality appears absolute. However, it becomes more complicated when examined at a different level. Some segments of society would argue that abortion is murder and is, therefore, immoral. Other groups would argue that a fetus is not a human being; thus, an abortion is not murder and, consequently, not immoral. There is certainly no absolute consensus on the morality of abortion. One's position is developed largely as a product of one's socialization (political, religious, and socioeconomic belief systems).

When exploring the issue of ethics, one's moral position and perspective of morality become key factors. A serious problem in dealing with ethics in policing is that there is a tendency to view ethical conduct in *absolute terms* which mirror statutory law and/or police policy. Certainly an officer is acting unethically when he or she does not arrest a person because of a bribe. Is it unethical if an officer does not arrest a person for a minor crime because it is near the end of a shift and the arrest would require a lot of paperwork and overtime? Is an officer unethical when he or she decides not to arrest a homeless person because that person committed a minor theft in order to eat? Most would agree that these circumstances vary on a "scale of morality," and thus the ethical propriety of the officer's decisions in these cases will also vary.

Our concepts of ethics in policing must expand beyond equating ethical behavior with statutory provisions or departmental policy. We must ask our officers to *think* and make decisions based upon what is moral (or right) in light of their professional and statutory obligations. This is particularly true as we increasingly ask officers to use problem-solving and community policing techniques. In the above examples, we will agree that the officer accepting a bribe was immoral and should be disciplined. In the second situation, depending on what the crime was, we may ask the officer to explore alternatives and look at the "cost-benefit" of arresting the person. Perhaps counseling the individual, or working out an option of having the person make reparations with the victim are preferable to an arrest. In the situation involving the homeless person, the most moral action may be for the officer to take the person to a homeless shelter for food and assistance.

If we want our officers to think about applying ethics to policing decisions, we must give them the framework to accomplish this. Increasingly, police departments are adopting *organizational values* as an avenue toward this end.

Values

An important consideration in maintaining police integrity as well as ethical decision-making is the inculcation of values in police personnel—both formally and informally.

> Values are the beliefs that guide an organization and the behavior of its employees. The most important beliefs are those that set forth the ultimate purposes of the organization. They provide the organization with its raison d'être for outsiders and insiders alike and justify the continuing investment in the organization's enterprise. . . . All organizations have values. One can see these values expressed through the actions of the organization—the things that are taken seriously and the things that are rejected as irrelevant, inappropriate, or dangerous.[19]

In this vein, the police department must develop a belief system among its officers to accept certain responsibilities and standards of conduct as being proper. This may be accomplished through leadership by example, ongoing training in values and value systems, and articulation of expectations and value statements. Importantly, the process of inculcating values must be consensual, not coercive. The process of integrating ethics, departmental mission, professional responsibility, fairness, due process, and empathy is long-term. A department which attempts to coerce values will meet with little success. Chief David Couper of the Madison, Wisconsin Police Department established a mission and issued the following statement of values "to drive and direct the organization:"

> WE BELIEVE IN THE DIGNITY AND WORTH OF ALL PEOPLE.
> WE ARE COMMITTED TO:
> Providing high-quality, community-oriented police services with sensitivity
> Protecting constitutional rights
> Problem-solving
> Teamwork
> Openness
> Planning for the future
> Providing leadership to the profession
> We are proud of the diversity of our workforce, which permits us to grow and which respects each of us as individuals. And we strive for a healthful workplace.

This statement clearly articulates both a managerial philosophy and behavioral expectations for officers. It establishes important values (e.g. belief in dignity, protection of rights, openness) that Chief Couper expects of his employees. It is a consensual statement, noting that "we" subscribe to these values in performing the job of law enforcement.

As another illustration, the Michigan State Police (MSP) developed a value statement to personnel as follows:

> The Michigan Department of State Police has been entrusted with duties and responsibilities to preserve, protect, and defend people and property and maintain social order. The public trust mandates that all members exemplify the highest standard of conduct both on and off duty. Departmental members shall uphold all laws and function in an ethical, courteous, impartial, and professional manner while respecting the rights and dignity of all persons.

The MSP value statement is more formal than the Madison one and specifically addresses off-duty conduct. Despite these differences, the MSP statement embodies the same fundamental concepts and expectations of employees.

The articulation of value statements is only the beginning. For the values to have meaning they must be taught and practiced by all personnel throughout the chain of command, regardless of whether a person is in an operational or administrative assignment.

The Newport News, Virginia and Houston, Texas police departments have statements of values which are significantly more detailed than the Madison and MSP examples. The notable difference is apparent through the strong sense of moral obligation the organization expects of its employees. On the matter of integrity, the Houston value statement contains supporting commentary:

> The integrity of the Department must not be compromised. There can be no question or suspicion among the citizenry regarding Department ethics. It is imperative that the Department maintain the highest levels of integrity and credibility, ensuring that its standards are sufficiently high so there is not even a perception among citizens that questionable practices exist. Professionalism, in this sense, means adherence to impeccable integrity and careful protection of all citizens rights. It also includes the maintenance of equally high levels of accountability from those authorized to enforce the law.[20]

This statement should leave no question in the minds of officers about the department's position and expectation concerning any form of improper behavior. Because of the "moral" implications of the values, proper behavior is urged, not out of the threat of discipline, but because this type of behavior is "right."

The inclusion of values and the adherence to a higher standard of integrity will make officers both role models for the public and more professional employees. Moreover, this will demonstrate to the community that the police department has identified fundamental principles which guide its responsibilities.

Value statements of two cities are shown on the upcoming pages.

A Higher Standard of Integrity for Police Officers?

An issue which has caused considerable debate is the question of whether there is a higher standard of integrity for police officers than exists for "average citizens." The thesis that police officers are obligated to a higher standard of behavior can actually be traced to the concept of the *social contract*. You will recall from chapter 2, under this philosophy, it is argued that in order to have an orderly society, the public relinquishes some of its social privileges to the government in exchange for control

NEWPORT NEWS, VIRGINIA POLICE DEPARTMENT STATEMENT OF VALUES

VALUE #1

The Newport News Police Department is committed to protecting and preserving the rights of individuals as guaranteed by the Constitution.

VALUE #2

While the Newport News Police Department believes the prevention of crime is its primary responsibility, it aggressively pursues those who commit serious offenses.

VALUE #3

The Newport News Police Department believes that integrity and professionalism are the foundations for trust in the community.

VALUE #4

The Newport News Police Department is committed to an open and honest relationship with the community.

VALUE #5

The Newport News Police Department is committed to effectively managing its resources for optimal service delivery.

VALUE #6

The Newport News Police Department is committed to participating in programs which incorporate the concept of shared responsibility with the community in the delivery of police services.

VALUE #7

The Newport News Police Department actively solicits citizen participation in the development of police activities and programs which impact their neighborhood.

VALUE #8

The Newport News Police Department believes it achieves its greatest potential through the active participation of its employees in the development and implementation of programs.

VALUE #9

The Newport News Police Department recognizes and supports academic achievement of employees and promotes their pursuit of higher education mechanisms which contribute to the maintenance of order. The government is a representation of the people and appoints agents (e.g. police, judges, government administrators) to enforce the social control mechanisms. The privileges granted to the government include permission by the people to develop strictly limited processes, for example, to deprive citizens of their liberty or use force to protect the rights of the broader society.

In exchange for this relinquishment of rights, society expects that the government will protect the citizens, that the citizens' rights will not be violated, and that the government will appoint agents who have the integrity to protect citizens and adhere to the premises of the social contract. It is, in part, based on this philosophical foundation that a free society must expect the highest standards of behavior and ethical conduct from those persons empowered to deprive persons of their basic liberties. That is to say, if the social contract is to remain a valid socio-philosophical principle, the public expects agents of the state (e.g. the police) to behave at the highest levels of integrity and to clearly obey the rules (laws) of society. It must be recognized that the precepts of law in both our civil and criminal justice systems are rooted in these principles. As such, the expectation of integrity and the observance of rules by law enforcement officers are clearly stamped in our social history.

The courts have been directly faced with this issue. In *Calvert* v. *Pontiac*, 288 Mich. 401 (1939), a Michigan court stated that a police officer is a person . . ." whose character must be above reproach and whose truthfulness must be above suspicion. [The officer's] veracity and integrity must be relied upon in the performance of [his/her] duties and the trial of criminal cases" (288 Mich. at 404). Similarly, in *Royal* v. *Ecorse Police and Fire Commission*, 75 N.W.2d 841 (1956), the court stated that a police officer, intent on retaining a position on the police force, can expect, as in the military, to be held to a higher standard of conduct in his or her behavior.

This concept was supported by a Supreme Court case in which a different and higher standard of conduct for military personnel was upheld. In *Parker* v. *Levy*, 417 U.S. 733 (1974), the Court upheld the court-martial's finding of "conduct unbecoming an officer" because of the need to foster an orderly and dutiful fighting force. The underlying theme of the Court's logic focused on the need for administrative controls that maintain organizational integrity in furtherance of the protection of the country. The conceptual relationship between the Court's logic in this case and the argument as related to police officers is based on two primary factors.

First, there is a recognition that most law enforcement agencies are organized as a paramilitary structure. Generally speaking, this includes a fairly rigid chain of command, ranks with defined organizational responsibility, stringent standards for personnel control, utilization of government resources to maintain order and provide service, highly structured administrative control mechanisms, characteristics of the traditional bureaucracy, and articulated expectations of personnel performance and behavior. These similarities have been noted in varying degrees by the courts and the literature. With the recognition that their mission and authority is different, similar standards of organizational behavior have been applied to both the military and the police—particularly with respect to the need to maintain organizational integrity in order to properly perform their respective missions.[21]

Second, because of the significant powers possessed by the police to arrest, conduct searches and seizures, and use force, there is a recognition that strong controls must be in place to minimize the abuse of these powers. Just as the Court found that the military needed to maintain a dutiful and orderly fighting force in *Parker* v. *Levy, supra*, the police need a dutiful and orderly force to fulfill their mission of protecting citizens and the democratic process.

HOUSTON, TEXAS POLICE DEPARTMENT PHILOSOPHY AND VALUES

The mission of the Houston Police Department is to enhance the quality of life in the City of Houston by working cooperatively with the public and within the framework of the United States Constitution to enforce the laws, preserve the peace, reduce fear, and provide a safe environment.

The articulated values of the Houston Police Department in support of this mission are:

- Policing the community involves major responsibility and authority. The police cannot carry out their responsibilities alone; thus they must be willing to involve the community in all aspects of policing which directly impact the quality of community life.
- The Police Department believes it has a responsibility to react to criminal behavior in a way that emphasizes prevention and that is marked by vigorous law enforcement.
- The Police Department adheres to the fundamental principle that it must deliver its services in a manner that preserves and enhances democratic values.
- The Department is committed to delivering police services in a manner which will best reinforce the strengths of the city's neighborhoods.
- The Department is committed to allowing public input in the development of its policies which directly impact neighborhood life.
- The Department will collaboratively work with neighborhoods to understand the true nature of the neighborhood's crime problems and develop meaningful cooperative strategies which will best deal with those problems.
- The Department is committed to managing its resources in the most effective manner possible.
- The Department will actively seek the input and involvement of all employees in matters which impact job performance and manage the organization in a manner which will enhance employee job satisfaction and effectiveness.
- The Department is committed to maintaining the highest levels of integrity and professionalism in all its operations.
- The Department believes that the police function operates most effectively when the organization and its operations are marked by stability, continuity, and consistency.

More recently, a Minnesota court of appeals upheld the firing of an officer on the grounds of his competency and fitness for duty based on the officer's off-duty behavior. In its decision that off-duty conduct can be regulated by a police department, the court of appeals stated that a police department can demand that its officers maintain a higher level of conduct than that which is expected from society, *Thompson* v. *City of Appleton*, 366 N.W.2d 326 (1985).

Although legal precedent on the issue is not exhaustive, there is sufficient evidence to suggest the genesis of a trend. This trend articulates the need for law enforcement officers to maintain a degree of integrity higher than the average citizen because of: (1) the powers the government invests in the police, and (2) the important responsibilities the police hold for public safety. Holding police officers accountable to a higher standard of conduct has important policy implications for all disciplinary matters. If a police department subscribes to this concept, the department is also responsible for informing officers, both via written directives and training, and enforcing those standards when officers are involved in misconduct.

The Environment for Integrity

Administrative mandates for high moral standards also exist in departmental codes of conduct. A *code of conduct* usually outlines behaviors, those which are proscribed and those which are prescribed for officers. If an officer violates one of these standards, then he or she is subject to disciplinary action.

A police officer is a public official with a particularly high moral obligation to not violate the law. This, while seemingly simple, provides a complex dilemma for officers. Even though it is unacceptable for any person to violate the law, it seems particularly offensive when a police officer does so. Does the officer compromise his or her integrity by violating a minor law? Are ethical standards abrogated by this behavior? The answers to these questions carry implications for public expectations, legal mandates, administrative guidelines, ethical constraints, and moral beliefs held by the officer.

As an illustration, let us say that an off-duty officer is at a party with a group of life-long friends. Some people are openly smoking marijuana and offer some to their friend—the police officer. With the marijuana in hand, the officer declines a "hit," but then passes it along to the next person. What has legally transpired? The officer witnessed marijuana being used, was in possession of a controlled substance, and passed (distributed) the drug to another person. Thus, the officer not only observed drug laws being broken, he or she technically violated possession and distribution laws. Were the officer's ethics and oath of office compromised? Should the officer be subject to discipline for drug possession and distribution? Should the officer be disciplined for not making arrests? Would the officer, given the circumstances, have caused greater problems (or perhaps embarrassment) for the department if arrests had been attempted under these circumstances? In practice, these questions do not have definite answers, yet, this exact experience has occurred. Fair and reasonable resolution of such a situation would require a difficult decision by police administrators.

The problems experienced by officers in similar circumstances contribute to ethical conflicts in the practice of policing. Through socialization, a person learns that certain behaviors, such as speeding or drinking alcohol in a public park, while unlawful, are not inherently—or morally—wrong. When a citizen is arrested for one of these law violations, there is usually embarrassment and inconvenience, but there is virtually no moral condemnation. However, should that law violator be a sworn police officer, the standards of acceptable behavior are more narrowly focused because expectations regarding the integrity of all aspects of the officer's behavior are on a higher plateau. This is a reality that most police officers recognize, but do not readily accept.

It has been argued by police labor leaders that holding officers to a higher standard of integrity is unjust and an unfair employment practice. Yet, this is a reality that has been supported by police leaders, the courts, and labor arbitrators as a result of the unique public trust held by police officers.

The Public's Perception

There are, unfortunately, several examples of how public opinion of the police changes based on publicized incidents of police misconduct. In McAllen, Texas, videotapes of instances where officers clearly used excessive force on prisoners were broadcast on both the local and network news. During the time of the initial broadcasts, public opinion of the police dropped significantly and the police department was subjected to ridicule. The drug-running scandals in New York's 77th Precinct left the NYPD at the center of distrust (almost fear) from the perspective of many citizens. Confessions by Miami police officers that they had participated in a violent drug ring brought criticism of the department's selection, training, and supervision of personnel. When four Los Angeles police officers charged with beating Rodney King were not convicted, violence and public outcry about racism and police "cover-ups" resonated across the country.

Each of these incidents represents police misconduct that was extensively publicized. Not only did the publicity affect local citizens' attitudes toward the police, but national opinion about the police was also being shaped by the events. Problems such as these call attention to the human frailties of law enforcement officers and bring into question the department's commitment to ethical behavior. Ethics and integrity must be more than a written code which is suitable for framing; they must be more than a subject in the police academy. Instead, they must represent the department's moral fiber in all aspects of its interaction with the public.

The two boxes which follow contain a model code of ethics and a code of conduct put forth by the International Association of Chiefs of Police (IACP).

POLICE DECEPTION AND LYING

Virtually every police officer will, sometime in his or her career, intentionally lie or deceive someone. Despite one's initial negative reaction to this statement, it must be recognized that there are different motivations for deception, some of which can be justified. But are these reasons ethical? To answer this, one must first understand the different types of police lies.[22]

Accepted Lying.   These are lies which are part of the policing working environment and are accepted because they fulfill a defined organizational purpose. In certain circumstances both administrators and officers agree there are times when lying and deceit are necessary tools for crime control. Even this has an ethical continuum that is problematic. For example, an officer who is working in an undercover capacity with a drug trafficking ring must not only lie, he or she must also become quite proficient at it in order to develop evidence and, in some cases, ensure personal safety. This, most would agree, serves an ethical purpose.

At the other end of the continuum, let us assume that the police suspect a person would, if offered, actively participate in a crime. There may be no known criminal offense at this point, only the suspicion that the person would willingly participate in a crime. Law enforcement officers can offer undercover "opportunities" for the person to commit a crime, but must stop short of inducements or solicitation (entrapment). Who determines the difference between an "opportunity for crime" and an "improper inducement"? Many times it is the officer involved in the case, the legality of the actions being highly dependent on how the officer "writes it up." In these types of discretionary matters, where police administrators know that officers must lie as part of their job assignment, it is of paramount importance that they understand their ethical obligations as well as the legal ones.

Accepted lying can involve other forms of deception as well. Let us say that two men are arrested for robbery. They are separated for interrogations, each being told that the other confessed to the robbery and was willing to strike a plea bargain in exchange for testimony against his confederate. While this is a common practice and

IACP LAW ENFORCEMENT CODE OF ETHICS*

As a law enforcement officer, my fundamental duty is to serve the community; to safeguard lives and property; to protect the innocent from deception, the weak against oppression or intimidation and the peaceful against violence or disorder; and to respect the constitutional rights of all to liberty, equality and justice.

I will keep my private life unsullied as an example to all and will behave in a manner that does not bring discredit to me or my agency. I will maintain courageous calm in the face of danger, scorn or ridicule; develop self-restraint; and be constantly mindful of the welfare of others. Honest in thought and deed both in my personal and official life, I will be exemplary in obeying the law and regulations of my department. Whatever I see or hear of a confidential nature or that is confided to me in my official capacity will be kept ever secret unless revelation is necessary in the performance of my duty.

I will never act officiously or permit personal feelings, prejudices, political beliefs, aspirations, animosities or friendships to influence my decisions. With no compromise for crime and with relentless prosecution of criminals, I will enforce the law courteously and appropriately without fear or favor, malice or ill will, never employing unnecessary force or violence and never accepting gratuities.

I recognize the badge of my office as a symbol of public faith, and I accept it as a public trust to be held so long as I am true to the ethics of police service. I will never engage in acts of corruption or bribery, nor will I condone such acts by other police officers. I will cooperate with all legally authorized agencies and their representatives in the pursuit of justice.

I know that I alone am responsible for my own standard of professional performance and will take every reasonable opportunity to enhance and improve my level of knowledge and competence.

I will constantly strive to achieve these objectives and ideals, dedicating myself before God to my chosen profession . . . law enforcement.

*Originally written 1957, amended 1989.

generally appears to be legal, there are nonetheless ethical questions about this form of deceit. The issue at this point is to make certain that officers understand their ethical obligations and apply their values to these situations.

Tolerated Lying. These lies are recognized by the police department as being untruths, yet are tolerated because they are "necessary evils." Situational, or "white lies," present a moral quandary even though the police may present a logical rationale for their use. When viewed from a moral perspective, they may appear "wrong," yet can be easily justified from an operational perspective. For example, the police may tell noisy teenagers "to move along or go to jail" when there is no actual criminal violation. In another illustration, a police chief, as a result of pressure from the Mothers Against Drunk Drivers (MADD) may tell the public that officers are enforcing driving under the influence laws against all drunk drivers. In fact, the police know they cannot enforce all the laws all the time.

An important point about tolerated lies is that they do not involve criminal wrongdoing or violations of the police code of conduct. Rather, they are lies of op-

POLICE CODE OF CONDUCT*

All law enforcement officers must be fully aware of the ethical responsibilities of their position and must strive constantly to live up to the highest possible standards of professional policing. The International Association of Chiefs of Police believes it important that police officers have clear advice and counsel available to assist them in performing their duties consistent with these standards, and has adopted the following ethical mandates as guidelines to meet these ends.

Primary Responsibilities of a Police Officer

A police officer acts as an official representative of government who is required and trusted to work within the law. The officer's powers and duties are conferred by statute. The fundamental duties of a police officer include serving the community, safeguarding lives and property, protecting the innocent, keeping the peace and ensuring the rights of all to liberty, equality and justice.

Performance of the Duties of a Police Officer

A police officer shall perform all duties impartially, without favor or affection or ill will and without regard to status, sex, race, religion, political belief or aspiration. All citizens will be treated equally with courtesy, consideration and dignity. Officers will never allow personal feelings, animosities or friendships to influence official conduct. Laws will be enforced appropriately and courteously and, in carrying out their responsibilities, officers will strive to obtain maximum cooperation from the public. They will conduct themselves in appearance and deportment in such a manner as to inspire confidence and respect for the position of public trust they hold.

Discretion

A police officer will use responsibly the discretion vested in his position and exercise it within the law. The principle of reasonableness will guide the officer's determinations, and the officer will consider all surrounding circumstances in determining whether any legal action shall be taken. Consistent and wise use of discretion, based on professional policing competence, will do much to preserve good relationships and retain the confidence of the public. There can be difficulty in choosing between conflicting courses of action. It is important to remember that a timely word of advice rather than arrest—which may be correct in appropriate circumstances—can be a more effective means of achieving a desired end.

Use of Force

A police officer will never employ unnecessary force or violence and will use only such force in the discharge of duty as is reasonable in all circumstances. The use of force should be used only with the greatest restraint and only after discussion, negotiation and persuasion have been found to be inappropriate or ineffective. While the use of force is occasionally unavoidable, every police officer will refrain from unnecessary infliction of pain or suffering and will never engage in cruel, degrading or inhuman treatment of any person.

Confidentiality

Whatever a police officer sees, hears or learns that is of a confidential nature will be kept secret unless the performance of duty or legal provision requires otherwise. Members of the public have a right to security and privacy and information obtained about them must not be improperly divulged.

Integrity

A police officer will not engage in acts of corruption or bribery nor will an officer condone such acts by other police officers. The public demands that the integrity of police officers be above reproach. Police officers must, therefore, avoid any conduct that might compromise integrity and thus undercut the public confidence in a law enforcement agency. Officers will refuse to accept any gifts, presents, subscriptions, favors, gratuities or promises that could be interpreted as seeking to cause the officer to refrain from performing official responsibilities honestly and within the law. Police officers must not receive private or specific advantage from their official status. Respect from the public cannot be bought; it can only be earned and cultivated.

Cooperation with Other Police Officers and Agencies

Police officers will cooperate with all legally authorized agencies and their representatives in the pursuit of justice. An officer or agency may be one among many organizations that provide law enforcement services to a jurisdiction. It is imperative that a police officer assist colleagues fully and completely with respect and consideration at all times.

Personal-Professional Capabilities

Police officers will be responsible for their own standard of professional performance and will take every reasonable opportunity to enhance and improve their level of knowledge and competence. Through study and experience, a police officer can acquire the high level of knowledge and competence that is essential for the efficient and effective performance of duty. The acquisition of knowledge is a never-ending process of personal and professional development that should be pursued constantly.

Private Life

Police officers will behave in a manner that does not bring discredit to their agencies or themselves. A police officer's character and conduct while off duty must always be exemplary, thus maintaining a position of respect in the community in which he or she lives and serves. The officer's personal behavior must be beyond reproach.

*Adopted by IACP in 1989.

erational expedience. Tolerated lies have different motivations. The ethical question is whether *motivation* for a tolerated lie can balance moral infringements.

Deviant Lies in Support of Perceived Legitimate Goals. These types of lies are told "to put bad guys in jail." They do not involve deception in support of a lawful organizational purpose (such as accepted lies). Instead, they are overt acts of perjury to "fluff up the evidence" in order to make a case stronger.

For example, an officer stops a car because the driver is "suspicious" even though there is no probable cause or reasonable grounds for the stop. The officer then searches the car "to see what's in there," once again without any legal justification. During the course of the search, the officer finds a gun and some illegal drugs. If the officer says that the car was stopped because the driver was "suspicious" and the car searched because the officer was "curious," the evidence would be excluded and the person released from custody. To avoid this, the officer "creates" probable cause for the stop—perhaps a nonexistent traffic violation. The officer may also say that "during the course of talking with the driver, what appeared to be the butt of a gun was observed sticking out from under the seat." With this "evidence" the officer would have reason to get the driver out of the car and look for the "possible weapon." Of course, while looking for the gun the officer observed the drugs lying in "plain view." With these lies the case may be prosecuted.

In the case of lies such as these, one can understand the rationale for the officer's behavior. Nonetheless, the lies are perjurious, being both unethical and unlawful. An ethical question for police administrators is whether disciplinary action should be tempered because the officer's motivation was in support of organizational goals even though the behavior was not. Does the organization bear any responsibility for the officer's behavior because of poor training or supervision? If so, this too must be considered in the disciplinary processes. A more important concern, however, is that the department must establish value-based behavior in all personnel so that these types of lies can be prevented.

Deviant Lies in Support of Illegitimate Goals.

Lies in this category are told in support of corrupt activities or to protect the officer from disciplinary action and/or civil or criminal liability. These lies clearly serve no legitimate purpose and they cannot be rationalized to support an acceptable purpose.

Most commonly, those who tell these types of lies are overtly involved in some type of misconduct. Interestingly, however, there are times when officers involved in no wrongdoing, per se, have been drawn into telling such lies as a result of the subcultural norm known as the "code of silence" or the "blue curtain of secrecy." Because of the peer rejection associated with being known as a "rat," one who speaks out against another officer, this norm is more like a police "code of omerta," akin to the code of silence in La Cosa Nostra. Thus, rather than experience this rejection, an officer will lie to protect another's wrongdoing.

The standard is clear. This type of deception is unethical. However, the true impact of the "blue curtain," which forces an officer to choose between lying or suffering peer rejection, is particularly tragic. One remedy for this is to continually reinforce values in order to change the organizational culture. The difficulty with this approach, however, is that it is a long-term effort, requiring a generation for such change to occur.

WHISTLE BLOWING

A college graduate with a degree in criminal justice finds employment as a probationary officer with a municipal police agency. During the six months' provisional period, this officer becomes aware, by observation, of various forms of unprofessional conduct among numerous officers: falsified reports, minor payoffs, "cooping," and the like. Should the officer report this to supervisors, perhaps even directly to the chief?

The officer is married, with two children. Police jobs are scarce in the area. The officer discusses the matter quietly with several trusted colleagues and with one police union official. All advise the officer "not to rock the boat." Only two weeks remain of the probationary period. Question: What would *you* do in these circumstances? Would you "blow the whistle"?

This is a fairly common ethical quandary, a case situation suggesting the possibilities in case analysis as an instructional method in teaching criminal justice ethics. The case focuses on the often sticky question of whistle blowing, defined by Sissela Bok as sounding "an alarm from within the very organization . . . aiming to spotlight neglect or abuses that threaten the public interest."[23] Obviously, whistle blowing is not a question confined to police organizations, but it invariably presents a high stakes moral dilemma. Here are some of the latent moral conflicts, as Bok identifies them:

- Deciding whether, other things being equal, speaking out is in fact in the public interest
- Weighing responsibility in the public interest against responsibility to colleagues, institution, profession
- Assessing the possible or probable results in retaliation, damage to career, and ability to support family[24]

At the conclusion of an insightful monograph, Bok writes:

> Whistle blowing is a new word for a very ancient practice. It is becoming more prominent now, as we learn to spot it in very different circumstances and as organizations grow in size, and offers an opportunity for a close look at individual choices, as well as possible institutional changes and professional standards. The teaching of ethics can benefit from and contribute to such inquiries, and can help to seek ways of protecting dissent and encouraging criticism, while cutting down on erroneous or harmful resorts to the panic button.[25]

We have all too briefly touched on a sampling of important ethical issues in policing. The community dimension in these issues has been evident in the frequent references to "the public interest." There are, of course, many other issues that may well be spotlighted for special attention under the general heading. We listed some of these issues as earlier discussed in this text, and there are still others that we have not dealt with at all, or dealt with only in passing—for example, surveillance, the insanity plea,[26] white-collar crime,[27] gun control,[28] and ethical issues in criminalistics and forensic science.[29] It is hoped that what we have done, albeit in sweeping and cursory fashion, will convey some idea of the intellectual smorgasbord that beckons those who are curious about ethics in law enforcement.

SOME CONCLUDING REFLECTIONS

In a stimulating book, David Duffee describes a community service model for criminal justice and observes that "our aim must be good societies, not crimeless ones."[30] He is talking about quality of life as a moral imperative. How does a police rookie fall into an ethical morass? Lawrence Sherman has an answer:

> The rookie discovers that police work is more social work than crime fighting, more arbitration of minor disputes than investigations of major crimes, more patching of holes in the social fabric than weaving of webs to catch the big-time crooks. The rookie's usual response is to define most of the assignments received as "garbage

calls," not *real* police work. Not quite sure whom to blame for the fact that he or she was hired to do police work but was assigned everything else, the rookie blames the police executive, the mayor and city council, and even previous U.S. presidents (for raising public expectations). But most of all the rookie blames the public, especially the poor, for being so stupid as to have all these problems, or so smart as to take advantage of welfare and other social programs.[31]

Ethics is the study of values and sometimes it's hard for police and a lot of other people to tell the difference between good values and bad. Still with the police rookie in mind, Sherman identifies some of the *questionable values* that might conceivably test the ethical mettle of this young officer.

1. Decisions about whether to enforce the law, in any but the most serious cases, should be guided by both what the law says and who the suspect is.
2. Disrespect for police authority is a serious offense that should always be punished with an arrest or use of force.
3. Police officers should never hesitate to use physical or deadly force against people who "deserve it."
4. Due process is only a means of protecting criminals at the expense of the law abiding and should be ignored whenever it is safe to do so.
5. Lying and deception are an essential part of the police job, and even perjury should be used if it is necessary to protect yourself or get a conviction on a "bad guy."
6. You cannot go fast enough to catch a car thief or traffic violator, nor slow enough to get to a "garbage" call; and when there are no calls for service, your time is your own.
7. Police do very dangerous work for low wages, so it is proper to take any extra rewards the public wants to give them.
8. The paramount duty is to protect your fellow officers at all costs.[32]

An appropriate appraisal of these values would, in itself, constitute an adequate agenda for a college course in police ethics. It should surely generate spirited polemics. But Carl Klockars has something to say about this:

> Spirited polemic is not a good rhetorical environment in which to talk about ethics. But it has its place in contemporary criminological trade ethics literature just as it did in the dialogue of *The Republic*. It will not cease to be a rhetorical environment for talking about ethics until an unimpeachable ethical argument comes along and all mankind agrees in unison to be impeached by wit. Until that time, as Socrates was obliged to demonstrate, anyone who would continue to speak of ethics must know how to make Thrasymachus eat his words.[33]

QUESTIONS FOR DISCUSSION

1. Explain the link between law and ethics in the United States.
2. What are some of the reasons for the apparent contemporary surge of interest in ethics and values?
3. How would you explain the community dimension of ethics in public affairs?
4. Define normative ethics and relate it to applied and professional ethics.
5. What ethical issue is raised in governmental paternalism?
6. How would you argue the morality of coercion in criminal justice?

7. What realistic value, in your opinion, is there to having a formal code of ethics which is recognized by the International Association of Chiefs of Police?

8. Discuss your opinion of whether there should be a higher standard of integrity for police officers than for "regular citizens." Provide a rationale for your position.

9. Distinguish between ethical principles and organizational values.

10. How would you argue the ethics of the use of deception by the police?

NOTES

1. Lawrence Sherman, "Learning Police Ethics," *Criminal Justice Ethics* (Winter/Spring, 1982): 18.

2. Michael Brown, *Working the Street* (New York: Russell Sage Foundation, 1981), p. 221.

3. Douglas Sloan, "The Teaching of Ethics in the American Undergraduate Curriculum, 1876–1976," in *Ethics Teaching in Higher Education*, Daniel Callahan and Sissela Bok, eds. (New York: Plenum Press, 1980), pp. 2–9.

4. Douglas Sloan, *Knowledge, Education, and Human Values: Toward the Recovery of Wholeness*. Critical Issues Symposium Series. Copyright © The Charles F. Kettering Foundation, in cooperation with Teachers College, Columbia University, 1980.

5. These are all fairly standard dictionary definitions of these terms.

6. Daniel Callahan, "Goals in Teaching Ethics," in *The Teaching of Ethics*, Callahan and Bok, op. cit., p. 62.

7. Ibid., pp. 64–69.

8. Ibid., pp. 69–72.

9. Ibid., p. 71.

10. Ruth Macklin, "Problems in the Teaching of Ethics: Pluralism and Indoctrination," in *The Teaching of Ethics*, Callahan and Bok, op. cit., pp. 81–101.

11. Alasdair MacIntyre, "How to Identify Ethical Principles," in *The Belmont Report* (Washington, DC: Dept. of Health, Education and Welfare Publication No. (OS) 78-0013), pp. 10–40. See also, by the same author, *After Virtue* (Notre Dame, IN: University of Notre Dame Press, 1981).

12. Bernard Gert, *The Moral Rules* (New York: Harper & Row, 1970).

13. These rules, ideals, and commentary reflect an adaptation of Gert by Albert C. Cafagna, associate professor of philosophy, Michigan State University.

14. For example, William F. May, "Professional Ethics: Setting, Terrain and Teacher," in *The Teaching of Ethics*, Callahan and Bok, op. cit., pp. 205–41.

15. Ibid., p. 220.

16. See Stuart Hampshire, ed., *Public and Private Morality* (Cambridge, England: Cambridge University Press, 1978); and Richard Wasserstrom, ed., *Morality and the Law* (Belmont, CA: Wadsworth Publishing Co., 1971).

17. Based on lecture notes of Albert C. Cafagna, associate professor of philosophy, Michigan State University, Professor Cafagna acknowledges help from his colleague, Professor Herbert G. Bohnert, in this formulation of variables.

18. Emile Durkheim, *Professional Ethics and Civic Morals*, translated by C. Brookfield (Glencoe, IL: The Free Press) p. 14.

19. Robert Wasserman and Mark Moore, "Values in Policing," *Perspectives in Policing* (Washington, DC: National Institute of Justice 1988), p. 1.

20. Houston Police Department (undated), *Statement of Philosophy and Values* (Mimeographed) p. 7.

21. David L. Carter and Darrel W. Stephens, *Drug Abuse by Police Officers* (Springfield, IL: Charles C. Thomas, Publishers, 1988).

22. This typology is based on previous research by the author. For a detailed discussion of the foundations for this categorization see Thomas Barker and David L. Carter, "Fluffing Up The Evidence and Covering Your Ass': Some Conceptual Notes on Police Lying," *Deviant Behavior* 1990 11:61–73.

23. Sissela Bok, "Whistleblowing and Professional Responsibilities," in *Ethics Teaching*, Daniel Callahan and Sissela Bok, eds., op. cit., pp. 277–95.

24. Ibid.

25. Ibid., p. 295. Also recommended reading are John Rawls, *A Theory of Justice* (Cambridge, MA: Harvard University Press, 1977); David Ewing, *Freedom Inside and Organization* (New York: E. P. Dutton, 1977); Ralph Nader, Peter Petkas, and Kate Blackwell, *Whistle Blowing* (New York: Grossman Publishers, 1972); and Charles Peters and Taylor Branch, *Blowing the Whistle* (New York: Praeger, 1972).

26. See Ernest VanDenHaag and Thomas R. Litwack, "The Insanity Defense," *Criminal Justice Ethics* 3, no. 1 (Winter-Spring 1984): 3–26.

27. See Andrew J. Reck, "The Concept of White-Collar Crime," in *Ethics, Public Policy, and Criminal Justice*, Frederick Elliston and Norman Bowie, eds., op. cit., pp 59–71.

28. See "Gun Control," an entire issue of *The (AAPSS) Annals* 455 (May 1981).

29. See William J. Curran, A. Louis McGarry, and Charles S. Petty, *Modern Legal Medicine, Psychiatry, and Forensic Science* (Philadelphia: F. A. Davis Publisher, 1980).

30. David E. Duffee, *Explaining Criminal Justice: Community Theory and Criminal Justice Reform* (Cambridge, MA: Oelgeschlager, Gunn & Hain, Publishers, 1980), p. 212.

31. Lawrence Sherman, "Learning Police Ethics," *Criminal Justice Ethics* 1, no. 1 (Winter-Spring 1982): 10–19.

32. Ibid., pp. 14–15.

33. Carl B. Klockars, "A Theory of Contemporary Criminological Ethics," in *Ethics, Public Policy, and Criminal Justice*, Frederick Elliston and Norman Bowie, eds., op. cit., pop. 419–58.

Part Two

THE PARADOX OF
POLICING

The Police Use of Force

ELIZABETH WATSON

*Former Chief of Police Austin, Texas Police Department and Houston,
Texas Police Department*

Discussions regarding the police use—or rather MISUSE—of force certainly are not new. What is relatively new, however, is the amount of open, objective discussion and research now being committed to understanding the issue. At the very least, the implications of this increased comprehension reach far beyond the traditional focus on recruitment and entry-level examination.

Police departments have long used psychological screening mechanisms, in part to identify overly "aggressive" personalities and screen them out of the pool of potential police applicants. Cadet training curricular nearly always contains comprehensive instruction in defensive tactics designed to gain compliance without injury. Further, there is the ubiquitous emphasis on the need to use "only the minimum amount of force necessary" to accomplish the police mission.

What, then, happens from the time of entry to the point at which an incident of excessive force occurs, and are there systems in place which work to diminish the potential for such occurrences? Indeed, it has been argued that such instances are rare, that police generally do exhibit restraint in the routine conduct of their business, as evidenced by the hundreds of thousands of arrests made in which force was necessary, but apparently not excessive. This evidence notwithstanding, however, increasing pressure is being exerted on police executives throughout the country to establish civilian review boards, which presumably would ensure impartial evaluation by disinterested persons of the community, whose purpose is to hold the police accountable when the use of force is questioned. Interestingly, however, in many localities which have used civilian review boards, it has been learned that penalties exacted by the board often are more lenient than those applied by police practitioners.

Undoubtedly, there exists a compelling need to discipline any officer who brings discredit to the police profession through the use of excessive force. The question which remains unanswered is to what extent discipline not only corrects individual transgressions, but also creates an environment in which future violations are less likely to occur. It appears unlikely that discipline alone can accomplish the latter objective for at least three reasons.

First, police rarely have the opportunity to learn from the mistakes of their peers. Instruction on the proper use of force usually occurs in a classroom setting, and pertains to the relatively abstract issues of law and/or ethics. When an officer is disciplined or fired for excessive use of force, a cloud of confusion forms amidst doubt and misinformation. Too often, that cloud materializes into defensiveness and a desperate search for justification, either of the officer's action (i.e., "I know Joe and he would never . . .") and/or management's reaction (i.e., "It must be politics . . ."). Case studies, shared among police departments, represent an untapped resource that could bring stark reality to the training component.

Second, for many years police executives have endeavored to shape a positive police image and encourage good performance by focusing on identification and punishment of negative behavior. There are two obvious shortcomings of this approach: First, it is reactive in nature; by the time the corrective action is necessary, it is, by definition, too late. Second, punishment does little to instill a positive tone in the organization or to encourage good performance. On the contrary, rather than instilling positive behavior, the emphasis on negative controls often manifests itself in the expression: "Nobody ever got fired for doing nothing."

In fairness, it must be pointed out that nearly all police executives acknowledge the need to recognize and reward outstanding performance. Unfortunately, however, established reward systems usually center around one heroic act and are dependent on the initiative of a conscientious citizen or supervisor to bring the action to light. Too often, routine police performance and the conduct of individual officers elude detection absent some overt signal, usually in the form of a commendation or complaint. Consider, for example, performance evaluation instruments used by many police supervisors in departments all over the country. Sergeants routinely look at the number of calls answered, reports written, and arrests made as indicators of police productivity. Seldom is there an effort made to determine the *quality* of the police-citizen interaction, yet therein lies the information most critical to assessing police performance. Because this critical pool of information is left untapped, opportunities to reward professional conduct are lost, as well as opportunities to detect poor or problem behavior before it escalates into gross misconduct.

Third, in most large cities, the police have become estranged from the citizens they serve. Unable to determine by sight the law-abiding from the law-breaking, some officers develop their own styles of interaction, which may or may not be conducive to positive and constructive outcomes. Operating with a void of information, both the officer and the citizen are handicapped, each not knowing what to expect from the other, and each perfectly willing—indeed, sometimes inclined—to expect the worst. It is arguably in these uncertain environments, fraught with misunderstanding, that problems are most likely to occur.

Recognizing this dilemma, many police executives are embracing community-based policing, partly because it helps reduce the ambiguity in many police-citizen contacts. Contrary to some critics, community policing does not require additional personnel. Rather, it is a more comprehensive, problem-solving approach to crime, which requires a wider range of skills. While the traditional focus on law enforcement is retained, community policing adds an analytical dimension to the policing role, which requires more sophisticated communication skills, reasoning ability, creativity, and initiative. It likewise requires police managers to be more resourceful in their use of existing staff, and to establish new systems that *routinely* encourage and reward positive behaviors. Community policing is as old as policing itself, but it forces re-examination of ideas and paradigms that may have been lost or forgotten over the years. For example, if we all can agree that the police exist to serve the community, why don't we recruit into the police *service*, rather than the police *force*? What's in a name? Perhaps more than we care to admit.

Chapter 5

THE ROLE DILEMMA
OF THE POLICE

Let us consider what many analysts perceive as the central, most fundamental issue affecting the relationship of police and community: the role dilemma of the police. Our considerations so far have suggested and anticipated this core issue. Role and goals: any discussion of police organization and activity obviously must begin with this.

Take, for example, Bordua's vision of the police as community leaders—or *managers*, to use this term. He is talking about role and goals. His notion is a far cry from the "strong back, weak mind" image of the police. By and large, American police have slowly met Bordua's challenge. Nonetheless, one can still generate a heated argument in police circles over the question of whether it is appropriate for the police to be out ahead of the community, rather than simply followers. The question is basically political, tending to portray the police as "wavemakers"—troublesome innovators. This portrayal is not one always welcomed by politicians.

Although not the first to discover the role issue, the 1968 National Advisory Commission on Civil Disorders (Kerner Commission) touched on the matter:

> The policeman in the ghetto is a symbol of increasingly bitter social debate over law enforcement. One group, disturbed and perplexed by sharp rises in crime and urban violence, exerts extreme pressure on police for tougher law enforcement. Another group, inflamed against police as agents of repression, tends toward defiance of what it regards as order maintained at the expense of justice.
>
> . . . police responsibilities in the ghetto are even greater than elsewhere in the community since the other institutions of social control have so little authority: the schools, because so many are segregated, old and inferior; religion, which has become irrelevant to those who have lost faith as they lost hope; career aspirations, which for many young Negroes are totally lacking; the family, because its bonds are often snapped. It is the policeman who must deal with the consequences of this institutional vacuum and is then resented for the presence and the measures this effort demands.[1]

Three decades have passed since this was written, yet the observations retain a ring of truth.

CONFLICTING EXPECTATIONS

In a marital relationship, suppose the partners have not simply different but sharply conflicting expectations of each other's role. Can such a predicament breed trouble? Amen. In student-teacher relationships, can conflicting role expectations spawn difficulty? Of source. How about in employer-employee relations? Yes, indeed. There are countless examples that might be cited to make the same point; it is elementary in understanding human relations problems.

Now complicate substantially these simple illustrations of role conflict and apply them to the relationship of the police and the communities they serve. Bear in mind that in sizable cities, a single police agency is politically accountable, and is required to be responsive in its services to many divergent "communities," not merely to one. Their expectations are not only different, but conflicting. *What* the police do and *how* they do it is probably the most important determinant of the status of police-community relations. What is the primary mission of the police? How are police organizational goals set? In establishing police policies and priorities, what community input is there, and what weight does this input have with decision-makers? Lohman used a soft term in Chicago when he was instructing police trainees about the causes of "dissonance" with the community. Many such instructors would agree that there is nothing more crucial in understanding this than the role issue. In fact, dissonance seems to be the norm in relations with the minority community.

As suggested earlier, the police have no monopoly on role conflict in a democratic society. It is, in fact, inevitable and not necessarily damaging in relationships. (It somewhat reflects the evolving nature of the social context.) Certainly many husbands and wives can and do find ways to reconcile their conflicting expectations. They achieve a reasonable, and at least minimal "working consensus." Positive relationships in marriage and in friendships often develop out of initially negative, conflict-laden interaction. Essentially, the process involved is political, as consensus is a political term that implies peaceful, cooperating, mediating resolution of differences. The stake in weighty issues may be the survival of a free society.

In police and community relations, role conflict is of cardinal significance. Why so? The police have extraordinary authority and power, as we have observed. They may, under some circumstances, deprive persons of their liberty. Sometimes they are *authorized* to use reasonable force, to protect the public interest. They may initiate the legal process. A social role with such repressive and punitive possibilities is bound to be the object of unusual public (and scholarly) interest and apprehension. Recall the parliamentary debate regarding Peel's proposal. The reluctance to create the Metropolitan Police was based on fears that the police would become *too* powerful, substituting their values for the community's.

HISTORICAL PERSPECTIVES

It is instructive to study the police role question in a historical perspective. In his first principle, Peel made his role position clear: the basic mission for which the police exist—to prevent crime and disorder as an alternative to the repression of crime and disorder by military force and severity of legal punishment. Reflected in this statement was the concept of English policing dating back centuries. Banton graphically indicated the two functional sides of police work and suggested the role dilemma as well when he referred to *law officers* and *peace officers*.

The Anglo-American system of civilian policing has brought together a variety of both explicit and implicit functions. Since 1829, in the United Kingdom, the primary functions have been the preservation of the peace and the prevention of crime, as suggested by Peel's first principle. Other functions have been regarded as ancillary. While it is generally assumed that civilian policing in the United States has followed the British model, American police typically have given apprehension the primary focus while peace keeping and crime prevention have been of secondary importance. Progressively, for each decade since the 1960s, this has slowly changed. The community policing movement has added greater balance to these priorities.

In analyzing the difference, the distinguished American social historian Oscar Handlin has cited "the exceptional diffusion of violence in our society." He points out that ours has been, from the beginning, a much more violent society than that of most European countries. Carrying arms and rounding up a posse were aspects of American history that are still glamorized in today's movies and television. Handlin also says that early American police forces had "undifferentiated functions." The police were public servants with duties pertaining to public health, clean streets, and all sorts of other odds and ends. Thus, it was easy to make scapegoats of the police for every problem. Until after 1900, the most important aspects of police work as we see it today were not performed by the police. Various private agencies took care of apprehending crooks, while the police busied themselves with menial chores, thereby cultivating the public impression that a police officer was a rather backward character, a more or less friendly simpleton.[2]

The literature dealing with British policing emphasizes the prevention of crime and the maintenance of peace as the two most important functions of the civilian police. On the other hand, American writers tend to emphasize the protection of security and the enforcement of law as the two primary functions. This difference is much more than a semantic incidental. It has a direct, practical application in the manner in which police agencies have been organized, the standards regarded as germane in recruiting, the kind of training that a police officer receives, and in beliefs and values considered important in the craft. Every police recruit inherits the ambiguities pertaining to the role—what he or she is expected to do and what the priorities are.[3]

The widespread confusion and lack of consistency or consensus among police officers themselves on the question of their role has been pointed out by many observers. One difficulty is the number of persons and groups professing some right to speak about what police officers do and how they do it. Police administrators and supervisors, police officers themselves (through their professional and fraternal organizations), legislative bodies, the courts, governmental executives, assorted bureaucrats, and of course "the people"—many different factions of the population, with different perceptions of and expectations from the police—all of these forces and others rightfully demand a voice and vote in the question of what the police should do and how they should do it. Thus, the police agency is in the position of attempting to accomplish the impossible—that is, to discern some consensus among the many disparate points of view and to develop an operating mode that is acceptable to most of the people most of the time.

To see the role predicament as basically political, and to see the key to its satisfactory resolution as correspondingly political, is to recognize that all public administration in democratic society faces and must settle the constant consensus questions via the same processes, if they are settled at all. In this respect, the administration of police and criminal justice agencies is no different from that of other entities. In totalitarian systems, if any question arises about the role of the police, it is much more expeditiously settled: the police do what political leaders tell them.

As to the American experience in the post-Peel period, it is interesting to note that the Boston police—as an example—in the 1840s were not mainly preoccupied with law enforcement. They were watchmen, as Roger Lane has described them, with their principal job being to maintain peace in the streets.[4] The Boston police were not fully armed at public expense until 1884. The shift in functional emphasis to crook catching came later. As James Q. Wilson describes it:

> What [led] to a change was twofold: the bureaucratization of the detectives (putting them on salary and ending the fee system), and the use of the police to enforce unpopular laws governing the sale and use of liquor. The former change led to the beginning of the popular confusion as to what the police do. . . . [the detective], and not his patrolman colleague, was the "real" police officer doing "real" police work.[5]

Because the public was sharply divided in opinion regarding liquor laws and such questions as Sunday closing of saloons—situations in which the police could initiate prosecutions on their own authority, rather than on citizen complaint—disastrous police-community relations problems were averted when the police simply chose to do no more than was absolutely necessary. Their motto was: better to do too little than too much. Wilson explains that the police began to provide various services to citizens who seemed likely to become instigators of public disorder. Thus, in the 1850s, the police in Boston, Philadelphia, and New York were heavily engaged in overnight lodging service, in addition to supplying coal for poor families, soup kitchens for the hungry, and jobs as domestics for girls they thought might be lured away from prostitution. Such social services by the police helped to soften their public image whereas liquor law enforcement hardened it. Eventually, however, the organized charities opposed this aspect of social services, ostensibly because they thought it inappropriate for the police to render such services, but more likely because it reflected unfavorably on them.

At the turn of the century, the maintenance of order was still the paramount function of the American police. But two early twentieth-century influences shifted emphasis away from maintaining order to that of enforcing law. One was Prohibition, which put police in the position "of choosing between corruption and making a nuisance of themselves," as Wilson phrases it; and the other was the Great Depression of the 1930s, which focused public attention "on the escapades of bank robbers and other desperadoes." Wilson observes:

> Police venality and rising crime rates coincided in the public mind, though in fact they had somewhat different causes. The watchman function of the police was lost sight of; their law enforcement function, and their apparent failure to exercise it, were emphasized.[6]

Then came President Hoover's appointment of the Wickersham Commission and their 1931 report. The Commission considered both police and politicians as principally blameworthy, and reform became the slogan. The argument was that since the police *can* prevent crime, intolerable crime rates mean that the police are not doing their job because of political influence. Wilson analyzed the consequences:

> If the job of the police is to catch crooks, then the police have a technical, ministerial responsibility in which discretion plays little part. Since no one is likely to disagree on the value of the objective, then there is little reason to expose the police to the decision-making processes of city government. *Ergo*, take the police "out of politics."[7]

All "superfluous" police services were questioned. These were not "real police work." The police were portrayed mainly as "crook catchers"; both the police view of themselves and the public's view of them were adjusted accordingly, over a period of several ensuing decades.

Yet this was a view of police work that really did not correspond with reality. The police knew that they were still handling family fights and troublesome teenagers. They also knew that they alone could not prevent crime. So they turned to manipulating crime records, to make things look better from the standpoint of public expectations. The "good pinch" and the "G Man" became symbols of "real police work." Rewards and incentives in the department—for example, "promotion" to detective—were geared to the crook-catching function. And the *means* of apprehending criminals were not always open to public scrutiny. Indeed, one summarization of the Wickersham Commission Report was published under the title, *Our Lawless Police*.[8]

In effect, the American police shifted their concept of their role from a predominantly watchman to a predominantly crook-catching emphasis, in accord with their reading of public expectations. As public demand was seen to be increasingly for more police attention to containing crime, the police moved in that direction—even as they realized that what they could do about this, unassisted by the community, had to be more pretense than actual performance. Peter Manning writes:

> It would appear that much of policing action is an attempt on the part of the police to dramatize certain of their actions and to conceal or make less than salient their other than frequent but less impressive activities.[9]

MORE PRECISELY, WHAT'S THE ISSUE?

A more precise statement of the dilemma of the police role is necessary here. So far, we have been talking around the issue. The President's Crime Commission (1967), the Kerner Commission (1968), and the National Commission on the Causes and Prevention of Violence (1969–70) all pointed out that the vast majority of the situations in which the police intervene are not crime situations calling for arrests. Another presidential commission, headed by former Pennsylvania Governor William Scranton, studied student unrest and college campus disorders in the aftermath of the Kent State University and Jackson State College tragedies of the spring of 1970. This commission also stressed the peace-keeping responsibilities of the police.

In the 1970s, the National Advisory Commission on Criminal Justice Standards and Goals added its voice to the debate on the police role. Its report on the police begins with consideration of the role question, tying it directly to community relations. This commission emphasized the importance for every police agency of developing both short- and long-range goals and objectives, and of securing maximum input in this process from within the agency and from all community elements.

More recently, the role conflict has been complicated with the addition of quality-of-life issues as a police responsibility. Certainly, this goes beyond the traditional view of the police as either a law officer or peace officer. What is more apparent is the police officers in the role of *problem solver*. Officers are being asked to be "proactive," that is, to aggressively look for broad solutions to crime, disorder and quality-of-life problems in the community.[10]

It is crucial, of course, in discussing the role question, to recognize that the debate is not over whether the police should be relieved of either of their principal

"Officers are being asked to be 'proactive'—that is, to aggressively look for broad solutions to crime, disorder and quality of life problems in the community."

functions. The argument is not one of law enforcement versus order maintenance versus problem-solving. It is recognized that police work includes all of these functions. The debate has to do, rather, with *emphasis*. If, for example, the police spend most of their time in keeping peace (often called *conflict management*), why should a police agency be organized as if this were not so? And why should police officers be trained as if most of their time were spent catching crooks, when most of their time is not spent catching crooks? What then is the desirable relationship between the major functions of the police, granting that these functions are not mutually exclusive? Sometimes, making an arrest helps to preserve civic peace; sometimes it can set off a riot. Is crime to be suppressed at any price? Such questions highlight the focus of the issue.

A general response is that any police agency should develop its role concept (goals and objectives) in accord with consensus expectations of the community it serves. But the problem is that major city police agencies aim to serve numerous, highly diversified communities, not a single entity, and consensus is exceedingly difficult to come by. As communities (neighborhoods, precincts, or divisions in big cities) differ in their cultural, ethnic, racial, socioeconomic, educational, occupational, and demographic features, so will their police service needs and requirements differ. The order of priorities among the jobs to be performed by the police should be set accordingly. But the demands are conflicting. Stated in only one dimension of the complexity of the issue, wealthy people want different services from the police than do poor people.

Moreover, there is the problem of community inputs. How adequate, how reliable, how representative are these inputs? Too often, police agencies play political and administrative games, pretending sincere interest in what poor and powerless segments of the community have to say while having no desire to serve their needs. Various excuses surface—for example, that "these people" were given an opportunity to speak their piece, but failed to appear. All of this contributes to the conclusion, long since reached by the powerless, that the police are first and foremost the police of the rich and the powerful. Indeed, the "apathy" of the poor and powerless is, more often than not, a sign that they have been completely "turned off" by the insincerity of public administrators. This often explains why they fail to appear or to speak up. The ownership these people, referred to as being "disenfranchised," feel toward their community and government is practically nonexistent.

RAMIFICATIONS

So we have the issue clearly described, and at least a start in considering its complicated tentacles. Time now to clarify some terminology.

Wilson defines *order maintenance* as the handling of disputes, or behavior that threatens to produce disputes, among persons who disagree over what ought to be right or seemly conduct, or over the assignment of blame for what is agreed to be wrong or unseemly conduct.[11] Examples of this would be a family quarrel, a noisy drunk, a bar fight, a street disturbance by teenagers, or gang members congregating on a street corner. Although a law may be broken in these examples of conduct, the police do not see their responsibility as simply the comparing of particular behavior to a clear legal standard and making an arrest if the standard has been violated. In many order maintenance situations, the legal rule is ambiguous. Blame may be more important to the participants than guilt.

There is, of course, some ambiguity about what constitutes a peaceful community. Some communities may appear disorderly to observers while maintaining a substantial degree of legality. The converse may also occur: order may be maintained amid questionable legality. More often than not in peacekeeping situations, the officer will not make an arrest, because most such infractions are misdemeanors, and in most states an arrest cannot be made unless the illegal act is committed in the officer's presence or unless the victim is willing to sign a complaint.

Law enforcement, on the other hand, is the application of legal sanctions, usually by means of an arrest, to persons who injure or deprive innocent victims; for example, burglary, purse snatching, mugging, robbery, or auto theft. Once guilt is established, there is no question of blame. The officer is expected either to make an arrest or to act to prevent the violation from occurring in the first place. The task is to apprehend or to deter the criminal. But in most instances involving crime, the officer lacks the resources to do so. Therefore, few cases are "cleared by arrest." Moreover, current studies reflect that a high proportion of crimes go unreported. Nobody knows how many crimes the police prevent, but the number is not thought to be large. And certain police tactics—such as "street sweeps"—in so-called high-crime areas that might have the effect of preventing certain types of crime may also place the police in conflict with some elements of the community.[12] Wilson believes that what the police do for crime prevention, they do as part of their regular law enforcement activities. Therefore, he does not consider crime prevention separately.

The police are frequently criticized for behavior that is, to a considerable extent, integral to "the system," or "the way things work"—such is the nature of a bureaucracy. Reform movements often concentrate on what should be done to improve police officers, rather than on what fundamental changes should be contemplated in the system itself. Police departments are often charged with such things as hiring unqualified personnel, manipulating crime statistics, condoning improper procedures on the street, and using patrol tactics that irritate people and heighten tensions. Community groups recommend solutions for these matters. Because their diagnosis is often that the problems are caused by incompetent, rude, brutal, and prejudiced police officers, the remedies they suggest usually included elevated recruitment standards, more and better education for police officers, tougher internal discipline, exterior review of police behavior, and other measures focusing on police officers.

But suppose that "better" men and women officers—that is, more college-educated police officers, more black officers, more police participants in the best "sensitivity training," and even more neighborhood control of the police—should suddenly become a reality. Under such conditions, deemed ideal by many critics of the police, the crime rate might well go up rather than down, at least temporarily, and such measures would not necessarily resolve the conflict in the community between those who want less police surveillance and those who want more. The ingredients that are often identified by community groups as important in creating better police-community relations must be carefully delineated and qualified.

These observations are no argument against better men and women in police work. They do suggest, however, the complexity of police-community relations problems. Something more fundamental than cosmetics (for example, "flashy" uniforms) and better qualified personnel is required if significant change is to occur. Commitment to the need for basic restructuring of police organizations should be a primary qualification for police work. Otherwise, police-community relations will continue indefinitely on the same old treadmill, along with other aspects of our system of law and justice.

THE BENCHMARK

On the basis of his analysis of the police role dilemma, Wilson directed a well-known study of the management of law and order in eight communities, and identified three styles of policing—the watchman, the legalistic, and the service—relating each style to local politics.[13]

His is the prevailing view of the essence of the police quandary. Other writers express it in somewhat different ways. Gordon Misner has noted, for example, that it has become increasingly fashionable for the police in various parts of the country to refer to themselves as "law enforcement officers." The intent, Misner believes, is to convey the impression to the public that they see themselves first and foremost as "real cops," not social workers. In Misner's opinion, doing so helps these officers live with the anger, frustration, and anxiety they feel about what they think is expected of them under current conditions.

"Law and order" is often a question of law *or* order, Misner says, and "the dilemma arises from the conflicting set of instructions society has historically given to the policemen." He continues, echoing Wilson:

> The policeman really has two role models from which to choose: he can conceive of himself as a "rule enforcer," or as a "guardian of the peace." He is helped in the choice by the role preferred by his chief and immediate superiors. In many departments, being a rule enforcer is viewed as a necessary stage of development in the growth of a mature policeman. . . . The older policeman hopes that the young prospect will realize eventually that strict enforcement of the laws is a gigantic inconvenience, not only to the public but also to the policeman himself. It is part of police folklore that an experienced policeman knows how to "stay out of trouble," and has necessarily learned that law enforcement is simply a means and not an end in itself.[14]

Misner agrees with Wilson also in the observation that the role concept of any particular policy agency largely determines how the agency is organized, the priorities prescribed for specific tasks, the kind of training police officers receive, and the system of rewards. As an example, Misner refers to the less than thirty percent proportion of patrol time and resources spent in criminal process activity in larger urban areas. He adds another point:

> There are situations when nonenforcement of certain laws or regulations may actually contribute to the peace and tranquility of the community. Enforcement, therefore, is a two-edged sword that must be used with a delicate sense of balance and timing. To suggest that "total enforcement" is a magic formula for reinstituting order in a troubled community simply lulls the public into a false sense of security. It also diverts public attention from seeking more basic, long-term solutions to social problems.[15]

Another widely respected police analyst, Herman Goldstein, one-time administrative assistant to the late Chicago police superintendent, O. W. Wilson, and now professor of law at the University of Wisconsin, substantially agrees with Wilson, Goldstein argues that the police must become more, not less, involved in noncriminal activities, if they are to be effective in dealing with civil disorder and civil disobedience:

> The police function in two worlds. They play an integral part, along with the prosecutor, the courts, and correctional agencies, in the operation of the criminal justice system. As the first agency in the system, their primary responsibility is to initiate a criminal action against those who violate the law. This is a highly structured role, defined by statutes and court decisions and subjected to strict controls.
>
> The second world is less easily defined. It comprises all aspects of police functioning that are unrelated to the processing of an accused person through the criminal system. Within this world, a police department seeks to prevent crimes, abate nuisances, resolve disputes, control traffic and crowds, furnish information, and provide a wide range of other miscellaneous services to the citizenry. In carrying out these functions, officers frequently make use of the authority which is theirs by virtue of their role in the criminal process. . . . Police spend most of their time functioning in the second of these two worlds. . . . Despite this distribution of activity, police agencies are geared primarily to deal with crime.[16]

Goldstein and his University of Wisconsin colleague, Frank J. Remington, drafted the chapter dealing with the role of the police in *Task Force Report: The Police* of the 1966 President's Crime Commission. They wrote:

> There are two alternative ways in which police can respond to the difficult problems currently confronting them:
>
> 1. The first is to continue, as has been true in the past, with police making important decisions, but doing so by a process which can fairly be described as "unarticulated improvisation." This is a comfortable approach, requiring neither the police nor the community to face squarely the difficult social issues which are involved, at least until a crisis—like the current "social revolution"—necessitates drastic change.
> 2. The second alternative is to recognize the importance of the administrative policy-making function of police and to take appropriate steps to make this a process which is systematic, intelligent, articulate, and responsive to external controls appropriate in a democratic society—a process which anticipates social problems and adapts to meet them before a crisis situation arises.

Of the two, the latter is not only preferable; it is essential if major progress in policing is to be made, particularly in the large, congested urban areas.[17]

Goldstein goes on to observe:

The contrast between what the police actually do and the provisions made for staffing and directing the police agency is but one of a jumble of contradictions and conflicts within which the police must work. As one delves more deeply into the various factors that shape police functioning, one finds that laws, public expectations, and the realities of the tasks in which the police are engaged require all kinds of compromises and often place the police in a no-win situation.[18]

Another insightful Goldstein comment in the same source bears repeating, although more relevant to our discussion in chapter 1:

The police, by the very nature of their function, are an anomaly in a free society. They are invested with a great deal of authority under a system of government in which authority is reluctantly granted and when granted, sharply curtailed. The specific form of their authority—to arrest, to search, to detain, and to use force— is awesome in the degree to which it can be disruptive of freedom, invasive of privacy, and sudden and direct in its impact upon the individual. And this awesome authority, of necessity, is delegated to individuals at the lowest level of the bureaucracy, to be exercised, in most instances without prior review and control.[19]

LAW AND ORDER

Jerome Skolnick approaches the police role question from a slightly different angle. In his writings, he emphasizes the distinction between law and order and, more specifically, the conflict between two goals that might guide police behavior. One is adherence to the rule of law: police attitudes and actions that give high priority to the rights of citizens and to legal restraints upon government officials. The other is managerial efficiency: the goal of maintaining order with an efficient, technically sophisticated police organization. Skolnick feels that police in the United States tend to emphasize order as their goal, at the expense of legality. For Skolnick, maintaining order means controlling criminal behavior. His use of these terms differs from Wilson's. Skolnick states his position this way:

The common juxtaposition of "law and order" is an oversimplification. Law is not merely an instrument of order, but may frequently be its adversary. . . . The phrase "law and order" is misleading because it draws attention away from the substantial incompatibilities existing between the two ideas. Order under law is not concerned merely with achieving regularized social activity, but with the means used to come by peaceable behavior—certainly with procedure but also with the law itself. . . . In short, "law" and "order" are frequently found to be in opposition precisely because law implies rational restraint upon the rules and procedures utilized to achieve order. Order under law, therefore, subordinates the ideal of conformity to the ideal of legality.[20]

Skolnick's analysis brings to mind Herbert Packer's two visions of criminal justice, the *Crime Control* model and the *Due Process* model. Both have the prevention and deterrence of crime as their primary goal. Other than this, the models are conflicting in assumptions, in policies, and in operational procedures.

Bruce Terris, who served on the staff of the President's Crime Commission, offers a summarizing view:

> Improved police-minority relations require a radical change in the conception of both the police and the community, of what police work is all about. . . . The situations in which police officers most frequently find themselves do not require the expert aim of a marksman, the cunningness of a private eye, or the toughness of a stereotyped Irish policeman. Instead, they demand knowledge of human beings and the personal, as opposed to official, authority to influence people without the use or even the threat of force. These characteristics are not commonly found in police officers because police departments do not consider these values as paramount. As a result, persons with these abilities are not attracted to police work nor rewarded by promotion or incentive if they happen to enter a department.[21]

Fortunately, this condition has changed dramatically during the past generation, and it appears that it will be little more than nostalgia by the millennium.

VIEWS FROM OTHER COUNTRIES

In Canada, a Task Force on Policing in Ontario filed a report with the Solicitor General reflecting the results of its comprehensive study and making some 170 recommendations. Among them were these:

> Objectives within each police force be defined in terms of that community's requirements for crime control, protection of life and property, and maintenance of peace and order.
>
> The reality of police judgment in the application of law be squarely faced in each police force, and that deliberate and continuing steps be taken to ensure that each police officer has the ability to exercise his judgments so as to support the objectives and priorities of the force.[22]

The British Royal Commission on the Police had some relevant things to say in its *Final Report:*

> Efficiency is not the sole end of a good and wise administration of the police, and that the apparently confused police system which this country has inherited reflects not merely the British habit of adapting old institutions to meet new needs, but the interplay of conflicting principles of great constitutional importance which human minds have always found, and still find, the utmost difficulty in reconciling.[23]

A former Chief Inspector of Constabulary for Scotland, David Gray, has referred to the future of police service. Some police officers think, he says, that the police should become a highly specialized instrument of crime detection and law enforcement. Others wish to see a service combining scientific and operational efficiency with a policy of police involvement in the community designed to cultivate public confidence. The Police Advisory Board for Scotland has endorsed the latter line of development. Acting on this principle, Gray established community involvement branches in Scottish police forces with the primary aim of crime prevention.[24] To prevent crime, as Michael Banton puts it, "the police officer needs to know and be at the service of all sections of society."[25]

In 1995, the British Sheehy Commission examined the structure of the police service in England and Wales. While many of its recommendations for reform were controversial, the Commission clearly noted the need for local accountability of the police service.[26]

John Alderson, former chief constable of Devon and Cornwall, speaking to an International Conference on Police Accountability at the University of British Columbia in Vancouver, said:

> Social change has altered the game since the authoritarian and stratified society has been dismantled and the more free, permissive, participatory society has taken its place. The institutions designed for the authoritarian society have to adapt within their essential character or take on new forms. Policing arrangements are no exception. The impact of such change on policing arrangements has been profound, since the authoritarian concept of the police role has been undermined.

Later in the same presentation, he called for what he termed "a new ethic of policing," concerned mainly with the prevention of crime through "communal policing" directed against social disorganization leading to crime. He went on to say:

> It seems, therefore, that in their own responsibilities for the prevention and containment of crime, the police operate at three levels. The primary level challenges their ability to harness the proactive forces in society, exemplified in social participation of the kind which I have described. This represents their contribution to what I have described as a new ethic of policing. At the secondary level, they have to guard, to patrol, and to enforce the law . . . if the primary function is embedded in the communities, the secondary and enforcement role will be seen to be complementary to it. The common good is witnessed as being served. The tertiary role of the police may be said to be their investigative function which will, in turn, be enhanced by their success in the primary or social participation role. . . .[27]

As evident in the *Statement of Common Purpose* of the London Metropolitan Police (Appendix A) the "Met" is placing a strong emphasis on community-based policing as an inherent part of their role. This is also occurring in the British provincial forces. For example, in the Staffordshire Constabulary the police have been strongly involved in broad-based youth activities as part of their role. Similarly, officers in Staffordshire, Northumbria, Thames Valley, and West Mercia are aggressively involved in crime prevention and problem-solving activities.[28]

Given the close heritage of American policing and that in England, we may not be too surprised to see a similar evolution in the role and philosophy of policing. However, this perspective on the role of the police goes much further. For example, the South Korean National Police have slowly begun re-evaluating their role. They will undoubtedly remain a strong, military-type organization, but they have nonetheless started to direct some activities from a community-based perspective. Many of the staff members from the Korean National Police College have received graduate degrees in criminal justice in the United States. As a result of their exposure to policing change in this country, coupled with their own long-term concerns about policing in Korea, the role of the police is beginning to change.

Perhaps one of the most interesting areas to look at change in the police role is eastern Europe. Following the dramatic sociopolitical change in the former Soviet bloc countries in the late 1980s and early 1990s, coupled with the dissolution of the Warsaw Pact and the reunification of Germany, the police in the eastern European countries saw their role and responsibilities radically altered. In the former East Germany, many of the police command personnel were political appointees with the responsibility of ensuring that the "party line" was continually enforced. Their concern was less centered on crime control than on social control and limitation of emigration. Following reunification, West German police officials had to carefully review

THE UNITED NATIONS INTERREGIONAL CRIME AND JUSTICE RESEARCH INSTITUTE (UNICRI)

FOCUS 5.1

The United Nations has been mandated by its member states to address the growth of international crime, drug trafficking, transnational organized crime, drug abuse, and other forms of criminality as well as oppressive law enforcement practices by various governments. As a result of this mandate, the UN created the United Nations Interregional Crime and Justice Research Institute (UNICRI). Since its establishment in 1968 (originally the United Nations Social Defense Research Institute), new investigative methodologies, instruments, skills, and information have been developed to explore the criminological issues of the Institute's mandate.

The objective of the UNICRI, as specified in Article II of the United Nations Statute, is

> . . . to contribute, through research, training, field activities, and the collection, exchange, and dissemination of information, to the formulation and implementation of improved policies in the field of crime prevention and control, due regard being paid to the integration of such policies within broader policies for socioeconomic change and development, and to the protection of human rights (1992:3.)

The UNICRI's primary activities have been developed through programs in support of the objective. These include

all police officials in the eastern portion of the country to scrutinize their competence and honesty. Those officers (of all ranks) who remained with the police had to be re-trained in law, operations, and role in order to change their behavior from that of an oppressive force to one which the community could turn to for assistance. (Of course, the citizens of East Germany also have to be re-socialized to trust the police—a process that will require time).[29]

In Russia, the police are also facing a wide variety of new challenges. With less repression by the government, the opening of borders, movement to a free market economy, and an environment of social, economic, and political chaos, the police face major problems. Crime is increasing and the police have found that they are ill-prepared to deal with it. They have increasingly looked to the West in order to re-define their role and responses to these social problems. In Hungary and the Czech Republic great strides are being made in "democratic" policing and crime control, while many problems—including widespread corruption—remain in other former Soviet bloc countries.

The strong respect for civil rights found in the Netherlands, the concern for local neighborhood communications and control found in Japan, and the growing concern for citizen safety and crime control in Brazil, all are indicative of a movement to rethink the police role.

1. The identification of appropriate strategies, policies, and instruments for the prevention and control of the phenomena so as to contribute to socioeconomic development and to promote the protection of human rights;
2. The establishment of a reliable knowledge and information base on social problems involving juvenile delinquency and adult criminality, special attention being given to new, frequently transnational forms of these phenomena;
3. The formulation of practical models and systems in the foregoing context aimed at support for policy formulation, implementation, and evaluation in an operational sense;
4. The provision of action-orientated research and training related to the United Nations program for crime prevention and criminal justice;
5. Designing and carrying out training activities at the interregional level, and at the request of interested countries, at the national level; and
6. The promotion of the exchange of information by maintaining an international documentation center on criminology and related disciplines.

Research from UNICRI has both academic and practical applications. Understanding the international dimensions of crime and various responses to criminality can provide a much broader understanding of criminal justice issues in a world society which is increasingly transnational.

Leone, Ugo, *United Nations Interregional Crime and Justice Research Institute—Program Description* (Rome, Italy: United Nations, UNICRI, 1992).

Americans are a provincial people. We tend to judge progress, problems, and social evolution based upon the experiences within our own borders. Perhaps this is because of our geographic isolation, size, and success as a sovereign. This provincialism tends to blind us about progress and initiatives occurring in other parts of the world. Suffice it to note in this brief passage, that the American police are not the only ones experiencing role conflict and role change. It is increasingly a global experience.

ROLE THEORY

Sociologists devoted to role theory are not satisfied with the generalizations in which we have so far indulged. A few have found the police role question of special research interest. They have their own terminology for dealing with the question, for example, *role, role reciprocal, role set, role concept, role expectations, role performance, reference group, role model, generalized other, role conflict, isomorphism,* and so on.

A systematic empirical study of the police applying sociological role theory was done more than a decade age by Jack Preiss and Howard Ehrlich.[30] Their study of a state police organization testified to the complexity of the question. They found that there is, indeed, a great deal of confusion and ambiguity in role perceptions by police officers themselves. Trial-and-error learning and "playing it by ear" are intrinsic elements of police role behavior. Preiss and Ehrlich agreed that certain dilemmas faced by police officers are part of the structure of the police organization itself. They found little consensus in role perception among police officers at the same or at different levels of the organization. In turn, there was little consensus in how police officers perceived what others ("audience expectations," "significant others," etc.) required of them in role performance. Often this left the police officer choosing from among behavioral roles without adequate guidelines.

An example of what occurs under such circumstances would be a police department that lacks clearly defined organizational goals. The result is a paucity of well-delineated departmental policy and procedures, and a correlative lack of effective supervision. As a result, the patrol officer is perplexed in attempting to determine his or her responsibilities. Unsure of requirements or of subsequent reactions, such police officers tend to be guided by informal communication among peers and are inclined to apply personal values and interests, as well as "situational opportunism," as criteria for decision making. If police officers are unsure of the standards being used to evaluate their performance, they are left to decide for themselves whether it is better to be technically proficient or decently sensitive to people. This kind of decision bears on the nebulous nature of personnel evaluation processes in police organizations.

In a comprehensive article, looking over fifteen years of studies and publications dealing with the sociology of policing, English sociologist Maureen Cain reflects that it "has been taken for granted that we 'know' what the police, as an institution, really is."[31] This "myopia," she writes, "precludes, of course, the raising of questions about what the police *might* be." In one stimulating paragraph, she asserts:

> Police, then, *must be defined in terms of their key practice.* They are appointed with the task of maintaining the order which those who sustain them define as proper. Such a definition makes it possible to raise a much wider range of questions about police (no longer "the" police) than has hitherto been typical of sociological work. Questions can be raised about the additional jobs they do, about how these affect their relationship with their employers and those whom they police, about the formal and unofficial ways in which limits are and are not set to the means they can employ, and about who sets these limits—the employers or the policed.[32]

CAN THE POLICE ROLE DILEMMA BE RESOLVED?

Is there realistic hope that the riddle of the police role can be managed? The conflict is to some extent endemic to "the system" in democratic societies, and we cannot simply repeat the old bromide that more research is needed.

A beginning, as a matter of principle, is the recognition that no single formula will settle the question for all communities. It is a question to be dealt with community by community, and—in big cities—neighborhood by neighborhood. In simple terms, the style of policing should reflect the style of the community. This is the situation that has been rather haphazardly arrived at in many urban communities today. It is now being addressed in a more reasoned method based upon what the police have learned in the past three decades of research.

How exceedingly difficult it is to bring about massive and radical change in a large, urban police agency was demonstrated by the Police Foundation's six-year project in the Dallas Police Department. The expressed goal of the project was the identification of the basic needs of the Dallas community and the structuring of a police role conforming to these needs. The project failed, according to a foundation report, because as executed, it could not achieve this goal. Among other difficulties was the resignation of the police chief and his key staff and advisers, in the midst of pressure, upheaval, and dissension. The plan was said to be visionary, but there was little change in the attitudes and performance of police officers. Yet it was generally acknowledged that much could be learned from the mistakes made in this project.[33]

At heart, the role conundrum of the police is a political issue, and its resolution is correspondingly a matter of political process. Understanding the dynamics of different community characteristics and responding with a proper politically acceptable action is a challenge that cannot be taken lightly.

QUESTIONS FOR DISCUSSION

1. Explain the sense in which the role dilemma of the police is basically a political question.
2. At the beginning of the twentieth century, American police were functionally geared toward "order maintenance." Why has this role orientation shifted?
3. What type of role dilemma do contemporary police officers find themselves in given the shift toward community policing?
4. Why has the traditional self-defined role of the police as "crime fighters" been misleading?
5. Why may the police be referred to as an "anomaly" in a free society?
6. Can the role of the police differ between communities? Support your response with your reasoning.
7. We are seeing police role changes occur not only in the U.S. but also in other countries. What are the prominent reasons for these changes?
8. If we say the role of a police officer is that of "problem solver," how does this differ from the traditional role vision?
9. Why does Jerome Skolnick argue that the phrase "law and order" is misleading?
10. Can the role dilemmas be resolved? If so, how? If not, why?

NOTES

1. U.S. National Advisory Commission on Civil Disorders, *Report of the National Advisory Commission on Civil Disorders (Kerner Report)*, (Washington, DC: U.S. Government Printing Office, 1968), p. 157.
2. Oscar Handlin, "Community Organization as a Solution to Police-Community Problems," *Police Chief* 32, no. 3 (March 1965): 18–19.
3. For a more detailed discussion of this point, see President's Commission on Law Enforcement and Administration of Justice, *Field Surveys IV* (Washington, DC: U.S. Government Printing Office, 1967), vol. 1, pp. 25–28.
4. Roger Lane, *Policing the City: Boston, 1822–1855* (Cambridge: Harvard University Press, 1967).
5. James Q. Wilson, "What Makes a Better Policeman?" *Atlantic Monthly* 233, no. 3 (March 1969): 132.
6. Ibid., p. 133.
7. Ibid.
8. Ernest Jerome Hopkins, *Our Lawless Police* (New York: Viking Press, 1931).
9. Peter K. Manning, "The Police and Crime: Crime and the Police," *Sociologische Gids*, Maurice Punch, ed. (May 1, 1978).
10. See Robert Trojanowicz and Bonnie Bucqueroux, *Community Policing* (Cincinnati: Anderson Publishing Company, 1990). Also John Eck and William Spelman, *Problem Oriented Policing* (Washington, DC: National Institute of Justice, 1988).
11. James Q. Wilson, "Dilemmas of Police Administration," *Public Administration Review* 28, no. 5 (September/October, 1968): 407.
12. Ibid., p. 408.
13. James Q. Wilson, *Varieties of Police Behavior: The Management of Law and Order in Eight Communities* (Cambridge: Harvard University Press, 1968), p. 3. Reprinted by permission.
14. Gordon E. Misner, "Enforcement: Illusion of Security," *Nation* 208, no. 16 (April 21, 1969): 488.
15. Ibid., p. 489.
16. Herman Goldstein, "Police Response to Urban Crises," *Public Administration Review* 28, no. 5 (September/October, 1968): 417–18. Reprinted with permission from *Public Administration Review*. Copyright © 1963, 1968 by The American Society for Public Administration, 1120 G Street, N.W., Suite 500, Washington, DC. All rights reserved. A classic description of the "soft" side of policing is

Egon Bittner's "The Police on Skid-Row: A Study of Peacekeeping," *American Sociological Review* 32 (1967): 699–715.

17. U.S., President's Commission on Law Enforcement and Administration of Justice, *Task Force Report: The Police* (Washington, DC: U.S. Government Printing Office, 1967), p. 18.

18. Herman Goldstein, *Policing a Free Society* (Cambridge: Ballinger Publishing Co., 1977), p. 9.

19. Ibid., p. 1.

20. Jerome H. Skolnick, *Professional Police in a Free Society* (New York: National Conference on Christians and Jews, 1967), pp. 10–11. Reprinted by permission of the National Conference of Christians and Jews.

21. Bruce J. Terris, "The Role of the Police," *Annals of the American Academy of Political and Social Science* 374 (November 1967): 67. Reprinted by permission.

22. Task Force on Policing in Ontario, *The Public Are the Police: The Police Are the Public*, Report to the Solicitor-General of Ontario (Ottawa: Office of the Solicitor-General of Canada, 1974).

23. Great Britain, British Royal Commission on the Police, *Final Report* (London: Her Majesty's Stationery Office, 1962). George E. Berkley reflects on European views of the police role in *The Democratic Policeman* (Boston: Beacon Press, 1969).

24. Quoted by Michael Banton in "The Definition of the Police Role," *New Community* 3, no. 3 (Summer 1974): 164–71.

25. Ibid., p. 171.

26. Sheehy Commission. *A Review of Police Organization and Practices in England and Wales: Executive Summary.* (London: Her Majesty's Stationery Office, 1995.)

27. See John C. Alderson and Philip J. Stead, eds., *The Police We Deserve* (London: Wolfe Publishing, 1973).

28. Charles Kelly, Chief Constable, *Annual Report of the Staffordshire Constabulary* (Stafford, United Kingdom, 1992).

29. David L. Carter, "A Forecast of Growth of Organized Crime in Europe: New Challenges for Law Enforcement," *Police Studies* (Fall).

30. Jack J. Preiss and Howard J. Ehrlich, *An Examination of Role Theory: The Case of the State Police* (Lincoln: University of Nebraska Press, 1966).

31. Maureen Cain, "Trends in the Sociology of Police Work," *International Journal of the Sociology of Law* (1979): 7, 143–67.

32. Ibid., p. 158.

33. Mary Ann Wycoff and George L. Kelling, *The Dallas Experience: Human Resource Development*, vol. 1 (Washington, DC: The Police Foundation, Inc., 1978).

Chapter 6

ROLE AND PROFESSIONALISM

Since the emergence of the reform movement, police leaders have spoken of the "professional" police officer. The term "professional" conjures up different perspectives. Ideally, if the police behave professionally and are perceived as professional, they will more effectively fulfill their role. Similarly, they will provide a better *quality* of service which, ideally, will also result in greater satisfaction by the public.

The character of a "professional police officer" has changed somewhat since the vision of August Vollmer. Given the early initiatives in the "reform era," the professional orientation was primarily focused on police administrators. Later it was directed toward the street officer, with the "ideal" being the thorough, impartial, unemotional officer (somewhat similar to *Dragnet's* Sergeant Joe Friday). Another image which evolved was that of the college-educated officer. This suggests that the distinction of a "professional police officer" is evolutionary and that we have made strides, but have not yet fully reached the goal.

This chapter will address these issues in greater detail from both philosophical and pragmatic perspectives.

THE IDEA OF PROFESSIONALISM

In contemporary police circles, "professionalism" is a favorite topic, in conversation, in publications, and in critical analysis. The assumption is that everyone knows what it means, and there is a further assumption that full-fledged professional recognition and status are highly desirable.

Logically, our idea of what it means to be a professional police officer is governed by our notion of the police officer's role in society. It could be argued that, if we emphasize the law enforcement function, professionalism means attributes conducive to this function, for example, courage, respect for superiors, reliability, and obedience. If, instead, we emphasize the peace-keeping side of policing, then professionalism means attributes such as intelligence, common sense, friendliness, courtesy, and patience. While this is admittedly an oversimplification of the issues, it illustrates the point.

There also appear to be both law enforcement and peace-keeping orientations for police-citizen interaction. A law enforcement orientation emphasizes what the community should do to assist the police in such activities as containing crime, catching crooks, and providing information about "suspicious persons." This has been popularly referred to as "romancing the police." A peace-keeping orientation for police and community relations is more likely to emphasize what the police and community can do together as partners. *Preventing* crime as well as disorder is seen as an important objective of this partnership. In this conception, receiving information and interpreting it are two-way processes.

For the police, a law enforcement orientation for police-citizen interaction tends to emphasize public relations, while a peace-keeping orientation emphasizes community participation. The essence of the peace-keeping orientation is mutual trust so that citizens may regard helping the police as, in effect, helping themselves to create a better community.

As generalized abstractions, these distinctions may be important only to theoreticians. In practice, a given police agency will probably have some of both orientations evident in its organization and activities. Inevitably, therefore, discussions of professionalism are predictably argumentative, as are discussions of role emphasis.

There are two general characteristics of professionalism, in any field, that should be mentioned. One is that professional recognition and status is a matter of *community attitudes*. What makes a profession professional is the public saying that it is. It is a public certification of competence. That is what "a license to practice" means. The other characteristic of professionalism is its *relativity*. Police Department A is more, or less, professional than Police Department B. Police Department C is more or less professional today than it was ten years ago. Police Officer Smith is more or less professional than Police Officer Jones.

There is also another element of relativity involved in professionalism. The judgments cited above are made relative to certain standards as to what constitutes professionalism. Inevitably these standards are role-related.

MARKS OF A PROFESSION

What marks do we look for in identifying a profession or a professional? One mark is that the constituency has arrived at some consensus regarding the "product" of the profession—the mission or social role. Another mark is specialized knowledge, proficiency and skills, attained through rigorous education and training—probably in specialized schools or academies, certified or accredited by professional standards monitors. Leadership is another mark expected of professionals. They should be teachers, sharing what they have learned.

There are numerous other marks of a profession. It is *client-oriented*. It has a *service* ideal. It caters to human needs, not wants. It is self-policing; it has an *ethic*. *Pecuniary profit* is not a primary objective. It tends to develop an esoteric language, a distinctive terminology. It also develops professional organizations and symbols, artifacts, and journals. Professionals enjoy considerable autonomy in their decisions—so-called professional judgments, not without some restriction, surely, but with comfortable latitude in exercising their discretion.[1]

We begin to see that our definition of professionalism, or of a professional, will depend considerably upon what we regard as important in a particular field—what priorities we feel ought to be emphasized by workers in that field.

The dictionary defines a *profession* as "a calling requiring specialized knowledge and often long and intensive academic preparation, used by way either of instructing, guiding, or advising others, or of serving them in some art."

Sometimes in discussions of professionalism, reference is made to what is called *attitude*, for example, in the aphorism "attitude makes the professional." Attitude, although elusive and difficult to define in a concrete way, becomes somewhat more manageable when it is applied to the relationship between a professional and a client. The late Alexander Woolcott had attitude in mind when he defined a professional as "someone who does his best job when he feels worst."

Now we might pause for a momentary exercise. Ask yourself which of these marks of professionalism, when applied to police work, seem to pertain more to the law enforcement side, which seem to pertain more to the order maintenance side, and which seem to pertain to both. Question: which role is the greater test of professionalism, that is, which role provides the greater opportunity for truly professional demeanor? Hold your answer a bit as we note that the Wickersham Commission tipped its hand in 1931:

> If the job of the police is to catch crooks, then the police have a technical, ministerial responsibility in which discretion plays little part. Since no one is likely to disagree on the value of the objective, then there is little reason to expose the police to the decision-making processes of city government. *Ergo*, take the police "out of politics."[2]

SOCIAL CHANGE AND PROFESSIONALISM

Before going on to consider professionalism more specifically with respect to the police, there are a couple more aspects of the subject. One is that there seems to be no limit today to the desire to be recognized as a "professional." Painters, carpenters, plumbers, building custodians, barbers, beauticians, electricians, television repair people—the list could go on and on. Everybody wants to be a professional! An increasingly technocratic and skill-conscious society has made it more difficult to distinguish between a technician and a professional. What's the difference between a doctor and a plumber, or between a lawyer and a trade union official—especially since some of the latter are also lawyers? How does either compare with a computer technician, in terms of knowledge, proficiency, training, etc.?

Once there were only a few recognized professions. Status as a professional was prized. Does a multiplication of professions water down this status? Does it blur distinctions once held sacred? Does it matter all that much? Bear in mind that in the world of fifty years ago, when a high school diploma was widely regarded as an unusual educational achievement, a college baccalaureate meant professionalism of some kind. This is changing. There are many bartenders today with baccalaureates, and there are quite a few city planners with doctorates in urban development. Our traditional concept of professionalism has been "turned upside down."[3]

BUREAUCRACY AND PROFESSIONALISM

Another relevant consideration, adding to the confusion, is the fact that it has become fashionable to equate bureaucracy with professionalism. Bureaucracy is a system of administration characterized by specialization of functions, by adherence to fixed rules, and by a hierarchy of authority. The more bureaucratic the organization, the more professional it is deemed to be. While the argument over the compatibility of bureaucracy and professionalism will continue endlessly, most analysts agree that these "models" clash at certain points. Several years ago, for instance, sociologist Harold Wilensky argued that the distinctive standards of a profession are its *technical* basis (systematic knowledge or doctrine acquired only through long prescribed training), and its adherence to *professional norms* (ethic, attitude, client relations, etc.). He emphasized *autonomous expertise* and the service ideal. Bureaucracy enfeebles the service ideal more than it threatens autonomy, Wilensky asserted, and he concluded that very few occupations will achieve the authority of the established professions. If we call everything a profession, he said, we obscure its meaning and make it less a prize to be earned only by meeting demanding requirements.[4]

The professional and bureaucratic organizational models clash at several points. For instance, professionalism means critical thinking, questioning, and inquiry. Bureaucracy suggests doing what one is told, lest one's loyalty to the organization be questioned. We shall return to this point momentarily in a discussion of the distinction between organizational efficiency and effectiveness.

PROFESSIONALISM AND THE POLICE

In the face of such arguments, it may well be wondered how important it is, really, to go on building a case for the police as professionals. Maybe the question has become largely academic. If a building custodian is a professional, then the security officer in the same building would appear to have some justification for awarding himself the same status.

Before his retirement as Washington, DC, police chief, Jerry V. Wilson struck a sobering note. "Somehow," he wrote, "in the transition from individualized to institutionalized professions, we have come to suppose that no one but 'professionals' perform important, worthwhile tasks. The truth is that more often than not, it is the 'non-professionals' of any given work unit who perform most of the productive work." Chief Wilson's definition of a professional seemed to include anyone doing productive work. If his view were generally accepted, there would be reasonable question as to whether the whole matter merited serious attention—which may be what he was suggesting.

If one goes back to earlier statements regarding police professionalism, at a time when perhaps the idea provoked more interest because far fewer people adorned themselves with the mantle, one finds some stimulating commentary. For example, in 1959, James Slavin—then chief of the Kalamazoo (Michigan) Police Department, later the chief in Denver and until his retirement, director of the Traffic Institute at Northwestern University—told the Fifth National Institute on Police and Community Relations at Michigan State University of a number of obstacles to the professional development of American police. One was the hesitancy to carry out vigilant internal monitoring of police practices. Another was his impression that some so-called professional police organizations and associations were indistinguishable from labor and craft unions. Slavin hastened to add, on this point, that he was not critical of labor and craft unions; he was merely calling attention to the difference that is generally assumed to exist between a union and a professional association.

Slavin pointed to "a most imperceptible progress in establishing documented standards for selection of police personnel from our citizenry." He said that little information was available describing what qualifications were necessary to predict a successful police career. Another shortcoming, according to Slavin, was the inadequacy of training for supervisory responsibility in police agencies. He advocated wider uses of training methods similar to those of business and industry. Slavin concluded: "The thing we fail to emphasize in our writings and discussions is that it is the characteristics that mark a profession that are worthwhile, rather than talking frequently as though what we want most of all is to be identified as a professional occupation."[5]

A few police officers who heard Slavin speak on that occasion took sharp exception to his view. Some still would today: surprisingly little has changed! A much more popular view with police officers, then and now, was expressed in an editorial in *The Police Chief*:

> I know of no period in recent history when the police have been the subject of so many unjustified charges of brutality, harassment and ineptness. It almost seems that the better we do our job enforcing the law, the more we are attacked. The more professional we become, the more effective we become and the more effective we are, the more we impinge upon the misbehavior of society.
>
> But for this we should offer no apology. A police force is established, among other things for the purpose of enforcing existing laws. In this respect, we are dutybound. Those who damn our actions in this regard must be made to understand that the police do not make the laws, that laws are the direct product of public desires, and if the public does not like those laws or believe them to be fair, then the public should change the laws rather than criticize the police. . . . We can no longer afford to answer unjust criticism with thinly veiled innuendoes and pusillanimous generalities. If we are right, let's say so.[6]

Interestingly, this 1964 editorial reflects many of the frustrations felt by the police as we approach the year 2000. Despite better relations with the community, more enlightened police leadership, and higher caliber officers, the humanity of officers is all too often overlooked by the public when an unfortunate incident occurs. All officers are therefore stereotyped.[7]

Some advocates of police professionalism see police officers as "healing physicians of a sick society," but the analogy probably loses some of its appeal when spelled out by Norman Cousins:

> Finally, the good [medical] doctor is not only a scientist but a philosopher. He knows that the facts of medicine will continue to change and that, therefore, his professional training can never be an absolute guide to good practice. It is his philosophy of medicine that has to serve as the solid base of his practice. The doctor's respect for life, his special qualities of compassion and tenderness—even under the most devilish of circumstances—these are the vital ingredients of his art. To such a doctor, the most exotic diagnostic machines are not more important than the simple act of sitting at the beside of a patient. In this sense, the ultimate art of the good doctor is to make good patients. He does this by making the patient a full partner in his recovery. Such a doctor is worth all the recognition and reward a society is capable of offering.[8]

Many police officers would regard this view of police work—in the sense of its "bedside manner with clients"—as going a bit far, although one might hope that "making the patient a full partner" would be quite acceptable. Indeed, we are moving toward this in community policing.

There is, of course, a vast literature on the subject of police professionalism. But our particular interest is in its role-related dimensions, about which several observers merit quoting, especially for the police-community relations implications.

First, and again, Jerome Skolnick:

> It is not surprising that the solution to "the police problem" in America has been
> frequently conceived as changing the quality of people, rather than the philosophies
> of policing. . . . Police reform means finding a new source of police, and police
> control is a matter of having the "right" sort of people in control. "Reform" of police
> means increasing the efficiency of police personnel. It is rarely recognized that the
> conduct of police may be related in a fundamental way to the character and goals of
> the institution itself—the duties police are called upon to perform, associated with
> the assumptions of the system of legal justice—and that it may not be men who are
> good or bad, so much as the premises and design of the system in which they find
> themselves.[9]

Next, Patrick V. Murphy, former president of the Police Foundation and career
police executive in New York City, Syracuse, Detroit, and Washington:

> The police alone cannot solve the crime problem. Neither can the combined police
> and criminal justice "system"—even if it were improved to merit the "system" label.
> But the police could do far better if they understood their potential, as well as their
> limits, and spoke clearly and honestly to the public about both. They have failed to
> understand. They have failed to educate the public. They have contributed more to
> the problem than to its solution by defending the status quo when basic change is
> needed.[10]

Writing in *Law Enforcement News*, E. J. Jenkins, Jr., editorialized:

> A general review of police recruiting practices shows that few police agencies seek
> the necessary character traits needed to fulfill the police mission. The bulk of the
> screening processes used in recruiting police officers demonstrates a rather
> cardboard reliance on basic intelligence and agility tests, with great emphasis put on
> education, especially at the college level. Relatively few police agencies seek
> applicants with character levels high in such areas as salesmanship and idealism, two
> most essential police qualities, the former needed to get along with and relate to
> people, and the latter needed to insulate the individual from corruption and a very
> frustrating judicial system. In fact, few police administrators look for character
> traits at all, but would rather stick to the traditional mode of selecting police officers
> despite the little job relevance these methods contain.[11]

James Q. Wilson's two-factor explanation of the early twentieth century shift of
American policing from order maintenance to law enforcement has a parallel sociological explanation by Peter Manning. Political pluralism and localism in the allocation of political responsibility, Manning feels, was one significant influence, and the
second was ethnic diversity. Thus, "rather than drawing on a central authority,
American police departments must operate within *local political contexts*. Local issues are reflected in the control and behavior of the police more in the United States
than in the United Kingdom. The symbolic canopy of authority is more problematic
in America for police organizations. They are implicated continuously in generating
and maintaining public support . . ."[12]

Manning continues:

> When one looks in fact at what the police *do*, it is clear that they are dirty workers
> . . . . They fight crime in the same sense that academics fight ignorance—in theory
> . . . . There is a contradiction between the public and the private role of the police:
> it is perhaps the very centrality of the police role to maintaining our sense of public

morality that requires it to be such a multivalent and contradictory role, requiring the management of such diverse duties, audiences, and behaviors.[13]

Manning refers, then, to the contradictory expectations bearing on American police as "dramatic dilemmas of policing."

ORDER MAINTENANCE RECONSIDERED

It may seem that we have strayed from our agenda of police professionalism and wandered back again to the matter of role. Not at all; what we have here are interwoven threads in a single tapestry. We are leaning toward a conclusion that the real test of professionalism for the police is much more in their order maintenance or peace-keeping role than in their law enforcement role. And in this exploration is to be found the guidance we need to respond to our earlier question about matching up the marks of professionalism with either of the two roles.

At this point, a breakdown of the peace-keeping side of the police job may be helpful. Egon Bittner[14] has identified five types of situations in which the police often become involved:

1. The regulation of various types of businesses that lend themselves to exploitation for undesirable and illegal purposes.
2. The handling of a wide variety of situations in which the law has in fact been violated, but the officer chooses to dispose of the situation by employing some alternative in invoking criminal process.
3. Intervention in an infinite array of situations—to arbitrate quarrels, to pacify the unruly, and to aid people in trouble.
4. Dealing with mass phenomena, such as crowds, where there is the potential for disorder.
5. Caring for those who are less than fully accountable for their actions, such as the young, the alcoholic, and the mentally ill.

Bittner notes that the police function is "only in a trivial sense determined by those considerations of legality that determine law enforcement."

If the police make their case for professionalism mainly in their order maintenance functions, to what lengths may this be extended? There are, of course, reasonable limits. There is a point in many situations where it becomes rather clear that referral is the appropriate action. To know at what point is a *professional* judgment: to back off for medical people, for counselors and psychologists and psychiatrists, for social workers of many types, etc. There should be no problem with this; a police officer delivers a baby only when there is no choice!

But there is often a functional gray area in order maintenance, as there is also in law enforcement. It appears that in this gray area, the two roles most logically blend together. James Q. Wilson and George L. Kelling discussed this in an article on a neighborhood foot patrol program in Newark, New Jersey, evaluated for its results by the Police Foundation some five years after the program's initiation. The article notes that the program did not seriously reduce the crime rate, to no one's surprise, but residents of the foot patrol neighborhood felt more secure than people in other areas and had a more favorable opinion of the police. Officers walking beats had higher morale, greater job satisfaction, and a more favorable attitude toward citizens of their neighborhoods than did officers assigned to motorized patrol. The question was, how can a neighborhood be "safer" when the crime rate had not gone down?

Wilson and Kelling concluded that what foot patrol officers did was to raise the level of public order—and this despite the fact that the officers were white and most of the residents were black. To understand this requires recognizing a difference between resident fear of real crime and anxiety created by a sense of a street being disorderly. Disorder and crime go together. Suppose a window in a building is broken and left unrepaired. All the rest of the windows will soon be broken. One broken window left unrepaired is a sign that no one cares.

Wilson and Kelling reason:

> We suggest that "untended" behavior also leads to the breakdown of neighborhood controls. A stable neighborhood of families who care for their homes, mind each other's children, and confidently frown on unwanted intruders can change, in a few years or even a few months, to an inhospitable and frightening jungle. . . . Such an area is vulnerable to criminal invasion.[15]

The analysis of this type of situation by Wilson and Kelling is lengthy and detailed, and we cannot do justice to it here. But their central point is that "the essence of the police role in maintaining order is to reinforce the informal control mechanisms of the community itself." To do this, they argue, is a vital police job. From the vantage point of public attitudes toward the police, effective police performance of this nature substantiates their "professional image."

EFFICIENCY VERSUS EFFECTIVENESS

Mentioning "effective" police performance leads us to another consideration, the distinction between organizational efficiency and effectiveness. Skolnick has much to say on this subject:

> The problem of police in a democratic society is not merely a matter of obtaining new police cars or more sophisticated equipment, or communication systems, or of recruiting men [sic] who have to their credit more years of education. What is necessary is a significant alteration in the philosophy of police so that police "professionalization" rests upon the values of a democratic legal polity, rather than merely on the notion of technical proficiency to serve the public order of the state.[16]

Skolnick again, later in the same reference:

> If the police are ever to develop a conception of legal as opposed to managerial professionalism, two conditions must be met: First, the police must accustom themselves to the seemingly paradoxical yet fundamental idea of the rule of law, namely, that the observance of legal restraints may indeed make their task more difficult. That's how it is in a free society. Second, the civic community must support compliance with the rule of law by rewarding police for observing constitutional guarantees, instead of looking to the police as merely an institution responsible for controlling criminality. In practice, regrettably, the reverse has been true. The police function in a milieu tending to support, normatively and substantively, the idea of administrative efficiency as an index of police professionalism. Steps must be taken to reverse this trend. The observance of the principles of legality will indeed be the hallmark of professional police in a free society.[17]

Numerous authors refer to the same point. Herman Goldstein, for instance, observes that increased operating efficiency in police agencies is truly a worthwhile goal. But "an increasing number of people," he writes, "have come to express dissatisfaction with the professional model and its commitment to efficiency as the *ultimate* goal of police reform."[18]

So how are organizational efficiency and effectiveness distinguished, granting that one is a means to the other, and thus that both are important? John Matthews and Ralph Marshall have done a good job in clarifying the distinction. Criminal justice organizations, they opine, are like other organizations in that they must serve both organizational and service ideals, the latter meaning client needs. Organizational ideals are internal, having to do with such matters as survival, growth, maintenance, internal conflict, and threats from the environment. Unfortunately, what happens too often is that disproportionate organizational resources are directed to these internal needs, and what is left are directed externally to serve client needs. Considerations of efficiency tend to subsume considerations of effectiveness. Moreover, "organizations tend to reward participants whose behavior focuses on organizational rather than client needs."[19]

A pertinent citation is:

> Now I would maintain that a profession serves *needs*, not *wants*. I don't particularly care about being a pal with my doctor, but I do want to respect him for his competence, his skill, and his attitude as a professional. I don't think he should go out of his way to be a pal to me either. When I need his help, I want something more from him than soothing assertions that he'll never let me down. . . . May I suggest [then] what I regard as the first implication of the professional concept [in law enforcement] for police-community relations: to woo the client's respect, not his favor—in short, to reassert authority as a necessary corollary to responsibility.[20]

Efficiency is doing the *job right*—providing "value for money" to our clients (the community). Effectiveness is doing the *right job* and includes rewarding officers who help attain the department's goals. It is preferred that an organization be both efficient and effective as long as the community needs are served and the boundaries of performance remain balanced.

SO WHAT'S THE MESSAGE?

Police officers reading this chapter may feel that the tone is antipolice. One can understand this reaction while at the same time calling it inexpedient. If the cause of police professionalism is to be taken seriously, it is essential that the police react professionally to critical review. Recall also that professionalism is a police-community transaction, including the hope and prospects for it. The police are not walking this beat alone!

What's the message? It comes down to this: police professionalism *without a human dimension* is not a very significant goal—as many analysts have indicated. If there were greater police and community consensus, community by community, about where the emphasis should be in the role of the police, the arguments about police professionalism would soon wane.

There is a sense in which police professionalism may not be a desirable goal. If all it means is more "hardware" and equipment, more military posturing, more bureaucracy, more impersonality in client relations, more isolation from the community on the grounds that citizens cannot possibly know as much as "professionals," more efficiency and less effectiveness—if this is what police professionalism means, let's forget it. On the other hand, if it means such things as positive attitude and quality service to all clients, ethics in police behavior, meeting human needs without "hangups" about whether it is police work or social work—if this is what police professionalism means, let's go all out for it. Remember, too, that not everyone who works in the police station has to be a "professional." There should be plenty of room and recognition for those who are technicians and, indeed, custodians.

Professionalism in any field is, at base, behavioral. It should not be viewed as an abstract concept for detached academic scrutiny and discussion. If it is to have any meaning, any activation, it must be in the manner of acting by officers in their daily, routine dealings with citizens, their clients. Officer attitude and behavior is what matters, not rhetoric and proclamations.

SOME REMAINING THOUGHTS

Earlier in this chapter, there was a reference to an analogy between the police and lawyers or medics. It is a frequently used buttress in discussions of police professionalism.

> Professionalism is a term that must be understood in a special sense when applying it to policemen. Generally speaking, a profession provides a service (such as medical aid or legal advice), the quality of which the client is not in a position to judge for himself; therefore, a professional body and a professional code must be established to protect both the client from his ignorance and the profession from the client who supposes that he is not ignorant. The policeman differs from the doctor or lawyer, however, in important respects: first, his role is not to cure or advise but to restrain; and second, whereas health and counsel are welcomed by the recipients, restraint is not. If this is true, then professionalism among policemen will differ from professionalism in other occupations in that the primary function of the professional code will be to protect the practitioner from the client rather than the client from the practitioner.[21]

Accountability looms large as a mark of professionalism, with self-monitoring as a means to this end. Accountability of the police is clearly increasing due to enlightened, responsible leadership and increased openness between the police and community. While the system is certainly not perfect, a series of conferences sponsored by the National Institute of Justice in 1997 observed that police integrity was at its highest level. Moreover, police executives were aggressively pursuing policies and practices to ensure high quality, responsible police service.

Another perspective refers to the police as having "turned to their own councils," as represented by police fraternal organizations. As William Brown puts it, "They [the fraternal organizations] are his unquestioning champions and today's policeman [sic] needs a champion." Thus it is that the police respond to current pressures "by withdrawing from the professional arena to the blue-collar world." With this goes apathy, "the classic reaction of a group to what it sees as a hopeless situation."[22]

In developing basically the same thought, John Pfiffner refers to the "isolation syndrome" of the police, and his diagnosis of the pressures that explain it is similar to Brown's. As a result, Pfiffner says, the police turn to what he calls "guild protectionism," born out of self-pity and the failure to make personal adjustments to extreme vocational tensions.[23]

What about the line officer and the service ideal of professionalism? Albert Reiss has observed that our larger American police departments have become major bureaucratic organizations. Many of their problems are, therefore, peculiar to bureaucracy. Reiss contends that most attempts to professionalize police work have led to a professionalization of the police department, to a lesser extent to the professionalization of those in staff positions, and only to a relatively minor extent to professionalization of the rank-and-file officer. He states that the nature of changes within police departments has tended to work against the professionalization of the line officer. The department has been professionalized, says Reiss, through bureaucratization, and the line officer accordingly becomes no more than a technician who takes orders. Reiss also maintains that broader societal changes work against professionalization of the line officer, primarily through redefinition of the police role. He argues that the nature of police work "coerces discretionary decision-making in social situations, and both the end and the means valued by our society require that in the long run at least part of the line must be 'professional'"[24] With the move toward community policing, line officers are becoming more professional, and the rules permit them to become more empowered. As a result, the officers are held to higher standards of accountability.

Reiss is particularly interested in the relationship of the professional with clients. He characterizes this relationship as technical, in the sense of specialized knowledge to be applied in practice. The client relationship, moreover, is moral and ethical. But its central feature is a decision about the client in which the professional decides something relating to the future of the client. This feature of the professional-client relationship is especially critical when the client has little choice about whether to abide by the decision of the professional.

To support his view that the professionalization of police departments through bureaucratization has worked against the professionalization of the line officer, Reiss points to three factors:

1. The increasing centralization of decision-making in departments. A bureaucratic system where decision making is decentralized to the line would be more consistent with professionalization of the line.
2. The tendency of specialization in police organizations to be more technical than professional. It has been more "professionalization of the organizational system" than it has been professional role specialization. Writing tickets in traffic enforcement, for example, is a work assignment, a technical job specialty. It does not involve professional decision-making by the line officer.
3. The making of decisions at the staff rather than the operating level of police departments, and the bringing in of professional specialists at the staff rather than the operating level. As an illustration, "human relations" in many departments is largely a staff function. It is handled through central orders, leaving little room for "professional treatment of clients" by the line officer.

Fortunately, these are precisely the issues addressed in community-based reform. Policing generalists with decentralized authority using creative approaches for community problem solving is the direction in which we are now moving. Assessing these criteria as a gauge of professionalism suggests that policing is moving closer to this ideal.[25]

Wilensky observed that the professional norm of selflessness is more than mere lip service: "The service ideal is the pivot around which the moral claim to professional status revolves."[26] It would be difficult to express more eloquently a major implication of police professionalism for police and community relations.

PROFESSIONALISM AND EDUCATION

One factor which is considered an important benchmark of a profession is the educational level of personnel—certainly it has been an issue in law enforcement. In the late 1960s there was flurry of activity related to higher education and law

"One factor which is considered an important benchmark of a profession is the educational level of personnel . . ."

enforcement. The impetus for this activity was a result of several factors: civil unrest; the way the police responded to this unrest and disorder; police relationships with minorities; increasing interest in law enforcement research; changes toward the "reform" management style in policing; and a vision of policing as "professionalism." Perhaps most significant, however, were the recommendations of the *President's Commission on Law Enforcement and Administration of Justice*, followed by passage of the *Omnibus Crime Control and Safe Streets Act* in 1968.

The President's Commission recommended that police educational standards be raised, with the ultimate goal of requiring a baccalaureate degree as a minimum standard for employment.[27] The basis for this recommendation was the increasing complexity of police tasks, coupled with police officers' need for a strong foundation on which to base many critical decisions while policing the community. In order to facilitate the series of educationally related recommendations of the President's Commission, a provision of the Omnibus Crime Control Act was the creation of the *Law Enforcement Education Program* (LEEP):

> LEEP was a program to stimulate criminal justice personnel to attend college. In the case of the police, the belief was that better-educated law enforcement officers would provide more responsive, more comprehensive, and more insightful police service. In the long term, as college-educated officers rose into police leadership positions, they would explore new approaches, with more creativity and better planning.[28]

Thus, the recommendations of the President's Commission and the financial incentives available through LEEP formed the nucleus of a movement toward increasing police educational levels. Colleges and universities developed law enforcement/criminal justice degree programs and police departments began to establish incentive pay, educational leave, and other educationally related policies. Overall interest in police education grew, characterized by increased research, growth in organizations related to criminal justice education, such as the Academy of Criminal

Justice Sciences, and large enrollments in criminal justice programs. Further incentive was given when the *National Advisory Commission on Criminal Justice Standards and Goals* set target dates by which police departments were to establish formal educational requirements.[29]

Why Higher Education as a Hallmark of Professionalism?

The trend toward college education in policing was gaining momentum. Higher education *seemed* to be a good idea for the police; it *appeared* to be a logical evolutionary step for a profession in its adolescence; many people *believed* that the college experience would make officers perform better. Observers of the "education movement" urged caution and contemplation, however, expressing concern that curricula and policy were based on emotion and intuition rather than on research. In fact, these criticisms were largely true. Arguments presented in support of the President's Commission recommendations, the LEEP standards, and the National Advisory Commission's goals were generally rhetorical rather than scientific.

Just as concerns were expressed about the general value of a higher education for the police, other criticisms were directed toward the quality of curricula and instruction in college criminal justice programs. Most noteworthy in this regard was the Police Foundation–sponsored *National Advisory Commission on Higher Education of Police Officers*. The essence of the Commission's inquiry—which came to be known as the "Sherman Report"—was that law enforcement education had serious limitations. It was suggested that even if the arguments in support of police college requirements were valid, the overall benefits of college would not be realized because of qualitative inadequacies in academic course inventories, course content, and faculty credentials.[30]

Once again, many of the Sherman Report's criticisms were true. Standards were low, police officers who were just starting college often received "life experience" credits, and in many cases police training hours were converted to academic credits. There were also charges of "academic profit-taking" where institutions were accused of taking advantage of LEEP monies and large criminal justice course enrollments to offset funding and enrollment shortages in other areas. Unfortunately, since law enforcement/criminal justice was not viewed as a "true" academic discipline, institutional standards for both faculty and students were lower than one would find in other fields. Were the charges of academic profit-taking true? Yes, probably to some extent.

As a result of these concerns, increased research on educationally related issues in law enforcement emerged, generally beginning in the early 1970s. Major issues studied relating to higher education included:

- Officer performance
- Officer attitude
- Discretion
- Professional identity
- Ethics
- Cynicism
- Authoritarianism
- Decision-making
- Deadly force
- Minority recruitment
- Police department policies

- The role of higher education in policing
- Criminal justice in the educational institution
- Faculty productivity
- Curricula, and
- Syllabus design[31]

This list does not purport to cite all the research on police education, but it did serve as an illustration of the wide range of inquiries over a relatively short period. The results of the research varied, but certain trends began to emerge. Although not conclusive, the research suggested that higher education provided a number of benefits for law enforcement. In sum, the research indicates that college education for officers:

- Develops a broader base of information for decision-making.
- Provides additional years and experiences for increasing maturity.
- Inculcates responsibility in the individual through course requirements and achievements.
- Permits the individual to learn more about the history of the country and the democratic process, and to appreciate constitutional rights, values, and the democratic form of government.
- Engenders the ability to handle difficult or ambiguous situations with greater creativity or innovation.
- Allows a view of the "big picture" of the criminal justice system and a fuller understanding and appreciation for the prosecutorial, judicial, and correctional roles.
- Develops a greater empathy for minorities and their discriminatory experiences. This understanding is developed through both coursework and interaction in the academic environment.
- Engenders understanding and tolerance for persons with different lifestyles and ideologies; translates into more effective communication and community relationships in the practice of policing.
- Makes officers appear less rigid in decision-making, encourages them to make their decisions in the spirit of the democratic process and to use discretion in dealing with individual cases rather than applying the same rules to all cases.
- Helps officers to communicate and respond to the crime and service needs of the public in a competent manner, with civility and humanity.
- Makes officers more innovative and flexible when dealing with complex policing programs and strategies, such as problem-oriented policing, community policing, and task force responses.
- Equips officers to better perform tasks and to make continuous policing decisions with little or no supervision.
- Helps officers to develop better overall community relations skills, including engendering the respect and confidence of the community.
- Engenders more "professional" demeanor and performance.
- Enables officers to cope better with stress and to be more likely to seek assistance with personal or stress-related problems, and thereby to be more stable and more reliable employees.
- Enables officers to adapt their styles of communication and behavior to a wider range of social conditions and classes.
- Tends to make officers less authoritarian and less cynical with respect to the milieu of policing.
- Enables officers to accept and adapt to organizational change more readily.[32]

The State of Police Education Today

Despite the recommendations of the national commissions, the growth of criminal justice programs, and aggressive research in the 1970s, the intense interest in higher education seemed to diminish in the 1980s. This is not to suggest that no research was conducted during this time, but the amount of research was significantly less. Moreover, in the early 1980s funding for LEEP was reduced drastically, and finally the program was dropped. At the same time, grant priorities changed, and the opportunity to gain financial support for research on issues related to police education became almost nonexistent. As compounding factors, criminal justice enrollments and curricula stabilized, while crime, such as violence and illegal drug traffic, became more visible. As a result, many of the previously debated topics in police education became matters of secondary, sometimes tertiary, importance in relation to other crime-related issues.

Because the Police Executive Research Forum (PERF) places an important emphasis on college education, it has had a continuing concern about educational issues, including the diminished attention given to police education over the past decade. Among the questions PERF was concerned about were:

- How many police agencies require formal higher education for employment?
- How many agencies give preference to college-educated applicants?
- How many have formal or informal requirements of college education for promotion?
- What kinds of existing policies provide incentives for higher education?
- What is the relationship between higher education and the recruitment of women and minorities?
- What college characteristics are important to officers seeking a degree?
- Has progress really been made in the implementation of educational policies since the President's Commission report and passage of the Crime Control Act over two decades ago?
- Is the education movement making progress or is it stagnant?

With financial support from the Ford Foundation, PERF commissioned a study of these issues.[33] The findings show that there has been a steady growth in police officer educational levels with an increasing number of departments requiring, sometimes informally, some type of college experience for employment or promotion. Yet, two fundamental issues continue to surface:

- Does college education make an officer "better"?
- Does a college requirement have a discriminatory effect on minorities?

Are College-educated Officers Better? This is a perennial question for which a straightforward "yes" or "no" answer is usually sought. Unfortunately, evidence from the research simply does not permit an easy response. Since studies have addressed the effects of college on a wide range of behavioral variables (as described above), conclusions about the effects of college on police performance have to be made based on a collective interpretation of these findings. People have different perspectives of what makes an officer "good" or "professional." For example, the research indicates that officers with college are less authoritarian and cynical. The authors feel this is a positive effect. Yet, some would argue that officers

POLICE EDUCATION AND RACE/ETHNICITY

The Police Executive Research Forum study found that white officers constitute 80.3 percent of sworn personnel. Blacks make up 12.3 percent, Hispanics account for 6.4 percent, and persons of other racial/ethnic backgrounds represent roughly 1.0 percent. Somewhat surprisingly, these proportions approximate Census Bureau demographic estimates of the United States. Because of the concerns about discrimination, educational levels of minorities were of particular interest. Mean educational levels of minorities were comparable to those of whites. Moreover, all minority racial/ethnic groups contained higher percentages of graduate degree holders than did whites.

When these data are viewed in conjunction with the finding that minorities' representation in law enforcement is similar to their representation in the general population, the findings regarding educational level become more relevant. It appears, overall, that law enforcement agencies can effectively recruit and retain minorities with a college education. The distribution of minorities in policing, however, appears to be skewed—primarily because of disproportionate minority distribution among cities and counties, but also as a result of differential recruitment and employment practices by various law enforcement agencies. Based on the data and site visits, we concluded that police agencies need to make more substantive and directed recruitment efforts to identify and employ minority police candidates with a college education.

Minority Representation and Educational Levels in Law Enforcement Agencies

| Race/Ethnicity | Percentage of Representation | | Educational Levels | | |
	Police (%)	National (%)	Average educational level (yr)	No college (%)	Some college (%)	Four-year or graduate degree (%)
Black	12.3	12.1	13.6	28	63	9
Hispanic	6.4	8.0	13.3	27	68	5
White	80.3	76.9	13.7	34	62	4
Other	1.0	3.0	13.8	19	73	8

Roughly one officer in eight was a woman. The data showed that 87.9 percent of all sworn officers in these agencies were male and 12.1 percent were female.

must be authoritarian and cynical (this being viewed as "not gullible"); therefore, college may be interpreted as having a negative effect on these factors.

The entire debate of the effect of college education on policing has an important new dimension which was not even an issue when the education movement took off in the 1960s—community policing. As noted in chapter 3, the community policing concept has experienced explosive growth. As a new philosophy encompassing both

When the mean educational level is stratified by gender, male officers averaged 13.6 years of education and female officers averaged 14.6 years—a full year more than male officers.

Educational Level of Police Officers by Gender

Level	Male	Female
Mean (yr)	13.6	14.6
No College (%)	34.8	24.1
Some Undergraduate (%)	61.7	45.1
Four-year or graduate Degree (%)	3.3	30.2

Significant differences become evident when the distribution is examined. Among male officers, 34.8 percent had no college credits, whereas 24.1 percent of female officers had not attended college. Conversely, 22.8 percent of all male officers had either a four-year or a graduate degree, whereas 44.6 percent of female officers held those degrees.

One may reasonably ask why the women's educational level was notably higher than the men's. One possibility is that police departments gave greater scrutiny—consciously or not—to female applicants. As a result, women with stronger credentials were hired. A second possible explanation is that women who aspired to enter law enforcement believed that they had to be more competitive to enter this male-dominated field. Therefore, they tended to complete their college education, and perhaps graduate school, before applying in order to have the strongest possible background. A third reason, for which we found some anecdotal evidence, is that women tended to enter law enforcement from another career that required a degree. The most common example was public school teachers, generally at the elementary and middle school levels, where most teachers are female. We found that a number of teachers left the field of education to enter law enforcement. For some the change was a result of frustration in the public schools; others found that teaching did not fulfill their career ideals; and for others it was a matter of job security, salary, and benefits.

In all likelihood, all of these reasons contributed to the higher educational level of women in law enforcement. Thus, education does not appear to be an employment barrier for women, although other social barriers remain, which must be addressed by police agencies seeking women officers.

David L. Carter and Allen D. Sapp, *Police Education and Minority Recruitment* (Washington, DC: Police Executive Research Forum, 1991).

operations and management, community policing has drastically changed the way law enforcement views itself and its approach to accomplishing goals. As a result, line-level police officers are given broader responsibilities and are charged with performing their jobs in creative and innovative ways. In addition, officers are urged to be proactive in program development in their duties and are given even broader discretion. In many ways, the community policing perspective of "professional" officers is far less paternal than was the traditional (or "reform") perspective of professionalism.

Given the nature of this change, the issue of college education is even more critical. The knowledge and skills that officers are being asked to exercise in community policing appear to be tailored to college preparation. Once again, the jury is still out—we do not have *the* answer, but it appears that college makes the officer more effective.

Is College a Discriminatory Requirement?   This is a sensitive question which has both philosophical and pragmatic implications. Philosophically, police administrators do not want to discriminate against minority groups, nor do they want departments that are not representative of the total community. Pragmatically, if the police organization has discriminatory policies, they are liable for a lawsuit.

The *complete* answer to this question is somewhat complex. Yes, college is a discriminatory requirement. The reason is twofold. First, minority group members have disproportionate access to a college education as a result of various social, economic, and political factors. Second, minorities tend to have lower college graduation rates as a result of poorer pre-college preparation in the public schools as compared to whites. Despite these discriminatory factors, a college education *can* still be required for police employment. In the case *Davis* v. *Dallas* 777 F.2d 205 (5th Cir. 1985), the Fifth U.S. Circuit Court of Appeals held that the Dallas Police Department requirement of forty-five semester hours of college with a "C" average was a Bona Fide Occupational Qualification (BFOQ) in light of the unique responsibilities of the police and the public responsibility of law enforcement.[34] This decision does not mean that discrimination is no longer an issue. Rather, law enforcement agencies must base a college requirement on a firm foundation of justified need. Moreover, innovative efforts should be made to recruit minorities who meet these requirements.

Interestingly, the findings of the PERF study showed that overall, minority representation in American law enforcement agencies approximates proportions of minorities found in the general population. Moreover, educational levels of minorities in law enforcement are virtually the same as those of white officers.[35] Thus, a college requirement *and* minority representation are not impossible mandates. A college-educated police force which is racially and ethnically representative of the community can be achieved. Such an accomplishment can only make the police department more effective and responsive to community needs.

Importantly, then, the role of education in professionalism is to ensure that police officers are informed decision-makers who base their actions on a logical interpretation of facts and application of diverse knowledge. Clearly, a consensus that higher education enhances the quality of police performance exists. By inference, we may also conclude that education contributes to professionalism, but does not guarantee it.

THE ISSUE OF POLICE UNIONS

The character of public-sector labor relations appears to be changing. While over the past two decades the presence of unionization appears to be slightly declining in the private sector, the reverse is true with respect to the police and fire services. Police labor organizations at the state and national levels have become increasingly sophisticated in providing bargaining advice and support to local collective bargaining units. Similarly, they have become influential through political activism and have been able to further their agenda through lobbying for passage of legislation that is beneficial to the labor movement.[36]

With the increase in police unionization, the question of professionalism becomes more clouded. Generally speaking, unionization is characterized by a divisiveness and distrust between labor and management; strict adherence to contractual provisions with minimal regard to the needs of the "customer"; and a greater emphasis on form than on substance with respect to the policing enterprise. Moreover, unionization is more closely aligned with craftsmanship, or "blue collar" work, while professional positions are more akin to "white collar" occupations. From another perspective, departments with collective bargaining tend to have less flexible management. Discretion tends to be limited, managers are often suspicious of employee motivations, and there is a greater tendency to manage by formalized procedures. Certainly these are generalizations, yet, overall they are valid.

Can a professional attitude flourish in such an environment? Probably, but it will take commitment by labor and management alike. Importantly, it is not the infrastructure of the organization which makes a person "professional," but the individual attitudes of workers toward their responsibilities, the attitude of leaders with respect to how they guide the organization, and the environment of the organization which encourages cooperative relationships in dealing with problems and controversies, rather than encouraging conflict. While a unionized police department can certainly be professional, it is not a natural state, but one which requires effort on both sides of the table.

WHERE ARE WE GOING WITH POLICE PROFESSIONALISM?

Police departments are increasingly better managed, are selecting higher caliber personnel, and are exploring alternate and innovative ways to serve the community. The fragmented nature of policing in America, with departments of all sizes and widely varying authority, virtually assures that "one" style of policing and "one" professional model will *not* evolve. Rather, we will likely see a *consensus* of a professional model which broadly encompasses beliefs about what the police should do, how they should do it, and the kinds of people who should be police officers. As a goal of professionalism—or perhaps quasi-professionalism—this is realistic.

QUESTIONS FOR DISCUSSION

1. Explain the link between role concept and professional concept. How is police professionalization related to police-community relations?
2. What does it mean to say that professionalism, in any field, is a matter of relativity?
3. What are some of the generally recognized marks of a profession? Which of these has special significance for the police?
4. How has social change in the past half century altered traditional views of professionalism?
5. Are professionalism and bureaucracy compatible? At what points do they clash?
6. Distinguish between organizational efficiency and effectiveness and relate this distinction to professionalism.
7. Is police professionalism a desirable goal? Why or why not?
8. Assuming you plan on entering law enforcement as a career, explains the benefits you feel the college experience will provide to you as a police officer.
9. If you were asked, "Does a college education make a police officer professional?" how would you respond?
10. Will the move toward community policing make officers more professional or less?

NOTES

1. For further discussion of these benchmarks of a profession, see Bernard C. Brannon, "Professional Development of Law Enforcement Personnel," in *Police and Community Relations: A Sourcebook*, A. F. Brandstatter and Louis A. Radelet, eds. (Beverly Hills, CA: Glencoe, 1968), pp. 302–16.

2. Cited in James Q. Wilson, "What Makes a Better Policeman?" *Atlantic* 223, no. 3: 135. Copyright © 1969 by the Atlantic Monthly Company. Reprinted by permission.

3. See Harold Wilensky, "The Professionalization of Everyone," *American Journal of Sociology* 70, no. 2 (September 1964): 137–58.

4. Ibid.

5. James M. Slavin, "How Can Policing Become a Profession?" *Proceedings of the Fifth National Institute on Police and Community Relations* (East Lansing, MI: Michigan State University, 1959). The discussion preceding the quote is based upon this lecture.

6. Quinn Tamm, "Police Professionalism and Civil Rights," *Police Chief* (September 1964): 30. Reprinted by permission of the International Association of Chiefs of Police, Gaithersburg, Maryland.

7. It should be noted that the feeling among many minorities is that the police have not actually changed at all. Instead, they have become better at hiding their "true character." This idea will be explored in a later chapter.

8. Norman Cousins, *Saturday Review* (August 22, 1970): 32. Reprinted by permission.

9. Jerome H. Skolnick, *Justice Without Trial: Law Enforcement in Democratic Society.* Copyright © (1966, John Wiley & Sons), pp. 4–5. Reprinted by permission of John Wiley & Sons, Inc.

10. Patrick V. Murphy and Thomas Plate, *Commissioner: A View From the Top of American Law Enforcement* (New York: Simon & Schuster, 1977), p. 260.

11. E. J. Jenkins, Jr., "Reaching the Goal of Maximum Police Efficiency," *Law Enforcement News* (September 11, 1978): 6.

12. Peter K. Manning, op. cit., "The Police and Crime: Crime and the Police."

13. Ibid.

14. Egon Bittner, op. cit., "The Police on Skid-Row," p. 701.

15. James Q. Wilson and George L. Kelling, "Broken Windows," *The Atlantic Monthly* (March 1982): 31–32.

16. Jerome H. Skolnick, "The Police and the Urban Ghetto," *Research Contributions of the American Bar Foundation*, no. 3 (1968): 11.

17. Ibid., p. 12

18. Herman Goldstein, op. cit., p. 7.

19. John P. Matthews and Ralph O. Marshall, "Some Constraints on Ethical Behavior in Criminal Justice Organizations," in *The Social Basis of Criminal Justice: Ethical Issues for the '80s* Frank Schmalleger and Robert Gustafson, eds. (Washington, DC: The University Press of America, Inc., 1981), p. 12. See also Michael Steinman and Chris W. Eskridge, "The Rhetoric of Police Professionalism," *The Police Chief*, LII, no. 2 (February 1985): 26–29.

20. Louis A. Radelet, "Implications of Professionalism in Law Enforcement for Police-Community Relations," *Police* (July–August 1966): 82. Reprinted by permission of Charles C. Thomas, Publisher.

21. James Q. Wilson, "The Police and Their Problems," 1962, pp. 200–11. Wilson relies here on a differentiation developed by Everett C. Hughes in *Men and Their Work* (Glencoe, Ill: Free Press, 1958), pp. 140–41.

22. See William P. Brown, "Mirrors of Prejudice," *Nation* 208, no. 16 (April 21, 1969): 498–500.

23. John M. Pfiffner, "The Function of the Police in a Democratic Society," *Occasional Papers: Center for Training and Career Development* (Los Angeles: School of Public Administration, University of Southern California, 1967).

24. Albert J. Reiss, Jr., "Professionalization of the Police," in *Police and Community Relations*, Brandstatter and Radelet, eds., 1968, p. 216. The discussion of Reiss's ideas is based on this same article.

25. David L. Carter, "Human Resource Management for Community Policing." A paper presented at the annual NIJ Conference, (Washington, DC).

26. Wilensky, "The Professionalization of Everyone," op. cit. p. 140.

27. President's Commission on Law Enforcement and Administration of Justice, *Task Force Report: Police* (Washington, DC: U.S. Government Printing Office, 1967).

28. David L. Carter, "Methods and Measures," in *Community Policing*, R. Trojanowicz and B. Bucqueroux (Cincinnati: Anderson, 1989) p. 167.

29. National Advisory Commission On Criminal Justice Standards and Goals, *Police* (Washington, DC: U.S. Government Printing Office, 1973).

30. National Commission on Higher Education for Police Officers, *Proceedings of the National Symposium on Higher Education for Police Officers* (Washington, DC: Police Foundation, 1979). See also Larry W. Sherman, and National Advisory Commission on Higher Education of Police Officers, *The Quality of Police Education* (Washington, DC: Josey-Bass, 1978).

31. For a comprehensive discussion of these research areas *see* David L. Carter, Allen D. Sapp and

Darrel W. Stephens, *The State of Police Education: Policy Direction for the 21st Century* (Washington, DC: Police Executive Research Forum, 1989).

32. David L. Carter, Allen D. Sapp and Darrel W. Stephens, "Higher Education as a Bona Fide Occupational Qualification (BFOQ) for Police: A Blueprint," *American Journal of Police* 1988 7(2): pp. 16–18.

33. David L. Carter and Allen D. Sapp. "The Evolution of Higher Education in Law Enforcement: Preliminary Findings From a National Study," *Journal of Criminal Justice Education* 1990 1(1): pp. 59–85.

34. *Ibid.* Carter, Sapp, and Stephens, 1988.

35. David L. Carter and Allen D. Sapp, *Police Education and Minority Recruitment: The Impact of a College Requirement* (Washington, DC: Police Executive Research Forum, 1991).

36. Allen D. Sapp, David L. Carter, and Darrel W. Stephens, *Law Enforcement Collective Bargaining Agreements: Preliminary Findings From A National Survey* (Washington, DC: Police Executive Research Forum, 1990).

Chapter 7

ROLE AND POLICE DISCRETION

As we approach the twenty-first century, we have seen a wide range of research and innovation occur in policing. Law enforcement has matured philosophically, administratively, and operationally. We urge dialogue with the community more than ever before and endeavor to be openly accountable to the citizens, the law, and professional ethics. Yet, controversy still surrounds police use of *discretion*—sometimes referred to as *invisible justice*. Certainly there have been blatant cases of poor, sometimes unlawful, decisions by officers in recent years. Cases of excessive force, poor judgment in "hot pursuits," and perjury with the intent of putting drug dealers in jail are only a few examples. In some cases, poor discretion is simply inexcusable; in other cases it is understandable, but no less tolerable. The "gray areas" between right and wrong or proper and improper are pervasive problems. These are the things that make discretion so problematic—and important.

It is said that ours is a government by law, not a government by people. This means, of course, that those empowered by the people, from whom their authority is derived, are not free to exercise that power by whim or caprice. They are held accountable to the people to discharge their responsibilities within the limits of established law. A police officer, for example, might describe his or her job (however naively) by saying that it is his or her duty to enforce the law equally for all, no more and no less.

If it was this simple, there would probably be much less concern for police and community relations. But the fact is that the law is not really so impersonal, not so detached from what people do with it, from how they interpret it, and from how police enforce it. Moreover, the law does not cover every situation in which police officers may find themselves. Sometimes where there appears to be applicable law, police officers may be well advised to conduct themselves as though ignorant of the law, for to attempt to enforce it might invite Armageddon.

For the law is not an end in itself. Properly understood, it is a means to higher ends in human affairs, such as good order, justice, and individual liberty. In complex societies, law is an indispensable instrument of social control. It comes to life through what people make of it and what they do with it. In a totalitarian social system, law is a mechanism of tyranny, dedicated to order as an end in itself, coldly efficient because it is little concerned with the means used to maintain peaceable, conformist behavior. In a democratic society, however, there is (or should be) as much attention to procedural law as there is to substantive law. As Jerome Skolnick puts it, "The procedures of the criminal law . . . stress the protection of individual liberties *within* a system of social order."[1] We are reminded of Jerome Hall's depiction of the police officer as "the living embodiment of democratic law."[2]

THE NATURE AND NEED FOR POLICE DISCRETION

Reduced to its most elementary and obvious trait, discretion as exercised by police officers means that choices are constant. Such decisions are integral to all aspects of criminal justice, but judgments made by police officers are particularly crucial since initial interpretations of law are involved. Moreover, the time factor is often critical; laws cannot be written to cover all situations that arise, and some laws are unenforceable all or part of the time. Additionally, there are such considerations to be taken into account as probable cause, when to use force and how much of it, and dealing with some persons (for instance, those with diplomatic or legislative immunity) differently than others.

Decision-making by the police is complex, and as with all true professionals, mistaken choices produce serious consequences. Often it is not so much a matter of a clearcut mistake as it is one of room for argument as to whether another choice may not have been preferable. The threat of malpractice suits hovers in the background. In the past, police administrators have tended to hide behind the publicized claim that their officers enforce all laws equally for all citizens—plainly false—or the equally droll insistence that an officer's judgment should never be questioned by a citizen because it undermines the majesty of the law. Fortunately, today's police leaders are less inclined to indulge in such comedy. They do, however, remain sensitive to charges of discrimination, capriciousness, and corruption.

The reasons for the inevitability and, indeed, the wisdom of the use of police discretion have been identified by Wayne R. LaFave, among others, beginning with the recognition of what full enforcement of the law would mean.[3] There is no need to repeat all this here, other than to note that the public does not expect, nor would it tolerate full enforcement. This is what police executives have also recognized. The police-community arguments about discretion focus on when it should or should not be invoked, and the manner in which it is applied. The fact that delegated power and public policy are involved is pivotal, so the factors the officer weighs in making a decision are important. Seriousness of the offense is most significant. Other influences are the apparent mental state of the offender, his or her past criminal record when known to the officer, whether weapons were involved, the relative danger to the officer, whether disrespect toward the officer was displayed, and sometimes other, less defensible matters, such as the race, social position, and style of dress of the offender.[4]

THE ISSUE

The character of a neighborhood or the community conditions will affect the character of discretion exercised by the police. Social class differences explain this in part, but there are other variables involved. The character of the neighborhood or community likewise tends to condition whether law enforcement or order maintenance is seen as the primary role of the police. It will also affect the types of crime prevention activities stressed as well as officers' general approach to community policing initiatives. There is clearly more latitude for the exercise of police discretion in order maintenance functions than there is in law enforcement functions. There-fore, its exercise is likely to be more problematic in order maintenance situations. The link between role and discretion is apparent, and the ultimate problem of dis-cretion as a police-community enigma becomes clear, namely, the problem of its con-trol, structuring, or accountability.

A common, complicating addendum is the fact that police management sees the structuring of discretion as its domain and too rarely is receptive to citizen partici-pation in this process. As one text puts it, "Once we recognize that police are crafts-men whose activities are directed by their self-conception of expertise and skill, by their interest in factual guilt rather than legal guilt, and by their perception of dif-ferences among individuals, it is not surprising that they have established techniques to evoke and circumvent the rules that would handcuff them in the performance of their craft."[5]

So it is that demands for community control of the police, in one way or another, are so often central in police-community tension. Such pleas are generally resisted by the police. Elements of racism tend to emotionalize the issue because minorities are almost always prominent among those calling for more community control over police exercise of discretion. Charges of abuse of power fuel these controversies. What is at stake is, "political control over police discretion."[6] Aggravating the con-troversies is the satisfaction that patrol officers derive from fighting crime—"the good pinch," not always with great concern about the legality of how they get it. Michael Brown develops the point further:

> The autonomy to act as professionals toward the community presupposed internal control over the actions of police [officers], which was to be accomplished through stringent discipline. Because the values of professionalism and the necessity of internal discipline are so closely tied to the legitimacy of police authority in professional departments, administrators are compelled to honor these values and to attempt to enforce discipline. Yet the uncertainties of police work and the consequent police culture serve to legitimize a distinctly different set of values than those of professionalism. The resulting conflict between the values of professionalism and the police culture is the root of the structured contradictions of police bureaucracies.[7]

What is salient in the discretionary choices made by patrol officers? Clearly, it is the way they "resolve and adapt to the demands of an uncertain, ambiguous task on the one hand, and to the equally uncertain demand for organizational discipline on the other."[8]

THE ISSUE ELABORATED

By law and in theory, the police are expected to enforce all laws, to arrest everyone they see committing an offense. Clearly, this is absurd. Everybody knows that ex-pecting the police to enforce all laws to the letter is an impossibility police officers perhaps most of all; but up until the recent past, this absurdity has been kept a se-cret. Now, at last, police leaders are beginning to acknowledge that officers cannot function without considerable latitude in the exercise of personal discretion. De-partmental policies and regulations have tended to ignore this elementary fact. Pros-ecutors and judges have reprimanded officers for exercising discretion, even as they wink at their own more extensive use of the same prerogative.

In short, police discretion is inevitable partly because the police cannot do everything, partly because many laws require interpretation before they can be applied, and partly because the community will not tolerate full enforcement of all laws all the time.

> In almost every public organization, discretion is exercised—indeed, from the client's viewpoint, the problem arises out of how and whether it is exercised—but the police department has the special property (shared with a few other organizations) that within it discretion increases as one moves *down* the hierarchy. In many, if not most, large organizations, the lowest ranking members perform the most routinized tasks and discretion over how those tasks are to be performed increases with rank. . . . [But in police organizations] the lowest ranking police officer—the patrol [officer]—has the greatest discretion, and thus, his behavior is of greatest concern to the police administrator.[9]

Reiss suggests that the central question is whether decision-making by patrol officers is of a kind that is "open to professionalization." He asserts, as have others, that the tendency has been to professionalize police organization rather than police practice—the department rather than the individual. Thus, the key question is whether the patrol officer's work requires truly professional abilities. If it does, then the patrol officer should have the professional autonomy corresponding with these abilities and responsibilities.

Reiss concludes that the evidence is mixed. He thinks that, in the long run, some aspects of police patrol work will require professionals, while other aspects of this work can be adequately handled by technicians. He insists that such differentiation in occupational specialities is necessary if we are to cope realistically with the question of police professionalism.

Skolnick believes that the issue of police discretion is the epitome of the problem of order and legality. The basic issue is whether there should be, in his language, "a loosening or a tightening of restraints on the decisional latitude of the police."[10] An important distinction should be made, he argues, between *authorized* and *unauthorized* discretion; most of the problems revolve around lack of clarity on what discretion is authorized—how much, under what circumstances, and so on. Again, this confusion suggests the importance of control by policy guidelines and other means.

Even when the useful distinction between authorized and unauthorized discretion is applied, however, some difficulties remain. Complexities in decision-making are still present even when discretion is clearly authorized, and they are compounded when discretion is unauthorized. Unauthorized discretion appears especially to be the issue in tense encounters where police officers exercise discretion and citizens contest their authority to do so. This exemplifies Banton's distinction between authority and power. The issue is reflected in the term *arbitrary police behavior*. For street police officers, however, the uniform constitutes authority and, as Skolnick says, they are "usually willing to back up a challenge" with all the force they can command, particularly if they perceive themselves to be in danger. At such a time, rules are no help.

The element of perceived danger is generally believed to be an important conditioner of police behavior. Banton discusses this point at some length, and Skolnick observes that, when street police officers feel they are in control of the situation, their behavior is apt to be more tempered. When they encounter hostility, they are tempted to make strong claims of authority, sometimes with frail, if any, legal justification.[11] Another influence upon their behavior is the history of prior relations with a particular type of suspect, the perceptual shorthand that identifies the "symbolic assailant," that is, the person who uses gesture, language, and attire that officers have come to associate with violence and danger. The point is this: street police officers are influenced in their discretionary determinations, subtly but firmly, by perceived threats to their survival. Whether or not they have been delegated authority, hence legal grounds, for a particular judgment seems to be of lesser importance.

DISCRETION VERSUS DISCRIMINATION

The exercise of discretion by the police sometimes deteriorates into discrimination, violence, and other abusive practices. While studies are inconclusive as to the extent to which race, gender, ethnicity, and age influence officer discretion, there is little question that it does happen. Personal judgments are often conditioned by emotional hangups and predilections. In specific instances, it is often extremely difficult to draw a reliable line between discretion and discrimination—and if the latter, to prove intent.

To illustrate this difficulty James Q. Wilson states that "the patrol [officer] believes, with considerable justification, that teenagers, [African-Americans], and lower-income persons commit a disproportionate share of all reported crimes." Simply to be in one of these population categories makes one, statistically, more suspect than another. If, in addition, a person identified with one of these categories behaves unconventionally, the tab of "suspicious person" is promptly applied. The police would regard it as dereliction of their duty if they did not treat such persons with suspicion (to be suspicious is an important quality of the police subculture, as we shall see later), routinely question them on the street (stop and frisk), and detain them for further interrogation if a crime has occurred in the area.[12] This is, in fact, stereotypic thinking, but it is a commentary on the "real world" of police officers for which they see no practical alternative. It is also a commentary on why some police administrators prefer to insist that officer discretion does not exist. To admit that it does may be interpreted as discrimination or corruption.[13] Expressions such as "street justice" and "alley court" convey the same impression.

Wilson and George Kelling ask the question point blank: How do we ensure that the police do not become the agents of neighborhood bigotry? They offer no wholly satisfactory answer to this important question, and they admit it. The best hope, they say, is that officer selection, training, and supervision will provide a clear sense of the limit of discretion.[14]

In this matter of discretion versus discrimination, however, it is easy to blame police officers and to overlook the factors that make their behavior more understandable, if not more acceptable. For example, the class composition of the particular community influences police behavior. Wilson has pointed out that, because relatively little public disorder occurs in middle-class suburban communities, it is rarely necessary for the police to intervene in situations of intense conflict in these areas.[15]

Wilson holds that harsh and unjust police treatment of blacks is as much a problem of social class as it is a problem of prejudiced police officers. He does not question that many police officers are racially prejudiced. But according to Wilson, even if all police officers were free of prejudice, blacks would still regard their treatment by the police as unjust. The reason is that a high proportion of violent crime is basically a lower-class phenomenon.[16] Blacks (and some other minority groups) are disproportionately lower class; therefore, a greater probability exists that blackness (or other visible signs of minority group status) will trigger the suspicion of police officers. As we have noted, this is a stereotypic reaction, but important in understanding police behavior in stressful circumstances. Skolnick has

said that the "disposition to stereotype is an integral part of the police [officer's] world."[17] It is also typical bureaucratic behavior, by no means confined to the police: *When you've met one, you've met them all!*

The behavior we are discussing involves something more complex than one-way stereotyping. There are also, for example, counter-stereotypes held by members of minority groups toward police officers. There is a tendency for minority group members to draw conclusions about the police based solely upon their personal experiences, their perceptions, or the stories of others. The accuracy of these conclusions may be as flawed as any stereotypes the police may hold about minority group members. This is a natural way for humans to explain behaviors of those with whom they have conflict. Despite its existence as "human nature," it is a dysfunctional phenomenon.[18]

THE CONTROL OF DISCRETION

The autonomy of the professional, in any field, is surely not absolute. The crucial question is *control*, or structuring. Obviously, there is no tougher question in police administration. The law, court decisions, legislative actions, organizational policies, and supervision—these and other influences harness discretion in law enforcement functions while, of course, leaving some unavoidable latitude to the judgment of individual officers. In order maintenance functions, the latitude is wider because there is no way to structure for situations that are unpredictable. Thus, the true test of officer professionalism is in order maintenance.

Control means guidelines, and there is no scarcity of suggestions—for example, the National Advisory Commission on Criminal Justice Standards and Goals produced an extensive list.[19] Many of the standards for law enforcement accreditation are explicitly stated policies that may be used for discretionary controls. These suggestions focus on policy, supervision, selection, and training, along lines mentioned earlier. Perhaps the most vital control mechanism is the rewards and incentives aspect of personal management. Performance evaluation is complicated by the absence of consensus regarding police role as well as by the disposition of police unions to have a voice in management decisions, especially in personnel matters.

Better education and training for police officers are thought of as relevant to the control of discretion in the sense of improving qualities of judgment, prudence, sensitivity, and wisdom. This seems on the face of it to be a logical assumption, but still largely unproven. No doubt, in individual cases, the assumption holds up, but there is nothing automatic about it. A college degree is not necessarily an antidote for prejudice, nor for emotional or moral immaturity.

To place limits on discretion, police departments are increasingly preparing voluminous policy and procedure manuals in an attempt to give guidance to officers in all critical decision-making situations. (Indeed, an entire industry exists of companies that write departmental manuals.) The fact that legalism and "doing it by the rules" are given greater credence in professional departments does not, apparently, outweigh the importance in officer behavior of norms coming from the police culture, generated by the uncertainties of police work. What is involved is a means-and-ends attitude: to pursue crime aggressively requires, in the view of some officers, sometimes taking liberty with law, regulations, due process, and community "whims." The point is essentially the same as one we noted earlier, namely, conflict between bureaucratic, administrative controls, and behavior norms governed by the police culture. Supervisors tend to lean one way in this conflict; officers tend to lean the other way. So it is that "the policeman as crime fighter is, in many ways, a far more dangerous character than either of his predecessors, the nightwatchman and the nineteenth-century beat cop. Both the nightwatchman and the beat cop had a capacity for crudity and corruption, but they were not given to crusades."[20] The nature of contemporary policing is that the qualities of officer judgment must be enlarged and that officers must become more responsive to the people they serve. But this optimism is tempered:

> Police work inevitably entails the arbitrary use of power: brutality, corruption, the violation of individual rights, and the penchant to take the law into one's own hands, to use it as a tool to right wrongs and attain "justice." It is misleading and naive to think these abuses of power can ever be entirely eliminated, for they are the products of an occupation based on coercion. And as long as the police continue to wield broad coercive powers, the relationship between the police and the communities they serve will be characterized by a dialectical process in which the demand for external control by the public is contradicted by an effort of the police to limit such control.[21]

Herman Goldstein takes generally the same critical position as Brown in assessing what the professional model has done for the control of discretion—and for about the same reasons.[22] Goldstein offers a thorough analysis of structuring, and observes:

> If discretion is to be exercised in an equitable manner, it must be structured; discretionary areas must be defined; policies must be developed and articulated; the official responsible for setting policies must be designated; opportunities must be afforded for citizens to react to policies before they are promulgated; systems of accountability must be established; forms of control must be instituted; and ample provisions must be made to enable persons affected by discretionary decisions to review the basis on which they were made.[23]

Goldstein argues for greater attention to the end product of policing, a substantive, problem-oriented approach, and less concern for organizational and procedural matters (Recall the earlier discussion of the distinction between organizational efficiency and effectiveness.)

> If the police are to realize a greater return on the investment made in improving their operations, and if they are to mature as a profession, they must concern themselves more directly with the end product of their efforts.
>
> Meeting this need requires that the police develop a more systematic process for examining and addressing the problems that the public expects them to handle. It requires identifying these problems in more precise terms, researching each problem, documenting the nature of the current police response, assessing its adequacy and the adequacy of existing authority and resources, engaging in a broad exploration of alternatives to present responses, weighing the merits of these alternatives and choosing from among them.[24]

LEGAL GROUNDS FOR POLICE DISCRETION

The law, under our system, unquestionably allows and indeed encourages discretionary evaluation and judgment throughout the criminal justice process, by the police officer, the prosecutor, the courts, and the correctional authorities. A cardinal principle is that each offender should be dealt with as an individual. The misuse or usurpation of delegated power in the system is not uniquely a police problem; judges and prosecutors have been known to stretch their discretion to unconscionable extremes of either leniency or severity.

DISCRETION AND ACCREDITATION

Law enforcement accreditation was designed to increase standardization of police practices, enhance accountability, and generally increase the quality of service provided by law enforcement agencies—in essence, to increase professionalism and to further maintain control. To accomplish these ends, standards were created which had to be met by agencies seeking accreditation. These standards largely required the creation of policies and procedures to guide the behavior of officers. The accreditation standards, which are both comprehensive and policy-based, resulted in police agencies creating exhaustive policy manuals.

Since policies and procedures are designed to guide behavior, they inherently limit discretion. As more controls are established to enhance accountability, the discretion officers have in performing their duties decreases. Although this was desirable during "reform policing," it may be inhibiting for community-based policing. Thus, while policing is philosophically moving toward a more discretionary environment, accreditation, in its current form, tends to limit discretion.

Accreditation is not mandated by any type of certifying body or agency. It currently has no special legal standing and it is neither encouraged nor discouraged by any governmental or regulatory organization. Instead, it is a voluntary, peer review process that symbolically infers organizational control and accountability based on the police department meeting standards in a prescribed process. The mass articulation of policies and procedures, a result of accreditation, forms a basis for administrative law and serve to assist an agency in its defense of certain types of civil lawsuits. Yet, the imprimatur of CALEA remains largely symbolic at this point, with no special legal status.

On a related note, both accreditation and the initiatives toward community-based policing are youthful movements. They are not inherently in conflict, but neither are they in complete synchronization. The fundamental point of conflict is the issue of limited discretion. Based on the current debate in the policing community, the accreditation standards need to be revised and the process must become more flexible if it is to survive.

Judges and prosecutors enjoy the luxury of time in their deliberations. The street police officer frequently has no such advantage. For this reason, legal scholars have become increasingly concerned with what Skolnick terms "introducing arrangements to heighten the visibility of police discretion to permit its control by higher authority."[25] Wayne LaFave states his primary premise as follows:

> From the point of view of either the individual suspect or the community as a whole, the issue is not so much whether police are efficient, or whether the corrections process is effective, but whether the system of criminal justice administration in its entirety is sensible, fair, and consistent with the concepts of a democratic society.[26]

LaFave joins those who contend that there has been a traditional failure to recognize the existence and importance of police discretion. His discussion of the reasons for this attitude includes such factors as overly strict interpretation of substantive criminal law, the assumption that only legislative and judicial bodies should decide what conduct is criminal, concern and uncertainty whether the rule of law is adequately safeguarded by police exercise of discretion, and the assumption that prosecutors are more competent to exercise discretion than are the police.

The question of police discretion has not received careful legislative attention. There is considerable evidence that legislative bodies either specifically deny police discretion, or consciously ignore it. Generally, appellate courts have not recognized the propriety of police discretion either. Where discretion is recognized as proper, courts have not indicated what standards ought to control the exercise of such discretion:

> The exercise of discretion by the police, which seems inevitable in current criminal justice administration, continues unrecognized. In practice, policies to guide the individual officer in deciding whether to make an arrest are not formally developed within the police agency, and no sustained effort is made to subject existing practices to reevaluation.[27]

There are several initiatives that could conceivably be taken that could help structure discretion while coping effectively with the issues involved. These measures include wider public understanding of the issue (with correspondingly greater likelihood that the public will support the principle of necessary, though regulated, police discretion); the elevation of the level of police professional competence; improved intradepartmental review and control of discretion through administrative policy, supervision, and discipline; more use of criminal action against officers who abuse their discretionary power; and more use by defendants of their constitutional right to equal protection—which would provoke challenges of the criteria used by the police in invoking criminal process.

As we have noted, the issue of discretion exercised by an individual police officer on the street in dealing with an individual citizen incorporates the question of dealing differently with various groups of citizens—for example, because of racial or cultural considerations, or social-class differentials—and of dealing differently with various neighborhoods or areas in a city. The policy questions involved are extremely complex, one reason they are seldom discussed.

> Notwithstanding the great importance and significance of these and other instances of discretionary enforcement, the police have failed to evaluate carefully such enforcement policies or even to acknowledge that such practices exist. Rather, most departments attempt to maintain the existing stereotype of the police as ministerial officers who enforce all of the laws, while they actually engage in a broad range of discretionary enforcements.[28]

This "head in the sand" approach is rapidly changing, however. More progressive police leaders, higher educational levels among officers, more thoughtful officer selection, adoption of the community policing philosophy, and the accreditation movement are all important factors in this changing attitude.[29]

Jerome Hall and Joseph Goldstein are among those who have taken a somewhat more conservative stance on the subject of police discretion. Hall subscribed to the thesis that there must be a sharp demarcation between police and judicial functions and that, therefore, the police should be strictly confined to so-called ministerial duties. It is not the police officer's job, he insisted, to decide whether a person under arrest is guilty of a crime; the police arrest only "on reasonable ground." Nor is it the job of the police he continued, to define or declare any general rules of law. And finally, he said, "whatever the police in our system may think the rules of law mean, their interpretations are not authoritative."[30]

However, most of those who have studied the issue of police discretion would probably agree with LaFave:

There are ways of recognizing police discretion and of controlling its exercise. Legislatures can give explicit attention to police discretion and prescribe criteria to guide the exercise of that discretion. This is the trend at the sentencing and correctional stages of the criminal process, and there is no reason to believe that this sort of legislation would be less appropriate at the arrest stage. Courts can subject police discretion to the kind of review which sometimes occurs in regard to economic regulatory agencies.

The development of an "administrative law" in the enforcement field is as important as it is in the field of economic regulation, but while the one has been given sustained attention, the other has been completely neglected. Greater legislative and judicial recognition of the importance of police discretion might in turn encourage police administrators to acknowledge its importance and attempt to devise methods of meaningful evaluation of existing policies.

The obvious complexity of the task of dealing adequately with police discretion at the arrest stage makes it all the more important that a start be made immediately.[31]

THE GRAVITY OF THE ISSUE

Taken collectively, the questions that arise in connection with the exercise of discretion by police officers constitute a major issue—it could be argued *the* major issue—in police and community relations. Human judgments about the use of such extraordinary delegated power are bound to attract critics—some righteous, some malevolent. The genius of checks and balances within the democratic system is again underscored.

It is a somewhat startling thought, but as the President's Crime Commission stated in *Challenge of Crime*, law enforcement policy is actually made by the patrol officer on the street. The commission referred to the criminal code, in practice, not as a set of specific instructions for police officers, but as "a more or less rough map of the territory in which police work. How an individual [officer] moves around that territory depends largely on his [or her] personal discretion." The commission said that a police officer is "an arbiter of social values."[32] The officer's assessment of probable gains and losses as he or she determines the manner of intervention in a particular situation is stated by the commission in practical terms: the legal strength of the available evidence, the willingness of victims to press charges and of witnesses to testify, the temper of the community, and the time and information at the police officer's disposal.

Communities and neighborhoods vary considerably in what they expect of the police. In effect, modern social conditions prescribe significant differences in both law enforcement and order maintenance, depending upon where one looks. In practical police terms, this means that a metropolitan police department works at its job with a different style in different precincts or divisions. This is hardly a novel organizational pattern, but little is said about it by administrators, for fear it will be interpreted as unequal protection or differential treatment. The distinctions that need to be made on questions of this kind are finely ground, and public administrators prefer to avoid them if possible. It should be understood that in sound police administration, a policy of different styles of policing for different areas should *not* mean that some areas will get poorer service than others.

We have insisted on maintaining the police as a responsibility of local government in order to assure accountability and an opportunity for local influence over so potentially powerful a government activity. Yet at the same time we have constructed various devices which, in attempting to protect the police from pernicious influences at the local level, effectively shield the police from the communities they serve. The net result of these conflicting aims is that considerable ambiguity exists as to who in fact is responsible for the many decisions that are made in the running of a police agency, and there is a great deal of uncertainty over how the public is supposed to control police operations.[33]

Despite our best efforts to change this problem, the conflicts remain.

DISCRETION AND COMMUNITY POLICING

As law enforcement agencies increasingly move toward the community policing (CoP) philosophy, the need for discretion is *increased*. With CoP, the authority of police officers is increasingly decentralized. This is necessary because we are asking officers to:

- Proactively identify problems
- Assess community needs
- Identify potential solutions
- Evaluate these options
- Decide which option is best and can be used, and
- Implement the chosen alternative

In some cases this may be a complex, time-consuming process while in other cases it is a quick, short-term initiative. Regardless of the complexity, officers must still be empowered to make these decisions—this is essential for CoP to be successful.

This need for increased discretion brings with it other responsibilities. The police selection process must ensure that the best people are hired as officers, people who have the intellectual capacity and judgment to wisely use discretion. Training that gives direction and ascribes limits to discretionary decisions must also be provided. Finally, supervision of officers must be used more meaningfully to ensure the accountability and propriety of discretionary decisions.

Related to the issue of discretion is the inherent need of police executives (and the community) to give officers the *freedom to fail*. If officers are asked to explore new ideas in dealing with community problems, it must be recognized that this is a process of experimentation. As such, not all ideas will work as envisioned. To tell officers they can try what they want but the new ideas "better work" is a sure way to inhibit creativity. However, if officers learn that creativity is encouraged and that they will be rewarded for initiative and effort, regardless of the results, experimentation will be stimulated. These elements of creativity, experimentation, and the freedom to fail are all inherently reliant on officer discretion.

EDUCATION AND DISCRETION

The use of discretion requires informed judgment, logical analysis of issues, the skill to research alternatives, and the ability to make reasoned decisions. This is true whether the issue is one which permits contemplation over time or one which requires immediate analysis and decision-making (such as the use of force). The research suggests that officers who are college educated tend to possess these characteristics.[34]

"The use of discretion requires informed judgment, logical analysis of issues, the skill to research alternatives, and the ability to make reasoned decisions."

Higher education in criminal justice has gone through a notable transformation. Early programs, particularly those stimulated in the late 1960s and early 1970s as a result of the Law Enforcement Education Program (LEEP), were vocational in nature. Many classes attempted to teach policing "skills," such as report writing, interrogation, patrol tactics, and even riot control and firearms training. This was largely done because there was no research foundation looking at the function of the police or research about higher education and law enforcement. As noted previously, it is ironic that college education for the police evolved largely on an intuitive belief that it was desirable, rather than on any scientific evidence.

In the late 1970s and early 1980s there was a significantly growing body of research on the policing function, focusing primarily on administrative issues, or at least the managerial perspective of operational issues. As a result of this research and the adoption of contemporary management principles by police leaders, educational programs tended to have a strong focus on management, supervision, and planning.

As law enforcement has philosophically evolved from the reform era to the community-based era, we are experiencing a transition in educational programs. College curricula in the 1990s are moving away from "broad field" or "functional" majors, toward more interdisciplinary course offerings. They have begun to emphasize socio-behavioral dynamics, which will help future officers in the *practice of policing*. Inherent in this growing approach is an emphasis on individual responsibility, problem solving, and professional interaction between the individual and the community. This philosophical evolution in higher education is clearly consistent with officer discretion.

Beyond the philosophical implications, there are a number of more concrete factors which support the relationship of higher education to the wise use of discretion.

College-educated officers receive fewer citizen complaints and tend to have fewer liability cases filed against them.[35] They are more open to alternatives for problem solving, more likely to explore nontraditional policing responsibilities, and generally more flexible in their approach to policing the community.[36] Perhaps most importantly, they have honed their analytic skills throughout the educational process. The experience of writing research papers, analyzing reading assignments for class discussion, and taking examinations all lead to skill development that can be applied to "real world" situations in their careers.

Discretion involves significant empowerment for the officer. As a result, law enforcement needs the best prepared people available in order to wisely use that authority.

CLOSING OBSERVATION

The stark reality is that discretion will always be part of a police officer's daily behavior. The decision of whether to stop a car, issue a citation, chase a car, conduct a search, or pull a trigger will always rely on one basic tenet—the judgment of the officer. It is imperative that we understand the philosophical issues and administrative debate surrounding the proper delegation of decision-making authority and the best way to maintain accountability and control. It is also imperative that we understand the pragmatic dimension of discretion—a decision that is typically made spontaneously, under some degree of stress, and no supervision. As a result, the most important ingredient is the type of people whom we employ as police officers to make those decisions.

QUESTIONS FOR DISCUSSION

1. Under what circumstances would you say that a police officer's exercise of discretion is a truly *professional* judgment?
2. Why is it that police executives are often so cautious, and even evasive, in what they say publicly about police discretion?
3. Why is discretion not only allowed, but encouraged with community policing?
4. In police work, discretion increases as we move *down* in the organizational hierarchy. What is meant by this?
5. What are some of the factors a police officer is likely to weigh in making discretionary decisions?
6. Indicate some of the environmental and situational influences on police discretionary judgments?
7. How would you distinguish between discretion and discrimination?
8. How does law enforcement accreditation limit discretion?
9. What is the relationship between higher education and police officers' use of discretion?
10. How does perceived danger figure in a police officer's discretionary decisions?

NOTES

1. Jerome H. Skolnick, *Professional Police in a Free Society* (New York: National Conference of Christians and Jews, 1967).
2. Jerome Hall, "Police and Law in a Democratic Society," *Indiana Law Journal* 28, no. 2 (Winter 1953).
3. Wayne R. LaFave, *Arrest: The Decision to Take a Person into Custody* (Boston: Little, Brown, 1965).
4. Larry J. Siegel, Dennis Sullivan, and Jack R. Greene, "Decision Games Applied to Police Decision Making,"

Journal of Criminal Justice (Summer 1974): pp. 131–142. Also Kenneth Culp Davis, *Police Discretion* (St. Paul, Minn.: West Publishing Co., 1975).
5. Charles W. Thomas and John R. Hepburn, *Crime, Criminal Law and Criminology* (Dubuque, Iowa: William C. Brown Publishers, 1983), p. 357.
6. Michael K. Brown, *Working the Street* (New York, NY: Russell Sage Foundation, 1981), p. 283.
7. Ibid., p. 286.

8. Ibid., p. 287.
9. James Q. Wilson, *op. cit., Varieties of Police Behavior*, p. 7. Reprinted by permission. (Cited in note 13, chapter 3.)
10. Jerome H. Skolnick, *Justice Without Trial*, p. 71.
11. Ibid., p. 90.
12. James Q. Wilson, *Police Behavior*, p. 40.
13. A. O. Archuleta, "Police Discretion v. Plea Bargaining," *Police Chief* (April 1974): 78.
14. James Q. Wilson and George L. Kelling, op. cit., "Broken Windows," p. 35. In the pages of *Justice Quarterly* 1, no. 1 (March 1984): pp. 75–89, Samuel Walker of the University of Nebraska–Omaha has criticized the Kelling-Wilson article on the ground that they misinterpret the history of American policing, 1930–1960. Whatever the validity of his critique, Walker admits that their concept of revitalized police patrol is nonetheless worthy of serious study today.
15. James Q. Wilson, "Dilemmas of Police Administration," *Public Administration Review* 28, no. 5 (1968): 411.
16. For documentation of this point see, for example, U.S. President's Commission on Law Enforcement and Administration of Justice, *Crimes of Violence*, prepared by Marvin E. Wolfgang (Washington, D.C.: U.S. Government Printing Office, 1967), pp. 166–169.
17. Jerome H. Skolnick, *Justice Without Trial: Law Enforcement in Democratic Society*. Copyright © (1967, John Wiley & Sons, Inc.), p. 83. Reprinted by permission of John Wiley & Sons, Inc.
18. This phenomenon was particularly apparent and directed toward the entire criminal justice system following the verdict in the O. J. Simpson case.
19. National Advisory Commission on Criminal Justice Standards and Goals, *Police* (Washington, D.C.: U.S. Government Printing Office, 1976), pp. 21–33.
20. Michael K. Brown, op. cit., pp. 287–288.
21. *Ibid.*, pp. 304–305.
22. Goldstein approaches the issue more from a management perspective, while Brown's view is more sociological.
23. Herman Goldstein, op. cit., *Policing a Free Society*, p. 110.
24. Herman Goldstein, "Improving Policing: A Problem-oriented Approach," *Crime and Delinquency* (April 1979): p. 236.
25. Jerome H. Skolnick, *Justice Without Trial*, p. 71.
26. Wayne R. LaFave, in the Foreword to *Arrest: The Decision to Take a Suspect Into Custody* (Boston: Little, Brown, 1965). Reprinted by permission. See also: Sanford H. Kadish, "Legal Norm and Discretion in the Police and Sentencing Processes," *Harvard Law Review* 75 (1962): pp. 904–31; Joseph Goldstein, "Police Discretion Not to Invoke the Criminal Process: Low-Visibility Decisions in the Administration of Justice," *Yale Law Journal* 60 (1960): pp. 543–94.
27. LaFave, *Arrest*, pp. 81–82.
28. Ibid., p. 494.
29. Roy R. Roberg and Jack Kuykendall. *Police Management*. 2d ed. (Los Angeles: Roxbury Press, 1997).
30. Jerome Hall, "Police and Law." (See note 2.)
31. LaFave, *Arrest*, pp. 494–5.
32. U.S. President's Commission on Law Enforcement and Administration of Justice, *The Challenge of Crime in a Free Society* (Washington, DC: U.S. Government Printing Office, 1967), p. 10.
33. Herman Goldstein, *Policing a Free Society*, p. 132.
34. David L. Carter, Allen Sapp, and Darrel Stephens, *The State of Police Education* (Washington DC: Police Executive Research Forum, 1989).
35. Victor Kappeler, Allen Sapp, and David L. Carter, "Police Officer Higher Education, Citizens' Complaints, and Department Rule Violations," *American Journal of Police*, vol. XI, no. 2 (1992): pp. 37–54.
36. Carter, et al., Ibid.

Chapter 8

THE SELF-IMAGE OF THE POLICE OFFICER

I t is commonly said that police officers are a cynical, authoritative, and isolationist group of people who have low self-esteem and feel they receive little respect. Just as in the case of any other generalization, there is some truth to this observation—but it is superficial. In fact, what we have learned over the course of the last three decades is that the self-image of police officers is changing. While there are still remnants of these characteristics, their impact is diminishing. Despite this, we need to be vigilant to understand the nature of poor self-image, factors which contribute to this belief, and the impact of poor self-image on officer behavior and relationships with the community.

Certainly self-image has again come into question in the 1990s as a result of the excessive force problems experienced in Los Angeles and Detroit as well as the corruption problems found in the New York Police Department. While these are isolated incidents, they chip away at the fabric of police professionalism across the country and, consequently, the image officers have of themselves, their department, and the police profession. Self-image is a sociopsychological phenomenon which is molded by one's personal experiences as well as one's experiences with different groups—both occupational groups and social groups. This chapter will explore these various psychological factors which have an impact on officer self-image.

The key concept in psychology is *behavior*. How better to understand it is a simplified statement of the main interest of the psychologist. Since all of us act out our attitudes, the union of attitudes and behavior is evident.

We have referred to the "police culture"—more accurately, perhaps, occupational subculture. We speak of the values and beliefs of this subculture, clearly role-related, and all of it attitudinal. This is our focus in this chapter: attitudes of police officers, of themselves—the self-image. A good way to begin is with a consideration of the morale problem of the police.

THE MORALE PROBLEM

What is commonly referred to as the "morale problem" of the police is as variously defined as is police professionalism, with a tendency to settle for rather superficial explanations; for example, that the police morale problem is largely a matter of money. Accordingly, improved police salaries and pension benefits are seen as the answer. There is certainly no opposition here to improvement of the financial security of police officers, but the problem is not that simple. This is increasingly evident as police salaries have become very competitive with the private sector over the past decade.

Morale pertains to the attitude, mental and emotional, that an individual has about the tasks he or she is expected to perform. What is called *good* morale is a state of well-being that stems from a sense of purpose and confidence in the future. It depends on role conception, role performance, and role satisfaction. Morale is intimately related to self-respect which, in turn, contributes to a positive self-image.

Simply defining morale in these terms provides a clue to the particular problem of the police officer. If morale is related to role, and if police work is a classic example of role conflict and role ambiguity, it follows that police officers must have a special kind of self-image problem.

How does a person learn who he or she is? Psychologists tell us that an individual discovers a large part of the answer to this question in the feedback he or she gets from others. To illustrate this point, we may say that people harbor certain attitudes regarding what a person does—his or her job or calling. This is what is meant by *ascribed status*. Some jobs have high status, others, low status, depending upon such attitudes. The status of a person's job or occupation is an important factor in the satisfaction he or she gets from it, but it is, of course, not the only factor.

What people do for a living is one basis of feedback for self-image, for learning who they are and how they rate in the status hierarchy of a given society. The feedback process means simply that we govern our actions according to the estimate we believe others are making. This may be tabbed the *social self*. An individual discovers who he or she is by seeing himself or herself reflected in the actions of others toward him or her. This has been referred to as "the looking-glass self."

We have said that occupation is one source of personal identity. Possessions, where we live, what we do for recreation, and what we wear are others. However, we tend to screen or filter the information that comes to us in the feedback process—to be selective in what we perceive and accept about ourselves. We tend to see and accept what is pleasant about ourselves and provides a positive image, to reject what is negative, and often to project on others what we cannot accept in ourselves. Some psychologists say that the closer our self-image is to the image that most people hold of us, the nearer we are to good mental health. Achieving this realistic appraisal of ourselves is the process and goal of personality maturation.

THE SOCIALIZATION PROCESS IN CHILDHOOD

A brief review of elementary childhood psychology is helpful here. Socialization begins with birth. The helpless infant identifies with surrounding adults for satisfaction of basic needs. In time, the child begins to see himself or herself through the eyes of adults. Through their behavior, the child develops self-confidence and self-respect, or the opposite. The child's actions are strongly affected by the picture of self thus formulated. As Oberlin College sociologist J. Milton Yinger puts it:

> Environments that fill a child with self-doubt and even self-hatred lay the basis for later attacks on one's self, in the form of alcoholism, drug addiction, mental illness, or irresponsibility—or attacks on the community, in the form of crime and disregard of the interests of others.[1]

Conscience and self-respect, then, are basic requirements in sound personality development. Needless to say, many children grow up without either. Clear, consistent standards of behavior and supportive affection are not provided by parents or by significant others. If a child is to be a successful adult, models of successful adults with whom to identify are needed. This is expressed, for example, in programs such as Big Brothers/Big Sisters. When such models are not available, crude and inadequate definitions of oneself are created, which may result in painful answers to the question, who am I? There is a self-perpetuating quality to this kind of pattern: children who have had a problem of identity become the parents of another generation for whom they cannot supply the proper balance of affection and discipline.

The most difficult task in growing up is in coming to terms with one's self, of learning who one is, what one can do, and how one stands in relation to others. For those in seriously disadvantaged environments, this task is especially difficult. Deeply insecure, self-hating, and frustrated, they often invent a cultural world of their own, a world in which they can be dominant and set the standards. This new culture may be the world of the gang, which is not necessarily a criminal group, but one in which youngsters try to salvage some sense of dignity and control. They search for the feelings that they are "somebody," at least to each other. The behavior is described in this way:

> The gang demands aggressive independence, a touchy and exaggerated virility, and a deep, protective secrecy. Acceptance by the gang provides almost the only source of security for its members, but such acceptance is conditional upon continual proof that it is merited, and this proof can only be furnished through physical aggressiveness, a restless demonstration of sexual prowess, and a symbolic execution of those illegal deeds that a "sissy" would not perform.[2]

Thus, socialization begins in our formative years, being shaped by the "significant others" who touch our lives. The attitudes, beliefs, language and lifestyles of family members, friends, and peers both shape and focus every aspect of one's values and belief systems. It is not a wonder that diverse attitudes and personal priorities are endemic among human beings. Understanding this important, yet basic, phenomenon provides an important foundation to not only understand self-image, but also the image others hold for the police.

OCCUPATIONAL SOCIALIZATION

Occupational socialization is a product of communications and social relationships within the organizations. Bombardment of terms, concepts, and belief systems which are part and partial of the organizational environment begins to shape attitudes and beliefs.[3] In some ways occupational socialization begins with the recruitment and selection process. There is a tendency to seek out future employees who fit the "image" one has of a police officer. If given free rein, recruiters would probably tend to identify potential police officers who matched their own personal characteristics. Indeed, there is good evidence that this occurred. Even today with affirmative action and good faith attempts to increase the diversity of America's police forces, new recruits tend to reflect the dominant attitudes and beliefs of the police organization. This is *not* unique to policing. It occurs in virtually every occupation.

The police academy represents the first overt process of socializing. New officers learn language, cultural norms, and associated factors which create the sociobehavioral infrastructure for policing. These factors interact and become reinforced by others, eventually leading to the development of attitudes and behaviors which are generally consistent with other police employees.

After the academy, the new recruit will typically be assigned to a Field Training Officer (FTO) for a period of time ranging from two weeks to six months (this varies greatly between police departments). The FTO's responsibility is to teach the new officer how to place the academy's classroom training into practice. The FTO will also monitor the progress and success of the recruit as well as make recommendations for future training, acceptance onto the force, or dismissal. The on-duty behaviors, attitudes, and policing styles of the FTO also are part of the socialization experience. The new officer will tend to drive the same way, interact with citizens in a similar manner, and even eat at similar locations as the FTO. These are not conscious actions by either the FTO or the recruit. Rather they are part of the socialization— hence, learning—process.

After successful completion of field training, the new officer is usually on a probationary period for six to eighteen months. During this time the officer is regularly reviewed by his or her supervisor (usually a sergeant) to keep track of the officer's progress and performance. The officer will typically know the expectations of the sergeant, including those which are unique, or personality-related, to the individual supervisor. The officer will then modify his or her behavior to conform with the sergeant's. For example, if the officer knows that a sergeant feels that traffic enforcement is important, then the officer will issue more citations. Similarly, if an officer knows that a supervisor rates community relations highly, then the officer will have more community contacts. These learned behaviors are the essence of occupational socialization.

It must be recognized that this process is both necessary and natural. It is not inherently "good" or "bad." A new officer must learn the tricks and tools of the trade from a wide variety of perspectives. The officer must know how to communicate with others, perform the tasks of the organization, and execute the responsibilities of his or her office. Occupational socialization becomes dysfunctional when the officer learns the "wrong things." For example, if erroneous or improper information is presented in the academy, if the Field Training Officer "teaches" improper techniques, or if supervisors fail to adequately monitor a probationary officer's progress, then occupational socialization will likely have undesirable results.

MULTIPLE ROLES, MULTIPLE SELVES

All of us belong to many groups, and each group judges us by different standards. The average adult plays a number of social roles in the course of a day, each involving a pattern of conduct that a person occupying a specific position in society is expected to follow. Being a parent, for example, is a social role. A person may be a spouse, a parent, a police officer, a student or teacher, a PTA officer, and a youth group leader and be active in sundry religious or civic organizations. Each involves a social role. Each implies a certain pattern of socially prescribed behavior. As we have seen, role behavior may involve conflict or ambiguity when standards are not clear or consistent. We have seen how this is exemplified in police use of discretionary power.

Multiple social roles mean, in effect, multiple selves. Thus, from adolescence onward, a person faces the problem of integrating the several different selves required by different and sometimes conflicting roles. Our perceptions of self depend on the context, varying somewhat with what has gone before and with whom we have been dealing, as well as the immediate situation. Another point worth noting is that we encounter and relate to different people in the various social roles we play. Some people see us exclusively in one role, others in another. Therefore, it is possible that the feedback will vary, so that a person may receive more favorable feedback in one role than he or she does in another. In short, one may be viewed as a more successful spouse or parent than as a police officer or teacher, or vice versa.

In the complex of the many selves of the individual, each one may be far from simple. A rapid shift in roles requires quick changes in habits, because roles standardize behavior, and often in attitudes and values as well. Adjustments to the requirements of changed roles are often difficult. Role changes frequently involve frustrations—for example, those experienced by civilians becoming soldiers or soldiers becoming civilians. Recognizing these facts helps us understand the different self-images we may hold for ourselves.

THE POLICE OFFICER'S SELF-IMAGE

With the above as a cursory review of some relevant general considerations pertaining to the self-image, our specific interest is in the self-image of the police officer. In a survey conducted by the International Association of Chiefs of Police (IACP), police officers from many departments, ranging in rank from patrol officer to inspector, were asked a series of questions as to how they saw themselves and their job.[4] Following are some of the questions and responses:

Survey Question	Percent Answering "Yes"
Do you feel tense and "under pressure" during duty hours?	47
Do you find your home life made difficult by annoyances, irritations, and aggravations which are a "hangover" from your job?	41
Is your physical condition suffering or deteriorating from duty requirements?	32
Is the police "image" favorable in your community as far as you can determine?	40
Do you feel that officers in your department are just "cogs in a big machine"?	60

It should be added that 90 percent of the same officers answered yes to the question, "Do you plan to make law enforcement your life career?" and 66 percent said that the dangerous aspects of police work seldom worried them. Two out of three believed that punishment was effective in crime control. Four out of five thought that punishment for crime ought to be more severe. Seven out of ten thought that the police did not have enough authority. Only 55 percent believed that the police should be concerned with social problems, such as education, jobs, and housing discrimination. But 90 percent asserted that the police should be involved in recreation programs for youth.

In their written comments on the same questionnaires, about one out of three officers complained about one aspect or another of their work, some with marked bitterness and defensiveness. Yet only a few admitted occasional shame at being a police officer. Many revealed characteristics of a persecuted minority: hypersensitivity, the feeling that everyone was against them, cynical despair, displaced aggression, and the like. When asked why they continued as police officers, the main reasons given were:

- The position offers good fringe benefits other than salary.
- It is an interesting job.
- It's steady work; I don't have to worry about layoffs, strikes, plant shutdowns, etc.
- I'm trapped. I'd quit if I didn't have so much time invested; I have to go on now until I retire.

On the whole, these officers in this 1969 survey seemed to value their job for its security, but many did not think that it rated very highly in conferring social status.

In the 1990s, the self-image of police officers changed on several fronts. In previously unpublished research by the author, as well as that done by the late Robert Trojanowicz,[5] we have learned that the self-image of police officers has risen as law enforcement has evolved toward a new generation. Officer stress does not seem to be as prevalent an issue as it was in the 1960s and 1970s. One reason is that officer duties are more clearly articulated and training is better. Similarly, as the police workforce has become more educated and diverse, officers have greater self-confidence in their abilities and perceive their social status as being higher. Also, salary levels of police officers have risen significantly—they are competitive with most occupations and tend to have better employee benefit packages. This leads to lower fiscal stress and greater perceived comparability to other occupational and social groups. On the matter of physical condition, officers tend to feel that they are in better physical condition than people in other occupations. This is a result of an increasing number of departments having health and wellness programs or, at the least, providing physical conditioning facilities for officers to use.

In departments which have moved toward community policing, officers report higher levels of job satisfaction, greater sense of purpose in their profession, and the feeling of accomplishment when they help resolve community problems. Although the empirical research on these factors is limited at this point, the anecdotal evidence strongly suggests that greater decentralization of police authority, greater autonomy of individual officers, and broader flexibility in officer discretion all contribute to more productive and more satisfied employees.

It was the rare individual in the 1990s research who reported "shame" at being a police officer—in fact, overwhelmingly the officers reported pride in their profession. Similarly, most officers, and particularly those with a college education, reported that law enforcement was their intended career choice.

Current findings, which are similar to the 1969 research, show that most officers plan to stay with their departments until retirement. Also, most officers are not overly concerned with the dangerous aspects of being a police officer. This may be somewhat surprising given the rising levels of violence, increased required use of body armor for police, and the trend of police departments toward adopting 9-mm semi-automatic handguns as service weapons.

WHY BECOME A POLICE OFFICER?

The 1969 IACP research found that a little over one-half of the police officers surveyed came into police work almost by accident: they had tried several jobs and finally settled on policing. A substantial majority stated that the job was different

". . . police officers and those entering policing view it increasingly as a profession . . ."

than they expected. An even larger proportion had given little or no thought to leaving policing, although officers with higher educational levels were more likely to report that they had considered leaving police work.

These findings contrast to officers in the 1990s in several ways. Currently, the vast majority of people in police work today entered the profession as a conscious, career-oriented decision, i.e., they had decided upon policing as a career and planned for it rather than entering it by accident. While job experiences were somewhat different than they anticipated, current officers seemed to have a greater understanding of the breadth of policing responsibilities. As in the earlier study, current officers have given little thought to leaving police work. A notable difference, however, is that officers with lower educational levels gave more thought to retirement or leaving the department than the higher educated officers. In fact, officers with a college education looked forward to promotions and a longer career in policing.

When asked why a person became a police officer, historical answers were "I want to help people," "It's exciting," "I don't want a job that's indoors," and "It's a secure job." All of these factors still seem to apply today—but with greater conviction. Thirty years ago police applicants' job options, if they were not selected for the police department, were such occupations as a butcher, baker, bank teller, carpenter, or other vocational positions, largely "blue collar" jobs.[6] Today's officers view job options in a different realm—teaching, business, law school, and other "white collar" professions. This is an important symbolic difference in self-image. Specifically, police officers and those entering policing view it increasingly as a profession, certainly as an occupation higher on the social strata than has historically been the case.

Historically, when stratified by race and ethnicity, minorities had slightly different reasons for entering policing. Blacks, for example, expressed the belief that policing was a possible avenue for obtaining a civil service job which would provide both job security and a middle-class income.[7] In New York and Boston, Irish-Americans felt that they had enhanced opportunities for promotion given the rich Irish traditions in those departments.

Today, minorities have essentially the same reasons for entering policing as do whites. However, there may be greater conviction of contributing toward community tranquility among minority officers. An increasing number of women have entered policing as a result of affirmative action initiatives. Women give virtually the same motivation as men for entering law enforcement. Interestingly, however, there is a greater tendency for women to enter policing after working several years in another occupation first. A common occupation for women to leave in order to enter police work was teaching. The reasons: police work was more rewarding and more secure (some also said policing was safer)![8]

SECURING QUALIFIED PERSONNEL FOR POLICE WORK

As noted earlier, there are those who say that nothing is to be gained by securing "qualified personnel" (whatever that may mean) for police work because, after a few years of experience in the field, "they become like all the rest of them." This is to say, the role shapes the self, as opposed to the position that a relatively immutable self shapes the role. Those taking the latter position would argue that personnel who are initially selected for high quality would substantially improve police service. The highest caliber people must be recruited into law enforcement.

The standards for "recruiting" by the Commission of Accreditation of Law Enforcement Agencies (CALEA) recommended that law enforcement agencies "identify and employ the best candidates available, not merely eliminate the least qualified."[9] Recruiting must be a proactive process that seeks to identify the best possible candidates and "sell" the potential candidates on applying to the police agency.

Barriers to Effective Recruiting. Law enforcement typically uses the approach of "hiring," not recruiting. Potential applicants either go to the police department or stop by a college recruiting table and say, "I'd like a job." The hiring officer then says, "Okay, let's see if you qualify." There is little "selling" of the department and even fewer attempts to overtly identify the best possible candidates. Instead, the departments tend to simply make themselves available and respond to inquiries. This is aggravated by the fact that recruiting is typically viewed as a low-priority function, with officers more frequently *assigned* to recruiting rather than being *selected* for the job. As a result, the officers are required to "fill training classes" so their attitude is more attuned to finding people who meet at least the minimum defined criteria in order to fill positions, rather than identifying and selecting the best possible people available.

Civil service regulations can also inhibit innovative recruitment and selection. Frequently, regulations stipulate that, regardless of other qualifying criteria, applicants are hired based on their ranking on a written examination. Other regulations, such as residency requirements or "points" for previous civil service employment (regardless of whether it was related to policing) may also inhibit aggressive recruitment. Although civil service regulations provide job protection and address historical employment inequities, many regulations have not been sufficiently revised to address the professional needs of contemporary law enforcement. Nor do such regulations address minority recruitment and factors that may place minority candidates at a competitive disadvantage on written examinations.

Based on research in this area, the author has identified three myths that influence recruiting activities:

- *Myth 1*: Law enforcement salary and benefits are not competitive.
- *Myth 2*: There are few college students who want to enter *local* law enforcement after graduation, and
- *Myth 3*: There are virtually no minority group members who are college educated and interested in local law enforcement.

A review of starting salaries in a sample of police agencies serving populations of 50,000 or more inhabitants showed that first and second year police officers typically earned $25,000 to $28,000 annually plus overtime, court time pay, and benefits. Conversely, other average starting salaries for college graduates tend to be lower. For example, retailing starts at an average of $20,909 annually, public school teachers at $21,428, and new management trainees at around $23,845. Other entry-level occupations commonly requiring social science backgrounds had an average annual starting salary of $23,310. (While comparable benefits are available, these positions typically have no overtime salary provisions.) Police salaries and benefits have increased over recent years, making law enforcement not only competitive but also desirable.[10]

With respect to the type of agency college students seek to enter, police administrators tend to feel that candidates desire to work for federal law enforcement rather than at the state or local level. Based on the author's experiences and discussions with colleagues at other colleges and universities, it appears that there is a significant body of students interested in a law enforcement career who prefer municipal or state agencies. There are several reasons for this: the most frequently given reason is personal preference for this type of work, i.e., they simply *want* to work in patrol. Additionally, federal law enforcement salary scales have not kept pace with those of state and local agencies. A new federal agent may earn around $25,000 a year (or less) plus overtime. In addition, the agent can be assigned to an area where the cost of living is high, thereby reducing "buying power." Another reason for preferring local law enforcement is that students want to stay reasonably near their home and recognize that federal employment will typically require relocation (sometimes several times). In this same vein, it should be recognized by state and local agencies that not everyone who applies to a federal agency will be employed by one. While employment with a federal agency may have been an initial career objective, the career *goal* remains to be in law enforcement, and candidates will apply to other organizations beyond their "first choice."

The third myth is that there is virtually no pool of college-educated, minority law enforcement candidates. Quite obviously, there are fewer black and Hispanic than white candidates. However, of the minority group members in college, a significant proportion are enrolled in the social sciences. Many of these students are in criminal justice programs and are interested in a law enforcement career.

As one example, in the 1997–1998 academic year, Michigan State University, Sam Houston State University, and Central Missouri State University each had approximately one thousand criminal justice students (undergraduate and graduate). The total percentage of minority criminal justice students at all three universities is nearly twice as high as the university-wide proportion of minority students. Moreover, the percentage of minority enrollment in criminal justice has increased dramatically over the past five years at all three institutions. Discussions with colleagues at other colleges and universities have indicated a similar trend. Thus, it appears that not only are there college-level minorities interested in criminal justice careers, but also those minorities are in proportionally higher numbers compared to other academic areas.

Police administrators must recognize and overcome these "mythical" recruiting barriers. Moreover, effective planning must be established in order to employ the best police candidates regardless of gender, race, or ethnicity.

Recruiting Plans. If recruiting is to mean more than simple "hiring," the police agency must develop a goal-oriented policy to meet this end. To secure the best people for police work, a three-phased recruiting plan may be desirable:

- *Short-term*: Police executives must establish recruiting as a priority for the department. High-quality people are the touchstone of high-quality police work. Select good people to work in recruiting. Give them some status and the tools they need to do the best job possible. Develop a marketing plan for recruiting that includes operational, tactical, and strategic objectives. Use recruiting models that have proven successful, including private sector techniques, other government methods, and successes in police recruiting. Recruiters must also be directed to focus on applicants whose career interest is on "service" rather than "adventure."
- *Medium-term*: Police departments should consider regional projects, in conjunction with other law enforcement agencies, to improve recruiting. The development of cooperative image enhancement programs, including public service announcements, publicity, and paid advertisements as well as a regional applicant pool can be beneficial to all law enforcement agencies. Many of the best officer prospects will be applying to several agencies, so each department must emphasize its strengths to appear as the most attractive. In addition, recruiters must always be looking for good prospects regardless of the current number of vacancies. Flexibility can be built into the selection process in order to employ the proverbial "cream of the crop" as police officers.
- *Long-term*: Look at the organization and the positions available (sworn and nonsworn positions). Consider the skills really needed to get the job done, especially in a department with community policing. Restructure positions as appropriate and consider hiring civilian specialists for positions that do not require law enforcement authority. Look at changes in policing responsibilities in the next five to ten years and recruit people who will be able to do the job then.

While specific plans must be developed to meet the unique needs of a given department, a contemporary perspective of recruiting must be conceived. The intent of this perspective is to ensure that the best quality police officers are employed, who have not only the desired credentials but also reflect the demographic characteristics of the community. The most important, longest term, and most expensive investment a police organization makes is its people. It should endeavor to get the best.

SEEING ONESELF AS A PROFESSIONAL

As earlier noted, obtaining "qualified" people for police work is complicated by role ambiguity in the sense that the yardsticks for measuring qualification are hazy. Consequently, hiring qualified people—by some standard—is not guaranteed to produce professionalism. Moreover, "good" people may become absorbed—swallowed by the values and pressures of what is—and forget their original commitment to basic structural, functional, and systemic change. Some would phrase this differently, suggesting that the young and inexperienced simply come to recognize that the old ways are best. The compromising of goals often results from the delicate interplay between the desire to make changes and the need to keep a job.

Police leadership must be concerned with the job survival of young careerists entering the field with a commitment to change. Conditions *ought* to be such that they are retained in the system long enough for their influence to be felt. But the fact is that *any* system tends to protect itself against change. The result is that young careerists with inspiration and competence to be agents of change are discouraged from entering the system initially, or become frustrated and drop out at some later point, or survive only to the extent that they compromise their commitment to change. Thus the system remains self-insulated and self-perpetuating, a haven only for those conforming to its standpat values. John Matthews and Ralph Marshall have coauthored an excellent description of what happens in police organizations to three types of employees: those who create problems, those who neither create nor solve problems, and those who solve problems.[11] The latter are innovative "wave makers," and they historically have not done very well in police work. Times, however, are changing.

A glimmer of hope for the change-minded comes from the possibility that the community served by the organization will demand change and insist upon the creation of conditions conducive to it. Where police work is concerned, this has happened far too rarely in the past. Sophisticated police-community partnership could bring it about more widely in the future. It is a healthy and dynamic state of organizational affairs for administrators to be pressured into periodic reexamination of goals, policies, practices, structures, and priorities. An old way may be better than a new way, in some instances. But to have to show empirical evidence to demonstrate it either way—that is the stuff of professionalism and better service to the community. And this, in turn, will have a bearing on problems of morale.

While more than attitude is required to make a professional, believing that one is a professional and striving to behave in a manner consistent with a professional model are surely important in making an earnest effort toward that objective. In a relevant study of this matter, James Leo Walsh discovered some interesting things about police attitudes.[12] Walsh observed police officers in four midwestern departments and conclude that officers who see policing as a profession have attitudes toward their work considerably different from those who see what they do as just a job. This contrast extends to attitudes toward minorities and to the use of force, as well as to other matters. Walsh found, for example, that the "professionals" were much more concerned about public approbation, respect, and support than were the "jobbers." The latter were more apt than the professionals to say that riots and the poor constitute the number one police problem. Nearly half of the jobbers felt that the use of force in police work actually helped their standing in the community, while 60 percent of the professionals said that the use of force, although sometimes necessary, was detrimental to their efforts to achieve professional status. The professionals were inclined to attach much more importance than the jobbers to public service in police work. The jobbers tended to stress physical size and strength as desirable qualifications for police work. The Walsh study also suggested that generalization regarding the values and beliefs of police as a group are hazardous.

David Bayley and Harold Mendelsohn, in their study of Denver police officers, observed that "very little credence is given by [officers] to charges that [they] treat minority people unfairly or improperly."[13] This has also been indicated by Skolnick. Walsh found that the jobbers were much more likely than the professionals to claim that unequal treatment was the fault of minorities themselves. Some 62 percent of the jobbers felt that the poor and minority groups actually get better treatment than the middle class. Another 23 percent of the jobbers felt that the poor and minority groups have problems because they are "too lazy" to improve their lot in life. Only a small percentage of the professionals subscribed to these notions. Walsh described a central hypothesis of his study as follows:

> To be proud of one's occupation and to view it as a profession enjoying positive standing in the community should lead to attitudes toward the work done by members of the profession different from those one would expect from other practitioners whose view of the occupation is that it is simply a job—something one does because he can't find anything else, or because it is the most secure position available, or something that anyone could handle with little or no training.[14]

ANOMIE AND CYNICISM

Various analysts have dealt with the Durkheimian concept of *anomie* in different contexts. The term means "normlessness" and its usual relevance in criminal justice is in discussions of crime and delinquency causation. There is a sense, however, in which the police officer may be caught in this web. Again, role ambiguity is a basic consideration. Charles L. Johnson and Gary Copus have probed this complicated conceptualization, relying heavily on Robert K. Merton. "Anomie," they declare, "arises when the equilibrium between cultural goals and societal means of achieving these goals is upset."[15] What are cultural goals? Merton's answer is "that organized set of normative values governing behavior which is common to members of a designated society or group."[16]

What emerges in this conceptualization, then, is what amounts to ethical dissonance—as represented by the departure of conduct from ethical norms. To the degree that this occurs in police work, as we have seen that it does, and perhaps quite frequently, normlessness is the result, thus anomie. Bear in mind that we have observed that such police departures from ethical norms are at least partially explainable as a reaction to the uncertainties of police work—in short, role ambiguity. Importantly, with role ambiguity there is a feeling of uncertainty, even futility, in the purpose of one's role. Consequently, this self-image leads to a cynical view of one's work and, by extension, cynicism toward those with whom officers' deal (i.e., citizens).

Anomie and cynicism go hand in hand. The following point by Arthur Niederhoffer is pertinent:

> . . . the new patrolman must resolve the dilemma he has learned at the academy and the pragmatic precinct approach. In the academy, where professionalism is accented, the orientation is toward that of the social sciences and opposed to the "lock-them-up" philosophy.[17]

So it is that "ethical codes become, if not irrelevant, at least placed in a perspective not related to the real world."[18] Reactions to a state of normlessness by police officers are manifested in one or more adaptive responses. conformity, innovation, ritualism, retreatism, and rebellion. There is some psychological stress in each of these adaptive patterns, and the cogency of cynicism is evident.

Cynicism may be a by-product of anomie in the social structure; at the same time it may also prepare the way for personal anomie or anomia. . . . As the cynic becomes increasingly pessimistic and misanthropic, he finds it easier to reduce his commitment to the social system and its values. If the patrolman remains a "loner," his isolation may lead to psychological anomie and even to suicide.[19]

Cynicism has always been part of the police officer's working persona—and will probably continue to be, but at a different level. The author would argue that a degree of cynicism is desirable for police officers. We do not want officers who are gullible or officers who would not question suspicious actions. We need, however, for that cynicism to be tempered with good judgment and a reasonable perspective of reality. As the levels of education, training, and supervision of our officers increase, the likelihood that cynicism will be balanced with perspective grows.

PSYCHOLOGICAL STRESS

There has been increasing attention in recent years to psychological stress in police officers. Literature on the subject is abundant. Training programs devote more and more time to it. The statistics reflecting divorce and family strain,[20] number of police officers undergoing clinical treatment with psychologists and psychiatrists, and police suicides are melancholy indications of the extent and severity of the problem.[21] Add to this "burnout," alcoholism, and drug addiction. Bernard Garmire, an "old pro" among police executives, writes that today's police officers suffer from conflicts between professed and practiced values, between how they want to be valued and how they are valued, and between the role they most value and that they least perform.[22] Anomie, cynicism, and psychological stress in police officers are closely related, as we have suggested, and the community has considerable stake and responsibility in the causes and cures. The pressures on the officer have their source in value conflicts within police organizations, and in value conflicts in community expectations.

As a response to stress, increasing numbers of police departments have established Employee Assistance Programs (EAP) and provided additional psychological treatment assistance as part of the officers' employment benefit packages.[23] Certain stressors are endemic—they are unresolvable—such as the constant exposure to the worst side of humankind, physical injury, and death, and inherent dangers related to policing. Other sources of stress—such as those imposed by shift work, financial problems, marital problems, and so forth—can be controlled through a variety of techniques. If the latter types of stress can be managed with the assistance of an EAP, the effects of endemic stress will be reduced.

Ironically, anecdotal evidence suggests that when officers are given broader responsibility and more discretion, as in the case of problem-oriented or community-based policing, stress may actually be *reduced*. The basic reason is that officers have greater contact with members of the "law-abiding community." As such, they receive positive feedback for their work, experience cooperation with the public instead of conflict, and earn feelings of accomplishment when community problems are resolved.

Interestingly, research interests in stress were notably absent for nearly two decades. However, recently interest has been rekindled. In fact, the National Institute of Justice set aside funding in 1997 expressly for research related to police work, including the effect of stress on officers' families. Unfortunately, at the time of this writing, none of the findings were available.

THE SUBCULTURE OF THE POLICE

Occupational socialization creates occupational subcultures. For our purpose, *subculture* may be defined as the meanings, values, and behavior patterns that are unique to a particular group in society. In larger police organizations, there will likely be several "sub-subcultures," so to speak: one at the line level, another at the supervisory and middle management level, and another at the upper administrative level. Some attitudes and values will be common to all levels, some will differ and even conflict, as we have observed.

Most communities seem to be unaware that they expect their police to perform impossible tasks. The police, quite naturally, are defensive in their reactions to community expectations that they cannot fulfill. They are too often reminded of their failures by people who do not understand the problems of the police. Moreover, they are often a scapegoat for the community's social and moral default. Because police officers are, by occupational prescription, inclined to be suspicious, they tend to isolate themselves from an unsympathetic, critical, untrustworthy, and uncomprehending community, and to form their own in-group alliances with fellow officers. This supplies needed emotional and ideological support with elements of secrecy and ritual, even a special language and other subgroup trappings— this creates the "Blue code of Secrecy" within the police subculture.

Former dean, Victor Strecher of Sam Houston State University's College of Criminal Justice, has described police subculture by utilizing a theoretical paradigm comparing the police with medical students.[24]

MEDICAL

The concept of medical responsibility pictures a world in which patients may be in danger of losing their lives and identifies the true work of the physician as saving these endangered lives. Further, where the physician's work does not afford (at least in some symbolic sense) the possibility of saving a life or restoring health through skillful practice . . . the physician himself lacks some of the essence of physicianhood.

Those patients who can be cured are better than those who cannot.

"Crocks" . . . are not physically ill and . . . are not regarded as worthwhile patients because nothing can be done for them.
(*Note*: To a medic, a "crock" is a hypochondriac.)

Students worry about the dangers to their own health involved in seeing a steady stream of unscreened patients, some of whom may have communicable diseases.

Perhaps the most difficult scenes come about when patients have no respect for the doctor's authority. Physicians resent this immensely.

POLICE

The concept of police responsibility pictures a world in which the acts and intended acts of criminals threaten the lives or well-being of victims, and the security of their property. The true work of the police officer is the protection of life and property by intervention in, and solution of, criminal acts. Further, where the police officer's work does not afford (at least in some symbolic sense) the possibility of protecting life or property by intervening in criminal acts, the police officer himself lacks some of the essence of police identity.

Those cases that can be solved are better than those that cannot.

Chronic neighborhood complainants are not worth taking seriously because there is no substance to their complaints, and nothing can be done for them.

Police officers worry about dangers to their own safety involved in approaching a steady stream of unknown persons, some of whom may have serious behavioral problems and intentions of causing them injury or even death.

When a citizen makes an officer sweat to take him into custody, he has created the situation most apt to lead to police indignation and anger.[25]

Beyond childhood and adolescent socialization, the police officer, Strecher asserts, undergoes a process of occupational socialization through which he or she becomes identified as an officer and begins to share all the perspectives relevant to the police role. There is substantial coherence and consistency among these perspectives. Moreover, because all police officers occupy the same social-institutional position, they tend to face the same kinds of problems arising out of the nature of the position. Therefore, the demands and inhibitions of the police role, as we have suggested, are decisive in shaping the kaleidoscopic perspectives of the police officer.

Strecher holds that police officers do not simply apply the perspectives that carry over from previous experience or backgrounds. He believes that background may have indirect influence in many ways, but goes on to say:

> The problems of the police officer are so pressing and the initial perspectives so similar that the perspectives developed are much more apt to reflect the pressures of the immediate *law enforcement* situation than of ideas associated with prior roles and experiences.[26]

Therefore, police subculture is a shorthand term for "the organized sum of *police perspectives* relevant to the *police role.* " Other researchers might argue with Strecher on the question of how important prepolice background is in explaining officer attitudes. "Background" is an all-encompassing term that covers a great deal of territory. Jerome Skolnick is interested in the sociology of occupations and devotes considerable attention to what he calls "the working personality" of the police officer—an analysis of the effects of the occupation on the personality of the officer. The literature dealing with the effects of one's work on world outlook is extensive. Skolnick suggests that:

> the police, as a result of combined features of their social situation, tend to develop ways of looking at the world distinctive to themselves, cognitive lenses through which to see situations and events. The strength of the lenses may be weaker or stronger depending on certain conditions, but they are ground on a similar axis.[27]

In another work, Skolnick observes that the police officer's attitude toward work is much like that of a combat soldier. For the working officer, life is "combat." People are either good or bad, the situation is safe or unsafe—the "we-versus-they" attitude. Like the soldier, the police officer is irritated by minor organizational rules, what he calls "legal technicalities," and long-winded, sociological explanations.

> Additionally, as one observes police, one notices their employment of two predominant models of discourse. One of these models, which might be termed "office language" or "working language," is frequently profane, loud, and good-humored. Transported into the cold light of print, the words might have a shocking effect upon delicate sensibilities. But such discourse would ring familiar to a steelworker or longshoreman, a ballplayer or a soldier. . . .
> Off the street, police frequently resort to an alternative model—"officialese"—out of fear that "working language" might spill out and offend officialdom. An outstanding example of police officialese is the substitution of the word "altercation" for "fight." . . . So the police [officer] is often not a graceful or moderate speaker or writer, and [this] inability or perhaps unwillingness to conceal true feelings get [the officer] into trouble.[28]

To relate these insights of Strecher and Skolnick to our initial point, we note the variables that influence personality: childhood development, the experiences one has had before taking a certain job, and the job itself, along with its particular organizational context. Each of these factors comes into play for an individual's developing self-image; the degree to which one factor or another may predominate depends on the individual and the situation.

If broken down into specific elements, the police subculture is characterized as being cynical, authoritarian, isolationist, and conservative. While these characteristics still remain fundamentally applicable, their impact is not as pervasive as it was during the reform era of policing. As in the case of the previous discussion of cynicism, authoritarianism is another factor which is not completely undesirable. We want police officers who will assert authority during crisis situations and when they encounter interpersonal conflict. However, we want that authoritarianism tempered with reason and responsibility. If it is not, then it will surely lead to abuses. As in the case of cynicism, education, good training, and effective supervision can be important counterbalances for authoritarian tendencies.

Isolationism became a particularly evident artifact of the reform era. With attempts to make officers more mobile, reduce opportunities for corruption, enhance a professional image, and make officers more aware of the threats associated with policing, isolationism increased. This was aggravated during the late 1960s and early 1970s when the police were frequently targeted as "symbols of oppression" by protesters in the Civil Rights movement and those opposing the Vietnam War. Efforts in police-community relations, notably in the 1960s, coupled with crime prevention activities in the 1970s and 1980s, attempted to turn the tide. Unfortunately, these initiatives typically only involved a limited number of officers in the department—those assigned to the community relations and/or crime prevention units. Community policing has begun to change this isolationism somewhat because it involves all officers and seeks to accomplish goals (solve problems) in cooperation with community members. With more broadly-based communications in support of cooperative efforts related to goal accomplishment, the bounds of isolationism are broken down. While isolationism remains, its dysfunctional effects are being reduced.

One factor of the police subculture which has not changed is conservatism. Historically, police officers tend to view the justice process as one which should be retributive rather than rehabilitative. Their feelings toward constitutional interpretations are narrow, as are their attitudes toward welfare and social assistance. Some evidence suggests that minority officers tend to be more liberal than their white counterparts when they join the police department, but become more conservative during their tenure as officers. This is an illustration of socialization into the subculture.

Why do police officers tend to be conservative? It is probably a function of several interactive factors, including:

- Frustration with the courts and corrections
- Repeatedly seeing the trauma of victims
- Regularly seeing the detrimental effects of social problems
- Seeing money "wasted on social programs" that are taken advantage of by repeat offenders
- Seeing the failure of rehabilitation
- Seeing the "welfare cycle" as being continuous and rarely broken
- Being accused of racism and bigotry when they are making sincere efforts to do their jobs fairly
- Being socialized into a long-standing culture of conservatism

This should not be viewed as being a negative characteristic but as a pragmatic observation of the police cultural environment. When examining the police subculture, the impact of peer pressure cannot be overlooked. The "Blue Code of Secrecy" and the "Blue Curtain" are common metaphors for the prevalence of peer pressure in the subculture.[29] It is a norm in policing that one officer does not "rat" on another. Officers are expected to tolerate, although not necessarily condone, misbehavior by other officers. To inform on another officer's improper behavior can result in ostracism. When asked directly about this subcultural norm, most officers say they do not like it: they feel it is stressful and dysfunctional, yet a "fact of life." Subcultural norms are developed over generations and reinforced through occupational socialization. Although many officers oppose certain norms—such as the "Blue Curtain"—it will still take a generation or more for this to change.

PERSONALITY TYPE AND POLICING

Researchers have been interested in the questions of why a person would want to be a police officer and whether there is an identifiable type of personality that gravitates to police work. It appears that the stereotypic assumptions of yesteryear, such as that there is such a thing as a "police type," are coming under careful scrutiny. Early research of this kind, reflecting a typical interpretation, proposes that certain personality traits established early in life were clues to whether a person would be able to stand the pressures of a police career.

> We find that the appointees most likely to remain in law enforcement are probably those who are more unresponsive to the environmental stresses introduced when they become officers of the law than are their fellow-appointees. These stresses include becoming a member of a "minority" (occupationally speaking) group, need to adhere to semi-military regimen, community expectation of incongruous roles and the assumption of a position of authority complete with the trappings of uniform, badge, holster, and gun, and all that these imply. The officers who remain in law enforcement may well be the sons of fathers who imposed a rigid code of behavior to which their children learned to adhere, and who do not feel a strong need to defy or rebel against authority.[30]

John Pfiffner suggests that the personality culture of the police affects their view of crime and criminals. He asserts that law enforcement officials generally subscribe to the classical theory of criminology. They tend to see the violator as a wrongdoer, morally responsible for his or her conduct, and therefore liable for the consequences. This school of thought maintains that the fear of punishment is a powerful deterrent to law transgression. Those who commit crime should be treated as enemies of society; "soft" treatment is regarded as a waste.

Pfiffner contends that there is fundamental conflict between the two schools of thought he identifies. One is oriented to force and intimidation, the other to kindness and "loving sensitivity." Of course, this is an oversimplification, as Pfiffner concedes, but he says it is nonetheless a handy theoretical construction. The question he poses is whether it may not be timely to redefine these roles. He asks: Does the welfare-therapeutic-bureaucratic society require a new concept of the police function? If so, will it be one in which the police participate more widely in the whole process of dealing with the problems of handicapped humanity? Will more of a team approach be demanded for these problems, in which the police role will be but one phase of society's cooperative effort to deal with the problems of personal and social disorganization?

Society will soon redefine the police role to include ideas, perceptions, and insights which will bring the police into the area of dealing with social pathology on a scale larger than the present holding and containing operation. That role has not yet been spelled out, and is not even dimly perceived by many police administrators; indeed, perhaps most would feelingly deny it to be within the police purview.[31]

Since Pfiffner's work over forty years ago, we know a great deal more about those who enter policing. Actually, his vision of the future was quite perceptive. The "social pathology on a larger scale" has been more precisely defined now to include quality-of-life issues and problem solving. Because of the changes in the police role, we are now seeking officers with the personality and characteristics that are consistent with this changing role. These changes are long-term, occurring over a generation. As noted previously, the impact of occupational socialization is recurring, but it too changes with a generation.

The task of policing is more complex today than it has ever been. Similarly, the responsibilities of officers are increasingly complex and challenging. These challenges, coupled with the increased social status and competitive salaries of policing, are attracting the most competent and professionally oriented cadre of people ever to law enforcement. Police leaders must be vigilant in pursuing subcultural changes while at the same time being tolerant, recognizing that desired changes are slow in being realized.

The manner and degree to which the police subculture is shaped and governed by organizational phenomena has been competently analyzed by Peter K. Manning in a number of articles and books in recent years.[32] Manning shows how the police mandate (role) has been gradually shifted from simple protection of citizens and their property from the "dangerous classes" to the paramilitary "crime fighting" of today. The myths and rituals surrounding police work, both within and beyond the police organization, are described by Manning as basic to what he calls the inherent contradictions of police-community relations. He contends that the police are not really in the crime-control business. What they spend most of their time doing, he says—but do not consider "real" police work—is supplying human services. As long as the police encourage the public to think of them as "crime fighters," Manning asserts—which in today's society they cannot be—and refuse to develop new modes of crime control and service delivery, they will be caught in the middle of public and political controversy.[33]

PREDICTING SUCCESS IN POLICE WORK

Past research attempted to develop a battery of psychological tests to predict whether a candidate would be a successful police officer.[34] The essential effect of these assessments was to determine characteristics which were *perceived as desirable* for a police officer, but were not strongly supported by empirical evidence of the actual tasks officers performed. That is, there was a tendency to test potential officers on psychological dynamics related to crime-control strategies and dealing with danger. However, little assessment was done on conflict resolution and virtually none on problem solving, communications, and creativity.

As police management became more sophisticated, there was recognition, even during the reform era, that officers were spending a great deal of time on noncrime related duties (typically referred to as "calls for service"). Consequently, management assessments, in the form of a *job task analysis*, became more common. The effort sought to explicitly determine the types of duties officers actually performed during their working hours. These analyses are extremely detailed and "behaviorally anchored." This means that the actual behavior is identified; it is not just a description of duties. Based on the job task analysis, assessors were able to articulate the *knowledge, skills*, and *abilities* required to do policing.[35] This process permits both the articulation of explicit educational and vocational needs as well as psychological characteristics desired for police officers.

Because policing varies widely based on the size and characteristics of a jurisdiction, types of police officer authority, philosophy of the police executive, nature of crime, demands of the citizens, availability of social or support services, and a panoply of other factors, a job task analysis is valid only for the department wherein the assessment is conducted. That is, a job task analysis of the police department in Tallahassee, Florida could not be used for St. Joseph, Missouri or McAllen, Texas because each of these three cities has varying characteristics and responsibilities.

The problem becomes exacerbated with the growth of community policing. As described previously, under the CoP philosophy, each department makes a proactive effort to tailor programs and all operational activity to the jurisdiction. When the increased discretion and broader responsibility are factored into this equation, the task identification for police officers becomes geometrically complex. This makes the need for comprehensive behavioral assessments not only more difficult, but also more necessary.

As we learn more about the effects of CoP and become more sophisticated in our management assessments (as well as goal-setting), our ability to articulate personnel needs will become stabilized. We will be able to more clearly and reliably define the types of persons needed as police officers and to confidently predict success. Needless to say, there is a long path ahead before we reach these levels.

MORE ABOUT POLICE VALUES

Studies dealing with contrasts among occupational value systems are fairly common in contemporary literature. One study of this kind probed the question of whether there were noteworthy differences between the values of police officers and those of representative samples of other black and white Americans.[36] The findings disclosed a somewhat larger value gap, on the whole, between police and blacks than between police and whites, but the gap was considerable in both cases. The police officers tested ranked high such values as *a sense of accomplishment, capability, intellect*, and *logic*. They devalued such modes of behavior as being *broadminded, forgiving, helpful*, and *cheerful*. They ranked *equality* significantly lower than a national sampling of whites and far lower than a national sampling of blacks. This ranking of equality was interpreted as an indicator of conservatism.

Other research has underlined the importance that police officers attach to respect for law and authority and, more specifically, to respect for the individual police officer. Several studies indicate that police officers feel that lack of respect for the police is America's primary law enforcement problem. We mentioned this in our discussion of discretionary use of police power. Officers attach symbolic importance to their uniform, especially when their authority is challenged—officers feel tested when they have to sweat to take someone into custody, and their anger is easily aroused under such circumstances.

Walsh, looking into the question of the meaning of the uniform to the police officers, asked the question of the officers he interviewed: "Some have suggested that police work could improve its image if it were to encourage officers to wear suits, not uniforms, while on duty. Do you agree?[37] Almost 90 percent of the respondents disagreed. Among these, the importance of the uniform as a "symbol of our identity or mark of distinction" went up as professional striving went up; the "professionals" were stronger in their disagreement with the question than the "jobbers." The latter saw the uniform as important, but mainly as a deterrent to those who might break the law.

Danger and suspicion are, of course, significant conditioners of the attitudes and behavior of police officers. Ironically, construction work and farming are more physically dangerous than policing; however, both the police and the public view law enforcement as the most dangerous occupation. This is not meant to diminish the danger but to place it in perspective. The unique aspect of danger in policing is that injuries are frequently *intentional* rather than accidental. The use of body armor, changes to semi-automatic handguns, and the increased use of survival training programs both reinforce and magnify the perception of danger. Certainly these factors affect attitudes and behaviors of officers. An illustration of the emotion can be found in the San Diego patrol car experiment (discussed in chapter 3), where one-officer cars were found to be safer than two-officer cars. Most officers rejected the findings as being "wrong" because of emotional reinforcement of the danger issue.

Sterling explored this matter in his study of police recruits. He observed that the prospect of danger in the work has little meaning for the police recruit. It is only incidentally covered in training; it is learned through the occupational socialization process. According to the research, perception of danger is related to length of experience as a police officer.[38]

To begin with, the recruit may have some vague notion, as training begins, that policing is more hazardous than barbering. Then he or she comes to recognize that the element of danger is, to some extent, predictable by specialization; a bomb specialist, for example, faces more danger than a training director. The recruit also learns that danger for the patrol officer is largely unpredictable. This is the point where "the message" begins to take hold.

> Statistically, the risk of injury or death to the patrolman may not be great in order maintenance situations, but it exists, and worse, it is unpredictable, occurring . . . "when you least expect it . . ." . . . the risk of danger in order maintenance patrol work . . . has a disproportionate effect on the officer partly because its unexpected nature makes him more apprehensive and partly because he tends to communicate his apprehension to the citizen.[39]

Danger may also be considered in its spatial and positional characteristics (the "ecology" of danger?); for example, so-called high-crime areas, office work as opposed to street patrol, and so on. Still another consideration is the danger potential associated with the appearance and conduct of people. This is where Skolnick's observation regarding the police stereotype of "suspicious persons" and the "symbolic assailant" are relevant. The perceptions involved and the related emotions are learned through experience.

Danger may also be considered in relation to situations. This aspect usually does get some attention in police training. For example, the recruit is told that disturbance calls are often dangerous. Westley alluded to the high danger level associated with family disputes, because the parties have a tendency to direct their hostility toward the officer. It may be noted in this regard that "Fear reactions in combat may be due, in part, to an attitudinal factor, the feeling that one has not had sufficient training."[40] Perhaps this is similarly true for the new patrol officer.

Skolnick described the police officer's picture of the "symbolic assailant": persons who signal danger, based upon dress, mannerisms, or language. They are to be even less trusted than average citizens. VanMaanen identified several types of citizens that officers feel are especially troublesome in the function of controlling the population: "suspicious persons," "assholes" and "know-nothings."[41] "Suspicious persons" are those involved in crime or who are on the periphery of crime. Whenever they are seen, the officer assumes they are "up to no good," and they are therefore treated accordingly. The "asshole" is a person who displays "a poor attitude" and "disrespect" toward the officer. These are people who need to be "taught a lesson" and are most likely to be the recipient of "street justice". Finally, the "know nothings" are the average citizens who have little understanding of the criminal world and cannot fathom the things that officers face. These people are usually treated with indifference.

CHANGE

We have had a panoramic and somewhat rudimentary look at a number of interesting facets of the self-image of the police. In some respects, this is the most fundamental aspect of the study of police and community relations. Surely it is one of the most important considerations if one is to understand the social-psychological dynamics of police-citizen interaction.

The subject of police self-image has broad implications. It is often regarded as marshy ground by the student because so much about it remains inconclusive. But research is increasingly concentrating on it and promises the dividends of scholarship.

Michael Brown has astutely analyzed the uncertainties of police work as mainly explanatory of the values and beliefs that guide the exercise of police discretion and what he calls the "ethos" of line police officers. The values of professionalism that have been pushed in recent police reforms have tended to reinforce organizational discipline and bureaucracy. But these values clash thus creating a bifurcated system of internal control—one derived from professionalism (bureaucratic model) and the other, from the police subculture. This conflict increases the officer's sense of uncertainty, as he or she is caught between internal and external pressures that cannot be fully reconciled. Morale problems and psychological stress problems are more understandable from this perspective.

> The police subculture, therefore, emerges as a formidable force—created in part by the impossible character of the police function and in part by the environment in which the police work—that determines the way in which much police business is handled. It is inclined to oppose strongly any proposed changes in policing that are seen as threatening the protective bond between officers.[42]

This resistance to change makes the police unusually vulnerable to criticism which in turn causes them to seek shelter in their own subculture. And this strengthens their hand in subverting change. Where does responsibility reside for doing something constructive about this seemingly indestructible paradox? It resides in the partnership of police and community. It also resides in evolving policing philosophies and enlightened police leadership. Basically, the paradox is attitudinal, and attitudes *can* be changed.

SOME FINAL THOUGHTS

Self-image is important because it relates to esteem and feelings of self-worth. Essentially, if officers feel their role is important, they are respected for their professionalism, and their work is appreciated—by the public and police administrators alike—they will perform better. Their attitude toward work will be more positive and, consequently, their efforts more productive. Beyond being operationally more effective workers and good organizational representatives to the public, there are pragmatic benefits. Officers with a strong self-image are more likely to have a higher level of job satisfaction, which, in turn, will lead to fewer sick days taken and a generally increased quality of life in the workplace. Police leaders must remember that their employees constitute an occupational community. It behooves us to recognize that community relations applies *within* the organization as well as external to the department.

QUESTIONS FOR DISCUSSION

1. What is "morale"? How is it related to self-respect?
2. Relate the concepts of *social role* and *social self*?
3. List the reasons why you would like to become a police officer. How realistic are your reasons? Do you think these may change after you begin working as an officer?
4. What is the difference between a police officer who views his or her job as a "professional" as opposed to those who may view themselves as a "jobber"?
5. Why can we say that the working environment of a police officer is a subculture?
6. Why are police officers generally conservative?
7. What "myths" exist among many police executives concerning the ability to attract qualified police recruits? Why are these myths?
8. What is meant by occupational socialization? How does it influence officers' self-image?
9. How might community policing influence an officer's self-image?
10. How might a potential police officer's success be predicted? What factors would be key in determining this?

NOTES

1. J. Milton Yinger, "Who Are We?" (Speech delivered to a Northern Ohio Institute on Police and Community Relations at Cleveland, OH, November 21, 1964).
2. John H. Rohrer and Munro S. Edmonson, *Eighth Generation* (New York: Harper & Brothers, 1960), p. 160. Reprinted by permission of Harper & Row, Publishers, Inc.
3. Mittie Southerland, "Organizational Communication." In Larry Hoover, ed., *Police Management: Issues and Perspectives*. Washington DC: Police Executive Research Forum, 1992).
4. Nelson A. Watson and James W. Sterling, *Police and Their Opinions* (Washington, DC: International Association of Chiefs of Police, 1969), p. 100. Reprinted by permission.
5. Robert Trojanowicz and Bonnie Bucqueroux, *Community Policing* (Cincinnati, OH: Anderson Publishing Company, 1990).
6. Patricia Lynden, "Why I'm a Cop: Interviews From a Reporter's Notebook," *Atlantic*, 223, no. 3 (March 1969): pp. 104–108. Copyright © 1969 by the Atlantic Monthly Company. Reprinted by permission.
7. Nicholas Alex, *Black in Blue* (New York: Appleton Century Crofts, 1969), pp. 34–35.
8. David L. Carter and Allen D. Sapp, *Higher Education and Minority Recruitment* (Washington, DC: Police Executive Research Forum, 1992). Data on salaries updated in 1997.
9. Commission on Accreditation of Law Enforcement Agencies, *Standards for Law Enforcement* (Alexandria, VA: CALEA, 1987).
10. L.P. Scheetz, *Recruiting Trends* (East Lansing, MI: Collegiate Employment Research Institute, Michigan State University, 1990), pp. 16–20.
11. John P. Matthews and Ralph O. Marshall, "Some Constraints on Ethical Behavior in Criminal Justice Organizations," in *The Social Basis of Criminal Justice: Ethical Issues for the 80's*, Frank Schmalleger and Robert Gustafson, (Washington, DC: University Press of America, 1981), p. 14 ff.
12. James Leo Walsh, "The Professional Cop" (Paper presented at the Sixty-fourth Annual Meeting of the American Sociological Association, September 1969).
13. David H. Bayley and Harold Mendelsohn, *Minorities and the Police: Confrontation in America* (New York: Free Press, 1969), p. 148.
14. Walsh, "Professional Cop," p. 1.
15. Charles L. Johnson and Gary B. Copus, "Law Enforcement Ethics: A Theoretical Analysis," in *The Social Basis of Criminal Justice: Ethical Issues for the 80's*, Frank Schmalleger and Robert Gustafson (Washington, DC: University Press of America, 1981), p. 42.
16. Robert K. Merton, *Social Theory and Social Structure* (New York: The Free Press, 1968), p. 216.

17. Arthur Niederhoffer, *Behind the Shield* (Garden City, NY: Doubleday and Co., Inc., 1969), p. 56.

18. Johnson and Copus, op. cit., p. 47.

19. Arthur Niederhoffer, *Ibid.* See also R. M. Regoli, *Police in America* (Washington, DC: University of Press of America, 1977).

20. A good reference is Arthur and Elaine Niederhoffer, *The Police Family* (Lexington, MA.: Lexington Books, 1975).

21. Among many relevant references are the novels of Joseph Wambaugh.

22. B. L. Garmire, "Value Shock," parts 1 and 2, *Texas Police Journal* 22, no. 12 (January 1975): pp. 17–21; and 23, no. 1 (February 1975): pp. 12–16. See also the entire issue of *The Police Chief* (International Association of Chiefs of Police) for April 1978, and articles in the May 1978 issue, pp. 42 and 73, are relevant.

23. Based on a 1992 study by David L. Carter and Allen D. Sapp on *Police Labor Relations* for the Police Executive Research Forum. At the time of this writing, the results on this issue have not been published.

24. Victor G. Strecher, "When Subcultures Meet: Police-Negro Relations," in *Science and Technology in Law Enforcement*, Sheldon Yefsky, ed. (Chicago: Thompson, 1967).

25. The last statement on the police side of this paradigm is Skolnick's.

26. Strecher, "When Subcultures Meet," pp. 703–4.

27. For example, see: Everett C. Hughes, *Men and Their Work* (Glencoe, ILL.: Free Press, 1958); Henry Borow, ed., *Man in a World at Work* (Boston: Houghton Mifflin, 1964).

28. Jerome H. Skolnick, *Justice Without Trial: Law Enforcement in Democratic Society* (New York: John Wiley & Sons, 1966), p. 42. Reprinted by permission of John Wiley & Sons.

29. See Thomas Barker and David L. Carter, eds., *Police Deviance*, 2d ed. (Cincinnati: Anderson Publishing Company, 1990).

30. Ruth J. Levy, "Predicting Police Failures," *Journal of Criminal Law, Criminology, and Police Science* 58, no. 2 (1967): p. 275.

31. John M. Pfiffner, "The Function of Police in a Democratic Society," *Occasional Papers: Center for Training and Career Development* (Los Angeles: School of Public Administration, University of Southern California, 1967). Reprinted by permission. Pfiffner's earlier work is reflected in his *The Supervision of Personnel*, 2nd ed. (Englewood Cliffs, NJ: Prentice-Hall, 1958).

32. Peter K. Manning, *Police Work: The Social Organization of Policing* (Cambridge: MIT Press, 1977).

33. Ibid., dust jacket.

34. U.S., Department of Justice, LEAA, *Psychological Assessment of Patrolman's Qualifications in Relation to Field Performance* (Washington, DC: U.S. Government Printing Office, 1968).

35. See Larry Gaines, Mittie Southerland, and John Angell, *Police Administration* (New York: McGraw-Hill, 1991).

36. Milton Rokeach, Martin G. Miller, and John A. Snyder, "The Value Gap Between Police and Policed," *Journal of Social Issues* 27, no. 2 (1971): pp. 155–171. See also Jacob Chwast, "Value Conflicts in Law Enforcement," *Crime and Delinquency* 11 (April 1965): 151–161.

37. Walsh, "Professional Cop"; Bayley and Mendelsohn, *Minorities and the Police: Confrontation in America* (New York: Free Press, 1969), pp. 50–51.

38. Sterling, *Changes in Role Concepts During Recruit Training*.

39. James Q. Wilson, "The Patrolman's Dilemma," *New York* (September 1968): pp. 19–20. Copyright © 1968 by The New York Times Company. Reprinted by permission.

40. Stouffer et al., *American Soldier*, p. 227.

41. Peter K. Manning and John Van Maanen, eds., op. cit., *Policing: A View from the Street*, p. 223.

42. Herman Goldstein, op. cit., *Policing a Free Society*, p. 11. The paraphrasing of Michael Brown refers to his *Working the Street*, (Russell Sage Foundation, 1981). Also recommended is the Foreword by Peter Manning in W. Clinton Terry III, ed., *Policing Society* (New York: John Wiley & Sons, 1985).

Chapter 9

THE PUBLIC IMAGE
OF THE POLICE

There is general agreement that the concept of the looking-glass self has substantial validity: what we think other people think of us has considerable influence upon our attitudes and behavior. Therefore, our self-image and our public image are complementary phenomena—how we see ourselves and how others see us. Or, put in a slightly different way, what we expect of ourselves is governed largely by our readings of what others expect of us. All of this is attitudinal; we act on the basis of these expectations, there are feelings involved, and the attitudes as well as the behavior are subject to change, sometimes swiftly. Quite simply, we do "judge books by their covers."

As individuals, as groups, organizations, business firms, as universities, and as police officers or agencies, we pay a lot of attention to our "public image." We are taught that respect for others begins with respect for self. And self-respect is built on what we think others think of us. Thus, an interaction between individual human beings takes place. Divested of all its complexity, the human equation depends upon how well we understand ourselves and others.[1]

We know that the process of building self-respect begins in childhood. If parents say to a child, "You are a fine child; we are glad you are ours; you are honest and generous," the child comes to see himself or herself in these terms. The child's public image is good; the feedback he or she is getting from the people who matter is favorable. The child's self-confidence and self-respect, or lack thereof, are not innate, but develop out of these basic early experiences. It is not, of course, simply the words of parents and others that count, it is the action toward the child that also influences the self-image.

There is also an action factor in the manner in which a business firm measures its public image. Are people buying the product? Check sales and profits. Simple enough. But suppose the product is a public service, such as that of the police department, and the operation is supported by taxes? The measures of the public image in such a case are not as concrete as in hard-product business firms. It is much more difficult to tell whether the customer is satisfied. In fact, in police work, as we have seen, it is sometimes very difficult to tell what citizens expect, particularly when they change their mind, sometimes rapidly, to suit the circumstances. Customers also tend to want one kind of service for other people and another for themselves. And

"Law enforcement is inherently designed to serve the public—that service goes beyond crime control and may include . . . dealing with an emergency, or helping in any of a myriad of other exigencies which a citizen may face."

there are many different kinds of customers to be served, often with conflicting expectations, as we have noted. Some examples of inconsistent public expectations of police:

- Don't bring your personal problems to work. But be "human."
- Get all the facts in the case. But respect privacy.
- Be visible, and be invisible.
- Be tough, and be compassionate.
- Stop all speeders, but not me.
- Control crime and arrest law breakers, but don't bother citizens.
- Take risks, but don't be uptight.
- Don't be prejudiced, but be suspicious of "peculiar" people and strangers.
- Know the law. Also be a social worker, psychiatrist, ombudsman, counselor, babysitter, and so forth.

Conflicting needs and demands, conflicting role expectations, and client satisfaction cannot be measured simply through statistics. But there are ways in which dissatisfaction can be expressed. Pressure can be brought to bear on the city council to squeeze the police budget. Some sort of extraordinary community control mechanism may be imposed on the police department. Or, more likely, the chief may be dismissed, or persuaded to retire—unless he or she has been contractually appointed for life.

If a business executive who sells yachts discovers that the product does not enjoy a good public image among families with an annual income of less than

$12,000, the executive does not worry much about it. It is viewed as being unfortunate but irrelevant. However, the police are in a somewhat different position. They are expected to be the police for *all* the people. Therefore, it should not be too comforting to be told by public opinion pollsters that most of the people approve of the police most of the time. The more heterogeneous the community served by a police department, the less likely it is that such soothing assurances will be forthcoming.

Public image is important because it influences the way citizens respond to the police, the support they provide for departmental funding, the cooperation given to the police in doing their job, and the degree to which they will participate in police programming. Law enforcement is inherently designed to serve the public. That service goes beyond crime control and may include providing protection, mediating conflict, resolving a crisis, providing assistance to solve problems, dealing with an emergency, or helping in any of a myriad of other exigencies that a citizen may face.

The public's image of the police will vary, positively and negatively, as a result of crises the police face, crime problems, and individual experiences of the public during specific instances. However, the overall image of the police is a collage of these experiences that occur and are reinforced over time. Moreover, the image is honed and influenced by factors which are only incidental to specific police actions. This chapter explores a range of specific issues, with the *caveat* that it is a holistic or cumulative effect of these factors that shapes the true public image of the police.

GENERAL AND SPECIFIC IMAGES

In recent years, there have been many public opinion polls and surveys undertaken in many places with the purpose of discovering the status of community attitudes toward the police. The usual finding, in general terms, is that most people are satisfied with the job done by the police most of the time.

The National Opinion Research Center reported to the President's Crime Commission in 1966 that only 8 percent of the people polled thought that the police do a poor job of enforcing the law. The Commission stated that "if the persons showing greatest skepticism toward the police were evenly distributed through all kinds of communities and neighborhoods, one might conclude that there was no serious police image problem."[2] While this remains basically true three decades later, greater dissatisfaction with the police now exists, particularly among minorities.

Overlooking methodological problems frequently encountered in such general inquiries[3] as well as their ephemeral nature, there may be some comfort for police executives in such results. Indeed, it may be too comforting, if the assumption is that all's well in what and how the police are doing things. The generalized public image of a police department is not very useful information administratively if the goal is really effective service to the whole community.

Much more useful is specific information about specific community audiences responding to specific questions. Examples: Which police services do employed black women, aged eighteen to twenty-four with a high school education, feel are satisfactorily provided? How do white or black youth in high schools feel about the quality of classroom instruction by police officers dealing with the topic of respect for law? What are the tasks that elderly citizens in the community think they could handle that would be helpful to the police?

Obviously, specific information of this kind goes far beyond general popularity polls in producing quality police service. It is a beacon for enlightened administration and sound police-community relations. Correspondingly, it is also politically astute. The criticism of generalized survey data is illustrated by the following quotation:

> . . . the overwhelmingly favorable picture of police-community relations reported by some may be a function of misinterpretation of items as well as a function of the level of specificity of the items utilized in the research. . . . on general items the public reports a favorable image of the police reflecting their support for the institutional foundation of this criminal justice agency. While on more specific items the favorable image decreases tremendously, reflecting a rather negative evaluation of specific police officeholders and practices. . . . most of the empirical literature assessing the mood of the public toward criminal justice agencies is not useful for informing policy decisions.[4]

The view that the police have no serious image problem appears to be substantiated by various research projects. Yet the United States Commission on Civil Rights and the Community Relations Service of the Department of Justice have been reporting a steady stream of civilian complaints of police misconduct and use of excessive force. At the same time, vicarious liability lawsuits against the police have increased dramatically, reaching record levels in the 1990s.

FACTORS THAT SHAPE THE PUBLIC IMAGE

As noted previously, the public image of the police is a complex phenomenon resulting from the interaction of a wide range of local and global factors. That is, some incidents which occur receive national attention, and this shapes public opinion about the police in general. Similarly, there are things which happen within the local community that help shape public opinion more specifically about law enforcement. It is important to recognize the *interactive* nature of these factors. Interim impressions about the police are influenced by transient incidents or experiences (whether they are good or bad). However, an actual "opinion" is a belief based on reinforcing factors that may be derived from multiple sources or repeated occurrences of similar incidents. The major factors that form public opinion are:

- Experience with the police, and
- The refinement of perceptions about the police

Experience with the Police

Clearly, an important factor shaping the public image of law enforcement is the personal experience that citizens have had. Two fundamental premises will have an impact on the image:

- The reason for the contact
- The character of the officer's behavior

The *reason for the contact* refers to the context of the interaction between a citizen and an officer. Such things as whether the contact was initiated by the officer or citizen, whether it was related to crime or service, or whether the contact was formal or informal, are examples of factors which will begin to focus the citizen's image. Simple logic applies: if the environment of the contact is inherently one of conflict, such as an arrest, this will contribute to a more negative image. Conversely, if the circumstances are of a cooperative nature, such as forming a Neighborhood Watch, the image is more likely to be positive. The interpersonal dynamics become more complex when intertwined with psychological dynamics that the citizen may be experiencing at the time of the contact: stress, grief, trauma, and relief are examples of intervening factors that will strongly influence one's perception of an officer and the propriety of the officer's actions.

Certainly, an equally important dynamic is the *character of the officer's behavior*. There is no doubt that the officer's body language, attitude, comments, and appearance will influence the citizen's image. These can be nearly as influential as the actions the officer takes to resolve the situation at hand. Even factors such as the officer's personality and general communications style will have a strong impact on image. Interestingly, as one means to deal with this, some police departments—such as McAllen, Texas; Tucson, Arizona; and Boston, Massachusetts—have sent officers through the Dale Carnegie course so they may learn effective communications and interpersonal techniques to help them be effective and authoritative without being offensive.[4]

During the reform era of policing, professionalism was envisioned as being detached and unemotional when dealing with the public. This resulted in the perception that the police were uncaring and not empathic to the problems of citizens. Similarly, routinization of many policing activities—such as responding to burglaries, issuing traffic citations, and handling stolen vehicle cases—resulted in the officer's demeanor implying that the problem at hand was "no big deal." To the citizen, these incidents are "big deals" indeed. When the officer forgets the trauma these incidents cause the citizen, it gives the appearance of indifference, perhaps even that the citizen is bothersome. Needless to say, these attitudes and behaviors are offensive to citizens paying hard-earned taxes for police services.

There are some specific types of experiences with police officers that seem to have a particular impact on public image.

Response Time.   As discussed in chapter 3, police response time has been examined in several comprehensive research projects. The important finding, with respect to the current discussion, was that citizens have certain *expectations* about the police. These expectations are formed from a wide range of influences—for example, word of mouth, movies, promises of politicians, or "intuition." If the police meet a citizen's expectations, the person is more likely to have a favorable image of the police. Problems arise when these expectations are not based on realistic criteria. For example, if a person comes home and discovers that he or she has been burglarized, the citizen calls the police, reports the crime, and the dispatcher responds with something to the effect of, "An officer will be there shortly." Unfortunately, the police and the citizen have different perceptions of how long "shortly" is. To the police, "shortly" may mean "within the hour." To the citizen it may mean "five to ten minutes." If an officer arrives in thirty minutes, the police may feel this is a fast response, but the citizen will perceive it as a slow response and have a less favorable image of the police because his or her expectations were not met. This can be further aggravated because of the citizen's stress associated with the victimization—stress which produces anger, frustration, and the perception that "time is moving slow."

The challenge for the police is to manage the citizens' expectations. That is, by giving the community realistic information on when they can expect the police, unrealistic expectations may be controlled. For example, a conversation between a citizen reporting a burglary and a police dispatcher may be, in part . . .

CITIZEN: My house has been broken into—I need the police.
DISPATCHER: Is the burglar still there?
CITIZEN: No.
DISPATCHER: Is anyone injured? Is an ambulance needed?
CITIZEN: No.
DISPATCHER: Did you see anyone leaving your house who might still be in the area?
CITIZEN: No.
DISPATCHER: So everyone is safe, just shaken up?
CITIZEN: Yes, that's right. Can you send a police officer?
DISPATCHER: Yes, an officer will come to your house. Right now our officers are tied up on calls requiring medical assistance so it will be a little bit before they can get to your house.
CITIZEN: A little while?
DISPATCHER: Yes—I would say about one hour. It is 2:30 P.M. right now, an officer should be there by 3:30 P.M. If no one has arrived by 3:30 P.M. or if you see a suspicious person, please call us back right away.
CITIZEN: Okay.

In the above scenario the dispatcher has ensured that a life-threatening circumstance is not present and that the burglar is gone. This conversation also helps reinforce to the citizen that he or she is safe, thereby reducing some of the stress. The dispatcher then lets the citizen know that an officer will respond, but it will not be right away because of calls which are potentially life-threatening—thus, the citizen is given a *reason* for the delay. While the citizen may not particularly like having to wait for the police, he or she understands the reason. The dispatcher then gives the citizen the *time expectation*—in this case one hour—which is reinforced by telling the caller what time it is and the time the officer can be expected. The citizen is also reassured that he or she can call the police back if necessary.

This relatively simple, yet important, communications exercise deals with the problem of response time and citizen expectations. Surprisingly, police departments have seldom communicated with citizens like this, let alone given them reasons for delays. As long as the police respond within the expectations they have established, the public will tend to have a favorable image, rating the police higher on competence and general satisfaction.

Traffic Control.   Traffic control is an area in which the police have the most frequent contact with the general public. It is also the police activity that generates some of the greatest criticism and ill will.

When directing traffic, officers often channel motorists in a direction they do not want to go. This occasionally develops frustrations among motorists, with the citizen viewing the officer as being "inflexible," a somewhat provincial view, since the driver is considering himself or herself rather than the traffic conditions. Similarly, citizens get frustrated when they receive a parking citation, even when they know the citation is justified. The frustration they have toward *themselves*—for getting caught—is transferred to the police. (Who wants to blame oneself for something that went wrong?) The tendency is to say something to the effect, "The cops must not be busy enough if they have time to write parking tickets." Of course, the same citizen would have a different view of the importance of a parking citation if there was a car blocking their driveway. Traffic direction and parking enforcement are two types of circumstances in which citizens tend to view the police as "nit pickers," rather than looking at the broader picture of police responsibilities.

By far, the biggest conflict between the police and the public occurs in the enforcement of traffic laws. When an officer issues a motorist a citation, the impact is multifold. First, the driver frequently recognizes that he or she is guilty and is frustrated at being caught. Once again, the frustration is psychologically transferred to the police officer as a defense mechanism against self-blame. Second, the citizen is embarrassed to be pulled over, particularly in an area where they may be recognized by friends or acquaintances. Third, the citation carries a financial impact. It is typically going to cost fifty dollars or more for the fine and court costs. This could increase significantly if the car is towed, the driver hires a lawyer, or if the motorist has to take time away from work to go to court. Finally, the citation may represent an increase in insurance costs, depending on the driver's history, which can also have a significant financial impact.

Because of these burdensome factors, traffic enforcement frequently results in citizens developing negative attitudes toward the police. For example, the driver may feel that the police have a "quota system," which requires officers to issue a specified number of citations. This conjures up images of unfairness, under the assumption that officers will issue a sufficient number of citations to meet their quota, then not issue any more for the remainder of the shift. One classic response of a police officer who was accused by a motorist of trying to fill a quota was, "No sir. We don't have a quota—we can write as many tickets as we want." Although the statement is true, it does not particularly warm the public image of the police.

It is the rare police department today that has a quota of traffic citations. Some departments may have "performance measures," which include "evidence of traffic enforcement activity." Even in these cases, there is rarely a specified number of traffic citations an officer is expected to issue. Even if a department establishes a formal quota, there is nothing unlawful about it. Rather, the practice seems to offend our sense of fairness.

There is one interesting case which is the opposite of a quota. Former Kansas City, Missouri Police Chief Steven Bishop announced to his officers and the public that the police should cut back on the number of citations they issue. He wanted officers to issue tickets only in those cases where driver behavior was unsafe and warranted the citation, not in every technical violation of the traffic laws. The city manager was enraged. He said this cutback in the number of citations issued would result in decreased revenue to the city, possibly by millions of dollars. The chief of police responded that he would then announce to the public that the police would, instead, keep issuing the same number of citations because the city manager wanted to keep the revenues coming in. Needless to say, the city manager was not pleased and decided to live with the reduced revenue. In this case, the police public image with respect to traffic enforcement was enhanced because of the actions of the chief.

The negative implications of traffic enforcement are compounded by several myths, factors that are accepted as "self-evident truths," but are largely fallacious. Citizens get particularly frustrated when an officer's behavior goes against this "conventional wisdom of traffic enforcement." The myths include:

- *Myth*: An officer cannot issue a citation if you drive onto private property.
  Fact: The officer is issuing the citation for violation of a traffic law on a public street. It makes no difference where the driver stops to receive the citation—public or private property.
- *Myth*: The police cannot leave their immediate jurisdiction to issue a citation.
  Fact: As a general rule this is not true; however, the law varies by jurisdiction. Typically, a municipal or county officer can issue a citation outside of their

jurisdiction as long as the "pursuit is fresh." Typically, an officer cannot leave the state and issue a citation; however, there are a few exceptions to this.

- *Myth*: A mistake on the citation—the wrong date or time or location—will negate the ticket. *Fact*: The citation is simply a written accusation that the driver violated the law. The prosecuting attorney (and sometimes the officer) can amend the citation to correct mistakes. Frequently, mistakes such as this are deemed "harmless error" and are not grounds for dismissal of the citation (although this is a judicial decision).
- *Myth*: The police cannot tow your car after issuing a traffic citation, unless it is a citation for Driving Under the Influence (DUI). *Fact*: In practice, the towing of cars is most greatly influenced by departmental policy, not law. If the officer has a reason he or she can articulate to tow the car, that is usually all it takes. Of course, the driver is responsible for the towing and storage charges for the car.
- *Myth*: The police cannot take a person to jail on a traffic offense unless it is a DUI. *Fact*: A citation is an arrest for violation of a traffic law. Like most arrests, the citizen is given the opportunity to post bond as a promise to appear in court or resolve the arrest. In most traffic cases, the bond is the motorist's signature. If the driver refuses to sign the citation's "promise to appear," the officer is obligated to take the person to jail or have them post a cash bond. A person can also be taken to jail if the officer, for some reason, decides not to offer the signature bond (this varies by jurisdiction).
- *Myth*: The vehicle cannot be searched when the driver is issued a traffic citation. *Fact*: There is a great deal of law on this, but suffice it to say it is possible to "search" a car in a traffic citation situation. There are several ways this can occur: if the driver consents to a search; if the officer has probable cause to believe the vehicle contains seizable property; or if the officer observes what is immediately recognized as contraband, the vehicle can be searched. If the vehicle is towed, it can be "inventoried," which is also tantamount to a search. Finally, if the officer reasonably believes that there is a weapon within the driver's reach and the officer can articulate the reason for this belief, a limited examination of the interior of the car can be made to look for a weapon.

The purpose of this discussion is not to provide a recitation in law, but to illustrate that many common assumptions are fallacious. When citizens have mistaken information on these issues, they feel their rights are being violated. As a result, their frustrations are magnified when their "conventional wisdom" proves not to be true—and the image of the police suffers more.

One element of traffic control which tends to produce a more favorable image of the police is the handling of traffic accidents. When collisions occur drivers experience several emotions—anger, frustration, stress, fear, embarrassment, and trauma (emotional and/or physical). The intensity of these emotions will vary with the seriousness of the accident, but they nonetheless exist. Permeating the conditions of a traffic accident is chaos: uncertainty of what to do next, possible injury to oneself and others, traffic congestion, and transportation if the car is disabled are some examples of the factors contributing to the chaotic environment. The arrival of a police officer at the accident scene symbolizes control. Citizens can rely on the officer to begin resolving the chaos and restoring normalcy. These conditions tend to produce a favorable image of the police unless the officer appears uncertain, or worse, incompetent.

Managing police so that their behavior will be competent, fair, and empathic during traffic encounters with the public can minimize the factors that contribute to a negative police image. Despite positive efforts in this regard, the reality is that regulatory activities, such as traffic, will inherently engender conflict which must ultimately be balanced by other factors in the police-community relationship.

Victimization.   In 1997, the FBI's Uniform Crime Report showed that index crimes *decreased* for the sixth year in a row.[5] Yet, most people perceive crime to be increasing. This perception is influenced by a number of factors, perhaps the most influential being reports and stories in the news media. Nightly "Police Beat" reports on the local news, national news stories on crime, and special focus programs on crime-related issues—most notably drugs—have a significant impact on public opinion. As one illustration, the preponderance of subjects on the CBS News program "48 Hours" deal with crime and policing issues. This is not to infer that the news stories and programming are erroneous, but rather to illustrate the frequency of instances in which the public is exposed to crime-related issues. The repeated exposure brings with it reinforcement, as articulated in learning theory, wherein the public develops a skewed perception on the frequency of crime.

If the police are viewed as the community guardians responsible for controlling crime, one would expect that their image would suffer with this perceived omnipresence of criminal activity. Interestingly, there is no consistency on this point. It appears that the public's opinion varies on the association between police activities and crime. In essence, sometimes crime influences the public's opinion of the police and sometimes it does not. Certainly the public recognizes that the police have crime prevention responsibilities, but there is some tendency to give a much stronger association to detecting and solving crime.

Based on several surveys of the public, the police generally receive good marks for solving crime. Whites and people with higher incomes were the most pleased with police crime-solving. Inner-city residents and minorities, people who are the primary clients of police services, were the least satisfied. However, even these groups felt the police did a pretty good job in solving crimes. The inference which might be made is that since the public perceives the police as being effective crime solvers, the police image is enhanced.[6]

Perhaps just as important is that the police presence at a crime scene represents the beginning of "re-normalization." The trauma experienced by citizens as a result of victimization starts to reverse when the police arrive. Officers instill a sense of safety and security. They represent overt action toward the resolution of the disorder caused by the victimization, and they provide demonstrable action toward identifying and dealing with the criminals. From the citizen's perspective these are positive actions, which will probably translate into a favorable image of the police. An important *caveat* is that the interaction with citizens after victimization is a fragile one. A poor attitude by the officer or the appearance of indifference can easily turn the image into a negative one.

Asking Officers for Information.   A common form of experience with the police comes through a citizen-initiated inquiry to an officer. The officer's demeanor, response, and language during a brief encounter can have a significant influence in shaping public opinion. The police are symbols of authority who have a wide range of responsibilities related to government and the law. The public tends to assume an officer will have answers to many questions ranging from how to register a car to the location of a given address. The knowledge of the officer, the effort an officer expends to find an answer to a question, and the way an officer's answer is communicated will shape the citizen's image about all officers in the department.

Following are examples of actual conversations between the author and officers in three separate police departments in an attempt to gain directions. The responses of the officers in each case give differing impressions, which may have influenced a citizen's perception about the department in general. Stereotyping is not an accurate way of developing impressions, but it is a social reality, one which can be based on something as innocuous as a short conversation.

In Las Vegas, Nevada, the author was attempting to locate a particular office. The address was on a short side street in a nondescript building with no clearly discernible landmarks nearby. The conversation with a Las Vegas Metro Police officer was as follows:

AUTHOR: Excuse me officer, can you tell me how to find this address?
OFFICER: Can you believe it, I've never heard of this street. Just a minute, let me ask someone.
[He asks another officer who was unfamiliar with the street and then asks the dispatcher. The dispatcher apparently located the street on a map and then gave general directions to the officer.]
OFFICER: I know where it is, but it's hard to explain. Why don't you just follow me and I'll show you.
[The officer guided us to the street, waved, and went on about his duties.]

In this case, the officer left a very positive impression. He was helpful, friendly, and made the "extra effort" to respond to a request. The resulting impression was obviously positive. Another experience was not as good.

After attending the North American International Auto Show in January, three of us left Detroit's Cobo Arena in search of a barbecue restaurant for which we had an address, but not a clue to its location. We approached a police officer standing next to a street barricade and had this conversation:

AUTHOR: Excuse me officer, we are trying to locate this restaurant. Can you tell us how to find this street and give us an idea on how to get to this address.
OFFICER: What do I look like? The f . . . in' Chamber of Commerce?

Besides our not finding the restaurant, the image of the police suffered as a result of the officer's response. The day was cold and the officer had apparently been outside a long time with little to do but stand beside the barricade. He was cold and bored on this Saturday and had undoubtedly been asked directions many times by auto show visitors. However, this does not excuse his demeanor. If he responded similarly to everyone he spoke with that day, the damage this one officer may have done to the police image could be substantial.

The final illustration is yet different. Two of us arrived in Philadelphia about 8:00 P.M., rented a car, and attempted to find our hotel on John F. Kennedy street. We had difficulty navigating and ended up in what was obviously an inner-city area with no idea of where our street was. We spotted a parked police car and pulled up beside the officer. He rolled down his window and we had the following brief conversation:

AUTHOR: Officer, can you help us? We are trying to find John F. Kennedy.
OFFICER: He's dead.

After a short pause (and seeing a puzzled look on my face) the officer laughed and gave us directions. In this case, the officer's response could have resulted in different reactions. People respond to humor—particularly so-called "black humor"—in different ways. Some citizens may have interpreted this response as offensive. Others—like us—would think it was humorous. In either case, a response such as this will provoke a reaction which can shape the public image.

People will always ask the police for information. Officers must recognize that the impact their words and actions have on citizens' perceptions is substantial. Regardless of the conditions at the time, the officer's personal comfort or state of mind, and the frequency the officer is asked the same or similar question, he or she must be prepared to respond professionally and with civility. The cumulative effect of negative interactions can have a dramatic effect on public image.

Going Into a Police Station.   Walking into a police station, regardless of the reason, will influence a person's perception of the police. If the station is dirty and cluttered, the perception may be that the police do not really care about their role or the public. If the station is "cold" and sterile, the perception may be that the police are impersonal and the citizen's presence is a trespass on officialdom. Conversely, if the paint, furniture, and layout of the police station's foyer are "warm" and comfortable, the image of the police will start on a positive note.

Police departments need to be concerned about security of the facility. However, some departments overreact in this regard. The security at a police station does not need to be the same as that in Fort Knox. Reasonable security measures that tend to be unobtrusive are far more desirable. The attitude and demeanor of the police employee who meets people entering the police station should be friendly, empathic, and professional. When citizens come into the police station, they need some type of assistance; recognition of this fact should permeate the attitude of the receptionist (whether this is a sworn officer or not).

If a lobby or waiting area of the police station also has amenities—comfortable chairs, smoking area, vending machines, and rest rooms—all play a subtle, but realistic role in shaping the public's image, particularly if citizens have a long wait at the station. The department should also take this opportunity to have materials available for the public to read and take with them. Information on crime prevention, the department's mission and goals, a history of the department, the department's annual report, and the process for making a complaint against an officer should all be available. Not only is this good public education, it is the public's right to know these things about their police department.

Collectively, both the overt and subtle environment of the police station send a number of messages to the public about the police image. It is only reasonable to capitalize on these factors to make the image as favorable as possible.

The Development of Perceptions

The second broad area that helps form the public's image of the police can be envisioned as perceptual development. This encompasses a variety of factors that build on each other, each reinforcing the other. As perceptions develop, they also become more selective. That is, once a person's vision of the police begins to solidify—whether positive or negative—the perception tends to focus on aspects which support that image.

Friends and Acquaintances.   "I have a friend who was stopped by a cop . . .". There are a wide range of conversations that have started in this or a similar manner.

When a person has an encounter with the police, regardless of the context, there is a tendency to describe this encounter to others. The way this interaction is described is going to be related to both the reason for the contact and the demeanor of the officer. People tend to present only their perspective of the encounter as well as their perception of the propriety of the officer's actions and behavior. Many times, the circumstances of the encounter are embellished to justify the citizen's own actions. The third party is likely to believe the person and may even pass the story along to others (with, perhaps, further embellishments).

"Word of mouth" can have a geometric effect, particularly when one considers the number of police officers who have multiple contacts with citizens each day. These types of experiences can have an indeterminable—and largely uncontrolled—effect on public image. What we *do* know is that if there are actual problems with officer behavior, then "word of mouth" will magnify the negative effects on image. This fact reinforces the need to have positive police-community encounters and resolve any problems in behavior or demeanor as soon as they are identified.

Media Reports.   Media relations will be addressed in greater detail in a later chapter. At this point it is important to recognize the tremendous impact media reports have on public opinion. The emergence of politicians providing "sound bites" during campaigns as well as the expensively crafted political commercials and carefully designed protocols for the presidential debates serve as strong evidence of the media's impact.

It is important to recognize that the police are under constant scrutiny of the media for several reasons. First, there is a constant public concern about crime and violence. Since the police have the primary responsibility for crime control, media attention is a logical extension. Second, the police possess authority for the use of force and deprivation of liberty which is unparalleled in the United States. Given the sanctity with which we hold individual liberties, scrutiny of the police by the media is also a logical extension. Finally, the public holds a fascination for the police. Whether it is the experience of vicarious excitement, curiosity about the unusual nature of police responsibilities, or concern about the authority embodied in officers, the fascination is clearly demonstrated by the frequency of news stories and numbers of police portrayals in the entertainment media.

Generally speaking, the public tends to generalize what it sees in media reports. For example, stories about police misconduct or abuse of authority help frame the police image in the public's mind of the police *in general*, not just those who were the subject of the story. Fortunately, the opposite is also true: favorable reports are also generalized. Police executives must be cognizant of these generalizations and understand their impact on image.

Historically, the police have been "closemouthed" with the media. They have resisted sharing information about crime and community problems, even that which has been deemed public information. Rather than viewing the media in terms of conflict, the police need to work cooperatively, share information which is appropriate, and view the media as a partner in public information and public safety.

Symbolism.   The police are awash in symbols: badges, uniforms, firearms, batons, arm patches, police cars, radios, and computers all symbolize elements of police authority. In recent years police departments have made increased efforts to have uniforms and vehicle markings reflect a professional and positive image. The reality is that we *do* judge books by their covers. As we have learned from marketing research, people draw conclusions about other people, places, and things based upon appearance. A competent police officer who has a slovenly appearance and is dressed in a dirty, unprofessional uniform will convey a significantly different message than the same officer with a professional looking uniform and appearance. In this same vein, over the past several years the trade magazine *Law and Order* has held competitions for design and appearance of police uniforms and vehicles. Innovative designs have been developed, which unquestionably enhance the professional appearance of the police.

Subtleties are important in symbolism. For example, a professional appearing police officer wearing mirrored sunglasses will present an image of a cold, isolated, authoritarian individual. An officer who smiles and says, "What can I do for you?" will present a far more favorable image than an officer who grimaces and says, "Yeah, what do you want?" when asked a question by a citizen. As simple as these things sound, they are the fundamental building blocks of image.

Overcoming a Negative Image: A Case Example

When a police department has a negative public image it cannot be simply changed through superficial modifications and public relations. Instead, change must address *substantive* matters as well as *symbolic* messages. Moreover, attitudinal change must be planned as a long-term endeavor. Short-term efforts may mollify immediate problems, but will have little lasting effect. The McAllen, Texas Police Department had a significant negative image problem—which was well-earned—that it changed to a positive image—also well-earned—over nearly a ten-year period. The department's experiences serve as a good case illustration.

McAllen is a city of nearly 100,000 people in south Texas just a few miles north of the Mexican border. The city's residents are about 65 percent Hispanic, although there is a "shadow population" of an additional several thousand people who are Mexican nationals in the United States as undocumented aliens. In the late 1970s the city had an "Anglo" mayor, city manager, and police chief. The police department of some seventy-five officers at the time (about 50 percent Hispanic) had a public image that ranged from neutral to poor. The department was a classic reactive organization which used aggressive tactics to "fight crime."

The chief of police of over twenty years had risen through the ranks and had changed virtually nothing during his tenure. The chief was essentially a recluse from his officers, the city commission, and the community. To illustrate, the chief never attended city commission meetings, but instead sent his assistant to discuss policing matters. When the chief retired, the most recent photograph of him that the local paper could find was about twenty years old. He refused to pose for or send a more recent photograph. When city officials gave the chief a retirement dinner, he did not attend. To further illustrate his isolation, one officer told the author that after working at the department for over a year, the chief spoke to the officer for the first time: as the officer walked down a small hallway in the police department, he met the chief of police who said, "Get out of my way!"

The importance of these characteristics lies at the essence of police-community relations: the chief of police sets the tone for the agency. If the chief is an isolationist, this is the model the agency follows in order to follow the department's "leadership." It is also the model officers must follow to demonstrate the characteristics that are most likely to get them promoted. Similarly, the philosophy the chief sets for the way policing is done will surely be followed by the officers. Thus, officers will perform their work in an aggressive, reactive manner. This was starkly reflected in a large number of civil rights violations filed against the police department for use of excessive force. When these cases were filed there was a tendency for the city to settle the cases out of court, paying damages to the plaintiff and not taking any disciplinary action against the officers involved. Among the officers, this was interpreted not just as tolerance for the behavior but support for it: aggression and "toughness" were viewed as being characteristics of "a good cop."

Organizational characteristics also played a role. The rank structure, chain of command, span of control, and deployment practices all were inconsistent with sound management practice. There were only a few written policies and procedures, sometimes in conflict with each other. Promotions were somewhat arbitrary, training was limited, and discipline was inconsistent.

In the early 1980s the environment began to change as a result of a specific civil rights suit which the city was unable to settle out of court. It was revealed during a trial that the department had videotapes, taken from a camera mounted in the booking room, which showed several cases of excessive force by officers against people who had been arrested, for typically minor offenses such as public intoxication. In this particular lawsuit, following the leadership of the attorney from the American Civil Liberties Union who was involved, the vivid videotaped images of officers beating prisoners inside the police station were broadcast on local and national television. This, coupled with the other problems of the department, led to a new low in the department's image. Officers were ridiculed and letters to the editor as well as editorial cartoons lampooned the department's credibility and competence. Officers would stop cars for traffic violations and drivers would say, "Are you going to beat me?"

Since the city could not settle this case with a monetary payment as it had in the past, it agreed to an injunction, which had two unique stipulations. First, the department had to provide eight hours of training every month to every officer (all ranks included) on issues related to civil rights, criminal law and procedure, human relations, cultural relations, ethics, and related issues. Second, the city had to create a "Police Human Relations Committee" (PHRC), which was a quasi-civilian review board to review accusations of police misconduct.

Although the city was resistant to both the training and PHRC—primarily because they were mandated by the federal court—it recognized the need for change. This recognition was stimulated by both the problems of the department and pressure from the public. Beyond those changes mandated by the court, the city felt the department needed new leadership and a reorganization. In three years, the department had four police chiefs; the last of the four, Alejandro (Alex) Longoria, the city's first Hispanic chief, remains in that position today. To help in the reorganization, the city contracted with outside consultants who had no vested interest in the department. The consultants were given the authority to develop a completely new organizational structure, new rank structure, and guidance on needed policies. In addition, the consultants were asked to conduct an assessment center as the means of staffing *all* of the ranks in the new organizational structure. This process was like conducting radical surgery on an organization—it was unprecedented in policing and remains as an unusual case study.

The city's commitment to these organizational changes, along with the training and PHRC required by the court, were a difficult environment for a new chief to deal with. As one might expect, there were transition difficulties and a period of time when little that was visible happened, although the impact of the change was being internalized by both the police and the community. The image of the department slowly improved with the changes and much of the controversy died down. Yet, Chief Longoria recognized that the department had to change its philosophy as well as become more proactive in order to improve its image and, more importantly, be more responsive overall to the public's needs. His leadership and recognition that change required time, commitment, and refinement were important factors in the new image of the McAllen Police Department.

Chief Longoria "fine-tuned" the organizational structure based on day-to-day experiences, but kept the bulk of the new structure intact. He began a process of reviewing and refining policies and procedures and automated the records system to provide more efficient service as well as to permit crime analysis. The chief also looked at the department's most important resource—its people. He felt that the training was inadequate and took several steps to change this. For example, he was unsatisfied with the basic training officers were receiving from the regional training academy. As a result, he developed and received state certification for an academy specifically designed for the McAllen Police Department. This gave him greater quality control and permitted the department to tailor the training to its own needs. The chief also explored in-service training *beyond* that required in the court order. He sent officers around the country, and in one instance to Germany, in order for them to get the best possible training.

The department increased its size to around 125 officers with the chief stressing the need for high quality, professionally oriented people to be police officers. He reached out to other law enforcement agencies in the region to participate in task forces and address regional policing problems as well as working with other aspects of city government.

Recognizing the need for both symbolic and philosophical changes, the chief took additional steps in the middle to late 1980s. He changed the markings on the police cars and made other symbols of the police appear more visible and professional. The chief also established a television show, with a local college professor as host, to discuss policing issues, both as a forum and as a public education medium. More importantly, Chief Longoria developed an expanded statement of the department's mission and wrote the department's first statement of values. At the same time he was moving increasingly toward a community policing (CoP) philosophy. In this regard, the chief began with discussions and exploratory training for officers to understand the concept and for the command staff to more clearly define the direction for community policing.

As part of the CoP initiative the chief received funding to establish community police centers in several areas of the city, particularly those which had traditionally received little attention not only from the police but also other city services, such as the street and health departments. Police employees helped establish parks, recreation facilities, public health seminars, and provided a range of social assistance. A nagging problem had been the victimization and service needs related to undocumented aliens. These people were easy prey to criminals and would not go to the police for fear of being arrested and/or deported. Chief Longoria addressed this problem by making a policy decision that the McAllen Police Department would deal with undocumented aliens just as they do citizens—that the aliens would *not* be taken into custody simply because of their status nor would the Immigration and Naturalization Service be told of their presence. This eventually led to a stronger acceptance of the police in the community.

By the early 1990s the image of the McAllen Police Department was the exact opposite of what it had been a decade earlier. The community relationship is strong, the department is viewed positively and professionally by both the community and other law enforcement agencies, and officers have pride in their organization. The metamorphosis of the police department was not easy and is never complete—change must be refined and re-balanced. New crises and challenges will arise and some personnel will always be resistant. Fortunately, Chief Longoria, the mayor, city commissioners, and the city manager recognized that change in the department would require a long-term commitment. Attempts at short-term change typically yield results that will not last.

The Lessons for Change

As noted in chapter 3, change is difficult for any organization. How does this change occur? While not definite, a general transition process appears to emerge. First is the recognition that traditional police approaches have not succeeded. Second, attitudes about the police function among administrators, line personnel, and citizens must change. Third, community assessments must be performed to identify new police responsibilities. Fourth, new organizational and operational approaches must be conceived to meet the newly defined police responsibilities. Fifth, the community must be enlisted to work cooperatively with the police to achieve the desired results. Finally, there must be a commitment both by law enforcement and the community to continue the initiative's growth. Managing change, therefore, requires police administrators to practice the lessons learned from the political environment.

Based on the lessons learned at McAllen as well as many other organizations (not just police departments), several points are critical in order for change to occur. In sum, the lessons for change are as follows:

- *There must be a stimulus for change.* This is a leader with a vision willing to take the first step in challenging the status quo; a "change agent". Importantly, this stimulus must be ongoing and widespread. Given this, there are two significant elements that a change agent must address: (1) vigilance in effort and (2) diversity in focus.
- *There must be administrative commitment.* The effective administrator must provide ongoing support for a new initiative or program; that is, providing consistency between what is said and what is done. If administrators are not willing to try such things as reallocation of resources, amending policies and procedures, or experimentation with new ideas, then there is little reason to believe the sincerity of their pronouncements. If commitment is not shown to either employees or politicians, the probability for success will be significantly reduced.
- *Any change must be grounded in logical and defensible criteria.* While it is somewhat of a cliché, it is worth noting that changing to simply "shake up" the organization will be dysfunctional rather than productive. If politicians and employees are going to tie their professional fortunes to change, they must be given good evidence to support the change. Moreover, since change consumes resources, it is wasteful to pursue it unless this change is well-grounded in logic and evidence.
- *People at all levels must be able to provide input.* The importance of team-building for a new endeavor cannot be understated. Any initiative must have participation from as many people as possible. Not only will this diverse input provide new insights, but team-building provides "ownership" and, hence, a sense of investment and responsibility by members of the team.
- *There must be sufficient time for experimentation, evaluation, and fine-tuning of any new program or idea.* When a new initiative is started, it will inherently have "bugs" in it; not every malady or problem can be anticipated, and some

ideas will not work as originally conceived. Just because operational problems arise, it does not mean the idea was bad. Administrators, politicians, and employees must be flexible, adjusting their activities until there has been sufficient time to actually evaluate the initiative's true effects.

- *Before change is introduced, the plan must be communicated to all persons and their support must be enlisted.* Politicians, citizens, and employees alike must understand clearly what is being done and why. There is a tendency to assume that everyone knows and understands the issues of a new endeavor to the same extent as those who are immersed in the planning. Lack of communication is something that can destroy a new activity but, fortunately, is fairly easy to avoid. Remember that communication is more than sending messages, it also involves gaining feedback from the messages. Be cognizant of the issue, recalling the admonishment, "don't leave people in the dark."

- *Change takes time in order to have an effect; major change may take a generation.* As has been noted, we are generally a short-term and impatient culture. However, when implementing major organizational and behavioral change such as community policing, a key ingredient is resocialization of employees, citizens, and political leaders. This is inherently a long-term endeavor that requires patience and stamina before positive results can be seen. This sense of time must be instilled in all involved in order to minimize frustration and impatience.

- *Recognize that not everyone will "buy in" to new ideas.* For virtually any endeavor that is proposed, we must recognize that complete support is improbable; it is the nature of the human psyche. One must take care, however, to avoid discounting people who oppose new initiatives as being "lost causes" or obstructionists. Listen to their concerns—they may raise some valid issues that need to be addressed. If their ideas are used positively, they may become part of the team. Realism dictates, however, that there will still be those who oppose the new system (frequently for emotional or personal reasons). In these cases, an administrator's options are: (1) continue to try to convince them to change; (2) ignore or avoid them; (3) place employees in an assignment where they can do little damage; (4) increase the quality of the relationship with those political leaders and employees who support the initiative; or (5) tolerate employees or politicians until they resign, retire, lose their influence, or die.

- *Be flexible and open in your view of organizational, philosophical, and programmatic change.* No matter how much thought is given to a new initiative and how much effort is invested in planning, we still must recognize that many ideas are "losers." However, we often will not know this until the idea has been tried and evaluated. Even in failure, we have learned something. Unfortunately, given the culture of our political environment, there is a tendency to mandate success—a practice that is tantamount to a search for mediocrity. Both within the police organization and the broader political system, we must maintain the "freedom to fail"—without this, creative new ideas will be few and far between.

- *The chance always exists that one may be placed "on the hot seat" from a political perspective.* It cannot be denied that any attempt at change carries risks—the more massive the change, the greater the risk. Questioning traditional orthodoxy is not easily accepted by organizations, particularly bureaucratic organizations as typically found in government. Thus, proponents of new initiatives must understand that when they are on the forefront of change, their political necks are on the line. In light of this, administrators must be supportive and empathic with the politicians and employees supporting the change.

- *Change requires challenging conventional wisdom or, at least, traditions.* Debating the value of traditions has not been a politically popular avenue for people to follow, yet it is a necessary one in order for new ventures to be undertaken. When conventional wisdom is challenged it will be met with resistance, criticism, and perhaps ridicule from doubters, dogmatists, and traditionalists. The astute leader must be prepared to deal with these reactions both personally and professionally. Importantly, when those who support the leader's ideas of change are ridiculed, the leader has the obligation to reassert that person's value and contributions to the organization.

- *The organization's personnel evaluation system must measure and reward effective involvement in change.* Since change requires a personal commitment, or investment, there must be some individual benefits that can be accrued from one's participation. Benefits do not have to be monetary, but they can include such things as positive reinforcement, job perquisites, creative freedom, recognition, and awards or commendations. Similarly, awards and expressions of appreciation must also be afforded to politicians and others who substantially help usher change. In essence, without rewards, failure is assured.

These lessons for change have broad applications to all types of organizations and initiatives. Recognizing their value can have a substantial impact on hurdling political roadblocks and attaining the desired result.

SURVEYING THE PUBLIC

As best as it can be determined, the earliest attempts to survey public opinion regarding the police were made in the 1950s.[7] The basic premise of these early studies was the recognition that no matter how well a police department is organized, or how efficient and honest its administration, it is judged by individual citizens and, consequently, by the nature of its public contacts. The studies concluded that actual contacts with the police are the single most important determinant of the public image of the police.

The basic survey instrument in these studies was a multiple-choice questionnaire. Random sampling was done by contacting respondents in groups carefully chosen to contain a variety of ages, economic levels, occupations, political viewpoints, educational levels, and cultures. All the multiple-choice answers pertained to the attitudes and beliefs of the general public toward police officers, on the premise that what people *believed* was important, even when not supported by facts.

Survey research has continued to be an important source of information for law enforcement in order to learn more about the community's experiences with crime, and the behaviors, concerns, and opinions of police service. While survey research lacks some of the methodological rigor of experimental and quasi-experimental research designs, it nonetheless can be controlled for validity and reliability. More importantly, for many of the issues in which the police are interested, surveying the public is the only way to obtain the desired information—if you want to know what the citizens think and feel, you must ask them.

One of the problems with this type of research is that police agencies will attempt to conduct a survey without understanding the research methods. On the surface survey research looks easy; however, there are many complexities involved in order to ensure that the findings are *valid*, i.e., that you have measured what you want to measure, and *reliable*, i.e., that the findings represent what you portray them to represent, or that they are dependable. Issues of question construction, sampling, and analysis are critical for survey findings to be useful.

The most comprehensive survey research endeavor in criminal justice is the National Crime Victimization Survey (NCVS) of the U.S. Bureau of Justice Statistics. The NCVS surveys a sample of nearly 100,000 Americans to determine their victimization experiences, behavior related to the avoidance of victimization, and the extent to which they report crimes. Interestingly, the NCVS findings overall indicate that actual crime may be underreported by as much as 65 percent. The reasons for this underreporting include belief that because of the nature of the crime the police will not be able to do anything about it, the feeling that the citizen will be bothering the police, and the conviction that the police do not care about the crime. This latter reason is particularly related to the public image of the police.

The Police Executive Research Forum has also utilized a series of survey research projects to learn more about topical issues in policing. Among the topics these projects explored were police higher education, toy guns and crime, labor relations, the homeless, police drug use, law enforcement accreditation, violent crime, police weaponry, and violence in the schools.

Beginning in the late 1980s as community policing became more widespread, police departments explored new ways to ascertain community needs and desires. At the same time, the police sought some way to measure how the public perceived the new community-based policing initiatives. As a result, police departments began surveying their citizens.

Madison, Wisconsin; Fort Collins, Colorado; Fort Pierce, Florida; Lansing, Michigan; and Aurora, Colorado were among the first police departments to explore this approach. Rather than being fearful of receiving "bad ratings" from the citizens (which could be politically disastrous) the chiefs envisioned the surveys as a tool to help "fine-tune" police service and as a resource for making decisions on how to focus police initiatives.

Police "customer" survey methods have varied with differing degrees of scientific rigor, breadth, and intent. Some departments will scientifically sample the community while others mail surveys with utility bills to all citizens. Similarly, some departments will send surveys to all people who have contact with the police whether they have been the victim of a crime, involved in a traffic accident, or been given a ticket. Regardless of the method used, the intent is the same: gain information from the public—the customer who receives police service. (See the Madison, Wisconsin survey as shown in the accompanying box.)

Some of the findings from these projects have been surprising. The public wants to have increased contact with officers in informal circumstances, such as simply talking to an officer on a regular basis or seeing the officer participate in community activities. This infers that citizens want to personalize their relationship with the police. Moreover, citizens want officers to have an investment—a personal investment—in the community they police. Some have phrased it as wanting individual officers to feel they have "ownership" in the community as a means to stimulate activities to enhance the quality of life.

Perhaps most surprising have been the priorities for police service identified by citizens. Consistently, citizens report that among their highest priorities they want the police to handle such things as barking dogs, abandoned cars, trespassing juveniles, and similar calls that the police would categorize as "minor." When asked

CRIME IN THE NATION'S HOUSEHOLDS

The fear of being victimized pervades many Americans' lives; however, the fear of being victimized in one's own home is particularly disturbing. The National Crime Victimization Survey (NCVS) uses survey research methods to determine the extent of victimization, the types of crimes involved, and whether or not the victim reported the crime to the police.

In 1990, the most recent NCVS data available, found that 24 percent of U.S. households were victimized by a rape, robbery, assault, theft, burglary, or auto theft. This was a decline from the 25 percent of households that in 1989 experienced a crime as measured by the NCVS. Despite the pervasive appearance of crime in 1990, this percentage of household victimization was the lowest annual percentage since 1975.

Among some of the 1990 findings

- Five percent of U.S. households had at least one person age 12 or older who was the victim of a violent crime.
- Five percent of all households experienced at least one completed or attempted burglary, and 17 percent a completed or attempted theft.
- As in previous years, households with higher incomes (29 percent of households in the $50,000-or-more income category) were more likely to experience a crime than households with less income.
- Households in urban areas (30 percent) were more likely to experience a measured crime than suburban households (23 percent) or rural households (17 percent).
- Twenty-eight percent of both African-American households and households of other races—Asians, Pacific Islanders, and Native Americans—were victimized by crime, compared to 23 percent of white households.
- Among the regions, the West continued to have the highest proportion of households touched by crime (28 percent) while the Northeast had the lowest (20 percent).

While the NCVS does not reflect the nation's "official" crime statistics—the official statistics are in the FBI's Uniform Crime Report—they do provide an additional measure of crime which goes beyond the Uniform Crime Report. This is particularly important since the NCVS, as a result of its survey research techniques, includes crimes which have not been reported to the police. These data can be useful for policymaking as well as understanding the community's concerns about crime.

Bureau of Justice Statistics, *Crime and the Nation's Households, 1990* (Washington, DC: U.S. Department of Justice, Office of Justice Programs, 1990).

MADISON, WISCONSIN POLICE DEPARTMENT CUSTOMER SURVEY

The Madison Police Department would like to do a better job serving you and others. You have been selected to help us. Please take a few moments of your time to fill out this questionnaire. If you wish to make additional comments, feel free to do so on the back of this questionnaire.

DAVID C. COUPER
Chief of Police

1. Number of contacts you have had with the Madison Police Department in the last 12 months:

   — One

   — Two

   — Three or more

2. What was the nature of the contact(s)? (Check all that apply).

   — I called the department to report an incident

   — I was a victim of a crime

   — I was a witness to a crime or incident

   — I was involved in a motor vehicle accident

   — I requested information from the department

   — I was arrested

   — I received a traffic ticket

   — Other (Specify) _____

3. How would you rate us on each of the following: (Check the appropriate box for each item)

	Excellent	Good	Average	Fair	Poor
Concern					
Helpfulness					
Knowledge					
Quality of service					
Solving the problem					
Putting you at ease					
Professional conduct					

(continued)

4.   How can we improve? (Please write your comments)

5.   To help us analyze this survey, we need some information about you. As we noted before, all information is anonymous.

   a. Sex

   __ Male

   __ Female

   b. Race/ethnic identity

   __ White

   __ Black

   __ Hispanic

   __ Other

   c. Age group

   __ Under 17 years

   __ 18–20 years

   __ 21–24 years

   __ 25–39 years

   __ 40 and over

   d. Family income group:

   __ Under $5,000

   __ $5,001–$13,000

   __ $13,001–$20,000

   __ $20,001–$35,000

   __ $35,001 and over

   e. Do you live . . .

   __ In the city of Madison

   __ Other

COMMENTS:

**THANK YOU FOR TAKING THE TIME
TO FILL OUT THIS SURVEY.
PLEASE RETURN IT IN THE ENCLOSED ENVELOPE.**

about serious crime, citizens responded that they were also concerned with these, but were adamant about the need to deal with the "annoyance" calls. The reason was that annoyance calls represented things which affected the citizens on a daily or continual basis. While victimization of crime was clearly a concern, it was a relatively rare occurrence unlike the annoyance incidents. This reinforces the community concerns about quality-of-life issues and the desire for the police to address these factors, perhaps as aggressively as crime is addressed.

A CLOSER LOOK AT CITIZENS' ATTITUDES

Public opinion surveys stressed the importance of citizen contacts with the police in shaping attitudes. Unpublished research by the author found that students who had been through the Drug Abuse Resistance Education (DARE) program had overall a more positive attitude toward the police than those who had not. Similarly, DARE students felt more comfortable with talking to the police and contacting them.[8]

Another study examined relationships among age, sex, occupation, education, minority-group status, and the degree and kind of contact those citizens had with the police. The most positive composite image of the police was found in middle-aged, married white, female college graduates who had had no contact with the police and whose husbands were engaged in a nonexecutive capacity in a white-collar occupation. By contrast, the most negative composite image was held by a somewhat younger nonwhite male manual worker with a grade school education or less, who had had some, but not extensive, contact with the police.[9]

There is more of interest in this study. Women, for example, were twice as likely as men to view the police as primarily a service organization, rather than one primarily responsible for criminal or traffic law enforcement. Women who had had some contact with the police tended to describe the police officer's demeanor as impersonal; men with experience in such contacts tended to see the officer as friendly. Somewhat surprisingly, this study found little significant effect of either education or occupation upon attitudes toward the police. A bit puzzling was the finding that persons with no contact with the police had the most favorable attitude (what is the source of their image?); persons with limited personal contact were next most favorable; those with considerable negative contact appeared to be more favorably inclined than those with only limited negative contact. Conjecturing the possible reasons for these responses makes a stimulating discussion.

Citizens' ratings of the honesty and ethical standards of police officers have traditionally been high, generally increasing from 1977 through 1990. However, notable drops in these ratings began in 1991 and 1994. White, college-educated Republicans earning over $30,000 per year rated the police highest on ethical and honesty standards. However, when stratified by race, education, politics, or lower income, these ratings of the police dropped.[10]

In some ways, these changes reflect a paradox. Despite the increasing educational levels of police officers, the movement toward community policing, increased responsiveness to citizen concerns by police executives, and the movement toward managing by values, respect for local police has declined somewhat. Similarly, over the past two decades, the police have been more open with respect to personnel problems, have urged the public to report police malfeasance, and have established a wide range of programs designed to manage problem employees. Yet, during this same time there has been a significant increase in the public belief that police use excessive force too frequently.[11]

Several likely reasons exist for these increasingly unfavorable ratings:

- There have been several high-profile incidents of police abuse of authority in cities such as Los Angeles, Detroit, Miami, and Houston.
- There is increasing public frustration with drugs and crime, which is frequently (and perhaps unjustly) directed toward the police.
- There is a general cynicism by citizens toward government in general and its ability to solve problems.

These problems present important challenges for law enforcement—operationally, administratively, and in community relations. Programming must be established to deal with legitimate concerns but also to correct erroneous perceptions. It is a human tendency to stereotype. Thus, when images of excessive force flash across the nation's television screens, people tend to generalize the behavior to all officers. While this may seem unfair, it is a real problem, which must be comprehensively addressed.

In a recent national study by the John Jay College of Criminal Justice, citizens were asked how they rated their local police on treating people fairly. Sixty-eight percent of the white respondents and 54 percent of the Hispanic respondents rated the police as either pretty good or excellent. However, only 38 percent of the black respondents rated the police as pretty good or excellent while 26 percent rated them poor. While over half of all the people surveyed rated their local police as excellent or pretty good on *not* using excessive force, the ratings of black respondents were again noticeably lower than whites and Hispanics.

There was one factor that all three groups generally agreed on—adjudication of officers charged with complaints. Consistently, regardless of race, ethnicity, age, income, or population, respondents clearly felt that an adjudication body made up of both civilians and police officers should be used. Significantly fewer felt that an all-civilian review board should be used and among all demographic classifications of citizens, seven percent or less of the respondents felt that a review board should consist only of police officers. These findings infer that the public feels the police are generally fair to citizens, but do not want them "judging their own" when allegations of misconduct arise.[12] There are two reasonable explanations for this. First, some distrust still remains with the public about law enforcement being able to police itself. Second, the public feels that the community should have input into the control of the policing function—essentially, maintaining police accountability to the community.

HOW MINORITIES VIEW THE POLICE AND VICE VERSA

In general, the studies show, not surprisingly, that blacks and other minorities perceive the police more negatively than do whites. Blacks were markedly more negative than whites in evaluating police effectiveness in law enforcement. On questions pertaining to police discourtesy and misconduct, the disparity between the attitudes of blacks and whites was even greater. About two-thirds of whites, but only one-third of blacks, thought the police were "almost all honest."[13]

While the surveys indicate that blacks are substantially more hostile to police than whites, blacks also strongly feel the need for police protection. The Michigan State University study for the President's Crime Commission revealed that the primary complaint of blacks against the police was of permissive law enforcement and inadequate protection and services in areas where blacks reside. This has been confirmed in studies by the United States Civil Rights Commission and others. The Michigan State study also found that Hispanics tend to "look upon the police as enemies who protect only the white power structure." The University of California survey in Philadelphia discovered that some Hispanic leaders felt even more alienated from the police than did blacks.[14] Various studies have shown that young people are generally more negative than older persons in their attitudes toward the police. Similarly, the poor have generally less favorable attitudes toward the police than the affluent.

It is interesting that a study conducted by Wayne State University's Center for Black Studies showed that affirmative action in hiring and promotions in the Detroit Police Department has improved citizen perceptions of the department: 81.8 percent of whites and 77.1 percent of blacks expressed satisfaction with police; 82.4 percent of those surveyed said they did not think police use of excessive force was a problem today, but 59.2 percent thought it had been in the past. An increase in the number of black officers was thought to be the main reason for this change in public perception.

James Q. Wilson makes the point that "the single, most striking fact about the attitudes of citizens, black and white, toward the police is that in general these attitudes are positive, not negative."[15] Yet he qualifies this apparent contradiction by adding: "But if a majority of blacks are not critical of police conduct, a significant minority are, and this minority is composed chiefly of the young."[16] All studies reveal that the most frequent complaint of blacks toward the police is inadequate protection and service in predominantly black neighborhoods.

There has been limited research on Hispanics and the police, but there are similarities with blacks with respect to their attitudes. Police attitudes toward Hispanic citizens appear to vary geographically throughout the United States. For example, in the southwestern U.S., where there is the largest proportion of Hispanic residents, officers tend to view them more suspiciously. There is a greater likelihood for officers to assume that an Hispanic is an undocumented alien, notably if the person is perceived to be of a lower socioeconomic class. Officers also tend to equate a strong Spanish accent with a lack of intelligence, a higher probability of being an undocumented alien, and/or the probability of being "criminal."[17] Stereotypical behavior such as this will obviously cause conflict and contribute to a poorer image of the police.

In looking at Hispanic citizens' attitudes, the research indicates that the image of the police *decreases* as fear of crime increases, frequency of contact with the police increases, and victimization increases.[18] The inference here is that police interaction with the Hispanic public needs to be examined more closely. Part of the problem appears to be that most officers neither speak Spanish nor understand the Hispanic culture. Further research findings suggest that Hispanic citizens feel they are routinely discriminated against by not only the police but also the entire criminal justice system. This feeling of discrimination was based upon the belief that the police would "do little or nothing" to deal with victimization or to help them resolve conflicts. In fact, a notable number of Hispanic crime victims said they did not report crimes to the police because:

- They felt the police would do little or nothing
- Their previous experience with the police was bad
- They did not want to "bother" the police, or
- They were afraid of the police[19]

These findings are aggravated by the fact that people who evaluated the police the lowest tended to be those who had the most frequent contact with their local law enforcement agency. Certainly, this bodes poorly for the public image of the police. There are important lessons to be taken from these results, which have implications for training in cultural understanding and relations, the phenomenon of stereotyping, and the need to increase the quality of communications, both lingual and attitudinal.

Hostility generates hostility. Typically, the animosity loses sight of original issues and focuses on who started it all, chicken-and-egg fashion. Hostile attitudes toward the police are likely to be reciprocated in hostile police attitudes toward those who "bug" them. William Westley concluded that it was a universal complaint of police officers that the public would not help them and in fact often hindered them in their duties.[20] Albert Reiss looked into several aspects of this and found that there are frequent instances in which a citizen is victimized by crime and yet does not report it to the police. The reason most often given is that the victim believes it is useless or futile to do so. This may be because victims think the police regard the experience as so minor that they do not want to be bothered. Past experience may support the victim's beliefs. For example, the police in big cities occasionally respond to breaking and entering complaints in slum areas by suggesting that the citizen buy a dog or a gun, or move.

Another reason given for failure to report crimes was that the citizen felt it too troublesome to do so. But the Reiss study produced little evidence that citizens' failure to report crime was due to a belief that the police were against them. And only one percent of those interviewed said they had failed to report an incident they had witnessed that looked as though it might be a crime.

> Quite clearly, citizens do not always feel the obligation to call the police to report a crime. . . . there does seem to be reason to believe that citizens do not call the police unless they regard a matter as something where they were seriously wronged or they are personally affronted, or where they have something personally to gain from it, such as gain from an insurance claim. But any gain has to be worth the effort of calling the police and "getting involved." Apart from such motivations to call the police, citizens are inclined to disengage themselves from any responsibility to call the police.[21]

In commenting about police views of citizens, Wilson cites studies indicating that the chief complaint of officers is the lack of public support for their efforts.[22] But Wilson thinks this may be a tilted perception because big-city officers do not have much contact with "average" citizens. They are more apt, by the nature of their job, to be "involved with the poor, the black, and the young." He adds:

> Blackness conceals, for some police officers, the important differences in social class and respectability among blacks. Because the urban class is today disproportionately black . . . a dark skin is to the police a statistically significant cue to social status, and thus to potential criminality.[23]

Additional complications in this mutual hostility syndrome may be illustrated by two factors. One is that the police are sometimes viewed as behaving too impersonally. In a demonstration situation, for example, the taunts of the demonstrators may not produce any perceptible police reaction. This can become irritating to the demonstrators, and in itself may provoke inflammatory behavior, because the police fail to act as they are expected to act; therefore, they are "inhuman," not because they overreact, but because they underreact.

The other factor pertains to police concern for uniform application of the law. Police officers wonder how they can function on the basis of the principle of equal justice if there are different standards of community conduct, and therefore of expected police behavior, in each community or neighborhood. The conflict here is more apparent than real for those who understand the distinction between equality and equity, as most police officers are well aware.

We have seen that the occupational socialization of police recruits includes both the adoption of standard modes of police behavior and the gradual shedding of behaviors that are inappropriate for the police role. The most important aspect of this socialization is the identification of role-relevant reference groups and the development of a sensitivity to their expectations and evaluations. This process is precisely the connection between police behavior and police public image. However, the role-relevant groups that the police recruit are seldom as diverse as the community he or she will serve, although this is clearly changing.[24]

POLICE AND POLICED AS ADVERSARIES

Whatever the proportion of time may be that police officers spend in law enforcement functions, this part of their role is clearly coercive. They are, in this sense, important agents in a social control apparatus that revolves around the use of force, when necessary to carry out its mandate. The effect is to curb, or to deprive people of their liberty. To citizens at large, the meaning of police and criminal justice processes resides in "no-no" symbolism: this you must not do, this you must do—or else.

To this extent, and with particular reference to the law enforcement side of policing, the relationship between police and policed may be said to be adversarial in nature. It involves inherent conflict. "The police [officer] in the routine case is often (though not always) dealing with his clientele as an antagonist, in that he issues summons[es], makes arrests, conducts inquiries, searches homes, stops cars, testifies in court, and keeps a jail."[25]

This may be the most telling observation that can be made regarding the public image of the police. A common expression of it, by police officers, is that they are not in business to win a popularity contest.

> It is unlikely that any single instance of police action has ever been completely satisfactory to everyone concerned; for no matter how efficient or brilliant the example of police work may be, it is not likely to be viewed with enthusiasm by the thwarted or apprehended offender or his family or friends.[26]

So it is that the best kind of programming to improve police-community relations cannot be expected to alter the adversarial element in the relationship. Yet it should be remembered that, in all their functions, the police carry out a responsibility assigned to them by the community they serve. Protecting people against themselves is part of the job. The main purpose of police-community programs is *not* to enable the police to win popularity contests.

Some analysts have gone on to say that the inherent conflict between police and policed is further aggravated by various other considerations. Discussions of this point have tended to fall into categories according to the particular academic or operational vantage point of the observer: sociology, psychology, politics, philosophy, anthropology, psychiatry—or civil rights, legalistic, judicial, and so on. Michael Banton's view on the subject, which is influenced by his English environment, is somewhat unique. Banton does not deny that, in dealing with certain types of criminals, or in a tough, urban neighborhood, "there may be justification for the view of police and public as adversaries." But in general, Banton rejects the adversary conception in three related arguments:

1. The police officer spends very little time "chasing people or locking people up." He or she spends most of his time helping citizens in distress.
2. It is misleading to describe a police officer's job as law enforcement. An officer's activities "are governed much more by popular morality than they are by the letter of the law."
3. Even criminals recognize the moral authority, as opposed to the power, of the police. When people grumble at the police, they are really "trying to make their violations seem excusable to still their own consciences."[27]

Banton goes on to make a key point in comparing British with American policing: that in the "comparatively more highly integrated society that Britain is, there is greater consensus about the right way to respond to given situations," (or greater predictability in police behavior, Banton says in another place). Then he adds, speaking as a social anthropologist:

> The moral authority of the police officer depends upon the level of social integration and moral unity of the community, and one cannot compare the work of British and American police without recognizing these differences in the context in which they have to operate.[28]

Quite clearly, the social and cultural environment strongly influences the degree to which citizens view the police as adversaries.

The American social historian Oscar Handlin recalls that the organized police force is a relatively recent historical phenomenon in England and the United States. He reminds us that there were opponents of this idea who thought that freedom and democracy would be jeopardized by a paid professional police force. Handlin believes that current American public attitudes toward the police are partly rooted in residuals of the historic past in Europe and America, when police were seen as agents of tyranny and oppression, as functionaries for "keeping people down" under the aegis of czars and emperors.[29]

A PSYCHIATRIC VIEW OF THE ADVERSARIAL RELATIONSHIP

Several psychiatrists have shown keen interest in police and community discord in recent years.[30] More than three decades ago, psychiatrist Chester M. Pierce addressed a Police-Community Relations Institute in Cincinnati and presented his diagnosis of police-citizen conflict. Pierce reported that psychiatrists and psychotherapists often deal clinically with police officers. He surmised that police officers are frequently perplexed about their public image. They would like to be thought of as benevolent, sacrificing, and strong protectors, but fear that they are seen, in extreme cases, as "weak, greedy flatfoots." From this observation, Pierce drew two inferences:

1. In police-citizen interaction, there is a "lock-key" arrangement. On the one hand, the police officer finds people whose personal problems facilitate the solution, although unsatisfactorily, of the officer's own problems. On the other hand, citizens invite their own catastrophes with police officers by using the officer to solve their problems, also in an unsatisfactory manner.

2. Police-community conflict reflects an ongoing modification related to the emancipation of women in our society. With the concomitant diminution in the importance of the father in the family prestige system, public attitudes toward police authority have changed, since the police officer is a father equivalent.[31]

Pierce's meaning may be clearer in the following passage:

> The police [officer] . . . must be conservative and sober in aims and objectives. Thus, he is timebound, and functions in an organized setting which is authority-centered and militaristic.[32]

In a sense, the police officer has the unpopular job of thwarting change. Law is, by definition, "an enlightened revision of custom," he says, and therefore demands a conservative, sober, objective approach to impartially protecting all spheres of the society. This means that a common public perception of the practical work of the police officer is that of conservative guardian of the status quo. Pierce continues:

> The citizens of a community are individually centered and supportive of independent assertion. Their approach to problems, in contrast to the police, would tend to be more individually subjective, more impressionistic, more impulse-ridden.[33]

Pierce believes that, to the police officer, the greatest strain in police-citizen relations is the failure of someone to observe the status quo. To the citizen, the greatest strain is failure of the officer "to exert kindly enough treatment of an individual."[34] Ironically, the research on this issue over the past three decades reinforces Pierce's observations.

OTHER VIEWS OF THE ADVERSARIAL RELATIONSHIP

From what we have said, it is evident that there has been no scarcity of police studies suggesting sociological, psychological, and political explanations for the adversarial relationship between police and community. All agree that the law enforcement part of the police task is adversarial. Then each theorist extends the point by saying, in effect: "Yes, and to make matters worse . . ."—proceeding to such reasons as role conflict, organizational/environmental factors, etc. Numerous psychologists have probed such questions as these:

- To what degree is police-citizen antagonism a matter of conflicting *perceptions*, for example, of the police role in today's society?
- In the sense of pre-police background, specifically in terms of attitudes, beliefs and values, what type of individual (personality) finds policing an attractive career?
- What happens to the "police personality" as a result of occupational socialization, in terms of attitudes, beliefs, and values?
- Are there significant personality differences, in the same terms, between police officers and members of other occupations?
- To what extent is the behavior of police officers the result of society's impossible expectations of them? What are the implications of this for the police self-image?
- Where do the police stand in the violence phenomenon?

In simple terms, rule enforcers are always at a disadvantage in creating their public image. The people in the striped shirts in football, hockey, and basketball, and the umpires in baseball are perennially the targets of scorn, hostility, and emotions run amuck, more often than not because they are interpreting and enforcing established rules in a manner that separates winners and losers. The nature of the job, in addition to the obvious fact that nobody wins all the time, is clearly adversarial. So the officials are accustomed to catcalls, screams of rage, accusations as to their ancestry or relatives, and sometimes worse treatment by paying customers. For the most part, they are professionals who stoically withstand such vituperative fan behavior.

In the case of the police, however, the matter is more serious because the majesty of the law, which they represent, is not merely a game. In a way, the police are their own clients, and this helps to explain their supermoralistic tendencies, as if they were engaged in a private war against crime. Even prosecutors and the courts are dubious allies, as viewed by the police, since both often reject decisions made by the police.[35]

Perhaps this helps to explain the tendency of the police to take almost personal offense at what they see as the failure of the public to assume appropriate responsibility in coping with crime. Many officers feel that their main problem is the indifference and apathy of the public toward problems that the police feel are of major importance. There is, of course, some basis for this feeling, but public apathy is not confined to matters of interest to the police. Apathy, moreover, is an effect rather than a cause. What causes apathy and what can be done about it—this is the question.

Another point to be kept in mind is that, these days, more and more people are direct victims of crimes against property and person. There is widespread concern for the victims of crime, resulting in crime victim compensation programs in many states. So it is that the attitudes of crime victims toward the police and criminal justice are an important barometer in assessing the public image of the system.

POLICE PERFORMANCE AND IMAGE

Repeating a point made at the beginning of this chapter, customer reactions to the police "product" are difficult to measure because this product is community service. Measuring police productivity involves both individual officer performance and police agency effectiveness, on a wide range of factors, many of which are difficult to measure.

Because the department's legally defined task is to enforce the law, the typical annual report of a police department contains statistical information on crime rates, arrests, crimes cleared by arrests, convictions, value of stolen property recovered, and the like. But the police themselves largely determine the criteria by which their success is measured. There are difficulties in interpreting the data to the public so as to make an acceptable case for success.

In a market-oriented society, police administrators must try to maintain public confidence in department productivity. Sometimes this leads to an overload in the reporting of statistics. The problem is further complicated because the police do not control the outcomes of cases they initiate in the enforcement process. Prosecutors and courts make the eventual determinations. The police officer's sense of justice is vindicated only through convictions, but he or she has little control over this. As Reiss and Bordua say, "While department arrest figures may define the police [officer's] success, acquittals in court may define failures." They continue:

> These dilemmas in defining success are partially resolved by the development of a complex bargaining process between police and prosecutors, the shifting of departmental resources in directions of maximum payoff from a conviction point of view, the development of a set of attitudes that define the police as alone in the "war on crime," and the elaboration of success measures that do not require validation by the courts.[36]

Public impressions of "the crime problem" are generally molded by police data and media reports. Although questions of staffing and budget often prevail, there is a risk that the police may be considered failures if the volume of crime is too high. Because police success is measured by arrests and convictions, and police law enforcement is separated from outcome, an element of friction between the police and the judicial system (*antagonistic cooperation*, it has been called) is inherent in the situation. The police want not only conviction, they want the guilty to be punished. They interpret this as vindication of their sense of justice, as appreciation for their efforts, and as upholding morality.[37]

It should also be kept in mind that activities which occupy uniformed patrol officers most of the time are not easily quantified. Time spent in visits with residents of a neighborhood, sometimes just talking and listening, is difficult to computerize, and it looks pretty vapid in an annual report. City councils, the media, and the public want evidence of something more exciting, often to fuel stereotypic notions of police work nurtured by banal television fare. So it is that the public image of the police, what they do and how well they do it, is largely myth. Further, the police tend to encourage this myth because it appeals to their own predominating perception of the main task and because they feel it politically expedient to avoid disturbing the public fantasies. It is not easy, for example, to explain publicly that effective police-community teamwork may, in at least the short run, cause the rates for certain crimes to go up rather than down, with more arrests, and so on.

In short, the contradictions in police work as well as the manner in which the police have attempted to adapt to, if not to exploit, these contradictions create a situation in which the public image of the police is a research nightmare. Accordingly, the numerous studies undertaken in recent years, aimed at "finding handles" in questions of police productivity, have been as slippery as a bar of wet soap. Yet it is widely agreed that such research is imperative, as the Police Foundation has emphasized, given "the critical dilemma created by the combination of the rapid increase in the volume of crime, the increasing demand for public services, and the limitation of the tax dollar."[38]

Performance measures most frequently used by police tend to be internally rather than externally generated. Supervisors, rather than peers, self, or clients, set performance standards. Therefore, these measures tend to conform to bureaucratic standards only indirectly related to the actual objectives of police work. The tendency is to measure how much or how many rather than how well. This kind of evaluation dwells on general qualities rather than on behavior in specific situations, and it is more concerned with law enforcement than with community service or conflict management. Furthermore, evaluation is used more to punish failure than to reward success.[39]

Police administrators have taken some steps to improve the quality of performance, in the face of heightened public and political pressures. Improvements in police technology are an illustration, along with such ventures as the 911 emergency system, increasing the workload of officers—often necessitated by budgetary cutbacks for personnel—and moves in consolidating police service, for example, sharing, pooling, and contracting. And while limited, there has been some increase in the number of consolidated (or regional) police agencies. Other developments include the increased use of civilian employees (rather than sworn officers) for support service functions in police agencies, the use of technology to expedite responsibilities related to crime reporting, and a gradually emerging recognition that citizens can be of great help to the police in crime control activities. Yet all these and similar moves to improve police effectiveness, worthwhile though they surely are, still fail to come to grips with fundamental issues and contradictions.

POLICE MISCONDUCT AND CORRUPTION

Another subtopic suggested by the general caption of the police public image is, of course, police misconduct and corruption. Quite aside from whatever the facts may be in a given department as to the actuality of unprofessional behavior, public impressions of the nature and extent of such behavior are important, politically and administratively. Such impressions, even though not supported in fact, can be a telling indication of community trust and confidence in the department. If in a question asked in a public poll, a large number of respondents express the belief that there is considerable corruption in the police department, it should certainly attract the attention of the chief—even if the chief is sure that there is no substance to the view.

An Overview of Police Misconduct

Police misconduct occurs when an officer violates a law or regulation of the police department. As illustrated in Figure 9-1, there are variations in the seriousness of these violations and, consequently, a range of penalties which may be imposed. A minor rule violation, such as not taking a police report when asked by a citizen, may result in the officer's suspension for a few days without pay. A more serious violation, such as falsifying reports or testimony may result in the officer being fired.

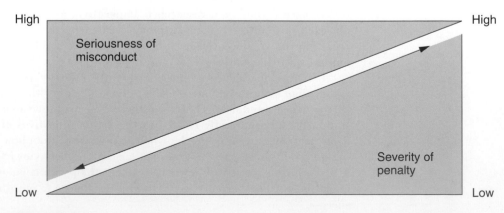

Figure 9-1

Overt criminal violations, such as corruption, may also include criminal prosecution of the officer. In these more serious cases of misconduct there is commonly a news report detailing the incident. Needless to say, these will help shape the public's image of the police—not in a favorable light.

Beyond the fact that some misconduct has occurred, the *type* of misbehavior has different implications for the development of image. For example, in some cases of excessive force the public response is that "the criminal had it coming"—there is typically little sympathy for the law violator. Even in the infamous LAPD-Rodney King case, there were a substantial number of citizens who acknowledged that officers "probably" used excessive force, but still felt that Mr. King "asked for it." Consequently these people had little condemnation for the police. Conversely, when officer misconduct involves a violation of the public trust or immorality, such as corruption or a sexual assault, public condemnation is much harsher. In these cases the police image suffers the most.

There are a wide range of behaviors which fall into the broad classification of "misconduct." Just to give a perspective on the variability of behaviors that constitute misconduct, some illustrations include:

- Accessing police records for personal use
- Abuse of sick leave
- Lying to supervisors and managers
- Perjury on reports and in court
- Commission of a crime
- Falsifying overtime records
- Excessive use of force
- Use of offensive language to citizens
- On-duty drinking
- Off-duty firearms incidents
- Failing to complete police reports
- Accepting gratuities
- Providing recommendations for an attorney, towing service, or bail bond service in exchange for personal rewards
- Failure to report misconduct of a fellow officer
- Failure to inventory recovered property or evidence
- Sleeping on duty
- Cheating on a promotional examination
- Sexual harassment or improprieties

Needless to say, the list could continue. It is important to recognize both the breadth of behaviors which are embodied under the label of "misconduct" as well as the obvious degree of seriousness. Some of the behaviors clearly have a greater impact on the public image than others. Beyond excessive force, discussed elsewhere in this text, two types of misconduct have become increasingly apparent in recent years, reflecting contemporary social dynamics. Both of these also have a significant effect on the public image and trust of the police: corruption and officer drug use.

Corruption

In the last decade, a number of incidents of police corruption received widespread publicity. Most of these cases involved drug-related corruption and large amounts of money. In one of the most notorious cases, known as the "Miami River Cops" case,

COMPLAINTS AGAINST THE POLICE

Because complaints against police officers in England and Wales are overseen by the centralized Police Complaints Authority (PCA) in London, the British are able to have comprehensive national records on allegations of police misbehavior. Cultural differences between the United States and Britain will likely have an effect on the frequency of different complaints; particularly with regard to the excessive use of force. Despite this, the nature of complaints appear to be similar overall. According to the PCA, the seven most frequent complaints against officers, in order of frequency, are

- Incivility
- Assault/excessive force
- Procedural irregularity
- Neglect of duty
- Irregularity of evidence
- Oppressive conduct
- Irregular stop and/or search

Interviews by the author at the British Police Complaints Authority.

---

a handful of officers were involved in a multimillion dollar drug operation. After this case was discovered, the chief of police requested the U.S. Department of Justice to conduct a research project exploring how corruption could be controlled in police departments. Based on this study, conducted by the International Association of Chiefs of Police (IACP), a number of important areas were identified as focal points for the control of corruption.[40] While drug corruption was the stimulus for the study, the findings apply to virtually all forms of corruption. The following is a summary of some of the IACP conclusions:

The Chief Executive Sets the Standard.   The police chief must establish a clear tone for the department that corruption will not be tolerated in any form. Corruption must be defined for the officers so there is no question about those acts which are prohibited. It must also be clear that officers are expected to act in a lawful and ethical manner, including the identification of officers involved in misfeasance. Furthermore, the chief executive must be firm in the commitment that disciplinary action and criminal prosecution will be swiftly and surely taken against offending officers.

Management and Supervision.   Managers and supervisors have the responsibility to reinforce the chief's tone of integrity, commend officers for ethical behavior, and lead by example. Supervisors and managers must also monitor officers, particularly those in assignments that are of a higher risk for corruption, to ensure their behavior is lawful. When any suspicion arises about a subordinate's behavior, the manager or supervisor must take immediate action to resolve the questions.

Supervisory Training. Supervisors need to receive training in such areas as recognizing the signs of corruption, employee assessment, and inculcating values in subordinates. Too often supervisors are given these responsibilities but are not told how to fulfill them. In-service training must also include "updates" on police policy, liability law, and related factors that change in the policing environment.

The Formal Internal Audit Process. The department should establish a system which monitors officer behavior to ensure all police personnel are following procedures related to stops, detention, arrests, storing evidence and recovered property, conducting computer checks, and any other aspect of police procedure that is subject to abuse. Irregularities should be more closely examined, particularly where patterns of irregularity exist.

Internal Auditing and Informants. Two corruption-related problems arise with informants: The improper use of departmental money to pay informants and the use of informants to perform improper acts on behalf of the officer. To avoid these problems, careful controls must be in place to audit both money and interaction between officers and informants. Any "secret" or "confidential" funds for informants and undercover operations must have rigid controls for accountability.

Internal Affairs. The Internal Affairs function within a police agency is designed to investigate allegations of wrongdoing by police officers. Internal Affairs investigators must be familiar with the different types of corruption that occur, know how to investigate corruption cases, and maintain vigilance in their investigations. Too frequently, these cases are difficult to investigate because of the unwillingness of people to testify.

Drug Enforcement Units. Because of the vast amounts of money involved in unlawful drug transactions, officers working in Drug Enforcement Units are particularly susceptible to corruption. Supervision, audit controls, and a policy of regular personnel turnover in these units will help reduce the potential for corruption.

Evidence Handling and Storage. While most police departments have procedures for marking and storing evidence to maintain the chain of custody for evidence in court, these procedures typically do not provide a comprehensive control of evidence. Procedures must be established to comprehensively control property beginning with the *time it is seized*, not when it arrives at the police station. Supervisors should also monitor officer conduct when property is seized. Care should also be taken to periodically monitor property in storage to ensure it has not been tampered with.

An Early Warning System. Based on the research related to officer corruption, we have learned that there are certain behaviors that are indicative of improper officer behavior. Purchases that appear to be beyond the officer's financial means, changes in the officer's social behavior, and allegations from informants that an officer might be "on the take" are illustrations of these indicators. Utilizing these types of information, the department may develop an "Early Warning System" that monitors the indicators—particularly for officers in highly susceptible assignments. In this way, corruption can be dealt with before it becomes extensive. Moreover, such a system will hopefully have a preventive element.

Training.   Officer training on matters related to corruption, integrity, and ethical responsibilities should be provided on a periodic basis to keep awareness of the problem omnipresent. For officers working in undercover assignments, training should be provided that explicitly addresses the threats of corruption in the assignment, the avoidance of corruption, and actions to take when corruptive advances are made toward the officer.

Discipline.   When officers are found to have been involved in corruption, discipline should be swift, sure, and substantial. This reinforces the chief's commitment to having a "clean" department and shows that there will be no toleration for corrupt behavior.

Corruption, perhaps more than any form of misconduct, undermines the public confidence in the police. It represents a complete violation of the public trust and an absolute abuse of the authority the public has vested in police officers. When corruption flourishes in a department, the integrity of the entire police department is drawn into question. As a result, stringent controls, such as those summarized above, play an important role in maintaining the viability of the police image.

The Special Case of Drug Corruption[41]

As noted previously, drug-related corruption of police officers has been particularly problematic. While overall incidents of corruption appear to have declined, the cases of drug-related corruption have notably increased. The reasons are complex and offer challenges for the police and community together in order to minimize their impact. To better understand the breadth of the problem, the author has developed the following typology.

Type I Drug Corruption: In Search of Illegitimate Goals.   The type 1 goals are defined as "illegitimate" in that an officer is seeking to use his or her position as a police officer simply for personal gain. Examples of this type of corruption would include:

- Giving information to drug dealers about investigations, undercover officers, names of informants, planned raids, and so forth in exchange for a monetary payment.
- Accepting bribes from drug dealers in exchange for actions such as nonarrest, evidence tampering, perjury, or contamination of evidence.
- Theft of drugs by an officer from the police property room or laboratory for personal consumption or sale of the drug.
- The "seizure" of drugs without arresting the person possessing the drugs with the officer's intent of converting the drugs to personal use.
- Taking the profits of drug dealers' sales and/or their drugs for resale.
- Extorting drug traffickers for money or property in exchange for nonarrest or nonseizure of drugs.

Research by the author indicates that there are two distinct behavioral cycles—not necessarily mutually exclusive—motivating type 1 corrupt acts. These motivations are classified as "cycles" because of a distinct recurring and reinforcing process. For example, after an officer's initial corrupt act he/she would fear being detected. After the fear decreased and another opportunity occurred, the officer would perform another improper act. Again, a period of fear of apprehension, albeit shorter, followed by another incident. The failure of being detected apparently reinforces the officer's feeling of invulnerability from detection. As times increases, the frequency of misconduct would cyclically increase until an undefined saturation point is reached and the officer feels that no further risks could be taken.

User-driven cycle—In these cases an officer starts as a "recreational" user of drugs, typically buying the substances for personal consumption from a dealer. The officer's behavior evolves to a point when he or she decides that instead of buying the drugs they can be "confiscated" from users/dealers or taken from the police property room. This decision appears to be the product of several interacting factors. One is the increasing cost of drug use. A second factor is opportunity: the officer concludes that it is cheaper to convert seized drugs for personal use rather than to buy them. Finally, officers begin to worry that their occupational identity may be discovered by drug dealers (if not already known), leading to blackmail.

Profit-driven cycle—Officers involved in this form of corruption include both users and nonusers of drugs. The intent in this form of corruption is purely monetary. The primary motivation for becoming corrupt is the vast amount of unaccountable and untraceable money involved in the illicit drug trade, coupled with the opportunity, by virtue of police authority, to seize these monies. This is further compounded by the fact that the source of the money is illegal activity. During the course of research on the topic, officers involved in corruption tended to make comments along the line that "it's not fair" or "it's not right" that drug traffickers had far more money than the officers who were "working for a living."

For perspective on the amounts of money involved, consider the comment of one former undercover narcotics investigator now assigned to a task force to investigate drug corruption: "When you're looking at ongoing [drug] deals of even medium to small quantities, $100,000 is a small score for a bribe in drug trafficking today." In another case, ten officers from one police department made two robberies of cocaine from drug traffickers. In just these two robberies, the officers made over $16 million among them. The amounts of money are staggering—and tempting.

Type 2 Drug Corruption: In Search of Legitimate Goals. Strikingly different is the second form of corruption—a search for legitimate goals. Since corruption is the abuse of one's position for personal gain, it may be argued that, in the case of drug corruption, "gain" is not only money, tangible goods, and services but may also be an organizational benefit—perhaps a form of "winning" or "revenge." Examples of type 2 corrupt behavior include:

- False statements to obtain arrest or search warrants against "known" drug dealers/traffickers
- Perjury during hearings and trials of drug dealers
- "Planting" or creating evidence against "known" drug dealers
- Overt and intentional entrapment
- Falsely spreading rumors that a dealer is a police informant, thus placing that person's safety in jeopardy

The characterization of "legitimate goals" is made from the perspective of the officer. There are persons who officers "know" are involved in drug trafficking. However, the police are consistently unable to obtain sufficient evidence for arrest. Similarly, there are "known" criminals who have been found not guilty in court because the government has not been able to prove its case—often because evidence has been excluded on "technicalities." The officers see these recurring circumstances and become frustrated because the trafficker is "beating the system." This is compounded by the tendency to perceive legal strategies during hearings and trials as "unfair manipulation of the law" by attorneys.

The type 2 corrupt officer's self-determined goal is to prosecute and incarcerate the drug traffickers. However, type 2 corruption occurs when the attempt to accomplish this *legitimate goal* is through *illegitimate means*. When the goal (conviction) is achieved the officer receives the satisfaction that he or she "won." This form of revenge is psychologically rewarding and, obviously, improper.

It is argued that in the case of type 2 corruption, the acts are not only for the personal psychological gain of the officer but also in support of organizational goals through which the officer may be rewarded by commendations, promotions, and/or recognition. It may also be argued that this form of corruption is for organizational gain via the arrest and prosecution of known, serious, and often dangerous drug traffickers.

Type 2 corruption is further compounded because this behavior is not traditionally perceived as being corrupt. There is a degree of informal organizational tolerance for behavior that gets "known" traffickers off the street or seizes the traffickers' cache of drugs. This tolerance complicates the determination of wrongdoing and undermines the commitment toward integrity that was discussed in the previous section.

An officer's exposure to drug-related situations as well as the opportunity for either type of corruption will be largely dependent on the officer's assignment. While the opportunity for corruption may be found in many assignments, clearly patrol officers and drug investigators have the greatest exposure to corruption-related situations.

Illicit Drug Use by Police Officers

Just as drug-related corruption has surfaced, the problem of employee drug use has emerged in law enforcement (just as it has in virtually every other occupation.) Although instances of alcohol abuse have been well documented as they relate to police officers, scrutiny of drug effects other than alcohol, have been less prevalent. The obvious distinction between alcohol and illicit substances is the unlawful nature of the latter. Not only must concern be directed toward the behavioral effects associated with drug use, but also the abrogation of duty and trust by the officer who has violated the law through drug possession. Furthermore, concern must be given to the threat posed by the association with drug dealers. This alone can place an officer in a compromising position.

Recreational Drug Use. The most frequent issue related to officer drug abuse is "recreational" use. Recreational use of drugs is a somewhat broad characterization. Admittedly, it is a term that may not be completely inclusive of all drug use, particularly in cases of addiction. For the present discussion, recreational use is defined as drug use that does not involve corruption and that was initially a product of the desire to experience the expected exhilaration, psychoactive effects, physiological effects, and/or mood changes associated with drug consumption. Under this definition, drug use may include both on-duty and off-duty use of illicit narcotic and non-narcotic controlled substances as long as corruption is not involved.

On-duty drug use—The extent of on-duty drug use by officers is simply not known. An intuitive assumption is that some on-duty use occurs; however, it appears to be relatively rare. When it does occur, the potential ramifications are widespread. The most serious implication is that an officer may use deadly force or be involved in a traffic accident while under the influence. Other effects of on-duty use include poor judgment in the performance of the officer's duties, an increase in behavior related to liability risks, participation in other forms of misconduct, and having a negative influence on co-workers and the community with whom the officer has contact.

In one case the author discovered during the course of research on the topic, a patrol officer in a major midwestern city was found using cocaine while on duty.[42] During the internal affairs investigation the officer admitted he had regularly used cocaine on duty for over one year. The officer said he felt co-workers would be able to tell from his behavior when he was "high," so each time after he "snorted" cocaine he would "chase it" with whiskey. He knew fellow officers would "cover for him" if they thought he was an alcoholic. Therefore, he masked the cocaine's behavioral influences with the odor of alcohol. This experience, which provides insight into the occupational culture of policing, serves as an extreme example of how on-duty substance abuse can occur without being discovered.

On-duty drug use can also occur if the problem becomes systemic within the work group. In one moderate-sized midwestern city, about thirty officers were identified as being involved in a "user's ring" (most of whom did not use drugs on duty). Drug use became so pervasive that there was tolerance for its use, even on duty. While some officers in the group did not like the on-duty use, they would not inform on those using drugs during working hours because of the strong implication they would be discovered as a drug user, albeit during off-duty hours. The implication from this experience is that in light of the police subculture, if off-duty use becomes pervasive, there is an increased likelihood of on-duty use among the officers involved.

In perhaps the only empirical study of the subject, Peter Kraska and Victor Kappeler discovered on-duty drug use during the course of working with a southwestern police department on another project. Through the use of unstructured self-report interviews, departmental records, and personal observations, they found that 20 percent of the officers in the department used marijuana while on duty twice a month or more.[43] Another four percent had used marijuana at least once while on duty. Moreover, ten percent of the officers reported they had used nonprescribed controlled substances (including hallucinogenic drugs, stimulants, or barbiturates) while on duty. (This may not be an additional ten percent of the officers; it may include some of the marijuana users.) Most of the officers involved in this behavior were between the ages of twenty-one and thirty-eight and had been police officers for three to ten years.

One may hope that the high incidence of on-duty drug use found in this study was an exceptional occurrence. If not, the problem may be greater than we believe. Certainly, the findings dispel the myth that drug use is a problem found only in the police departments of the nation's largest cities. Based on this and other research, it is also reasonable to assume that those agencies that have had more serious drug-related problems, notably corruption, have also experienced on-duty drug use.

Drugs of choice—In cases where police drug use has been documented, marijuana appears to be the most common drug used. The preference for marijuana is most likely because of its comparatively minor addictive nature, its limited long-term effects, the ease of obtaining it, its comparatively low cost, and, importantly, the lesser social stigma associated with the use of marijuana compared with use of other drugs. Cocaine is clearly the second most frequently used drug and appears to be fairly prevalent. The best explanation for this seems to be its availability, its prevalent use in many social situations, and a generally greater exhilaration of cocaine compared to marijuana.

There is also some evidence of abuse of nonprescribed or falsely prescribed pharmaceutical substances. Amphetamines and barbiturates fall into this category, typically where officers have used the drugs as a way of coping with various personal problems. In some cases, stimulants have been used to help keep officers "alert" (or awake) when they have been working excessive hours in a second job or going to school. This form of substance abuse appears to have different dynamics than marijuana or cocaine use. Interestingly, officers showed greater tolerance for protecting officers who used amphetamines and barbiturates as opposed to other controlled substances, despite the fact that the use of those substances is illegal. There were no indications of a significant problem with synthetic hallucinogenic drugs or heroin.

As a final note, some police administrators have expressed concern that an increasing number of officers may be using illicit anabolic steroids. Their concern, while somewhat focused on the illegal use, is primarily directed toward the reported behavioral effects of steroids. Specifically, some research has indicated that regular steroid users become violent and aggressive. The implications of these effects in law enforcement are obvious. Interestingly, new police programming may indirectly contribute to this problem. With more departments participating in competitive physical competitions, such as the Police Olympics, which include weight lifting, martial arts, running, and similar activity, in addition to rewarding physical fitness, the appeal of the conditioning effects of steroids is powerful. This is an important area for police executives to carefully explore.

Substance Abuse as a Job-Related Condition.
Questions have arisen of whether officer drug use could be a job-related condition. There have been two primary arguments on which this assertion is based: police stress and the officer's job assignment.

The rationale that the stress argument posits is that, as a result of the high levels of stress in policing, some officers have resorted to drug use as a coping mechanism. Despite the wide array of research on police stress, there is no scientific evidence to support this claim. In fact, the author would argue that drug-abusing officers would experience *greater stress*, since there is always the fear that an officer's drug abuse may be discovered. This, of course, would likely end in discipline or termination. If stress was, in fact, a major cause of police drug use, then it is likely that higher levels of drug use would have been discovered over the past two decades. Furthermore, evidence from police disciplinary actions and labor arbitrations where officer drug use is at issue does not suggest that stress was a cause.

The second issue of job-relatedness is more problematic. This argument states that officers who are working undercover drug investigations with frequent and ongoing exposure to drugs may become socialized in the "drug culture." Constant interaction in the environment of drug use and transactions reduces the adverse social and moral implications of drug consumption, while at the same time reinforcing the permissibility of its use.

It is clear that undercover officers do, in fact, become socialized into the drug culture based on language, dress, and other behaviors, and these carry over to the officer's off-duty time. Officers who work undercover in prostitution, gambling, and bootlegging tend to hold a diminished view of the social impact and "wrongfulness" of these behaviors. Given these factors and our knowledge about the socialization process in general, it is reasonable to assume that officers could be similarly assimilated into the drug culture. This is reinforced by the knowledge that if an officer is going to be accepted into a social group, he or she must appear to ascribe to that group's norms. While the process may begin as a masquerade for the officer, constant exposure to the culture combined with the stress of the environment may reasonably lead to acceptance of drug use (and other improper behaviors) at the social level even though the officer recognizes that they should not be accepted at the legal level. Generally, the longer an officer is in such an environment the more acceptable that group's values and norms become. While empirical research is virtually nonexistent on this issue, anecdotal evidence from research conducted by the author gives credence to the occurrence of this process.[44]

Based on an analysis of drug use and corruption, the author has identified six factors of the police occupational environmental that contribute to drug involvement.

Opportunity structure—The nature of the policing environment provides officers with opportunities to exploit situations for "profit." Answering calls where a business has been burglarized, stopping a person and finding drugs in their possession, or finding a person with stolen property in his or her car are all examples of situations where officers could capitalize on both their authority and the opportunity the situation presents to gain property or money. Even the fact that the police come into contact with many criminals—and people who are on the periphery of crime—provides additional opportunities. Fortunately, only a few officers exploit these opportunities. In the case of drug use, officers have the opportunity to seize drugs from "the street" and convert them to their own use.

Rationalization—Observing that "everyone uses drugs," "I'm not hurting anyone," and "what I do on my own time in my own home is no one's business," illustrates how officers rationalize drug use. The process of rationalization is a psychological mechanism people use to justify behavior that they know is improper. When accused of wrongdoing, the rationalization changes to displacement wherein others are blamed for one's own improprieties. Obviously, the fallacy in rationalization is the failure to acknowledge one's responsibilities.

Invulnerability factor—Essentially, this is the perception that because of the officer's position and authority, he or she can avoid becoming implicated in improper behavior. Easy access to information, camaraderie, and the power to influence the behavior of drug users and dealers are contributory factors to this feeling of invulnerability. This is epitomized in the statement of one officer who was accused of drug use by a drug dealer, "Who's going to take the word of a junkie over a cop?"[45]

Abrogation of trust—It is clear from the research, case law, and ethical standards of policing, that there is a higher standard of integrity required for police officers than for "average citizens."[46] With this higher standard of integrity coupled with the oath of office an officer takes to uphold the law, any unlawful behavior violates the public trust embodied in the officer's oath.

Blue Code of Secrecy—Peer pressure is a strong social phenomenon that has dramatic influences on people's decisions. The "Blue Code of Secrecy" is a manifestation of peer pressure in the police occupational culture. Essentially, this norm infers that an officer should never "rat" on the behavior of another. The norm has little to do with the nature of the behavior. Rather, the fact that one officer would inform on another is a violation of this sacred occupational trust. Honest, hard-working officers may realize others are violating laws or regulations, but tend to "look the other way" instead of reporting them. This does not mean the honest officer condones the improper behavior, but feels the strength of the Blue Code overpowers the obligation to inform. Thus, improper behavior, such as drug use, is perpetuated. Certainly, honest officers will distance themselves from the dishonest ones, but the code is seldom violated except in the most notorious of cases.

THE POLICE AND CRIME

When discussing crime there is a tendency to view it as a singular phenomenon—an ominous cloud over the community that the police must strive to disperse. However, to understand crime and the community, it must be dissected into various elements. Broadly speaking, we will look at the *fear of crime* and at *actual crime*. Actual crime is somewhat selective—that is, it is much more prevalent in certain geographic areas of a city or county than in others. Even the characteristic of selectivity changes with the type of crime. Some crime, that which instills the greatest concern in the community, is violent or predatory in nature. Homicide, assault, robbery, and sexual assaults fall into this category. Thefts are the next worrisome form, and these include burglary, larceny, and auto theft. The third band on the crime continuum consists of nuisance offenses ranging from vandalism to trespassing. This three-point typology does not attempt to encompass all crime, but to provide a perspective on those which instill the greatest community concerns. Other crimes, such as fraud or illegal dumping of waste, evoke concern among citizens, but little fear.

While actual crime may be geographically selective, fear of crime is far less so. If the crime rate increases in a community or if there is a particularly heinous crime, the fear will tend to increase somewhat uniformly across the community. People tend to view crime in very personal terms, which are internalized, leading to fear.

Because of the different dimensions of crime, the police must recognize that variable approaches to crime fighting are needed. Thus, any "war on crime" must have different battle lines or strategies. Just as importantly, the community must recognize this also. The following discussion is not meant to be a comprehensive treatise on crime, but a guidepost to issues regarding how crime affects the police-community relationship. The way crime is viewed in a community and the way police respond to perceived crime problems will have some influence on the public image of the police.

Fear of Crime

Fear of crime, a tenuous factor with which the police must deal, has an intangible quality. It is based on citizens' perceptions of safety, perceptions of the frequency of crime in their neighborhood, feelings of vulnerability, and the general quality of life they are experiencing. Although it is intangible, it is a very real concern as evidenced by the growth in private security firms, crime prevention devices, and personal safety products over the past decade. When an underlying fear exists, it takes little for it to become pervasive.

Research on the issue has found that over one-half of the people in the United States said they were fearful of being a crime victim in the 1990s, with women being the most fearful (even though the crime rate dropped from 1991 to 1997). Interestingly, young adults, aged eighteen to twenty-four, are the most fearful, and older Americans are the least fearful.[47] This is a notable change over recent years, when older Americans had the greatest fear of crime. Increased mobility, greater social decentralization, and higher levels of exposure to crime and violence—both in the news and entertainment media—among younger adults have most likely contributed to this fear. This is reinforced by the steadily increasing perception of rising crime rates and increasing "uneasiness" of being alone at night reported by citizens.[48]

These fears represent some important problems the police must face. Conceptually, it is argued under the community policing philosophy that the police have the responsibility to address all community concerns that contribute to a deteriorating quality of life. Pragmatically, if the public is fearful about victimization, they are more likely to feel the police are not doing their job; hence, their satisfaction with the police will decrease. Regardless of the perspective, fear of crime remains a problem the police must face.

Crime prevention checklists, Neighborhood Watch, Operation Identification, and public education programs address some fears. These kinds of activities, however, are somewhat superficial. The most effective way to reduce the fear of crime is to change the environment of the neighborhood. Eliminating the "signs of crime"—abandoned cars, overgrown lots, rubbish, and other symbols of neighborhood decay—will have a longer-lasting effect. Similarly, such things as ensuring that burned out street lamps are replaced, condemned buildings are torn down, and specific crime trends are addressed reinforce safety and a higher quality of life in the neighborhood. While many of these activities may be nontraditional for the police, they nonetheless reflect the roots from which the fear of crime grows.

SUMMARY

What should be apparent from this discussion is that there are a wide range of factors that influence the public image of the police. Many of these factors are rooted in fact and experience, while others are based on perceptions: some are accurate and some are not. The public perception is important for obtaining cooperation and support. If a police department is moving toward community policing, it is essential that lines of communication be open and that support from citizens be solidly in place. If the image is that the police are corrupt, insensitive, or incompetent, it is going to be much more difficult to enlist citizen participation. Conversely, if the police image is positive, professional, and cooperative, the public will be much more enthusiastic and less suspicious of police motives related to public involvement.

If the image is poor, the police must take *substantive* initiatives to improve that image. Mere public relations will not accomplish this. In addition, the police must be patient and realize that changing the image will require not only effort, but time. If the public image is positive, the police must remain vigilant to maintain that image. A positive image is fragile. Thus it must be continually reinforced through administrative control, community-based programming, and professional officer behavior.

QUESTIONS FOR DISCUSSION

1. Describe some of the ways that experience with the police can shape a citizen's image of all officers.
2. Explain the conceptual foundation of the "lessons for change" in organizations.
3. What is the relationship between the police public image and role expectations?
4. Discuss why some people do not report crimes to the police.
5. What contributions to policing have been made through the use of survey research?
6. Was it surprising to you that citizens' ratings of the honesty and ethical standards of the police have traditionally been high over the past fifteen to twenty years? Why or why not?
7. Why is the view of minorities toward the police different than that of whites?
8. Do you feel that when cases of police misconduct are publicized citizens view this as "an exception to the rule" or as a generalization to all officers? Explain your position.
9. Herman Goldstein has said that "corruption is endemic to policing." What is meant by this? Do you agree or disagree?
10. Have you found it surprising that a notable number of police officers have been found to use drugs? Why or why not?

NOTES

1. Those doubting this "self-evident truth" need only look at the research in advertising and marketing—superficiality sells!
2. U.S. President's Commission on Law Enforcement and Administration of Justice, *Task Force Report: The Police* (Washington, DC: U.S. Government Printing Office, 1967), p. 146. See also D. C. Couper, *How to Rate Your Local Police* (Washington, DC: Police Executive Research Forum, 1983).
3. Mervin F. White and Ben A. Menke, "A Critical Analysis of Surveys on Public Opinion Toward Police Agencies," *Journal of Police Science and Administration* 6, no. 2:204–18. Copyright © International Association of Chiefs of Police, Inc.
4. This is based on the initial findings of research for a master's thesis by Joanne Ziembo, School of Criminal Justice, Michigan State University (1993).
5. *Crime in the United States 1996.* (Washington, DC: Federal Bureau of Investigation, 1997).
6. See: *Sourcebook of Criminal Justice Statistics.* (Washington, DC: U.S. Bureau of Justice Statistics, 1997).
7. Surveys were not common because (a) police did not rely on research in those years and (b) the police never gave much thought about the public's concerns.
8. David L. Carter, "Student Attitudes Toward the Police," unpublished research findings, 1997.
9. Jack J. Preiss and Howard J. Ehrlich, *An Examination of Role Theory: The Case of the State Police* (Lincoln: University of Nebraska Press, 1966), p. 124.
10. Timothy Flanagan, et al. *Sourcebook of Criminal Justice Statistics*, (Washington, DC: U.S. Government Printing Office, 1996).
11. *Ibid.*
12. "Public Solidly Favors Mixed Police/Civilian Review Boards," *Law Enforcement News*, October 31, 1992, pp. 1, 6.
13. U.S. President's Commission on Law Enforcement and Administration of Justice, *Field Surveys II, Criminal Victimization in the United States: A Report of a National Survey* (Washington, DC: U.S. Government Printing Office, 1967).
14. U.S., President's Commission on Law Enforcement and Administration of Justice, *Field Surveys V*, p. 30 and *Field Surveys IV*, vol. 1, p. 105 (Washington, DC: U.S. Government Printing Office, 1967).
15. James Q. Wilson, *Thinking About Crime* (New York: Basic Books, 1975), p. 99.
16. Ibid., p. 100.
17. See David L. Carter, "Hispanic Interaction With the Criminal Justice System" *Journal of Criminal Justice*, vol. 11, (1983) pp. 213–27.
18. David L. Carter, "Hispanic Perception of Police Performance: An Empirical Assessment," *Journal of Criminal Justice*, vol. 13, (1985) pp. 487–500.
19. *Ibid.*
20. William A. Westley, "The Escalation of Violence Through Legitimatization," *Annals* 364 (March 1966), p. 126.
21. President's Commission on Law Enforcement, *Field Surveys III*, vol. 1, p. 69.
22. For example, Peter H. Rossi, et al., "Between White and Black: The Faces of American Institutions in the Ghetto," in *Supplemental Studies* of the 1968 Kerner Commission, p. 104.
23. James Q. Wilson, op. cit., *Thinking About Crime*, p. 107.
24. Anecdotally, as a result of a series of technical assistance site visits made by the author in 1997 for the COPS-funded Regional Community Policing Training

Institutes, it was found that police executives were increasingly aware of the need for resocialization.

25. James Q. Wilson, "The Police and Their Problems: A Theory," *Public Policy*, Yearbook of the Harvard University Graduate School of Public Administration (Cambridge, 1963), pp. 191–92.

26. *Public Relations and the Police* (Houston study), p. vi.

27. Michael Banton, "Social Integration and Police," *Police Chief* (April 1963) pp. 10–12. Reprinted by permission of the International Association of Chiefs of Police, Gaithersburg, Maryland.

28. Ibid., p. 12.

29. Oscar Handlin, "Community Organization as a Solution to Police-Community Problems," *Police Chief* 32, no. 3 (March 1965) p. 18.

30. Karl Menninger was a consultant to the President's Crime Commission in 1966 and also a consultant to the development of the Lemberg Center for the Study of Violence at Brandeis University. See his book *The Crime of Punishment* (New York: Viking Press, 1968).

31. Chester M. Pierce, "Psychiatric Aspects of Police-Community Relations," *Mental Hygiene* 46, no. 1 (January 1962), pp. 107–15.

32. Ibid., p. 111.

33. Ibid.

34. Ibid., p. 112.

35. Albert J. Reiss, Jr., and David J. Bordua, "Environment and Organization: A Perspective on the Police," in David Bordua, ed., *The Police*, 1974, p. 30.

36. Reiss and Bordua, "Environment and Organization," in David Bordua, ed., *The Police: Six Sociological Essays* (New York: John Wiley & Sons, 1967), p. 36. Reprinted by permission of John Wiley & Sons.

37. Jerome H. Skolnick treats various aspects of this matter in *Justice Without Trial: Law Enforcement in Democratic Society* (New York: John Wiley & Sons, 1966). See also Jerome H. Skolnick and J. Richard Woodworth, "Bureaucracy, Information, and Social Control: A Study of a Morals Detail," in David Bordua, ed. *The Police: Six Sociological Essays* (New York: John Wiley & Sons, 1967).

38. Joan L. Wolfe and John F. Heaphy, eds., *Readings on Productivity in Policing* (Washington, DC: The Police Foundation, 1975), p. i.

39. Gary T. Marx, "Alternative Measures of Police Performance," in Emilio Viano, ed., *Criminal Justice Research* (Lexington, MA: Lexington Books, 1975), pp. 179–93.

40. International Association of Chiefs of Police, *Building Integrity and Reducing Drug Corruption in Police Departments* (Washington, DC: U.S. Department of Justice, Office of Justice Programs, 1989).

41. This discussion is based on research conducted by the author and originally reported in, David L. Carter, "Drug Related Corruption of Police Officers: A Contemporary Typology," *Journal of Criminal Justice*, vol. 18, no. 2 (1990).

42. David L. Carter, "An Overview of Drug-Related Conduct of Police Officers: Drug Abuse and Narcotic Corruption," in *Drugs, Crime and the Criminal Justice System*, Ralph Weisheit, ed. (Cincinnati, OH: Anderson Publishing Company, 1990).

43. Peter Kraska and Victor Kappeler, "Police On-Duty Drug Use: A Theoretical and Descriptive Examination," *American Journal of Police*, 7:1 (1988) pp. 1–28.

44. Ibid., David L. Carter, "Drug Related Corruption . . . ".

45. Ibid., David L. Carter, "An Overview . . . " p. 95.

46. David L. Carter and Darrel W. Stephens, *Drug Abuse By Police Officers: An Analysis of Policy Issues* (Springfield, IL: Charles C. Thomas, Publisher, 1988).

47. Timothy Flanagan, et al. *Sourcebook of Criminal Justice Statistics* (Washington, DC: U.S. Government Printing Office, 1996).

48. Ibid.

Part Three

PERSISTENT PROBLEMS

The Impact of Civil Liabilities Litigation on Policing

ROLANDO V. DEL CARMEN, LL.B., LL.M., M.C.L., J.S.D.

Professor
College of Criminal Justice
Sam Houston State University

Getting sued is a fact of life and an occupational hazard in modern-day policing. American society is litigious, and the police are a popular target because of the sensitive nature of their task and the immense authority they wield. Police officers are unique in that they alone are authorized by the state to use force, including deadly force, in their work. Use of force is indispensable in policing, but it also carries immense responsibility. The effect of the use of force can be traumatic and devastating; hence, lawsuits arising from police-induced damage or injuries are common and predictable.

The effects of lawsuits on police departments are considerable and can be permanent. Ironically, despite antagonism from the police and general adverse perception, the long-term impact of lawsuits may be positive for the general public and the agency. More than any single factor in the last fifteen years or so, liability lawsuits have accelerated professionalization in police ranks throughout the country, while fostering greater awareness among law enforcement agencies of the responsibilities inherent in policing in a free society. Professionalization escapes easy definition, but it generally includes better training, upgraded recruitment, and promulgation of and strict adherence to prescribed agency rules. All three have attracted more attention in policing as a result of liability lawsuits.

Fear of lawsuits has led to better training in most areas of police work. It no longer suffices that officers simply be trained prior to assuming responsibilities. The type of training given must be current, task-responsive, and properly documented.

High on the list of improved and more intensive training needs in any police department is the police use of deadly force. Other concerns include use of force in general, automobile pursuits, searches and seizures, arrests, care of arrested persons, and police-community relations. Training enhances competence which, in turn, reduces liability risks. As is the case in most public agencies, however, training funds are the first to go in times of financial exigency. Liability lawsuits bolster the case for more training money as it has become shortsighted for cities and municipalities to cut training funds to meet financial shortfalls. The "pay now or pay later" reality now applies to police training.

Along with better training, liability lawsuits have brought about a need for upgraded police recruitment. A study by Carter and Sapp on the effect of higher education on liability concludes that police liability risks may be reduced if officers obtain higher education, saying that "while the evidence is indirect, the argument suggests that higher education may reduce liability risks." They maintain that college-educated police officers communicate better with the public, write better reports, perform more effectively, show more initiative in performing police tasks, use discretion wisely, and are more professional (Carter and Sapp, 1989:154). Recruitment of officers who know the limits of police authority has gained higher priority in many departments. Along with this is more reliable psychological screening—measures which identify applicants who are more likely to create liability problems for the agency. The strictly law enforcement-oriented mind set, which is more likely to lead to excessive use of force, is slowly giving way to a service orientation. This reduces conflict between police and the public and decreases liability potential.

A third effect of lawsuits is more pervasive use of manuals in police agencies. There is hardly any police agency in the country, rural areas included, whose day-to-day operations are not governed by a manual. The days when administrators "flew by the seat of their pants," and got away with it because nobody scrutinized what they did, are gone. Through liability lawsuits the courts are constantly looking over the shoulders of police administrators and second guessing their decisions on crucial matters. Police administrators realize that a manual insulates them from liability for what their officers do; at least in lawsuits based on the negligent failure to direct and supervise.

Manuals narrow police discretion in that officers must "go by the book" and in the process be held accountable for their action or inaction. Police use of firearms serves as an example. In the recent past the only guidance some supervisors gave to their officers was the macho message, "Never take your firearm out in anger, never put it back away in shame." That has changed. Now the advice given by supervisors is for officers to follow manual provisions strictly. Failure to adhere to agency rules invites internal investigation and subsequent administrative sanction. Many police departments have detailed policies on the use of force, which specify the level of force that can be used in certain situations.

Professionalization is crucial in the ranks of police administrators because they set policies and make decisions that can insulate the agency and officers from liability or expose them to it. Bad policies increase the chance of lawsuits; conversely, well-designed policies reduce liability potential. Administrators bear legal responsibilities for both their employer and subordinates. While courts have decided that the supervisor can be made liable for what subordinates do, they have also held that public agencies can be made financially accountable for policies promulgated by duly authorized policymakers. A negligent police administrator who lays back and lets subordinates run the department does both the subordinate and the agency a disservice—not to mention a flirtation with liability. He or she exposes the agency and subordinates to as much liability as one who stands still and refuses to evolve with changing times. Lawsuits have therefore made the role of supervisors even more central to policing.

Other results from liability lawsuits against the police are less evident yet equally difficult to measure and document. The rash of litigation directed toward policing has caused anxiety about who will represent the police if sued and who pays damages if imposed. Most states have laws authorizing state representation of public officers who are sued, as long as they acted within the scope of their authority. Most police officers, however, are not covered by this provision because they are local employees. In the absence of written policy, representation and indemnification are uncertain in most police departments. While most agencies, by practice, will represent officers and pay damages, such assistance may be withheld, with no recourse available to the officer.

Internal police investigations stemming from police actions have become a focus of concern, as have rights related to dismissal. Widely publicized use-of-force cases, such as the Rodney King incident in Los Angeles, result in an internal investigation, which may be followed by suspension and dismissal. These proceedings have led to lawsuits by officers against the agency and consequent heightened consciousness of officers' rights during internal police investigations. During the last few years, courts have been asked to resolve issues concerning police job-related rights, and case law is still evolving.

The role courts play in policing now looms even larger as a result of liability lawsuits. Court decisions have traditionally set the parameters of police work, but the consequences of violations have been generic to policing rather than being officer-specific. For example, the 1966 Miranda decision has governed police procedure when interrogating suspects, but a violation of the Miranda rules brings no direct adverse consequence on the officer. Instead, the immediate effect is on the prosecutor who fails to secure a conviction because crucial evidence is inadmissible. Liability lawsuits, on the other hand, can mean individual liability for the officer either in blatant cases or when the agency refuses to provide counsel or indemnification. As a result, the effects are more direct and personal.

The spate of headlines over alleged police misuse of force has spawned proposals designed to curb police abuse of authority. One proposal requires the Justice Department to keep accurate data (there is no such requirement or practice at present) on the use of excessive force nationwide by the police. A second suggested remedy provides for the enactment of a Police Accountability Act that authorizes the Justice Department, on behalf of the person injured, to file civil lawsuits challenging department-wide patterns or practice of police abuse. This is in addition to the authority now granted by federal law to criminally prosecute errant officers. A third proposal seeks to empower police-abuse victims to sue for injunctive or declaratory relief. Under a current Supreme Court decision, it is difficult for a victim to sue for system-wide reforms (instead of for damages) because of the requirement that whoever sues must have "standing"; meaning that such a plaintiff must be able to show that he or she is likely to be harmed again by the police. A fourth proposal authorizes victims of police use of excessive force to sue local governments that employ the officers instead of holding local governments liable only if the injury resulted from agency policy or custom, as is the case law at present. The common theme in these proposals is deterrence of police misconduct along with greater accountability through active federal monitoring and intervention. It is safe to assume that these goals have been achieved in varying degrees, at least in departments that have been sued, of which there have been many.

CONCLUSION

A review of available studies leads to the conclusion that no reliable data support the often-heard claim that liability lawsuits have assumed crisis proportions in this country. The problem, however, is not to be taken lightly. Police officers, administrators, and agencies are fully aware of the liability risks that policing entails. The publicity generated by high-profile, use-of-force cases make civil liability a growing concern at present and in the immediate future. Despite understandable and predictable police antagonism, there is reason to believe that the long-range impact of court intervention augurs well for the public in that it places in perspective the responsibilities officers have when policing a free society. That is the way it should be in a country where the judiciary is entrusted with the task of maintaining the delicate balance between governmental power and individual rights and where the courts are expected to afford redress to members of the public when everything else fails.

David L. Carter and Allen D. Sapp, "The Effect of Higher Education on Police Liability: Implications for Police Personnel Policy," *American Journal of Police*, vol. III, no. 1 (1989): 154.

Chapter 10

PERCEPTION, ATTITUDES, BELIEFS, AND VALUES

In the preceding two chapters, dealing with the self-image and the public image of the police, we have been analyzing attitudes. It is appropriate therefore, that we review some elementary psychology, to be sure we understand the nature of attitudes.

Psychology is concerned primarily with three basic behavioral processes: learning, motivation, and perception. All systems of psychology are interested in these processes, although with different emphases. Some psychologists emphasize learning, while others emphasize perception or motivation. They have different perspectives, but all agree that these processes are closely related.[1]

For example, if one regards learning as most important, one conceives of behavior as resulting from a stimulus that may be inside or outside the body; therefore, in this context, motivation is discussed largely in terms of stimulus. If one regards motivation as fundamental, one might analyze body changes and conditions that give rise to certain behavior. Motivation is concerned with the *why*—the reasons for behavior. It involves what are called value judgments and includes the inculation of norms and attitudes.[2]

It is not necessary for our purposes to review these behavioral processes in detail. Very briefly, then, the psychologists who stress learning (often called behaviorists) foster an objective, detached, scientific approach to the study of behavior. It is essentially stimulus and response, "input" and "output," that interests them; the school of thought they represent is often associated with conditioned reflexes. It is a cause-and-effect approach to behavior; a given cause produces a given (largely predictable) result. In this theory, emotion is a conditioned response to environmental elements.

Psychologists who concentrate on motivation (often called psychoanalysts) tend to look inside the person to identify the needs, impulses, and emotions that cause behavior, with special attention to subconscious and irrational elements.

Then there are those psychologists who study the process of perception (sometimes called phenomenologists). They assume that individuals relate to and give meaning to the world around them. How does the individual come to understand and deal with this world? For this school of thought, behavior is a response to the world *as it is perceived*. The assumption is that humans are rational creatures. One individual may see the world in terms that seem irrational to another, but once it is discovered *how* it is seen, the other's behavior becomes understandable.

Each of the three schools of thought has produced evidence to support its views, and each has been applied to significant problems. All three schools are represented in reputable professional psychotherapy and on university faculties. Consequently, we rely on all three perspectives to discuss issues involved in this psychological dimension of police-community relations.

THE PERCEPTION PROCESS

We have discussed how police officers perceive themselves and how others perceive police officers. As a behavioral process, perception begins with the assumption that people—at least from their own point of view—behave in a rational, purposeful, logical manner, depending upon how they perceive the objective world. Each of us responds to the world according to the way he or she perceives it. Fortunately for human welfare and progress, we do not all see the world in the same way. Yet however we see it, each of us will behave rationally *within that framework*. The basis of our individual point of view is the nature of the self, as we have seen, and not necessarily what really happens in the world outside the self. Each of us helps to create a personal reality. And perhaps the ultimate maturity and wisdom, for each of us, is the recognition that the world we perceive is not the only world there is.

Perception involves "intake" or awareness through any of the senses, not merely visual. The process is made vivid in a story of a conversation among three experienced major league baseball umpires. One said, "Some are balls, some are strikes, I call 'em as they are." The second umpire retorted, "Some are balls, some are strikes, I call 'em as I see 'em." And the third one mused, "Some are balls, some are strikes, and *they ain't nothing until I call 'em*."

If we combine elements in the different approaches of the umpires, we might conclude (1) that we respond to things in accordance with the physical realities out there in nature; (2) that the physical reality is perceived in accordance with some possible distortions in our subjective processes; and (3) that we enter into a transaction with the energies of nature and abstract components that we integrate with our perceptual processes to create the world within which we operate.

More simply, the pertinent ideas may be arranged in the following sequence:

1. When we talk or write about something, what we describe is something that happens inside us as much as what happens outside.
2. What each of us can talk or write about is only a very small part of reality.
3. Many of our problems in communication arise because we forget that individual experiences are never identical.
4. Since each of us perceives the world in bits and pieces, we tend to communicate about it in bits and pieces. To a certain extent, our individual experience teaches us *what* to see and hear.
5. Communication is a human transaction. It depends upon symbols—words, gestures, etc. But the symbols do not have the same meaning for others with different experiences, resulting in a "communication breakdown."[3]

Perceptions and the Self. How we perceive the world, then, is based upon the *self*: our own unique experience. Each of us actually has many selves, not just one. These selves are related to our positions in the social scene, our social roles. Our perceptions of self depend upon the context at the moment, varying with what has gone before, who or what we have been thinking of, and the immediate situation we face. If we are short of funds, the bank on the corner looms large. If we are en route to a final exam, professors are not heroes or heroines. If a police officer rescues us from the locked-the-keys-in-the-car predicament, cops are marvelous people!

Because our roles are social, the word symbols we use to designate them often denote reciprocal human relationships *(transactions)*. The associations are often implied "pairings"; for example: man–woman; boy–girl; lecturer–audience; parent–child; teacher–student; writer–reader; police officer . . . what? How one completes this pair will probably reveal his or her perception of the principal role of the police. Police officer and law breaker? Police officer and lost child? Police officer and derelict drunk?

For efficient functioning, flexibility is required of all of us, as we shift from one self to another. Thus, we should strive to be open-minded in our perceptions of others, not only to be sensitive to the role they are playing at the time, but also so we can empathize with them. We limit perception when we insist on dealing with others in terms of our own fixed ideas as to what they are. It is important also to keep in mind that we perceive others, and they perceive us, in only one or two or three of the roles we play. Most people see a police officer only in that role; they have no opportunity to see him or her in other roles.

Each of us tries to maintain a stable world in spite of evidence to the contrary. We tend to shape things according to our conceptions and our purposes. This tendency, of course, varies by individuals. Some people are relatively more rigid or dogmatic than others and take a long time to accept and adapt to reality. Some people are relatively adaptable and easily shift and adjust to changing situations. It is a question of how much stability a particular individual needs, regarding either his self-image or the outer world. Some individuals resist the forces of exterior change, inappropriately, by forcing a posture of outer stability. This repeats what we said earlier about the difficulty some individuals have in adjusting to rapid and drastic changes in social role; for example, civilian to soldier, soldier to civilian, single to married, married to divorced, and so on.

Consider again the first two umpires. So long as we think there is a real world out there, we may kid ourselves into believing that we adapt to it reasonably well: "I call 'em as they are." However, if we recognize the truth in what the third umpire said, we should recognize that our "reasonable adaptation" may reflect a greater ability to distort the real world than to adjust to it: "They ain't nothing until I call 'em."

Rigidity and Flexibility. Let us say that a certain professor has in class a student who the professor *knows* is cheating during examinations. The student has not been caught at it (the student being very clever), but the professor is nonetheless sure that the student is guilty. The professor knows this because of the way the student sits and looks around the room and at the ceiling during exams. The professor is certain that some day the student will blunder and be caught red-handed.

Could the professor be wrong in this judgment? "Just a hunch," "based on years of experience" may be the professor's response, which could be right. And then again, the professor could be wrong. Lots of people get fixed ideas about other people for which there is no factual evidence. It is a human trait to maintain our images of self and of others, to seek consistency and stability and the comfort of predictability. It requires much less effort to think stereotypically than to think in individualistic terms. "If you've seen one, you've seen them all!" Stereotyping is a form of perceptual shorthand.

This tendency is something each of us must learn to control. We must stretch our perceptions to enable us to see the contrary evidence, the unfamiliar, the unexpected. True, it is difficult to do. People of different backgrounds not only see things differently; they also *fail* to see things, even though presented right before their eyes. An abundance of psychological research and numerous tests, exercises, and even party games provide convincing evidence of this fact. For example, an individual's tendency toward a closed mind (dogmatism) can be scientifically measured. Basically, it is a blocking of perception.[4]

We see the accustomed and the familiar; we see those things that are not emotionally threatening, those that agree with our special professional training, and those that support our own point of view. Contrary or conflicting reality is filtered out of our perceptual orbit. We cannot stand to face this about ourselves, perhaps, or about others in the world "out there." As the critic puts it, "Don't confuse me with the facts. My mind's made up!"

Perceptual Shift.   Studies have shown that when people are asked to evaluate material that carries strong social and personal importance for them, they will displace the material from what should be its true scale placement.[5] The psychological term for this is *displacement*; a popular term is *perceptual shift*. Perhaps an example will best show what these terms mean.

John Q. Trustworthy considers himself a completely law-abiding citizen. He will not knowingly violate a law. He thinks that major violators are evil and minor violators are bad. He is annoyed by people who do not obey parking regulations or who ignore no-littering admonitions. John Q. is also a dog lover, and when he walks his Border Terriers, their requirements are quite important to him. In his entire life, John Q. has received but one summons from a police officer and that was for creating a public nuisance with his dogs.

John Q. does not see how his dogs' activities could possibly be construed as a nuisance. But a police officer saw it that way. As a result, John Q.'s perception of the police shifted. John Q.'s feelings about law enforcement were more than a little changed, at least temporarily. This is displacement, and any experienced police officer would have no trouble in supplying further examples. Law-abiding citizens often tend to be in favor of strict observance of the law—when it applies to *other people*.

In another illustration, some black activists have forcefully argued that Acquired Immune Deficiency Syndrome (AIDS) is a product of a governmental plan conceived years ago. This plan was allegedly plotted by white government leaders who were attempting the genocide of blacks. The perception of most whites is that this theory is an outrageous distortion of reality—it is inconceivable. The perception of some blacks is that there could be some merit in this theory. Given the diverse social-psychological development of whites and blacks, it is not likely that their perceptions of the viability of this theory will ever enmesh. This illustration addresses the inherent element of perceptual shift. Perceptions are individualistic, yet culturally based.

PERCEPTION AND ROLE PERFORMANCE

What is the relationship between perceived role expectations and actual role performance? We have given some attention to this question. Despite the growth in departmental policies and more intensive training provided for line officers, there remains a great deal of discretion in officers' decisions. This is particularly true in the practice of community policing. Most new officers, however, have little to base their discretionary decisions on except intuition, observations of other officers, and limited supervision, all on a foundation of training and policy. Thus, to become socialized into the role of a police officer still requires learning by experience and "playing it by ear."[6]

"Playing it by ear" seems to be an intrinsic element of the police officer's role behavior, as it is with all occupational subcultures. It exemplifies role performance governed by perceived audience expectations, although the actor does not necessarily conform to the expectations of any given audience. To the extent that one does not, there will probably be tension in some facet of police-community relations, caused by opposing or conflicting perceptions of role. Logically, the solution to this problem will be found in more *consensual* agreement in the role perceptions (hence, expectations) of diverse audiences, as suggested in an earlier chapter—essentially a political dynamic. Some minimal consensus on goals is obviously necessary for any social system to function as a system. Diversified perceptions flowing from cultural, economic, political, racial, and other experiential differences must be reconciled so as to fashion, insofar as possible, a view of the police by all community factions as *our* police. This process is fraught with difficulty, frustration, and imperfection because such conflicting human perceptions are involved. But this is the metabolism of politics in a pluralistic, democratic society.

Perceptions and Police Work.

Additional illustrations of the relation between perception and role enactment may be helpful. An aspect of perceptual development that should be mentioned again pertains to the manner in which perceptions of role attributes change. The assumption is that training and education are among the variables that affect role perceptions. If a police recruit at the start of training conceives of police work as consisting largely of physical tasks carried out in a hostile environment, he or she will logically see such role attributes as physical strength and courage as essential for the work. After training, if the recruit comes to recognize an important role for the police in performing various public service tasks and sees that people can be influenced more readily through verbal rather than physical skills, he or she will value more highly such role attributes as verbal skills, courtesy, and "people knowledge." With police education levels continually increasing throughout the 1990s, recognition of these attributes is becoming the status quo.

Niederhoffer made some additional points that are relevant here:

1. The police have been perceived, by members of minority groups, as a symbol of white oppression. Members of minority groups are perceived by the police as symbolic assailants and suspicious persons. On both sides, there are experiences to bolster the perceptions. But both perceptions are nonetheless stereotypic, and the stereotypes are mutually reinforcing, especially if there are no breakthroughs of significant contrasting experiences on either side.
2. Having more minority group police officers on the force may be one important possible breakthrough, with vital effect upon perceptions of the police department.

On the other hand, the black police officer may be perceived as an "Uncle Tom," as a traitor, as demanding from his own group a standard of behavior more stringent than that expected of others.

3. Certain people in the community simply do not perceive the police as trustworthy; conversely, the police do not perceive certain people in the community as trustworthy. This is *credibility*. Obviously, it is a problem of perception.[7]

Hans Toch refers to police officers who often cite their "experience" in support of sundry opinions. But, he says, the kind of person one is (including the kind of job one holds) has much to do with what one experiences, as opposed to what anyone else might experience in the same situation. A police officer is supposed to be good at spotting trouble. Yet the ability to spot trouble does not necessarily mean that one understands the reason for it. Some might even argue that the police need not understand the causes of crime—that their job is enforcement.

If one takes this position, then on what basis can police officers lobby for the death penalty, or criticize probation officers, or insist that sex offenders should be kept in prison? Certainly they may express their views as interested citizens. But they should keep in mind that their police experience does not bear on these matters, by their own role definition.

> . . . the police officer's "experience" is highly specialized, and no more conducive to an *accurate* picture of people than that of other observers. It is, of course, experience that is relevant to police work . . . but even here in a rather narrow way. If the professional police officer dealt with the public courteously, fairly, and effectively, his relevant experiences would be a string of courteous, fair, and effective dealings with people. Unfortunately, many "experienced" officers find themselves substituting for this requirement an imposing string of tense encounters, displays of confidence, "conning" talks, transparently patronizing intimacies, bluffs that may or may not have worked, and force that did. This sort of "experience" may give the *illusion* of competence to deal with people, but the people involved have not been consulted in arriving at this illusion.[8]

Of course, the same could be equally applicable to "experts" on any subject—all of us have a capacity for arranging the world in such a way that incorrect perceptions are confirmed. We see, selectively, what we want to see, what we expect to see, and weight it with our values: good–bad, true–false, acceptable–unacceptable, and so on. Thus, we have the sorting process, separating the "good guys and the bad guys," the "white hats and the black hats," the "ins and the outs." Whatever the particular terms, it's *we* and *they*.

The self-fulfilling principle is also operative in our perceptual transactions. Because we tend to see what we expect to see—blocking out evidence that does not fit our preconceived picture—there is a tendency to see only what substantiates our predisposition. Persons thought of as suspicious therefore act suspiciously; police officers thought of as brutal act brutally.

Even stereotypic "bad" traits that we attribute generally to a group of "bad guys" stems from some impulse that all of us have. We accuse some groups of being belligerent and hostile, others of being dirty, and others of grabbing all they can get. We were taught in childhood that these are undesirable qualities; therefore, "bad" people are so characterized. We forget that the real war is between the "good guys" and the "bad guys" *within each of us*. Both good and bad feelings are in each of us, and the crucial task is to use those that are appropriate to the reality in which we find ourselves. Refinement of our own perceptions in such a manner helps to modify the perceptions others have of us.[9]

Indeed, differing philosophies of police work and of judicial and corrections activities seem to spring from differing philosophies about the nature of humans and society. A tendency to sort people into good and bad produces a point of view toward such work that contrasts with the view produced by recognizing the capacity for good and bad in each of us. There are also different views regarding the nature and source of authority in society. These are grounded in theology and metaphysics, and reflected in social anthropology. As can be seen, perceptual influences are complex and wide-ranging.

Factors in Perceptual Distortion. Because perception is a behavioral process, it is well to be aware of the sources of perceptual distortion. Some important ones are these, their relative importance varying with individuals and situations:

1. Personal rigidity or dogmatism; relative difficulty in adjusting to the forces of change.
2. Emotional "loading." Illustrated by perceptual shift (displacement) in the example of the dog lover.
3. Experiential limitations—difficult sometimes to recognize and accept realistically—but part of the human condition.
4. Cultural myopia—sometimes called "tunnel vision." Our perceptions are weighted by the attitudes, beliefs, and values we accept as part of our ethnic, racial, and social class, and other similar affiliations.

PERCEPTION AND ATTITUDES

Perceptual distortion or "tilt" suggests consideration of the link of perception, attitudes, beliefs, and values in personality structure. As we have noted, perception or awareness begins with sensory input: visual, audio, olfactory, etc. Perception is the meaningful interpretation of sensations as representative of external objects—*apparent* knowledge of reality.[10]

Yet perceptions and sensations are distinct. A color (sensation) differs from a specific colored object (perception). Thus, when evaluating people and programs we must endeavor to measure true relationships and behaviors, not simply our perceptions.[11] This is difficult to do since we tend to conclude that our perceptions represent "truth."

Perceptions are the sole internal representatives of reality; they are the mind's reflection of matter. Aristotle noted, "Nothing is in the mind that does not pass through the senses," and Leonardo da Vinci declared, "All of our knowledge has its origins in perceptions." Few contemporary psychologists would challenge this. Most would agree that perception is an interpretation of sensations; a few would say that perceptions are "invariants" of sensations.[12]

In any event, our perceptions are the basis for our opinions on any given subject. These are ideas we may or may not have thought out; they are open to dispute and subject to relatively easy change. But some of our opinions assume a certain constancy. They take deeper root, and we are less willing to change them. They become convictions on which we are prepared to act. These convictions are *attitudes*. The basis of our attitudes is in social experiences, as perceived. A *belief*, in turn, is a kind of attitude. So is a *value*. To distinguish, let us say that one takes the position that people with green hair should not be permitted to live in a certain neighborhood. This is an attitude. Or simply to say, "I can't stand people with green hair." If, however, one goes on to add, "because people with green hair cannot be trusted," one thereby cites a *belief* to explain the attitude. This is the seemingly plausible *rationalization* for the attitude. The *value* is implicit: the quality of not being trustworthy is evil, wrong, undesirable. A value is a norm of behavior, an index of good and bad. Basically, a value is itself an attitude and a belief—based upon perception. And as we have observed, our perceptions are subject to possible distortion.

To understand all this is to realize that, to a certain extent, we are taught what we perceive. To enter the realm of our awareness, what's "out there" has to pass muster with the attitudes and values we have already adopted. Few of us deal comfortably with value conflict, a point we shall note again as we discuss cognitive dissonance in a subsequent chapter. The possibility of communication with another person develops as we discover commonality of experiences, although our interpretation of individual experience may differ. The ink blot test is based on this idea.

Attitudes develop primarily because they tie an individual to a group that a person feels can aid in attaining important goals. Thus, the choices a person makes, such as to affiliate with this organization rather than that, to join this party rather than that, or to read this newspaper rather than that, are often decisions based on a certain set of attitudes, beliefs, and values. We tend to prefer what coincides with what we already believe. Our perceptions of opposing attitudes, beliefs, and values tend to support what we already believe. Therefore, our attitudes, beliefs, and values tend to be self-insulating and reinforcing, because we shut out of our perceptions any contrary or opposing evidence. The alternative creates internal *value conflict*, which can be very upsetting, because it involves the recognition that a cherished belief may need some qualification.

In addition to an action factor, an attitude tends to be emotionally loaded. An attitude usually involves strong feelings about something or somebody. This point provides an important clue for attitude change.

An illustration of value conflict and attitudinal differentiation is occurring in policing today. Police reformers and researchers have been "leading the charge" in support of the community policing (CoP) movement. Yet, many line-level officers have expressed suspicion and rejection of the concept because, based on their experiences as police officers, "it won't work." The occupational values the officers hold are based on their socialization and consequent attitudes of doing police work in a given (traditional) way. They become dogmatic, resistant to change, when new values and organizational standards are imposed that are notably different from their experience. This dogmatism is a natural psychological phenomenon, which must be dealt with if change is going to occur. As long as it is approached in a logical and rational manner and sufficient time for inculcation is provided, change may begin to occur. If, however, it is addressed from an *emotional* perspective—as it often is— any change will be as difficult as Dorothy Guyot's analogy to "bending granite."[13]

COMMUNICATION

Problems of human relations are frequently referred to as "communication" problems. There is some validity to this characterization, but the complexity of the communication problem is not always grasped. Sometimes it is suggested, for instance, that "talk sessions" will cure the problem, communication being defined simply as "talk." If the parties can be brought together in conversation, all will be well.

A clear implication of what we have said in this chapter is that the communication problem—for instance, in police and community relations—will not be so easily solved. This is true for several reasons, each emphasizing that mere messages do not usually produce mutual understanding. We may summarize our analysis by indicating a few of the reasons the communication problem is so formidable:

1. Any message in a communications situation may touch upon at least three levels of meaning. A message may contain seeming *fact*—a report of reality *as the communicator sees it*. A message may also contain *inference*. And it may also contain *judgment*. Thus, a message may report an event: it may include conclusions drawn about the event; and it may include a personal evaluation of it. Much argument takes place between people and groups at all three of these levels of meaning—the latter two directly and the first implicitly.

2. A second important barrier to clarity in communication may be in the *difference of values*. This pertains to the "value gap." It pertains to differences in the conditions of life—age, education, occupation, experience, sex, social class, ethnicity, culture, race, religion, and so on—that, as we have seen, vitally influence our perceptions and, consequently, our attitudes, beliefs, and values. This is, of course, a common cause of difficulty in intergroup communication. So ingrained and deeply rooted are our values that we seldom have occasion to identify them specifically, even to ourselves. Thus, when confronted with groups of persons who evaluate differently, we are likely to think of them as strange, primitive, stubborn, inferior, or even badly motivated. Moreover, *unstated* values lie behind stated attitudes and beliefs. Indeed sometimes the speaker or actor may not be fully aware of these values and the degree to which they influence what is said or done.

3. Difficulties in intergroup or interpersonal communication are created by our *defenses against reorientation*. One such defense is selective perception: we see what we want to see, what we expect to see. Another is selective retention: we consciously retain only a very small fraction of our perceptual input— usually that in which we have a personal interest. For example, if someone we do not like says something with which we agree, we tend to remember the statement but to forget who said it.

4. Still another communication obstacle is the tendency *to place too much emphasis on the message*. All communication systems comprise a source, a channel, a message, and a receiver. The relationship between the source and the receiver merits much more attention than it ordinarily gets. This is the essence of the so-called credibility question. In a nutshell, *we believe people whom we trust*. The place, then, to begin establishing more effective communication between police and community is not with the message to be communicated, or even the system by which it is to be communicated. The place to begin is with existing attitudes between source and receiver: the police and community audiences. It is the quality of this relationship that will be decisive.[14]

Although in our society we rely heavily in communication upon spoken and written symbols, we also communicate significantly in many nonverbal, nonsymbolic ways. Under some circumstances, silence is communication. Color is communication: what, for example, do we mean by a "warm" color? Space communicates: for instance, how large is your office? Does it have a window? It is on the top floor? In many organizations, the importance of one's role may be determined by the "hierarchy of carpets." That is, the carpet becomes more decorative and plush the higher one is in the organizational hierarchy. Those lowest in the hierarchy typically have a tile floor!

People from other cultures attach different meanings to these things. "Culture-bound" is the common term, and it certainly generates communication problems. Assuming that everyone knows what I am talking about, and assuming that I know what others are talking about—without asking questions—can cause short-circuits in communication. Meanings are in people, not in the medium. A stick figure drawing is given meaning by whatever we ascribe to it; in itself, it is meaningless. And the meaning we ascribe to it comes from our individual experience. Refrain from saying "there are two sides to everything." The fact is that there are more than two. We are not born with communication skills; we *learn* them.[15]

Dialogue is the term recently employed to convey the real meaning of interpersonal and intergroup communication. For it is apparent that discussion does not always cast light on problems. The French scholar, Marcel Deschoux, has offered this explanation. In most discussions, each side enters the discussion "with guns loaded." Each insists that experience is all on their side. We ask others to wake up and see the truth, to "let the facts speak for themselves." The difficulty is, of course, that the facts do not speak. So we presume to speak for them. That our neighbor might possess some precious particle of the truth hardly occurs to us. We ask others only to accept our terms for a solution.

This is a combatant approach to problem solving. True dialogue has no chance. The aim is to vanquish others involved in the discussion, to disqualify them, even to embarrass and humiliate them and attack their personhood. Anything goes: smug statements, pretended indignation, mockery, shrugging of the shoulders, irony, plays on words, intended ambiguity, pomposity, inflammatory gestures, and the like. We gloat over reducing to silence someone with whom we started out to have a discussion. Forceful argument becomes more force than argument. Deschoux concludes:

> It is the spirit of peace that is the condition for authentic dialogue, War, attack, violence . . . have no place here. The essential thing is to accept fully the presence of someone else, and to open ourselves to his influence. What makes a dialogue is reciprocal presence and actions based on recognized equality. In both the action and the presence, there is mutual involvement. Dialogue is related to propaganda as love is to rape. For any authentic dialogue, therefore, there is work to be done first within ourselves. For it is, after all, *truth*—as Emerson insisted—that is the third party in dialogue.[16]

PREJUDICE

We have set the stage for a discussion of prejudice. It lurks in the very fabric of police and community relations, of interpersonal and intergroup relations more generally, and in every institution of society.

The late Louis Radelet once spoke to a group on the subject of prejudice. Following the talk, several listeners gathered around the speaker. One lady said: "That was a delightful speech. But we are fortunate not to have these problems in our town. We have no X, Y, or Z people here, and we probably never will have, because they know they wouldn't be welcome here!"

She had unknowingly made a power statement about the nature of prejudice. This is a subject about which a library full of books and articles has been written and countless speeches and exhortations have been delivered. The last of these is not in sight. One hesitates to be critical of high-minded evangelism, yet one may venture the observation that so much of the rhetoric about prejudice seems to deal with *other* people's prejudices rather than with one's own. Sometimes one wonders if there may not even be such a thing as prejudice against those whom one regards as prejudiced!

Definition.   Recall what we have said about the relationship between perception and attitudes. Prejudice is a kind of attitude. The word means "to prejudge." It is an attitude formulated with reference to objects, persons, groups, or values on the basis of limited information, association, or experience. Because prejudice is an attitude, it involves an *action* element (discrimination) and an *emotional* element (strong feelings about the object of prejudice). All attitudes are wholly *acquired*. We are not born with our prejudices, although various studies have indicated that prejudicial attitudes are acquired at an early age. One such study, of preschool-age children in Philadelphia, revealed that these subjects had already developed some clearcut we-and-they differentiations in their play patterns.[17]

Multiple Faces.   Prejudice is usually thought of in racial, religious, ethnic, age, or sexist terms. Not so common these days is the differentiation that was once made between a "city slicker" and a "hick" or "hayseed." Then there was the contrast drawn between the folks who lived "on the other side of the tracks," and those who lived "on the hill." There are "hillbillies," "Indian givers," and "skinheads." In industrial relations, there are epithets such as "union goons" and "titans." In police and community relations, it is "the man," "the pigs," "the freaks," "the jocks," and worse. And in other types of intergroup relationships, there are distinctive ways by which the parties brand each other as reprehensible, barbarian products of questionable parenthood. One speculates that even armchair psychiatrists may be working off their hostilities on the people whom they amateurishly diagnose. Ethnic jokes are still making the rounds, with the nationality shifting according to the teller, the listeners, and the circumstances: "I don't know if you like Polish jokes, but I heard one the other day . . ." The same is true with jokes about blondes, "red necks," and almost any other identifiable group about which a stereotype might be made.

The victims of prejudice become quite adept at recognizing behavior intended to mask prejudice. For example, there is the patronizing, condescending manner of those who begin a conversation with: "I'm not prejudiced. In fact, some of my best friends are ———, but. . . ." Or another version: "*You people* really are happier by yourselves, aren't you? You don't really want all this agitation and stirring things up." Or another: "Haven't I always taken good care of *you people* and looked out for you?" (This wording was particularly problematic for Independent Presidential Candidate Ross Perot in the 1992 Election Campaign.)

The many faces of prejudice suggest that racial differences are important chiefly because of cultural attitudes that make them important. Race is a symbol of one type of group differentiation, although anthropologists testify that scientifically, it is not a very significant differentiation. In some cultures, racial differences are simply disregarded. In American society, the ultimate goal may be expressed as making race no more important in sorting out people than whether they have freckles.

Prejudice and the Police.   Not surprisingly, there is evidence that the police, like many people, have treated people of diversity in a discriminatory manner. Some of this behavior is based on deep-rooted racial, ethnic, religious, or lifestyle prejudice developed through the socialization process of their lifetime. Other prejudices are developed through occupational socialization and are related to factors which

"Not surprisingly, there is evidence that the police, like many people, have treated people of diversity in a discriminatory manner."

are "policing-specific." For example, occupational experiences show that a significant number of persons with whom the police come into contact on official matters (other than traffic) are minorities. This is largely because a disproportionate number of minorities are of a lower socioeconomic status and reside in high crime areas, and consequently have more contact with the police through victimization, calls for service, and criminal arrests. Since this increased contact is with people who have "police problems," the officer tends to lose the perspective that many of the people are victims in need of general police service; they are not all criminals. Thus, the officer's decision-making process in dealing with diverse people is based on a fallacious, stereotypical correlation between race, ethnicity, or lifestyle and criminality.

One way police departments have tried to deal with stereotyping and prejudice is through periodic human relations, cultural diversity, or multicultural sensitivity training. These programs typically involve no more than a few hours of pre-service and in-service training during the course of an officer's career. There is, however, a major problem with this approach: the assumption that ingrained attitudes of prejudice can be changed with a few hours of police training on human relations. While the intent of such training programs is desirable, it must be recognized that these programs are not based on either sound theory or an operationally tested foundation. They are too commonly developed on premises which have not been scientifically examined and are frequently a reaction to some specific incident. The compounding effects of these problems are:

- Better human relations are typically not achieved
- Officer attitudes are not changed, and
- Cost-effectiveness of the organization is reduced because resources are wasted on ineffective training

Prejudice is an aversive attitude toward an individual or group because of certain characteristics which are deemed to be objectionable. This definition may not be comprehensive, but it illustrates a pervasive characteristic of prejudice. It is a generalized attitude or, as implied by its root word, prejudice is a "prejudgment." This prejudgment, which is typically observed in only a few people, is generalized (or stereotyped) to the entire group.

A great deal of prejudice is based simply on a lack of knowledge, or understanding without malice, per se, toward other persons or groups. What this means is that people learn, through socialization, different norms and values which are an individualistic social experience. Thus, any variance from these standards leads to the assumption that anything which is different is "incorrect." Therefore, those who have "different" values, beliefs, and behaviors are more likely to be discriminated against. This is similar to cultural conflict, but it exists at the interpersonal level rather than on an intergroup level.[18]

Although most research on prejudice focuses on the "recipient group," such as minorities, prejudice is also influenced by the personal characteristics of the assessor. This observation is supported by the author's research finding that the Hispanic male trait of *machismo* predisposed a prejudicial attitude toward females.[19] In these cases it was the characteristic of the assessor (i.e., Hispanic male) that precipitated the prejudice against women.

These findings infer that the understanding of prejudice must focus on an individual's characteristics as they interact with the perceived characteristics of the recipient group. Moreover, it appears that observations of minority separatism—skin color or language—may be viewed as a threat to the dominant society as perceived from the individual's socially defined position. If this is the case, then prejudice and discrimination may be a reactive mechanism to offset that threat.

The Development of Prejudice

An attitude is the cumulative product of the perception process. When phenomena are perceived, that perception is interpreted with a self-definition of "acceptability" and "nonacceptability" as a product of socialization. This process is universally applied by the individual, who assumes that his or her values and beliefs are "right" and any deviation from those attitudes is abnormal. Thus, humankind views phenomena selectively based on socialized perception. This process, by which we attach our individual values in order to determine the levels of acceptability of that which we observe, leads to prejudgment of people and behaviors. The outcome of this process is prejudice. Based on this developmental model, the earlier definition of prejudice may be modified by describing it as an emotionally based attitude about persons, objects, or locales founded on values which are universally applied to phenomena on the basis of one's own life experiences. It is important to understand that prejudice is an *attitude* which can predispose behavior.

The variability of a person's prejudicial attitudes is directly related to the manner in which the prejudice was acquired. The author, based on previous research, suggests that prejudice can be explained as a product of either normative or cognitive development. *Normative development* means that prejudice is the result of perceiving values which are inconsistent with our own, that is, value conflict. As the diversity of the values increases so does the intensity of the prejudice. This is a dynamic process in that a person's prejudice changes with his or her norms.

Cognitive development means that prejudice is learned through the direct teaching or observations of others, notably significant others. For example, if a child's parents are avid followers of the Ku Klux Klan, the child will directly learn prejudice against blacks. Occupational socialization will shape a person's attitudes in a like manner. For example, police training and the formal instruction of a Field Training Officer, as well as informal instruction, will have a significant influence on a police officer's attitudes and behaviors. Cognitive development is also value-laden, but it is less subtle than normative development and more difficult to change.

A description of prejudice is more precise when it is examined as part of a person's broader attitude. In this regard, the author suggests that there are four types of prejudice:

- *Sycophantic prejudice.* Prejudice shown toward another in exchange for friendship, acceptance, favors, or self-gratification. For example, a person endearing himself or herself to another for selfish reasons.
- *Homeostatic prejudice.* The desire to maintain behavior and attitudes in a manner consistent with one's social group standards; that is, maintenance of the social "steady state." Those who do not conform with the defined *status quo* will experience prejudice. As variance from the *status quo* increases, the intensity of the prejudice will increase. Peer pressure and peer acceptance are illustrations of this.
- *Normalized or institutionalized prejudice.* This occurs when custom, policy, or law discriminates against individuals or groups. The prejudicial attitude becomes a convention of institutional behavior without the sanction of moral legitimacy. The prejudices of the dominant social group become ingrained as a defined facet of acceptable behavior within organizations.
- *Phrenetic prejudice.* This is overt bigotry or frenzied and fanatical prejudice typically directed toward racial, ethnic, religious, lifestyle, and/or ideological minorities. In the former types of prejudice the motivations are largely value-laden. In phrenetic prejudice the motivation appears to be pathological hatred.

Tools. Stereotyping or overcategorization is one of the working tools of prejudice. It is a sweeping generalization regarding an entire group or category: Norwegians are giants, Englishmen lack of a sense of humor, police officers are corrupt, and so on. The stereotype may be viewed as "a picture in the head," "a shortcut for thought," or as "looking at all members of a group as if they were alike." Gordon Allport argued that a stereotype is not a category, but "often exists as a fixed mark of a category." "Police officers" is a category; "corrupt" is the stereotype. Stereotypes may or may not be based on a morsel of truth; they aid people in simplifying categories; they are used to justify hostility; and sometimes they serve as "projection screens for our personal conflict." Stereotypes are often socially supported—by the mass media, novels, short stories, newspaper items, movies, radio, and television.[20]

Jokes and anecdotes might also be added to the list of things that would fall flat without stereotypic props. Comedians have made much of this, particularly in lampooning their own group. Andrew Dice Clay's comments about women, Jeff Foxworthy's jokes about "red necks", and a wide array of comedians who use stereotypical affectations and language of minorities and gays all serve as illustrations. Some comedians defend lampooning in the name of humor, terming it "laughing at ourselves," "not taking ourselves too seriously." But as Mark Twain wrote: "'Tis said that a fishhook doesn't hurt a fish . . . but it wasn't a fish who said it."[21]

No aspect of prejudice has been more thoroughly researched than that pertaining to stereotypes. Gilbert, for example, worked with what he called the "fading effect" of stereotypes, years ago at Princeton. Hartley asked several groups of college students to mark, on a standard social-distance scale, their attitudes toward a large number of groups. He included the names of three groups that never existed. Those who revealed the most intolerant attitudes toward groups that do exist tended to display similarly intolerant attitudes toward the nonexistent groups. One conclusion was that prejudice does not necessarily require actual contact between groups. It may be based simply on contact with attitudes about groups.[22]

Another mechanism or tool of prejudice is called *projection*—more generally known as *scapegoating*. It means that we all tend to look for the causes of our failures outside ourselves; we blame the police officer for catching us speeding. *Projection* may be defined as "the tendency to attribute falsely to other people motives or traits that are our own, or that in some way explain or justify our own."[23] Scapegoating in itself is not an adequate theory to explain prejudice, but it is closely allied with stereotyping (for example, to hold that one did not secure a promotion because of the characteristic cunning of a certain group combines scapegoating and stereotyping).

Another tool of prejudice is rationalization: an accommodation of an attitude and an overgeneralized belief. Few people know the real reasons for their prejudicial attitudes. The reasons they invent are usually rationalizations, efforts to make the attitude seem plausible. All of us have trouble recognizing the difference between our *verbalized* reasons for behavior as we do toward others and the *real* reasons: the emotions from which the latter frequently spring may not be understood or acknowledged. Most of us are unaware of the psychological function that prejudice serves in our lives. It is a kind of crutch, to prop up our feelings of insecurity and inadequacy, and to serve as an outlet for feelings of frustration, aggression, and guilt. Nonetheless, such prejudices will guide conclusions, particularly about race, crime, and disorder.[24]

Causes. Prejudice has many causes. As with crime, no single theory of causation is adequate, and the causative factors are undoubtedly interactive. One school of thought regarding causation tends to emphasize *personality* factors. The focus is on the prejudiced person himself or herself. Another theory stresses *social structure* as an explanation for prejudice. The focus is on power arrangements in society. Prejudice is seen as an economic and political weapon. A third concept emphasizes the *cultural* causes of prejudice. Folkways nurture prejudice; social conformity motivates it. This theory of causation holds that prejudice is simply accepted, without challenge, as a cultural norm.[25] Any single prejudiced individual may reflect all the causes of prejudice because of the mutually reinforcing pattern of these factors.

Having identified three broad causes of prejudice, it may be well to touch on a few specific examples from the literature. Proponents of the personality theory of causation include some who stress that prejudice is a product of frustration. They argue that the blocking of goal-directed behavior frequently generates hostile impulses in the individual. This hostility may be directed toward self, or it may be "stored up" (repression), or it may be directed toward an innocent target (projection or displacement). Stereotyping, scapegoating, and rationalization are the tools, as we have noted. Personality factors are reflected, too, in the projection of impulses that we have trouble controlling in ourselves onto the supposed behavior of an out-group, for example, feelings about sex or the use of violence.

The whole gamut of repression, guilt, and projection is exemplified in the conversation-stopper: "Would you want your daughter to marry one of them?" Fear is at the base of it, fear that "one of them" will ask one's daughter, that the daughter might accept, or even that it might eventually be discovered that an inter-racial marriage is no great social catastrophe.

> It [the marriage issue] comprises a fierce fusion of sex attraction, sex repression, guilt, status superiority, occupational advantage, and anxiety. It is because intermarriage would symbolize the abolition of prejudice that it is so strenuously fought.[26]

The theory that personality is the cause of prejudice was given considerable impetus by *The Authoritarian Personality* studies. The central hypothesis of this research was that prejudice is often a symptom of a basic personality problem. The general finding was that prejudice is directly related to rigidity of outlook, to intolerance for ambiguity, to superstition, and to suggestibility and gullibility. Subsequent studies substantiated this theory.[27]

Such research suggests that prejudiced persons look for hierarchy in society. They like definite power arrangements, something predictable. They like authority and discipline; they tend to distrust other people and to see the world as a hazardous place.[28] They are the Archie Bunkers in our midst. But again, amateur diagnosticians can cause havoc by going about gleefully pointing to these behavior patterns in others and failing to see that their own behavior in so doing is questionable.

The effect of prejudice—for the prejudiced, and for the victims of it—has had the attention of numerous writers.[29] It is difficult to separate the causes of prejudice from its effects. What is a gain and what is a loss are questions tied to the values of the prejudiced, the values of the victims of prejudice, or the values of those who make a judgment, including those who write on the subject.

The preceding reference to those who prefer hierarchical, predictable, and definite power arrangements in society illustrates the point that theories of causation for prejudice blend together. So-called authoritarianism in personality pattern accommodates most easily to a highly ordered and orderly social structure. This suggests the second of the broad schools of thought regarding the causes of prejudice: the social structure emphasis. In this theory:

> The scale of hierarchy of prejudice in settled or stable times flows from the politically, economically, and socially strong and eminent down to lower hierarchies of the established order. . . . The most elaborate "race" superiority doctrines are products of already existing organizations of superiority-inferiority relationships and exploitations. The superiority doctrines have been the deliberate or unconscious standardizations of the powerful and prosperous groups at the top and not the ideas of the frustrated and deprived majority at the bottom.[30]

Prejudice exists, according to this theory of causation, because a person is convinced, deliberately or unconsciously, that he or she gains by it. The doctrinaire Marxist holds that the fundamental cause of prejudice is class conflict. In police and community relations, there appears to be an increasing tendency to believe that there can be no significant improvement, where such relationships are at their worst and most incendiary, unless and until there are basic changes in existing economic and political power arrangements. Dialogue and community organization are regarded by those of this belief as the preoccupations of "do-gooders," having little or no effect upon attitudes or behavior or upon aspects of the system that are thought to be unjust. Militancy even to the point of violence, massive voter registration drives, separatism as a strategy for identity and power and even increased multiculturalism in school curricula—these have become identifying characteristics of the power or social structure school of thought regarding prejudice. Its proponents are little affected by pleas to contain violence and to maintain law and order. Their retort is to call attention to how little is done to deal constructively with the human misery and injustice that precipitate violent behavior.

With reference to the school of thought that holds that prejudice has its roots mainly in the perpetuation of the cultural heritage, ten sociocultural conditions are offered that seem to encourage prejudice:

1. Heterogeneity in the population
2. Ease of vertical mobility, erratically distributed
3. Rapid social change with attendant anomie
4. Ignorance and barriers to communication
5. The relative density of minority group population
6. The existence of realistic rivalries and conflict
7. Exploitation sustaining important interests in the community
8. Sanctions given to aggressive scapegoating
9. Legend and tradition that sustain hostility
10. Unfavorable attitudes toward both assimilation and cultural pleuralism[31]

The overlapping of theories regarding the causes of prejudice is apparent in this listing. Moreover, their effects and dynamics have not changed over time.[32]

Self-Hatred.　The rejection of self, or of one's group identification, is a fascinating aspect of the study of prejudice. In our earlier discussion of self-image, we observed how the motivations for childhood behavior become increasingly social as the child grows. Gradually, children absorb into their own behavior and attitudinal motivations the values of the people around them. They learn from others what they should want to do, what they should want to be, and what is more (and less) important in life.

One does not go very far in studying motivation in human behavior without recognizing that anticipated reward figures prominently in it. A child who is motivated to do his or her best in school, to show some consideration for the interests and feelings of others, to postpone immediate satisfactions for larger and later satisfactions is a child who has experienced some rewards for such behavior. But what happens when a society more or less systematically cuts off parts of its population from the opportunity to know and share in the rewards for careful preparation and responsible work? Obviously, social motives for good behavior do not flourish in such circumstances. It is therefore fruitless to say: prove yourself a responsible, well-motivated individual, and opportunities will then materialize. Responsible motivations develop only in an environment in which these opportunities are present.

Self-rejection, then, is basically a question of identity. It bears on the answer to the query, who am I? If the answer comes back, "I am a nobody—and nobody cares," we may come to accept prejudice against ourselves as a fact of life, or prejudice against others as a way of dealing with our own sense of inadequacy. While there are many causes of prejudice—political, economic, social, and so on—deeply prejudiced people have often had a childhood filled with threat.[33] People who have difficulty in finding a satisfactory answer to the question, who am I? will sometimes take steps to establish who they are not. Among adolescents, this often takes the form of clannishness, of overidentification with a clique or gang. Forthwith, everything the gang does is good. The relationship to delinquency, crime, and other socially deviant behavior is evident. These are ways of lashing out or of striking back at others and at society in general, out of feelings of insecurity, frustration, hostility, bitterness, hopelessness, and ultimate despair.

The matter may be summarized in this way:

> To an important degree, prejudice is a way of trying to deal with a negative picture of one's self. The world seems threatening, because of early experiences filled with unpredictability and unhappiness. Members of another racial or nationality group were not the cause of a person's problems, but if he has been taught a prejudice, he may use it to control his own feelings of threat by blaming and attacking them. Prejudiced persons are often characterized by what psychiatrists call a weak ego. They are fearful of their own impulses; their picture of themselves, which has been reflected back to them by the behavior of others toward them, is an uncomplimentary one, and they are afraid of it. They may love their parents, but because their parents have given them a negative picture of themselves, they also hate them, but they cannot admit their hate. They repress it, and transfer it to the minority group against whom they are prejudiced. Because they are insecure, they become rigid-minded in an attempt to get some stability and predictability in life. Any suggestion that the relationship between the dominant group and the minority group might be changed is rigidly rejected.[34]

Social Conformity. We have said that common prejudice is cultivated by our desire for social acceptance. How strong is this influence? Various research experiments have been conducted to find out. The answer has been loud and clear: stronger even than self-preservation, under certain conditions. Paratrooper trainees jump off training towers under threat of being called "chicken" if they do not. It is a truism that society often encourages evil by legitimizing it, by condoning it through norms, laws, and folkways that sanction man's inhumanity to man.[35]

In one study, the idea was to discover the extent to which the subjects had an individual conscience, as against mechanically responding to commands from authority figures regardless of the morality of the commands. In the experiment, simulated electric shocks were administered to a subject who was really an accomplice of the experimenter. The actual subjects were third persons (taken singly) who were to administer shocks to the accomplice. Of course no electricity was actually transmitted: it was merely set up to appear so. The experimenter issued a series of commands to the accomplice. Each time the accomplice failed to comply with a command, the real subject was asked to administer a shock to the accomplice; each shock was apparently graduated in intensity, with 30 volts for the first button pushed, 60 for the second, 90 for the third—all the way to 330 volts, which was labeled: "Danger, severe shock." Each time a shock was administered, the accomplice (a gifted student of drama) screamed with increasing apparent pain. The real subject assumed that shock was actually occurring. It was startling to find that 65 percent of the real subjects, both students and adults, pushed all the buttons, obeying orders all the way. The subjects were all of middle-class background. Evidently, many people will condone evil when it is socially legitimized. This is sometimes called "the Eichmann syndrome."

None of us likes to be thought of as an oddball. If social pressures, particularly from people whom we wish to impress favorably, seem to condone a certain type of attitude or behavior, it is extremely difficult to rebel against the prevailing pattern. Indeed, there is often some reward for conforming and penalty for failure to conform. One frequently hears references to "dead heroes" or "unemployed crusaders." The pressures are often subtle, vicious, hard to prove, shrewdly and adroitly fabricated. If one speaks out in protest, he or she may be accused of being a lunatic or a troublemaker. One may be laughed at, or made to look ridiculous. Social heroes and heroines are often lonely, and sometimes pay a dreadful price for their heroism. This is evident in the policing culture when peer pressure exerts a significant influence on behavior. As mentioned in the previous chapter, an officer who does not succumb to this pressure and "rats" on a fellow officer will likely be quietly ostracized.

The Transition Between Prejudice and Discrimination

Prejudice evokes both attitudinal reactions, i.e., emotions and feelings, which may precipitate behavioral reactions, i.e., discrimination. If a person decides to *behave* in a manner consistent with their prejudice (attitude), there is discrimination. Conversely, if the disposition to behave *does not* come to fruition, there is no discrimination.

Based on the author's previous research, it is suggested that the characteristics of discrimination can surface at either the intragroup or intergroup level. With respect to policing, intragroup discrimination would occur within the police subculture. As examples these would include a white supervisor discriminating against a black subordinate (individual level), detectives discriminating against patrol officers (organizational level), or federal officers discriminating against municipal officers (social level). The permutations for such behaviors are geometric. However, a fundamental element remains consistent: there is the ever-present link of occupational culture, which binds the officers together as a cohesive group when confronted by or having to deal with "non-police" groups. Discrimination in the latter case would therefore occur as an intergroup phenomenon.

Intergroup discrimination by the police can take two forms. The first is *external discrimination*, the police (Group A) versus defined community collectives (Group B). The discrimination is based on an observed or perceived status as defined by either the normative or cognitive development of prejudice. The behavior focuses on defined demographics such as race, ethnicity, religion, age, sex, socioeconomic status, or sexual orientation.

The second form is *circumstantial discrimination*. Based on an officer's perception of another person's values, attitudes, and beliefs, the officer may discriminate. The perception is developed by the circumstances surrounding the encounter with the citizen and does not necessarily rely exclusively on demographic traits. Moreover, this form of behavior is the type to most likely surface as harassment. In its concept, circumstantial discrimination is closely akin to Van Maanen's three-point descriptive typology reformed to as, the "know-nothing, suspicious person, and asshole," scheme used by a police officer to classify an individual on perceived characteristics with the outcome of a police-citizen encounter to be defined by that perception.[36]

When examining police discrimination there is also a need to assess the role of the *victims of crime* and the *complaints against officers*. If crime victims are identifying minority groups members as criminals with greater frequency than whites, then the police are going to concentrate their enforcement efforts toward those minorities based on the victims' identifications. Similarly, we must consider the racial and ethnic composition of the community with respect to allegations of police discrimination. If most officers are white, and the preponderance of community members are black or Hispanic, any interaction between the police and the community may have the *appearance* of discrimination. In both cases, discriminatory actions may largely be perceptions rather than actual discrimination.

Some research suggests that the bulk of police prejudice is *not* an overt, malicious attitude toward racial and ethnic minorities.[37] Instead, other dynamics exist:

- Prejudice is based on our perception of others, which permits the classification of a person into an occupationally experienced category (e.g., "troublemaker," "suspect," "asshole," "transient," etc).
- While racial and ethnic prejudices exist, they are not any more pervasive among police officers than among other social or occupational groups. They are more critical, however, because of the authority we have vested in the police.
- Police discrimination is largely an unconscious phenomenon precipitated by homeostatic prejudice, which tends to be habitual behavior rather than an intentionally malicious act.
- Officers' discriminatory actions tend to be "good faith" beliefs that they are performing a legitimate police function, such as the "stop and frisk" of a person the officer defines as "suspicious," but are based on a stereotype, rather than intentional harassment of a minority group member.
- Police officers attempt to avoid occupational discrimination because of organizational, legal, and social sanctions. This avoidance is most likely not altruistic, but motivated by threat of punishment.
- Efforts by police administrators to control officer prejudice are largely ineffective. The initial focus of change should be toward behavioral change, i.e., avoiding discrimination, with long-term strategies for attitudinal change, i.e., obliterating prejudice.[38]

This last point has important implications for controlling police discrimination. If a police executive seeks to control this behavior, realistic remedies must be introduced. Most police efforts to minimize discrimination have attempted to accomplish this through the use of human relations training in the hope that academy instruction will change attitudes. Such a goal, however, is unrealistic in light of the evolutionary process by which attitudes are developed. It is simply unrealistic to attempt attitudinal changes during an academy training program. While behavioral change, e.g., discrimination, may be accomplished, it will probably not be lasting without a motivational influence that is either in the form of reward or punishment.

In a universal sense, changing prejudice and discrimination may occur only through education and legislation. While these may be philosophically acceptable remedies, they lack the pragmatic framework required in the organizational environment. Ultimately, change will rely on leadership employing stringent supervision, commitment to values, and the choice of highly qualified people as police officers.

MINORITY GROUPS

A society's favorite scapegoats are referred to as "minorities." What, exactly, is a minority group? This question may be answered by identifying six characteristics of a minority group:

1. Ease of identification of members of the group enables picking them out of a crowd on sight or through casual contact.
2. The out-group is defined by the slowness with which it is assimilated into the total population, that is, how long "difference" persists in the public mind.

3. The minority group's identity is fixed by the degree to which it exists in such numerical strength in a community that it irritates just by constant presence.
4. Minority groups' numbers and demands for recognition place them in a position of threatening the dominant group's notions of its own superior status, prior claim to desirable jobs, or unchallenged control of political affairs.
5. The intensity of dominant group reaction to the minority group can be measured by the history of emotional contact between the groups, flowing from such things as labor strikes, teenage gang outbursts, sensationalized crimes of violence involving members of minority groups, and even carry-over from Old World conflicts.
6. The number and kind of rumors that circulate are many and emphasize the criminality, sexual depravity, or diabolical plotting of the minority group.[39]

This characterization of a minority group blends the various schools of thought regarding the causes of prejudice. Most observers approach the determination of a minority group in terms of power. It has little to do with numerical considerations, as in electoral processes where the majority system is operative. The vital question is, where is the source of power? Who makes the decisions that matter? In these terms, the really significant relationship is that between the *powerful* and the *powerless*.

The literature suggests typical patterns of minority group reaction to their status:

1. Adjustment, adaptation, accommodation, repression, etc.
2. Submission, with consequent sacrifice of individuality, incentive, and ambition
3. Resistance, in various ways:
   a. to excel
   b. to repel
   c. to rebel[40]

What about the typical behavior patterns of the prejudiced? One model offers two types of classification, the first of which focuses on how individuals act out prejudice:

1. *Antilocution.* People tend to talk about their prejudices with like-minded others. Many people never go beyond this talk stage.
2. *Avoidance.* When a prejudice is more intense, people will go to considerable trouble to avoid contact with the group they dislike.
3. *Discrimination.* The prejudiced person makes detrimental distinctions of an active sort, i.e., Exclusion in employment, education, housing. Segregation is an institutionalized form of discrimination, enforced legally or by common custom. Obviously, it is a form of social stratification.
4. *Physical attack.* Under conditions of heightened emotion, prejudice may lead to violence or riots.
5. *Extermination.* Lynching, massacres, and genocide may occur.[41]

Another classification focuses on how conflict is handled:

1. *Repression.* Illustrated by the individual who says: "Now I'm not prejudiced, but . . ."
2. *Defensive rationalization.* To marshal "evidence" seemingly supportive of the prejudice. This is aided by selective perception.
3. *Compromise solutions.* Illustrated by *alternation*: turning prejudice on or off, depending on the situation, i.e., one kind of behavior in church, and another at a stag party.

4. *Integration*. True resolution beyond repression, rationalization, and compromise to embrace wholeness; to bring into common and equal membership.[42]

The sociological term for integration is *assimilation*. It is a process of blending one culture with another. Years ago, we spoke of America as a "melting pot." However, it is now recognized that this metaphor had an unfortunate connotation. It conveyed the idea of an eventual goal of *complete* assimilation, with the consequent disappearance of unique and distinctive cultural traits of the many peoples who compose our population. Insistent Americanization of our minorities, with the implication that their ways are unacceptable, has come to be recognized as an undesirable way to define the goal. The term "cultural pluralism" is now thought to be preferable; It is supposed to signify *unity in diversity*; however, its post influencing is still detested.

As we move toward the year 2000, an increasingly growing voice against prejudice is being heard from the gay-lesbian-bisexual community. "Homophobia" is the watchword for those who discriminate against gays and lesbians. This has become a complex social issue as a result of competing interests in domestic and civil rights law. Moreover, religious beliefs and governmental policy have become embroiled in the controversy. Opening of the military to gays, permitting legal recognition of gay marriages, hiring gay police officers, and teaching about gay lifestyles in school sex education classes are all issues that have resulted in strong emotional perspectives. The dynamics of prejudice directed toward homosexual men and women are very similar to those involving racial and ethnic minorities. Ironically, prejudices associated with sexual preference—on both sides of the issue—cross racial and ethnic lines.

We have been discussing *intergroup* prejudice and relations. What about *intragroup* prejudice and relations? Prejudice may be expressed by a minority group toward the dominant group, toward another minority group, or within the same minority group by some of its members toward other members. The latter is intragroup prejudice.

The prejudice of a minority group toward the dominant group is at least partly a matter of reciprocity and reaction, a result of dominant group prejudice and, at the same time, a reinforcing cause of the same. The prejudice of a minority group toward another minority group is, in part, displaced prejudice—using another minority group as a substitute target for hostilities—and in part a reciprocal prejudice.

The prejudice of a member of a minority group toward other members of the same group (shanty Irish versus lace-curtain Irish) is usually a matter primarily of social class differentiation, although other factors may contribute to it; for example, religious and political considerations (again, Irish versus Irish) or more subtle criteria of "acceptability." Among Puerto Ricans, for instance, there is a term, *troigaño*, which is used to refer to another Puerto Rican who is perceived as an acceptable prospective friend or spouse. The term has no relation to differences in skin pigmentation, religion, or family wealth. Apparently, it is a general term for a composite of likable personal characteristics.

RUMOR AND PREJUDICE

Rumor and prejudice are invariably companions.[43] Rumors explain, augment, and justify prejudices and hostilities. It has been said that no riot ever occurs without the aid of rumor.[44] Rumor enters into the pattern of violence at several stages:

1. Stories of the misdeeds of the hated out-group, accusing it of conspiring, plotting, storing up guns and ammunition, preying on women and children, and so on. Rumor is a kind of barometer of community tension. A rumor in itself may be the spark that ignites the powder keg: "Some white cop beat hell out of a black kid, cut his head open and all, because the kid wouldn't tell where he lives." In short order, this may become: "Ten white cops raided this hangout where some black kids were shooting craps, and six of the kids are in the hospital." A bit later, it might be: "A bunch of cops shot up the neighborhood and killed two black kids, looking for some dudes who knocked off a liquor store."

2. General and preliminary rumors build up to "marshalling" rumors, for example, "Something is going to happen tonight in the park by the river."

3. During a riot or disorder, rumors sustain the excitement—sometimes to a point of utter hallucination.[45]

A rumor is a verbal expression of hope, or fear, or of hate. Thus, the story that a promotional list has been posted on the bulletin board at the police station may engender hope. The story that "usually reliable sources" are predicting an earthquake may engender fear. The story that cops have gunned down three Hispanic teenagers may engender both *fear* and *hate*. And so on.

The discrediting of rumors is important, therefore, in controlling tension in the community. Recognizing this, communities where intergroup tensions are rife often establish tension control centers, the chief function of which is to provide factual information to the public in circumstances where rumors are rampant. Newspapers, radio and television stations, human relations agencies, and sometimes police departments have provided facilities and auspices for such centers. The exposure of rumors, in itself, probably does not change any deep-rooted prejudices. It does warn those of mild or negligible prejudice that wedge-driving rumors contribute substantially to community disruption by aggravating and sometimes triggering violence.[46]

HOSTILITY AND THREAT

Prejudice implies *hostility*—a sense of *threat*—with we-and-they differentiation at its base. "We" are better than "they" are (attitude), because we got here first (belief), or because the Bible says so (at least as we interpret it), or because they are "subhuman." If one grants the premise, for example, that "they" are "subhuman," prejudice and discriminatory behavior seem justified. Thus, humanity is arranged in an arbitrary hierarchy, to support one's perceptions, and one feels very strongly about it. So strongly, indeed, that one will not entertain even the possibility of compromise.

Just as with the self-image, in which the individual has a generalized self as well as multiple specific selves, each of us has both general and specific attitudes. A person has a general attitude or outlook toward life, toward the world in general, and toward other people. Terms such as introvert and extrovert, optimist and pessimist, dude and loser refer to such generalized attitudes. A person also has specific attitudes regarding specific things. Psychologists agree that a person who is prejudiced toward one group will usually be prejudiced toward other groups: it becomes a generalized pattern of thinking. Some peoples' entire lives are profoundly committed to values that take for granted, without any question, the innate inferiority of certain others.[47] This is particularly true with groups who blame others for their own limitations.

Our feelings of superiority about "our" group, as opposed to other groups, are called *ethnocentrism*. Oliver Wendell Holmes described it as the conviction that "the axis of the earth runs down the center of the Main Street of our town.[48] Around "our town," we build a high wall, so to speak, by our selective perceptions of reality. The pattern tends to be self-perpetuating: perceptual input is governed by determinations based on attitudes, beliefs, and values for which we will admit no challenge.

The hostile feelings that are the basis of prejudice tend to be most marked when directed against people who are seen to be socially nearest those harboring the prejudice. This implies the threat element. In the one hundred fifty years or so of the history of immigration to this country, there has been ample evidence of this. For example, during the significant growth of immigration in the early 1990s from both the Caribbean and the Pacific rim, hostilities and social pressure toward immigrants significantly increased. Philip Hauser observed, "The problem of hostility and distrust and prejudice was never the monopoly of any one group in our history. It was democratically available to everybody." He continued:

> As a matter of fact, one way to tell pretty much whether a people has yet made the grade in terms of disappearing into the community has been the attitude that they have toward the newest newcomer. Normally in our history, the 150 percent Americans were those who had not yet quite made the grade themselves—they had to have someone to look down upon. After they had been here long enough, they could relax and . . . become just 100 percenters.[49]

DEALING WITH PREJUDICE

The treatment of prejudice should be tailored to the particular causes in a particular situation. The literature on treatment is even more extensive than that on causes. The many civil rights and intergroup relations organizations in this country, though they work in different ways and with different philosophies, share the common purpose of combating prejudice and discrimination. Some are committed to broad educational-type programs, others to political action.

Because prejudice is so often thought of in intergroup relations terms, numerous programs foster rather far-reaching activity in community relations and community organization. National promotions, such as Brotherhood Week and Black History Week, have sought to make the overt expression of prejudice unpopular. Generally speaking, the trend in organizationally promoted programs has been to try to cope with prejudice as a group or societal problem. To emphasize that it basically comes down to the *individual* would seem to be too threatening, as so-called sensitivity training quickly establishes. It is also less threatening, as we noted earlier, to focus on the other fellow's prejudices, rather than on one's own.

Rather than attempting to catalog the various types of programs that have been undertaken to cope with prejudice, we will footnote several pertinent references where such information may be found.[50] Robert Merton has provided a useful classification of four types of persons, for each of whom a different treatment would be appropriate:

1. The unprejudiced nondiscriminator, or all-weather liberal. (Merton comments: "Beware of such liberals, 'who talk to themselves' about prejudice—[obviously, other people's]—and produce all sorts of false assumptions, e.g., that things are getting better—or worse, as the case may be. This is the fallacy of privatized solutions.")
2. The unprejudiced discriminator, or fair-weather liberal. Despite his own lack of prejudice, he will support discrimination if he sees it as profitable.
3. The prejudiced nondiscriminator, or fair-weather illiberal. This is the reluctant conformist, for example, the bigoted business person who profits from the trade of the

minority group. To convert him or her, discrimination must be made costly and painful.

4. The prejudiced discriminator, or all-weather illiberal. He believes that differential treatment is not discriminatory by discriminating. He is consistent in belief and practice. He may be moved toward Type 3 by legal and administrative controls, but such movement will be reluctant.[51]

Intergroup education in schools has been an important facet of antiprejudice programs for the past four decades in the United States, with organizations such as the National Conference of Christians and Jews and the Anti-Defamation League of B'nai B'rith in the vanguard.[52] Such "old line" organizations as the National Association for the Advancement of Colored People, the National Urban League, and the American Jewish Committee go on with their programs, as they have for more than half a century, without any sign that the reason for their existence is any less compelling than it was initially. In fact, there are ominous signs of growing prejudices and intergroup conflict in America today.

One of the most dynamic principles to emerge from intergroup relations programs during the past half-century holds that prejudice (unless deeply rooted in the personality of the individual) may be reduced by equal-status contact between majority and minority groups, in pursuit of common goals. The effect is greatly enhanced if this contact is sanctioned by institutional supports, and if it is of a sort that leads to the perception of common interests and humanity between members of the groups.[53] An assumption of this approach is that conflict of interest is inevitable in the free, pluralistic society. This point merits further analysis.

That interpersonal and intergroup conflict can and must be directed to constructive and positive ends, if a pluralistic society is to remain free, is a thought at first somewhat startling. The idea is that conflict is both inevitable and, in some measure, indispensable. Capitalism is based on it. So are the so-called checks and balances of political power—legislative, executive, judicial.

> The image of "order" in our culture is an image of peace and harmony. . . . These images of order create a culture where people are inexperienced and terribly frightened when conflict does break out. Because people try to exclude disorder from their daily lives, it seems as though the abyss is opening up whenever a difficult conflict arises. Because people do not know much about how to act in a situation of social conflict, they can only fear the worst.
>
> This naivete about disorder leads in two directions. It leads people to believe that conflicts not easily solved must inevitably escalate to a violent level and that, in order to prevent this, the forces of law and order must use preventive violence first.[54]

One institutional response to prejudice and conflict has been Affirmative Action. The intent of the concept is admirable: When two people are *equally qualified* for employment or promotion (or admission to college), the minority candidate would receive the appointment. Unfortunately, many employers applied the concept as a quota, missing the spirit of the plan. The results have been growing conflict and accusations—including lawsuits—of "reverse discrimination".

CONSTRUCTIVE CONFLICT

Many social analysts maintain that progress in dealing with social problems comes only as a result of tension-producing conflict. By this concept, wars and riots have an eventual, socially redeeming feature. Marxism has its roots in class conflict. Utopia is often built on ashes! Community organizers subscribing to the conflict resolution philosophy of the late Saul Alinsky induce cooperation among adversaries and clearly assume that conflict is potentially of great personal and social value. This theory contends that conflict prevents stagnation, stimulates interest and curiosity, and is a medium through which problems can be aired and solutions arrived at; it is the mainspring of personal and social change.

Various psychological theories are aimed at a utopia of conflict-free existence. But fortunately none of us has to face this prospect. The question is not how to eliminate or prevent conflict, but rather how to make it productive and how to prevent it from being destructive. Morton Deutsch speaks of *mutual gain* and *mutual satisfaction* for the parties to the conflict, not of conflict that is productive for the winner and destructive for the loser. His interest is in what he calls "impure conflict," that is, a mixture of cooperative and competitive elements.

What, he asks, is the difference between cooperative and competitive processes in conflict resolution? Concerning perception, Deutsch avers that a cooperative process tends to encourage the perception of similarities and common interests while minimizing the salience of differences. It stimulates a convergence or conformity of beliefs and values. A competitive process, on the other hand, tends to increase sensitivity to differences and threats, while minimizing the awareness of similarities.

Deutsch considers at length the conditions that give rise to either cooperative or competitive processes in conflict resolution, whether interpersonal or intergroup. Regarding the latter, of special interest in police and community relations, he suggests some general propositions:

1. Any attempt to introduce change in the existing mode of relationship between two parties is more likely to be accepted if each expects some net gain from the change than if either side expects that the other side will gain at its expense.
2. Conflict is more likely to be resolved by a competitive process when each of the parties in conflict is internally homogeneous but distinctly different from one another in such characteristics as class, race, religion, and political affiliation than when each is internally heterogeneous and they have overlapping characteristics.
3. The more coincidental conflicts there are in other areas between two parties, the less likely a conflict in any given area will be resolved cooperatively; the more cooperative relationships there are in other areas, the less likely it is that they will resolve a conflict in any area by a competitive process.
4. A competitive process of conflict resolution is less likely as the exchange of memberships between the groups increases.
5. The institutionalization and regulation of conflict increases the likelihood of a cooperative process of conflict resolution.
6. Conflict is more likely to be regulated effectively when the parties in conflict are each internally coherent and stable rather than disorganized or unstable.
7. Conflict is more likely to be regulated effectively when neither of the parties in conflict see the contest between them as a single contest in which defeat, if it occurs, would be total and irreversible with regard to a central value.
8. The anticipation of a hopeless outcome of conflict, such that nothing of value is preserved, makes the effective regulation of conflict less likely.
9. Conflict is less likely to be regulated effectively if the rules for engaging in conflict are seen to be biased, and thus themselves the subject of conflict.[55]

In intergroup conflict situations, what functions are performed by a third-party mediator? These are some that can be identified: helping to remove blocks and distortions in communication (translate and interpret); helping to reduce tension between the two sides by careful listening, blunting or narrowing the issue in conflict; reducing stereotypes; reducing the sense of threat; helping to establish norms for rational interaction; helping to determine what solutions are possible; helping to get the issue redefined so that different aspirations may be realized; helping to make a working agreement acceptable to the parties, for example, to establish conditions in which retreat is possible without loss of face; and helping to make the solution attractive and prestigious to interested audiences.

Clearly, there is a kind of science of conflict resolution; more accurately, conflict resolution is an extremely important facet of social psychology, with great relevance for police and community relations. In recent years, some big-city police agencies have moved away from the nomenclature of police-community relations, preferring to call it conflict management or crisis intervention. There is both an organizational strategy and an academically respectable philosophy behind this change. This discussion of the constructive possibilities in social conflict serves as a bridge to the next chapter.

QUESTIONS FOR DISCUSSION

1. Describe briefly the three behavioral processes of main interest to psychology.
2. Cite some basic principles regarding perception.
3. Explain the personality traits of rigidity and dogmatism.
4. Explain displacement or perceptual shift.
5. Explain how perception, attitudes, beliefs, and values are related.
6. Define prejudice and describe some of its common characteristics.
7. Distinguish between prejudice and discrimination.
8. Discuss the characteristics of a minority group and how these may contribute to police attitudes toward minority group members.
9. What is meant by ethnocentrism?
10. Explain how prejudice and rumor are related.

NOTES

1. This part of our discussion is based generally on two presentations made by Eugene L. Hartley to the National Institute on Police and Community Relations at Michigan State University in May 1961 and May 1965. Hartley was then head of the Department of Psychology at City College of New York.
2. The impact of these values on our decisions and attitudes is significant—it is the reason that personal and organizational change is so difficult.
3. These ideas are effectively presented in "Communications," an issue of *Kaiser Aluminum News*, house organ of the Kaiser Aluminum Company, vol. 23, no. 3, 1965. See "Points on Perception," in *The Police and Community: Studies*, Louis A. Radelet and Hoyt Coe Reed (Beverly Hills, CA.: Glencoe, 1973), pp. 69–79.
4. Milton Rokeach has been prominent among psychologists researching this matter. See, for example, his study *The Open and Closed Mind: Investigations into the Nature of Belief Systems and Personality Systems* (New York: Basic Books, 1960).
5. See, for example, George L. Kelling and Catherine M. Coles, *Fixing Broken Windows* (New York: Free Press, 1996.)
6. *Ibid.*
7. Arthur Niederhoffer, *Behind the Shield* (Garden City, NY: Anchor Books, 1969), pp. 182 ff.
8. Hans Toch, "A Note on Police 'Experience'," *Police* 11, no. 4 (1967): 89. Reprinted by permission of Charles C. Thomas, Publisher.
9. These ideas are adapted from Mildred Peters, "A Look at Ourselves: Elements of Misunderstanding," in *Police and Community Relations*, Brandstatter and Radelet, eds., pp. 58–61.
10. Jozef Cohen, *Sensation and Perception*, Eyewitness Series in Psychology (Chicago: Rand McNally, 1969), pp. 5–6.
11. See Larry Hoover, ed., *Program Evaluation* (Washington: Police Executive Research Forum, 1998).
12. For example, James J. Gibson contends, in his book *The Senses Considered as Perceptual Systems* (Boston: Houghton Mifflin, 1966), that sensory inputs generate sensations and also information about the exterior world. Changing information is not perception; only permanent, stable, invariant information is perception.

13. See Robert C. Trojanowicz and Bonnie Bucqueroux, *Toward Development of Meaningful and Effective Performance Evaluations* (East Lansing, MI: National Center for Community Policing, 1992); Gerald Whitaker, et al. See also Jack Greene and Ralph Taylor, "Community Based Policing and Foot Patrol: Issues of Theory and Evaluation," in *Community Policing*: *Rhetoric or Reality?* J. Greene and S. Mastrofski, eds. (New York: Praeger Press, 1988).

14. This summary is, in part, dependent on an article by William R. Carmack, "Practical Communication Tools for Group Involvement in Police-Community Programs," *Police Chief* 32, no. 3 (March 1965): 34–36.

15. Don Fabun, "Communications," op. cit., *Kaiser Aluminum News*.

16. Marcel Deschoux, *L'Homme et Son Prochain*, originally a lecture presented at the Eighth Congress of the Sociétés de Philosophie de Langue Français, held in Toulouse, ca. 1960 (Presses Universitaires de France).

17. Helen G. Trager and Marian Radke Yarrow, *They Learn What They Live*: *Prejudice in Young Children* (New York: Harper & Brothers, 1952).

18. David L. Carter, "Hispanic Interaction with the Criminal Justice System in Texas: Experiences, Attitudes, and Perceptions," *Journal of Criminal Justice*, 11:3, (1983) pp. 213–27.

19. Ibid.

20. Walter Lippmann, *Public Opinion* (New York: Harcourt, Brace, 1922), pp. 59 ff; Gordon W. Allport, *The Nature of Prejudice* (New York: Addison-Wesley Publishing, 1958), p. 158.

21. Samuel L. Clemens (Mark Twain), *The Writings of Mark Twain*, author's national ed. (New York: Harper & Brothers, 1917).

22. G. M. Gilbert, "Stereotype Persistence and Change Among College Students," *Journal of Abnormal and Social Psychology* 46 (1951): 245–54; Eugene L. Hartley, *Problems in Prejudice* (New York: King's Crown Press, 1946), p. 26.

23. Gordon W. Allport, *The Nature of Prejudice* (New York, Addison-Wesley, 1954 & 1958). p. 360. Reprinted as a Doubleday Anchor Book (Garden City, NY, n.d.). See also by the same author, *The ABC's of Scapegoating* (New York: Association Press, n.d.).

24. Ibid., Kelling and Coles.

25. Stuart H. Britt, *Social Psychology of Modern Life*, rev. ed. (New York: Rinehart, 1949). The three-way classification of the causes of prejudice used here is borrowed from Simpson and Yinger, *Racial and Cultural Minorities*.

26. Allport, *Nature of Prejudice*, p. 354. For a classic analysis of sexual factors in American race relations, see John Dollard, *Caste and Class in a Southern Town*

(New Haven, Conn.: Yale University Press, 1937); for a personal account, see Claude Brown, *Manchild in the Promised Land* (New York: Macmillan, 1965).

27. T. W. Adorno et al., *The Authoritarian Personality* (New York: Harper & Brothers, 1950); Milton Rokeach, *The Open and Closed Mind*: *Investigations into the Nature of Belief Systems and Personality Systems* (New York: Basic Books, 1960).

28. Allport, *Nature of Prejudice*, p. 382.

29. See Simpson and Yinger, *Racial and Cultural Minorities*; Dollard, *Caste and Class*; S. A. Fineberg, *Punishment Without Crime* (New York: Doubleday, 1949); *Emotional Aspects of School Desegregation*, Report No. 37 (New York: Group for the Advancement of Psychiatry, 1967).

30. Muzafer Sherif, *An Outline of Social Psychology* (New York: Harper & Row, 1968), p. 343. Reprinted by permission.

31. Allport, *Nature of Prejudice*, p. 233.

32. See Kelling and Coles, 1996.

33. Selma Hirsh, *The Fears Men Live By* (New York: Harper & Brothers, 1955), p. 110.

34. J. Milton Yinger, "Who Are We?" (Speech delivered to a Northern Ohio Institute of Police and Community Relations at Cleveland, Ohio, November 21, 1964). Reprinted by permission.

35. Milton Rokeach, "Police and Community—As Viewed by a Psychologist," in Brandstatter and Radelet, eds., *Police and Community Relations*, pp. 50–53.

36. John Van Maanen, "The Asshole," in *Policing*: *A View From the Street* Peter K. Manning and John Van Maanen, eds. (Santa Monica, CA: Goodyear Publishing Company, 1978).

37. David L. Carter, "Hispanic Perceptions of Police Performance," *Journal of Criminal Justice*, 13:6 (1985).

38. See Thomas Barker and David L. Carter, eds., *Police Deviance* (Cincinnati, OH: Anderson Publishing Company, 1991).

39. Adapted from Harold A. Lett, "A Look at Others: Minority Groups and Police-Community Relations," in *Police and Community Relations*, Brandstatter and Radelet, eds., pp. 123–24. Reprinted by permission.

40. Ibid., pp. 125–26. See also Simpson and Yinger, "The Consequences of Prejudice: Types of Adjustment to Prejudice and Discrimination," a chapter in *Racial and Cultural Minorities*.

41. Allport, *Nature of Prejudice*, pp. 14–15.

42. Ibid., pp. 316–21.

43. See "Points on Rumor," in *The Police and the Community*: *Studies*, Louis A. Radelet and Hoyt Coe Reed, (Beverly Hills, CA: Glencoe, 1973), pp. 92–98.

44. Gordon W. Allport and L. Postman, *The Psychology of Rumor* (New York: Henry Holt, 1947). See also E. T. Fitzgerald, "The Rumor Process and Its Effect on

Civil Disorders," *Police Chief* 38, no. 4 (April 1971): 16–32.

45. Graphically described by Alfred McClung Lee and Norman D. Humphrey in *Race Riot* (New York, Octagon Books, 1967).

46. Allport, *Nature of Prejudice*, pp. 61–63.

47. Gordon W. Allport, *ABC's of Scapegoating*, Freedom Pamphlet (New York: Anti-Defamation League of B'nai B'rith, 1948), p. 39.

48. Oliver Wendell Holmes, *The Autocrat of the Breakfast Table* (Boston: Houghton Mifflin, 1891), p. 126.

49. Philip M. Hauser, "Implications of Population Trends for Urban Communities" (Paper presented at an Institute on Metropolitan Problems, University of Wisconsin at Milwaukee, February 1, 1958).

50. See, for example, part 3 of Simpson and Yinger, *Racial and Cultural Minorities*. Also part 8 of Allport, *Nature of Prejudice*, and periodic reports and publications of the U.S. Commission on Civil Rights.

51. Robert K. Merton, in *Discrimination and National Welfare*, R. M. MacIver, ed. (New York: Harper & Row, 1949), p. 104. Reprinted by permission.

52. See, for example, various publications resulting from the Intergroup Education in Cooperating Schools project, sponsored by the American Council on Education in cooperation with the National Conference of Christians and Jews.

53. Allport, *Nature of Prejudice*, p. 267. A similar approach to community problem solving is called the normative sponsorship theory, developed by Christopher Sower of Michigan State University. See his *Community Involvement* (Glencoe, IL: Free Press, 1957); see also Robert C. Trojanowitz and Samuel L. Dixon, *Criminal Justice and the Community* (Englewood Cliffs, NJ: Prentice-Hall, 1974).

54. Richard Sennett, "The Cities: Fear and Hope," *New York Times* (October 20, 1970): 43. Copyright © 1970 by The New York Times Company. Reprinted by permission.

55. Morton Deutsch, *Conflict and Its Resolution*, Technical Report No. 1, National Science Foundation Grant No. G5–302 and Office of Naval Research Contract No. NONR–4294 (October 1965).

Chapter 11

POLICE, DEMOGRAPHY, AND MINORITY ISSUES

I t has been established that police roles in contemporary society include crime control, managing fear of crime, responding to problems of neighborhood decay, contributing to an enhanced quality of life, and helping to resolve a wide array of social problems. All of these roles involve both sociological and psychological dynamics. Moreover, the need for these roles is greater in urban areas, changes as the demographic characteristics of America change, and involves minorities disproportionately.

The interacting factors that contribute to the social milieu faced by the police tend to be interdependent, evolving with the fluid nature of our society. Many of the factors discussed in this chapter affect the police in subtle ways. All of the factors shape the characteristics of our communities and the attitudes of citizens who live there.

GROUP RELATIONSHIPS

Psychologists and sociologists, all interested in human behavior, differ in focus. The psychologist tends to concentrate on *individual* behavior, and the sociologist, on *group* behavior. Social psychology represents the blending of these disciplines. Distinctions among the behavioral and social sciences are thin, as may be illustrated by the question: Is human personality a social product? To deal with this question adequately, one would delve into sociology, psychology, anthropology, and biology. For our purposes, it is sufficient to say that, as our analysis shifts slightly, and perhaps imperceptibly, from psychological to sociological considerations, we shall focus somewhat more on group relationships.

Just as there are psychological processes in human behavior—perception, motivation, and learning—there are also social processes in group interaction. When two or more people meet, the ensuing interaction, if sustained to any extent, assumes some sort of pattern. This pattern of interaction is always erratic and inconsistent, but over a period of time, it can be plotted and given an identifying label. Many interpersonal or intergroup contacts do not go beyond small talk, if indeed that far. But often enough, there is some exchange of opinions and ideas, some sociability, and a dynamic interplay of personal and social forces is set into motion.[1]

Which pattern predominates in social interaction—cooperation or conflict? Complex systems of social theory have been built around this question, most holding that cooperation is the dominant social process, a few holding that competition and conflict are dominant. To what extent is it a "dog-eat-dog" world? If one takes an extreme position on this question, how does one explain that people do, in fact, live together in harmony, mutual aid, and trust? Civilization survives and thrives precisely because of helping and sharing and trusting. We seldom think about the extent in everyday life that individual self-monitoring prevails in holding society together. By and large, we trust the people—though we never met them—who build the structures and the automobiles and the aircraft, to the point of placing our lives in their hands, so to speak. More about this in a moment.

Social relations are, of course, an extension of individual human nature: a mixture of positive and negative, love and hate, good and bad, cooperation and conflict. Historians and anthropologists tell us that there are cultures and societies that have emphasized one far more than the other. Our society contains many examples of limited cooperation among competitors, which exemplifies the practical admixture of the processes.

SOCIAL PROCESSES

In the sociological sense, *competition* is the struggle for what are seen as desirable but limited goods: wealth, customers, or profits, prestige, jobs, promotions, parental affection, and the like. Prevailing cultural values establish what is regarded as desirable. People reared in a noncompetitive culture find it difficult to adjust to highly competitive conditions. Unregulated competition easily becomes destructive and takes unfair advantage of others. The U.S. airline industry is an example of this. After deregulation, a significant number of airlines became bankrupt, and many are in financial trouble. Thus there develops wide recognition of the need for ethical and legal controls. If the parties to the competitive process are of unequal strength, exploitation and injustice are likely results. Again, the ancient political question is asked: How much individual freedom, how much regulation, to achieve the common good?

Competition is usually impersonal and unconscious. It may exist without personal contacts. People may not be aware that what they acquire through competition may deprive someone else. But sometimes the scarcity of the good is only a *felt* scarcity, as with parental love, when theoretically there is no actual scarcity.

When competition becomes conscious and personal, it is *conflict*. Sometimes it is difficult to distinguish one from the other. Conflict may be internal, as in the concerns of the psychologist or psychiatrist. Sometimes internal conflict is caused by external forces; for example, in the case of value conflict. What sociologists call *contracultural conflict*, the clash between the values of *differing cultures*, illustrates this point: it may cause what has been called *personality disorganization*.[2] Then there is interpersonal conflict, for instance, when people disagree or in prolonged, close associations of human beings. There are also intergroup conflicts, as when groups compete for limited goods. And there are international conflicts, nation against nation.

Cooperation is a social process in which two or more persons or groups work together in mutual helpfulness. It exemplifies associative social interaction: the parties are inclined to want to work with one another, to join together, to gravitate toward each other, to pool their resources. The ultimate of this social process is love. Interaction may, on the other hand, cause individuals or groups to draw apart, a dissociative tendency. The ultimate of this is hate (war). Between these poles, there are varying degrees of association or dissociation.

Conflict tends to be an intermittent rather than a continuous social process. As we noted previously, conflict can be, often is, and must be turned to constructive, positive, cooperative ends. This is just another way of saying that individual behavior is sometimes cooperative, sometimes anything but cooperative. Social equilibrium, to the degree evidenced in a conflicting, pluralistic society, is often maintained through some form of *accommodation*. This is a process of limited cooperation—cooperation under certain conditions. *Coercion*, or forcing people to act contrary to their wishes, is the lowest level of accommodation. It is outward conformity in order to escape a penalty regarded as worse. Less demeaning to human dignity is *compromise*, a form of accommodation in which each of the conflicting parties agrees to give some ground and accept some losses. Conciliation, mediation, and arbitration are formalized types of compromise.

Toleration is a type of accommodation in which differences cannot be compromised, but are accepted for what they are, and are subordinated to cooperation and mutual participation. *Conversion* is the settlement of a conflict situation by a shifting of a person's beliefs, loyalties, or emotional attachments. ("If you can't lick 'em, join 'em!")

The difference between conversion, as a form of accommodation, and *assimilation* is slight. The latter is a process through which persons or groups acquire the habits and values of other persons or groups and become parts of a common system. It is a blending or fusion of two or more cultures. Anthropologists use the term *acculturation* to refer to this process. The sociological concept of *marginality* refers to persons who participate partly in two different cultures. They may not be fully accepted in either. (We particularly see this in young, second generation immigrants). Such ambivalence, when translated into behavior, makes one subject to conflicting role expectations that are not easily reconciled.

Amalgamation is a biological term, no longer much used, for the social process whereby races or cultures are merged through intermarriage. Biologically, amalgamation creates no problems. The principal barriers to it are culturally prescribed: ethnocentrism, caste, class, and the like. *Stratification* is the division of society into horizontal levels, evaluated and arranged hierarchically on the basis of such standards as learning, sex, occupation, age, effectiveness in war, social class, caste, race, and religion. The standards for stratification are many, often quite subtle, frequently pernicious and arbitrary, and are commonly imposed by law, public opinion, custom, and tradition.

Increasingly, we hear of cultural plurality or multi-culturalism. This refers to a renewed emphasis of various ethnic and racial groups to learn and stress the dynamics of their particular cultural roots rather than to view history and "mainstream" American culture as being singular—one which is predominantly based on Western European heritage. The multi-culturalism issue is causing significant social debate. Proponents claim that, in emphasizing the Eurocentrism, the predominantly white culture is discriminatory, robbing minorities of their cultural identity. Opponents to cultural plurality argue that American culture is a blend of many cultures, which has been shaped over the past three centuries. They argue that the multi-culturalism movement is divisive, not serving the best interests of the United States as a whole.

As in many arguments, both extremes represent some valid points, with reality occurring somewhere in the middle of the continuum. Increasingly, this conflict is having an effect on our social institutions—most evident currently is the growing move toward private ethnocentric schools. Resolving this conflict is difficult because neither one side nor the other is "right"; rather, each position is a belief. It is fueled, however, by historic discrimination against minorities. The thorny question that results asks, "Is it proper and/or in the best interest of American society to make changes in the current social and legal systems to mend past wrongs?" There is no easy answer.

The United States is said to be an open-class system. This means that shifting of social class (which is largely dependent on economic factors) is supposed to be possible for all. Many lower-class people may feel that the system is actually quasi-caste, which means that the chances of change are remote. Stratification in terms of social class is the point of departure for Marxism. Stratification in terms of gender is the point of departure for the women's movement. Stratification in terms of age is the point of departure for gerontology and activist senior citizen's groups such as the Gray Panthers. Some form and degree of stratification may be cause or effect of competition and conflict; in somewhat more subtle fashion, it may also be the result of accommodation. Whether it is a positive or negative social arrangement varies according to one's criteria.

SOCIAL CONTROL

Viewed as a whole, social interaction is based on the assumption that the participants will usually act rationally and predictably. It is, in this sense, coordinated. Another term for this is *social integration*. This goal is achieved through *social control*, a variety of techniques, means, and pressures by which society brings the behavior of individuals and groups into some measure of conformity. There are institutionalized or formal means of social control and noninstitutionalized, informal means. The law is an example of the former; public opinion, art, ceremony, praise, flattery, rewards, gossip, and ridicule are examples of the latter. The basic idea is to maintain behavior patterns within a certain range of acceptability, called "normality." What is acceptable or normal varies according to the culture, the circumstances, and the impact of social change. Advertising, propaganda, name calling, pressure groups, and lobbying are further examples of common social control mechanisms. A political campaign involves all of these and many more.

Law as a means of social control is, of course, of special interest in criminal justice. Law is the expressed will of the state and consists, in the United States, of the common law, statutory law, and court decisions. The prohibitions of law are an index of the range of behavior that the people of a democratic society will tolerate. Law is a society's ultimate weapon in controlling the conduct of its members. For law carries with it, as does any other mechanism of social control, a sanctionary element: rewards for conformity and penalties for deviance. Both the rewards and the penalties reflect shifting standards of public opinion, as evidenced in the history of penology.

In the matter of social integration, something should be said about a *social system*. This may be defined as an orderly arrangement of interrelated roles. An ordinary watch conveys the idea. Each part has a particular purpose and function contributing to the general purpose: to keep time. Any part may become dysfunctional, thereby making the "system" dysfunctional. The interrelationship of the parts determines whether the result is integration or disintegration.

Applying this simple concept to criminal justice, the police and other parts of the criminal justice system are, in fact, part of several social systems, and these systems overlap and conflict at certain points. Police are part of a political and governmental social system, and operate in interrelated roles with legislative, executive, and judicial branches of government. Within this system, as suggested earlier, the police are influenced in what they do and how they do it by federal, state, and local law-making bodies, by city managers and mayors, by corporation counsels and city planners, and by the courts. As an illustration of conflicts between interrelated social systems, what a state legislature may decide about some aspect of the treatment of offenders may not coincide with the judgment of professional corrections personnel. As another illustration, a number of state legislatures enacted mandatory arrest statutes for domestic violence, yet the research results are mixed regarding whether or not this is a viable policy.

A social system also includes familial, educational, political, religious, and economic institutions and the mass media. Clearly, what the police do and how they do it is influenced by this network of social institutions.

The police represent our society's institutional form of social control. Social control is possible to the degree that human behavior is in large measure predictable. Most people will conform to behavioral norms most of the time. Law defines the relationships of individuals and groups. Reactions to deviance constitute the core of social control.[3]

Not all behavior is controlled, in any society. Law is a very limited means of social control, tending to be overused for inappropriate purposes in solving all manner of social problems. We have seen an "explosion" in our civil courts because of an overreliance on the law to resolve conflicts between individuals. In the matter of sanctions for behavior deemed to be deviant, some are more severe than legal penalties—for example, ostracism, loss of a job or promotion, divorce, verbal abuse, excommunication, disinheritance, and boycott.

SOCIAL CHANGE AND SOCIAL CONTROL

Relatively few laws are needed in a culturally homogeneous society in which everyone respects the existing informal norms, especially if there is little spatial and social mobility. But in a complicated, technological, and culturally heterogeneous society, such as ours has become, many laws are required. The trend toward legal controls increases as basic institutional means of control, such as the family and religious bodies, diminish in influence. In short, social change and social control are intimately related. The study of police-community relations is, in one sense, the study of issues created by the effects of social change on the criminal justice aspects of social control.

Law observance is self-imposed social control—self-policing as we have called it. The question of whether people abide by the law because of consideration for others, or because of fear of penalties, has sparked debate down through time. Again, the various answers to this question are grounded in differing theories as to the nature of man and society. Plato, Machiavelli, and Hobbes were preoccupied with questions of social order and control. So, too, are many modern political and sociological theorists.

The prevalent anthropological view is that people mainly condition their behavior (and thus accept authority) in rational deference to social and moral considerations. Obviously, this means that all of us sometimes act for fear of consequences. But the more positive motivation usually prevails.[4]

> The communities with the highest level of social control are small, homogeneous, and stable . . . In such communities, social control is maintained to a very large extent by informal controls of public opinion, and there is little resort to formal controls such as legislation or the full-time appointment of people to law enforcement duties. . . . The small society with a simple technology can afford to have its "village idiot"; the large and complex one cannot, for many people would not recognize him and he might easily hurt himself or create havoc in the affairs of others. . . .[5]

Some police officers today imply that they have made a remarkable discovery when they say, "Being a cop today is a lot tougher than it used to be!" Yes, indeed, and the same is true for school teachers, the clergy, medical practitioners, social workers, and storekeepers. The police officer is an agent of society's system of social control. And social change, in many ways, has made the social control function infinitely more complicated than in the society of yesteryear. Among the obvious evidences are the computer revolution, high-speed communications and data transmissions, and the increased mobility of our society. But some of the marks of social change are less discernible, as for instance, in the matter of community relations.

THE COMMUNITY AND SOCIAL CONTROL

Social control is a function of the status of social relations in a given situation. Its level is determined by the kinds of social relationships that exist among individuals and groups who make up a society. This has been described in terms of relative social integration or disintegration. This is the essence of a functional definition of *community*. An ideal community is socially integrated; it encompasses a sharing of common experiences and a sense of belonging.

> The community that is our goal is a community of COMMON UNITY. It is a community which dignifies the right to be different. It is a community in which there is no penalty or sanction exacted upon those who protest. It is a community disposed in spirit to the dialogue. It is a decent society in the sense of Jacques Maritain's emphasis, viz., a society which helps people to be *persons*, i.e., "bearers of values." . . . the root of the idea of community is *participation*; not condescension, not patronage, not rescue, but the dignity and worth that men and women on any level of life experience when they are part of what is important to their fellows.[6]

Our main point here is to understand the relationship between social change and social control and to emphasize that social control and community relations are interdependent. As change occurs in people-to-people relations, in the transition from a simple to a complex society, social controls are more apt to be imposed by formal mechanisms.

When someone asks, "What has happened to community?" or declares, "We must restore a sense of community," it is well to keep in mind what we are talking about. A community is not simply a place or a location. It is not necessarily a small town or a big town. It can be rural, suburban, or urban.[7]

> In contrasting village society with the big industrial nation, it is difficult not to convey a false impression. Even in the small-scale stable society, consensus is never perfect; it is only relatively high. An even greater mistake would be to imply that consensus is absent under urban conditions. Certainly in some urban situations, the moral controls are weak and the formal organization has to impose strict penalties, but there are many basic issues—such as ideas of duty to kinsfolk, workmates, and neighbors—where popular morality remains powerful. In many urban residential neighborhoods, there is a very real sense of community, even if informal social controls are less extensive than in the village. Police [officers], being subconsciously aware of their dependence upon these mechanisms of control, prefer to work as peace officers and to see their role in these terms.[8]

This suggests that police officers in modern urban settings often play the umpire role, even to the functions of mediation and arbitration. So we are back again to "order maintenance," or work as "peace officers," and what others today have in mind when they refer to conflict management, preventive or proactive policing, crisis intervention, and the like.

POPULATION TRENDS

Social change has many meanings. We have referred to it in the sense of spatial and social mobility. Because this is so important with reference to the police officer's "umpire" function in social conflict, it merits further attention.

In the early 1900s social demographers predicted that the population of this country would reach a maximum of 165 million toward the end of the century, remain stationary for a time, and possibly decline thereafter. What has actually happened, of course, is that population passed the 165 million mark in 1955. In the 1990 census, the population was over 265 million and is estimated to reach 290 million by the year 2000. Whatever the reasons, including the post–World War II "baby boom," it is evident that the early estimates were significantly off.

There are several contemporary demographic trends that are of special interest to law enforcement. One is the increasing *concentration* of population in large cities—what the Bureau of the Census calls Metropolitan Statistical Areas (MSA's). An MSA is defined by the Census Bureau as a large population nucleus together with adjacent communities that have a high degree of social and economic integration with that nucleus. The Consolidated Metropolitan Statistical Area (CMSA) is an urbanized area with a central city or central population core, and contiguous closely settled territory, which, combined, have a total population of at least 50,000. Before 1983, the CMSA was called a Standard Metropolitan Statistical Area (SMSA) and was defined slightly differently, yet some comparisons of data trends may be made between the SMSA's and the CMSA's.

In the early 1900s, about 33 percent of our population lived in an MSA. By 1950, this had become 57 percent of the population living in 168 MSA's. By the 1970s, about 70 percent of the population lived in 220 MSA's, and in 1980, a little over 75 percent of the population lived in 275 MSA's. By the 1990 census, some 77 percent of the population lived in 283 Metropolitan Statistical Areas.[9]

This trend reflects increased urbanization in two ways. First, there is an increased *concentration* of the population in urban centers. Second, there is an increase in the number of these metropolitan centers. In some areas—Southern California; Dallas-Fort Worth, Texas; Miami-Dade County and Broward County, Florida; and the greater New York City area, to name a few—the metropolitan areas have become so geographically merged that the areas have been referred to as a "metroplex" or "megalopolis."

The implications for all government services, not just the police, are demanding. Concentrated population means not only growth, but also greater interpersonal and intergroup conflict, lower levels of communication within communities, and a greater probability for urban decay. This is by no means an unmanageable problem, but it is certainly challenging. With population growth and concentration, creativity in police service delivery and response to public concerns about crime and disorder are increasingly required.

The increase in MSA's also reflects greater decentralization of local governments. As more cities grow and geographically converge, the line between jurisdictions becomes increasingly difficult to discern. Since crime and the demand for police service do not respect governmental boundaries, this creates both operational and logistical problems for police agencies.

Another trend has to do with the *qualitative nature of the decentralization trend* in metropolitan areas. The suburbs of central cities tend to provide more desirable residential areas than the core city itself. Many American cities are seeing more affluent residents moving to suburban residential communities. Crime is lower, the quality of life is higher, and schools are often better funded in these communities. New businesses, particularly retail stores and consumer services, follow the residential trends to provide more convenience for their potential customers. This sociodemographic phenomenon has become known as "white flight" because the people following this mobility pattern tend to be white, while poorer people who must stay in the cities tend to be minorities.

Many times the poor cannot afford to buy their housing, so they must rent. Experience has shown that the quality of rental housing is frequently poor, contributing to a feeling of disenfranchisement from the community. When this occurs, the "signs of crime"—neighborhood deterioration—increases as do the associated problems of urban decay. The problem is exacerbated because the people and businesses who move away typically paid the most in taxes to support city services. The poor who remain cannot afford the taxes, yet they are the most frequent clients of police services and governmental assistance.

This general pattern has reached a point where vast sections of our inner cities have deteriorated to an ugly mix of small local business; old residences converted to dilapidated, multiple-family units; and heavy industry. As a result, urban renewal programs have flourished, notably beginning with President Lyndon Johnson's "Great Society," and continuing through to the "Weed and Seed" program of President Bush, and similar initiatives from President Clinton (notably the COPS agency.) The results of these programs have been mixed, but largely unsuccessful to any significant degree.

The cycle is difficult to break because it requires creativity and the commitment of government and citizens working together to change the characteristics of urban decay. This phenomenon strongly affects the police. With deteriorating neighborhoods come increases in crime as well as increased demand for police services. Yet, the police, too, are victims because budgets are reduced as a result of the fleeing tax base.

Residents, even transient ones, must first develop "ownership" in their community. By this we mean a social-psychological commitment to participate in community affairs and take action to help resolve community problems. Increasingly, community police officers are serving as the catalysts and organizers for these residents. The officers are taking ownership in the neighborhoods they police and are stimulating changes in attitudes. This type of leadership, that of changing attitudes and spurring community action, is a necessity before funding programs directed toward urban renewal will have a realistic opportunity to work.

Given the nature of the distribution of wealth in our society and the tendency of all people to congregate—socially and residentially—with others who share the same culture, race, language, and religion, the cycle of population migration contributes to continued segregation in our communities. In examining socio-demographic trends, there is little to suggest that this will change toward greater homogeneity. In fact, as noted previously, some evidence suggests a growth in multi-culturalism in the United States, which will likely lead to greater separation among races and ethnic groups. With the addition of substantial increases in immigration, notably from countries on the Pacific Rim, there is likely to be an increase in the number of distinct communities. Thus, it appears we are not experiencing increases of diversity *within* communities; instead the number of communities that are *diverse* is increasing. In essence, early demographic trends in the 1990s suggest increases in cultural and racial separation. These factors continue to challenge the ability of the police to respond to public demands and manage social conflict—particularly during a time when the police have received widespread negative attention associated with excessive force.

There are some additional demographic developments to be noted because of their bearing on people-to-people relations and on policing:[10]

- In looking at the year 2000, the biggest gains in population will occur in Florida, Georgia, and the Carolinas followed by California, Oregon, and Washington. The western migration will continue, but slow down compared with recent years.
- By 2000, the population is projected to be slightly over 278 million people and near 349 million by the year 2025.
- The number of persons aged 24 and younger will decline somewhat by 2000, yet the number of teenagers will remain about the same.
- "Baby boomers"—persons now aged 35 to 50—will be pushing toward retirement in 2000 and be well into retirement by 2025.
- A dramatic increase is occurring among people aged 75 and older as a result of advances in medical technology and overall better physical fitness among Americans.
- More than 49 million women will be in the workforce by the year 2000, an increase of nearly 11 percent over 1980 and 4 percent over 1990.
- The total number of households—separate living units of one person or more—will rise from slightly over 94 million in 1990 to nearly 106 million in 2000. The average household size will remain about the same—2.5 persons— or may even decrease somewhat as the number of single-person households increases from more than 25 million in 1990 to some 29 million in 2000.
- African-Americans will increase both in numbers and as a proportion of the population, giving them increased political and economic strength. In 1990, African-Americans constituted 12.4 percent of the population. By 2000, it is estimated that African-Americans will constitute 13.1 percent of the population and 14.6 percent by 2025.
- Asians constituted 3.5 percent of the population in 1990. In 2000, the Census Bureau estimates Asians will represent 4.3 percent (over 10 million) and 6.5 percent of the population in 2025.
- The U.S. Border Patrol apprehends roughly 900,000 people each year who try to enter the country illegally.
- The so-called "strip cities" or "metroplexes" continue to grow rapidly. Growth is particularly apparent in southern Arizona, south Florida, the Texas Gulf Coast, the Salt Lake Valley, and the Colorado Plateau. The explosive growth in Southern California is slowing notably.
- Slightly over 70 percent of America's population lives in a Metropolitan Statistical Area.
- African-Americans and Hispanics have made significant political gains over the last fifteen years, with all likelihood that their empowerment will grow along with their population.

Understanding the Trends[11]

For many Americans, the word "immigrant" evokes two vivid images: (1) the waves of Europeans flooding through Ellis Island in the early 1900s, and (2) the metaphor of America as a "melting pot" of cultures. These two visions often converge in a romanticized view of the past as a time when those "poor, hungry, huddled masses" from other countries required only a generation or two for their offspring to become full-fledged, empowered Americans. However, a closer look shows that many immigrant groups found the path to full assimilation into American society difficult. For many this meant struggling to find ways to blend in without losing their unique cultural identities.

Our past experiences forewarn us that race and ethnicity constitute a significant barrier to full participation in the American dream. In particular, the black experience has been unique from the beginning since most blacks, unlike European immigrants, did not come to the United States seeking freedom or greater opportunity, but were brought to this country as slaves. The lingering problem of racism still plays an undeniable role in preventing blacks from achieving full participation in the economic and social life of America.

Although legislation, court decisions, and policy changes have significantly reduced discrimination—at least institutional discrimination—*de facto* segregation persists in keeping many minorities trapped in decaying crime- and drug-riddled inner-city neighborhoods. The phenomenon of "white flight," discussed previously, only serves to aggravate the problem.

The role of race as an obstacle to full assimilation and participation is of obvious concern since almost one-half of all legal immigrants over the past decade have been Asians—Chinese, Filipino, Indian, Korean, Vietnamese, and Kampucheans (Cambodians)—and slightly more than one-third of our immigrants have been from Latin America. Though nine out of ten people of Hispanic ethnicity are "white," there is no doubt about the discrimination they face as a result of their ancestry. At the same time, only 12 percent of immigrants in the past decade have been Europeans.

Research by social demographers finds that as a result of cultural norms, birth rates of minorities will continue to be higher than whites. As a result, minorities still constitute an even larger percentage of young people in the United States in the future. Based on these trends, it is expected that by 2020 a majority of children in New Mexico, California, Texas, New York, Florida, and Louisiana will be black, Asian and Hispanic.

Power and wealth in America have traditionally been held by white males. Over the past three decades, in particular, both minorities and women have made significant gains, particularly in the business world. Yet women and minorities will earn significantly less than their white male counterparts—the "glass ceiling"—and they have yet to attain leadership roles in the public and private sectors in representative numbers.

Collectively, these changes evoke some interesting questions:

- Will the power and wealth of white males erode as their numbers decline or will they assert their influence to maintain their roles?
- Will minorities band together as a new coalition or splinter apart into competing social interests?
- Will growth of power among racial and ethnic minorities reduce strides made by women?
- Will there be changing "mainstream" attitudes and values and what impact will these have on policy and law?
- Are we embarking on a new era of tolerance and cooperation or a new era of hostility in which various groups will battle each other for status, money, and power?

The answers to those questions pose challenges to the police-community relationship.

The Challenge for Law Enforcement

With respect to the growing number of minorities and immigrants, the temptation to generalize from the few to the many is a particularly critical problem for police. Each immigrant, whether legal or illegal, and each minority group is not only part of a larger group but also an individual with unique gifts and faults.

Particularly where newcomers come together in poor neighborhoods with high crime rates, the police must guard against stereotyping, making assumptions about behavior of an entire group based on personal characteristics of an individual. Some new immigrants may be too timid to interact widely in their new communities, yet they may have to contact the police. Law enforcement, therefore, has a tremendous responsibility to respond to their needs equitably, professionally, and fairly. Many immigrants come from places where the police are feared, not respected, and the last thing they are likely to do is ask an officer for help or to share information with the officer. It is unreasonable to expect new immigrants to absorb the array of cultural and legal characteristics in a few years that Americans have learned over a lifetime.

Because police departments are a microcosm of society, it would be naive to assume that everyone who wears a uniform is free of bias. In addition, the statistics verify that there is link between race and the incidence of crime, but the mistake lies in seeing this as cause and effect. In a similar vein, research shows that African-Americans are arrested for violent crime at rates four times higher than their overall numbers would justify; Hispanics at rates two and one-half times what they should be. These factors lead both the police and public to make erroneous assumptions that African-Americans or Hispanics are "more criminal." In this regard, even more recent questions have arisen of whether institutional stereotypes have contributed to more arrests of minorities for crimes—notably drug arrests of African-Americans. Perhaps the increasing number of minority group members will help make American society more colorblind.

Each of these trends and demographic changes offers a challenge for law enforcement. They will shape the way law enforcement responds to the community as well as the types of services that will be provided. The police must become increasingly flexible, communicative, and sensitive to changing social needs. The characteristics of new police employees, training programs, and overall administrative philosophy of police executives are all factors that must respond to the changes in American society.

BLACKS IN THE METROPOLIS

Looking back over the past several decades, with particular reference to the relations between the police and the policed in American cities, special attention should be given to certain demographic facts regarding black citizens. In terms of numbers as well as for unique historical, sociological, and political reasons, blacks have figured most visibly in confrontations with the police in many urban localities. There are, of course, other minorities in such settings whose relations with the police have also been tense, but the police-black story is instructive, taken as a dramatic example of minorities in general.

Between 1790 and 1820, blacks made up about 20 percent of the population of the United States. By 1930, this proportion had dwindled to 10 percent of the total.

Today, it is estimated to be between 12 and 13 percent for the country as a whole. Just before the Civil War in 1860, 92 percent of all blacks in this country lived in the South. In 1910, 89 percent still lived there. The first large migratory wave of blacks from the South to the North occurred during World War I. The reasons were basically economic: the need for workers in northern war-production industries, and the virtual end of European immigration as a source of the needed employees.

World War II brought a similar internal migration of blacks, generally from rural to urban localities, and from the South to the North and West, although many blacks also moved to southern cities. The changing proportion of nonwhite to white residents of urban communities is evident in these figures: in 1940, 48 percent of the nonwhite population of the country and 57.5 percent of the white population was urban; by 1950, this had become 59 percent for each; by 1960, 70 percent of the white population was urban, as compared to 72 percent of the nonwhite population.[12] In 1997 those numbers were 80 percent and 83 percent, respectively.

How well prepared were black migrants for life in a metropolis? Within the span of a generation and a half, a people from a folk culture in the rural, economically depressed South were catapulted into metropolitan living. For immigrants to this country, the adjustment and adaptation process was one of assimilation, acculturation, or just plain "Americanization." But blacks were in a rather peculiar situation. Many have been Americans longer than many whites, but only in the past fifty years or so have they found themselves suddenly transplanted into the urban way of life. This process of adjustment has not been "Americanization" in the traditional sense, but rather one of urbanization or metropolitanization. Adapting to the demanding patterns of big-city living has been, for many blacks, a struggle against monumental disadvantages that few whites are able to comprehend.

There are those who ask, "Why can't they do what various immigrant groups did—lift themselves up and prove their worth by hard work and iron-willed determination?" Aside from the ethnocentric and chauvinistic implications of such a question, there are two points to keep in mind. One is that many Americans have inherited from their European cultural background a bias against people with darker skins. The other is that no other immigrant group coming to this country found itself shackled for almost 250 years by a highly institutionalized system of slavery. To be reminded of these considerations is still regarded in some quarters of our country, North and South, as highly inflammatory. But the question with which this paragraph began is equally inflammatory to black citizens.

In the matter of the urbanization problems of blacks, it is also pertinent to note that, as recently as 1950, the average schooling of blacks in the rural South was 4.8 years. This is below the level of functional literacy, the level at which a person can read a daily newspaper easily. Although this condition has been improved, it should be observed that the parents and grandparents of many black teenagers in the inner cities today have this level of formal education. Yet it should also be noted that during the 1970s, black youngsters in the nation's elementary and secondary schools made big strides in reading ability. For example, black low achievers in the fourth grade rose 8.4 percent during the decade, while white low achievers in the same grade scored 4.6 percent better.[13] By 1980 the median education level of blacks was 12 years, and it was 12.8 years in 1990.

Chicago is typical of what has happened as a result of population shift. Between 1950 and 1960, about 600,000 whites left the central city and moved to suburbia. During that decade, the central city's net white population loss was 400,000, because there was an excess of 200,000 white births over deaths. The black population increased by about 350,000 in the same period, from slightly more than 500,000 to almost 850,000. The black population of Chicago was 30,000 in 1900; by 1920, it was 120,000. The nonwhite population of Chicago quadrupled between 1900 and 1920, increased by more than 28 times between 1900 and 1960, and by more than 7 times between 1920 and 1960. By 1960, blacks constituted 14 percent of the population in the six counties of northeastern Illinois and 23 percent of the population of the city of Chicago.[14] The 1990 census showed that Chicago has lost 10 percent of its total population since 1980, with 20.7 percent of the city's population being black. The state of Illinois increased by 9 percent in total population during the decade.

THE PLIGHT OF OUR CITIES

We have noted a number of population trends that affect the social environment, as we put it, of intergroup relations, including police and community relations. To this should be added some description of what is happening to our cities, on the premise that police-citizen encounters most often occur in urban settings. Some urbanologists are saying that no amount of money can possibly solve the economic woes of our cities. Instead, the foundation must lie in a philosophy for urban renewal.

Perhaps the most overt symbol of problems in our cities was found in the aftermath of the 1992 riot in south central Los Angeles. Residents of the area brought to light the problems of poverty, limited job opportunities, physical and social decay, high crime and disorder, as well as a plethora of other social and economic problems. The residents felt they had been abandoned by city government and ignored by the criminal justice system. Ironically, the riot destroyed business and residences of the area which, in turn, created more chaos and fewer opportunities.

In an effort to repair the damage and strengthen the social fabric of this area, a private, nonprofit initiative was created named "Rebuild LA." The purpose of Rebuild LA was to draw the community together, using the resources of private businesses and professionals (both of which donated time and money) along with residents and business owners in south central Los Angeles to rebuild the community. The initiative was started within days after the riot. Yet, it was all but abandoned by mid-1993, with its chairperson, Peter Uberroth, resigning because of frustration.

Rebuild LA's lack of success does not appear to be a problem of resources or technical competence. Rather, changes in the physical and economic structure of the community were attempted without establishing clear support for the *social infrastructure* of the community. If commitment, trust, and input are not developed among those living in the community, there is little hope that meaningful change can occur. The people must develop an innate sense of "ownership," of community values looking at the best interests of the whole, not just oneself—or, as Mr. Spock from Star Trek would say, "The needs of the many outweigh the needs of the one." Without the sense of ownership and desire to build a better quality of community life, purely physical efforts will have little success.

This phenomenon is further illustrated in public housing projects throughout the United States. Many public housing facilities rapidly fall into disrepair and decay after a short amount of time. Crime increases and disorder is apparent. It is not the demographic characteristics of the people who live in these projects that inherently cause the problem; rather it is the philosophy by which these projects are managed. A manager of one public housing complex in a midwestern city told the author that his job was to "provide a warehouse for the poor." He further said that, ". . . these people don't care about the way they live, so why should I?"

His method of repairing damage was to use lots of concrete and metal "because these couldn't be broken." This man's attitude ignored the positive strides that

FOCUS 11.1

TOOLS TO INVOLVE PARENTS IN GANG PREVENTION

Because of increased concern about the growth of gangs, the U.S. Bureau of Justice Assistance funded a joint project to develop a mechanism to help minimize the chance of a youth joining a gang. The *National Crime Prevention Council, Boys and Girls Clubs of America*, and the *Police Executive Research Forum* jointly developed a kit of reproducible materials, which provides informational and educational tools to help communities with emerging gang problems enlist parents in:

- Preventing individual children from joining gangs
- Preventing gangs from gaining a foothold in a community, and/or
- Helping to drive gangs out of a community

The kit's messages are based on the knowledge, experience, and judgment of law enforcement and other criminal justice personnel, youth workers, youth program staff, concerned parents, and others experienced in working to prevent or rid the community of gangs. The kit contains three sections of information. The first is directed toward parents, with two publications entitled *1-2-3: A Parent's Guide to Gang Prevention* and *Parents Today*. The first portion presents the essential points and concepts, such as tips on recognizing gang involvement, more effective parenting as a prevention strategy, and working with other parents against gang penetration of the community. *Parents Today* provides general information on parenting, gang prevention, dealing with gang threats, and working cooperatively with others to deal with a gang problem.

The second section of the kit is directed toward younger children. It has a series of materials in a workbook called *Growing Up Strong: McGruff Helps Kids Get Decision Power*, which can be used in a classroom setting, in a youth center, or in other settings, particularly when parents and children can work together. The illustrated book is designed to help children ages five through eight learn about internal strength, sound decision-making skills, their unique value as individuals, and ways to resist negative peer pressure.

The third section is guided toward older children, ages nine to twelve. Included are educationally based paper and pencil games, a word search, crossword puzzle, and mini-posters. The kit also contains information on enlisting media support as well as key national resources where additional information and assistance can be obtained to deal with gang prevention.

For more information, ask for *Tools to Involve Parents in Gang Prevention*, National Crime Prevention Council, 1700 K Street, N.W., Second Floor, Washington, DC 20006-3817, telephone (202) 466-6272.

could have been made by building a consensus among residents about the behavior and values that would be tolerated in the housing project. Managing this way creates ownership, which, in turn, establishes a social-psychological investment in the community that leads to commitment and action. Exemplary programs at public housing projects in St. Louis and Chicago have shown that this approach works. Success, however, requires time and effort, commodities many are not willing to readily give.

Generally speaking our major core cities are experiencing increased taxes, poorer public services, deteriorating schools, higher crime, a reduced tax base, and physical decay of buildings and other elements of the infrastructure. If the trend is not reversed, a city—or at least neighborhoods—will die. East St. Louis, Illinois and Benton Harbor, Michigan illustrate this all too well. New York City; Newark, New Jersey; and Detroit, Michigan also serve as examples where these problems are taking their toll on city resources and citizens' emotions.

What do all of these things have to do with police and community relations? It has increasingly become a police responsibility to organize and stimulate the community toward change. Community policing attempts, among other things, to develop that sense of ownership and facilitate activities in support of community desires. The plight of our cities and the particular ways in which people are caught up in problems beyond their individual control directly affect the dynamics of what occurs in police-citizen interaction.

POVERTY AS A SOCIAL FORCE

Poverty is everywhere endemic to minority group status. The 1960s were marked by a declaration of war on poverty at the highest executive and legislative levels in this country. It became evident, however, that the war was declared without sufficient education as to the nature of the enemy. Poverty, like many social problems, suffers from many myths and misconception. Among them are:

- The myth that poverty is inevitable.
- The myth that poverty is simply a matter of being without money or other resources. This leads to the faulty conclusion that poor people are "just like us," except that they lack resources. Of course there are people who are temporarily "down on their luck." But the *culture of poverty* is much more complex. Moreover, the discount-store phenomenon operates on the assumption that the poor do have some resources. And one may question that some of the poor really want to be "like us."
- The myth that the poor are blacks, and that blacks are poor. This entire concept is false. Blacks belong to many classifications. Twenty-five percent of the population of this country are persistently poor, so obviously many are white. However, having said this, one may proceed to assert that there are many blacks in poverty—also [Native Americans], Southern Appalachian migrants, [Hispanics], Puerto Ricans, and even some white police officers. No one group should be used as a model for the whole.
- The myth that the poor are without culture. One thinks of such expressions as "the culturally deprived," "the culturally disadvantaged," etc. This is patent nonsense. The simple fact is that the poor live in a *different* culture. The Navajos of New Mexico are poor, but no one would suggest that they are "culture-poor."
- The myth that poverty breeds crime. Laws define crimes, and laws are made by dominant groups and provide maximum protection for those who make them. Even crime statistics are largely culturally derived. Where there is an apparent coincidence of crime and poverty, one must look beyond poverty for the cause of crime.[15]

Other, minor myths about the poor include that poverty causes family disruption; that the poor are dependent in spirit as well as in sustenance; that the poor are inarticulate.

What are some of the significant truths about poverty? Some have been implied above.

> Poverty is more of a culture or subculture than it is a social class. Identifying the poor with the lower class is similar to identifying the upper class with the rich. The difficulty is that a central middle-class concern, that is economic resources, is taken as the measure of two groups for which it is not a central concern.

> Poverty is socially invisible. It is overwhelmingly taken for granted as part of the scenery. Poor people tend to be seen as picturesque natives, living in the only way they know.

> Poverty means institutional nonparticipation. The poor do not make our institutions and they do not manage them, but they are subject to them. They are expected to live by a moral code established by people with quite a different experience. To be poor is to live in someone else's world.

> Poverty means immediacy. To be poor, as it is said, "to live from hand to mouth." The poor are not much concerned with the long ago, and even less with the distant future. Thus, the values of the poor are often difficult for others to understand. If fortune smiles, the poor man buys his automobile or television—today. Tomorrow will take care of itself; it can't be any worse than yesterday. To be poor is to live continuously in the now.

> To be poor is to have identity. Poverty has a place for everyone, and everyone is in his place. The feeling of lack of identity, of dislocation, of disassociation, of alienation is not a product simply of being poor. The poor know who they are; as with crime, we must look beyond poverty for the causes of disaffection.

Studying the poor in the United States by following roughly 5,000 families over a period from 1968 to 1975, the University of Michigan's Institute for Social Research has reported some interesting findings, based on the official poverty definition:[16]

- Education is the single, most important factor in determining whether a family is poor.
- Disintegration of families is a major factor in the movement of people into poverty.
- Rural residents run a bigger risk of being poor than city dwellers.
- Blacks are much more likely than whites to be poor.
- Relatively few "hard-core poor" stay that way year after year.

The study reveals that one of every eleven American families may be rated as poor in any one year, but 25 percent remain poor over a five-year period. Whites benefit from schooling more than blacks. Unemployment itself is not a major cause of the poverty problem, according to these researchers. It does, however, compound the problem. A family headed by a female is more than twice as likely to be poor, and stay poor, as one headed by a male. Besides being less educated and earning less than whites as a group, blacks more often are poverty-stricken because black families tend to have more children and more families are headed by single women, according to the study.

The police are, of course, not to blame for poverty. But there is little question that the police deal more continuously with various behavioral, physical, mental, health, housing, and welfare phenomena related to poverty than perhaps any other occupational group, including social workers. Indeed, it is this side of routine police work in our cities that accounts for so much of the job as to solidify the impression that police work is mainly social work. Whatever the proper name for this may be, it certainly requires special qualities of professionalism and personhood. If one test of the character of a nation is in how it cares for its needy, police officers carry a major share of the burden of proof. As we enter the twenty-first century, poverty will remain in our society—and police officers will remain responsible for many of the behavioral consequences of it.

THE POLICE AND MINORITIES: A CLOSER LOOK

During the past forty-five years or so, every social institution of our society has felt the effects of the Civil Rights movement. In the political arena, the movement has focused on changing the balance of power and the status quo, restructuring "the establishment," increasing voter registration and exercise of the vote, and the like. Black and ethnic businesses attest to the effects of the movement in economic institutions, and so does the emergence of tougher equal opportunity laws and of affirmative action in personnel administration.

With religious institutions, the effects have been spotty and erratic. Some religious bodies have earnestly endeavored to take a position in the vanguard of social change, while others have continued to debate the relative merits of admitting minority members, or have hidden behind a facade of ostensible openness in policy while actually discouraging the participation of "certain people." Suburban churches have been especially adept at playing this game. It is fair to say in general terms, however, that religious institutions in this country, especially in the past decade, have become markedly more cosmopolitan in policy and practice.

Educational institutions have been interested in intercultural or intergroup matters since the early 1940s, when the first specialized human relations workshops for teachers were held, coinciding with the earliest police training programs with a similar focus. Schools and colleges have been in the vortex of the Civil Rights movement during the past fifty years. Their involvement has ranged from the enactment of fair educational practices legislation to power battles regarding administrative control, curriculum matters, and busing.

Music and the arts, organized sports and recreation, and other leisure-time institutions also have had an uneven record relative to civil rights, with some of these demonstrating exemplary leadership for change while others are still engaged in conflict or are striving to duck the issue. As late as 1993, the Rev. Jesse Jackson met with major league baseball owners about issues of discrimination against blacks in professional baseball management.

Voluntary civic-social organizations also have had a checkered record regarding civil-rights questions; many of them skirt and dodge such matters at all costs. Lively arguments still take place as to whether one should or should not join a club or society where one can be "among one's friends" and "with people of similar interests." Perhaps most pernicious of all these days, in questions of racial justice, is the tendency to deny racial or ethnic connotations to positions taken on such issues as busing, affirmative action, and red-lining in housing. Closely akin to this is the position that Senator Daniel Patrick Moynihan has called "benign neglect": simply ignoring problems and, indeed, referring to those not inclined to share this posture as "trouble-makers," "dewy-eyed liberals," and the like. The ways and means of prejudice and discrimination have become more subtle and more ingenious as the law and prevailing public opinion have made overt expression illegal or unpopular. But these attitudes are still in the fabric of our social institutions.

The Police and the Civil Rights Movement

Police work and other aspects of the administration of justice have also been vitally affected by what has happened in civil rights and race relations. Some would contend that the police have been particularly affected, but this conclusion may be the result of measuring the effects in terms of street encounters. The Civil Rights movement contributed substantially to widening the opportunities for police officers to demonstrate creditable professional behavior—or its opposite.

For many nonwhites in the inner city, the white world remains rather remote and inaccessible, but traditionally the white police officer has made his or her presence felt in neighborhoods where all or most of the residents were minority members. The officer has been visible and is *there*, but frequently perceived as an "occupying force." Therefore, the police officer takes the brunt of frustrations, anger, hostility, and bitterness. The officer is seen as a symbolic agent of injustice, never to be trusted under any circumstances.

Evidences (and there are actually many) of compassionate, humanistic policing tend to be dismissed as rare exceptions. The apparent preoccupation of civil rights organizations with police conduct stems from the frequency of intimate contact between the police and minorities. There is an underlying implication that, if the police and the criminal justice system cannot adhere to the equal protection principle, it is fruitless to expect it in employment, education, housing, and so on.

In short, the police officer is a convenient target of the displaced hostility of minorities, however stereotypic the image may be. Much of the criticism directed against the police by minorities is really intended for the larger white power structure, but is displaced to a more readily available, identifiable mark. This explains the sometimes inflammatory nature of minority complaints against the police. As with any stereotype, there are fragments of truth and, often enough, actual experiences to bolster it. There *are* some corrupt, brutal, inhuman police officers, and there are memories (or stories that are believed) of harrowing experiences with such officers.

The police tend to see themselves as caught in the middle—trying to protect the system while garnering the trust and support of minorities. A factor that tends to warp many big-city police officers' outlook on questions of minority rights is the difficult and dangerous job of trying to contain what is erroneously referred to as "black crime," or "Hispanic crime," or "fill-in-the-minority crime." There is, of course, no such thing. There are crime-breeding social conditions that happen to predominate in areas where blacks and other minorities live in great numbers. The elimination of these social cesspools is one way of easing crime problems.

In the inner city, some minorities are involved in criminal and peace-threatening behavior, and it is easy for a white officer to conclude that minorities and trouble are irrevocably linked. This racial theory of crime causation has long since been rejected by criminologists. But the police officer on a ghetto beat has his or her own ways of identifying those who give the officer a bad time. If most of the people living in the neighborhood are black or are otherwise ethnically identifiable, it follows—in the officer's way of thinking—that the source of trouble is that particular group. As an agent of a bureaucratic organization that tends, as with all bureaucracies, to deal with people and situations stereotypically, the officer comes to associate problems with skin color or cultural differences.

The stereotype of the white police officer, is seen simply as the visible, ever-present enforcer of "white man's justice." On the other hand, the officer's perception of the people of the ghetto is often just as stereotyped, as we have noted. It is a picture-in-the-head embossed by racial and ethnic explanations for crime and other deviant deportment. The perspective on both sides is narrow and limited. The mutually reinforcing character of this dual stereotyping is central to understanding the police-minority relationship in typical big-city circumstances. It is further reinforced by the fact that the police officer seldom resides in the area of his or her beat. Officer and civilian may know each other, even well, and yet the relationship never goes beyond the superficial, the mutually distrustful.

Further, the attitudes are, typically, self-fulfilling. The reciprocal perceptions are selective, shutting out evidence contrary to the stereotypic images. Savagery in stereotype seeks and finds savagery to support itself. On either side, attitudes are justified on the ground that "you can't afford to take a chance. It's better to be wrong a hundred times than dead once."

ABUSE OF AUTHORITY AND EXCESSIVE FORCE

The most emotion-packed complaint directed against the police is that of "brutality," but little thought is given to its meaning. The assumption is that everyone knows what it means and that everyone attaches the same meaning to it. Stated another way, people cannot define it, but "they know it when they see it." As will be illustrated, this bit of conventional wisdom is often not valid.

As noted throughout this book, the spectacle of excessive force by the police has been omnipresent in the past few years. Even the stoic British constables, known for their subtle, caring, nonaggressive nature, have been criticized throughout England and Wales for use of excessive force. The British Bobbies blame increases in violence, increased assaults against officers, and general drunken "hooliganism" as the reason for their more physical encounters with the Queen's subjects. In the United States, officers also blame increased violence as well as a greater tendency for people to disrespect authority and resist police efforts in doing their job. Civil rights and community activists in both the United States and United Kingdom say the reason for cases of excessive force is racism and discrimination. There is some degree of truth in all of these observations, but the fact remains that the problem is much more complicated than any of these straightforward "conclusions" indicate. To oversimplify the problem will lead to ineffective solutions and, in the long run, greater problems.

In situations where excessive force charges are leveled against the police, there is frequently a communication problem created by definition differences. These situations are further complicated by emotional outbursts on both sides, by charges and countercharges, and by media stories that often accentuate the negative. It is difficult to bring reason to bear on the matter and to get at the question of exactly what is being contested. Police officers sometimes make the point that the public is quick to accuse an officer of excessive force, but not so concerned when the officer is attacked, insulted, or killed.

The ticklish excessive force question is a symptom that something is seriously wrong in police-citizen transactions. Being philosophical about it is not very helpful in the heat of the situation. After all, it is not very comforting to a hospitalized police officer, or to a hospitalized victim of an officer's wrath, to be told that there was really nothing personal intended, that it was merely symbolic warfare, springing from dual stereotyping. Such an explanation does not pay medical bills. Actually, drawing fine lines of definition in excessive force charges is largely an academic exercise. It is a rational approach, just as police responses may be rational. But when police-community relations descend to the level of excessive force charges, often accompanied by clamor to establish a citizens' review board to oversee police conduct, the situation has been

allowed to deteriorate emotionally to a point where rational dialogue is extremely difficult. It becomes a playground for hotheads. Under such circumstances, some sort of
moratorium or psychological icepack may be the only sane course.

There is no question that there are police officers for whom beating up or de-
faming people are grim means of job satisfaction. For some such officers, this may be
why they joined the force; for others, it is more a result of what happens to them
after they join. With some, it is plain fear in the face of "statistical danger," a perception and interpretation of what seems necessary for survival. And it is true that
the abuse and provocation absorbed by police in line of duty is little known and far
from appreciated. The mendacity, defiance of law, family abuse, impulsive and immoral conduct, alcoholic and drug-addicted behavior, and other socially destructive
acts that police officers witness are more than a little discouraging to the maintenance of a balanced and constructive perspective about their jobs and about the
people with whom they most frequently come in contact. The warped and cynical attitude often evident in police officers who have long worked in depressed areas is a
great obstacle to their understanding of and sympathy for the goals of social justice.

When a case of excessive force is publicized, the words *police brutality* ring out
with a violent mental image. The author attempts to avoid this label for three critical reasons. "Brutality":

- Is an emotional term, stirring fervor rather than stimulating a logical analysis
  and response to an important problem. With such emotion comes increased
  conflict, resistance to remedies, and reactions based on intuition rather than
  logic.
- Does not permit us to adequately distinguish between qualitative levels of force
  used by officers. The use of force is based on a continuum, which justifies
  when force can be used and the *degree of force* that may be used. As will be
  discussed later, the issue is not simply one of "using force or not."
- Is a label that does not adequately address the peripheral behavior of force,
  which is improper but does not *appear* to be excessive.

In empowering police officers, the law essentially authorizes officers to use that
amount of force which is necessary to effect a lawful arrest or search, but no more
force than that. Moreover, officers may use force to protect themselves or others
from injury; deadly force in the case of serious bodily injury or death. Keeping these
points in mind, we can understand that circumstances arise which may *appear* to be
a case of excessive force, but are not. Conversely, there are instances where an officer may be using excessive force, but a person watching may not know it.

To expand on this point, an illustration is useful. The use of excessive force,
while illegitimate, is not necessarily injurious. A police officer who maliciously tight-
ens an arrestee's handcuffs too tight in order to inflict pain (a punitive action) would
be using excessive force. A person who observed this treatment might not know the
force was excessive nor see it as "brutal." From another perspective, let us say an
officer is attempting to arrest a person who resists aggressively. The officer uses his
or her baton, perhaps striking the person, and brings the arrestee under control, at
which point the officer handcuffs the person and no further force is used. This would
be lawful and not excessive, yet the visual image to a bystander may appear that the
officer was "brutal." The significant point to note in these two cases is that the visual
impression of the incidents would be quite different, and the term "brutality" fails
to accurately describe either.

To better understand this phenomenon, the author has characterized excessive
force as part of a broader typology relating to the abuse of authority.[17] "Abuse of au-

thority" may be defined as any action by a police officer without regard to motive, intent, or malice that tends to injure, insult, trespass upon human dignity, manifest feelings of inferiority, and/or violate an inherent legal right of the public being policed. It is important to note that an abuse of authority does not have to be an intentional act; it may also be reactive behavior. Nor is abuse limited to a physically injurious act.

There are three types of abuse in this typology:

- *Physical Abuse/Excessive Force*. This classification includes (a) any officer behavior involving the use of more force than is necessary to effect an arrest or search; and/or (b) the wanton use of any degree of physical force against another by a police officer under the color of the officer's authority.
- *Verbal/Psychological Abuse*. These are incidents where police officers, relying on authority inherently vested in them based on their office, verbally assail, ridicule, harass, and/or place persons who are under the actual or constructive dominion of the officer in a situation where the individual's esteem and/or self-image is threatened or diminished. Also included in this category is the threat of physical harm under the supposition that a threat is psychologically coercive and instills fear in the average person.
- *Legal Abuse/Violation of Civil Rights*. This form of abuse probably occurs more frequently than the other types. Legal abuse is any violation of a person's constitutional, federally protected, or state protected rights. Although the individual may not suffer any apparent physical or psychological damage in the purest sense, an abuse of authority has nonetheless occurred.

As illustrated above, physical abuse encompasses a wide range of behaviors: assaults with fists, kicking, spraying of concentrated tear gas, i.e., Mace™ or "Capstun," assaults with a flashlight or baton, use of deadly force, or lesser forms of physical actions, such as over-tightening handcuffs, "bumping" a person's head as they enter a police car, or any of a wide variety of other physical acts. Remember, physical abuse, i.e., "brutality," occurs when force is used which goes beyond that which is necessary. The test is *not* the inherent nature of the force, but the collective response to three critical questions:

- Did the circumstances warrant the use of force?
- Was the amount of force used reasonable in light of the actions of the suspect?
- Did the officer stop the use of force when control of the suspect was gained or when a search was completed?

Even with specific questions such as these, the "answers" require an assessment of qualitative factors on continuums of behavior, absolutes such as "yes" or "no" typically failing to emerge. Given the complexity of these factors, one can see that determining whether physical abuse has occurred is not as apparent as one may intuitively assume.

While verbal/psychological abuse may not be as apparent as physical abuse, it has been recognized since 1966 in the noteworthy case *Miranda* v. *Arizona*.[18] In this case, Ernesto Miranda was interrogated for several hours about a rape. He was held incommunicado and not permitted to contact an attorney during repeated questioning by the police. Finally, Miranda confessed and was convicted. In overturning the conviction, the U.S. Supreme Court observed that the "police-dominated atmosphere" Miranda was subjected to was as coercive from a psychological perspective as it would have been if the officers had been using physical coercion.

Verbal and psychological abuse represent officer behavior that goes beyond the authority of investigation, enforcement, and control. It tears at the fabric of humanity under the guise of law enforcement authority, creating damage to the psyche—injuries that are far less difficult to observe and far more difficult to repair than physical injury.

In virtually all cases of physical abuse, and most cases of verbal abuse, there will also be a legal violation. Moreover, legal abuse can occur in a wide variety of other circumstances. Stopping cars, conducting searches, interrogating persons, and taking people into custody, all without legal grounds, are examples of legal abuse. Also, discrimination against a person based upon race, ethnicity, sexual preference, gender, or

FOCUS 11.2

POLICE CHIEFS' REACTION TO THE EXCESSIVE FORCE CONFLICT IN LOS ANGELES

Following the "not guilty" verdict of the Los Angeles police officers charged with assault in the case of Rodney King, there were statements by both public officials and private citizens that the "verdict was wrong" and that the "system didn't work." The civil disobedience and violence occurring in the wake of the verdict also brought outcries. A week after the verdict, the Police Executive Research Forum met in Washington for its annual meeting. At this meeting the chiefs felt there was a need to express their sentiments about the incidents and voted to accept the following statement as their position on the situation.

> The members of the Police Executive Research Forum (PERF), an organization of progressive law enforcement chief executives who collectively serve more than 35 percent of the nation's population, condemn the conduct of the police officers involved in the beating of Rodney King. Yet, PERF members must accept the jury's verdict in the King case because the jury is the key institution of our criminal justice system, and that system supports our government as a constitutional democracy.
>
> The review of police conduct by appropriate local, state, and federal officials is not over: the police department has yet to resolve the disciplinary issues; the King case will be heard in a civil court; and, the case is under investigation by the United States Department of Justice. Like all Americans, PERF members are anxious to see these actions proceed as expeditiously as possible.
>
> Though PERF members can understand the outrage generated by the King incident and the 'not guilty' verdict, the lawlessness and destruction that followed cannot be condoned.
>
> PERF members believe that the events of the past week are symptoms of far more serious underlying problems that contribute to the unacceptable level of crime, violence, and drug abuse in this nation. Politicians, law enforcement executives, and community leaders must improve their

religion, as well as sexual harassment are further examples of legal abuse. Like psychological abuse, legal abuse is difficult to see and control. Vigilance by supervisors, training of officers, and the willingness of "victims" to file formal complaints, including lawsuits, when legal abuse occurs are the primary remedies that must be relied upon.

What Causes Abuse?

We seek simplicity in answers to difficult questions. Straightforward, easily understood, intuitively acceptable explanations to problematic issues are easy to offer and accept. Unfortunately, experience has shown that most problems are more complex

understanding of the issues associated with the racial tensions that exist in America. More must be done to improve relations between the police, community, and government at all levels so that America's energy and resources can be more productively expended solving the problems critical to the quality of life in all communities. As thoughtful and responsible police executives, PERF members continue to accept responsibility for addressing these problems. To that end PERF members are committed to the following:

- In the police departments we lead, and to the utmost extent of our professional and personal influence, we will continue our efforts to develop and maintain a working environment that is free from the unnecessary use of force and inappropriate treatment of citizens.
- When gross misconduct occurs, we will move swiftly to seek appropriate remedies to include criminal prosecution and dismissal from police service.
- As an organization committed to the improvement of policing through research, PERF is conducting a study on the use of force by police under a grant from the National Institute of Justice. PERF will continue to vigorously pursue knowledge that will help guide the development of policies and practices that minimize the occasions in which police must use force.
- PERF will continue to promote the adoption of a philosophy of policing in which the police and the community work together in the prevention and resolution of crime, violence, fear of crime, drug abuse, and disorder problems.
- As an organization that has been in the forefront of addressing racial problems in policing, PERF will continue work on developing an environment in policing that reflects equality under the law in our relationships with the public we serve, and within our law enforcement agencies.

For PERF members to do less would betray our organizational principles, the trust of the communities we serve, and our commitment as professionals to work toward the improvement of policing in America.

than they appear on the surface; consequently, the solutions are also complex. Thus, allegations that discrimination, authoritarianism, indifference, or any other generalization about police behavior are the "causes" of police abuse are superficial.

The body of research evidence suggests that there is a range of factors that selectively interact with a police officer's job activities, decision-making, and organizational life that contribute to the abuse of authority. These factors—which the author characterizes as *stressors*—do not "cause" police misconduct, per se. Problems arise when an officer begins to experience multiple stressors without a legitimate release mechanism. These stressors continue to accumulate until a release opportunity occurs. The officer's action may be either intentional or simply a reaction to circumstances. Regardless of the case, it results in misconduct. These incidents are typically not the calamities we see in headlines, but are nonetheless abusive. The critical factors are:

- *Life-Threatening Stressors.* These are the embodiment of the constant potential for injury or death. A particularly important aspect of these stressors is the knowledge that violent acts against officers are intentional rather than accidental behaviors. Ironically, such things as body armor, the change to semi-automatic weapons, and training programs that teach about violence, all reinforce these stressors.

- *Social Isolation Stressors.* Included in this category are such factors as isolation and alienation from the community; authoritarianism; cynicism; and cultural distinction, prejudice, and discrimination. Hopefully, these stressors will increasingly diminish with the growth of community policing.

- *Organizational Stressors.* These deal with all aspects of organizational life— both formal and informal. Specific stressors include administrative philosophy, peer pressure, poor role models, misdirected performance measures, the pressure for upward mobility, changing policies and procedures, job satisfaction, lack of training, specialization, morale, inadequate supervision and administrative control, internal organizational jealousies, and other factors that create conflict in organizational life.

- *Functional Stressors.* Related to the actual performance of policing duties, these include role conflict, the use of discretion, the application of law and legal mandates, decision-making responsibilities in the use of force, resolution of problems and disputes, and similar activities. If an officer does not have a good understanding of his or her responsibilities and is ill-prepared to handle them, stress will increase.

- *Personal Stressors.* These stressors are based in the officer's off-duty life and include such things as family problems, illness, problems with children, marital stress, and so forth, or financial constraints. Personal problems cannot be left at home; they will inherently influence a person's daily behavior, including work decisions.

- *Physiological Stressors.* A change in one's physiology and general health may also affect both decision-making and tolerance (or intolerance) of others' behavior. Fatigue from working off-duty jobs; the physiological impact of shift work, illnesses, and physiological responses to critical incidents, i.e., getting "pumped up" for a call, are all examples of this form of stress.

- *Psychological Stressors.* The impact of most of the other stressors will also contribute to psychological stress. Other factors include constant exposure to the worst side of humankind, the impact of resolving situations that are of a repulsive nature, such as homicides, child abuse, or fatal traffic accidents, and internalization of fear about policing-related responsibilities.

These stressors are not mutually exclusive. It is their interactive nature which lends support to their cumulative effect on police behavior. As exposure to the stressors increase in both time and intensity without a control mechanism, the more the officer's self-control is eroded.

Police administrators have the responsibility to employ administrative measures that can address the problems of abuse from both preventive and follow-up perspectives. Such measures include:

- A clear statement of organizational philosophy
- Ethics and values
- Training
- Adequate supervision with regular training for supervisors
- An open complaint system supported by effective internal investigations
- Meaningful performance evaluations
- The availability of an Employee Assistance Program
- Clearly stated policies and procedures
- Trouble-shooting and prevention programs

In 1981 the United States Civil Rights Commission issued an important report entitled *Who's Guarding the Guardians?* which addressed wide-ranging issues associated with the abuse of authority. The report offered extensive findings and recommendations, some of which are particularly instructive in light of the above discussion.

FINDING	RECOMMENDATION
Serious underutilization of minorities and women exist in local police agencies; they remain too largely white and male.	Development and implementation of effective affirmative action [and recruitment] programs.
Current personnel selection standards in many police agencies are not adequately job-related, which disproportionately disqualifies minorities and women.	Review of selection standards to increase their job-relatedness.
Psychological screening of police applicants does not play a strong role in selection.	More emphasis is needed on these aspects of police training.
Police training programs do not give sufficient attention to human relations and the social service functions of the police.	Strengthen the use and professional competence of psychological screening of applicants.
Insufficient training and management attention is given to police stress.	Much more attention to officer stress in training and management programs is needed.
Police procedures for citizen complaints have improved but still need considerable perfecting.	The recommendation is implicit in the finding.

While important strides have been made in each of these areas, they nonetheless remain as valid today as they were when written over a decade ago. We know far more about these issues as a result of research. Similarly, we have seen the emergence of innovative police programming which addresses these factors. If our progress continues as it has thus far, we can be optimistic about the future.

COMPLAINTS BY MINORITIES AND COMPLAINTS BY THE POLICE:
"NEVER THE TWAIN SHALL MEET"—PERHAPS . . .

If a cooperative spirit between the police and community is to emerge, both must recognize the concerns of the other and make strides toward resolving their differences. Concerns will vary among communities, based on the characteristics of the police department, the community, and any unique factors in a given community's police-community relationship. Despite this variability, some generalities can be made based on the collective trends of research.[19]

Among minority complaints about the police (in order of concern by the citizens) are:

- Poor police protection
- Poor service to the inner-city residents
- An expectation of unfair treatment by the police
- Harassment and verbal abuse
- Stereotyping, particularly in "stop and frisk" cases
- Excessive force, and
- Discriminatory police personnel practices

The police typically respond to these criticisms by saying that the community "does not understand" the demands placed on the department. Indeed, most police resources in any given jurisdiction are devoted to inner-city areas. Fear of crime and the expectation of potential victimization most likely contribute to the feeling that more protection is needed from the police. In cases of stereotyping, one white officer who worked in a predominantly black area stated to the author, "I am accused of being discriminatory because most of the people who I stop are black. Yet, 95 percent of the people who live in my beat are black. Of course most of the people I stop will be black—just like most of the people I help are also black." Misperceptions are real, but the fact also remains that there is a basis for some of the community concerns. Law enforcement must be alert to monitor and remedy problems associated with these concerns as well as educate the public about misconceptions.

The police also have their favorite complaints directed toward minorities. Among them are:

- The public is apathetic toward crime problems, willing to complain about them, but not wanting to work with law enforcement to deal with those problems.
- The public expects too much of the police—calls for service that are noncriminal in nature often leave the police with little formal authority to resolve the problem at issue, yet the public expects a solution.
- Many of the charges made against the police by "vocal minorities" are perceived to be patently unfair because "the whole accurate story" is not known, frequently because of rumors and the lack of full reporting by the media.
- Many police officers strongly resent what they regard as the overemphasis on the rights of the individual at the expense of the rights of society in general and victims in particular.
- The police view themselves as trained professionals and resent increased imposition of civilian authority over police actions, with particular concerns about civilian review boards.

"If a cooperative spirit between the police and community is to emerge, both must recognize the concerns of the other and make strides toward resolving their differences."

- Many officers express great concern over what they perceive as the loss of values in society. This places the police on a collision course with segments of the population who perceive the police to be oppressive and anachronistic.

In sum, most police officers tend to see themselves as "trying to do good," by "fighting crime and evil" in the streets of the United States. They feel hurt and unappreciated by the storm of criticism that breaks around them and by what they consider a "nobody cares" public attitude. The police are also victims of stereotyping by the public who make generalizations about all officers based on the recalcitrant behavior of a few.

Both the police and the public feel powerless to change conditions that basically make the police-community relationship so hostile, so sterile. They blame each other for their many problems and thereby freeze communications further. In reality, the burden falls on the police to begin a dialogue to resolve these reciprocal complaints. Hopefully, with more enlightened community-based initiatives by law enforcement, the edge can be taken off some of these criticisms.

COGNITIVE DISSONANCE

The theory of *cognitive dissonance*, first proposed in 1957 by Leon Festinger and elaborated in 1962 by Brehm and Cohen, is based on "the notion that the human organism tries to establish internal harmony, consistency, or congruity among his opinions, attitudes, knowledge, and values. There is, in short, a drive toward consonance among cognitions."[20] The relation between pairs of cognitive elements can be incongruent, that is, they do not support each other and are therefore *dissonant*; or the relation can be congruent and therefore *consonant*, that is, one element supports the other. Thus, dissonance refers to the strain or tension between two items of knowledge, two attitudes, opinions, or values.

Contracultural conflict is a collective form of cognitive dissonance. There are five general conditions under which cognitive dissonance occurs:

1. Dissonance almost always exists after a decision has been made between two or more alternatives.
2. Dissonance almost always exists after an attempt has been made, by offering rewards or threatening punishment, to elicit overt behavior that is at variance with private opinion.
3. Forced or accidental exposure to new information may create cognitive elements that are dissonant with existing cognition.
4. The open expression of disagreement in a group leads to the existence of cognitive dissonance in the members.
5. Identical dissonance in a large number of people may be created when an event occurs which is so compelling as to produce a uniform reaction in everyone.[21]

The magnitude of post-decision dissonance varies with the importance of the decision, the relative attractiveness of alternatives not chosen, and the similarity of both chosen and unchosen alternatives.

> The magnitude of the dissonance resulting from an attempt to elicit forced compliance is greatest if the promised reward or punishment is either just sufficient to elicit the overt behavior or is just barely not sufficient to elicit it.[22]

The presence of dissonance gives rise to pressures to reduce that dissonance. Reducing dissonance calls for changing one of the dissonant elements of knowledge, opinion, attitude, or value; adding new, consonant elements to support the decision taken; or decreasing the importance of the dissonant elements.

What is the relevance of this theory to police-minority relations? Cognitive dissonance as synonymous with *culture shock*, a familiar concept in such activity as training personnel for Peace Corps service.[23] There are four generally recognized stages in the culture shock syndrome.

1. A kind of "honeymoon" period, during which the individual is fascinated by the novelty of a strange culture. He [or She] is polite, friendly, etc.
2. The individual settles down to a long-run confrontation with the conditions of life in the strange culture and the need for him to function effectively there. He [or She] becomes hostile and aggressive toward the culture and its people. He [or She] attributes his difficulties to trouble-making on their part. He [or She] develops elaborate, stereotypic caricatures of the local people.
3. Here the individual (if he [or she] has survived Stage 2) is beginning to open a way into the new cultural environment. He [or She] may take a superior attitude but will joke about local behavior rather than criticize it. He [or She] is on the way to recovery from shock.
4. The individual's adjustment is as complete as it can be. He [or She] accepts the other's customs as just another way of living and doing things.[24]

Thus, when officers go into a new cultural environment, they encounter customs, language and behaviors that are unique and, very likely, unfamiliar. Fascination with the culture begins to fade as officers increasingly feels their cultural separation from the group. As a defense mechanism—probably spiced with some stereotyping—an officer's attitude can become increasingly hostile. If the relationship cannot be directed back on track, it may become difficult to salvage.

As one example, the author interviewed a white officer in Texas who had been assigned to work as the community police officer in a public housing complex where the residents were primarily black. Through hard work, the officer got to know many of the residents by name, gained their confidence, and worked to resolve not only crime problems in the complex but many quality of life issues as well. At first the officer was uncomfortable with certain aspects of the residents' culture. However, her close relationship with them was also an educational experience, so that she began to be accepted surprisingly well in social groups, even being invited to functions of the residents, such as weddings, birthday, and graduation parties. Problems began to arise when her assimilation reached the point that the residents were very open about their attitudes towards the police and in some cases their attitudes toward whites. She was confused about a proper response. On the one hand, she was almost fully accepted into the social group she was trying to work with and help. On the other hand, both her occupational group and cultural group were being criticized, and she felt defensive. Her reaction was to remain friendly, but to withdraw from many organized social situations and work with the residents in a more "official" capacity. In this case, the officer's response appears to have worked well. The experience, however, begs the questions: "To whom should the officer show allegiance? One's occupational group? One's racial/ethnic group? The community group with whom you are working?" The answer is that some form of social balance must be sought.

MINORITY POLICE OFFICERS

Blacks and other minorities have been seriously underrepresented in the personnel of many police organizations in the country. There has been widespread concern about this among police administrators and civil rights agencies, who have tried to cope with the situation by using imposed formulas or public relations gimmicks that have often produced disappointing results. Equal opportunity legislation and affirmative action programs have made significant inroads on this problem in the recent past, but there is a long way to go.

Police departments today are, of course, generally required by law to operate on the basis of a merit system in employment and personnel practices. However, the general complaint of police administrators with respect to minority-group applicants has been that not nearly enough are qualified. On the face of it, this is a plausible and defensible administrative posture, widely assumed in various facets of public affairs and usually crowned with the statement, "and we certainly can't *lower* our standards." Getting qualified applicants of any background for police work today is something of a challenge, and the difficulty is much more acute in the case of the black or the Hispanic applicant. What is the problem?

It is astonishing that there should be so much apparent difficulty in understanding what the problem is. The factors explaining it are fairly obvious. Yet various recruitment campaigns and promotions are mounted in a manner to suggest that the instigators really believe that such things as television and radio spots and billboard posters will get the job done. There is consternation when these ploys simply do not work.

As with any other problem, solutions must be meshed with causes. What, then, are the causes of the problem of underrepresentation of minority people in police agencies? Following is an outline of some of the more important considerations:

1. Until the mid-1980s, minority-group applicants had not been aggressively sought by police agencies.

2. Minority-group young people have not viewed police work as an attractive or inviting career because they have seen police organizations as predominantly white, English speaking, and so on, and also because what they have seen of police in so-called high-crime neighborhoods hardly elevates their estimate of the occupation.

3. In the minority communities, especially in low-income areas, to aspire to be a police officer is frequently to be regarded by one's peers as a traitor. One pays a high price for such aspiration.

4. The preceding point suggests the difficult problem of marginality—for example, for the black police officer.[25]

5. The complex question of qualifications for police work is currently undergoing reexamination and reevaluation. What should it take to qualify? The qualities that are most useful in today's police function may not be measurable in such terms as years of formal education, or how tall an applicant is, or what he or she weighs, or how sharp his or her eyesight is. The important question is: What are the *relevant* qualifications? We too easily succumb to doing it the easy way, for example, requiring more formal education, which we equate with "elevating standards." Assumptions of this type urgently need rethinking, to reveal the superficiality of the administrative stance: "We can't get enough qualified applicants"; "We can't lower our standards." White, middle-class bias taints much that is said and done about this.

6. Minority people have reason to doubt that they are really wanted in police agencies, because they have reason to know that there is considerable racial prejudice and discrimination therein.[26]

7. As a result of past educational discrimination and present civil-service-type "merit examinations" for police service, minority people are in fact at a disadvantage in regard to the educational requirements. Also, because many such testing instruments are tilted by culture and social class and weighted with paper-and-pencil and reading skills, minority people are further handicapped. Across the country, numerous suits involving the development of nondiscriminatory tests of "merit" have been in litigation. Who decides the criteria for "merit"? This is a key question.

8. For *social* rather than racial reasons, numerous young blacks—again as an example of the typical minority situation—have a criminal record, making them technically ineligible for police service. This, too, calls for reevaluation, with careful attention to the individual applicant and the particular nature of the crime, rather than reliance on broad, no-exceptions, bureaucratic classifications, coughed up by computers.

9. Attitudes within police organizations toward minority-group personnel often create problems internally, a significant factor in the difficulty of retaining such personnel even when initially secured. One indication of this is the development of defense organizations to protect the interests and rights of minority-group police officers, for instance, the Guardians, the National Society of Afro-American Policemen, the Council of Police Societies, and

Officers for Justice. Their purposes are more serious than fraternity and fellowship. There is one theory that some of the negativism among police rank-and-file directed against actual or prospective minority-group colleagues is grounded in the self-image problems of some officers. They fear, for example, that police work will increasingly come to be regarded as what they call "nigger work." It should also be noted that, historically, there has been an attitude sometimes evident in the white community (and occasionally in the black community) that "a black cop is not a real cop."

10. Many educationally better-qualified blacks have taken positions in business, industry, and the professions rather than in public service, simply because salary and other incentives are far better.

While some of these factors are gradually fading, the change is far from swift. There is no question that the minority police officer is a very important figure in police and community relations. This recently acquired importance is a telling symptom of the gravity of police and minority group polarization. It is probably true that there is a resultant "counter-momentum," a tendency for police departments to expect too much from the minority officer, almost to a point of suggesting that, if only there were enough black police officers, all problems of police-black relations would evaporate. Some black police may be able to do certain things better than some white police in a predominantly black neighborhood, but the same thing is also true in a predominantly white neighborhood. In the long run, it may be recognized that blackness or whiteness is not a very important determinant of an effective police officer. It comes down to individual traits of personality, sensitivity, attitude, knowledge, and the like.

A 1991 research project of the Police Executive Research Forum[27] found, not surprisingly, today's typical police agency is white and male. Table 11-1 depicts the current police agency profile in terms of the racial and ethnic representation of sworn officers. White officers constitute 80.3 percent of all sworn officers in the nation's police departments that serve populations of 50,000 and more. Blacks make up 12.3 percent, Hispanics account for 6.4 percent, and persons of other racial/ethnic backgrounds represent roughly 1.0 percent. (The same study also found that some 12.8 percent of all police officers are women.) Somewhat surprisingly, these proportions approximate Census Bureau demographic estimates. While variations exist throughout the country, the data nonetheless suggest that police departments are doing a better job employing minorities than we may have intuitively believed.

TABLE 11-1.	Minority Representation in Law Enforcement Agencies that Serve Populations of ≥ 50,000 Compared with General U.S. Population	
Race/Ethnicity	Police (%)	National (%)
Black	12.3	12.1
Hispanic	6.4	8.0
White	80.3	76.9
Other	1.0	3.0

MORE ON AFFIRMATIVE ACTION

As with other facets of public service, criminal justice has been involved in the continuing debate regarding the merits and demerits of affirmative action. As mentioned earlier, police departments in many places have been targeted in legal suits to test personnel policies and practices, first by various minority defense organizations, and more recently by police unions and line fraternal groups. The Bakke and Weber cases were as closely watched in police circles as in colleges and businesses. There is little question that affirmative action and equal opportunity programs, persuasively mandated by Department Justice regulations, have had something to do with the improvements that have occurred in minority representation in criminal justice staffing.

The Supreme Court's five to four decision in both the Bakke and Weber cases was indicative of the political climate bearing on the issue. This rather accurately reflected the dilemma of the basic issue itself and clearly predicted an extended future of continuing litigation. Can preferential treatment on racial grounds ever be benign? Is the problem of discrimination best dealt with by compensatory treatment after it occurs, or ought we as a society to be asking more fundamental questions about the distribution of all opportunity?[28]

It is probably fair to say that affirmative action has been *the* focal point of public debate over civil rights in this country during the past three decades or so. The heart of the controversy is the apparent conflict between means and ends: means that deliberately use race, sex, and national origin to achieve ends that preclude any such consideration. The battle cry commonly employed is "reverse discrimination."

The arguments about affirmative action have centered on specific plans calling for quotas and preferential treatment. There are some thorny questions involved—for example, what is the difference between a goal and a quota? What kinds of affirmative measures should be used when and for what reasons? How long should these plans be continued? How can job seniority or civil service testing for job competence be reconciled with affirmative action?

Affirmative action means any measure adopted to correct or compensate for past or present discrimination or to prevent discrimination from recurring in the future. It is discrimination, then, that is the *raison d'être* for affirmative action, in the public interest. The bedrock of it is in the history of prejudice based on notions of white or male or ethnic/cultural superiority. There remain today many examples of such prejudice, not only in individuals but permeating our institutions and organizations.

Discrimination feeds on itself and creates its own momentum. In education, it curtails the credentials to get good jobs. In employment, it denies the economic resources to buy desirable housing. In housing, it confines minorities to school districts providing inferior education, and the cycle is closed. Lack of opportunity produces lack of accomplishment, which in turn is cited to confirm the original prejudice, or to engender new ones.

Civil rights legislation in recent years has aimed to call a halt to this sorry disaster. Generally, the federal courts have been supportive of affirmative action, including the Supreme Court in a series of decisions. But there has been, nonetheless, a lack of agreement on standards among the justices. During the past few years, the Justice Department has seemed to be seeking judicial softening in affirmative action decisions, highlighted in cases involving police and/or firefighters in such cities as Boston, New Orleans, and Detroit. In a six to three decision in June, 1984, the Supreme Court—in a case involving Memphis firefighters—ruled that seniority systems, as long as they are unbiased, may not be disrupted to save the jobs of newly hired minority workers. Speculation hinged on whether the Court might be moving toward new boundaries on judicial remedies for past discrimination. The question was, with the answer not at all clear, what did this decision mean in terms of affirmative action doctrine? With a number of other, similar cases still in the litigation pipeline, the future of affirmative action as public policy appeared to be at stake, although voluntary programs would undoubtedly continue.

And changes continue. In 1996 California voters passed a proposition prohibiting race as a factor that could be used in such government actions as awarding contracts and awarding admission to state schools. In 1997 the U.S. Supreme Court upheld that proposition. While opponents decried this as unfair and the death of affirmative action, many supporters of the proposition were minority group members. The debate continues.

In policing, the key to workable affirmative action is effective *recruitment* of new officers. Law enforcement agencies should identify and employ the best candidates available, not merely eliminate the least qualified. Unfortunately, most departments do the latter, as described in chapter 8.

QUESTIONS FOR DISCUSSION

1. What is a social process? Identify some of the social processes and indicate whether each suggests positive or negative social interaction.
2. Define social control and relate it to the other social processes. How is it related to social change?
3. Define social system. How do the police fit into the social system of a community?
4. Urbanization trends are being affected by increased *concentration* and the *qualitative nature of the trend*. What is meant by this?
5. Identify several population trends in this country that are of special interest to police-community relations.
6. In metropolitan areas, as the population of the central city has declined, serious crime has increased, and the tax burden has become overwhelming. What does this have to do with police and community relations?
7. What is meant by the comment that citizens must develop ownership in their community in order to develop a social infrastructure?
8. Explain some of the popular myths about poverty.
9. What are the main complaints of minorities against the police? What is the main counter-complaint of the police?
10. Discuss police use of excessive force and why it is of such topical concern today.

NOTES

1. Any standard introductory textbook in sociology covers these matters in detail. Our aim in this chapter is to elicit principles relevant to relationships of the police and the community.
2. John J. Kane, "Personal and Social Disorganization," in *Police and Community Relations: A Source Book*, A. F. Brandstatter and Louis A. Radelet, eds. (Beverly Hills, CA: Glencoe, 1968), pp. 61–66.
3. Jack P. Gibbs, *Social Control*, module 1 (Andover, MA: Warner Modular Publications, 1972), pp. 1–17.
4. See, for example, Talcott Parsons, *The Social System* (New York: Free Press, 1951).
5. Michael Banton, *The Policeman in the Community* (New York: Basic Books, 1964), pp. 2–11. Copyright © 1964 by Michael Banton. Reprinted by permission of Tavistock Publications, Ltd., Publishers, London.
6. Louis A. Radelet, "The Idea of Community," in *Police and Community Relations*, Brandstatter and Radelet, eds. p. 82. Reprinted by permission.
7. Roy R. Roberg and Jack Kuykendall, *Police and Society* (Belmont, CA: Wadsworth Publishing Co., 1993).
8. Banton, *The Policeman in the Community*, p. 7.
9. U.S. Bureau of the Census. *Statistical Abstract of the United States 1992*. (Washington, DC: U.S. Government Printing Office, 1997).
10. Ibid.
11. Based on previous research of the author. See Robert C. Trojanowicz and David L. Carter, "The Changing Face of America," *FBI Law Enforcement Bulletin*, January (1990), pp. 6–12.
12. Paul Mundy, "The Implications of Population Trends for Urban Communities," in *Police and Community Relations*, p. 67. Brandstatter and Radelet, eds. See also "The Negro Population of the United States," in *The Police and the Community: Studies*, Louis A. Radelet and Hoyt Coe Reed, (Beverly Hills, CA: Glencoe, 1973), pp. 101–108.

13. National Assessment of Educational Progress, National Institute of Education, U.S. Dept. of Education.

14. Ibid., Paul Mundy, p. 68.

15. William R. McKenzie, "The Face of the Enemy: A Brief Introduction to the Theory and Practice of Poverty" (Paper presented at the Midwest Philosophy of Education Society meeting held in Chicago, December 4, 1965). See also U.S. Department of Health, Education and Welfare, *About the Poor: Some Facts and Fictions*, by Elizabeth Herzog, Children's Bureau Publication No. 451-1967 (Washington, DC: U.S. Government Printing Office, 1978).

16. As reported in *U.S. News World Report*, November 8, 1976, pp. 57–58.

17. David L. Carter, "Theoretical Dimensions in the Abuse of Authority by Police Officers," in *Police Deviance*, 3rd ed., T. Barker and D. L. Carter, eds. (Cincinnati, OH: Anderson Publishing Company, 1993).

18. *Miranda v. Arizona*, 283 U.S. 436, 86 S. Ct. 1602 (1966).

19. Based on an analysis of wide-ranging data reported in Timothy J. Flanagan and Kathleen Maguire, eds., *Sourcebook of Criminal Justice Statistics* (Washington, DC: U.S. Government Printing Office, 1992).

20. Leon Festinger, *A Theory of Cognitive Dissonance* (Palo Alto, CA: Stanford University Press, 1957), p. 260.

21. Ibid.

22. Ibid., p. 263.

23. Victor G. Strecher, "When Subcultures Meet: Police–Negro Relations," in *Science and Technology in Law Enforcement*, Sheldon Yefsky, ed. (Chicago: Thompson, 1967).

24. Gunnar Myrdal, *An American Dilemma: The Negro Population in the U.S.* (New York: Harper & Brothers, 1944), pp. 50–64. Reprinted by permission.

25. See, Roy R. Roberg and Jack Kuykendall, *Police Management*, 2d ed. (Los Angeles, CA: Roxbury Press, 1997).

26. See President's Commission on Law Enforcement, *Task Force Report: The Police*, pp. 167–175; also the same commission's *Field Surveys V*, pp. 19–20. See also National Advisory Commission on Civil Disorders, *Report*, pp. 165–166. Some police departments have tried cadet and precadet programs for minority youth as young as 14 or 15 years of age in an attempt to overcome long-standing suspicions regarding police work.

27. David L. Carter and Allen D. Sapp, *Police Education and Minority Recruitment: The Impact of a College Requirement* (Washington, DC: Police Executive Research Forum, 1991.)

28. "Affirmative Action: Confronting the Dilemmas," *Phi Kappa Phi Journal* (Winter 1978)

Chapter 12

VIOLENCE, COLLECTIVE BEHAVIOR, AND DEADLY FORCE

Public interest in the police-community relationship surges at times when civic peace and order are threatened by violent crime or some form of collective disorder. In the case of violent crime the police are sought for protection, yet may be blamed for permitting the violence to flourish. Similarly, in some cases of collective behavior, the police have the responsibility of protecting protesters—even for very unpopular causes—while ensuring that peace is maintained. In other cases of collective behavior when the police use force to control disorder, they will invariably be criticized by one faction for using too much force while being labeled as "soft" by an opposing faction. Others will make judgments based on what they see on television for a few seconds during the news.

Regardless of whether the paradox exists as a result of violent crime or collective disorder, the police are visible and become part of the controversy. This is truly a pervasive problem for community relations. As a result, an understanding of the issues and dynamics is important.

VIOLENT CRIME

Violence in America clearly appears to be on the rise. An anecdotal review of news stories shows an ever-increasing number of drive-by shootings, senseless random shootings of innocent people, and the violence associated with the illicit drug trade.

As a vivid illustration, during one weekday evening ride on patrol in the Los Angeles Police Department's Newton Division the author heard six calls on drive-by shootings and, on several occasions heard gunfire while patrolling the streets. On the other side of the nation, a U.S. Capitol police officer told me, "Every night when I work on the north side of the Capitol, I hear gunfire throughout the evening. Usually a few shots here and there; occasionally machine gun fire."

Over the last two years this researcher has conducted site visits at a large number of police departments from San Diego to New York City. In every case, at some

". . . in some cases of collective behavior the police have the responsibility of protecting protesters—even for very unpopular causes—while ensuring that peace is maintained."

point during the visit, officers expressed their concern about guns on the street and the threat they pose to officers and citizens alike. Preliminary evidence indicates that communities are not immune from the violence regardless of size, character of the community, or geographic location. Moreover, it's not just criminals carrying guns. Illustrations will help exemplify these issues:

Los Angeles, California—Investigators with the Los Angeles Police Department's Scientific Investigation Division observed that shootings are so prevalent in certain areas of the city that at shooting scenes they sometimes have difficulty finding the correct expended shell casings for the offense being investigated and so many bullet holes exist they have difficulty in calculating trajectory.

Independence, Missouri—A high ranking police official told the author that so many citizens have purchased firearms to "protect their property" and that so often officers encounter the armed citizen when responding to prowler calls that dispatchers have been advised to tell citizens to stay in their houses until they are contacted by the police.

Detroit, Michigan—Since 1986 nearly 200 youths under age eighteen have died from gunshot wounds and over 430 more youths in this age group have been injured from gunfire.

San Francisco, California—Officers report increasingly encountering citizens and drug dealers alike who are wearing body armor because of the ever-present threat of gunfire.

Washington, DC—In one twenty-four-hour period, fourteen people were shot; three of them died. Medical facilities in the District of Columbia have been overtaxed with shooting victims to the point that a major hospital emergency room had to close because it was full.

Houston, Texas—A U.S. Bureau of Alcohol, Tobacco, and Firearms (BATF) special agent told the author that there were an extraordinary number of MAC-10 "assault" pistols on the street. He stated that these weapons are so easily converted to fully automatic that he was surprised to seize one recently that had not been converted.

Santa Ana, California—A police sergeant observed that within three days two people died in this city from gunfire, one for spilling another man's beer, the other for owning a cowboy hat another man wanted.

St. Petersburg, Florida—A police official stated that his department was seizing so many guns they were literally running out of space in the property room to store seized firearms. The number of gun seizures has been so high that an additional person was hired by the police department just to process handguns.

Tulsa, Oklahoma—A patrol sergeant told the author that shootings had become so commonplace in some of the public housing complexes that they had the appearance of war zones. The sergeant said, "If you don't hear a few shots go off during your shift you get uneasy—no shooting is unnatural."

Alexandria, Virginia—Some officers report they have never seized a "Saturday Night Special" handgun or seen a homemade "zip" gun. The same officers, however, have been involved in the seizure of Uzi machine guns, MAC-10 and TECH-9 "assault pistols," and a wide array of costly handguns made by reputable manufacturers.

Lansing, Michigan—The police reported that one man was knifed and seriously injured in a disagreement over a barbecue grill, while in a separate incident, a man outfitted with cowboy boots repeatedly stomped another on the head over a checker game.

Sacramento, California—Incidents of violence on the state's highways have become so prevalent that the California Highway Patrol began collecting statistics on highway violence in 1988.

New York City—When asked about violence, a New York City narcotics officer told the author, "You can't separate drugs and guns—the drugs make you popular, the guns make you bad. It seems like anymore a dealer's got to pop (shoot) somebody just to show he's legitimately in the dope business."

Sadly, these illustrations could continue. It is important to note that these acts of violence are not just occurring in the ghettos of the nation's largest cities. They are also happening in middle-class, moderate-sized cities in America's heartland. Many people would share the beleaguered observation of one Kansas City, Missouri citizen speaking to a reporter following a homicide, "There's so much shooting around here it's like living in Beirut."

A Perspective

Discussions by law enforcement personnel at professional meetings and in news stories and public clamor have addressed mounting concern about violence in communities nationwide. Specifically aggravating the concerns about violence by firearms is the prevalence of guns in the illicit drug trade. Reasons for this appear to relate to the mounting cash and territorial conflict associated with drug trafficking. One DEA agent in Las Vegas told the author, "It's a surprise at a (drug) raid if we *don't* find some guns." Another DEA official also stated that in addition to the money involved, the effects of crack cocaine appear to trigger the most violent reactions in people.

Various assertions have been made about the dynamics of firearms incidents. Many of these assertions, having been popularized through media attention, become "self-evident truths." Yet, these "truths" have had little scrutiny to determine their veracity. Among the more critical fallacious assertions are:

- Firearm violence is largely an inner-city "black problem."
- The carrying of firearms by citizens in inner-city areas is commonplace.
- Assault weapons are prevalent and involved in many shootings.
- Many of the shootings that occur are a result of random gunfire.
- Shootings involving multiple victims are generally the product of a person who is mentally deranged.
- Shootings are, to a large part, a result of either gang conflict or drug deals gone bad.

The questions remain: Are these "self-evident truths" valid? What are the dynamics of gun-related incidents? Preliminary inquiry into these issues during the course of the author's research has found that these assertions may have only limited veracity. Furthermore, a number of wide-ranging trends in violence have been identified in the author's research.

An important aspect inherent in any exploration of violence is the realization that the phenomenon of drugs and guns in our society is too extraordinarily complex to address through a singular analysis. Thus, the issues must be broken down into "basic blocks" and examined individually to understand the pieces of this complex puzzle.

Characterizations of Violence

When speaking of violent crime, there is a tendency to refer to violence as a one-dimensional problem. However, as illustrated in figure 12-1, violence can occur in many forms. Importantly, the *motivation* for these various forms of violence differ. For example, gang members may be involved in a drive-by shooting for revenge against another gang. A robber may shoot someone in order to escape from the crime scene. A black man may be assaulted by a racist for no other reason than the color of his skin. Or a depressed, frustrated employee who is fired from a job may seek revenge against the employer by taking a gun to the workplace and shooting people.

All of these actions are obviously violent, yet the reasons *why* the crimes were committed varied greatly. The importance of this lies in both our ability to prevent violent crime and our approach to investigating the offense. Different crime-specific strategies are needed to deal with different problems. For example, as described in Focus 12-1, a Family Violence Task Force was created in the Beaumont, Texas Police Department to deal with domestic assaults. The operating practices, expertise of officers, and organizational characteristics of this Task Force were explicitly designed to deal with this form of violence. Across the state in El Paso, Texas, the police department was facing a significant increase in another form of violence: drive-by shootings (Focus 12-2). An entirely different organizational response was needed to deal with this problem. The basic lesson, of course, is to recognize the multidimensional nature of the problem.

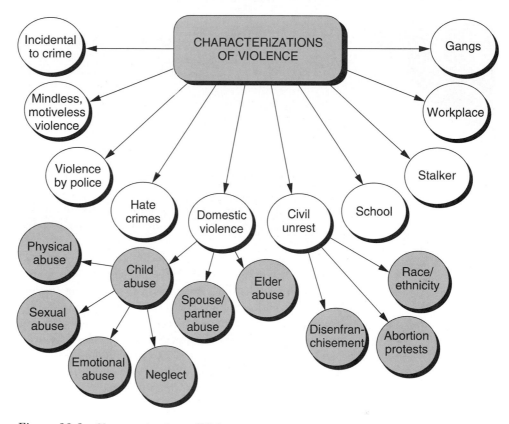

Figure 12-1   Characterizations of Violence

Why Do People Use Weapons Against Others?

If there are changes in the types of circumstances in which people use weapons against each other, then it is beneficial to understand the reasoning for weapons' use. While there is generally no conclusive, singular reason, among the explanations are:

- *Protection* (the weapon permits the citizen to avoid victimization or the criminal to safely escape the crime scene)
- *Perseverance* (the weapon allows criminals to continue the illegal activity should they be interrupted by the police or a citizen)
- *Autonomy* (the weapon permits a criminal to maintain control over a situation through its implicit threat)
- *Defense of others* (the weapon permits protection of a family member, friend, or criminal colleague)
- *Contempt* (the weapon is directly or symbolically used to express one's hatred for another person or group)
- *Intimidation* (the weapon permits the exercise of power that the individual could not otherwise achieve, often for psychological gratification)
- *Retribution* (the weapon is used as a means to "get back" at another; it is used as a form of punishment)

An analysis of the anecdotes presented earlier shows that the motives in the weapons' incidents can be classified in one or more of these categories. Within this

BEAUMONT, TEXAS FAMILY
VIOLENCE TASK FORCE

The Family Violence Task Force is functionally assigned to the Investigations Division of the Police Department. It is comprised of two patrolman grade investigators, a supervising detective sergeant and a civilian case specialist. The three sworn officers investigate all cases involving family violence with the exception of homicides. The case specialist functions as a liaison with the District Attorney's office as well as other agencies, such as Family Services, shelters, etc. (Currently the case specialist position is funded under a grant from the Violence Against Women Act.)

The task force is physically located at a site completely separate from any police facility. The intent of this was to make it easier for victims to meet with police and support personnel, since many feared going to the police station. Informal feedback from the victims reinforced the importance of this decision. In addition, a site was selected that was centrally located at a major intersection on the grounds of a large city park with a bus stop located in front of the offices. These factors were deliberate in order to provide an aesthetic, nonthreatening environment which was easily accessible.

The purpose of the unit was twofold:

- Investigate cases of reported family violence as quickly as possible in order to prosecute the offender and prevent future victimization from that offender.
- Provide education and intervention alternatives in high-risk circumstances to prevent victimization.

All cases involving family violence (except homicide) reported to the police department are forwarded to the task force for investigation, cases are then assigned to individual investigators. Every attempt is made to assign related cases to the same investigator, since they are already familiar with the people involved as well as the conditions in the family. All family violence cases are referred to the

context, the research indicates that rationalization for weapons' use has become more prevalent as has the frequency of use of weapons and, implicitly, more rapid decisions to actually use a weapon rather than just threaten its use.

What Are the Trends?

As part of a wide range of research conducted over the past several years, the author has attempted to identify and validate (to the degree possible) trends in violence across the United States. The research has encompassed every region of the United States and included discussions with law enforcement officers at all levels of government. Some initial trends emerged, with potentially significant im-

District Attorney's office, which has one Assistant District Attorney assigned exclusively to work domestic violence cases.

The Family Violence Task Force has taken the lead in establishing a strong relationship with various groups and organizations such as Victim's Assistance, the Women's Shelter, and the Violence Intervention and Education Program, as well as the specialist assistant District Attorney. These relationships have been important in expediting investigations and helping provide safety and social assistance to victims.

In the first year of the Family Violence Task Force's existence, the three task force officers investigated 1,487 cases. Over 82 percent of the cases investigated were disposed of and convictions jumped from 21 percent to 61.2 percent of all cases referred.

Critical Factors

A number of critical factors were identified to support the success of the Family Violence Task Force. These included:

- The unit's physical location must be separate from the police department in a place that is easily accessible by public transportation.
- Investigators need to establish a strong working relationship with critical support organizations, such as the Office of Victim's Assistance, Women's Shelters, Family Services, etc., and develop a good reputation among judges and justices of the peace.
- Support of the District Attorney's office is critical to not only thoroughly examine and review cases but also to aggressively prosecute these cases.
- Patrol officers must be trained on matters related to responses to family violence calls, such as:
  —Identifying all witnesses immediately (including name, address, phone, etc.)
  —Obtaining witness and victim statements as soon as possible.
  —Taking photographs of victims to demonstrate injuries.
- Cases should be assigned to investigators *immediately* because the victim is more likely to cooperate.

plications for police operations and officer safety. While no definitive measures of reliability can be attached, several trends were consistently noted. These include the following:

- There appears to be an increase of firearms being illegally carried by those involved in criminal transactions or those on the periphery of crime.
- There appears to be an increase in the number of "law-abiding" citizens who are carrying handguns—on their person or in their vehicles—as a result of fear of crime.
- There has been an increase in the number of police assaults in drug-enforcement situations—most frequently undercover "buy and busts."

EL PASO, TEXAS DRIVE-BY SHOOTING RESPONSE TEAM

As a result of escalating gang activity, in 1990 the EPPD tactical section was essentially made into a gang unit and given the responsibilities of investigating all gang-related crimes (except murder), enforcement, intelligence, and diversion. From 1990–1993, the gang task force was called out on drive-by shootings only if serious bodily injury was reported. In 1993, there was a substantial increase in the number of drive-by incidents. The gang unit was changed to an "all enforcement" unit. Essentially, fifty to sixty uniformed officers worked nights, saturating gang areas with stops and enforcement action. During this time, all gang investigations were assigned to the "crimes against persons" detectives. These changes had only a negligible impact on the growing gang problem.

In 1995, the Drive-by Shooting Response Team (DSRT) and the gang intelligence unit were created. Intelligence keeps track of the different gangs and gang members and trends in gang activities and provides on-going information and status reports on all gang-related activity in El Paso. The DSRT is responsible for all gang-related investigations, except murder; however, they provide substantial support in homicide cases. All five DSRT members work days, but are on a twenty-four-hour call-out basis and typically work cases "straight through" until arrests are made.

The DSRT and gang intelligence are centralized units working city-wide cases. In addition, the police department created CRASH units (Community Response Against Street Hoodlums) in each of the five regional commands. Working exclusively within their command areas, the CRASH units are uniformed officers working in marked cars who work during the nights in aggressive enforcement against gang members.

An important element in the success of gang suppression is constant communications and information sharing between the DSRT, CRASH units, and intelligence. In addition, the DSRT is physically located next to the Juvenile Probation and Juvenile Services offices, with which there are strong working relationships and communications.

Experience proved that, when a drive-by shooting occurred, gangs responded in several ways. One constant factor was that the victimized gang would immediately plan retaliation for the incident. This, of course, became an ever-broadening circle in which one assault could turn into ten assaults simply through on-going retaliation. Another factor was that assaulting gang members would get together to "get their stories straight"—all would tell the police essentially the same thing during interviews, thus potentially complicating the investigation. A third factor was that weapons would frequently disappear, thereby making it more difficult to link the suspects to the crime. Finally, gang members would intimidate witnesses, threatening both witnesses and their families, so that investigators interviewing witnesses would end up with "dead ends."

It was felt that the best way to overcome these factors was for investigators to make a rapid response to the crime scene. A key element was also to have the first responding patrol officers or CRASH units immediately "freeze" the crime scene and keep all witnesses present and secure (including keeping gang members separated from each other and from other witnesses).

The original intent of the DSRT was to investigate any drive-by shooting. However, it became apparent that as DSRT members and the intelligence unit became familiar with gang members, their graffiti "tags," and general gang behavior, that it was most effective for the mandate of the DSRT to be broadened into what is essentially a specialized gang crimes investigation unit. In this regard, the full DSRT would be called out and immediately begin the investigation when one of the following conditions existed:

1. There were injuries.
2. There was serious property damage.
3. The situation had the potential to escalate.
4. There were good investigative leads.
5. The field supervisor at the scene deemed it necessary to include the DSRT.

At its peak, there was an average of twenty-one drive-by shootings per month. After the DSRT was formed, drive-by shootings dropped by 50 percent in a seven-month period. Roughly 90 percent of the DSRT's arrests occur within twenty-four hours of the call-out and a significant number of cases result in a confession by the suspect. In addition, relying on asset forfeiture laws, the DSRT has seized a number of cars and other property associated with gang crime.

Critical Factors

The success of the DSRT is tied to several critical operational and policy factors. Among these are:

- An immediately "frozen" crime scene and control of witnesses by the first officers responding to the scene.
- A fast response to the crime scene by the DSRT, regardless of the time of day or night.
- The ability of DSRT investigators to work "straight through" a case.
- Good on-going intelligence and information-sharing between all police department units having gang responsibility as well as the juvenile probation department.
- Investigators getting to know gang members and their families, and "showing respect" when talking to gang members, whether during the course of an investigation or whenever they happen to see a gang member.
- On-going development of reliable confidential informants.
- Developing a strong, mutually respectful relationship with the county attorney and district attorney.
- Having support from administrators to operate freely and creatively.
- Having dedicated personnel who are willing to "go the extra mile" in their work effort.

- Most guns are handguns, relatively few shotguns and sporting rifles. The most common "long gun" appears to be the sawed-off and butt-modified shotgun; however, the frequency of finding these weapons is relatively low.
- There appears to be an increase in the *quality* and *style* of handguns being carried by persons. Related to this, trends appear to be:
  1. The handgun of preference is a semi-automatic of either a 9-mm or .45-caliber.
  2. The handgun is manufactured by a reputable, established company—there are relatively few "Saturday Night Specials."
  3. When "Saturday Night Specials" are seized, they are most frequently found in family disturbances and are likely to be "hand-me-down" weapons.
  4. Seizure of homemade "zip guns" is rare—more toy guns are seized than zip guns.
- There appears to be an increase in *both*:
  1. The number of shooting incidents that occur, and
  2. The number of rounds fired in each shooting incident.
- There appears to be an increase in the use of body armor among both criminals and civilians. Some evidence indicates that drug dealers are the most likely to wear body armor.
- There appears to be an increase in "motiveless and mindless" violence involving firearms. In some incidents, it appears to be "violence for the sake of violence."
- There appears to be an increase of younger people being armed with firearms, mostly handguns—even thirteen-, fourteen-, and fifteen-year-olds. For the younger persons who are armed, a more common weapon appears to be the .25-caliber automatic handgun.
- When speaking to officers about firearms violence, two words seem to be inextricably related: *guns* and *drugs*.
- There appears to be an increase in the use of—or at least interest or fascination in—"bladed" weapons, notably:
  1. "Survival" knives
  2. Martial arts weapons, particularly "throwing stars"

The Cycle of Progressive Violence

Although it is unlikely that a "root cause" of these trends can be identified, one may characterize the cause as a "socio-political-cultural-psycho-economic dope problem." The point of this tongue-in-cheek description is to emphasize that the progression of violence is a complex phenomenon, requiring a number of programmatic, educational, and legislative actions over the long term to reverse these trends. Figure 12-2 illustrates this dynamic in diagram form.

This phenomenon may be characterized as the "cycle of progressive violence" because it is a self-reinforcing progression fueled by a number of factors:

- The presence and relative ease of access to a wide range of weaponry
- Increased fascination with weaponry of all sorts
- Depiction of sophisticated and exotic weaponry in the entertainment media
- Cult-like followings of particular weapons' types or technologies
- Increasing tensions between racial and ethnic groups, including reactionary ideologies that form in response to programs such as affirmative action and busing

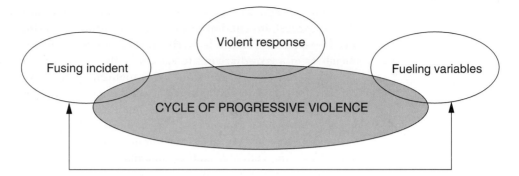

Figure 12-2   The Violence Cycle

- The lack of coping skills to deal with confrontational and stressful situations as well as the fear of crime
- Violence associated with the market forces of drug transactions
- Changing values influenced by the drug "econo-culture"

There is precedent for the concept of progressive violence at the individual level (as opposed to the social level discussed above). Research on serial rapists conducted by the FBI's National Center for the Analysis of Violent Crime (NCAVC) has found that serial rapists become progressively more aggressive and violent in their sexual assaults. Behavior that was "gratifying" in previous incidents is insufficient, so the rapist escalates the level of violence in succeeding assaults. When the assault results in a brutal homicide and the level of violence can no longer be escalated, the frequency of violence may increase, along with increasingly perverse behavior during the course of the rape-homicides. One may reasonably ask, if such a progression of violence can occur at the individual level, can it not also occur at the social level? This is what the cycle of progressive violence suggests.

On an optimistic note, all crimes, including violence, continued to drop from 1991 to 1998, but we must keep these data in perspective. Even at its lowest level during these years, the crime rate was still nearly three times higher than in the previous decade.

COLLECTIVE BEHAVIOR

Collective behavior is defined by sociologists as relatively unstructured social behavior that is not fully controlled by cultural norms—such as that occurring in crowds, riots, revivals, and even sometimes with rumor and fads. It brings into play emotions and unpredictable personal interaction.[1] For obvious reasons, collective behavior is of major concern to the police.

There are many different classifications of societal groups. Some groups are established, some are casual. Examples of the former are vertical and horizontal groupings, in-groups and out-groups, primary and secondary groups. Casual groups include crowds, mobs, and assemblages. Then there are related types of group behavior, such as social movements, social epidemics, fashions, fads, and crazes.

A *crowd* is a temporary gathering of people engaged in some type of collective behavior, ranging from casual strolling to a riot. It differs from an *aggregation*, which is simply an assemblage of individuals in spatial proximity. In a crowd, the individuals are also in psychological contiguity. Crowds often begin as aggregations, evolving through an interactive process known as *circular stimulation*. This means the reciprocal stimulation of individual emotions, causing behavior responses that are less deliberative and less critical than would normally be expected. As a result, members of a crowd are apt to act under the influence of commonly felt emotion.

An *audience* is a type of crowd responding primarily to a single source of stimuli while engaging in only minimum social interaction. Thus, in an audience, there is little circular stimulation. Attention tends to be focused on a performance rather than on other crowd members. A *mob*, on the other hand, is a crowd with a purpose often contrary to law, highly emotional, and with the irresponsible courage conferred by anonymity. A mob is sometimes characterized as an *acting crowd*, with considerable circular stimulation and an aggressive attitude toward a common object. It feels bound to no conventions and acts solely on the basis of aroused feelings. Collective excitement submerges critical thought and deliberate conduct even more than in a crowd. Appeals for rationality usually fall on deaf ears in a mob scene.

The element of psychological suggestibility present in a mob easily leads to violence. There is even a tendency, as in lynch mobs, to hold violence justifiable, so intense is the feeling about righting a supposed wrong. Cowards feel brave in a mob. A *riot* is mob behavior that erupts into public violence, tumult, and disorder.

> Riots are the products of thousands upon thousands of little events that have affected the habits and emotions of thousands upon thousands of people, both future rioters and future innocent bystanders.[2]

What occurs in a riot is always subject to debate. In a mob and riot situation, there are no completely trustworthy observers. Objectivity is lost in the stampede. Power and righteousness are felt to abide in the surge of the impassioned mob.

The art of crowd control is important to the police. Typical tactics include directing attention away from the common objective, efforts to divide members of the crowd physically and psychologically, and attempts to divert the leaders so as to dilute their integrating influence. The primary aim is to relieve the emotional tension caused by circular stimulation.[3]

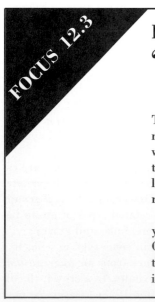

FOCUS 12.3

HENNEPIN COUNTY, MINNESOTA'S "DROP YOUR GUNS"

The *Drop Your Guns* program grew out of a particular concern shared by many members of the community in and around the Twin Cities: the increase in weapons-related incidents among youth. The goals of the program are to reduce the number of guns carried by teenagers, to educate the public about new state legislation that makes it a felony offense for a minor to possess a handgun, and to raise public awareness about the problem of gun-carrying teenagers.

Although the "gun turn-in" program is aimed primarily at Hennepin County youth, anyone can participate in the program. For every gun turned in, the County Attorney pledges amnesty from prosecution and a $50 voucher, "no questions asked." Participants place their unloaded weapon in a clear plastic bag, tie it, and take it to one of twenty-four designated drop-off sites in the county. A fire-

A *social movement* is a collective attempt to bring about a change in existing practices or institutions. The feminist and civil rights movements serve as examples. It implies dissatisfaction with some phase of existing social organization.

A *fashion* is a movement characterized by vertical ascent or descent through social classes. It is imitation throughout a social structure of a particular "elite," in clothing, manners, art, or ideas. Distinction, novel experience, and conformity are among the motivating forces.

Fads, *crazes*, and *social epidemics* are types of fashion movements. They are usually more eccentric than fashion, more localized and of shorter duration, and pertain to frivolous things not of great importance to the total culture.

Members of a social movement often have high morale, which is dependent on belief in the absolute rightness of their purpose and in the possibility of ultimate attainment of their goal. It takes on the character of a sacred mission. Often the members of a social movement see all opposing forces as evil.[4] "If you're not for us, you're against us!" The objective is so right and necessary that it cannot possibly fail. Parades, rallies, and "pep meetings" provide ceremony and ritual and help enhance the feeling of being a select group with a "manifest destiny." A feeling of personal exhilaration comes from association with others (rapport) in the movement. Sometimes special uniforms, slogans, hymns, and gestures help "turn people on to the movement's cause."

The Police and Collective Behavior

We tend to think of police action in collective behavior situations in terms of protecting society against disorder, pandemonium, violence, and unlawful activity. Just as important, however, are the activities of groups engaged in nonviolent demonstrations, which are not illegal, but which nonetheless require police action to protect the demonstrators in the exercise of their rights to assemble and speak freely.

Police, of course, are sympathetic to the philosophy that the best way to deal with a riot is to prevent it. Therefore, the "triggering incident" receives considerable

---

fighter accepts the weapon and issues the $50 voucher, which is redeemable for cash at local banks. (There is a limit of three guns from any one individual.) All the guns are dismantled by the crime laboratory staff and then melted.

The Hennepin County program is just one of several across the country seeking to address problems of handgun violence in their communities. Critics of the programs maintain that they only serve to give money to people for stolen or broken guns. Supporters argue that at least some guns will be taken off the street and that the programs provide important educational benefits.

There have been no formal evaluations of any of the programs such as *Drop Your Guns*. Thus, conclusions about their effectiveness cannot be made. Perhaps one of the more important aspects of these programs is that they serve as a symbol of the growing frustration with increased violence in our society— violence that traditional approaches to crime control have been unable to keep in check. Moreover, law enforcement officials, through such programs, are enlisting the community to provide input, assistance, and support in dealing with the problem.

attention in police training. It is recognized that the triggering incident is the culmination of what is usually a long series of events, occurring in an inflammable social situation. But the incident that sets off the conflagration may be quite innocent and may have no direct connection with the real issue. Many police departments have had to confess: "We looked for something to happen here, and instead of that, it happened way over there, where we least expected it!" Sometimes the action is calculated more to test the police than anything else. So the police must be wary lest they "get suckered."

Thus, a major disorder is almost always the culmination of a building-up process. Planning for control of disorder is based on a combination of conventional police mobilization tactics and *an understanding of the community*.[5] Tension control centers, such as those used in the 1960s riots, carried out such functions as:

1. Receiving and evaluating reports of tension
2. Getting background; fact finding; area surveys
3. Diagnosing the problem (identifying causes)
4. Setting up programs to relieve tension, stressing *communication* and *interpretation*, two basic processes in tension control.

The prevention of riots is not the responsibility of the police alone. A just social order for all is the ultimate answer, and reaching for this goal is a vital responsibility of an entire society. Law is oriented more to the behavior of individuals than to groups. A police officer arrests only individuals who violate the law. This is one reason group behavior is difficult for the police to handle.

> Police cannot take into court a whole group and present evidence against them en masse. If the police are unable to identify and arrest individual violators and present evidence of the specific violation, case by individual case, all they can do is suppress the violence. It is inevitable that in large-scale disorder, many violations of the law will go unpunished. This makes it doubly important to devise preventive programs involving all interested segments of the community.[6]

Police methods in dealing with collective behavior situations will vary according to circumstances, time, geography, area in a given community, the socioeconomic and cultural variations among people, and other such conditions. It must be emphasized that the importance of flexibility in police policies and operational procedures in heterogeneous, social conflict–laden communities is essential.[7]

Police approaches to the control of crime, violence, and disorder must be designed to match the varying psychological and sociological circumstances of the people involved. This is the principle that we enunciated earlier: that dealing with people in their individuality does not easily conform to mass-oriented, bureaucratically processed classifications and "no-exception" practices. A school system, a university, or a police department cannot be administered in this way in today's American society without encountering turbulence. The evidence of this is widespread. No one should make a case for democracy on the basis that it is necessarily efficient or tidy.

Symbols and Symbolic Behavior

Crowds, mobs, and social movements often employ various types of symbols and symbolic behavior. Mentioned earlier were parades, rallies, uniforms, slogans, hymns, and gestures. A raised clinched fist, display of the confederate flag, and the chanting of slogans all illustrate elements of a special language, which can be used to stimulate behavior in collective disorders.

To pursue for a moment one interesting facet of this a bit further, there is the constitutional question as to whether the First Amendment places a limitation on the power of school administrators to control student behavior exhibited as a symbolic expression of belief. A series of court decisions has dealt with this issue, in questions regarding the wearing of armbands, headbands, buttons, and the like.[8] At another level, in 1992 the Supreme Court held that destruction of the American flag as a means of expression was a protected right, effectively invalidating the federal statute on desecration of the flag.

Symbols and symbolic behavior are endemic to collective behavior. They represent an effort to structure disorganized situations in some small degree, a way for participants in social movements to communicate with each other in a rapport-building manner and to impart a sense of common cause. The same thing occurs, for basically the same reason, in all subcultures, including that of the police.

The symbols used in collective behavior usually carry strong emotional undertones that can quickly arouse people to irrational responses, particularly in group settings. Demagogues play on these feelings and manipulate gatherings in support of their particular purposes, which are sometimes socially questionable— right wing extremists groups particularly come to mind.

Symbols are often based on group stereotypes. Whether positive or negative, the symbol tends to perpetuate and lend credence to the stereotype. Take police-minority relations in the ghetto. So much of what passes for communication here is symbolic: language, gestures, name calling, insignia or dress, and the like.

So it is that many symbols tend to be dysfunctional in genuine human relationships because they encourage categorization of people and events.

Learning from Past Civil Disorders

The large-scale civil disorders that occurred in the United States during the 1960s were exhaustively studied by special commissions under presidential mandate. In the preface to the 1967–68 report of the National Advisory Commission on Civil Disorders, President Lyndon Johnson wrote:

> The only genuine, long-range solution for what has happened lies in an attack—mounted at every level—upon the conditions that breed despair and violence. All of us know what those conditions are: ignorance, discrimination, slums, poverty, disease, not enough jobs. We should attack these conditions—not because we are frightened by conflict, but because we are fired by conscience. We should attack them because there is simply no other way to achieve a decent and orderly society in America.[9]

Another study was conducted in 1968–69 by the National Commission on the Causes and Prevention of Violence. This commission declared:

> In our judgment, the time is upon us for a reordering of national priorities and for a greater investment of resources in the fulfillment of two basic purposes of our Constitution—to "establish justice" and to "insure domestic tranquillity."[10]

Still another study of collective behavior was made in 1970 by the President's Commission on Campus Unrest, which asserted:

> Too many Americans have begun to justify violence as a means of effecting change or safeguarding traditions. We believe it urgent that Americans of all convictions draw back from the brink. . . . Students who bomb and burn are criminals. Police and National Guardsmen who needlessly shoot or assault students are criminals. All who applaud these criminals acts share in their evil. We must declare a national ceasefire.[11]

In an analysis written for the National Commission on the Causes and Prevention of Violence, Jerome Skolnick stated that collective behavior has come to mean the behavior of outsiders, the disadvantaged and disaffected. "Panicky" and "crazy" are terms usually reserved for social movements and insurrections. Skolnick questioned typical governmental responses to civil disorders, which—he claimed—have historically combined long-term recommendations for social change with short-term calls for better strategy and technology to contain disruption. He offered five reasons for so questioning:

1. As the Kerner Commission stressed, American society urgently requires fundamental social and political change, not more firepower in official hands.
2. We must set realistic priorities. We must carefully distinguish between increased firepower and enlightened law enforcement.
3. Police, soldiers, and other agents of social control have been implicated in triggering and intensifying violence in riots and other forms of protest. A nonlethal weapon is still a weapon, and it does not solve social problems.
4. Riots are not merely pathological behavior engaged in by riff-raff. Neither are they "carnivals." They are spontaneous political acts expressing enormous frustration and genuine grievance. Forceful control techniques may channel grievances into organized revolutionary and guerrilla patterns.
5. In measuring the consequences of domestic military escalation, we must add the political and social dangers of depending on espionage as an instrument of social control, including its potential for eroding constitutional guarantees of political freedom.[12]

Skolnick further observed:

> If American society concentrates on the development of sophisticated control techniques, it will move itself into the destructive and self-defeating position of meeting a political problem with armed force, which will eventually threaten domestic freedom. The combination of long-range reform and short-range order sounds plausible, but we fear that the strategy of force will continue to prevail. In the long run, this nation cannot have it both ways: either it will carry through a firm commitment to massive and widespread political and social reform, or it will become a society of garrison cities where order is enforced with less and less concern for due process of law and the consent of the governed.[13]

Police action is unquestionably an important aspect of social response to collective behavior. Jerome Hall recalled that the posse is historic in our culture, but he reminded us that a critical situation provides an excellent opportunity to actualize the ideal of self-policing. He pointed out that several hundred citizens were deputized as peace officers in the 1919 Harlem riots, and voluntary service by socially minded white and black citizens has frequently emerged in civil disorder situations.[14]

The gravity of mob disorder is reflected in the prohibition under criminal penalty of two less serious situations that tend to culminate in riot: unlawful assembly and rout. While it is generally true that preparation to commit a crime is not a crime, this is not true with unlawful assembly or rout, in which the incipient stages of riot are recognized and prohibited.

> The police are familiar with arrest for assault and battery and for disorderly conduct, but they have ignored other available controls and legal measures, which can be taken before crimes are committed or before serious aggressions occur. First among these is the peace bond, used in family disputes and in rural areas, but ignored as a control of incipient symptoms of serious disorder. . . . There are other noteworthy legal controls which were designed to check criminal conduct in its incipient stages. At common law, a threat, privately made, was not criminal unless it amounted to extortion. But under many statutes, a threat uttered publicly in conditions tending

toward a breach of the peace is "disorderly conduct,". . . . More serious is the common law crime of solicitation or incitement to commit a crime, and incitement to riot is one form of that offense. Conspiracy extends incipient criminal behavior to the conduct of two or more persons; there are reported cases where convictions of conspiracy to commit a breach of the peace were upheld.[15]

The police should, of course, be familiar with these and other possible legal controls, but the greater wisdom is knowing when and how to apply them. A well-intentioned police action to maintain or to restore order has been known to result in volcanic violence and disorder.

Riots and Collective Disorder

Mounting evidence suggests that riots may again emerge in the U.S. within the next decade. While the 1960s riots were focused on institutional change related to the Civil Rights movement and the Vietnam War, the impetus for riots in the coming decade will be different. Deteriorating economic conditions, growing chasms between white America and people of color, decaying urban America, and growing political power of the affluent at the expense of the shrinking middle class and the poor will be the precursors of future riots. Moreover, the evidence suggests, as discussed later in chapter 17, that the riots of the future will eclipse those of the 1960s in duration, intensity, and violence. In the past several years there have been civil disorders in Miami, Shreveport, New York, Virginia Beach, and Los Angeles. The signs of stress are clearly emerging on our campuses and in our cities. The police must be prepared to deal with stress through both preventive strategies and control programs.

By prevention, we mean that police agencies must communicate more closely with the communities to determine problems and stressors within the community that may contribute to civil disorder. With this information, problem-solving strategies may be developed to reduce the stress. This activity will hopefully prevent civil disorder or, at the least, minimize its effect. For example, the civil disorder of south central Los Angeles following the not-guilty verdict of the LAPD officers accused of assaulting Rodney King may serve as an illustration. If the LAPD had better lines of communication with community members, they would have known of the potential for civil disorder and been able to institute plans to control it. Furthermore, if the police had a reputation for public assistance instead of one as an "occupying force," the public may have been more responsive to control techniques. This, of course, is hindsight, yet it provides a reasonable foundation for understanding the different roles the police may have in civil disorder.

There is a tendency in human nature to say, "That won't happen." If we believe that civil disorder "won't happen," then the likelihood that prevention and control strategies will be developed is practically nonexistent. Who would have believed in 1960 that in the following decade the United States would have assassinations, large-scale riots, domestic terrorism, and significant public disorder? To shrug off this experience in the 1990s, saying, "It won't happen again," is both naive and irresponsible.

Civil Disobedience

Collective behavior often reflects noncompliance with generally accepted norms. One of its methods or strategies may be civil disobedience: the deliberate violation of a law, or of a regulation having the force and effect of law, which is believed to be immoral or unjust. It is a deliberate challenge of civil authority, with the expectation of incurring sanctions, by persons whose values compel their loyalty to what they see as a higher order of authority. It is not anarchy—not utter rejection of all authority—but a choice of authority priority. The 1960s and early 1970s witnessed numerous civil disobedience acts for numerous causes. While there was a decade of relative quiet, demonstrations returned with increasing frequency in the late 1980s and have continued into the 1990s.

Civil disobedience challenges what the majority deems acceptable and puts social conscience to a test. Little wonder, then, that acts of civil disobedience are repugnant to many people. The police are especially disturbed by civil disobedience, one reason being that it puts them squarely in the middle between conflicting moral positions on what is usually an emotionally charged issue. For example, when the police must protect the participants in a Ku Klux Klan demonstration, they find themselves in the discomforting position of protecting people who stand for a cause the officers find morally repugnant.

Discussion of the topic of civil disobedience in conferences on police and community relations has been known to become so dominated by feelings as to produce a recommendation that all civil disobedience should be prohibited by law. This is equivalent to insisting that it is illegal to do anything illegal. To alleviate some of the tension, some important distinctions should be made in conversations about civil disobedience. To begin with, it is not always a question of deliberate violation of law. It may also be a way of protesting a court order. It may be more a matter of taking issue with the way a law is enforced than with the substance of the law itself.

Other distinctions are in the domain of logic. Is civil disobedience illegal? Obviously it is, most of the time. (It could be a protest against a policy, rather than a law.) Is civil violence illegal? Yes. But civil disobedience is not the same as civil violence. Not all illegal acts involve violence, nor is all violence illegal. It is surprising how frequently discussions of civil disobedience bog down in exactly such seeming minutiae, which, on closer examination, are seen to be important distinctions.

Another distinction was advanced by John Morsell of the NAACP, who stated in 1964 that a restaurant sit-in or a freedom ride was *not* an act of civil disobedience. He argued that these actions were based on the premise that exclusion from a licensed public facility on the ground of race was a violation of constitutional right. If these acts violated local laws, it was the local laws, not the freedom rides or sit-ins, that defied the law of the land. A school boycott, on the other hand, is civil disobedience. But the boycott of a business firm accused of discriminatory hiring practices is not civil disobedience, for there is no law requiring anyone to patronize that store.[16]

The relationship between civil disobedience and collective behavior may be described as "disorderly fallout." To illustrate, reactionaries against civil disobedience may form a mob, and a riot is possible. Most law enforcement is done by the people, not by the police. It is a matter of law observance by most of the people, most of the time. In connection with civil disobedience, however, even when the plan and intentions of the participants are peaceful, nonparticipants may become involved with participants emotionally, and then physically. Suddenly and spontaneously, there is disorder and violence. The police must move in to protect property and persons of whatever persuasion, participants and nonparticipants alike.[17]

Many law enforcement officials feel that a tragic result of civil disobedience is that it encourages people to adopt an attitude of general disrespect for the law and all public authority. Yet this is largely speculative: evidence is lacking to prove that there actually is such a transfer. In fact, there is a counterargument that acts of solemn and considered civil disobedience actually cultivate greater respect for *just* law.

> The object of civil disobedience is to call attention to a condition which the participants want to have changed. Naturally, the more widely and dramatically the acts are publicized, the better for the purpose. Unfortunately, this publicity often

makes the police look bad, especially if violence breaks out. And not only that, it also gives the officers a lot of hard and unpleasant work to do. And not only that, the cases are often dismissed and the officers then feel that their work was all for naught. So I think we can conclude undeniably that civil disobedience is quite unpopular with the police.[18]

The Philosophy and Rationale of Civil Disobedience

It is evident that civil disobedience is a fascinating and complicated philosophical subject. Henry David Thoreau and Mahatma Gandhi are among many eminent philosophers of civil disobedience. Gandhi tested and changed his ideas on the subject time after time in the course of a lifetime of experiences; Thoreau spent one night in jail and telescoped his thinking into one great essay, *On the Duty of Civil Disobedience*. The following is an attempt to chart a sampling of the main ideas of these two thinkers:[19]

THOREAU	GANDHI
We should be men [sic] first, and subjects afterward. Undue respect for law is dangerous.	The citizen's obligation to the authority of the State depends upon the extent to which the laws of a State are just and its acts nonrepressive. Submission to the State is a price paid for an individual's personal liberty, but it is always a conditional price.
I do not wish to be the agent, through the State, of an injustice to another, or to pursue a neutral life that lends support to the State in some sense.	The very notion of authority implies that the individual is an author and is morally autonomous in some sense; otherwise authority cannot be distinguished from force or power.
There are times when the injustice is so great that a calculus of consequences of civil disobedience is not required—no possible consequences outweigh the obligation to resist the injustice.	The validity of one's appeal to one's conscience is wholly independent of social recognition.
The State has no real utility. In fact, I pity it because it does not know friend from foe. The State does not have a decent, civilized purpose. To go to jail is a way of withdrawing from it. Jail is the only proper place for the just man.	Noncooperation and passive resistance are distinct from civil disobedience; the latter is a last resort by a select few—a deliberate breach of immoral statutory enactments where one invokes the sanctions of the law and invites penalties and imprisonment.
Civil disobedience is a form of political action. Going to jail is a means of communication, with some hope for its public effectiveness.	Civil disobedience presupposes the habit of willing obedience; if a man is not respected generally as law abiding, his act of disobedience is less authentic.
	Civil disobedience is despicable if it is a mere camouflage for some other goal or end, such as a cover for concealed violence.
	The civil resister is not an anarchist; he wishes to convert, not to destroy. True civil disobedience is reluctant, it is defensive, and very rare in the well-ordered State.
	Mass civil disobedience in the pure sense must be spontaneous, not organized, not manipulative.
	The prerequisites for civil disobedience include concern for the justice of the cause; strict nonviolence in thought, speech and deed; the capacity and willingness to suffer; moral discipline; humility; and above all, self-purification by good works among the people on behalf of whom one offers resistance.

It is apparent that Thoreau's arguments were not analytically strong, but Gandhi recognized "that the power of civil disobedience was that it did not use entirely rational persuasion but a symbolic behavior, because there is a more immediate means of moving a person than simple rational argument."[20]

A Question of Law

Consider what is most often challenged by an act of civil disobedience: the law. The standard definition of law is familiar: it is a rule of reason directed to the common good and promulgated by proper authority. There are questions inherent in each part of this definition. Is a given statute truly *a rule of reason*? Who determines this? By what special insights? By whose reason? Is a given statute truly *directed to the common good*? Again, who determines this? By what standards? Is a given statute truly *promulgated by proper authority*? Whence does this authority spring?

Scott Buchanan, a former resident scholar of the Center for the Study of Democratic Institutions, reminds us that there are those who take seriously the theory that lawmakers *discover* rather than make law, finding that genuine law is what the people *ought to want*.[21] This means that such things as justice, peace, freedom, and order are discovered as products of continuing dialogue among people of diversified background, interests, and perceptions—and this is what "the consent of the governed" in democratic, pluralistic nations should ideally mean.

Buchanan borrows from the theology of the late Martin Buber, who set out to show how the Old Testament—the Torah—could be interpreted as a continuous dialogue between the people and God. It was through this dialogue that the Jews became the chosen people, "the people of the law." The law was not imposed by a tyrannical God, for the people talked back to Him. Buchanan concludes that the Torah is "the demonstration in dramatic form of the doctrine that law is a teacher." The law, therefore, is not dogma; it is "a question to be pursued."[22]

This conception of law has implications for civil disobedience. This is not to suggest that any act of protest, purportedly for "good cause," is ipso facto justifiable.

> In grammatical terms, laws are obviously imperative sentences; they are, in positivistic terms, commands issued by an authority to be obeyed by subjects on pain of punishment. But if the subjects are free persons who can object, talk back, and disobey, there is at least a moment when the law is a question. . . . If the moment is extended, there will be an argument with many more questions, questions about the jurisdiction of the law, about the meanings of killings, stealing, lying, and adultery, about the purpose of the law and the common good. These are familiar questions in the courts and *mutatis mutandis*, for the legislature and the executive. In fact, whenever the law is in operation, it is itself a question and is up for questioning.[23]

This is not a new doctrine, nor was it invented by Buber or Buchanan. It is cited in the works of Plato, and Gandhi lived it out. Our First Amendment freedoms of speech, press, assembly, and petition are important as individual rights, but under this concept of the law, these freedoms become the apparatus of the continuing dialogue through which laws "become imprinted in the habits and hearts of the citizenry. *They are the means by which the laws are continually improved and adjusted to change.*[24] Clarence Darrow, the famous criminal lawyer of the 1920s, felt that laws should, like clothes, be made to fit the people they are meant to serve.

This perspective on law certainly makes it no easier for a police officer to deal with a limp civil disobedient. However, there is a certain social and moral drama in what the officer does under such circumstances, and how he or she does it, for in effect we are learning law by acting out justice or injustice in the streets.

The authority of law in a democratic society is the consent of the governed, freely given, and their willing compliance. However, dialogue and questioning as to what the law should be, and how it should be interpreted and implemented, constitute the essential dynamic of participatory democracy. This is what sociologists refer to as a consensual concept of authority in society, of particular importance in comparison with autocratic societies.

Merging Philosophy and Law

Civil disobedience is basically a question of morality. Challenges to government, law, or policy are inherently threatening and invariably produce questions as to the authenticity, sincerity, or morality of a given action. How can "the real thing" be tested or evaluated? What are the conditions that distinguish ordinary infractions of the law from civil disobedience? "If everyone were to disobey the law, the results would be disastrous; consequently, nobody has that right." True or false?

Such a question goes to the heart of the concept of civil disobedience. To repeat a point made earlier, there are many popular misconceptions of civil disobedience. It should be recognized that many protest actions are not civil disobedience. Some, in fact, are civil *obedience*—for example, distributing literature and parading or picketing with a permit. Another point: civil disobedience is not anti-law; it is in the democratic tradition, and, in the sense of the law as a question, perfectly compatible with the dignity of law. Indeed, one may argue that it enhances this dignity.

From the point of view of simple morality, the question of testing a civilly disobedient action may be approached in a manner similar to the question of deciding if a war is just. Some of the queries in such an approach would be:

- Is the issue truly a grave matter? (One does not commit an act of war or an act of civil disobedience frivolously.)
- Have all other reasonable, feasible, possible, conceivable means of resolving the issue been explored?
- Is the act merely an excuse for violence—as Gandhi put it, "a camouflage" for some other purpose? (Does the act have an ordinary criminal intent?)
- Is the act a chosen course, not accidental?
- How clear is the purpose? (To call public attention to injustice, to bring about a change, etc.) Is there a reasonable chance for success in achieving the purpose?
- Is one prepared to accept the consequences of the action? (One should not be surprised if one is arrested and jailed.) What harm may come to other parties as a result?

It is interesting to set these questions beside the conditions delineated by Sidney Hook under which individuals—on ethical grounds—may refuse to obey a certain law:

1. It must be nonviolent, peaceful not only in form but in actuality.
2. Resort to civil disobedience is never morally legitimate where other methods of remedying the evil complained of are available.
3. Those who resort to civil disobedience are duty-bound to accept the legal sanctions and punishments imposed by the laws.

4. Civil disobedience is unjustified if a major moral issue is not clearly at stake.
5. Where intelligent men of good will and character differ on large and complex moral issues, discussion and agitation are more appropriate than civilly disobedient action.
6. Where civil disobedience is undertaken, there must be some rhyme and reason in the time, place, and targets selected.
7. There is such a thing as historical timing. Will the cumulative consequences of the action, in the current climate of opinion, undermine the peace and order on which other human rights depend?[25]

Martin Luther King, Jr., who certainly understood the philosophy of civil disobedience, in his *Letter from Birmingham Jail*, wrote pertinently in this passage:

> You may well ask, "Why direct action? Why sit-ins, marches, etc? Isn't negotiation a better path?" You are exactly right in your call for negotiation. Indeed, this is the purpose of direct action. Nonviolent direct action seeks to create such a crisis and establish such creative tension that a community that has constantly refused to negotiate is forced to confront the issue. It seeks so to dramatize the issue that it can no longer be ignored. . . . I have earnestly worked and preached against violent tension, but there is a type of constructive nonviolent tension that is necessary for growth. Just as Socrates felt that it was necessary to create a tension in the mind so that individuals could rise from the bondage of myths and half-truths to the unfettered realm of creative analysis and objective appraisal, we must see the need of having nonviolent gadflies to create the kind of tension in society that will help men rise from the dark depths of prejudice and racism to the majestic heights of understanding and brotherhood. So the purpose of the direct action is to create a situation so crisis-packed that it will inevitably open the door to negotiation.[26]

In consideration of these various philosophical and jurisprudential foundations to civil disobedience, there are some distinguishable precepts in the application of civil disobedient actions:

1. Civil disobedience is a recognized procedure for challenging law or policy and obtaining court determination of the validity thereof.
2. Theories of jurisprudence recognize the propriety of nonviolent challenge to law or policy.
3. The obligation to obey the law is not absolute but relative, and allows for some forms of nonviolent challenge.
4. Protests and civil disobedience should receive protection under the First Amendment.
5. Even if the act of protest or disobedience is found to be a technical violation of law, the purpose of the disobedience should in some instances cause the punishment to be nominal.[27]

If civil disobedience were never justified, it would deaden moral and democratic sensitivity and prevent legal change. Many laws are disobeyed in that they are simply ignored, without any active concern by the state. As to the argument that it would be disastrous if everyone disobeyed the law, this is an illogical deduction from the specific to the general. The civil disobedient does not urge disobedience of all laws, nor does the disobedient argue that one disobedience justifies all such actions.

How far is a society willing to go in the latitude it permits for dissent? The minimum level is tolerance, or forbearance without approval. A somewhat greater indulgence would be at the level of peaceful coexistence. However, going somewhat further, a society might say that the individual has a *right* of dissent (and of civil disobedience) because of the advantages to society of free and open discussion.[28]

CIVIL DISORDERS

As we have noted, many disorders can hardly be called civil disobedience, in a proper sense. For one thing, violence is prominent. The use of violence by and against the police is the matter of interest here. Violence involves physical harm to others and the values of our society frown on it, to say the least. Yet we authorize the police to employ violence to cope with those who would do harm to others. Thus, the paradox "of causing harm to stop or prevent harm."[29] In point of ethics and justice, violence as a response to violence is deemed by most people to be right, indeed mandatory—to protect society, as it is said. So then the question in police use of force becomes one of standards for its use: in what precise circumstances, what type of violence, how much? In short, what constitutes its misuse? The implication is restraint, control, minimal use to accomplish a righteous purpose.

The task of bringing control to bear on what is sometimes a mob beyond control is a task assigned by society to the police, and if necessary, the military. Restraint is governed by reason, by what is called "good judgment," and a mob scene is the antithesis of this. So we are back to square one.[30]

Can the police do anything to prevent violence? The evidence is that they can. They can discipline their own use of it by policy, supervision, and training, and by sanctions for its misuse.[31] All this assumes standards—*professional* standards—defining acceptable and unacceptable behavior. Going beyond this, effective community relations helps to prevent civil disorder. Better police records of violent crime and weapons arrests is another factor. More effective gun control in the community, by one means or another, is another strategy.[32]

On the other side of this, the police frequently are confronted by individuals "fighting for their honor," with a crowd looking on. The individual takes on the officers to save face. In rough neighborhoods, the individual's honor is vital to self-image. Attack may be seen as the only recourse available.[33] Hans Toch thinks, on the basis of his research with the Oakland, California Police Department, that police resources and expertise can be mobilized in such a manner as to curb citizen violence directed against the police.[34]

When a police officer kills a civilian, the psychological impact on the officer can be devastating. As to typical organizational reactions, John VanMaanen refers to it as "a messy matter." He writes:

> Police kill people. It is not a part of their job descriptions, a part of their routine procedures, a part of their administratively urged activities, or a part of their socially esteemed and appreciated tasks. Ordinarily, they do not kill with malice and forethought as a part of some organizationally defined mission. When they do kill, it is usually without grand logic or preformulated strategy, but as an individualized response to an immediate, particular, and always peculiar situation. These contextual details allow a curious legitimatizing rhetoric to emerge within police agencies such that episodes involving the loss of a citizen's life at the hands of the police can be bracketed, accounted for, and thus understood by the police in only certain ways.[35]

The prevention and control of disorder must be a collaborative effort of citizens, government, and the police. Some of the more important questions for consideration are these:

- What are the indicators that can be regularly assessed for the purpose of developing a picture of neighborhood tension levels?

- What formal mechanisms do the police have for the collection, assessment, and use of information about the levels of tension in the community?
- How are levels of tension in the community analyzed, reviewed, and discussed by police and other governmental policymakers?
- Are the police avoiding confrontational tactics in congested and tense neighborhoods?
- Do the police have reliable sources of information in the community on which to base disorder planning?
- Does disorder planning provide for mobilization of resources and tactics to respond to a range of disorder problems?
- Has attention been given to a plan for limiting confusion and curbing rumors in a disorder?
- Have the media been made part of the team in disorder planning?

TERRORISM

Given the omnipresence of concern about terrorism in our society, a text of this nature would be incomplete without some attention to the subject. Physical evidence of our concern about terrorism is most evident in Washington, DC: a stroll around the White House or the U.S. Capitol shows barriers which have been erected—albeit tastefully—to prevent terroristic attacks. Similarly, as one enters virtually any public building in the nation's capital, including the various museums of the Smithsonian Institution, one can observe baggage checks, barriers, and in some cases, metal detectors and x-ray machines, all employed to prevent terrorism.

During Operation Desert Storm in the Persian Gulf in 1991, virtually all of the airports with commercial flights in the United States, even in the smallest cities, implemented anti-terrorism procedures. These measures included such things as restricting access to departure lounges to ticketed passengers, prohibiting parking in front of terminals, removing baggage lockers, and removing trash containers from public areas. Certainly these procedures illustrate a concern for terrorism that affects both the community and the local police.

Beyond the pragmatic reasons for discussing terrorism here, there are also two philosophical reasons:

- Terrorism tests the basic political values, structures, and processes of liberal democracies, as well as the balance between security and liberty.[36]
- In a more focused sense, terrorism tests criminal justice processes—police, courts, and corrections—in their social-control reactions to deviance.

Explaining Terrorism

Terrorism is the calculated use of violence or threat of violence to attain goals, often political, religious, or ideological in nature, by instilling fear, intimidation, or coercion. It involves a criminal act, often symbolic in nature, intended to influence an audience beyond the intended victim. We are familiar with a number of highly prominent terrorist incidents—the explosion of Pan American Airlines flight 103 over Lockerbie, Scotland the 1993 bombing of the World Trade Center in New York and the bombing of the federal building in Oklahoma City are vivid examples. Many terroristic attacks occur throughout the world, but we hear little about them, particularly in this country. For example, there are several terroristic attacks or threats in London every month from the Provisional Irish Republican Army (PIRA). The scant public reporting—or sometimes the downplaying—of many terroristic threats in Europe and the Middle East is due to two factors: one, the frequency of the threats, and the other, limited media coverage defeats the intent of the terrorists.

Immediately apparent from the illustrations given above is that most terroristic incidents occur abroad. There have been relatively few international terrorist attacks in North America due to our comparative geographic isolation, effective intelligence operations, prevention initiatives, and limited number of sympathizers with the ideologies of Middle Eastern terrorist groups (which are generally the most active). These groups have found that targets in the United States are simply too difficult and expensive to attack. The Irish Republican Army generally has no desire to stage terrorism in the United States because it receives contributions and support from some members of the Irish-American community and the PIRA does not want to offend its supporters. Abroad, terrorism remains an ongoing problem. U.S. targets—embassies, military bases, and citizens—remain more vulnerable, but still, attacks have been relatively rare. Given the changes in world politics, the threat of international terrorism against the United States appears to be somewhat reduced.

Domestic terrorism in the United States is different, but still relatively rare. This encompasses violent behavior by groups in the United States who oppose American laws, policies, and sociopolitical trends. In the 1960s, extreme political left groups—the Weathermen and Students for a Democratic Society (SDS)—were responsible for various terrorist acts. (Government offices and military ROTC facilities on college campuses were among their primary targets.) While these groups are gone, they have been replaced by political ideologues on the extreme right and those with narrowly defined "causes."

By all indications, some forms of domestic terrorism can be expected in the coming years. However, it will *lack* the frequency and intensity seen in many international terroristic acts. Thus, terrorism in the United States will be of a generally different nature than elsewhere in the world, but it does pose unique concerns for law enforcement.

Right Wing Extremists

Over the past few years, there has been a growing awareness about right wing extremist groups, their ideologies, and their influence on crime and justice issues. Many people in both the public and law enforcement community initially dismissed these groups, feeling they posed no serious threat to public safety. However, this perception rapidly changed in the wake of the 1995 bombing of the Murrah Federal Building in Oklahoma City. This was followed by revelations about militia groups as well as the Freemen in Montana and members of the Republic of Texas, both of whom maintain that the federal government has no authority over them and that the U.S. courts have no jurisdiction to hear cases against them. The public was inundated with information about these groups. And as is frequently the case, a broad brush was used to describe these various groups simply as extremists.

As depicted in Figure 12-3, right wing groups can be broadly categorized into three groups:

- The Christian identity movement
- Super patriots
- White supremacists

Just as the case with any group, membership and involvement is measurable on a continuum. Some people will believe the basic tenets of the ideology, but that is the

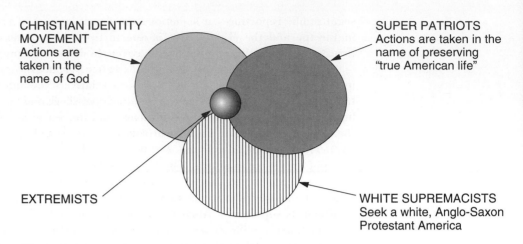

CHRISTIAN IDENTITY
MOVEMENT
Actions are
taken in the
name of God

SUPER PATRIOTS
Actions are taken in the
name of preserving
"true American life"

EXTREMISTS

WHITE SUPREMACISTS
Seek a white, Anglo-Saxon
Protestant America

Figure 12-3   Right-Wing Group Ideologies

extent of their involvement. Others may attend some meetings or read the literature, while yet others will become more active, the most aggressive of which will try to take action to make the change occur that the philosophy seeks. Indeed, that was the case of Timothy McVeigh and his motives for bombing the federal building in Oklahoma City. It is the true believers and the true ideologues who are the extremists that we must be concerned about.

Christian Identity Movement.   As implied by the label, members of these groups—such as the Covenant, the Sword and the Arm of the Lord, or CSA—base all of their actions in religion. They believe in a rigid, Protestant ethic, and often cite the Bible as justification for any actions they must take. They employ literal interpretations of the Bible, frequently citing those passages that can be expressly interpreted to support their beliefs. Identity members are highly anti-Semitic and anti-gay. They also vehemently oppose any cause or movement that could be classified as being politically liberal: the women's movement, abortion rights, affording benefits to partners of gay employees, Planned Parenthood, and so forth. They regularly reinforce their core beliefs in their religious services and outlets, including some radio stations. They are increasingly politically active, attempting to get laws and regulations changed to support their vision and supporting political candidates who they feel will support their cause.

White Supremacists.   Members of these groups are pure racists. While the most well-known group is the Ku Klux Klan, there are many others who are far more aggressive. They believe that all non-Anglos are intellectually and socially inferior and that the presence of Jews and minority group members in positions of power or authority will lead to the destruction of the United States. Their goal is to have an America that is all WASP—white Anglo-Saxon Protestant. Interestingly, while many of the christian identity ideologues are also racist, the white supremacists are not particularly religious. These groups have committed robberies for money to support their causes and burglaries for developing caches of weapons, as well as being aggressive in using the Internet to spread their message. The White Nationalist Party, neo–Nazis, and skinheads fall within this category. In addition there is the Aryan Nation, which is a racist group with strong religious undertones.

Super Patriots.   In a combination of beliefs, these groups tend to believe that the federal, and sometimes state, government is unlawful. In their own interpretations of the Constitution they believe that all legitimate authority is local, thus they proclaim all other forms of government as unconstitutional. Moreover, they often argue that since current county and municipal governments receive federal funds and those officials often work with state and federal agencies, the current local governments have been tainted and are also unconstitutional. As a result, new governments must be formed by members of the groups.

The less extreme group members are typically distrustful of the federal government and feel they must stockpile weapons and develop contingency plans in case the U.S. government attempts to take control of individuals' lives. Super patriot groups include the militias, Freemen, and Republic of Texas, in a wide array of positions on the continuum of extremism. They tend to see themselves as modern-day revolutionaries, fearing America has moved too far away from its founding principles and values. They fear conspiracies and are constantly pursuing rumors, such as "black helicopters" operated by the United Nations, which are gathering information on people and surveilling group members in preparation for the "new world order". They, too, use the Internet extensively, mostly for communication, and hold "preparedness expos," which include military hardware demonstrations and survival skill training programs.

A Perspective on Right Wing Groups. Right wing extremists are "true-believers" or ideologues. Many are willing to sacrifice themselves and their families in support of their beliefs—that makes them particularly dangerous. Like any other terrorist or ideologue, they rationalize their actions and truly believe they are right. There is a notable amount of "crossover" between the different categories of extremists, but most find an ideological home in one of the categories that represents their basic fears and beliefs. All of the right wing groups can be found in every state, with sympathizers in several foreign countries. Racist groups are particularly active in Germany, Austria, and South Africa, and there is evidence that they communicate regularly with the American groups.

Given their distrust in government and involvement in criminal activity, these groups are threats to both the police and the community. Of course, when they are simply exercising their right of free speech or conducting a lawful demonstration, the police are obligated to protect them just as they are any other citizen. The complexity of this interplay frequently leaves the police in a difficult position, requiring even greater communication with the community.

Narco-terrorism

Frequently in news reports there are references to "narco-terrorism." The term refers to violence used by drug trafficking organizations to expand their reach and increase profits. In Columbia, illustrating the most extreme example, narco-terrorism has been directed against judges and political officials to change national policies related to drug problems. Narco-terrorism is also used by rival drug trafficking organizations to gain control of the "turf" where drugs are sold here in the United States.

The reality is that drug trafficking is an economic venture, not an ideological one. As a result, violence associated with narcotics is not terrorism in its truest sense. While serious levels of violence occur, it is somewhat more easy to identify and address. In essence, narco-terrorism is really violence associated with organized crime.

The Abortion Controversy

The argument over abortion has permeated public debate and political maneuvers, particularly over the past two and one-half decades. Both pro-choice and pro-life advocates have been aggressive in the advocacy of their beliefs and both have resorted to violence in some form. Both sides are emotionally charged with the omnipresent belief that their position is correct. Success by the "other side" is seen as having important sociolegal implications, whether it is for the mother or the unborn child. Abortion is not only a legal issue, it is one with personal moral and philosophical implications. The result is that sincere advocates on both sides of the issue may resort to ironic strategies in order to emphasize their point and influence public policy. It is ironic because we have seen people on both sides of the "right to life" debate become involved in violence and property destruction in support of their position.

While terrorism of activists on the abortion issue may not reach the magnitude seen with groups such as the PIRA, they nonetheless have participated in activities that cause problems for other citizens and local police. Well-organized civil disorder and protests, defiance of court orders, burglaries of abortion clinics, arson, and assaults on people who have opposing views characterize some of the acts committed.

Animal Rights Activists

The United States has experienced an apparent increase in demonstrations and actions by people concerned about animal rights. Two particular organizations are at the heart of this controversy: the People for the Ethical Treatment of Animals (PETA) and the Animal Liberation Front (ALF). The arguments presented by these groups are that humans have abused animals—violated their "rights"—for product testing, medical research, fashion (fur coats), and hunting.

Animal rights activists argue that legislation has inadequately protected animals from abuse and exploitation by commercial and research interests. As a result, they have resorted to some forms of "terrorist" activities to assert their position. Activists have thrown paint on people wearing fur coats and harassed hunters lawfully pur-

FOCUS 12.4

THE NATIONAL DRUG CONTROL STRATEGY

As part of the Anti-Drug Abuse Act of 1988, the Office of National Drug Control Policy (ONDCP) was created—the so-called "Drug Czar." The intent of the ONDCP was to coordinate the efforts of all federal agencies that have responsibility for some aspect of drug control in the United States—law enforcement, eradication, interdiction, treatment, or education. Each year, beginning in 1989, the ONDCP has published a document entitled the *National Drug Control Strategy*.

The strategy details priorities wherein the federal government will devote its resources and support local initiatives in an effort to "win the war on drugs." The current national priorities on drug control are:

- Deterring new and casual drug users
- Freeing current drug users
- Focusing on drug trafficking organizations
- Focusing on drug supply and money laundering networks
- Focusing on the street dealer

suing their sport. In 1992 the ALF broke into animal research laboratories at Michigan State University, setting the facility on fire and destroying ten years' worth of data and research records of two professors. (Ironically, the professors' work was directed toward finding alternatives to live animal testing in research.) This, and similar attacks at research facilities, both at universities and corporations, have been a tactic of the more radical animal activists and serve as a somewhat unique form of terrorism in America.

Terrorism and the Police-Community Relationship

In discussing terrorism from the viewpoint of police-community relations, several questions are relevant:

- What are the causes and motivations for various types of terrorism?
- What are some of the typical strategies and tactics of terrorism?
- Is terrorism ever morally justified? If so, under what conditions?
- What counter-strategies and tactics are open to government and security forces?
- How do we balance the need for prevention and control strategies without infringing on the rights and liberties of citizens?
- What are the dangers of underreaction and overreaction to potential terrorism?
- What countermeasures might be taken locally, nationally, and internationally?
- What standard should guide news media in the release of information in terrorist incidents?

Terrorism is likely to become somewhat more common in the United States. It requires attention, study, and understanding. Its presence is an overt threat to the

---

The designation of "High Intensity Drug Trafficking Areas" is an effort to target locales that are of particular risk or concern as a result of the presence of drug-related problems. Ideally, the federal agencies will work in concert with state and local authorities to address the problems in these areas.

The ONDCP is not universally accepted. It has a small budget and little authority. As a result, its effectiveness is measured by the skills of the staff as negotiators and coordinators between the myriad of agencies involved. This is not always easy because of problems of "turf" and the need to "be visible" as a means of securing continued funding levels. Conversely, efforts to coordinate all national drug control initiatives were sorely needed. Moreover, previous national priorities were extremely diverse because they reflected the specific concerns of the agencies involved, such as the Drug Enforcement Administration, Coast Guard, Customs Service, Department of Education, and National Institute of Drug Abuse, to name a few, rather than a *coordinated* effort that capitalized on the strengths of all the agencies.

The greatest impact of ONDCP has perhaps been its ability to integrate the issues of drug control and articulate these in annually published strategies. The greatest weakness of the office has been its lack of authority to ensure that agencies expend their efforts in support of the strategy.

safety and security of our citizens. Its prevention and control may also pose threats to the rights and freedoms Americans hold as sacred. Because of this, effective communication with the community is a critical element in achieving the balance needed to deal with this problem.

DEADLY FORCE

With reference to the police, do violence and force mean the same? Clearly not. Force means coercion, as in enforcement. Violence is often irrational, and it is vehement, turbulent, ferocious. Going back to what we said earlier in the text, force is power, violence is might. For the police to restrain by arrest is force. When this restraint involves killing someone, force becomes violence. Democratic social control theory insists upon limiting the use by the police of force and violence.

The heart of the issue is again the question of the control of force. What constitutes excessive use of lethal force under varying circumstances? It is a question of clashing judgments. An officer's decision to use a weapon is historically grounded in strict legal terms based on society's views of what is reasonable and just. But in stark reality, a street incident provokes a decision based on little more than what a particular officer on the scene perceives as reasonable and just. Compounding the problem is a lack of uniformity in state laws and police policy applicable to the use of force in apprehending felony suspects.

Civil rights organizations have charged that racial and ethnic bias too frequently taints officer judgments in the use of deadly force, and that as a result, blacks, Hispanics, or other minorities are disproportionately represented among victims. In short, the issue is often stated as whether the police have one trigger finger for whites and another for minorities. Obviously, discussions of this issue quickly become heated. Departments, policies, and individual officers differ greatly, and so do particular situations and communities where deadly force becomes a hot topic. The nature of this emotion centers on the finality deadly force represents. If the officer's decision to use deadly force is based on incomplete information, biased emotions, or poor judgment, the bullet cannot be recalled if it is determined the officer's decision was wrong.

In a "typical" deadly force situation an officer confronts a person as a result of a call or some other behavior drawing police attention. As the officer attempts to gain information about the situation or control of the person, there is some action (or collection of actions), which the officer interprets as life-threatening. Based on these observations and interpretations, the officer must decide whether deadly force is the only reasonable alternative to respond to the life-threatening situation. If so, the officer draws the weapon, gives a final warning to the person, and if the person does not respond, the officer shoots—typically, the officer "shoots to kill."

All of this occurs faster than the time it took you to read it. The officer must perceive, interpret, and analyze this entire scenario in a matter of seconds under conditions of stress and make a decision of whether to shoot or not. Unfortunately, not all of the decisions are correct ones. Officers misinterpret information or see only part of the picture and an innocent person is shot. While it is imperative that we scrutinize the finest details of shooting incidents to learn "what went wrong," we must remember to temper that scrutiny in the framework of the officer's knowledge at the time the shooting took place. In cases where the officer's decision was based upon good faith, but was nonetheless wrong, the death of the innocent citizen is ruled an "excusable homicide." Essentially this means that the death was a tragic accident, but there was no misfeasance or malice on behalf of the officer involved.

The ruling that a police officer's mistaken shooting of a person is "excusable" is an emotional one, which produces controversy and frequently vocal criticism of the police among community members. They argue that the police are "covering up" discrimination and incompetence. Throughout our history, both of these have occurred, yet the fact remains that today's American police officer is the best trained and most accountable that we have seen in our history. All officers recognize the ramifications of using deadly force, and even the least professional and ill-prepared officer will not use deadly force indiscriminately if, for no other reason, than the personal accountability an officer will face. This is not to infer that wrong judgments are never made. Rather, it is to illustrate the solemnity of the police attitude on this issue.

The research on deadly force suggests that often the targets of that force are people who have committed less serious crimes. Moreover, concerns have been expressed that a "shoot to kill" policy is inhumane, that police have not been adequately trained in the use of deadly force, and that police shootings show a pattern of discrimination against minorities, notably blacks.[37] These issues require a closer examination.

The "Shoot to Kill" Policy

Most police departments have a policy that when an officer decides to use deadly force, he or she must "shoot to kill" rather than try to disable the person by shooting at the arm or leg. The admonition so frequently heard in old television westerns when the sheriff told a deputy to "wing 'em," simply is not an option in the real world. While the police recognize the need for a "shoot to kill" policy, it is not one which is publicized widely. This lack of publicity is not because the policy is improper, but it does present a cruel image to those who do not know the reasoning for it.

To start, the handgun is not an inherently accurate weapon. Moreover, as the distance between the weapon and the target increases, the accuracy diminishes. This is compounded by the fact that while police officers are competent and safe handgun users, they are not all expert marksmen who can place a shot at any place they like. During shooting competitions and "range firing," officers typically shoot at a stationary target. However, a criminal suspect will generally be running or moving and this makes the target even more difficult to hit. Compounding this reality is the stress of the situation, which also affects the officer's ability to take slow, steady, and accurate aim. Needless to say, if the target is an arm or a leg, this is smaller than the "body mass" and more difficult to hit. If the officer misses the target, the person will obviously not be disabled and will continue to pose a threat. In addition, the stray bullet could conceivably strike an innocent bystander. Thus, "shooting to wound" is not pragmatic reasoning.

Finally, deadly force is, by its very nature, intended to cause death. In light of this, if the officer decides that the situation is sufficiently serious to warrant deadly force to protect the life of the officer or others, then it is serious enough to take the ultimate action in order to protect the innocent. The stark reality is that as a society we have vested police officers with the authority to take the life of a dangerous person under certain circumstances. In those cases, officers have the obligation to fulfill the "shoot to kill" policy for protection of others from a dangerous threat.

Police Weaponry and Training

Most American police departments supply an officer with a "service handgun" and ammunition, which the officer carries on-duty. Virtually all departments have a regimen of firearms training, which includes classroom instruction on the safety, care, and use of firearms; the police department's firearms policy, specifying when deadly force may be used; legal issues of excessive force; and factors related to making the decision of whether to shoot or not. This is followed by firearms practice on a range (or other facility) wherein the officer must meet defined shooting standards—called "qualification"—before he or she can graduate from the police academy. Most departments also have 12-gauge shotguns in patrol cars that officers must also qualify in order to use.

Traditionally, police sidearms have been .38 or .357 caliber six-shot revolvers. Beginning in the late 1980s, a trend developed for police departments to change to semi-automatic weapons, most commonly a 9-mm caliber, each of which would hold nine to sixteen bullets. In a national study of the nation's largest law enforcement agencies for the Police Executive Research Forum on firearms policies and practices, some interesting findings were noted.[38] The most common reasons given for changing to the 9-mm weapon were the increased violence on the streets, the availability of more rounds of ammunition to officers, and to increase officer morale. Interestingly, safety, accuracy, and dependability of the semi-automatic handgun in comparison to the revolver were the least concerns. The change to a semi-automatic is also expensive. The weapons and ammunition cost more, and all personnel have to be retrained before they can be issued the new weapon.

With respect to officer training, the bulk of the police departments required officers to requalify with handguns every four to six months. Most departments (63.6 percent) required officers to shoot their qualifying course "cold," not permitting officers to practice ("warm up") first. The reasoning for this is to more closely simulate a condition under which the officer might actually use the weapon. This is a fallacious assumption, however, because the nature of the qualifying course is significantly different from the real world situation. In fact, only 15 percent of the departments reported they used any type of stress conditions when officers requalified with their handguns. Not surprisingly, departments tended to require officers to qualify with the actual weapon they carried on duty as well as with the same type of ammunition carried.

Some of the other PERF study findings related to police armament include:

- Of those agencies still using revolvers, the most common caliber was .357 (70.6 percent) compared with the .38 (29 percent).
- Nine agencies (1.7 percent) said that officers could use *any* weapon of their choice for a duty weapon.
- 162 agencies (31.2 percent) said officers could use *any approved* weapon as a duty weapon.
- The average length of time the current weapon had been in use was 6.6 months—a relatively short time period, reflecting the large number of agencies that had changed to a semi-automatic handgun.
- 316 agencies (60.8 percent) had a limit on the number of ammunition rounds officers could carry, with the average being 26.9 rounds.
- 118 departments (22.7 percent) were considering changing their handguns.
- All 118 of those considering a change were switching to a semi-automatic handgun.

Interestingly, the research by police departments considering a change of weapons tended to focus on which brand of 9-mm handgun would be purchased. Virtually no research was done on the cost-effectiveness and value of a change in handguns by the police departments.

Deadly Force and Discrimination

"Virtually all of the studies that have examined the race of civilian victims of shootings by the police have shown that blacks are shot in numbers disproportionate to their proportion in the local population."[39] These findings immediately give rise to the inference that police shootings nationwide are inherently discriminatory. Certainly, cases have been found in which discrimination was a fundamental influence on an officer's decision to shoot, both in justifiable and nonjustifiable situations. However, making generalizations about a small proportion of cases provides limited understanding. Other factors must be explored to fully understand the issues.

In the most comprehensive research on the issue, William Geller and Michael Scott observed that there is a very close match between the percentage of black and Hispanic persons arrested for serious felonies and the percentage of blacks and Hispanics who were shot or shot *at* by the police.[40] This finding somewhat dispels the notion that there is no correlation between the shooting of minorities and arrest patterns.

Despite this correlation, the issue of discrimination in police shootings must still be addressed. In fact, the research shows some positive strides by the police. In the fifteen years from 1970 to 1984, there was an "enormous reduction" in the number of civilians killed by big-city police, due almost entirely to the reduction in the number of blacks killed.[41] Geller and Scott concluded from this data and their independent research that the ratio of blacks to whites killed by the police dropped from 7:1 in 1971 to around 2.4:1 in 1989.[42] This suggests that when both the shooting ratio decline and arrest correlation are considered, discriminatory elements in police shootings turn out to be marginal. Beyond these national trends in police shootings, individual analysis of shootings in Chicago, Dallas, and Los Angeles reveal similar results.

These findings are not meant to infer that race and ethnicity have *no* relationship to police shootings, but they do provide a contemporary perspective. First, in terms of what is disproportional racially, overall police shootings have dropped dramatically as a result of greater police awareness of the issue, better police training, and better qualified officers who make more judicious shooting decisions. Second, the disproportion of police minority shootings reflects a similar disproportion of arrest rates. The reality we must face is that "street crime" remains disproportionately represented by minorities. This is a product of historical economic, social, and political factors that are slowly changing but will most likely remain well into the twenty-first century.

Third, prejudicial influences on officers are most likely the product of unconscious factors instead of overt decisions. Officers do not see a black person involved in a life-threatening situation and say to themselves, "That's a black man, I had better shoot him." Rather, officers unconsciously may take a racial stereotype into consideration along with a myriad of other factors in assessing the life-threatening nature of a situation. While this tendency is certainly less overt, it is also more difficult to change.

The police must remain vigilant in their control of deadly force. Indeed, law enforcement has made great strides in this vigilance. However, the community must also recognize the realities of crime and the responsibilities of the police. Police officers are asked to make difficult decisions, with limited information, under trying conditions. For public officials or community members to *summarily* conclude that an officer's decision to shoot was a product of racial discrimination is not only inherently unfair to the police, it is irresponsible.

IMITATION GUNS AND POLICE ENCOUNTERS[43]

Over the past several years news stories have reported tragic incidents involving a person with an imitation gun being mistakenly shot by a police officer who thought the gun was real. In other tragic cases, young people were playing with toy guns, a retarded person was acting "suspiciously" with a toy gun in their possession, people (including adults) were just "joking around" with a toy gun, and one or two attempted to commit a crime with an imitation gun—all of whom died from a police shooting. It is difficult for the public to understand how these tragedies could occur since "anybody can tell a toy gun from a real one." Consequently, the police are accused of being discriminatory, incompetent, or "trigger happy."

As one illustration, Lansing, Michigan police officers were called to the scene of a disturbance near a local motel at around 1:00 A.M. on a winter Sunday morning. The location was in a part of town were police calls were common. Information from the caller said that there was an Hispanic man armed with a gun threatening to shoot another person. When the police arrived at the scene, they saw the man with the gun in his hand. He was instructed to drop the weapon, but did not comply. After further instruction the man raised the weapon and officers fired. Only after approaching the man, who later died from the gunshot wounds, did the officers learn the gun was an imitation. The shooting was ruled excusable by the department's internal investigation as well as by a separate district attorney's investigation. The Hispanic community maintained that the shooting was a product of police discrimination because of the victim's ethnicity. Under pressure from the Hispanic community, the mayor appointed a special commission to investigate the case. This investigation also concluded that the shooting was tragic, but excusable under the conditions at the time. The Hispanic community continued to assert that the shooting was a product of discrimination, an assertion which contributed to strong feelings of conflict between the police and community.

At the heart of this and related controversies is the fact that a significnat number of imitation guns have been manufactured to look realistic. Unfortunately, many of these imitations have become involved in crime or confrontations with the police. The similarity is by no means accidental. Some of the toys and imitations are specifically manufactured to resemble real guns. Particularly popular firearms which serve as models for toys include the Uzi machine pistol and both the Colt and Smith & Wesson .357 revolver models.

The only research ever conducted on this issue found that in a four-year period, 458 police departments (65.5 percent of the population in this study) reported 5,654 robberies known to be committed with an imitation gun. Robbery investigators who were interviewed in this research estimated that, on an average, 15 percent of all robberies were committed with imitation guns. Additional findings from the study showed:

- In the same time period, police departments reported 8,128 known assaults with imitation guns.
- A reported 31,650 imitation guns seized in the four-year period were involved in some type of crime or incident. (This number does *not* include recovered stolen imitation guns.)
- One hundred eighty-six police departments reported 1,128 incidents in which an officer warned or threatened to use force and 252 cases in which actual force had been used against a citizen, based on the belief that an imitation gun was real.

The number of cases involving an imitation gun is surprisingly high. The complexity (perhaps confusion) inherent in all of the incidents studied in this project could be broken down into two fundamental factors: the *nature of the incident* and the *nature of the weapon*.

Nature of the Incident

The incident refers to the reason and circumstances surrounding the police and some type of involvement with an imitation gun. It was either a direct encounter with the police or a third party calling the police under the belief that an observed gun was real. The different types of incidents that were identified included:

- *The commission of a crime* with an imitation gun being intentionally used as an instrument of the crime by the criminal.
- *Mistaken encounters* when a citizen and/or officer encountered a person with an imitation gun but, as a result of the gun's appearance and the circumstances at the time, the people involved reacted as if the gun were real.
- *Officer-involved shootings in noncriminal situations* in which the circumstances facing the officer appeared reasonably threatening and/or criminal in light of the information known by the police officer at the time.
- *Commission of a crime and/or the brandishment of a toy gun as a real weapon, resulting in an officer-involved shooting.* In these cases the suspect was involved in a crime (or a criminal attempt) and tried to dissuade an officer's intervention by acting as if the imitation weapon were real.

Circumstances of this type occurred in a wide range of examples in the study's report. In all cases, officers reacted as if the imitation gun was real because they could reasonably believe that it was in light of the information they had. Citizens must understand that there is always an apparent police-related matter which precipitates an officer's encounter with a person possessing an imitation gun.

Nature of the Weapon

Obviously, in the imitation gun incidents an inherent element is the observation of what appeared to be a firearm. There are three broad types of imitations which were found in the study:

- *Toys.* These are imitation weapons designed with the specific intent that they are for play. They include a wide array of games, such as "cops and robbers"; a toy children use in concert with their imagination, water guns; toy guns designed for some type of "target practice"; and the more sophisticated games such as "laser tag."
- *Pneumatic Guns.* In this category are the types of guns which use pneumatic pressure to propel some type of projectile. The propellant system may be operated through an internal pump, be hand-operated by the person using the gun, or use a compressed CO_2 air cartridge. BB guns and pellet guns are the most prevalent types in this category.
- *Replica Guns.* These guns are models of actual weapons, accurate to minute details including moving parts and weight. Replica guns are full-size "working" reproductions of firearms, but are manufactured so they are unable to fire (and cannot be converted to fire).

Many of these guns are so realistic that in some cases, close inspection is required to distinguish the imitation from a real gun. In other cases, the difference can be determined with a quick look. However, during the stress of an encounter with a possibly armed person as well as under poor environmental conditions, it becomes amazingly difficult to distinguish between the real and the fake.

Complicating Factors

Beyond the nature of the incident and nature of the weapon, there were a number of critical factors identified in the study which influenced the officer's decision to shoot. These were:

- *The nature of the dispatched call.* The information given to the officer from the dispatcher, the tone of the dispatcher's voice, and the location of the call all contribute to both heightened awareness and stress, inferring a life-threatening incident at the call.
- *Expectations of the officer.* Based on the information received from the dispatcher, knowledge of problems in the area, known characteristics of the neighborhood, observations of the officer enroute to the call, and a wide range of other experiential factors, the officer develops defined expectations of what might be encountered at the scene of the call. Usually, as a safety factor, the "worst case scenario" is expected, including the belief that the officer will encounter an armed person.
- *Environment at the scene of the incident.* Upon arriving at the scene of the call or incident, the officer evaluates the behavior of the people involved and makes other observations indicating a possible threat. These judgments interact with both the nature of the dispatch and the officer's expectations, placing the officer in a situation wherein the likelihood of using deadly force increases.
- *Shape/design of the gun.* A finding repeated in every incident investigated in the study was that the shape or design of the gun was a paramount factor in the officer's decision to shoot. Even the guns made of plastic and with distinct colors were frequently indistinguishable from real guns, particularly under low light conditions. Moreover, officers tended to only take a "quick glance" to observe the weapon, thereby concentrating their attention on the overall behavior of the "armed" person in order to perceive threatening actions. This behavior is consistent with their training and remains as the proper approach to the situation in order to maximize officer safety.
- *Actions of the person(s) involved in the incident.* In the shooting incidents examined in this study, the factor ultimately influencing the officer's decision to shoot was the action of the individual. These actions were more than simply pointing the weapon at officers or other persons, but included such things as overt threatening movements, shouting, and even acting as if they were going to shoot the gun.

These factors collectively illustrate the complexity of imitation gun incidents faced by the police. Unfortunately, the community does not recognize these things. Instead, questions arise about the motives of police actions and the recurring issues of discrimination or officers being overly willing to shoot. Citizens, quite innocently, ask, "Couldn't that cop tell that gun was a toy?" Obviously not when there is a shooting involved.

In comparison to all crimes of violence and police-involved shootings throughout the United States, the proportion of cases involving imitation guns is small. The nagging element of the "toy gun problem" is that many of the incidents seem particularly tragic: a child is involved, a mentally disturbed person does not recognize the gravity of his or her actions, or a person simply uses poor judgment. The impact on a community can be dramatic, as seen in the earlier case in Lansing. There must be communication and education to understand this unique problem. The community must also recognize that a seemingly simple issue becomes geometrically complicated when all facets of the problem are analyzed. The experiences we have had with imitation guns are a manifestation of the larger problem of violence in our society. All of the problems are serious and none of the solutions are simple.

SUMMARY

Violence is a learned phenomenon which becomes part of the behavioral pathology of a culture. It has been molded by a series of complex, interactive patterns over a generation and cannot be changed with short-term programs and initiatives. As a result, it is unlikely that levels of violence will decrease in the next few years. In fact, they will probably increase, albeit at a slower rate, in the coming years, until institutional change reshapes the psycho-behavioral patterns of the next generation. Violence, and the fear of it, will inherently affect the community. Citizens will continue to turn to the police to deal with it, but its control is well beyond the reach of the police alone.

QUESTIONS FOR DISCUSSION

1. What are some of the major trends in violence in America today?
2. What is your opinion of "gun buy-back" programs such as Hennepin County's *Drop Your Guns* program?
3. Define collective behavior. Why is it often a special concern for the police?
4. Relate collective behavior to symbols and symbolic behavior.
5. How are collective behavior and civil disobedience often linked?
6. Define civil disobedience. Why is it troublesome for the police?
7. Define terrorism and explain how it is a concern of police-community relations.
8. Explain why there seems to be growth in right-wing extremism.
9. What is the core issue in police use of deadly force?
10. How can imitation (toy) guns be a problem for the police, both operationally and for police-community relations?

NOTES

1. Definitions used in this section are from William J. Goode, *Vocabulary for Sociology* (Flushing, NY: Data-Guide Distributing Corp., 1959). Deviant behavior is defined as action that violates a group norm or rule.
2. Alfred McClung Lee and Norman D. Humphrey, *Race Riot* (New York: Octagon Books, 1967), p. 5.
3. Raymond M. Momboisse, "Demonstrations and Civil Disobedience," *Police* 12, no. 2 (1967): 76–82.
4. Herbert Blumer, "Collective Behavior," in *New Outline of the Principles of Sociology*, Alfred McClung Lee, ed. (New York: Barnes & Noble, 1946), pp. 203–211.
5. William P. Brown, "The Police and Community Conflict," in *Police and Community Relations: A*
Sourcebook, A. F. Brandstatter and Louis A. Radelet, eds. (Beverly Hills, CA: Glencoe, 1968), pp. 322–334.
6. Nelson A. Watson, "Group Behavior and Civil Disobedience," in *Police and Community Relations*, p. 108. Brandstatter and Radelet, eds. Reprinted by permission.
7. While there is frequently criticism of police responses that are akin to paramilitary actions, one must recognize that sometimes that is the only way a situation can be controlled. Unfortunately, the visual appearance of such operations gives the *perception* of an excessive response.
8. *Tinker* v *Des Moines Independent Community School District*, 393 U.S. 503 (1969); *Hernandez* v School

District No. 1, Denver Colo., 315 F. Supp. 289 (D. Colo. 1970); *Aquirre v Tahoka Independent School District*, 311 F. Supp. 664 (N.D. Texas 1970).

9. U.S. National Advisory Commission on Civil Disorders, prologue to *Report* (from an address to the nation on June 27, 1967).

10. U.S. National Commission on the Causes and Prevention of Violence, preface to *The Politics of Protest: Violent Aspects of Protest and Confrontation* (Staff report written by Jerome H. Skolnick) (Washington, DC: U.S. Government Printing Office, 1969).

11. U.S., President's Commission on Campus Unrest, *Report: Campus Unrest* (Washington, DC: U.S. Government Printing Office, 1970), p. 1.

12. Jerome H. Skolnick, *Politics of Protest*.

13. Ibid.

14. Jerome Hall, "Police and Law in a Democratic Society," *Indiana Law Journal* 28, no. 2 (1953): 133 ff.

15. Ibid.

16. John A. Morsell, "A Rationale for Racial Demonstrations," in *Police and Community Relations*, p. 148, Brandstatter and Radelet, eds.

17. Watson, "Group Behavior," p. 112.

18. Ibid., p. 113.

19. Adapted from Raghavan N. Iyer, "Gandhi," and Harry Kalven, Jr., "Thoreau," in *Civil Disobedience* (Santa Barbara, CA: Center for the Study of Democratic Institutions, 1966). Reprinted by permission.

20. Kalven, "Thoreau," p. 28.

21. Scott Buchanan, "Martin Buber," in *Civil Disobedience*, pp. 29–32.

22. Ibid., p. 29.

23. Ibid., p. 30.

24. Ibid.

25. Sidney Hook, "Social Protest and Civil Disobedience," *Humanist* (Fall 1967).

26. Martin Luther King, Jr., *Letter from Birmingham Jail* (Philadelphia: American Friends Service Committee, 1963).

27. Harrop A. Freeman, in *Civil Disobedience*, pp. 5–10.

28. Immanuel Kant and William Wordsworth, quoted by Freeman, in *Civil Disobedience*, p. 10.

29. Lawrence W. Sherman, "Perspectives on Police and Violence," *The Annals* 452 (November 1980): 2.

30. The complexity of this matter is indicated in the reports of and for the U.S. National Commission on Causes and Prevention of Violence (U.S. Government Printing Office, 1969). See also Arnold Binder and Peter Scharf, "The Violent Police-Citizen Encounter," *The Annals* 452 (November 1980): 111–121.

31. An elaboration of this point is provided by Carl B. Klockars, "The Dirty Harry Problem" and by Peter K. Manning, "Violence and the Police Role," both in *The Annals* 452 (November 1980): 33–47, 135–144.

32. James Q. Wilson, "What Can the Police Do About Violence?" *The Annals* 452 (November 1980): 13–21.

33. William Ker Muir, Jr., "Power Attracts Violence," *The Annals* 452 (November 1980): 48–52.

34. Hans Toch, "Mobilizing Police Expertise," *The Annals* 452 (November 1980): 53–62.

35. John Van Maanen, "Beyond Account: The Personal Impact of Police Shootings," *The Annals* 452 (November 1980): 145–156.

36. P. Wilkenson, *Terrorism and the Liberal State* (Somerset, NJ: John Wiley and Sons, 1977). See also Sandra Stencel, "International Terrorism," in *Crime and Justice* (Washington, DC: Congressional Quarterly, Inc. 1978) pp. 21–44.

37. Lawrence W. Sherman, "Execution Without Trial: Police Homicide and the Constitution," in *Police Deviance*, 2d ed., Thomas Barker and David L. Carter (Cincinnati, OH: Anderson Publishing Company, 1991).

38. David L. Carter and Allen D. Sapp, *Summary of Contemporary Police Issues: Critical Findings* (Washington, DC: Police Executive Research Forum, 1992).

39. William G. Geller and Michael Scott, *Deadly Force: What We Know*, (Washington, DC: Police Executive Research Forum, 1992), pp. 147.

40. *Ibid.*

41. Lawrence W. Sherman and Ellen G. Cohn, *Citizens Killed by Big-City Police, 1970–1984* (Washington, DC: Crime Control Institute, 1986).

42. *Ibid.*, Geller and Scott, pp. 148–149.

43. The information for this section is based on research by the author for the Police Executive Research Forum under a cooperative agreement with the U.S. Bureau of Justice Statistics. For a comprehensive review of the issue see the project report: David L. Carter, Allen D. Sapp, and Darrel W. Stephens, *Toy Guns: Involvement in Crime and Encounters With the Police* (Washington, DC: Police Executive Research Forum, 1989).

Chapter 13

COMPLAINTS AND THE POLICE

Nearly every day one can read the newspaper or watch the news and learn about some form of misconduct by police officers. These reports are not limited to particularly notorious cases—they also include those that are less dramatic. These incidents become publicized not only because of media attention but also because there is an open process of accepting complaints by law enforcement agencies. Historically, police departments discouraged complaints against officers, feeling that the public "didn't understand" the stresses facing the police. This attitude has changed for a variety of reasons—managing by values, increased professionalism, and community policing, to name a few—and departments are now urging citizens to report abuses of police authority. It must be clear: overall, police agencies *want to know about officers whose behavior is improper*. Philosophically, this is important because of the responsibility the police have to the community. Pragmatically, it is important because of the department's image and the liability police officials can face if they permit abuses of authority to continue.

When Sir Robert Peel said that the police are the public and the public are the police, he was saying something important about police accountability for police actions. We have noted that policing in democratic society is a public, political function. The police are ultimately and clearly answerable to the public for their every move. Because the source of police authority is the community, the responsibility for controlling police behavior also lodges in the community. Police administrators are expected to see to it as an important part of their delegated prerogatives. Should they fail to do it, to community satisfaction, there are predictable rumblings. Thus, how a police agency deals with complaints about officer behavior is a critical police and community relations consideration.

The police are seldom questioned when they operate in a manner clearly supported by community consensus; their *authority* is recognized and generally accepted. But when they operate, as they sometimes must, in a manner involving their *legal power*, and where community support for the particular police action is questionable, there may well be citizen complaints. Power is not necessarily morally rightful. Authority, on the other hand, includes a moral element. If someone has power over someone else, he or she can force a certain action; if someone has authority, then commands will tend to be obeyed voluntarily.[1]

Under social circumstances, therefore, in which authority systems and authority figures are challenged—and questioned especially as to the arbitrary exercise of power—it is predictable that police conduct will come under closer scrutiny by the public. This is what has occurred in recent years. Logically, police behavior will tend to be particularly scrutinized by elements of the population (generally speaking, the powerless) who are insisting more and more emphatically that they be counted as part of the community to whom the police are accountable. For the police are expected to serve *all* the people, as with any public institution. Citizens and taxpayers in our society today have acquired the knack of "raising hell" with any and all public officials and agencies with whom they have a grievance—as a matter of right and duty. Police have become acutely aware of this.

A BASIC PHILOSOPHY

What would be some of the beams and trusses in a police philosophy regarding citizen complaints? We should make clear that in this context, we mean a grievance. In police vocabulary, there is some semantic difficulty with the term. When a citizen calls to charge that a neighbor is disturbing the peace, the police practice is to record the call as a complaint. The complaint is against the neighbor, not against the police. This is not our meaning in this chapter. We mean a grievance of (1) a citizen against the department; (2) a citizen against one or more police officers; (3) a departmental employee against the department; or (4) a departmental employee against another employee. Hence, (1) and (2) are *external* complaints, while (3) and (4) are *internal*.

A proper police philosophy regarding external complaints begins with the point already made: that the police should be held accountable to the public for their behavior, with no equivocation. This means all of the public, the powerless as well as the powerful. While it is not the best reason for this position, history is replete with lessons as to how quickly the powerless can become the powerful. By diligent and astute effort in community relations, the authority base of the police can be expanded and strengthened so as to maximize public support. The single, most important facet of this effort is to render quality service to all elements of the community.

So much, then, as the beginning of a philosophy regarding citizen complaints. Now to add to it.[2] Traditionally, the administrator of a police organization has the responsibility for supervision and discipline of personnel. This administrative prerogative is conditioned, to some degree, by public opinion—in a vague, general way. It is somewhat more specifically and directly influenced, at the municipal level, by city councils, commissions or other legislative bodies, by mayors, city managers or other executives, and by police or public safety boards, commissions, civil service bodies, and so on. It is a general working principle to keep interference with proper administration at a minimum. What does "proper" mean? Recall what we said earlier about the difference between efficiency and effectiveness. When organizational efficiency becomes an end in itself, look for troubled waters in community relations. There is a direct link between the number and type of external complaints and the level of public confidence in a police organization. As a general rule, in a community where there are numerous complaints against the police and accompanying clamor for establishment of a civilian review board or some other external mechanism for control of police behavior, there are police-community relations problems and usually other problems of a serious nature. The demand for civilian review is typically a telling symptom. And the likelihood is that the mechanism proposed for dealing with complaints against the police will strike more at the symptoms than at the roots of problems. We will elaborate on this point shortly.

SOME MANAGERIAL GUIDELINES

As a start in developing police managerial guidelines for dealing with external complaints, consider the following points:

1. Recognize that some citizens truly believe that some officers do sometimes mistreat some citizens. Incidents happen often enough to make the belief plausible. To respond to this with resentment is worse than no response at all. The belief that it does occur is real to some people, and the mistreatment itself may be. So how are mutual trust and confidence to be developed? This is the decisive question. Certainly it cannot be done through reciprocal excoriation.

2. Refrain from being judgmental regarding individuals who complain. To dismiss a complaint cavalierly, simply because of a judgment that the complainant is a "screwball" or a "pain in the ass" is to blow the whole ball game. Yes, complaints do require infinite patience and various other virtues. But in police work, this goes with the territory.

3. Consider these basic questions: *Should* the police control police? *Can* the police control police? If the answer to the first question is yes, then it is clear where the burden of proof lies with respect to the second question.[3]

4. Initiative for improvement of complaint procedures should come from police administrators, ideally in circumstances where it is not likely to be interpreted publicly as defensive or reactionary, or as "crisis oriented," or as an opportunistic gimmick to relieve political pressure.

5. If persons who believe they have been treated unjustly have no forum that they trust to explore their claims, their attitude of distrust is never dispelled.

6. There is an inconsistency between police lamenting, on the one hand, the apathy of the public regarding problems that loom large for the police, and on the other hand resisting the right and obligation of citizens to complain about what they perceive as improper police conduct. However negative a citizen complaint may be initially, it is a way by which the citizen has a say about governmental service and participates in democratic political process. With a positive police philosophy regarding complaints, the matter can often be turned to positive good for police service and for police and community relations. Some complainants may eventually become staunch allies of the police and valuable contributors to worthwhile programs and projects, as experience shows.

A final point is the reminder to police managers that municipalities are no longer held immune from suit if a municipal policy can be shown to induce civil rights violations. The number of civil suits of this nature have been increasing in the wake of amendments to the Federal Civil Rights Act permitting the awarding of lawyers' fees to plaintiffs who prevail in cases against cities. The number of civil rights cases continues to increase—as do the amounts of money in damage awards—with most cases alleging some excessive force. And the scope of the suits has been growing so that cities and supervisors may be held liable for failure to properly select and train police officers.[4]

THE CONTROL OF DELEGATED POWER

The control of delegated power may well be the most crucial element in a democracy. Our entire system of checks and balances as well as clear separation of governmental power testify to the importance of this principle. Because the police have a particularly sensitive delegated power, the problem with them is especially touchy. Control of their behavior most frequently becomes a matter of public contention under circumstances in which confidence in them is shaky.

This attitude is further embellished by stereotypic perceptions of the police officer as a "tough bully-boy," and by the fact that "we have given the police a job to do, but we haven't told them what the rules are." As an illustration, the Supreme Court upsets convictions because the police work is held to be unconstitutional and thus places the police in a bad light. The police are, in effect, held accountable on a Monday for violation of a rule established on Sunday that—it is decreed—should have guided their conduct the previous Saturday. This is the type of thing that is sometimes apparent in citizen complaints against the police, and it is the type of thing that at least partly explains why so many police are defensive about complaints. Keep in mind, however, that few of us, indeed, bear up well in the face of complaints about our behavior!

How is the use of police power to be controlled? *Quis ipsos custodes custodiet?* Who will watch the watchers? "The trouble that the police and the rest of us are now in is largely the result of our improvident reliance on the criminal sanction to perform a lot of messy social tasks for which it is not especially suited." What business does the Supreme Court have trying to educate or discipline the police. He suggested that this is happening because no one else is doing it. Who else could? The police themselves might do it, but they often have not. Most of the professional progress in police work in recent years has been in reducing corruption and in increasing efficiency. While these are certainly worthwhile achievements, "the revolution in rising expectations among urban minority groups and the due process revolution in the courts will not be satisfied with efficiency."[5]

Who else might police the police? Legislatures might do it, and Herbert Packer contended that such bodies are best suited for it—far more so than the courts— and he indicated why he believed this. But the fact is, he continued, that legislatures have utterly abdicated this responsibility. Packer thought that the Supreme Court's performance in the criminal procedure area had been increasingly unsatisfactory as its constitutional interpretations had become more legislative in tone. He questioned whether the familiar sanction against the police represented by the exclusionary rule of evidence is adequate. The exclusionary rule seeks to discourage police misconduct in the handling of suspects by court refusals to admit evidence. It also frequently frees the malefactor so he or she may again victimize some innocent person. It does not compensate the victim of police misconduct. In short, it has little to commend it, although it has probably had some small impact on police procedures.

The question of sanctions is basic, but what might "the stick" be? One possibility might be the right to file suit against the governmental unit that employs the police officer, accompanied by provisions for recovery of minimum or fixed damages, counsel fees, and the like. The strategy would be "to build respect for due process into the police officer's model of efficiency. Police officers who persistently violate the norms cost their employers money and are therefore seen as inefficient." As we have just noted, this situation is increasingly coming to pass.

THE DISCIPLINARY PROCESS[6]

The disciplinary process is critical for organizational control. It is the mechanism through which personnel who have violated department procedures and rules are sanctioned. The sanctions may be viewed as positive/remedial or negative/punitive. *Positive/remedial* sanctions are primarily intended to be *corrective* in nature. Ideally the sanction will have a learning effect so that the behavior will not occur again. *Negative/punitive* sanctions are intended to be *retributive* in nature. The intent is to punish the officer for violating rules.

Whether a sanction is positive or negative is largely dependent on two factors. The first is the *ideology of the police executive*. If the police chief's ideology toward employee motivation and control is that employees must be threatened and coerced to do the job, the sanctions are most likely to be negative/punitive. On the other hand, if the police executive believes that mistakes occur because of inadequate training or supervision or a lack of comprehension regarding organizational expectations, there will be a greater tendency toward positive/remedial sanctions.

The second factor is the *nature of the infraction*. As the seriousness of the infraction increases, the more likely the sanction will be punitive (if not in spirit, certainly in practice). This points to an important element in disciplinary philosophy: neither positive nor negative discipline represents a pure model. The sanctions will exist on a continuum. However, the general practices employed in most disciplinary cases weight the continuum toward either the positive or negative approach. The purpose of both forms of discipline is to encourage proper behavior. Positive discipline attempts a cooperative approach to this end, while negative discipline uses a coercive approach.

With complex civil service regulations, complicated collective bargaining agreements, evolving case law, appellate processes, and political factors—public opinion and scrutiny of the police or political negotiation in the city council—it is difficult to be conclusive about the status of disciplinary processes. This is aggravated by the fact that each law enforcement agency in the United States creates its own disciplinary structure and processes. Despite this, some general observations can still be made.

Grounds for Discipline

To initiate the disciplinary process, the most basic needs are to have *grounds* and *notice* for discipline. The grounds for discipline are written as organizational rules (or regulations), which either require or prohibit forms of behavior. The rules are supported by organizational policy, which states the police department's philosophy on various responsibilities and tasks. Rules and regulations do not have to be as precise as the criminal law but need to be sufficiently clear so that employees can reasonably distinguish between which behavior is acceptable (or required) and which is not.

All organizational rules, policies and procedures should be part of the department's manual—frequently called the "General Orders"—and each employee should have a copy. Providing employees a copy of the manual, including the disciplinary process and potential sanctions, establishes *notice* of behavioral expectations. With this type of notice the employee has greater difficulty contending that he or she was unaware that certain actions were prohibited or that the proscription of behavior applied.

If action is contemplated against an officer for misconduct, the *grounds* for the action must be carefully evaluated. If the department relies on unwritten customs or broad categorization—such as "conduct unbecoming of a police officer"—rather than rules that specifically prohibit defined forms of behavior, then problems may arise. Without having specific disciplinary charge categories, it is difficult for an adjudication body to make conclusive judgments.

It is imperative that standards of *substantive due process of law* be adhered to when administrative rules are broken, creating disciplinary grounds. That is, any rules must be clear, specific, and reasonably related to a valid public need. The administrative rule must be fundamentally fair in and of itself and not impose any unrealistic burden on the officer as a result of his or her police employment. Nor may the rule violate any of the officers rights.

Having the administrative framework in place is only one element of establishing the grounds for misconduct. Before any other element of the disciplinary system can be initiated, there must be an *allegation* that the officer violated an organizational rule or procedure. The allegation may be in the form of a complaint from a citizen, observations from a supervisor, or observation of another police officer. Importantly, the department must have some form of reliable information indicating that an officer may have been involved in misconduct before any administrative action should take place.

The Internal Investigation

After an allegation has been made, the department has the responsibility to investigate the allegation. Under the "pure model," a department has an independent Internal Affairs Division (IAD) investigate the facts and allegations of the complaint. The presence and structure of an IAD depends on a number of organizational variables:

- Agency size
- Overall public service demands of the department
- Available resources
- Number of complaints received, and
- Structure of the department's disciplinary process

The IAD function may be performed by specially full-time assigned personnel, an individual assigned IAD responsibilities on a case-by-case basis, a supervisor, command officer, or even an outside agency. Once again, size and complexity factors determine the investigative configuration.

Regardless of the structure, the factor of paramount importance is that the investigation be thorough and impartial. Importantly, the IAD function is merely *fact finding*—the IAD investigator should not be given authority to draw a formal conclusion on whether or not an allegation is true.

The internal affairs investigation is procedurally very similar to a criminal investigation. Physical evidence, if any, is collected and analyzed, witnesses are interviewed, applicable records are obtained for evidentiary use, and the accused officer is interviewed. The investigator then collates the information into a logical case report with supporting evidence and statements.

The significant distinction between an internal affairs investigation and a criminal investigation is the rules of evidence. Although there is a clear recognition that an officer who faces an administrative disciplinary hearing has procedural due process rights, the extent and precise nature of those rights remain debatable. Of particular concern to procedural due process are the Fourth Amendment prohibition against unreasonable search and seizure and the Fifth Amendment privilege against self-incrimination.

Generally speaking, during the course of a disciplinary investigation the Fourth Amendment guarantees apply to an officer at home and off-duty just as they would to any other citizen. However, lockers at the police station, a police car, and other elements related to on-duty performance may not be protected. Moreover, it appears that even if an unlawful search occurs, the fruits of that search *may* be used in a disciplinary hearing but not in a criminal trial.

With respect to the Fifth Amendment, the U.S. Supreme Court held in *Garrity* v. *New Jersey*, 385 U.S. 483 (1967) that statements compelled during the course of an internal investigation may be used in a disciplinary hearing but are not admissible in a criminal trial. Based on this decision, many departments have formalized the process of "Garrity Interviews" in IAD investigations to compel testimony as a way of "getting at the truth." These then can be admitted into evidence at the disciplinary hearing.

Adjudication of the Complaint

The adjudication process is the point at which a determination of the facts is made. All evidence developed during the course of the investigation is submitted to the adjudication mechanism for a determination of the validity of the allegation. There are a wide variety of adjudication mechanisms used by U.S. police departments, based on civil service regulations, collective bargaining agreements, administrative policy, or simply custom. Based on my previous research, adjudication mechanisms can be broadly categorized as follows:

Command Discipline/Review.   That disciplinary process wherein officer culpability is reviewed and sanctions, when warranted, are imposed by the department's command structure rather than through a hearing or board of inquiry. Typically, the results of a complaint investigation are formulated in a written report documenting the incident. This is forwarded through the chain of command to a designated command level where a determination is made and, if the complaint is sustained, a sanction is imposed. The command level adjudicating the complaint varies depending on the nature of the complaint and size of the agency.

Hearings/Proceedings.   There are three types of proceedings in which the veracity of allegations against an officer are adjudicated.

- *Adversarial*—the proceeding is closely akin to a court trial. Formal rules of evidence are followed, testimony is presented, evidence is introduced, cross-examination is permitted, and transcripts are recorded. In adversarial proceedings both the police department and accused officer are typically represented by counsel.
- *Quasi-adversarial*—The trial board or hearing body has only limited presentation of evidence (beyond the IAD report), most typically statements by those parties directly involved in the allegation. The proceeding also has very limited cross-examination and informal evidentiary rules. Direct testimony is frequently used only to clarify questions in reports and to permit the accused officer to make a statement on his or her behalf. Generally, the accused officer is permitted the right to counsel.

- *Nonadversarial*—No testimony is presented in this type of hearing. The adjudication board typically functions in a closed proceeding somewhat similar to a committee meeting. Only IAD reports, the initial complaint, and the service record of the accused officer are reviewed. Typically, the accused officer may submit a written statement to also be reviewed by the board. Generally, the accused officer is not present during the deliberations.

These broad categories are not meant to be conclusive, but serve as a "snapshot" of alternate adjudication models. Needless to say, many hybrids exist.

The adjudication process in most agencies does not issue a finding of the officer's "guilt" or "innocence." Instead, it simply attempts to determine, based on the evidence presented, whether or not the complaint or allegation against the officer can be *sustained*. The reason for this is twofold: first, administrative disciplinary hearings are conducted under relaxed rules of procedure, evidence, burden of proof, and disposition. As such, findings of "guilt" may go beyond the permissible scope of constitutional limits. Second, (and more pragmatically) the approach of "sustaining" or "not sustaining" complaints may afford the department some insulation from liability.

Disciplinary Sanctions and Alternatives

If a complaint is sustained after the review, then the reviewing body assesses the sanction (penalty) for the rule violation. Disciplinary alternatives usually depend on the seriousness and circumstances surrounding the rule violation, aggravating and mitigating factors, and the officer's personnel history. Several potential sanctions are available.

Termination of Employment.   This is complete severance from the police department, including salary, benefits, and any other reciprocal relationship between the officer and department.

Demotion/Loss of Rank.   Loss of rank refers to demotion from a formally recognized organizational position with authority over other members. As a penalty, loss of rank is a significant sanction because it represents a loss of earnings, a loss of status (in both the formal and informal organization), and a liability in career growth.

Punitive Suspension.   In a punitive suspension an officer is barred from work without salary for a designated period, usually not exceeding four weeks. During the suspended period the officer carries no authority as a police officer and in most jurisdictions the officer cannot work an "off-duty" job that may require police authority. While the officer has no authority or salary, typically personnel benefits are still accrued. A punitive suspension has an effect similar to a monetary fine.

Punitive Probation.   This is when the officer remains on duty receiving salary and benefits; however, his or her status is significantly altered because a subsequent sustained misconduct allegation of the same nature may result in suspension or termination.

Reassignment.   The sanction of reassignment is most appropriately used in cases in which an officer has been involved in misconduct associated with his or her current assignment. The reassignment may involve taking an officer out of a specialized position or, in the case of patrol, moving the officer to another shift and/or location.

THE POLICE OFFICERS' BILL OF RIGHTS

An ongoing issue in the review of police complaints is the rights of police officers during the complaint investigation. Police labor organizations have been particularly active in implementing steps to help protect officer rights. One measure which has been taken in this regard is development of a "Police Officers' Bill of Rights." In several states, the bill of rights is a matter of state law. In many jurisdictions the bill of rights is built into the collective bargaining agreement between the Police Officers' Association and the department.

While there are several different specifications in the various bills of rights, the following is a summary example of the typical provisions:

- Interrogations of officers accused of rule violations shall be done in a timely manner.
- Accused officers must be informed of investigating officers and the officer in charge of the internal investigation.
- An officer must be informed of the nature of the investigation before an interrogation begins.
- The length of interrogations must be reasonable and include rest breaks.
- Officers cannot be threatened with transfer, dismissal, or other disciplinary action as a means of obtaining information during the interrogation.
- Officers may have counsel or a representative of the employee organization present during the interrogation.
- The interrogation must be recorded with no "off-the-record" questions.
- Officers accused of criminal offenses must be advised of their Miranda rights.
- Officers being investigated may receive an exact copy of any written statement he or she signed or a copy of the interrogation recording.
- An officer cannot be ordered to submit to a polygraph examination.

This alternative is notably appropriate in cases in which the circumstances of the working environment contributed to the misconduct.

Mandatory Training.   If the officer's misconduct was a product of misfeasance, a reasonable sanction may be to provide the officer with additional mandatory training on the subject(s) of issue related to the misconduct. It is conceivable that the misconduct was a function of not being adequately prepared to perform the required functions of the job, therefore the department must recognize some of the responsibility and provide remedial action.

Reprimand.   A reprimand for the record is when the officer is officially admonished for his or her behavior. The admonishment is in written form with a copy placed in the officer's personnel record. The purpose of the reprimand is to serve as a record (and notice) of the incident and a warning about future misconduct. The reprimand may be considered in promotional evaluations as well as in punishment decisions in any future misconduct incidents. Reprimands may be expunged after several years if no other misconduct has occurred.

Disciplinary Appeals

Most police departments offer some avenue for appeals or reviews of sustained complaints. While appeals have not been specifically mandated in minimal due process standards for administrative hearings, the implication is clear that some form of review should be available. Police departments under a civil service system typically have the most formal appellate structure, many times with review occurring outside of the police organization.

The purpose of an appeal is to review the facts and evidence to determine if the complaint was properly sustained. Some appeals may also review the disciplinary penalty to determine if it is "appropriate." However, this is a minority of the cases.

CIVILIAN REVIEW[7]

Civilian review of police behavior and police accountability to civilian authority have been constant emotional topics. The police argue that civilians cannot understand the stresses and difficult circumstances faced by police officers in their daily activities. As such, civilians do not have an adequate foundation on which to make informed judgments about police actions. On the other hand, civilians point out that the police derive their authority from the community and as such must be accountable to the public for their actions—like it or not.

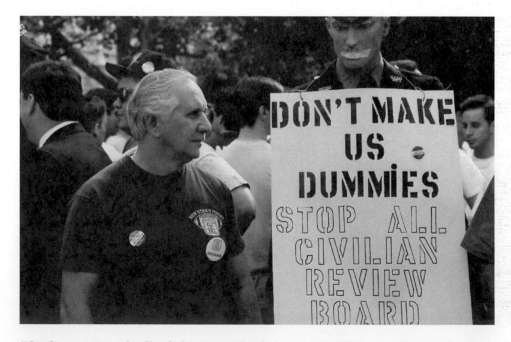

"Civilian review of police behavior and police accountability to civilian authority have been constant emotional topics."

The first and loudest calls for civilian review of the police occurred in the late 1960s following the riots. Since that time, the issue has regularly surfaced—whether on a national or regional basis—depending on events involving the police. One of the most recent calls for police accountability to civilian authority came following the "Rodney King incident" and its aftermath in Los Angeles (see the appended *Christopher Commission* report).

A wide range of approaches to civilian review/civilian accountability have been attempted throughout the United States. A brief review of some of these attempts will illustrate the diversity of ideas that have been explored.

Philadelphia, Pennsylvania Police Advisory Board.

The Philadelphia Police Advisory Board (PAB) was formed in 1958 as a result of campaign promises made by a newly elected reform mayor. Its nine-year life saw controversy and never any clear support from the police department. The eight board members were all citizens appointed by the mayor. The PAB did not have its own investigative staff. As a result, its investigatory options were either for the executive secretary (the only salaried employee) to attempt informal resolution of matters or refer the investigation to the police commissioner who assigned the Community Relations Division to look into the matter. If, following the investigation, it was concluded that a hearing was necessary, then an adversarial hearing would be held, generally with both the complainant and accused officer having representation of counsel.

The decision of the PAB on the veracity of the allegation was based on a majority vote. Normally, no formal opinion would be written concerning the decision. Following hearings wherein the allegation against the officer was sustained, i.e., "guilty," the PAB would send a disciplinary recommendation to both the police commissioner and mayor. The commissioner normally followed the board's recommendation, and if a disagreement occurred, it would be informally arbitrated by the mayor.

New York City Civilian Complaint Review Board.

The New York Civilian Complaint Review Board (CCRB) was created in the summer of 1966 following the election of a reform mayor who promised change in the NYPD. The new CCRB was essentially a transformation of an existing internal police review board. Because of this, and as a concession to opponents of the CCRB, the mayor decided that the board would not be entirely civilian. As a result, the CCRB consisted of seven members—four civilians appointed by the mayor and three police officials appointed by the police commissioner. All four civilians were full-time salaried staff. Police officers were assigned to work exclusively for the CCRB to carry out investigations. Rather than representing a true civilian review of complaints, the CCRB was a joint police-civilian approach to complaint review.

Conciliation of complaints was attempted whenever possible, usually in situations where an officer was clearly guilty of the allegation, but where the injury to the complainant was minimal. When conciliation was inappropriate, an investigation would be conducted. The CCRB would meet to discuss the outcome of the investigation and determine whether a hearing was warranted. Hearings were adversarial in nature with both sides having counsel, although rules of evidence were relaxed. Decisions were based upon a majority vote. If the complaint was sustained against the officer, the CCRB was not empowered to recommend disciplinary action. Instead, discipline remained the sole responsibility of the police commissioner.

The CCRB experienced a highly publicized, hectic yet controversial life of only four months. receiving over 400 complaints during that time—twice as many complaints as the police department's internal complaint review board had previously been averaging each year.

The NYPD police union was enraged with the CCRB. It felt that civilians had no role in the complaint review process and could not adequately make informed decisions about police officer behavior. As a result, the union started a publicity campaign against the CCRB in order to have a referendum on the CCRB placed before the public. The effort was successful and the CCRB was defeated by the public in a vote on the referendum.

Kansas City, Missouri Office of Citizen Complaints.

Kansas City's Office of Civilian Complaints (OCC) was established in 1970. It has a staff of five civilians and is located in an office building, which is physically separated from the police department. The OCC serves as a central clearinghouse for all citizens' complaints, whether made directly to the OCC or to the police department. Following receipt of a complaint, the OCC director may attempt conciliation, which, if successful, leads to the case being closed. If conciliation is not used (or if it is not successful), the case is forwarded to the police department's IAD for investigation. Completed investigation reports are returned to the OCC for review and analysis. At this point the OCC director may require additional investigative work if deemed necessary. After making a determination on a case, the OCC forwards its finding and recommendation to the police chief. This recommendation merely constitutes a suggested disposition to the case. Authority for all disciplinary sanctions remains with the police chief. Appeal of cases can be made to the Board of Police Commissioners, a civilian board appointed by the governor of Missouri. (Interestingly, both the Kansas City and St. Louis police departments are under state control, rather than being under the authority of their respective municipal governments.)

San Jose, California Office of the Ombudsman.

The San Jose Ombudsman's Office was created in 1971, partly in response to community pressure for some form of external review of the police following a series of allegations about serious police misconduct. Complaints against officers may either be filed with the police department's IAD or with the Ombudsman. If filed with the IAD, the Ombudsman does not carry out a full investigation, but is empowered to monitor the IAD investigation. If a complaint is filed directly with the Ombudsman's Office, a copy of the complaint is sent to the IAD and both units conduct an investigation. The Ombudsman monitors disciplinary outcomes and mediates a resolution when discrepancies exist (which is rare). Despite its independence from the police department, the San Jose Ombudsman has not been able to overcome skepticism from the community with respect to its impartiality.

Berkeley, California Police Review Commission.

Established in 1973, the Berkeley Police Review Commission (PRC) both investigates and convenes hearings on citizen complaints against the police. The PRC has nine members with each member of the city council appointing one of the PRC commissioners. The commissioners serve two-year terms and are part-time and unsalaried. In addition, the PRC has two full-time salaried investigators and therefore do not rely on the police department for investigations. The department retains its IAD to conduct its own investigations of citizen complaints as well as other misconduct allegations. PRC findings are only advisory for the city manager, police chief, and city council. If there is a discrepancy between the PRC findings and the IAD investigation, then the city manager will mediate the case with the police chief with respect to recommended discipline.

Detroit, Michigan Board of Police Commissioners.

In 1974 the city of Detroit established a Board of Police Commissioners—consisting of five mayoral appointees—responsible for overseeing a wide range of police practices, including the investigation of citizen complaints. To handle misconduct complaints, the board created the Office of Chief Investigator (OCI) which has twelve staff members to act on behalf of the board. The Board of Police Commissioners deals with three types of complaints: original complaints, reviews, and appeals. All original complaints are forwarded to the board's executive secretary. Those which cannot be resolved informally are referred to the OCI. The OCI staff will then either refer the case for investigation to the accused officer's supervisory staff, to the police department's Professional Standards Section (which is the same as IAD), or the OCI will investigate the case itself. This decision is generally based on the nature and seriousness of the complaint. The OCI will monitor all cases referred to the police department for investigation. Upon completion of any case investigation, the OCI director will decide the case disposition. When allegations against an officer are sustained, a recommendation for discipline is forwarded, via the Board of Police Commissioners, to the chief of police. The board has additional authority to review and then either set aside or affirm the chief's disciplinary sanctions.

Chicago, Illinois Office of Professional Standards.

In response to a growing public legacy about excessive force and misconduct going back to the 1960s, the Chicago Police Department created the Office of Professional Standards (OPS) in 1974. The OPS was established as a civilian body primarily intended to investigate allegations of excessive force, although it also acts as a recipient and registrar of complaints. Less serious complaints continue to be investigated by the department's IAD.

The idea of using civilians to not merely oversee the complaint process but to actually conduct the investigations was a unique feature at the time. The superintendent of police staffed the OPS with thirty civilian investigators and four supervisors, the majority of whom were former military personnel or investigators with other government agencies. Interestingly, the OPS was established not as an external body, but within the police department, directly responsible to the superintendent. Unfortunately, this administrative arrangement brought allegations that the OPS lacked real independence from the police department. Although civilians are employed as investigators in the OPS, they have no input into the disciplinary process once an investigation has been completed. The responsibility for hearing complaints and recommending discipline to the superintendent is the internal police Complaint Review Panel, which is generally composed of a lieutenant, a sergeant, and an officer of the same rank as the accused.

Portland, Oregon Police Internal Investigations Audit Committee.

Civilian review in Portland became an issue following public outrage at police misconduct in 1981. Based on the recommendation of a civilian task force investigating the police department, the city council created an eight-member civilian subcommittee of the city council called the Police Internal Investigations Audit Committee (PIIAC). The creation of the PIIAC was provisional pending the outcome of police union efforts to put the issue to a referendum before Portland voters. The police union waged a publicity campaign in opposition to the PIIAC and the mayor publicly announced his opposition to the committee. Despite these facts, the referendum passed and the PIIAC began operation in late 1982.

The PIIAC has three specific functions: monitoring police internal investigations of complaints, making findings of their reports public, and providing an avenue of appeal for citizens who are dissatisfied with the outcome of their complaint. The PIIAC is not a complaint review process, per se, reviewing individual complaints. Instead, its responsibilities are to review and monitor police procedures in the investigation of complaints.

McAllen, Texas Police Human Relations Committee. As a result of a pattern of civil rights cases involving excessive force against the McAllen Police Department, as well as dramatic evidence in one particular case, the Federal District Court for the Southern District of Texas issued an injunction to remedy the problems. Among the mandates of the 1981 injunction was the requirement to establish a police complaint review board called the Police Human Relations Committee (PHRC). The PHRC was composed of five members. Three were unpaid citizens who reflected the demography of the city and were appointed by the city council. The two remaining members were police officers appointed by the chief. In an attempt to solidify its authority and autonomy, the PHRC was charged with developing its own procedures to review cases. Investigations were the responsibility of the police department, which would turn all investigatory reports over to the PHRC. The committee would then make recommendations for discipline in cases where the allegation was sustained. Actual disciplinary decisions remained with the chief, however.

There are two unique distinguishing features of the PHRC. First, the committee was established by a federal court order, not by a decision of the department or by a mandate of the public or elected officials. Second, the PHRC was given the autonomy to develop *all* of its operating procedures—a process which caused notable indecision and delays.

The Commission on Accreditation of Law Enforcement Agencies and Complaint Review

As noted previously, the Commission on Accreditation of Law Enforcement Agencies (CALEA) standards are designed to provide a foundation for good practice in policing. A number of CALEA standards relate to complaints against the police and disciplinary practices. Since the accreditation process only applies to law enforcement agencies, internal rather than external review processes are addressed. Accreditation standards are continually reviewed and revised to meet changing law and practice in policing. As a result, it is likely that future standards (at least optional ones) will address external review. At the least, the CALEA standards represent important minimal benchmarks for investigation and review of police complaints.

International Association for Civilian Oversight of Law Enforcement

In 1985 the International Association for Civilian Oversight of Law Enforcement (IACOLE) was created to assist those persons involved in civilian review of police agencies. IACOLE's general membership is open to persons who are not sworn law enforcement officers and who work for or constitute agencies established by legislative authority to investigate and/or review complaints against the police. Membership includes not only civilian review authorities from throughout the United States but also an extensive international membership from Australia, Canada, Great Britain, Northern Ireland, and Nigeria. Although IACOLE is still a comparatively new organization, it has a healthy and thriving membership, which actively participates in the organization's annual meetings.

Some law enforcement officials are skeptical of IACOLE, fearing it has a "hidden agenda," while other police officials fully support the organization. Ideally, IACOLE will serve as a professional standard which best serves the interests of the *entire* community—police and public alike. Early indicators suggest that IACOLE is moving along this path.

Professional Police Organizations and Complaint Review

Certainly the myriad of professional law enforcement organizations are concerned about complaint review, discipline, and accountability to the public. The Police Executive Research Forum (PERF) established a forward looking model policy on complaint review in the early 1980s in addition to conducting research on various complaint-related issues over the years. The International Association of Chiefs of Police (IACP) has addressed misconduct review through training programs, forums at its national meetings, and through special publications. The National Organization of Black Law Enforcement Executives (NOBLE) has conducted research and consultation on the issue as well as co-sponsoring (with PERF) special conferences on police-race relations, which address complaints. The National Sheriffs' Association (NSA) has also provided training programs and discussion sessions on the issue at its national meetings.

It is important to note that the professional law enforcement organizations recognize the importance and controversy associated with complaints against the police. They are taking positive steps to deal with the issue in a cooperative spirit with the community.[8]

EXCESSIVE FORCE AGAIN

In an earlier chapter, we discussed abuse of authority, looking at the several types thereof and the communication problem that the charge of excessive force symbolizes. Physical and verbal abuse of authority are the grounds of most allegations in citizen complaints against the police. Many incidents involve street confrontations, often in situations in which the police are accused of apprehending a subject for disorderly conduct, then going on quickly to providing "street justice"—also known as "thumping"—for resisting arrest. The universality of a person an officer may describe as an "asshole" embodies a profile of a person who does not respect police authority, who will not respond in a manner the police think he or she should respond, and who is involved in some unlawful act (or perceived unlawful act). This is the person who is likely to be "thumped" and least likely to lodge a complaint against an officer. Why? As one officer told the author, "Assholes know who they are. They also know the rules of the game."

The heart of the police officer's trouble with "the assholes" is the "can't win" nature of the encounter. If the officer physically abuses a citizen, he or she faces criticism and possible counterattack, probable insolence, and the chance of enhancing the standing of the "asshole" in the eyes of the latter's peers.[9] If, on the other hand, the officer avoids forceful and aggressive tactics, he or she is subject to the insults of the "asshole," possible jeers and taunts of bystanders, and loss of respect on all sides, including that of other officers.

One study found that a high proportion (80 percent) of the police officers who strive to be professional felt that physical force was most apt to be used by an officer when dealing with this type of person. Adding to the officer's resentment was the expectation that the "asshole," if arrested, would soon be released by the courts and returned to the street to give the officer further trouble.[9] This is dirty work that the police wish they could escape but know they cannot, and it becomes a contributing factor in their cynicism.

Police agencies today, taken generally, are doing a better job than was the case ten or fifteen years ago in the statistics and records of citizen complaints. Computers have helped. So have community pressures. Yet the attitude of the police about complaints is still in large measure defensive. Some of this reaction is typically human, and the police have no monopoly on it. Complaints are by their nature threatening, or at least are perceived that way. But some of this attitude is also a carryover of a past when it was considered useful to perpetuate a certain mystique about what was going on, "behind the scenes," at the police station.

Another point worth noting is the difference between *actual* cases of excessive force and what segments of the community *believe* is happening. This latter belief cannot be dismissed lightly by police managers. The belief is a reality, especially among the poor and minorities. It is, as we have earlier noted, a symbolic term for their generally unfavorable attitude of distrust toward the police. Moreover, there is sufficient evidence of actual abuse of authority, physical or verbal, to lend credence to this belief and to fuel the conclusion that excessive force is more common than it really is. The roots of this attitudinal phenomenon are in mutual distrust, as police officers are also the victims, sometimes, of force, both physical and verbal.

RECOMMENDATIONS OF NATIONAL COMMISSIONS

The first detailed examination of complaints against the police occurred in the spate of national commissions beginning in the late 1960s. Interestingly, even though these issues were addressed over a quarter of a century ago, the points are still valid and worth recalling. In its general report, *The Challenge of Crime in a Free Society*, President Johnson's Commission on Law Enforcement and Administration of Justice recommended that every jurisdiction should provide adequate procedures for full and fair processing of all citizen grievances and complaints about the conduct of any police officer or employee.[10] The *Task Force Report: The Police* of the same commission discussed in some detail procedures within a police organization, including internal investigations, citizen complaints, external review, court appeals, civil remedies, civilian review boards, and the ombudsman system.[11]

A more specific analysis of the functioning of the grievance systems in the San Diego and Philadelphia police departments was provided in *Field Surveys IV* of the same commission. This included a thorough description and evaluation of the Philadelphia Police Advisory Board, originally called the Philadelphia Police Review Board, created in 1958.[12]

The National Advisory Commission on Civil Disorders (Kerner Commission) expressed particular concern in its 1968 report for opening channels of communication between government and urban ghetto residents. It recommended establishment of joint government-community neighborhood action task forces and formal mechanisms for the processing of grievances relating to the performance of city administrators. The commission did not specify the form of such mechanisms, but did identify certain criteria of adequacy:

- The grievance agency should be separate from operating municipal agencies.
- The grievance agency must have adequate staff and funding to discharge its responsibilities.

- The grievance agency should have comprehensive jurisdiction, bringing all public agencies under scrutiny.
- The grievance agency should have power to receive complaints, hold hearings, subpoena witnesses, make public recommendations for remedial actions, and in cases involving law violation, bring suit.
- The grievance agency should be readily and easily accessible to all citizens.
- Grievants should be given full opportunity to take part in all proceedings and to be represented by counsel. Results of investigations should be reported to grievants and made public. Expanded legal services should be made available to ghetto residents in various types of legal-aid-to-the-poor programs.[13]

The same commission emphasized that making a complaint should be easy and convenient. The procedure should have a built-in conciliation process to attempt to resolve complaints without the need for full investigation and processing. Excessive formality should be avoided. Because many citizen complaints pertain to departmental policies rather than to individual conduct, information concerning complaints of this sort should be forwarded to the departmental unit that formulates or reviews policy and procedures. Information concerning all complaints should be forwarded to appropriate training units so that any deficiencies correctable by training can be eliminated.

The National Commission on the Causes and Prevention of Violence stated emphatically that aggrieved groups must be permitted to exercise their constitutional rights of protest and public presentation of grievances. To enable the less affluent to obtain effective and peaceful redress of grievances, this commission recommended additional steps to meet their needs for legal assistance and encouraged state and local jurisdictions to experiment with the establishment of grievance agencies to serve all citizens.[14]

The President's Commission on Campus Unrest said in its 1970 report that the most urgent task for government must be to restore faith of Americans in their government, in their fellow citizens, and in their capacity to live together in harmony and progress.[15] This commission recommended reforms in the governance of institutions of higher education to include special attention to such things as:

- Increased participation of students, faculty, and staff in the formulation of policies.
- Procedures for dealing with grievances, to insure that such are promptly heard, fairly considered, and—if necessary—acted upon.

This commission went on to declare that many grievances are legitimate and correctable, but even when they are not—even when they are but a pretext for disruption—they often arouse emotions that are more than ephemeral. Within the limits of practicality, every complaint should be investigated and answered by as informal a process as may be appropriate in particular instances. Unwarranted charges should be repudiated, policies misunderstood should be explained, unfounded rumors should be dispelled, and facts should be provided.

The same commission observed that campus grievance committees generally have not worked very well. Problems with such committees have been the polarization of their members, a tendency to handle grievances on the basis of policies rather than merit, and slowness of response. Variations on the ombudsman system have been tried on some campuses. To be successful in such circumstances, the ombudsman must have both great autonomy and the support of top university administration. He or she must not be penalized by the administration if findings and recommendations embarrass university leaders. Some institutions have appointed special student affairs administrators or advisory bodies to act as liaison between students and administration.

In their *Report on Police*, the 1973 National Advisory Commission on Criminal Justice Standards and Goals joined the chorus calling for immediate implementation in every police agency of procedures to facilitate complaints alleging employee misconduct, whether the complaint is initiated internally or externally. The commission spelled out some of the principles that should apply, for example, that making a complaint should not be accompanied by fear of reprisal or harassment, that all complaints should be promptly and thoroughly investigated, and that a police agency should keep the public well informed of its complaint procedures.[16] In all citizen grievance procedures, the rights of individual police officers should be carefully protected.

CHECKPOINTS FOR COMPLAINT PROCEDURES

We have mentioned the need for systematic, periodic evaluation of complaint machinery. What guidelines or checkpoints may be suggested for this purpose? Depending on local community and departmental differences, the following questions may be helpful:

1. Is there policy or law requiring that all complaints reported be recorded at a central point to insure proper data retrieval?
2. Is there policy or law that prohibits employees from attempting to discourage any civilian from making a complaint?
3. Does the department make conscious efforts to cause complainants a minimum of inconvenience and embarrassment?
4. Is the machinery for hearing and processing complaints fair, impartial, and objective?
5. Is the machinery adequately publicized and interpreted so that all citizens know of it and can get further assistance if they need it?
6. Are all complaints adequately investigated?
7. Are there reports to the party making the complaint so that he or she is aware of developments from the time the complaint is made until the time of disposition?
8. Does the department have a reputation for integrity with the entire community? (Do all members of the community consider it *their* police department?)
9. Is there an avenue for formalized appeal of police decisions or findings?[17]

With some input from randomly selected citizens on some of these checkpoints, the police administrator will acquire a fairly reliable gauge as to the adequacy of complaint procedures. The ninth question, of course, takes procedure outside the department—to a police or safety commission, to the city council, to the city's community relations commission, to an ombudsman, to the prosecuting attorney, or to the courts.[18]

INTERNAL COMPLAINTS

Up to this point, we have focused on external complaints. More often than not, a police agency in trouble with external complaints will also have its headaches with internal complaints. In complaints of employees against the department, it is usually unfair practices that are involved. The belief is growing that a police department has an obligation to provide suitable channels through which all employees may offer criticisms and recommend changes, without peril. Much more attention must be devoted to this than in the past. Police unions are now well established, and administrators have pretty well learned to deal with unions realistically and constructively. Contractual obligations generally include procedures for airing the complaints of employees against employers (known as grievances). More rare, however, are established procedures for the processing of grievances of subordinates against superiors, and of employees against others of the same rank.

Subject to local and departmental differences, some key checkpoints for internal complaints follow:

1. All employees must be held strictly accountable for their behavior.
2. Supervision is the crucial function relative to internal (and external) complaints. The supervisor must have authority commensurate with responsibility. But if supervisors abuse this authority, they should be held strictly accountable. Guidelines are useful in prescribing and proscribing supervisor responsibilities.
3. Administrative directives should clearly delineate the rights and responsibilities of employees at every level in the department. Such policies should also clearly indicate available grievance and appropriate disciplinary procedures. Top administrators in the department should not be handling minor rule infractions while line supervisors are handling more serious matters.
4. Administrators also should have authority commensurate with their responsibilities. As a general rule, this includes discipline to the point of terminating an officer's service, subject only to the limitation of advisory consultation with the chief executive of the particular governmental jurisdiction, and the right of appeal by the officer to a civil service or other board of review. The latter should *not* have the power to overrule the police administrator, but only to review the administrative action and to make their findings public.
5. Members of the organization at all levels should know that they can call attention to the improper conduct of other employees without incurring organizational penalties. Indeed, this should be made clear in departmental regulations.
6. Some method or system of staff inspections should be routine, with reports made directly to the chief administrator.
7. Some sort of internal staff unit for the investigation of charges of employee misconduct is desirable in departments of sufficient size to justify it.
8. *Departmental trial boards can be administratively advantageous in departments of appreciable size.*[19]

The importance of carefully defined, widely disseminated, and adequately interpreted employee grievance procedures should be emphasized again. Due process provisions of such procedures should be loud and clear. It bears repeating that problems of internal relations in an organization inevitably are projected in external relations.

A FEW ADDITIONAL POINTS

There are a few points to be added on this extremely important matter. One is that a patrol officer on the street ought to be something of a neighborhood ombudsman. Unless there is reason for an individual officer to be avoided, people will tend to look to this officer for information, direction, assistance when in trouble, a helping hand in rain or snow, a listening ear in frustration, some friendly counsel, or referral to the agency or persons appropriate to a particular need. If the officer turns them off or turns them away, many people have no idea where they may find assistance. Police officers on street duty are accustomed to hearing complaints about many things. Most of the time, they are able to offer something: a suggestion, a word of advice, a cautionary note, a bracing thought, an encouraging idea. The best of police-community relations is not done through big projects, committees, and programs. It comes down to the one-to-one contacts of a police officer and a citizen.

Neighborhood organizations with the purpose of improving the quality of life in the neighborhood—whatever their name or more specific objective—often function as complaint processing mechanisms. The mediation of many such grievances can be handled informally in most cases, without recourse to more formal, more cumbersome, more adversarial procedures. A police officer, for example, may earn the respect and trust of residents in a neighborhood by such elementary virtues as honesty, helpfulness, friendliness, and commitment to service to people in need. In such circumstances, citizen complaints diminish in number and substance.

Finally, we should consider whether minority leadership and representation has aided relationships between the police and the community. Eight or ten of the nation's largest cities and numerous smaller cities currently have black chiefs of police. Does it make a difference, in the attitude of minorities toward the police and in terms of citizen complaints? There is no statistical basis for a response to this question because it is so difficult to factor out race, but it is safe to say that it certainly has symbolic political importance, in both internal and external relationships of a police agency.

QUESTIONS FOR DISCUSSION

1. Distinguish between external and internal complaints for a police agency.
2. Explain this proposition: If persons who believe they have been treated unjustly have no forum they trust within which to explore their claims, their attitude of distrust will never be dispelled.
3. Explain how a citizens' review board works in dealing with complaints. Discuss its strengths and weaknesses.
4. Briefly explain the general *process* of how complaints against police officers are handled.
5. What do roles of professional organizations and accreditation play in police complaint review?
6. Which of the civilian review approaches discussed in the chapter do you think is most workable? Explain your choice.

7. What are some of the most common criticisms of police complaint procedures?
8. Why do you think so few of the recommendations from the national commissions of the 1960s and 1970s have been fully implemented, even in the 1990s?
9. What are some of the checkpoints in evaluating the adequacy of procedures for dealing with internal complaints in a police agency?
10. *Accountability* and *responsiveness*. What do these terms mean in professional policing with specific concern related to complaints?

NOTES

1. Michael Banton, "Social Integration and Police," *Police Chief* (April 1963): 12.
2. Parts of this chapter rely on chapter 4, "Police Conduct and the Public," of U.S. President's Commission on Law Enforcement and Administration of Justice, *Field Surveys V: National Survey of Police and Community Relations* (Prepared for the Commission by the National Center on Police and Community Relations, Michigan State University, School of Police Administration and Public Safety) (Washington, DC: U.S. Government Printing Office, 1967), pp. 128–257. That chapter was written by John E. Angell.

3. Walter Gellhorn, "Police Review Boards: Hoax or Hope?" *Columbia Forum* 9, no. 3 (Summer 1966): 10.
4. Victor Kappeler and Michael Kaune, "Legal Standards and Civil Liability of Excessive Force," in Roger Dunham and Geoffrey Alpert, *Critical Issues in Policing*, 2d ed. (Prospect Heights, IL: Waveland Press, 1993), pp. 526–536.
5. Herbert L. Packer, "Who Can Police the Police?" *New York Review* (September 8, 1966). See also by the same author, *The Limits of the Criminal Sanction* (Stanford, CA.: Stanford University Press, 1968); also see Herman Goldstein, "Administrative Problems in Controlling the Exercise of Police Authority," *Journal*

of Criminal Law, Criminology and Police Science 58, no. 2 (1967): 160–172.

6. This material is based on original research by the author initially reported in Carter, David L, "Police Disciplinary Procedures: A Review of Selected Police Departments," in *Police Deviance*, 2d ed., T. Barker and D.L. Carter, (Cincinnati: Anderson Publishing Company, 1994). The current discussion is significantly modified and updated.

7. This material is based on joint research by the author and that of Paul West, *A Comparative Analysis of British and American Police Complaint Review Schemes* (Unpublished Master's thesis), School of Criminal Justice, Michigan State University (East Lansing, MI). Mr. West currently holds the rank of Superintendent with the Durham, England Constabulary.

8. See also Allen E. Wagner and Scot H. Decker, "Evaluating Citizen Complaints Against the Police," in Dunham and Alpert, 1993, Ibid., pp. 275–291.

9. *Ibid.*

10. U.S. President's Commission on Law Enforcement and Administration of Justice, *The Challenge of Crime in a Free Society* (Washington, DC: U.S. Government Printing Office, 1967), p. 103.

11. U.S. President's Commission on Law Enforcement and Administration of Justice, *Task Force Report: The Police* (Washington, DC: U.S. Government Printing Office, 1967), pp. 193–204.

12. U.S., President's Commission on Law Enforcement and Administration of Justice, *Field Surveys IV*, vol. 1, pp. 167–175; vol. 2, pp. 195–284.

13. U.S. National Advisory Commission on Civil Disorders, *Report of the National Advisory Commission on Civil Disorders* (Kerner Report) (Washington, DC: U.S. Government Printing Office, 1969), pp. 151–152.

14. U.S. National Commission on the Causes and Prevention of Violence, *To Establish Justice, To Insure Domestic Tranquility* (Washington, DC: U.S. Government Printing Office, 1969), p. 10.

15. *Report: Campus Unrest* (Washington, DC: U.S. Government Printing Office, 1970), pp. 202–206, 215.

16. National Advisory Commission on Criminal Justice Standards and Goals, *Report on Police* (Washington, DC: Government Printing Office, 1973), pp. 480–494.

17. President's Commission on Law Enforcement, *Field Surveys V*, pp. 228–229.

18. One possibility regarding such appeals is described in "A Model for Handling Citizen Complaints," in *The Police and the Community: Studies*, Louis A. Radelet and Hoyt Coe Reed, (Beverly Hills, CA: Glencoe, 1973), pp. 145–150.

19. Though somewhat dated, the Michigan State Study for the 1966 President's Crime Commission suggested some guidelines for the last two recommendations. *Field Surveys V*, pp. 235–245.

Part Four

SPECIAL ISSUES

The Work Experiences of Policewomen: Still a Minority

MERRY MORASH, PH.D.

Director and Professor School of Criminal Justice Michigan State University

Two decades ago, policewomen were employed almost exclusively in gender stereotypical jobs, such as working with juveniles and women. Since that time, they have increasingly worked in the most common type of job, the patrol work that forms the core of police activity They have been in the mainstream of police activities long enough to have moved into specialized units and higher administration. Yet, women still make up only 15 percent of all police officers nationally, and they hold very few administrative positions.

Many studies have laid to rest concerns that women cannot do police jobs as well as men can, and in fact some people assert that women can do some parts of the job better. Policewomen may place more emphasis on the skills of negotiation and conflict resolution than the use of physical force, and they are cut off from workplace peer networks that support employee corruption. But, given their minority status and their underrepresentation in top management, what is the workplace like for policewomen? How do women try to shape police work to fit their own images of themselves, and to change individuals and departments in an effort to maximize their contributions to policing? If policewomen have special problems at work, how do they cope, and what is the result of their coping styles?

THE RESEARCH

For several years, with the cooperation of the Police Executive Research Forum, I have been engaged in research intended to explain policewomen's experiences in the workplace. The study began with observations, conducted over seven years, of women in a state organization for policewomen. Because the organization's purpose was to provide support and advocacy, the meetings were characterized by a great deal of spontaneous discussion of workplace problems and strategies for coping with these problems. In a sense, the observations provided a window through which one could see the problems women considered to be important as well as their various responses to these problems.

The observations served as the basis for developing a questionnaire used to measure workplace problems and responses to those problems among women and men in twenty-five departments that volunteered to take part in the study. Survey findings are based on questionnaires returned by 1,191 police officers. Thirty percent of these officers are women.

STUDY FINDINGS

Police officers experience a variety of workplace problems: lack of influence over work operations, ill-suited equipment, sexual harassment, overestimates and underestimates of physical capabilities relevant to police work, limited opportunity to advance, lack of recognition of one's presence and contributions (invisibility) and overt hostility from other officers (being ridiculed or "set up"). Different from the offensive romantic advances, threats, attacks, and exposure to pornography that characterize sexual harassment, there was also language harassment, consisting of offensive profanity and jokes about sex. Racial and ethnic harassment involved negative comments and jokes, too, and some officers reported a general bias involving prejudicial treatment. Finally, some officers reported they were stigmatized because of appearance, experiencing negative comments about size or attractiveness.

Police officers used several distinct methods for coping with problems at work: toleration of problems, trying to get co-workers to like them, changing job assignments, formal actions (including legal and professional help), keeping written records, drawing on co-workers for support, and expressing their feelings.

Men and women often have the same difficulties at work. Many police officers, for example, feel they have little control over the way policing "gets done" on a day-to-day basis. But women also have special problems, with the most persistent being sexual harassment at work. Women reported harassment in many forms, including superiors' looking at pornographic material in their presence, making unwanted comments about their being homosexual, and trying to have a romantic (or at least sexual) relationship with them. From co-workers, they reported physical touching, unwanted jokes about their attractive appearance, and attempts at intercourse. Agencies with high levels of harassment from co-workers also had high levels from superiors.

Interestingly, women more often than men responded to problems at work, including harassment, with *toleration* rather than action. Men more often tended to take formal action, such as filing a grievance or obtaining legal help. Initial findings indicate that over the course of a career, workplace problems are not likely to decrease if the main coping response is "toleration"—a finding that has clearly negative implications for policewomen.

IMPORTANCE OF ORGANIZATIONAL CHANGE

If the workplace is so uncomfortable that some talented individuals leave, or have their energies taken up dealing with difficulties such as bias, then police agencies are not only liable, but they suffer from a loss of needed resources. In many different settings, it has repeatedly been demonstrated that leadership from the top is what it takes to make the workplace hospitable to women and other underrepresented groups. Certainly, increased numbers of women in leadership positions would send a clear signal that policewomen are not outsiders in the profession. Employee assistance programs to improve coping skills, as well as organized advocacy groups, are all part of the solution to the problem of women's continued underrepresentation and the rejection of their presence in at least some police agencies. It is particularly important to recognize that the problem lies not with the individual women who are affected and who try to respond but with the organization as a whole, which loses valuable resources and is diverted from getting the work of policing done in the most effective way possible.

Chapter 14

ISSUES RELATED TO SPECIAL POPULATIONS

Special populations" is a term used to describe groups of people who have unique needs with respect to the police service. They are frequently disenfranchised, easily taken advantage of, and have little vested ability to resolve their situation. In many cases, the police serve as their only source of assistance, yet even then, they are frequently reluctant to call, sometimes not recognizing the seriousness of their own situation. As guardians, the police have an important responsibility to proactively identify and respond to the needs of these special citizens.

POLICE AND YOUNG PERSONS

Young people in our society, of whatever racial or ethnic characterization, are the victims of discrimination in some respects. This has been graphically reflected in criminal justice processes, where due process for juvenile offenders has had a somewhat tortuous history. Taken generally, young people have been treated in some of the same ways as a minority group, while not strictly qualifying for this label in some other ways. Again in general terms, there are special problems in police-youth relationships, and when young people are poor and black, Puerto Rican, Hispanic, Asian, or Native American, encounters with the police may be especially volatile.

In analyzing this situation, we discover that the attitudes of young people of middle-school age (eleven to fifteen, approximately) are of special interest pertaining to authority figures and authority systems, including their attitudes toward the police. An assumption, supported by a fairly strong body of attitudinal research, is that youthful attitudes toward the police may vary according to the age and probably the gender, socioeconomic status, and racial-ethnic background of particular young people. It may be, too, that police attitudes toward young people also vary according to the situation and tend to interlock reciprocally with youthful attitudes toward the police.

The reciprocal attitudes of young people and the police are crucial in police-community relations currently and in the future. Most police agencies recognize this and give special attention to youth programs in schools and in the community. Delinquency prevention is one purpose of these activities, but there is also a broader, attitudinal and educational purpose, as for instance in law-related curricula in schools in which police officers participate.

ATTITUDES TOWARD AUTHORITY

Recall what we said in an earlier chapter about the development of attitudes toward authority. We discussed the process of socialization and its effects on self-image and identity. We said that the manner in which authority is imposed upon the child early in life sets a pattern for how the child will view people in authority later in life. Without getting into the relative merits of "discipline" and "permissiveness" in rearing children, we are interested at this point in some underlying reasons for the changing attitudes toward authority and social controls, and the changing role and functions of social institutions. Their relevance to the present subject requires repetition of several points made earlier.

In a simple, homogeneous, folkway society, where primary group restraints are strong, attitudes toward authority are simple and efficient because there is a single, dominant code or norm of behavior. Nonconformity in such a society is rare, and when it appears, the sanctions for it are immediate and often quite harsh. On the other hand, in a complex, heterogeneous society, there are many dissonant attitudes toward authority, and social controls are correspondingly numerous and intricate. In such a society, there are numerous competing and conflicting codes or norms of behavior.

What about change in the social institutions that have such a vital influence on attitudes and behavior—including, of course, attitudes toward authority? Consider, for example, the family of yesteryear in just one respect: it was multifunctional as to social, economic, religious, and educational requirements, compared with the family of today. Or take what a person did for a living. Once, work in our society was a moral calling, a way of life, and an important means of self-identity. Today, a person specializes, works as a cog in a bureaucracy, or loses identity on a production line. Yesterday, government was a local affair centering in the town meeting, and the citizen had voice and vote in decision-making. Today, decisions are made remotely, by "experts" (despite the calls for town meetings via remote telecommunication). Further, education beyond the early grades was once regarded as the privilege of a few rather than the expectation of most young people. And so on.

What then, in the kind of society ours has become, is the "proper" attitude toward authority and authority figures? Who decides this and how, and on the basis of what standards? Who is really to say that the attitudes of today's young people toward authority are worse—or better—than yesterday's? If one contends that today's young people have less respect for law and authority than yesterday's—and that this is bad—it may reveal more about the values of the contender than it does about the values of young people. Certainly the question of values has emerged extensively, as evidenced in the rhetoric of the 1996 presidential campaign. The program discussed in the following box is an example of values education.

An eminent child psychologist, Urie Bronfenbrenner, wrote that children *used to be* brought up by their parents. He asserted that de facto responsibility for upbringing has shifted away from the family to other settings in society where the task is not always recognized or accepted. As Bronfenbrenner stated it:

> While the family still has the primary moral and legal responsibility for developing character in children, the power or opportunity to do the job is often lacking in the home, primarily because parents and children no longer spend enough time together in those situations in which such training is possible. This is not because parents don't want to spend time with their children. It is simply that conditions of life have changed.[1]

Research has systematically compared the daily life of children growing up in a small town with the lives of children living in a modern city or suburb. The differences were significant. Other studies have pointed to how little we know about the influence of the peer group—or of television, for that matter—on the lives of young children. As for adolescents:

> The aspirations and actions of American adolescents are primarily determined by the "leading crowd" in the school society. For boys in this leading crowd, the hallmark of success was glory in athletics; for girls, it was the popular date.
>
> Intellectual achievement was a secondary value. The most intellectually able students were not getting the best grades. The classroom wasn't where the action was.[2]

The general conclusion to be drawn from such references is that "school culture" and "peer culture" (and probably "television culture") have become exceedingly important influences on youthful behavior and attitudes—probably more important, by and large, than "family culture" or "religious culture." What are the implications of this for youthful attitudes toward the police? There are numerous indications that appropriate "citizenship training" is not being managed very well in our society. Witness, for example, the proportion of people who do not vote in general elections. Witness the ignorance of the public in police and governmental matters. Witness what has been called "the philosophy of irresponsibility and unaccountability."[3]

POLITICAL SOCIALIZATION

We have said that youthful attitudes toward the police are part of a larger context of attitudes toward authority and political institutions.[4] From political socialization of a large sample of public school children, research on it was concluded:

> Every piece of evidence indicates that the child's political world begins to take shape well before he [or she] even enters elementary school and it undergoes the most rapid change during these years. . . . The truly formative years of the maturing member of a political system would seem to be those years between the ages of three and thirteen.[5]

Until the recent past, much citizenship instruction in the primary grades in this country was in the form of patriotic rituals and rather superficial civic instruction.[6] Relatively few experimental programs at this level departed from the usual pattern. In Los Angeles, an exception was the Patrolman Bill program, which reinforced civics lessons on safety, responsibility, law, and law enforcement.

One study hypothesized a greater degree of antipathy toward police on the part of pupils of low socioeconomic backgrounds, and a positive change in perception of the police on the part of those low socioeconomic status pupils who took part in the Patrolman Bill program. Third-grade public school pupils from three divergent ethnic and social-class categories were asked to draw pictures of the police officer at work, as an art class assignment. One low socioeconomic status group from the Watts neighborhood was asked to draw the pictures two weeks prior to Patrolman Bill's visit and on the third day following the visit. Each picture was then evaluated by four independent raters on a seven-point scale for the degree of aggressiveness, authoritarianism, hostility, kindness, goodness, strength, or anger expressed in the picture. An additional rater, working separately, performed an item analysis of police task performance on the basis of the picture's content. Comparison of ratings yielded no significant difference between the item analysis and the evaluation by the four raters on the entire field of the picture.[7]

From the results, the image held of police behavior fell into four categories:

- *Aggressive:* fighting, chasing, shooting
- *Assistance* (with negative overtones); unloading a paddy wagon, searching a building, in a car with prisoners, giving traffic tickets
- *Neutral:* walking, riding in a patrol car, directing traffic
- *Assistance* (with positive overtones): talking with children, giving directions

In the pre- and post-test group, there was a significant shift of responses from neutral or negative to positive assistance, which tended to verify the hypothesis that "personal contact with police under informal, nonthreatening conditions significantly reduces children's antipathy." Significant differences also appeared between the three highly diverse groups tested: one predominantly black and of low socioeconomic status; one predominantly Spanish-speaking and of low socioeconomic status; and one suburban, middle-class white. The group from Watts expressed less antipathy toward the police after the Patrolman Bill program than was originally expressed by the most positive (white, middle-class) group. Whether similar gains would hold with children of other ethnic or socioeconomic backgrounds is uncertain. Just how permanent was the attitude change resulting from the program is another

"PEDAL PATROL" FROM *KIDSBEAT*: HELPING EDUCATE YOUTH ABOUT THE POLICE

An example of a tool to help educate young people about the police is the publication KIDSBEAT. The concept for the publication emerged with the hope of upholding the integrity of law enforcement while arming officers with hands-on information that children can put to work in their schools and neighborhoods. When young people get involved in helping their police and community, they build not only a sense of personal responsibility and social concern but also a sense of respect for the profession. Officers can use KIDSBEAT as an educational tool in the schools, a Neighborhood Watch meetings with parents, and for community outreach programs, such as mall displays and public gatherings. It can be beneficial not only for crime prevention units but also school resource units, horse patrols, bike patrols, public affairs, and storefronts.

The following is an example of a portion of one KIDSBEAT issue dealing with police bicycle patrol.

PEDAL PATROL: GEARING UP FOR TWO-WHEELED ACTION

Some police officers have a curious habit of racing bikes down cement staircases, tearing through alleys, whirling through shopping centers, and jumping curbs. But it's not always fun and games.

(continued)

These energetic men and women represent a growing force of crime-fighting cyclists known as bike patrols or bike units. With the help of sturdy mountain bikes, cops all across the country are making their way into those "hard-to-get" places, like alleys and sidewalks, where patrol cars usually can't go.

When a bike cop spots someone in an alley selling drugs, he or she can easily sneak up on the suspect quietly and quickly. A patrol car, however, may not fit down a narrow alleyway. Even if it could, traffic congestion could keep the car from getting there fast enough. Besides, car engines are noisy and could ruin the element of surprise.

'There's always a lot of excitement when you're making an arrest,' says Officer Tom Henshaw of the Seattle, Washington Police Department's mountain bike patrol. 'But you always think about your own safety as well as the safety of the citizens. A lot of times, these people carry guns and knives, and they can be real dangerous.'

Officer Henshaw works in the congested area of downtown Seattle. He typically rides his bike up and down the sidewalks in front of offices, restaurants, and markets. Most of his time is spent around people, allowing him to see and hear all kinds of things. Just like officers in the old days, Officer Henshaw has a chance to meet the residents in his community and really get to know about them and their concerns. By being close to citizens, he learns a lot about the crime problems of the area. These citizens trust him and try to help by providing information about people who cause trouble.

Some bike patrols also depend upon officers perched on nearby rooftops to look for illegal activities through binoculars. When a crime is taking place, these 'watchdogs' immediately radio Officer Henshaw and other bike officers on the ground, who take off in a flash. Their adrenaline starts pumping as they shift their bikes into high gear.

'There's a need for an immediate burst of energy,' Officer Henshaw says, 'You usually don't feel the energy expended when you're rushing to a call. But after things are under control, you usually realize how tired you are, and you start to feel it.'

Pedaling up to 40 miles per hour during emergency calls, bike cops know the meaning of a good workout. That's why it's important for them to stay in tip-top shape. They ride an where from 10 to 30 miles per day. In Seattle, that can be extra-challenging because the area is so hilly.

In 1987 Seattle officers Paul Grady and Mike Miller came up with the idea to use bikes in their jobs. Both of them enjoyed biking after work and knew the benefits of moving in and out of traffic on two wheels rather than four. They convinced their captain to let them start the first police bike unit in the United States, and the idea has turned out to be a popular one.

Now, about 200 police departments across the country have created bike patrols because of their ability to maneuver so well. But larger cities, like Seattle with 500,000 people, aren't the only ones benefiting from cops on bikes. Smaller towns, such as Ocala, Florida, with 45,000 citizens, have seen how useful they are, too.

'The drug dealers fear the bike patrol,' says Officer Johnnie Johnston of the Ocala Police Department. 'They're used to looking at police cars. They don't expect us to sneak up on them with bikes.'

While bikes have been very helpful in catching drug dealers they are also used in responding to bank robberies, assaults, and thefts. Without a sound, bike patrol cops can pop up from nowhere.

Besides major crimes, bike officers also pay attention to bicycle safety—not only for themselves but for all bicyclists. They have a good understanding of the possible dangers when not using the proper signals or failing to follow the rules of the road.

Each officer always wears a helmet. Officer Henshaw says that is extremely important if a biker is ever hit by a moving vehicle or loses control of his bike.

Officers usually wear shorts for easy movement, except when its raining or cold. In wet weather, they wear long pants and special rain gear. And Seattle has more than its share of rain.

'If were not comfortable, warm, and dry, we're just going to be miserable, and we're not going to get a lot of work done,' says Officer Henshaw. 'You have to be somewhat comfortable and dry to stay out there for eight hours a day. That's why jackets and other equipment are real important to a bike program.'

Sometimes the rain slows officers down when they're responding to a call. Because of slippery roads, they can't travel as fast. They have to allow more space between their bikes and the vehicles ahead of them. Fortunately, Seattle's bike officers have never been seriously injured.

'We have to get to our calls safely,' says Officer Henshaw. 'If we crash on the way, then we aren't doing any good at all.'

The illustration in Figure 14-1 shows how an officer on bike patrol is outfitted.

BIKE PATROL FASHION

Bike patrol officers sport a different look than most police officers. Comfort and safety are important. Shorts are cooler and allow them to move easier.

Gloves protect their hands from blisters and burns. They also let officers keep a stronger grip on their handlebars for better control.

It's especially important for bike officers to wear comportable shoes because they pedal a lot of miles during the day. Soft-soled shoes allow them to keep a good grip on their pedals. These shoes are easier to run in, too.

A helmet offers protection from head injuries and is one of the most necessary parts of the uniform. Glare from the sun makes it hard to see sometimes, which is why officers wear wraparound glases.

Figure 14-1.   Bike Patrol Officer Wearing Uniform Shows Off Gear

FOCUS 14.1

TIPS—TEACHING INDIVIDUALS PROTECTIVE STRATEGIES

This project, sponsored by the U.S. Department of Education, is designed to help school-aged young people make responsible decisions. TIPS addresses problems such as disruptive behavior in the classroom, vandalism, victimization of young people, and disrespect for authority, through a decision-making curriculum for grades kindergarten through eight. As an early prevention program aimed at both perpetrators and victims of crime, TIPS has two major aims. One is to build responsible conduct by reducing victimization. To that end, TIPS alerts young people to their vulnerability of becoming a victim in various situations at home, at school, and in the community, while educating them on simple and safe protective measures they should take. Activities focus on such things as responsible behavior in dealing with strangers, awareness of dangerous situations, and ways of avoiding them, and the importance and "how to" of proper identification.

question: "Experience of others who have researched attitudes and attitude changes suggests that changes of this nature last only until further negative experiences."[8]

A program similar to Patrolman Bill called Officer Friendly was initiated in Chicago elementary schools. This program was subsequently launched in a number of other school systems throughout the country. The stated goals of the Officer Friendly program were:

1. Providing the opportunity to develop understanding of the rights, responsibilities, and obligations of living in the modern urban environment.
2. Developing rapport between the child and the uniformed officer.
3. Developing a wholesome image of the police department (and other public service agencies) in the mind of the child.
4. Reinforcing basic rules and regulations which govern experiences and activities within the child's environment.
5. Promoting interest in establishing goals and seeking positive and immediate ways of building toward their attainment.[9]

The Officer Friendly program consisted of three phases, encompassing an entire school year. The first phase was orientation, where pupils and teacher became acquainted with the program by meeting Officer Friendly and by reviewing materials that laid the groundwork for phase two. The second phase was an instructional period in which Officer Friendly, the teacher, and the pupils participated in a structured teaching-learning experience in keeping with the purposes of the program. Phase three was a reinforcement lesson and included a merit award presentation conducted by Officer Friendly. At the conclusion of this final phase, all materials went home to be shared with family and friends, to acquaint those around the child with the program.

Most recently, programs such as DARE, TIPS, and GREAT have been instituted. While there are substantive differences in the orientation of these programs, they have important characteristics which are similar. Patrolman Bill and Officer

The other focus of the program is to find responsible solutions to conflict situations rather than perpetration of a crime. By examining a variety of conflict-producing situations and offering guidelines for effective settlement, TIPS assists in improving interpersonal relations and reducing irresponsible behavior.

Underlying the program is the assumption that in order to stop the escalating spiral of crime and conflict, there must be a means to produce attitudes that will improve behavior and lead to rational decision-making. TIPS provides an opportunity for formally and consistently analyzing attitudes toward such fundamental concepts as: the need in a just and orderly society for rules and laws arrived at through the democratic process; the purpose of authority; and the responsibility a person holds both to oneself and to society.

Throughout the curriculum, young people are challenged to take responsibility for their own behavior, to apply rational decision-making despite peer pressure, and to take an active role in assuring the democratic processes work to protect the rights of all citizens.

For more information, contact: TIPS Program, Educational Information and Resource Center, 700 Hollydell Court, Sewell, NJ 08080, telephone (609) 582-7000.

Friendly were based on opening lines of communication and teaching youth about the police, generally in short-term exposures. The officers attempted to personalize the police and reassure school-aged youth that they could rely on law enforcement to help them.

Conversely, DARE, TIPS, and GREAT rely on principles of *education*, not public relations. Officers teach a complete curriculum, not simply make appearances. Course outlines include not only material about law enforcement, but information about decision-making and responsible citizenship. The programs are designed around learning theory with the hope of having a long-term effect not only on attitudes toward the police but also to help the youth become better citizens.

In one major study of early political socialization involving over 12,000 grade-school children in four regions of the United States, Hess and Easton found that the phenomenon in the realm of politics most apparent to most children is the existence of an authority outside the family and school; this external authority is specifically represented in the presidency and in the police officer. The child becomes increasingly aware of other institutions of authority, such as courts, Congress, and local elected officials, as he or she grows older. Emotional rather than rational processes explain these cognitions of external authority; favorable feelings are developed, for instance toward the presidency, long before concrete knowledge of it materializes.

It is theorized that reciprocal role relationships are the key to political socialization, that the child learns to see behavior in relation to that of some other person or institution, and that role expectations are learned. The child learns the rights and duties of the individual in relation to the rights and duties of the system. Early political socialization begins with an attachment to the nation, which is stable, basic, and exceedingly resistant to change. Authority figures and institutions are perceived by the child as powerful, competent, benign, infallible, and to be trusted. Laws are just and unchangeable, with punishment inevitable for wrongdoing.[10]

FOCUS 14.2

GREAT—GANG RESISTANCE EDUCATION AND TRAINING

In 1991 Phoenix law enforcement formed a partnership with local educators and community leaders to develop an innovative, comprehensive anti-gang program. The result was GREAT (Gang Resistance Education and Training), supported by funding from the U.S. Bureau of Alcohol, Tobacco, and Firearms.

Like DARE, the GREAT program goes into the classroom to prevent young students from getting into trouble and to stop them from joining gangs. Specially trained, uniformed police officers teach GREAT during the regular school year. During 8 one-hour classroom sessions, students learn how to act in their own best interest when faced with peer pressure. GREAT provides kids the necessary skills an information to say no to gangs and become responsible members of society.

The child's points of contact with the system are persons—the president and the police officer. These later become institutions, abstractions, and the roles played by the persons. The points of contact—the president and the police officer—are also the visible authority figures, and compliance with authority and law is mediated through these figures. Not surprisingly, the family can also strongly influence attitudes toward authority, roles, and compliance. While the family and strong authority figures influence attitudes, the school appears to be the primary source for content, information, and concepts. For children of low socioeconomic class status, it may be the only such source. The research indicates that the school is a "central and dominant force in the political socialization of the young child," and that the period between grades three and five is especially important in acquiring political information.

Where and how, then, do significant attitude changes occur? First, there is a fund of positive feeling for the government, especially for the president, that extends to include law, as we have noted. Second, the child's socialization occurs through a "core of respect for power wielded by authority figures, especially police. But some strain in this image gradually develops. While the school presents a positive image of the police, the child discovers early that the police have the duty, not only to capture lawbreakers, but also to punish lawbreakers. This discovery leads to mixed feelings about the police, a beginning of what we earlier identified as the adversary concept. There follows, third, experience in compliant roles at home and school, and finally, normative belief that all systems of rules are fair.

Other research on political socialization was directed as it related especially to the police officer.[11] Borrowing from earlier research, a free-drawing exercise was used as an exploratory instrument in which more than 600 elementary school children drew pictures of various authority figures. Evaluation of the pictures was done on the basis of content; for example, whether the police officer was seen as performing a protective, prohibitive, or punitive activity. Over 50 percent of the resultant drawings emphasized prohibitive or punitive activity, which suggested that the officer's capacity to direct and punish emerged as salient to the child. The police officer

This is accomplished through the eight weekly topics: (1) overview and introduction; (2) crimes, victims, and rights; (3) cultural sensitivity and prejudice; (4) conflict resolution; (5) meeting basic needs; (6) drugs and neighborhoods; (7) diverse responsibilities; (8) and goal setting.

GREAT was designed to strengthen the effectiveness of its in-classroom lessons after school is out. The police agency can supplement the GREAT curriculum with a summer recreation program and education program that reinforces positive attitudes toward authority, and against gangs. Parental involvement is paramount to the success of any gang prevention program, so GREAT can also be expanded to allow officers to contact the parents of suspected gang members and refer them to existing social programs for families facing a problem with gangs.

More information on GREAT can be obtained from the local U.S. Bureau of Alcohol, Tobacco, and Firearms Field Division Office or contact: Community Relations Bureau, Phoenix Police Department, 620 West Washington, Phoenix, AZ 85003, telephone (602) 262-7331.

also appeared in the drawings as physically dominant, being drawn several times larger than such comparison objects as an automobile or other people. The officer was also portrayed as physically and verbally active. Crime detection and prevention activities seldom appeared in the drawings, which suggested that the children were not aware that the police played such roles.

On a questionnaire rating, 78 percent of the second graders and 68 percent of the third graders thought the police officer "can make many people do what he wants." Of the fourth graders tested, 66 percent thought the police officer "can punish many people." It was concluded that "the child is impressed with the presence of a power over and beyond that of father or mother and one that even parents, as potent as they may appear to the child, cannot escape." Police are seen as the "seed out of which a sense of the legitimacy of the authority structure springs." Through the police, the child "is encouraged in the belief that external authority should and must be accepted," which reinforces a similar posture he or she is earlier encouraged to adopt toward the president and the government.

Lending further legitimacy to the police officer in the child's eyes is the affective impression of benevolence and dependability. However, these feelings were highly ambivalent, as indicated by the way the children rated the police officer on the questionnaire. For example, while 71 percent of second graders thought the police "would always want to help me if I needed it" and another 14 percent said "almost always," they rated the police officer very low in such statements as "I like him" and "is my favorite."

The conflict here is between the punitive cognitive image and the affective impression of benevolence and dependability. Nonetheless, they concluded that the children in general had a fairly high level of respect for the police officer.

School-Based Programs: D.A.R.E. and G.R.E.A.T.

Drug Abuse Resistance Education (D.A.R.E.) and Gang Resistance Education and Training (G.R.E.A.T.) are comprehensive preventive education programs intended to stop drug use, violence, and gang participation by educating children about the

DARE—DRUG ABUSE RESISTANCE EDUCATION

DARE (Drug Abuse Resistance Education) is a drug-abuse prevention education program designed to equip elementary school children with skills for resisting peer pressure to experiment with tobacco, drugs, and alcohol. Developed in 1983 as a cooperative effort by the Los Angeles Police Department (LAPD) and the Los Angeles Unified School District (LAUSD), this unique program uses uniformed law enforcement officers to teach a formal curriculum to classroom students. DARE gives special attention to fifth and sixth grades to prepare students for entry into middle school, junior high school, and high school, where they are most likely to encounter pressures to use drugs.

This innovative program has several noteworthy features:

- *DARE targets elementary school children.* In the past, middle school, junior high, and high school drug education programs have come too late to prevent drug use among youth. Therefore, substantial numbers of young people; report first use of alcohol, tobacco, and marijuana while in middle school or junior high school.
- *DARE offers a highly structured, intensive fifth and sixth grade curriculum* developed by Dr. Ruth Rich, the LAUSD health education instructional specialist, in cooperation with experts in the field. A basic precept of the DARE program is that elementary school children lack sufficient social skills to resist peer pressure to say no to drugs. DARE instructors do not use scare tactics or traditional approaches that focus on the dangers of drug use. Instead, the instructors teach children a variety of techniques to resist peer pressure. As a result of the instruction, children gain good judgment

threats and consequences associated with these behaviors. Specific emphasis is given to curricula that focus on self-esteem, taking responsibility for one's own behavior, resisting peer pressure, and making responsible decisions. A desired side benefit of the programs is that they offer students an opportunity to get to know and trust a police officer who has taught the courses in school. In this regard, the curricula were written by educators specifically to be presented to school children by specially trained uniformed police officers.

The benefits of developing an educational avenue as part of the policing mission can be seen in an illustration. In recognizing the need to employ a more contemporary and effective approach to law enforcement, the Mission, Texas Police Department refocused its drug and gang control emphasis. (Focus 14.4). In South Texas, just minutes from the Mexico border, Mission (a city of about 30,000 people) has an extremely high level of drug trafficking activity, including both the transit of drugs through the area and drug abuse, as well as gang activity. In discussing his reasoning for a heavy emphasis on school-based programs, Chief Leo Longoria stated, "the police department has taken away the 'big stick approach' [to deal with youth-related crime] and replaced it with education." In a significant shift of resources, the department has placed nearly one-fourth of its seventy-four sworn officers in the by learning skills in assertiveness, self-esteem, and decision-making and are thereby given alternatives to tobacco, alcohol, and drug use. In many instances the DARE curriculum addresses learning objectives of the state's Department of Education in addition to conforming to health education standards.

- *DARE uses uniformed law enforcement officers to conduct the class.* Uniformed officers as DARE instructors not only are role models for impressionable children but also have high credibility on the subject of drug use. Moreover, by relating to students in a role other than that of law enforcement, officers develop a rapport that promotes positive attitudes toward the police and greater respect for the law.

- *DARE represents a long-term solution to a problem that has developed over many years.* Many people believe that in time a change in public attitudes will reduce the demand for drugs. DARE seeks to promote that change. Equally important, DARE instructors instill in children decision-making capabilities that can be applied to a variety of situations as they mature.

In 1988 the Bureau of Justice Assistance of the U.S. Department of Justice actively supported DARE by awarding grants to fund four regional training centers to facilitate the effective development of DARE programs. There is widespread support for DARE among law enforcement, the school system, and the community. At this point there has been limited evaluation of the effects of DARE largely because the program is still comparatively new in terms of longitudinal evaluation research. At this time, the National Institute of Justice is conducting a national assessment of DARE with the desire to seek information on the long-term effectiveness of the program.

Bureau of Justice Assistance. *An Introduction to DARE: Drug Abuse Resistance Education* (Washington, DC: Office of Justice Programs, U.S. Department of Justice, 1991).

city's three school districts. In the fourth and fifth grades, officers teach D.A.R.E., in the middle school, officers teach the G.R.E.A.T. curriculum; and in each of the three high schools, the department has an Education Resource Officer (ERO) assigned. This approach, in the police chief's experience, has significantly improved relations between the police and community as well as contributing to fewer "police problems" and increased arrests as a result of more open (and trusted) communications.

The basic paradigm that there must be an integration of effort among the police, schools, and parents for school-based programs to achieve success can be extended to community policing. Alone, none of the three are likely to have complete success in directing a child's behavior toward a constructive, responsible end, simply because of the diverse experiences children have and the reality that parents have significantly less contact time with their children than they did a generation ago. Of the three groups, the police typically have the least influence on children. Yet, law enforcement officers can serve as a catalyst to both the parents and schools through programs like D.A.R.E. and G.R.E.A.T.—an effort that is only enhanced when the department is "driven" by a partnership and problem-based customer orientation, as found in community policing.

For example, the Kansas City, Missouri Police Department's use of D.A.R.E. has served as a vehicle for various activities in Kansas City that go beyond the in-school curriculum. Specifically emerging from ideas of D.A.R.E. officers were several new programs:

- A new community-based program called *The Park Hill School District Community Drug-Free Task Force* was created from the interest and concern of parents, the police, and schools.
- The idea for *Drug-Free Tailgate Parties* at various high school football games was created and successfully sponsored.
- An "adult prom" was sponsored as a fundraiser for drug abuse programs and community awareness of drugs and related problems that affect children.
- D.A.R.E. officers and students developed a docudrama for drug resistance, which was presented to students during high school prom week.
- Through leadership of school-based officers, a chapter of *Turning Resources and Energy in New Directions* (TREND) was developed in two middle schools and one high school.
- School officers helped develop a *Teaching and Reaching Youth* (TRY) program.

What has become increasingly evident is that school-based programs have provided important links to the community that were previously weak or nonexistent.

Socialization.   An important dynamic in any educational initiative is the socialization process. Socialization essentially includes everything a person observes and experiences throughout their lifetime, which shapes their attitudes, values, and beliefs. Our political beliefs, our perspective of "right and wrong", our priorities in life, and virtually every other aspect of the human experience is shaped by socialization.

Informal socialization occurs through a person's incidental exposure throughout life. For example, a young person is riding with his or her parents and the car is stopped for speeding. Whether the officer is pleasant and professional or unpleasant and overbearing will probably have some influence on that child's attitude toward the police. When the family continues on their way, if the parent who was driving is indignant toward the officer, calling him or her names, or if the parent is positive, saying that the officer was doing an important job to help keep people safe, will also be absorbed by the child. The interaction of these brief experiences will be a factor in the child's developing attitude toward the police. The single brief encounter has a limited effect on the child's value system, nonetheless it is a "planted seed". Subsequent encounters with a police officer may reinforce previous experiences—whether positive or negative—or could provide conflicting information, which the youth has to judge. For example, if the first experience was negative, yet the second was positive, then the child will be making judgments about his or her attitudes toward the police. Other factors color that judgment, such as comments by friends or teachers, observations on television, or any other type of input the youth may receive. Simply stated, the predominant type of input—or socialization—one receives on a regular basis has the greatest influence on the child's developing attitudes and beliefs.

Formal socialization occurs when specific information is directed toward an individual with the intent of shaping their values and beliefs. The school, church, job training, and to some extent, court sentences are focused on teaching a person behaviors and beliefs as well as substantive skills. Ironically, informal socialization appears to be somewhat more influential than formal socialization. Despite this, there is a clear interaction between the two types.

With respect to school-based programs, constant positive exposure to a police officer over a sustained amount of time helps shape a positive attitude toward the community, its values, and the police. Consequently, the programs may help to develop good citizenship in the students who participate. The extent to which any given young person will be influenced is dependent on his or her previous socialization, the quality of the program instruction and experience, and the amount of follow-up, or "reinforcement", the young person receives concerning the police, whether it is from parent, friends, teachers, or other police officers. Importantly, D.A.R.E. and G.R.E.A.T. can serve as significant opportunities to open the door to young people and plant the seeds of responsible citizenship—factors that the police department can build on in their community policing initiatives. This, interestingly, can influence both the child and the parents.

For whatever reason—values, peer pressure, rebelliousness, religion, and any combination of these and other factors—the acceptability of human behavior moves on a continuum. For example, some young people never use drugs or seriously entertain the idea of participating in an unlawful act. Others, unfortunately, may be destined for involvement in some unlawful activity. These extremes represent research questions that criminologists have studied for years. What we know about these conditions is that they are the product of a complex interaction of physical, environmental, and social-psychological factors that can be influenced by socialization—positive and negative—toward either extreme.

As illustrated in Figure 14-2, a substantial portion of young people seem to be in the middle of this continuum, vulnerable to some type of influence that will edge them closer to one end or the other. School-based programs and positive interaction with the police as a result of a community-based orientation—either through direct instruction or through its indirect effects—can socialize those in the middle of the continuum toward the end of greater responsibility.

Benefits of School-Based Programs for Community Policing and Community Relations. Building on the ideas that have been discussed thus far, several factors become evident when the benefits of school-based programs are examined as related to community policing. In a project for the U.S. Bureau of Justice Assistance, the author interviewed a number of police officers who had worked with D.A.R.E. Their experiences on the benefits of the program are evident in their comments:

- *It "humanizes" the police—that is, young people can begin to relate to officers as people, not as a uniform or institution.* A D.A.R.E. officer in Massachusetts told the author, "I have had countless kids tell me that they never thought they would speak to a cop. It shows you that they viewed us [the police] as robots or

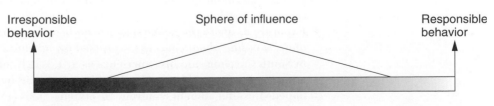

Figure 14-2. Continuum of Responsibility

some untouchable force. If I hadn't had these kids in class, most would probably still view us that way."

- *It permits students to see police officers in a helping role, not just an enforcement role.* A Georgia D.A.R.E. officer had a fifth-grade student tell him, "I didn't know you did good things, I thought you just put people in jail." Showing all sides of policing responsibilities can be an important educational tool.

- *It opens lines of communication between youth and the police.* In Michigan, an officer said, "When I worked patrol, I rarely said over a half a dozen words to kids and they certainly had little to say to me. Now, [after working in D.A.R.E.] I talk to kids all the time—even ones who graduated from the program several years ago—and it's amazing some of the things they tell me."

- *It opens lines of communication between the school district and police to deal with a wide range of issues, such as violence in the schools, drug abuse, or any other problem for which there is mutual concern.* One Texas police department had a relationship with a school district which could best be described as contentious. The district did not want the police to come on campus unless they were specifically called and then under fairly controlled circumstances. Moreover, the police department had difficulty getting much cooperation from the school except under the most extraordinary circumstances. The Chief of Police said that after the D.A.R.E. program started, the relationship with the school system completely turned around. Not only did the D.A.R.E. officer serve as an important "common ground" but the school officials developed a greater understanding of police procedures and needs, just as the police department learned more about the school district's concerns.

- *It serves as a source of feedback to the police department to better understand the fears and concerns of young people to help the police develop problem-solving efforts that extend beyond drugs.* A D.A.R.E. officer from a rural Missouri town said, "I was surprised to learn how scared many of these kids were about different types of crime. They would hear about gangs and homicides occurring in Kansas City and were convinced that was a problem [here] also. I can't ever remember a homicide [in our town] and I would be surprised if we ever had a gang member pass through here. So, I found myself explaining things to kids about all kinds of crime in addition to drug resistance."

- *It places the police in a different light with respect to many adults within the community; specifically parents, teachers, school staff, administrators and school board members.* A Michigan parent told the author, "At first I wasn't too sure that having a cop teaching kids in school was a good idea. I thought they'd try to turn the kids into informants or something. But after talking with my daughter about the [D.A.R.E. instruction] and listening to her enthusiasm and talking with [the officer] at her graduation, it changed my mind. It has good lessons about personal responsibility which should be continued in the schools and at home."

- *Exposure to life in the public schools can broaden officers' perspectives and understanding about concerns expressed by community members.* An officer in South Carolina said his experience as a D.A.R.E. officer gave him a greater appreciation for problems school teachers face and how these problems impede the education of children. He stated, "This [experience] has not only helped me in my job, but it has made me a better parent and citizen."

- *D.A.R.E. training is an instrument of socialization that introduces officers to a philosophy that measures success by community acceptance and support rather than the numbers of crimes and arrests.* A California police captain observed that officers returning from D.A.R.E. training have ". . . a definite change in character.. The officers demonstrate greater sensitivity to the needs of people in the community, and an eagerness to interact with the community and teach what they have learned. Such changes in police attitudes provide a firm foundation upon which police-community partnerships can be established."

- *Using D.A.R.E. officers as a resource, the department can become more creative in developing problem-solving initiatives.* A California police manager stated, "We've found D.A.R.E. officers to be an excellent source to help identify community problems [that] need to be solved because [these officers] learn so much in the schools. They're also a good resource for viewing new programs from a slightly different light, because they seem to understand many things about our community that many of us have lost touch with."

- *D.A.R.E. officers can serve as a conduit to provide information to young people beyond drug-related matters, particularly in question-and-answer sessions.* A Florida officer stated, "I get questions about traffic laws, search and seizure, the accuracy of TV police shows, crimes in the news, local gossip about crimes and criminals, the Mafia—just about anything you can think of. There's certainly lots of misconceptions in these kids' minds. Hopefully, I'm straightening some of them out."

- *D.A.R.E. can serve as a stimulus for youth to become more involved in other responsible activities, such as the Police Explorers Police Athletic League, or other youth-oriented initiatives.* A Texas police manager observed, "D.A.R.E. gets many young people enthused about the police, which leads to their interest in about anything we're involved with. The more young people we can get to participate in positive, character-building activities, the better citizens they will be. Over the years, D.A.R.E. will probably plant the seed for many of these young people to enter a law enforcement career."

- *D.A.R.E. reduces peer pressure and balances values as related to all types of responsible behavior.* An officer from Florida observed, "Most kids want to do what is right, but the peer pressure to conform is unbelievably strong. What they learn in D.A.R.E. discussion sessions is that there are lots of other kids who share their values to do 'what's right'. That lesson goes far beyond drug resistance and gets to the heart of being a good citizen."

School-based programs foster the same kind of close and prolonged contact with the community that is fundamental to community policing. The officer is removed from the patrol car and interacts closely with school administrators, teachers, parents, community members and young people over an extended period of time, developing a rapport that fosters communication and problem-solving on issues extending beyond any specific program curriculum.

The interaction between school officers, community police officers, and the citizens with whom they have contact becomes very strong. A police supervisor in Massachusetts stated, "Every student and parent views 'their DARE officer' as being 'the best one', much the same way people view 'their' community police officer as being the best officer on the department". These perceptions by the public have important implications for gaining support and developing partnerships for crime control and problem-solving. Given the benefits that can be gained from these linkages, the po-

SCHOOL-BASED PROGRAMS OF THE MISSION, TEXAS POLICE DEPARTMENT

The Mission Police Department in conjunction with the Mission Consolidated Independent School District (CISD.), the Sharyland Independent School District (ISD.) and the La Joya Independent School District have joined efforts in an attempt to curb increasing youth gang violence and substance abuse. As a result of these joined efforts, the organizations have formed the Youth Services Education Division. The division consists of specially trained police officers that provide three unique programs to the elementary, junior high, ninth grade Mission campus, and senior high schools. The programs include Drug Abuse Resistance Education (D.A.R.E.), Gang Resistance Education and Training (G.R.E.A.T.), and the Education Resource Officer (ERO) programs.

The police department has a total of sixteen officers assigned to the Youth Services Education Division. Fifteen are officers in the schools, and there is one supervisor for all the officers at all the campuses. This translates to 21.6 percent of the sworn full-time Mission police officers being assigned to the schools. Personnel management points of interest related to this division include:

- The school districts pay the officers' salaries for the school year (177 days)
- During summers, officers receive . . .
  —State mandated in-service training
  —Special training required for their assignments
- During summers, when not in training, Youth Services officers are assigned to the patrol division—the purpose is to:
  —Renew the officers' expertise and awareness of "the street"
  —Help keep avenues of communication open with other officers
  —Help cover time for vacationing officers

Officer Selection

Officers are volunteers and must have a minimum of two years experience in the police department. There is a departmental review of the officer's work record and fitness report to determine how the officer's work experience and demeanor blend with the requirements of the school-based assignments. Following these steps, the officer appears before an oral selection board, which is exclusively made up of representatives from the administration and staff of the school district where the officer will be assigned. The applicant officer is introduced by an officer already working in the schools and the school's review board selects the officer.

Agreements with the School Districts

D.A.R.E. and G.R.E.A.T. officers will perform their curricular teaching tasks as trained. All officers work with both the Penal Code and the Education Code for investigation and enforcement. The police have jurisdiction over crimes against children during travel to and from schools, even if the offense occurs outside of the agency's immediate geographic jurisdiction.

Relationship Between School-Based Officers and Those in More Traditional Assignments

Not surprisingly, initially school-based officers were viewed as "kiddie cops." Patrol officers and detectives thought school-based officers did not do "real police work." With experience, however, generally attitudes of other officers have evolved. Now, school-based positions are viewed as an assignment just like any other position in the department. Indeed, most officers view the school-based officers as a good resource, mainly because they recognize that the school-based officers have a great number of contacts, which can be used in investigations and problem-solving.

School Management Relations Issues

Each principal is in charge of his or her own campus and wants to have control over officers, thus a mutually agreed upon arrangement had to be developed. The principal has direction over all curricular matters officers are involved in while the police supervisor has direction over all police activities. Occasionally negotiation is required over authority to direct an officer; however, this is usually accomplished without much problem. There have been very positive reactions from school staff, teachers, students, and parents with respect to having officers in the schools. Some comments by and about Education Resource Officers include:

- "Many kids contact me for non-police activities—at least half. In fact, the [high school] counselor refers many kids to me, even though there is no criminal activity involved."
- "I provide career advice. I also try to work with the parents a great deal."
- "School staff members make me feel like I belong here. There is camaraderie."
- "Teachers love these programs. They like the officers and they like the security of the officer in the school."
- "The [school programs] are political animals. We have to meet the needs of the schools and community but not go too far."
- "A Mexican National student attending school in Mission stated to an ERO: "I see the police here to help us. She has warmth and says `Hi' to us by our first name."

The EROs also challenge the students academically. For example, in one school, students who do well on their TAAS (Texas Assessment of Advanced Skills) tests get the opportunity to dunk the officer in a water tank. The first contact back at school for students who are suspended is the Education Resource Officer, as a rule of school discipline.

Effects of the School-Based Programs

While a formal program evaluation has not been done, there are some particularly evident effects of the school-based programs. Among these are:

- Notably fewer gang problems in the schools.
- Fewer crime problems, in general, in schools and on school property.

continued

- Better liaison with the schools for identifying and resolving crime-related problems.
- Wider range of sources of information among school-aged youth to help solve crimes and problems.
- Significantly increased avenues of communication between the police and community via students who get to know officers, which helps in crime prevention, problem identification, and problem-solving.
- Generally increased public relations for the police department, which has resulted in greater respect and appreciation for the department that has also translated into better budget appropriations from the city council.
- The school-based initiatives appear to have displaced much of the youth crime and gang-related activity out of Mission, mostly into neighboring McAllen.

Special Programs in the Mission Police Department

A number of other special programs have been implemented in Mission, which either directly or indirectly support the school-based programs. These include:

- Summer youth camp: Operated by D.A.R.E. officers, the camp targets "at-risk" kids, ten to thirteen years of age. It involves activities such as familiarization with the police and fire departments; field trips to boot camps, jails, courts, and other criminal justice facilities; and a general education and awareness program.
- Citizens' Police Academy
- CAAT—Citizens Against Auto Theft: Citizens volunteer to have stickers placed on their car, which give police consent to stop the car at night to determine if the owner is driving the vehicle.
- "Danger Stranger": A danger awareness program for children
- Participation in the TRIAD Program for senior citizens
- Citizen volunteer enforcement program for handicapped-space parking violations.
- Mobile Community Centers
- Monthly Neighborhood Watch meetings, city-wide "from the colonias to the rich side of town"
- Joint police and fire presentations for the Public Housing Authority
- Public Information Officer position created; a "customer-directed" position

lice should strive to build on any avenue of communications and cooperation that can be developed.

Both community policing and school-based programs are evolving initiatives that endeavor to respond to changing social problems and demands. Like any other effort they will have to rise to meet the challenge—many of which are based in "human nature."

Criticisms of D.A.R.E. and G.R.E.A.T.   Despite the popularity and benefits of these programs, a number of criticisms have been offered. The predominant criticism argues that it is unrealistic to believe that the comparatively short exposure students have to the programs will have any lasting effect on their behavior. Relying on learning theory, critics observe that for D.A.R.E. and G.R.E.A.T. to be successful, they must be included in a multi-year curriculum, providing substantive reinforcement in order to re-socialize the attitudes, values and beliefs of young people. (While multi-year curricula are available, most schools use the programs for only one or two years.) Critics tend to argue that the issue is not whether the programs have value, but whether they are achieving their stated goals of drug, violence, or gang resistance.

Another criticism of the programs is that despite the existence of gang, violence, and drug abuse problems, special curricula in the schools are not warranted. Supporters of this argument state that there are many social and behavioral problems that may effect young people; however, it is not feasible (nor is it the school's job) to address all of these potential problems through a structured curriculum. They argue that whenever a new curricular element is added, something must be sacrificed, thus "robbing" the student of educational opportunities to become proficient in educational fundamentals. Indeed, persuasive arguments can be made in this regard; however, the final responsibility rests with school officials and parents about whether it is a prudent use of curricular time to provide instruction in these programs.

A final criticism simply asks, "Is it the job of the police to teach classes such as these in the schools?" This question has philosophical, resource-based, and political implications for the chief of police. Philosophically, the chief of police must look at the police department's mission and role to assess the propriety of placing a police officer in the schools as a teacher for the duration of the program's curriculum. Is this activity consistent with the public's desires, the goals of the department, and the problems within the community? Related to this is the resource question: How much are the programs going to cost the police department both in "real" dollars and indirect costs? Will any other police activity have to be sacrificed in order to support the programs? If so, what are the comparative priorities of D.A.R.E. or G.R.E.A.T. and the sacrificed program? What are the "cost benefits" of the program?

These questions are not easy to answer because of the political dynamics. In the hierarchy of actual problems in a community, drug abuse or gang involvement may be low. However, if public concern is high and the public wants the programs, the chief of police may be politically forced to implement them, despite the philosophical and resource questions. One police chief told the author he felt that if had not started the D.A.R.E. program, it could have cost him his job. While this is an extreme circumstance, it illustrates the power of a politically charged environment.

Neither D.A.R.E. nor G.R.E.A.T. offer a panacea. They are tools that have a great deal of support from the police and public alike in dealing with the pervasive problems of drugs and violence. Certainly they can help solve some problems, increase communications between the police and public, and provide an avenue for broadening the police-citizen relationship. Recognizing the strengths and weaknesses of such programs is essential in order to keep their value in perspective.

Gangs

Gangs were traditionally viewed as social clusters of predominantly young males who congregated for social- and esteem-related reasons. "Social," with respect to gangs, meant that the young persons had a defined mechanism for recreation and interaction, albeit frequently illegitimate. Cultural norms of the gangs evolved, just as in

VICTORIA, TEXAS POLICE DEPARTMENT GANG SUPPRESSION PROGRAM

As a result of a growing gang problem, including a few drive-by shootings, this program was created to both investigate gang activity and prevent the growth of gangs in the city. Two officers were assigned to develop programs and coordinate activities: One is a sergeant who is a School Resource Officer and the D.A.R.E. supervisor and the second is an investigator who works primarily in public housing. In determining gang activity, the department relies on the Texas Penal Code definition of "criminal street gang" in Title 11, Chapter 71, Section 71.01 (d):

> "Criminal street gang" means three or more persons having a common identifying sign or symbol or an identifiable leadership who continuously or regularly associate in the commission of criminal activities.

Victoria's gangs are predominantly "territorial" in nature and generally Hispanic. They are not a recent phenomenon; indeed, in some cases, there are third generation gang members. Changes in the gang situation—predominantly growing violence and increased fear among the young people—fueled a new approach to gang control by the police department.

The current gang initiative has eight components, some of which are more structured than others. These are described below (in no particular order).

Graffiti Education and Eradication

Patrol officers, school officials, and other members of the community have received training programs to recognize gang graffiti and report it. When reported, the graffiti is photographed by an investigator, and then adult community service officers or probationers immediately cover it with heavy paint. The surface is later painted over to match the original surface.

Before the training, some parents reported they had gang symbols on their property and did not realize it. Similarly, after the education programs, some parents reported recognizing tattoos that were gang signs on their children.

Gang Education (Community and Schools)

Having a slightly different orientation, this initiative has several facets. For example, gang and violence issues are included in the D.A.R.E. curriculum; the School Resource Officer talks with young people who show interests in joining a gang to give them a realistic perspective of gang life. Officers also speak to junior high and elementary school children in small groups or assemblies about gangs.

This portion of the program also provides education to teachers and parents to recognize gang signs, clothing, and behaviors. Previously, the officers reported, teachers and parents had no idea about the meaning of gang symbolism; therefore they did nothing about such symbols. After the educational programs, teachers and parents alike call the police to report the symbolism and take action to get rid of it. Interestingly, many middle and upper class families whose children were involved in gangs were among the most difficult to deal with.

Adopt-A-Gang

This is a program that has intentionally not been "pushed," but permitted to evolve. Patrol officers in each of the city's five zones may voluntarily Adopt-a-Gang as a means to help youth who are in the gang as well as to develop intelligence. Experience has shown that this initiative requires both dedication and patience on behalf of the patrol officers. The first step is that they must develop trust among the gang members. The trust is to show that the officers will listen to the young people and help them when they can. The Victoria officers have a wealth of examples of when this has occurred. There is no deceiving of the gang members, who know that an officer will take any enforcement action as necessary. The program permits the officer to get to know gang members and their families, so that officers can learn more about gang members' behavior as well as who they associate with.

Retaliation Reaction

A significant fear of many gang members (as well as non-gang kids) is retaliation for a gang event. Such diverse factors as a territorial trespass, an insult, an assault, or a homicide against a gang typically results in some form of retaliation by the victimized or the offended gang. As one investigator observed, "Because of retaliations, one assault can turn into ten." Retaliation is an inherent part of the gang culture, and perhaps even more intense in Hispanic gangs as a result of *machismo*. As a result, the police department has used this initiative to suppress retaliation after a known incident. Using diverse tactics ranging from the use of gang informants to "spreading the word" that the police are watching and will take harsh action against retaliation to the use of directed patrol, the police tailor their reaction to control retaliation.

Gang Grand Jury

One of the most effective strategies to suppress gang activities was a special Gang Grand Jury, which investigated and indicted numerous gang members for a variety of offenses. Even gang members who were "hardened" were intimidated by the Grand Jury process. Moreover, the code of silence among gang members was effectively taken away because all testifying gang members assumed that the others were providing evidence; thus, they did too. While the Grand Jury is not viable on an on-going basis, it served as an effective tool for dealing with gang-related crime during extended peak problem times.

Personal Protection Classes

This was specifically designed as a summer program, initially directed toward children who were at-risk of becoming gang members. The school resource officer taught martial arts classes to students with a social contract that the students would not become involved in youth gangs. Since the students were aware of "gang colors" the program promoted their interest in "colors" in terms of the colors of martial arts belts. The classes were also intended to promote mentorship for students who could not get involved in other activities, such as football, band, etc. The Personal Protection Classes were intended to provide a group where the

continued

students could "belong" and have a basis for kinship with others, without turning to a gang as a social outlet.

Schools-Malls-Community Anti-Gang Programs

As a means to minimize the visibility and the "copy cat" aspect of gang appearance, the police provided information to the schools and malls about the types of dress and behavior that were characteristic of gangs. As a consequence, the malls developed rules to exclude gang members and gang apparel on their property. Similarly, the schools—beginning with the alternative school—implemented a more restrictive dress code, which included:

- No earrings
- No "baggy" pants
- Shirt must be tucked in
- Students must wear a belt
- No emblems of such things as gangster rappers, alcohol, drugs, smoking, or sexual connotations
- No "unusually colored" hair

Effective in fall of 1997, the school district's dress code is even more restrictive, essentially a type of broad uniform. While these restrictions will not cause an individual to leave a gang, it minimizes the presence of gangs and appears to largely eliminate the "wannabes."

Promotion of "Legitimate Large Gangs"

Under the assumption that many young people are gang members because of the social aspects and have a need for peer group membership, this strategy is to both promote and recognize membership in legitimate large groups, such as sports teams; band; Boys and Girls Clubs; Y.O.U. (Youth Opposed to Using); and similar organizations. Gang specialists from the police department feel that this approach has helped to positively sway some children who were "on the fence" about gang membership. For those kids, the Boys and Girls Clubs has been particularly important.

The gang officers stated that the most important aspect of any program was to "get to know the kids". The most effective tool was communication after building a bond of trust. The gang officers spent a great deal of time—including off-duty time—getting to know the gang members and their families. They also observed that showing "genuine interest" in the young people, not just a "police interest", was an essential foundation for effective communication. The open lines of communication were important not only for diverting some youth from gang involvement, but also as an intelligence tool. On several occasions gang members would contact the officers about potential gang violence or retaliation. Interestingly, while the gangs would "talk tough" and show their *machismo*, most of the young people were fearful of the violence. It was the observations of the gang officers that many of the youth were involved in gangs simply for the kinship and mutual support derived from the group. Offering other group membership options sought to fulfill this social need.

The programs in Victoria have clearly been effective in reducing gang violence. Gang membership has dropped a little, but gangs are still prevalent, although not as visible. The gangs are also less likely to be involved in criminal enterprises and are mostly territorial, with occasional violent confrontations erupting over territorial issues. The police department credits the various initiatives for reducing the violence, appearance, and criminality of the gangs. The gang officers cautioned, however, that the police had to "keep the pressure" or the gang problem would again become pervasive.

the case of any subculture, to include language and dress as well as display of the "colors" and symbols, which uniquely identify a gang.

Historically, gangs were involved in identifying and protecting "turf" as well as involvement in petty crimes, usually some type of theft. During the mid-1980s, the gang orientation began to change drastically. Increasingly, gangs have become involved in drug trafficking, theft, extortion, and other crimes at the local, regional, and national level. It is difficult to make any meaningful generalizations about gangs as an emerging form of organized crime simply because they vary so much; nonetheless, this is an emerging trend in law enforcement.

Gangs tend to be neither very sophisticated nor well-organized (this includes the much publicized "Crips" and "Bloods" moving across the country from Los Angeles). Gangs largely exist along racial or ethnic lines and tend to cooperate predominantly with similar ethnic groups. Alliances are generally short-term and informal. Despite these factors, a growing number of gangs are taking on the characteristics of continuing criminal enterprises. Sometimes a distinction is made between *cultural* and *instrumental* gangs. The former is characterized as being the more traditional, while the latter has evolved with the expressed purpose of drug trafficking and other criminal enterprises. The distinction between these categories appears to be marginal as gangs expand.

In a project sponsored by the Office of Juvenile Justice and Delinquency Prevention (OJJDP) of the U.S. Department of Justice, an eight-step process called IDENTIFY was developed to involve the criminal justice system, schools, parents, and community in gang control.[12] The elements of the process are:

- I*dentification of the problem*—Define the who, what, when, where, and why of the problem in order to isolate it and understand it.
- D*efine the system components*—Articulate what agencies, organizations, and initiatives have primary authority and responsibility for dealing with the problem.
- E*numerate policies, procedures, practices, programs, and resources*—Applicable directives that address the problem are specified and resource needs are assessed as they relate to the problem.
- N*eeds clarification*—A comparison of the problem's characteristics with existing resources to determine additional policy, procedures, practices, and program and resource needs.
- T*arget strategies*—Refine the programmatic elements needed to address the problem and integrate these into an overall strategy to resolve the problem.

- I*mplementation plan*—Develop a plan that defines specific objectives, tasks, and resources to be contributed by each participant agency and organization for placing the resolution strategy into action.
- F*ocus agency responsibilities*—This is a process of refinement. Relying on initial feedback from the strategy, the team of agencies "fine tunes" their contribution to the overall strategy in order to have the greatest impact on the problem.
- Y*ell*—Used in the metaphorical sense (and to provide the "Y" in IDENTIFY!), this refers to evaluation and overt assessment of the strategy to assess its impact and needed changes.[13]

Developed explicitly to address gang problems, this OJJDP project follows a process similar to problem-oriented policing. Importantly, it attempts to overtly enlist the various groups which can have an impact on gang problems and provide a framework for them to approach the issues in a comprehensive and integrated fashion. Since gang problems frequently involve juveniles, the process of dealing with offenders becomes complicated. IDENTIFY endeavors to make this process easier.

YOUNG PEOPLE, THE POLICE, AND THE COMMUNITY

Every community (and every police agency) worries a lot about its young people. Adults spend considerable time and money on programs aimed at helping children, "to keep them out of trouble." Adult pundits in every generation are sure that "kids ain't what they used to be." One can agree or disagree with such a statement without knowing what it really means, because there is no way to research it.

Worry about children, then, may be the same old generational cycle merely repeating itself. On the other hand, there may be something really special this time around. No one can be sure. While avoiding any such judgment, these are examples of the kinds of events that cause the worry:

- More young people are being arrested for serious crimes, state by state. But public funds to finance juvenile programs are being reduced. In 1974, congress passed a Juvenile Justice and Delinquency Prevention Act. Nearly three decades later, there is little evidence that it has had any impact.
- Nobody knows how many youthful Americans have tried marijuana, but there is little doubt that the number is high. Data from both the "PRIDE" and "Monitoring the Future" drug surveys indicate that in the years 1994 to 1996, roughly 80% of the nation's high school seniors had tried marijuana at least once.
- Derelicts on urban skid rows are younger, on the average, than they were years ago. More and more are in their twenties; without skills or even a high school diploma, many are unemployable. Alcohol and drugs are pervasive problems.
- Runaway and "throwaway" youngsters are roaming the country in numbers hitherto unthinkable. (A throwaway, or "push out," is an unwanted child who is encouraged by parents to leave home.) Joblessness is a factor; so are increases in divorce and in emotional instability of the type reflected in child abuse.
- The hydralike problems of young people include several curious paradoxes. For example, there is the matter of schooling. On the one hand, it is estimated that there are two million American children who want to go to school but are forced out by school officials and policies. If a child is truant, the penalty is often suspension. Some cannot attend because of conditions related to poverty. Others seem to be out because they are black, or Spanish-speaking, or in some other way different from the

majority. Some are adjudged retarded without having been tested. At the higher levels of education, there are frequent reminders that discrimination has by no means disappeared. A major national commitment made during the 1960s to increase the number of blacks attending college seems to have been forgotten; black college enrollment has been proportionately going down.

- To complete the paradox, there is the kind of dropout who is out of school because he or she doesn't want to go. This side of the problem is also of grave concern.

Much remains to be done in the area of children's rights, including the question of the procedural rights of children under the law. In Michigan, as in many states, seventeen is referred to as "the witching age" for youth in trouble: there are no programs, no funds, and no facilities to help the teenager who is neither child nor adult; therefore, the courts are looked to for assistance, prompting fresh interest in the juvenile code.

In numerous states, despite controversy about it, children under eighteen can be punished for so-called status offenses, crimes that would not be crimes if committed by an adult. Truancy and running away are examples, along with smoking, drinking, curfew violations, ungovernability, waywardness, and others. The National Council on Crime and Delinquency sees status offenses as unfair on the grounds of denial of due process. There is movement in various states to revise the juvenile code to eliminate status offenses in a way supportive of children's rights. In the view of those backing such change, the essential issue is equal protection. The movement for children's rights has precipitated lively debate, at base an argument over the concept of parental authority.

However, children's rights is not a new issue. In 1967, the U.S. Supreme Court, in a single decision (*in re* Gault), brought about a reexamination of the entire relationship between children and the state. The result has been accommodation of constitutional due process standards in juvenile proceedings, making such proceedings more adversarial in the manner of legal machinery for adults. The question of whether teenagers should be able to secure medical services without involving their parents on such controversial issues as abortion and prescription of birth control pills is causing widespread argument.

Supreme Court decisions in the past decade or so (typically by five-to-four margins) heralded the end of schools' unquestioned control over students (known as "in loco parentis"). One such decision argued that students "don't shed their constitutional rights at the schoolhouse gate."[14] Another held that students have a constitutional right to prompt notice and hearing for punishment even in a case as minor as a single day's suspension. Public education was judged a property interest protected by the due process clause of the Fourteenth Amendment. In still another case, a month later, the Supreme Court made it easier for students to sue school board officials who deprive them of due process rights. Many educators have said that these decisions still do not go far enough. Others retort that an increasingly adversarial relationship is being engendered among students, teachers, administrators, and parents.

The juvenile code and litigation in cases testing the perimeters of children's rights and parental authority are matters of interest in the arena of children-police-community relations. But these matters excite adults much more than young people, as the latter have interests of higher priority. For college students, the prevalent question is, will I be able to get a decent job when I graduate? Other matters seem diversionary.

VIOLENCE IN THE SCHOOLS

In late January 1993, a *USA Today* story reported that a fifteen-year-old Los Angeles student, who carried a .357-caliber magnum handgun because he feared gang violence, accidentally killed one student and wounded another in a high school classroom. The same day, an Associated Press story reported that in Lorain, Ohio two junior high school girls, aged twelve and thirteen, were charged with planning to kill their English teacher. The thirteen-year-old said she wanted to kill the teacher because "the teacher yelled at her." The twelve-year-old said her reason was because "she sends me to the office all the time." To make this case more unusual, the girls' classmates had bet about 200 on whether or not the girls would actually kill the teacher.

Both of these stories illustrate tragic circumstances that occur in our schools far more often than most of us may envision. In the first case, the student's fear of crime was so obsessive that he felt the need to carry a gun. The fact that the student had access to a loaded weapon and had the wherewithal to carry it to school for "defense" is also a symbolic comment of changing values. Even more telling is the belief by the two junior high school girls that the way to deal with a student-teacher problem was to kill the adult. That other students knew about the plan and bet on it is further evidence of deteriorating values.

According to a special report from the Bureau of Justice Statistics, an estimated 9 percent of students, aged twelve to nineteen, were crime victims in or around their school over a six-month period. Fifteen percent of the students said their school had gangs and 16 percent claimed that a student had attacked or threatened a teacher at their school. The same report found that up to 25 percent of the students had a fear of "being attacked" *while at school*—compared to 11 percent who feared being attacked in travel to and from school.[15]

A 1993 national study by the Police Executive Research Forum explicitly looked at police experiences with violence in the school.[16] Police agencies reported that over the past three years crimes at public schools had been increasing. Of the most notable increases:

- 80.4 percent reported an increase in assaults
- 76.3 percent reported an increase of firearms possessions in the schools
- 75.0 percent reported an increase of bladed weapons possessions
- 71.7 percent reported an increase in the destruction of property
- 66.3 percent reported an increase in violence at school-related functions
- 55.6 percent reported an increase in the number of assaults against teachers
- 54.3 percent reported an increase in the number of drug arrests

Overall, 83.5 percent of the police departments rated crimes in general as a problem in the schools, and 64.0 percent indicated that firearms-related crimes were a problem. An important question, given these findings, is, "What impact is this environment having on the educational process and socialization of these youth?"

There is good reason for concern about school crime and violence. A survey by the Centers for Disease Control and Prevention found that among students in grades nine through twelve, nearly one in twenty carried a firearm within the thirty days preceding the survey.[17] Similarly, the FBI's Uniform Crime Report data recorded in 1990 alone that there were 2,348 murder victims between ages fifteen and nineteen. The same year, there were 31,991 juveniles charged with possessing or carrying a weapon.[18]

The problems of crime and violence in the schools have a long-term deteriorating effect on society in general. It resocializes young people toward the belief that violence is a viable response to conflict. Moreover, crime—and fear of it—significantly disrupts the learning environment, thereby inhibiting the academic enterprise. Since education is a building block process, the entire educational career of students can be derailed through crime experiences at school.

Fighting and threatening conflicts have always been a part of school life. Most of us—male and female alike—recall "bullies" during our formative school years who intimidated other children, particularly those who were smaller and less assertive. Similarly, many of us recall conflicts among other students wherein disagreements were resolved physically, rather than through negotiation.

Many of these encounters are normal experiences during growth, which may be referred to as *maturational combat*. That is, the behavior is a rudimentary means to resolve conflict when interpersonal negotiation and reconciliation skills have not been developed. Rather than "talk through" an argument, a more primal response of physical aggression is used. This is normal developmental behavior, which varies in intensity among people. Importantly, however, it is a component of the socialization process through which we normally evolve. Most of us "grow up."

The current issue is not focused on this transient combat of adolescence. Rather, concern is directed toward more aggressive behavior, many times involving some type of weapon, which grows from factors beyond what one may call "typical" conflict during maturation.

An important *caveat* is warranted at this point: the author does not propose that "maturational combat" and "school violence" are either mutually exclusive or dichotomous. Rather, these behaviors are on a continuum (illustrated in Figure 14-3). The continuum illustrates several critical factors. First, it recognizes that not all persons will be involved in physical encounters. Of those who are, most of the physical conflict will be limited to maturational combat. For some, however, behavior extends further to intentional aggression or violence. These individuals use physical conflict as a means of manipulation, dominance, and personal aggrandizement with respect to their relations with others. While the aggressive characteristics of some will not evolve beyond this point, others will adopt physical aggression as a primary means of resolving conflict or realizing personal desires. As such, this behavior is repetitive and becomes part of a behavioral pattern.

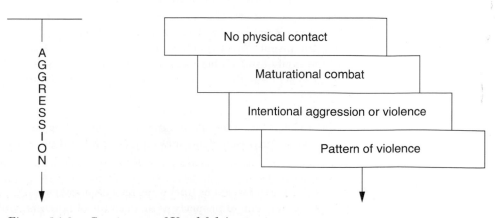

Figure 14-3. Continuum of Youthful Aggression

A person's evolution on this continuum is dependent on a variety of factors which are socially, economically, and demographically interactive. Unfortunately, many of these characteristics converge in an environment that is too complex for a school system—particularly with constrained resources—to realistically deal with. This is not to infer that all hope is lost. Rather, it is to give a realistic balance.

To deal with this, a two-pronged model is offered to address school violence. The first prong is *diagnosis*. It attempts to provide a framework to understand the problem. The second prong is *intervention*. This offers alternatives to remedy, or at least manage, the violence.

Prong 1: Diagnosis

To understand—or diagnose—school violence, one must understand the dynamics of the behavior. If violent behavior at either the individual or aggregate level can be correlated to defined "causal" factors, then a target exists toward which intervention strategies can be directed. Diagnosis of school violence must address four elements:

- The nature of the relationship
- A manifestation of violent behavior
- The constructs of conflict
- Compounding variables

Nature of the Relationship.   To understand and resolve school violence, one must first understand the nature of the relationship between the parties involved. The student's relationship in violent transactions involves different categories of people. Characteristics of the violence and precipitating factors consequently vary depending on the interpersonal relationship. These may be viewed as "contributory causes" of violent behavior. Importantly, there is no singular "cause"; rather, a number of relevant variables constitute the formula for violence. Moreover, the social pathology of these factors seems to be viral; that is, they interact and "infect" the judgment patterns of young people which, in turn, not only aggravate the behavior, but also make it more difficult to control. Importantly. the nature of intervention is strongly related to the relationship between those involved in the violent behavior. Thus, effective diagnosis with respect to the nature of the relationships can be an important element for preventing future problems.

Manifestation of Violent Behavior.   The process of diagnosis must also determine the nature of the aggression or violence. What were the characteristics of the incident? What was the apparent intent? Was there just a threat? If so, how "real" was the threat? Was the behavior symbolic, e.g., vandalism? If so, what is the nature of the symbolism? If there was injury, how serious was it? Was a weapon used? If so, what type? Was the violence a product of an individual act or was it a group dynamic?

The answers to these questions are vital to understanding the breadth and depth of the violence as a foundation for victim counseling and development of intervention strategies. Aggressive behaviors may be exhibited in any of a number of ways:

- Threats
- Display of weapons (including imitation weapons)
- Destruction of property as an example of potential violence (e.g., "trashing" a locker; vandalism)

- Influencing the victim through intimidation
- Individual physical assault
- Gang physical assault
- Sexual assault
- Assault with firearms
- Assault with weapons other than firearms

As is readily evident, the seriousness and motivations of these behaviors vary. The basis of this variance is largely influenced by the *constructs of the conflict*.

Constructs of Conflict.

Constructs are factors identified during the study of a problem that appear to be important contributors—or at least correlates—to the violence. In the current case, a series of constructs have been identified through the author's empirical research, literature review, and discussions with school officials.

Based on these findings, significant factors that contribute to the outgrowth of youth violence include:

- Sexual relationships
- Friends in a dispute
- Drugs and drug deals
- "Turf Battle"
- A "Power Relationship" (e.g., general assault, sexual assault)
- Theft (particularly for symbolic trend attire, such as tennis shoes, leather jacket, or jewelry)
- Jealousy
- Peer abuse (e.g., "picking on" or "making fun" of a youth)
- Racism
- Gangs
- Competition (for attention, for a position, for friendship, for notice, for reinforcement)
- Values (what is "right" and "wrong")

As illustrated in Figure 14-4, the constructs do not exist independently. Rather, they interact with each other to precipitate violent acts. These constructs are primary indicators that must be analyzed based upon their interrelationship with *compounding* variables and the manifestation of the violent behavior.

Compounding Variables.

Compounding variables are antecedent or intervening factors that influence the constructs. Antecedent variables occur *before* the constructs become interactive, leading to the aggressive behavior. *Intervening* variables occur during the interaction of the constructs. While others may certainly exist, the following have been identified as being among the most important of the compounding variables:

- Nature of home environment
- Nature of social relationships
- Economic issues of the child and the home environment
- Nature of discipline (or lack thereof) at home
- The child's victimization, including child abuse, neglect, or sexual assault
- Peer influence and lifelong socialization

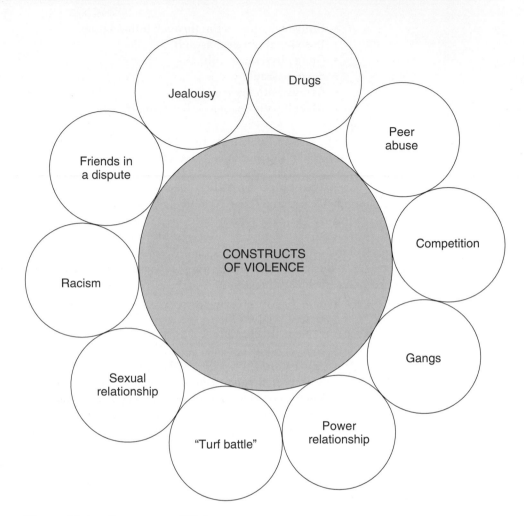

Figure 14-4.   Constructs of Violence

The compounding variables serve to give direction to a youth's behavior. That is, while the constructs play important roles in "setting the scene" for violent behavior at school, the compounding variables can influence the youth's actual behavior as related to the constructs. Importantly, the constructs are primarily related to the youth's school environment and "macro group" behavior. Conversely, the compounding variables are primarily related to the youth's personal environment, including both individual and "micro group" behavior. These distinctions are not dichotomous but exist on a continuum. Clearly they all interact to a large degree, yet their degree of influence is notably different.

Prong 1—Summary.   Identifying these elements serves as guideposts to begin understanding the total environment that contributes to violent behavior. Thus, school officials experiencing problems of violence—and specifically *patterns* of violence—can begin to develop a "picture" of the behavioral causal features by examining these factors. The purpose of identifying these elements is to develop a blueprint for intervention strategies that reduce the probability of violence occurring.

Prong 2: Intervention

The concept of intervention implies that programming will be developed that can minimize the probability and effects of violent behavior. Intervention can generally be viewed from two perspectives: first is the *philosophy* of intervention. This perspective attempts to define the intended purpose and goals of a given strategy. In this regard, the intervention philosophies may be

- *Control*—This endeavors to control the students and their environment in order to prevent violence from occurring and/or minimizing the impact of violence.
- *Punishment*—When a person is identified as being involved in aggressive or violent behavior, punitive sanctions are imposed as a means of making the individual "pay" for improper behavior. Ideally, under this philosophy, the punishment is of a nature that the individual will not want to involve himself or herself in the behavior again, in order to avoid the punishment.
- *Rehabilitation*—This philosophy attempts to identify factors that caused a person to be involved in violent behavior. With this knowledge, the intervention strategies attempt to alter those causal factors so the person will not participate in future violent behavior.

On the surface, the philosophies appear fairly straightforward; however, as researchers have learned in the field of corrections, the application of these concepts is extraordinarily difficult and evaluation results are inconclusive. While these different approaches are not always cooperative, they are not mutually exclusive. Undoubtedly there should be programming that addresses each type of philosophy to some degree. Yet, one philosophy is typically dominant in any intervention programming. Sometimes the dominance of a philosophy is for a practical reason. For example, if there is widespread violence in the school, simply gaining *control* of the problem will be the underlying philosophy. In other cases, an administrator may have a particular philosophical foundation, which correlates with his or her educational philosophy. As such, any intervention program will necessarily reflect this.

The second perspective of intervention is based on *strategy*. This is much more pragmatic because it addresses specific operational foundations of an intervention program. The intervention strategies focus on procedural issues, which serve to structure the implementation of the program. The foundations of intervention strategy include concerns that are:

- Educational/behavioral
- Administrative
- Legal
- Physical

The *educational/behavioral* strategy teaches young people about appropriate and acceptable behaviors. More importantly, this approach attempts to resocialize young people in order to change their values with respect to the propriety of certain behaviors. Thus, it is important to not only educate about *what* is proper but *why* certain behaviors are proper. An important advantage to this strategy is that it can have long-term, lasting effects on behavior. A significant disadvantage is that this is a slow, labor-intensive method for changing behavior, which requires continual reinforcement as a means of resocializing the individual.

FOCUS 14.6

THE STAFFORDSHIRE, ENGLAND "SPACE PROGRAM"

In 1981, Chief Constable Charles Kelly of the Staffordshire, England Constabulary modestly initiated the SPACE Program—*Staffordshire Police Activity and Community Enterprise*. The program's primary purpose is to provide a wide range of activities and opportunities for young people, to prevent their involvement in crime, drug use, and other inappropriate activities during the summer months when they are not in school. In addition, the program serves to bring the police and community closer together as well as to integrate the police with other government agencies and the private sector.

The program typically attracts over 20,000 children from ages ten to sixteen. Twenty-nine centers throughout the county are used to provide sporting, educational, recreational, historical, and leisure-based activities. Supervision of the program is provided by regular officers, members of the special constabulary (reserve officers), civilian police employees, and some 1,000 citizen volunteers from the county. Arrangements have been made with local bus companies to provide free travel for participants to one of the SPACE centers. Assistance is also provided by the armed forces, including the Royal Marines and the Royal Air Force.

Administrative strategies are incorporated into most schools. These are simply the procedures for identifying and processing students who are involved in improper behavior. Importantly, these strategies need to be codified and enforced with consistency regardless of the philosophy employed. Closely related to administrative issues are *legal* issues. These ensure that students' rights are maintained and that standards of equal protection and due process remain intact. Strategic legal issues go beyond procedure and also address legal sanctions—civil or criminal—which may be imposed as necessary to deal with problem students.

Finally, *physical* strategies concern changes in environmental design and implementation of environmental precautions as a means to control behavior. Physical strategies typically do not have any long-term behavioral impact and generally do not have any effect outside of school. Despite these limitations, physical strategies can be imposed relatively quickly and help ensure safety and security on the school grounds.

None of these strategic factors can occur in isolation. They, like all other factors, must be viewed interactively as part of a violence intervention package.

Operational Concerns for Intervention.   Intervention programs to control and prevent violence include participation by the parents, school district, and criminal justice system as well as the young people themselves. Realistically, there are limitations to institutional programs of intervention, particularly when the dysfunctional influences are centered outside of the school and when there is no reinforcement of socially accepted values in the home. With this *caveat*, practical elements of any intervention policy must include several fundamental elements.

First, policies must be *prevention-directed*. That is, a fundamental goal of any policy is to keep violence from occurring (to the extent that it is possible). Second,

Beyond providing general information about opportunities for young people, special arrangements are also made. For example, The Staffordshire Police Cadet Camp offers a one-week residential camp to sixty children to learn a wide range of "outward bound activities," such as rock climbing and "rough camping." Supervision and instruction for the camp is provided by the police training staff. Special efforts are made to include kids from minority groups as well as handicapped kids, with the focus of activities being to integrate these young people with all other program participants.

In conjunction with the daily SPACE activities, there are also events such as the *Rural Crime Patrol Country Fair, Carnival Day, International Day,* a large-scale bicycle race, classic car show, and many other events and booths. While people of all ages participate, the underlying focus is always the children, with a consistent theme: crime prevention, drug prevention, and the availability of the Staffordshire Police as a resource to help with solving problems and gaining assistance regardless of the nature of the problem.

Although the SPACE program was designed to meet the specific needs of Staffordshire County, England, it has served as a model for other police forces, not only in the United Kingdom but also in other European countries, as an avenue to bring the police and community closer together.

Kelly, Charles. *Community Involvement Report of the Chief Constable of Staffordshire for 1992* (Stafford, England: mimeographed report of the Staffordshire Constabulary, 1992).

policies must have some element to *impose sanctions* for violations of standards of conduct. Regardless of whether the sanctions are punitive or rehabilitative in philosophy, some means of imposing sanctions must be available in order to maintain control of the environment. Third, policies must have some element of *protection.* That is, there must be means—behavioral and/or physical—to maximize the protection of children from victimization.

Types of Intervention Programs.   A wide range of alternatives exist for specific intervention programs, all of which depend on the nature of the violence problem within a school, the grade levels involved, resources available for programming, the number of students and staff involved, capabilities and ability of law enforcement to participate, and a wide array of individual characteristics associated with the school. Regardless of these factors, the foundation for intervention policies must first be established by philosophy, followed by specific programming. Among the types of policies and programs for managing violent behavior that may be implemented are:

- Codes of conduct that prohibit gang association and colors
- Swift and sure enforcement of code standards
- Reinforcing positive values and behavior in curricula
- Close liaison programming between the schools and law enforcement agencies on gang, drug, and violence matters
- Close work with parents by both law enforcement and the schools
- School policies that impose sanctions when parents permit children to violate standards

- Close monitoring of school campuses for signs of gang behavior (student behavior and symbolism)
- Policies for searching lockers and/or students whenever there is any reasonable grounds to believe there are weapons or drugs present
- Automatic expulsion and referral to juvenile court for students found with weapons
- Work with police on:
  —Community policing
  —Drug Abuse Resistance Education (DARE)
  —Investigative activities
  —Interaction between the schools, the community, the police, and juvenile authorities regarding suspected violence, drug, and/or gang activity
- Prohibiting the display of clothing or adornment that indicate gang membership on school property and at school-sponsored events
- Strict monitoring of visitors to school campuses
- Reducing the emphasis of simply passing all students from grade to grade and enforcing academic standards
- Strong support by school administrators for teachers who enforce discipline; similarly, school board support of administrators
- Open discussion in class of violence problems with respect to the problem, student concerns, and consequences

It is not suggested that this is an exhaustive list. These are simply among the types of intervention programs that can meet the philosophical goals and strategies of dealing with school violence.

Applying the Intervention Model.   Effective intervention is specifically dependent on effective diagnosis. The process begins by identifying the causal or correlational behavior (as discussed above) that is instrumental in precipitating the violent behavior. The nature of those factors varies between school districts. Thus, the diagnosis must be individualized not only to the different school districts but also the individual schools. An analytic process identifies the more influential factors within the targeted school, i.e., provide the diagnosis. Based upon this analysis, alternate intervention strategies are explored to determine:

- Their effect on the correlational variables identified in the diagnosis
- Their reasonable availability for implementation
- Their potential effect on the correlational factors (i.e., their efficiency and effectiveness as an intervention strategy)
- The "costs and benefits" (which are not just monetary concerns) of the intervention
- The reasonable potential for the interventions to be effectively implemented over a long term

All of the elements of an intervention program as discussed thus far can be visualized in a problem-solving model as illustrated in Figure 14-5. A *caveat* is warranted at this point. While it is relatively easy to understand a model such as this, its implementation is quite a different story. Resources must be allocated, a significant planning effort must be completed, coordination must occur, and approvals from appropriate officials must be gained. Once programs are developed and approved, personnel training must be performed to ensure everyone understands the intent and application of the program.

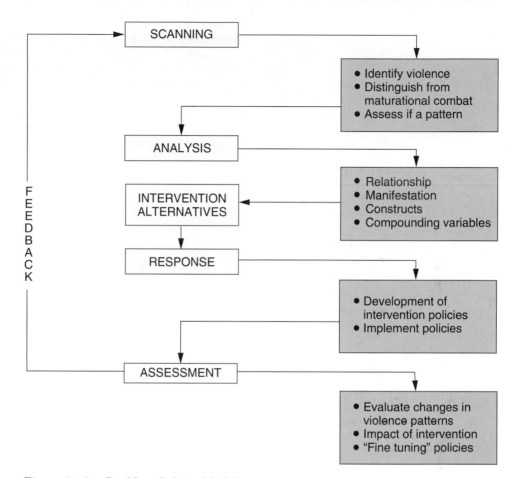

Figure 14-5.   Problem-Solving Model

The problem of violence in the schools is one in which there is great potential for the police to have a positive impact. For this to be achieved, however, a strong relationship with the schools must be established, followed by police leadership in a cooperative, community-based spirit to stimulate problem analysis and intervention.

WOMEN AS POLICE OFFICERS

It may be observed that the rights of women in our society have been a much more engrossing popular issue than that of the rights of children and youth. The choosing up of political sides regarding women's rights, leading to the nomination of a woman for the office of vice president of the United States, is a labyrinthian subject, one clearly beyond our scope here. But there are a few aspects of it that are clearly of special interest in criminal justice-community relations. We touched on one such aspect in the discussion of affirmative action, and it is appropriate to follow up on this now.

Sexism and racism have some common attributes—in the dynamics of prejudice and discrimination, in scapegoating and stereotyping, and most significantly, in the elements of power.[19] Something of the flavor of this is conveyed by Lucy Komisar, former vice president of the National Organization for Women (NOW), in these rather cryptic terms:

The definition of manhood that judges masculinity on a scale of power, dominance, toughness, violence, and aggression is anathema to feminists, partly because women have been its chief victims. Rather than insist that women, too, ought to feel free to express these traits, feminists assert that males and females ought to develop a new human ethos based on an end to hierarchies, dominance, and force.[20]

In a narrower sense, what is the present status of women in law enforcement? A national study sponsored by PERF found that roughly one officer in eight in the nation's largest jurisdictions was a woman.[21] The data showed that 12.1 percent of all sworn officers in these agencies were women. On a related note, when the mean educational level of police officers is stratified by gender, male officers averaged 13.6 years of education and female officers averaged 14.6 years—a full year more than male officers (Table 14-1).

One may reasonably ask why the women's educational level was notably higher than the men's. One possibility is that police departments gave greater scrutiny—consciously or not—to female applicants. As a result, women with stronger credentials were hired. A second possible explanation is that women who aspired to enter law enforcement believed that they had to be more competitive to enter this male-dominated field. Therefore, they tended to complete their college education, and perhaps graduate school, before applying in order to have the strongest possible background. A third reason, for which some anecdotal evidence was found, is that women tended to enter law enforcement from another career that required a degree. The most common example was public school teachers, generally at the elementary and middle-school levels, where most teachers are female. Teachers reported leaving the field of education to enter law enforcement for a variety of reasons. For some the change was a result of frustration in the public schools; others found that teaching did not fulfill their career ideals; and for others it was a matter of job security, salary, and benefits.

What are the prospects for women who want to become police officers? Generally good—increasingly, police departments are seeking women to fill the ranks. The reasons for this vary. Some evidence suggests that women have better interpersonal communications skills than men, are more adept at problem-solving, and have greater tolerance for diversity than men—all characteristics desirable for police officers. Another reason for increased recruitment of women is the recognition that women have been discriminated against in police employment and that this historical wrong must be corrected. A final reason is less philosophical than the previous two. Some police administrators feel that if they do not increase the number of women officers, they will be sued. Regardless of the motivation, the job prospects for women in policing are good. While promotions of women have still lagged behind men, this too is changing.

TABLE 14-1	Educational Level of Police Officers by Gender	
Education Level	Male	Female
Mean years	13.6 years	14.6 years
No college	34.8%	24.1%
Some undergraduate	61.7%	45.1%
Four-year or graduate degree	3.3%	30.2%

It appears that we are past the most emotional phase of the movement for equal rights in criminal justice. The old arguments are still heard, it is true—perhaps even fairly often—but the tone today sounds more and more like that of a losing argument, just as in other facets of professional employment. Should women in police work be generalists or specialists? The answer is the same as it is for men: *both*—depending upon individuals, circumstances, and departmental needs.[22]

A Police Foundation study of women on police patrol remains definitive, although done nearly three decades ago.[23] This study addressed three decisive questions:

1. Is it appropriate, from a performance standpoint, to hire women for patrol assignments on the same basis as men?
2. What advantages or disadvantages arise from hiring women on an equal basis for patrol work?
3. What effect would the use of a substantial number of policewomen have on the nature of police operations?

The major findings are listed as follows.

Assignment

- New women were assigned to regular uniformed patrol less often than comparison men.
- The type of patrol units to which new women and comparison men were assigned was frequently different. In particular, men were less often assigned to station duty and more often assigned to one-officer cars.

Performance

- Comparison men handled somewhat more patrol incidents per tour, primarily because they initiated more traffic incidents (usually, issuance of written citations).
- New women patrolling alone tended to handle more service calls assigned by police dispatchers than did men patrolling alone.
- New women and comparison men responded to similar types of calls while on patrol and saw similar proportions of citizens who were dangerous, angry, upset, drunk, or violent.
- New women obtained results similar to those of comparison men in handling angry or violent citizens.
- Arrests made by new women and comparison men were equally likely to result in convictions.
- New women and comparison men worked well with their partners in two-officer units. The partners shared the driving about equally, took charge with about the same frequency, and were about equal in giving instructions to the other.
- New women and comparison men received the same amount of backup, or assistance, from other police units.
- New women and comparison men showed similar levels of respect and general attitude toward citizens.
- New women and comparison men received similar performance ratings from the police department in its standard review of police officers after the first year of performance.

- Police officials in an anonymous special survey gave new women lower ratings than comparison men on ability to handle domestic fights and street violence, and on general competence. Women were rated equal to men in handling upset or injured persons.
- There was no difference between new women and comparison men in the number of sick days used.
- There was no difference between new women and comparison men in the number of injuries sustained or the number of days absent from work due to injuries.
- There was no difference between new women and comparison men in the number of driving accidents in which they had been involved since joining the police force.
- Comparison men were more likely than new women to have been charged with serious, unbecoming conduct.
- Citizens showed similar levels of respect and similar general attitudes toward new women and comparison men.
- Citizens interviewed about police response to their calls for assistance expressed a high degree of satisfaction with both male and female officers.
- Citizens who had observed policewomen in action said they had become somewhat more favorably inclined toward policewomen.

Attitudes

Citizen Attitudes

- Citizens of the District of Columbia, regardless of their race or sex, were more likely to support the concept of policewomen on patrol than to oppose it.
- Citizens believed that men and women were equally capable of handling most patrol situations, but they were moderately skeptical about the ability of women to handle violent situations.
- The police department was highly rated by citizens, and this rating has not been affected by the introduction of women into the patrol force.

Police Attitudes

- Patrolmen doubted that patrolwomen were the equal of men in most patrol skills.
- Patrolwomen felt that their patrol skills were as good as patrolmen's in most cases.
- Patrolmen, patrolwomen, and police officials agreed that men were better at handling disorderly males, that women were better at questioning rape victims, and that there was no difference between men and women in skill at arresting prostitutes.
- Police officials agreed with patrolmen that patrolwomen were not as likely to be as satisfactory as men in several types of violent situations.
- Patrolmen had a definite preference for patrolling with a male partner. Patrolwomen had a slight preference for patrolling with a male partner.
- Patrolwomen felt they received a greater degree of cooperation from the public than patrolmen did.
- Patrolwomen felt that police supervisors were more critical of patrolwomen than of men. Patrolmen felt there was no difference.
- Black police officials and black policemen were somewhat less unfavorable toward policewomen than white, male officials and policemen.

- Male patrol officers who said that women "should not be a regular part of the patrol force" had less formal education and were more likely to believe in arrests as a performance measurement than other patrolmen.
- Police officials were somewhat more positive toward policewomen in 1973 than they had been during the initial months of the experiment in 1972.
- There was little change in the attitudes of patrolmen toward policewomen between the start and the conclusion of the experiment.

There have been many more recent studies of women on patrol, all generally concluding that women do the job adequately. However, some research has indicated that the research on this subject is flawed.[24] Since all of the evaluations of women on patrol compare female and male officers, the focus is on gender differences.

> Our analysis suggests that the studies of women on patrol have repeated many of the problems associated with social science research on gender differences in the work place. Furthermore, given the dominance of male values in public policing, the studies of women on patrol fail to adequately explore alternative police styles, particularly those that emphasize dispute resolution and the deescalation of authority and interpersonal violence.[25]

So the familiar refrain: more and better research is needed! Generalizations colored by male stereotypes are not good enough, nor are data tainted by other methodological shortcomings.

The National Council on Crime and Delinquency had adopted a strong policy statement, urging all criminal justice agencies "to implement procedures aimed at removing all restrictions to equal opportunity" for women, including management positions.[26] Both the President's Crime Commission and the Commission on Criminal Justice Standards and Goals sounded the same theme. A number of significant benefits have been identified that accrue from assigning women a broader police role:

1. A probable reduction in the incidence of violence between police officers and citizens when women are assigned to patrol.
2. A probable improvement in an agency's crime-fighting capability, since women have demonstrated proficiency in certain facets of investigative work.
3. Women in the patrol function probably improve police and community relations, as the public sees the police more as public servants.
4. An overall improvement in patrol work probably results from more emphasis on social services.
5. Police agencies hiring women for patrol duty are likely to be more responsive to the community because their personnel are more representative of the population.
6. By introducing women into jobs that have been held exclusively by men, departments are likely be forced to rethink and reevaluate other traditional policies and "conventional wisdom."
7. Hiring women on the basis of equal opportunity is in accord with the law, therefore of particular importance in law enforcement agencies in terms of public attitudes.[27]

Yet not all analysts agree with this positive evaluation.[28] Policing is a multifunctional agenda. Male officers, as individuals, handle certain functions more capably than they handle others, mainly having little to do with being male. Why should not the same be true of female officers?

A final important issue to be considered in this section is *sexual harassment*. A woman officer from a midwestern police department told the author, "I don't see the extent of sexism I used to. Particularly younger men coming to work (in policing) seem to accept women as equals—that is, until older officers change their minds." As inferred in the *Perspective* by Dr. Merry Morash at the beginning of part four, the amount of sexual harassment in law enforcement is difficult to determine for several reasons. One problem is *defining* its presence. In extreme cases, such as a male touching the breasts of a female, or an officer telling a driver that a ticket will not be issued in exchange for sex, the presence of harassment is obvious. In other cases, it is more problematic.

Let us say that a male officer goes to the same restaurant regularly and casually knows a waitress whom he sees there. If the officer says to the woman, "You look nice today," is this harassment? What if the officer says, "You look sexy today," or "You look *hot* today." Do these changes in wording constitute harassment? The determination of harassment is not easy and, in this example, would depend on several factors. For example, the nature of the rapport between the officer and waitress will make a difference, as will the interpretation of the officer's words and actions by the woman. In some cases, the officer's comments would be harassment; in other cases, they would not. We can say that in most cases the officer's latter comments would surely be poor judgment.

A complicating factor in determining harassment is the social pathology of law enforcement organizations. The occupational culture of policing is based on the values and eccentricities of a male-dominated environment. To a large extent, it is characterized by *machismo* in behaviors exemplified by such things as aggression, taunting, "horseplay," and sexually related conversation and innuendo. Despite significant increases in the number of women in policing, the generally higher caliber (and better-educated) people entering law enforcement, better training in ethics, and implementation of policies to control harassment and related factors, the long-established characteristics of the occupational culture largely remain. Since survival in the informal organization requires adherence to the cultural norms, women tend to tolerate these values. Men tend to misinterpret culturally related behaviors of women officers—largely holding them to a double standard—and men cannot understand why they are accused of sexual harassment. Initiatives already in place to deal with this problem must be continued and refined. Slowly the culture is changing, but vigilance in education and reinforcing proper behavior must be maintained to minimize sexual harassment both among police personnel and the public.

DOMESTIC CRIME

Historically, domestic crime received limited attention by the criminal justice system. A large part of the reason was because it was "hidden" from public view. It occurred within households, and victims rarely sought assistance outside of the home. Unfortunately, the old adage "out of sight, out of mind" applies to this problem. Another problem with domestic crime is that it inherently involves the family; government has been reluctant to interfere in family matters except in the most extreme cases.

Most of this has changed as a result of evolving victims' attitudes, research, and the generally growing awareness of the problems. Domestic crime remains an extraordinarily complex problem with many difficulties which must be resolved to ensure safety and fairness without overtaxing the capabilities of our criminal justice and social systems.

There are three broad areas of domestic crime that are of concern:

- Child abuse
- Spouse and partner abuse
- Elder abuse

Child Abuse

This is a broad label that encompasses a wide array of behavior that is physically and psychologically threatening to a child. To better understand the issues involved, child abuse may be divided into four categories.

The first is *physical abuse*, perhaps the most widely perceived type of child abuse. Essentially, this is the physical assault of a child and includes such behavior as striking, kicking, and even burning children. The rationalizations offered by physical abusers are typically related to the need for "discipline," but tend to be a product of the adult's weakness to control his or her own behavior rather than a failure of the child to "behave." A child's misbehavior or crying or insolence frequently sparks abusive aggression, but this is not always the case. Incidents have been reported in which an adult's frustrations with his or her own life are "taken out" on the child. Unfortunately, evidence suggests that these abusive patterns may emerge as learned behavior, with the child assuming that this is "normal" and, consequently, growing to become a physical abuser himself or herself in adulthood.

The second category, *sexual abuse*, includes any type of sexual assault on a child, including rape, sodomy, fondling of the genitals, or other sexually oriented behavior involving the child. Increasingly, there appears to be little correlation between sexual abuse and physical abuse since the motivations of the adult's behavior are entirely different. The sexual abuser, motivated by a psychological aberration, seeks abnormal sexual fulfillment. As in the case of physical abuse, the sexually abused child typically feels that the behavior was his or her "fault," thereby making discovery of the crime even more difficult.

A third category is *emotional abuse*. A child who is physically and sexually assaulted is also emotionally abused; however, emotional abuse can occur separately. Berating a child, not giving a child proper emotional support for growth, failing to acknowledge a child's accomplishments, constant verbal abuse, and "name calling" are all forms of emotional abuse. While not as scarring as physical abuse, "emotional assaults" cause psychological damage, which is extraordinarily difficult both to identify and remedy. Despite the crippling effect that this can have on a child's life, emotional abuse is the most difficult for the police to deal with. At what point does the abuse occur? How can evidence of emotional abuse be obtained? Who is to judge that certain behavior is, in fact, abusive? Surely, the need to deal with this problem requires patience and creativity in order to overcome the negative impact emotional abuse can have on a child.

The final category, *child neglect*, poses different problems. Neglect embodies the failure to care for the safety, security, and life-sustaining needs of a child. Importantly, child neglect does not inherently relate to a lack of food, clothing, shelter, or a safe environment. It must be viewed in relation to the total economic and social condition of the family. For example, a homeless family has significant limitations on what can be provided to children. Yet, if the family treats the children as well as their circumstances permit, this is not neglect. On the other hand, if a wealthy family lets children do what they want when they want with virtually no parental supervision, this may be neglect. Unfortunately, it is easier to focus on the lack of tangible evidence related to child growth than it is on the more lasting characteristics of caring and well-being.

One of the tragic elements of child abuse is the inability of the victims to care for themselves and seek outside assistance to help them out of their situation. Moreover, abuse and neglect of children contribute to psychological deterioration and maladjustment, which, in turn, shape their persona as they approach adulthood. Not only does caring for abused children aid helpless victims, it may also change the life course of a person and prevent his or her becoming a "police problem" as an adult. The challenge for law enforcement is substantial and effective problem-solving and communications skills are essential.

Spouse and Partner Abuse

Spouse and partner abuse occurs when one party of a couple living together assaults the other party. The people may be married or simply living together; they may also be either "straight" or gay. The key element in these cases of abuse is that the couple have an emotional relationship, typically not just a friendship of people living together for convenience. The most typical circumstance is a physical assault or threat. However, emerging laws and research suggest that sexual assault is also a problem in some of these cases. While the assailant in a spouse and partner abuse case is most commonly a male, some evidence suggests that there may be more male victims than are intuitively assumed.[29] Spouse abuse is underreported; however, cases where men are victims are especially so.

When the police encounter a spouse or partner abuse situation they have several options.[30] First, they may *arrest* the person making an assault. There is disagreement among police officials and researchers as to whether arrests should be mandatory or left to the officer's discretion. This and other questions regarding police handling of spouse abuse cases were tested by a Police Foundation study in Minneapolis and by a PERF study in Albuquerque, Memphis, Charleston, and Newark. The Minneapolis study initially concluded that arrests worked best for deterring spouse abuse, measured by the criterion of police being called back to the same addresses. The widespread publicity on the initial results of this study led to a significant number of police policies being changed to make arrests *mandatory* in domestic assault cases. The PERF study concluded that a more flexible arrest policy worked best in the four cities it studied. Controversy emerged after the Minneapolis study with respect to the methodology and reporting of its findings. Some evidence suggests that the Minneapolis findings may be erroneous either as a result of methodological errors or simply as an aberration. Consequently, many of the mandatory arrest policies are now being rethought in favor of greater officer discretion.[31]

Since arrest is not the only—or best—alternative to deal with spouse abuse, other options should also be considered. The officer should seek the disposition alternative that is most congruent with solving the problem of the particular people involved. A second option that may be considered is *mediation*. This involves the use of different ways to "talk out the problem." The approach varies with the individuals, the officer, and the specific circumstances at the time. An important element of the officer's decision is to determine that the threat of a further assault is not imminent. Once assured, the officer mediates the dispute to reduce the tension, help establish reciprocal understanding between the parties, and develop a mechanism to minimize the probability of further disputes.

A third option, which is frequently an outgrowth of mediation, is *referral*. If the officer identifies a specific problem (or two) that "sparked" the abuse, he or she may be able to make a referral to assist in dealing with the problem. If the problem is financial, perhaps referrals for food stamps, welfare assistance, job retraining, employment service, and/or financial planning may be helpful. Referrals for other problems may be to alcohol and substance abuse centers, psychological counseling, marriage counseling, or any other special need for assistance.

Another commonly used option in domestic violence cases is *separation*. Frequently, a "cooling off" time is needed for the parties to compose themselves in order to discuss the issues in a civil manner. Officers responding to a domestic disturbance often find that the parties simply cannot communicate. Tempers are hot and emotions are frayed; the chance that reason will prevail is minimal and the potential for violence may be high. The officer's judgment may be that an arrest is not warranted, but separation may be. As a result, the officers suggest that one of the parties leave for a few hours or perhaps the night, in order for calm and reason to return. In the extreme case of spouse or partner assault, separation may include taking an abuse victim to a shelter for safety and care.

A final option is *no action*. Typically in these cases, the officers find that the parties have resolved the conflict themselves, either through their own mediation or separation. In some cases, notably if the intensity of the conflict has been reduced when the officers arrive and particularly on a "busy night," the officers may simply warn, "Stop the arguing and fighting. If we get a call back, somebody's going to jail." In these instances, the officers have certainly solved no problems and have done little to promote police-community relations.

Elder Abuse

This problem has received significantly less attention than child abuse and spouse/partner abuse. It typically involves the neglect or emotional and, at times, physical abuse of senior citizens. Most frequently the abuse is by relatives, notably children. The reasons for elder abuse are not definitively known. However, three primary factors seem to have emerged. First, some people who have assumed the responsibility of caring for the elderly begin to feel that this duty is an "inconvenience" in light of other responsibilities they have. Second, the expense of taking care of the elderly, particularly for those with small fixed incomes, provides extra stress. This becomes even more problematic during times of economic constraint. Finally, a frustration emerges when the demands of dealing with aging parents disrupts the family lifestyle or infringes on time that would otherwise be devoted to leisure and recreation. It appears that these factors interact and result in frustrations being "taken out" on the elderly living with them. While there is no definitive research, some evidence further suggests that people who were child abuse victims are more likely to be elder abusers (as well as child abusers).

It is difficult for the police to learn about elder abuse because the victims tend to feel helpless and scared. Consequently, they are not likely to report the abuse. The fear senior citizens experience results from the recognized need for financial support to help them survive. Moreover, victims of elder abuse also appear to have a distorted perception that they need to continue to protect their children from any type of punishment—even if this contributes to continued abuse.

Dealing With Domestic Crime

As noted previously, the police face a number of dilemmas in attempting to identify and deal with domestic crime. Certainly there is a need to encourage reporting of all types of incidents. This can be done through public education, enhanced means to facilitate reporting, and enlistment of community support to help identify cases.

Policies, procedures, and strategies must be developed to facilitate intervention programs. These measures may range from arrest to referrals to counseling. When prosecution is being sought, the police must have effective means to develop evidence and encourage testimony. This is problematic with domestic crime victims and requires officers who have special training and empathy and who are able to establish a strong foundation of trust with these victims. In this same vein, the police must also develop alternatives for caring for victims. While law enforcement cannot be responsible for all aspects of this care, it can serve as a community-based stimulant to assist in the development of resources and facilities for care.

Whatever response and intervention policies are developed, the police must recognize the need for short-term reactive policing and long-term problem solving. Certainly the police need a variety of social resources to help them deal with domestic crime. Community-based responses help them fill this need.

HOMELESS PERSONS

The continually growing awareness about homeless persons in our nation's cities is stimulating questions about how the government should respond to the problem. Food, shelter, physical illness, mental illness, substance abuse, physical safety, child care, education, and skill development are among the needs that must be fulfilled. Yet, most locales have no twenty-four-hour-a-day social service agency to address even the most fundamental needs of these people except the police. Moreover, since the police are the only agency "on the street," one would assume that they are the most likely to encounter homeless people.

Media attention directed toward the apparent growth of homelessness in the United States provides a wide range of anecdotal evidence about the problem. Somewhat surprisingly, empirical research on the presence and problems of street people is fairly limited. News accounts documenting homeless persons tend to focus on the "worst cases," such as families living out of cars, children separated from their parents, or cases of homeless teens. While these cases are indeed tragic and are in need of a social response, they appear to represent the exceptions to homelessness rather than the rule.

Repeated questions focus on underlying factors such as criminality, mental illness, and substance abuse as related to chronic homelessness. If a social response to the problem is to be developed, it is important to understand the actual role of these factors. The literature provides some useful insights.

With respect to criminal behavior, homeless persons have a higher overall arrest rate than the general population. However, the majority of offenses for which they are arrested are public intoxication, theft/shoplifting, violation of city ordinances, and burglary.[32] While some evidence suggests that ostensibly serious offenses such as assault, larceny, and burglary are committed by homeless persons, the actual crimes tend to be petty thievery, entry into vacant buildings, and other acts aimed at maintaining subsistence in the absence of housing.[33]

On the issue of financial viability, not surprisingly, economic conditions play an important role in homelessness. However, one researcher concluded that ". . . many homeless people are too personally deteriorated to respond to a more favorable economy."[34] Some research indicates that, although the homeless, as a whole, engage in relatively high levels of illegal activity, for many this is an adaptive response to dealing with severely limited resources.[35] The impact of financial resources cannot be ignored, but it is an oversimplification to state that jobs and financial assistance effectively deal with the problem. As one researcher observed, "the path to homelessness for many was paved by years of crime, drug abuse, and/or mental illness."[36]

Fortunately for most, homelessness is a temporary condition that is economically related. These people appear to be the most resourceful. They locate shelters, food

"The continually growing awareness about homeless persons in our nation's cities is stimulating questions about how the government should respond to the problem."

kitchens, and even are able to find part-time employment until they "get back on their feet." The homeless in this category are rarely involved in crime and have little inter-action with the police. On the other hand, the *chronically* homeless are the most likely to be dysfunctional and involved in the criminal justice system.[37] In this regard, one researcher observed that "although poverty underlies virtually all homelessness, when one also has personal problems such as mental illness, chemical dependency, or physical health problems, one's chance of becoming homeless increases."[38] The re-search suggests that temporary homelessness is predominantly an economic issue, while chronic homelessness involves mental illness and substance abuse. Therefore, social responses to homelessness should provide an integrated approach of mental health treatment, substance abuse counseling, social service, and employment assis-tance all in one setting—ideally a shelter. Unfortunately, most communities do not have any resources that have all of these services in one location. In fact, many com-munities are fortunate to have simply a shelter for an overnight stay. As in the case of many social problems, the police are frequently called to help the homeless, regard-less of the availability of resources, and they must find assistance in some form.

In a national study of homelessness, somewhat surprisingly, less than one-half of the police executives in the nation's largest cities indicated they did *not* see the pres-ence of street people as a very significant problem in their communities. This might be explained, however, by the finding that the police view homelessness in light of *all* their responsibilities, not as an individual problem.[39]

Some further insights were gained that provide inferences as to why street peo-ple are not viewed as a major problem. Over 90 percent of the police chiefs surveyed stated that street people are generally viewed as a "public nuisance." Indeed, most indicated that the police responsibility was simply to remove these people from the streets, or at least from public view.

There were two predominant concerns about the homeless that were expressed by police executives. First, it was strongly perceived that their presence increased the fear of crime among citizens. Second, it was felt that the living conditions of the homeless posed a public health hazard. Consequently, police contact with street people was just as likely to focus on these concerns as any other.

When the police *do* have encounters with the homeless, the three most common reasons are that:

- Citizens have reported the presence of a homeless person to the police.
- Officers observe a person in a problematic situation.
- The police receive complaints from the business community about the presence of homeless people.

The inference from this is that the police typically do not initiate contact with homeless people unless there is some specific reason indicating the need for police intervention. This may range from victimization to the need for medical care to a complaint of panhandling near businesses. Conversely, it appears the *mere presence* of the homeless will not draw police attention—or at least police action—leaving them to seek the aid of social service organizations on their own. This is not meant to infer nonfeasance by the police. Rather, it is a realistic interpretation of police policy related to priorities that are both self-imposed and those mandated by the community.

The police tend to feel that assistance is available for street people to aid them with food, shelter, medical assistance, and alcohol or drug dependency problems. This view may imply that the United States is doing a better job of dealing with the homeless than has traditionally been thought. This is not to say that improvements cannot be made, nor is it intended to understate the magnitude of social conditions related to homelessness. Rather, it appears that from a social assistance perspective, the picture is not as bleak as we may have intuitively assumed.

It was noted earlier that the police tend to view homeless people as a public nuisance. This appears to be the product of two primary factors. First, street people generally do not commit crimes (at least not serious ones), but come to police attention because of calls, substance abuse, panhandling, or participation in behavior which is problematic, but not inherently criminal. Second, the police fairly regularly receive calls from businesses about the homeless, leading to the "public nuisance" label. These matters, added to the "fear of crime" and "health hazard" issues, appear to be simply a product of the presence of homeless people on the street.

Given the attention that homelessness has received in the media, these somewhat contradictory research findings pose several questions, which should be addressed:

- Are police executives misinformed about the presence of street people or the degree of homelessness in their jurisdictions?
- Are regional variations in the numbers of street people and the availability of services significantly distinct to make homelessness a selective policy issue?
- Are social assistance organizations doing a sufficiently good job in dealing with street people so that the police are only involved in the "worst cases?"
- Do the police lack sensitivity to the problem because of the lack of good reporting on matters related to street people?
- Do the police lack sensitivity to the problem because of a lack of concern about street people?

As a special population with whom the police must deal, homeless persons represent unique challenges. As a result, law enforcement must fully understand the problems, issues, and responsibilities.

ELDERLY PERSONS

Persons aged sixty-five and older comprise the largest part of the nation's live-alone population, and this proportion is growing steadily. Often these older people are trapped in shoddy hotel rooms or apartments, fearful of venturing out. The prevailing problems of the aged are many and need not be detailed here. The over-sixty-five age group has nearly one in six persons living in poverty, compared with one in ten of those under age sixty-five. Nearly 60 percent are women.

Elderly persons are frequently the victims of serious crimes. More often than not, they are *helpless* victims. Their circumstances and problems call for special study and understanding by the police as well as by other public and private services. Fortunately, many programs for the aged have been developing in cities across the country, ranging from reduced public transportation fares to so-called outreach centers to assist elderly persons with their problems. Interest in their situation is growing as a larger proportion of our population is aging, but there still remains a long way to go in local, state, and federal action.

In this regard, the American Association of Retired Persons (AARP) has been active. AARP established a section called Criminal Justice Services that, among other things, has training programs and model policies which law enforcement agencies can use to select and train senior citizen volunteers. The AARP has been active in other areas as well. For example, each year they co-sponsor, with the Federal Bureau of Investigation and the International Association of Chiefs of Police, the "Triad" conference that addresses issues of mutual concern to the police and senior citizens. The AARP was also instrumental in influencing passage of the *Age Discrimination in Employment Act*, which affects Americans in all occupations, including criminal justice.

The talents, wisdom, and experience in a wide range of career fields of many senior citizens are potential resources that police agencies would be well advised not to overlook. With budgets as they are, administrators should consider older persons for volunteer duties in crime prevention, communications, records, and crime analysis.[40]

HANDICAPPED PERSONS

In the typical urban setting—or rural, for that matter—how many types of people with special needs are there, calling for some sort of informed and understanding assistance from the police? The range is staggering, from mothers with infant children who are without homes or resources to the physically and mentally handicapped. There are many others, but the handicapped are so often ignored and so little understood in our society that we should pause to consider them within the theme of this text.

Rights for the handicapped have been enlarged dramatically over recent years. A major stride forward occurred with passage of the *Americans With Disabilities Act* (ADA) in 1990. The ADA not only prohibits discrimination based upon handicapped status, it provides "handicapper rights" and removes many obstacles for access of handicappers to buildings, communications devices, and entertainment.

Such developments reflect society's recognition of and accommodation to the special needs of the physically handicapped. What has this to do with the police?

Generally, police officers everywhere have always treated handicappers with appropriate deference. What seems to be happening is that society is now catching up to the police with a perspective and level of sensitivity long overdue.

For mentally handicapped persons, the situation is somewhat more complex, the condition more difficult to recognize. Some mentally ill individuals are potentially dangerous and no one can predict their behavior, not even experts. More mentally handicapped people are involved in community treatment programs than in past years, and properly so, but community attitudes toward them tend to be apprehensive. Behavior perceived as "suspicious" or "bizarre" prompts 911 calls. Ordinarily, police officers are not well-trained in dealing with the mentally ill. Indeed, even for experts, it is sometimes difficult to distinguish the symptoms of drunkenness and epilepsy, as an example.

For the police, then, dealing with mentally handicapped people is often a ticklish problem. Well-intentioned but mistaken judgments can produce serious consequences. The National Institute of Mental Health has long been aware of this and has encouraged more attention to the matter in well-designed police training and publications. But even trained police officers can make mistakes in this perplexing domain, just as can psychologists and psychiatrists. Public understanding is much to be desired.

SUMMARY

"Special populations" offer challenges to the police in diverse ways. Understanding changing emotional and physical needs as predicated by the natural processes of human life are one dimension. Special needs imposed as a result of interpersonal and intergroup relations throughout the human social community represent another. And anomalies imposed on people as a result of genetic or external factors, which affect physical and/or mental capacities, reflect yet a third dimension of the special challenges for police.

Because of the humanity inherent in our culture and the affinity the police hold for "special people," the contribution law enforcement makes to the quality of life of those citizens is likely to be substantial.

QUESTIONS FOR DISCUSSION

1. Why are youth attitudes toward the police a matter of special interest?
2. What is the intent of programs like TIPS, D.A.R.E., and G.R.E.A.T. and how do they differ from past initiatives by the police directed toward children?
3. Discuss teen gangs and concerns they pose for the police.
4. Why do you feel that violence in the schools has increased in recent years? What are the ramifications of this problem?
5. Discuss the "compounding variables" related to children's violence. What do they mean?
6. What is meant by "intervention" as related to the problems of children's violence?
7. What are some of the major issues that have to be addressed with respect to women police officers?
8. How can the police address the relatively hidden offenses of domestic crime?
9. What major issues face the police with respect to older Americans?
10. How might community policing change the relationship between the police and "special populations" (as compared to traditional policing methods)?

NOTES

1. Urie Bronfenbrenner, "The Split-Level American Family," *Saturday Review* (October 7, 1967): 60. Reprinted by permission.

2. James S. Coleman, *The Adolescent Society* (New York Free Press, 1971).

3. Fred E. Inbau, "Lawlessness Galore," *Vital Speeches* 32 (November 15 1965): 96.

4. The growing emphasis on police youth programs illustrate this. Whereas in years past, youth programs were viewed as being secondary, they are now a primary focus.

5. David Easton and Robert Hess, "The Child's Political World," *Midwest Journal of Political Science* 6 (1962): 229–246.

6. See Fred I. Greenstein, *Children and Politics* (New Haven, CT: Yale University Press, 1965).

7. Robert L. Derbyshire, "Children's Perceptions of the Police: A Comparative Study of Attitudes and Attitude Change," *Journal of Criminal Law, Criminology and Police Science* 59 (1968): 183–190.

8. Ibid., p. 188.

9. *Officer Friendly* Resource Unit, available from the Sears Roebuck Foundation, Skokie, IL.

10. U.S. Department of Health, Education and Welfare, Office of Education, *The Development of Basic Attitudes and Values Toward Government and Citizenship During the Elementary School Years*, part 1, CRP1078, prepared for the Bureau of Research by Robert Hess and Judith V. Torney (Washington, DC: U.S. Government Printing Office, 1965).

11. U.S. Department of Health, Education and Welfare, Office of Education, *Development of Attitudes Toward Government*, Final Report CRP1078, prepared for the Bureau of Research by David Easton and Jack Dennis (Washington, DC: U.S. Government Printing Office, 1968).

12. Dan Bryant, *Community-wide Responses Crucial for Dealing with Youth Gangs* (Washington, DC: Office of Juvenile Justice and Delinquency Prevention, 1989).

13. Kären M. Hess and Henry M. Wrobleski, *Police Operations* (St. Paul, MN: West Publishing Company, 1993), p. 380.

14. *Tinker* v. *Des Moines Independent School District et al.*, 393 U.S. 503 (1969).

15. Lisa D. Bastian and Bruce M. Taylor, *School Crime: A National Crime Victimization Survey Report* (Washington, DC: U.S. Department of Justice, Bureau of Justice Statistics, 1991).

16. David L. Carter and Allen D. Sapp, *Violence in America's Public Schools: Critical Findings* (Washington, DC: Police Executive Research Forum, 1993).

17. Reported in M. Elaine Nugent, "Why Johnny Carries a Gun to School," *NCTAP News* (Alexandria, VA: Institute of Law and Justice, 1992).

18. *Uniform Crime Report*, Washington, DC: U.S. Department of Justice, Federal Bureau of Investigation, 1990.

19. Robert Terry, "The White Male Club," *Civil Rights Digest* 6, no. 3 (Spring 1974): 69 ff. See also U.S. Commission on Civil Rights, *Social Indicators of Equality for Minorities and Women* (Washington, DC: U.S. Government Printing Office, 1978).

20. Lucy Komisar, "Where Feminism Will Lead," *Civil Rights Digest* 6, no. 3 (Spring 1974): 6.

21. David L. Carter and Allen D. Sapp, "Police Education and Minority Recruitment: The Impact of a College Requirement." *A PERF Discussion Paper* (Washington, DC: Police Executive Research Forum, 1991).

22. Clarice Feinman, "Policewomen: The Crisis in Identity," *Criminal Justice Columns* (Allyn and Bacon/Holbrook Press), vol. 2, no. 3, p. 3.

23. Peter B. Bloch and Deborah Anderson (of the Urban Institute), "Policewomen on Patrol: Final Report" (Washington, DC: The Police Foundation, Inc., 1974). See also Catherine Milton, *Women in Policing* (Washington, DC: The Police Foundation, Inc. 1972).

24. Merry Morash and Jack R. Greene, "Evaluating Women on Patrol: A Critique of Contemporary Wisdom" (Paper presented at the annual meeting of the Academy of Criminal Justice Sciences, Chicago, March 1984).

25. Ibid.

26. Board of Directors, National Council on Crime and Delinquency, *Crime and Delinquency* (January 1976) pp. 1–2.

27. Lewis J. Sherman, "A Psychological View of Women in Policing," *Journal of Police Science and Administration* 1, no. 4: 383–394. Copyright © 1973 by the Northwestern University School of Law. See also Bernard L. Garmire, "Female Officers in the Department," *FBI Law Enforcement Bulletin*, (June 1974); Glen Craig, "California Highway Patrol Women Officers," *The Police Chief* (January 1977); Peggy E. Triplett, "Women in Policing," *The Police Chief* (December 1976); and William O. Weldy, "Women in Policing: A Positive Step Toward Increased Police Enthusiasm," *The Police Chief* (January 1976).

28. For example, see Anthony Vastola, "Women in Policing: An Alternative Ideology," *The Police Chief* (January 1977).

29. Maureen McLeod, "Women Against Men: An Examination of Domestic Violence Based on an

Analysis of Official Data and National Victimization Data," *Justice Quarterly,* vol. 1, no. 2 (1984).

30. See Samuel Walker, *The Police in America: An Introduction,* 2d ed. (New York: McGraw-Hill, Inc., 1992) pp. 116–117.

31. For greater detail on these studies see: *Law Enforcement News,* (November 21, 1983); Lawrence W. Sherman and Richard A. Berk, *The Minneapolis Domestic Violence Experiment* (Washington, DC: Police Foundation, 1984); Lawrence W. Sherman and Richard A. Berk, "The Specific Deterrent Effects of Arrests on Domestic Assault," *American Sociological Review,* vol. 9 (April 1984): 261–272.

32. David A. Snow, Susan G. Baker, and Leon Anderson, "Criminality and Homeless Men: An Empirical Assessment," *Social Problems* 36:5(1989): 532.

33. Pamela J. Fischer, "Criminal Activity Among the Homeless: A Study of Arrests in Baltimore," *Hospital and Community Psychiatry* 39:1(1988): 46.

34. Brent B. Benda, "Crime, Drug Abuse, Mental Illness, and Homelessness." *Deviant Behavior* 8:4(1987): 371.

35. Andrea Solarz, *An Examination of Criminal Behavior Among the Homeless.* (A paper presented to the annual meeting of the American Society of Criminology, San Diego, CA, 1985.)

36. Op. cit. Benda, p. 371.

37. John R. Belcher, "Are Jails Replacing the Mental Health System for the Homeless Mentally Ill?" *Community Mental Health Journal,* 24:3(1988): 185–95.

38. Martha R. Burt, and Barbara E. Cohen, "Differences Among Homeless Single Women, Women with Children, and Single Men," *Social Problems.* 36:5(1989): 521.

39. David L. Carter and Allen D. Sapp, "Police Experiences and Responses Related to the Homeless," *Journal of Crime and Justice* (1993).

40. See Gerald J. Dadich, "Crime, the Elderly, and Community Relations," *The Police Chief* (February 1977); George Sunderland, "The Older American: Police Problem or Police Asset?" *FBI Law Enforcement Bulletin* (August 1976); Ordway P. Burden, "Enlisting Senior Citizens to Stretch Police Budgets," *Law Enforcement News* (September 11, 1978).

Chapter 15

POLICING AND THE POLITICAL ENVIRONMENT

Policing and other criminal justice processes in a democratic society are public, political functions. These processes span the three divisions of government. Legislative bodies create law. The executive branch, with the police as its major instrumentality, is responsible for the enforcement of law. The judiciary, including the prosecutorial function, interprets the law, passes judgment on violators, and sentences those convicted to correctional treatment of some kind.

All of this is subject to civilian oversight, with the community ultimately responsible for all the processes dealing with crime and criminals. Thus, what happens is public, and inevitably political. It has to do with the use of authority and power.

What the police are, what they do, and what is expected of them, how well or how poorly they fulfill these expectations, what can be done to improve police services—these are, in considerable measure, political questions. They are also in some sense sociological, social, psychological, and economic questions, depending on the eye of the beholder. Historically, however, policing has tended to be viewed primarily as a political institution, inextricably tied to the function of governing through the executive responsibility for enforcement of laws enacted by legislatures and interpreted by courts. Given this orientation, it is surprising that police and community relations programs have devoted so little specific attention to the political aspects of police work.

So policing is inevitably political. To call for "taking the police out of politics" is absurd. But "politics" has a taint to it, in public opinion. It has come to be regarded as "dirty," "contaminated," "corrupt," "unethical," "dishonest." When the Wickersham Commission in 1931 proposed taking the police out of politics, it meant politics in this jaded meaning. The commission recommended "professionalizing" the police, as an antidote for the despicable "disease" of politics. Forthwith, discussions of professional policing have made it appear that professionalization and depoliticalization go hand in hand. There is some nonsense in this, and ie has caused widespread public confusion.

POLITICAL POLICING

One lamentable result of this confusion has been a reluctance to speak openly and frankly about the politics of policing and of police-community relations. "Nice people do not talk about such things." This has played into the hands of those who would use a police department or police officers as political pawns, as instruments for political chicanery of one kind or another. So the question of the police and politics is not as simple as it appears at first blush. James Q. Wilson has even argued that having the police as part of a political spoils system has not been all that bad.[1]

In other than a partisan, political sense, it should be evident that the police have a perfectly legitimate, respectable, and indeed indispensable political role to play. But history—even contemporary history—is replete with examples of the police playing the role of enforcers of political tyranny. Terms such as "police state" and "secret police" symbolize political policing at its frightful worst. For many Americans, there is more than one reason for reluctance to contemplate the police as a political entity. But look at it this way: the management of a police agency is surely in the realm of public administration. A police chief plays several social roles, but the political role is unquestionably one of the most vital of these roles. Yet this is different from being a politician, although the chief must be this in some sense too, as a matter of survival.

Moreover, a patrol officer also carries out some interesting political functions. As we have noted earlier, the officer should be a kind of neighborhood ombudsman—fielding complaints and playing mediator in all sorts of disputes. In the routine exercise of discretion, the officer, in effect, makes policy on the street. Clearly, this is a political function. Stated in the simplest terms, a police officer is a powerful person. The criminal justice system is a coercive system. This is the "stuff" of politics.

William Ker Muir has brilliantly developed this thesis in a widely applauded work.[2] His research was done with twenty-eight police officers in a sizable American city. His conclusions cannot be fully appreciated, taken out of context. But—with risk and apology—they were these, on the questions of how the use of coercion by political persons might be for the general welfare, in the face of personal danger, without becoming radically Machiavellian:[3]

1. The more a powerful figure enjoys talking, the less cynical his perspective and the more comfortable he feels about using coercion . . . a pleasure in using language to associate with others . . . [is] absolutely essential in escaping the depleting effects of power.
2. The more exposure a political figure has had to the contemplation of human suffering, the less cynical his perspective.
3. The longer his political apprenticeship, the more comfortable the political figure will feel about using coercion.
4. The more emphasis the legal system places on liberty, the more comfortable a political figure will feel about being in a position of authority. Coercion is the instrument of equality and the enemy of liberty . . . The law, insofar as it effectively harmonizes the civilized morality responsive to liberty and the coercive morality responsive to equality, functions to prevent corruption of power.

To translate these conclusions properly, the reader is asked to see the police officer as a political figure. To Muir, police officers are powerful persons. His main interest is in the effects of coercive power on human personality.

The police must, we have stressed, be responsive and accountable to the community. To be so, the police must be able to distinguish between corrupting political pressures and the needs of the larger community. In an era in which private and factional interests are everywhere being presented and pressed in a manner either ignoring the public interest altogether, or gratuitously assuming that private and public interests are coterminous, the distinction is, in fact, often difficult to draw. The International City Management Association deals with the point as follows:

> The complexities of the police function in the environment in which policing occurs place great pressure on the police administrator to maintain a balance between professional competence and responsiveness to legitimate political pressures which are reflective of the needs of the community. The police chief must have a basic commitment to maintaining a position of neutrality when political issues are involved. Within the context of accountability through the political process, the chief must insure that partisan interests are separated from community priorities.[4]

We have referred often to the politics of discretion in police patrol, for it pertains to the use and control of power; power delegated by the community. Make no mistake, discretionary decisions that officers make on a daily basis have political implications for the police—particularly when those decisions are made injudiciously.[5]

AGAIN, THE ROLE QUESTION

Politics and policing are integral. This is our point of emphasis. Earlier we discussed the public image of the police and said repeatedly that it is how the police are *perceived* by the public that is important. Perception has great meaning in politics. It is akin to the old adage, "How will it play in Peoria?" What candidates for political office say and how they say it are carefully weighed to determine how the public will perceive what is being said. Every move creates impressions that affect voting behavior.

Inescapably, we must return again to the matter of police role. As earlier implied, the role question is, at heart, a *political* question. Police officials count votes, just as Supreme Court justices do. Consensus is a political phenomenon. Police officers size up their reference groups and reach decisions on how to act depending upon how they weigh factors of influence and power in the community.

As one chief told the author:

> I have to understand what the mayor wants, what the city manager wants, what the council members want, what each segment and interest group of the community wants, and what I feel we should do given the research and changes which are occurring in policing. Then I mix these different "wants" together to get an optimum work [role] which addresses most needs in light of what we can afford. Then I try to get the officers to do it. That's why I look older than I am![6]

In a similar vein, in his consideration of three styles of policing (watchman, legalistic, and service), Wilson observes that the particular style that prevails in a particular community is not explicitly determined by community decisions, although a few of its aspects may be so determined. In Wilson's language, "the police are in all cases being governed by it."[7] He goes on to say that the police do not distinguish to any great extent among issues that are actually quite different in principle, whether it be a city manager's efforts to reform the department, a council member's efforts to name a new deputy chief, or a civil rights organization's efforts to establish a civilian review board. All such issues are interpreted by police as a struggle by "outside forces" for control of the department, and all officers see them all as "politics."

A general conclusion is that understanding the political life of a community will not provide an adequate explanation of existing police policies. To a considerable extent, such policies are left to the police themselves. Many segments of the community apparently prefer not to push their own interests unless a crisis develops. There may be public pressure for the police to "do something" about some problem. But what to do and how to do it is left to the police.

THE "SEXUAL ASSAULT GUARANTEE": A CUSTOMER-ORIENTED APPROACH TO POLICE SERVICE

Increased crimes on college campuses have led to a reexamination of the problem including mandated crime reporting and the delivery of more comprehensive services to the university community. The Department of Public Safety (DPS) at Michigan State University was the first university police department to employ Community Policing on its campus. Successes with this, under the leadership of DPS Director Dr. Bruce Benson, led to other innovations, many of which were the ideas of line personnel. One such idea was the "Sexual Assault Guarantee" originated by Sergeant Dorothy Rietzler. Because sexual assault, and notably "date rape," is such a concern on college campuses, the guarantee provides reassurances to the victims and a stronger "comfort level" between the police and the community. A written guarantee to sexual assault victims hoped to accomplish several objectives . . .

- *Stimulate awareness, discussion and reporting of the "hidden" and often unreported crime of acquaintance rape.*
- *Help put sexual assault victims more at ease in accessing and working with their local police officers.*
- *Emphasize a strong organizational commitment by the Department of Public Safety to sexual assault victims.*
- *Enable DPS to reach out to sexual assault victims, who have already suffered much trauma, to provide help so that they are not further victimized by the criminal justice system itself.*

With these in mind the MSU Department of Public Safety, with input from groups and specialists throughout the university, developed the following Sexual Assault Guarantee.

Sexual assaults, including date/acquaintance rape, are a very serious concern of DPS. If you feel you are the victim of a sexual assault on campus, your Department of Public Safety will guarantee you the following:

1. We will meet with you privately, at a place of your choice in this area, to take a complaint report.
2. We will not release your name to the public or to the press.
3. Our officers will not prejudge you and you will not be blamed for what occurred.
4. We will treat you and your particular case with courtesy, sensitivity, dignity, understanding, and professionalism.
5. If you feel more comfortable talking with a female or male officer, we will do our best to accommodate your request.
6. We will assist you in arranging for any hospital treatment or other medical needs.
7. We will assist you in privately contacting counseling, safety, advising, and other available resources.
8. We will fully investigate your case and will help you to achieve the best outcome. This may involve the arrest and full prosecution of the suspect responsible. You will be kept up-to-date on the progress of the investigation and/or prosecution.

9. We will continue to be available for you, to answer your questions, to explain the systems and processes involved (prosecutor, courts, etc.), and to be a listening ear if you wish.

10. We will consider your case seriously regardless of your gender or the gender of the suspect.

If you feel you are a sexual assault victim, call your Department of Public Safety at 355-2221, and say you want to privately make a sexual assault complaint. You may call any time of day or night. If we fail to achieve any part of the above guarantee, the Director of Public Safety, Dr. Bruce Benson (355-2223), will meet with you personally to address any problems. DPS wants to help you make the MSU campus safe for students, faculty, staff, and visitors.

To make the university community aware of the guarantee, the DPS placed advertisements, made press releases, posted the guarantee in residence halls and buildings, and made presentations to student groups. In addition, the DPS gave presentations on the concept at various professional meetings, including a special meeting at the FBI Academy dealing with campus crime. Reactions have been positive from the university, various professional and civic groups, and the Michigan legislature. Innovative programming such as this leads to better service and more open communications between the police and their community.

Police work is carried out under the influence of a *political culture*, though not necessarily under day-to-day political direction . . . with respect to police work—or at least its patrol functions—the prevailing political culture creates a "zone of indifference" within which the police are free to act as they see fit.

The most important way in which political culture affects police behavior is through the choice of police administrator and the molding of the expectations that govern his [or her] role.[8]

In sum, the community (or "political culture") influences law enforcement in a broad sense, but this influence is ordinarily indirect and indecisive. Many people feel that any kind of an alliance with the police spells trouble. The vast majority of citizens prefer to "keep their distance" from the police. They seem content to leave policing to the police. An officer signals trouble, to be avoided if possible. Thus, serious efforts to ally police and community more closely require ambitious public, political education as an integral part of problem-solving projects.

Another basic aspect of the politics-police integration is that the police play a subtle role in preserving and protecting a particular lifestyle or environment in a community.[9] Law is, after all, a reflection of societal values; and so, too, is what is defined by law as crime. Law making is a fundamental political process; so, too, is law enforcement. In one illustration, a Texas police chief told the author that the greatest concern of his residents was that vandals were "tearing up" the greens of the local golf course. This upper class community surrounded the golf course, which served, in many ways, as the town's social center as well as the informal political center. The chief of police observed that to many people this problem may seem inconsequential. However, it was important to his citizens and the political leaders, therefore it was important to him also.[10]

In a classic work, *The Honest Politician's Guide to Crime Control*, Norval Morris and Gordon Hawkins developed a comprehensive plan that they guaranteed would reduce crime substantially.[11] They asserted that it is not lack of knowledge but rather a failure of political responsibility that supports our "luxuriant" crime rates. Hence, their program "is directed to the politicians and to the concerned citizens who are responsible for them." The main features of their program are:

1. Decriminalization of such "crimes" as public drunkenness, possession of any drug, gambling, disorderly conduct and vagrancy, and sexual behavior between consenting adults.
2. The professionalization of the police, along lines Morris and Hawkins describe in detail.
3. Overhaul of the entire corrections system, including abolition of the money bail system, community-based treatment of offenders in the vast majority of cases, reduction of the size and number of prisons, creation of integrated state jail systems, and greater use of probation and parole.
4. Elimination of juvenile status offenses.
5. More adequate psychiatric and psychological treatment of offenders.

The political role of the police is changing again in the community-based era. Community policing focuses on substantive issues of crime, community problems and quality of life in neighborhoods—factors which effect residents on a daily basis. When officers solicit input from the community and enlist them to cooperatively deal with these problems, citizens begin to develop expectations about how the police will improve the overall conditions in the community. As this process becomes more structured, it begins to take shape, a bond—perhaps something akin to a formalized social contract—is developed, which places the police more definitively in a position to respond to those expectations.[12]

If the police fail, the police community relationship will surely suffer as will general support for the police. However, if the police are successful in resolving the problems that are of primary concern to the community, then a different political dynamic will emerge. In these cases, the police become politically empowered by the citizens. The police represent that aspect of government which has actually responded to the *people in the neighborhoods* (as opposed to the rich, the "politically connected," and special interests). The people become satisfied not only with police service, they become *advocates* for the police in the political process. Not surprisingly, this becomes somewhat of a paradox for elected officials who are not comfortable with the fact that "employees" (i.e., the police) have stronger support from the public than do elected representatives.

Perhaps the most significant political dynamic of community policing relates to *policy*. When the police ask the community about their concerns, when they ask the community to participate in problem solving, and when they substantively act on this input, then the community is being brought into the policymaking process of the police department.[13] This is not only virtually unprecedented in our history, it enhances accountability far beyond civilian review boards, police commissions, or advisory councils. What better demonstration of commitment to effective police-community relations can be found than to give the public a *real voice* in what the police do?

POLITICAL PERSPECTIVES

Once it is established that politics and policing in any society, whether democratic or otherwise, are integral, one can identify certain aspects or perspectives of special interest for study. To call these "forms" of political policing would not be quite accurate because this conveys more hard-and-fast categorization than in fact is the case. The aspects tend to blend together.

We have already touched on perspectives. One is political policing in the sense of the Wickersham Commission's condemnation: in effect, the police are a "knee-jerk" instrument of partisan, conniving, machine politics. This style of political policing is, for the most part, unprofessional. Although some might argue that it has some redeeming features, by and large, this is a perspective of political policing generally rejected as a model by contemporary scholars. While this type of political policing has diminished significantly in the last three decades, it is still uniquely found in many small elected sheriffs' departments.

A second perspective that we have noted is that policing is coercive. Coercion is power. Power corrupts because it is inevitably abused. In this sense, this perspective is not so different from the first perspective. The corruption is in the abuse of power, and it takes many forms. It is both individual and organizational, and it is nurtured by the police subculture and its values. As we have earlier suggested, its effects on community relations are devastating. It is, perhaps, the most fundamental of perspectives regarding politics and policing. We touch on it lightly here only because we have examined this perspective at considerable length in earlier chapters, notably with respect to drug corruption.

A third perspective of political policing, also mentioned earlier, is the police-state perspective. Again, corruption is evident: abuse of power to the point of might, despotism, tyranny, with the police as the "muscle" in the political purpose of totalitarianism. The major distinction, in comparison with the police in democratic societies, is in controls on the use of power and in civilian review.

A fourth perspective is represented by so-called radical criminology. Its proponents point to what they view as the corruption of capitalist socioeconomic class structure, with the police as principal agents for its perpetuation. What constitutes crime in this view is class oriented. The questions of who is arrested, convicted, imprisoned, or executed are all class tilted. The law itself is an instrument of the powerful, aimed at powerless victims. This is the abuse-of-power element in the lexicon of radical criminologists. The Marxist solution is a classless society, a "dictatorship of the proletariat."

Ironically, in each of these political perspectives, there is a fundamental community relationship that is addressed. Although that relationship may be coercive or abusive in some models, it must nonetheless be reckoned with.

POLITICS AND POLICE ADMINISTRATION

A fifth perspective is that of politics and police administration. To administer is to manage and to direct. One administrative function in a police agency is formulation of organization goals, ideally employing a process of securing input from inside and outside the organization. Among other things, this means community participation in this process, a process that is essentially political. Organizational policy development, implementation, and evaluation are also prime administrative functions, also essentially political because the process is closely allied with the goal-setting process. A national study for the Institute for Social Analysis concluded:

> . . . it was apparent that although the police policy-setting process clearly has implications for the nature of police-community relations in any particular city, very little evidence was found indicative of a relationship between formal police-community relations programs and citizen participation in the police policy-setting process.[14]

Public administration involves the exercise of discretion. So does police work. To exercise discretion is to exercise power, as we have seen, and in policing, the power is extraordinary. All of this is a commentary on the inevitable political nature of policing. The President's Crime Commission recommended that the police must assume a larger role in the development of law enforcement policies: Figure 15-1 is a reflection of this principle.

The "administrative process" and administrative flexibility, expertise, and, most important, administrative responsibility are as necessary and as appropriate with respect to the regulation of deviant social behavior as they are with respect to other governmental regulatory activity. This seems perfectly obvious. Yet the common assumption has been that the police task is ministerial, this perhaps reflecting an assumption that administrative flexibility and "the rule of law" are inconsistent. This assumption seems invalid. The exercise of administrative discretion with appropriate legislative guidance and subject to appropriate review and control is likely to be more protective of basic rights than the routine, uncritical application by

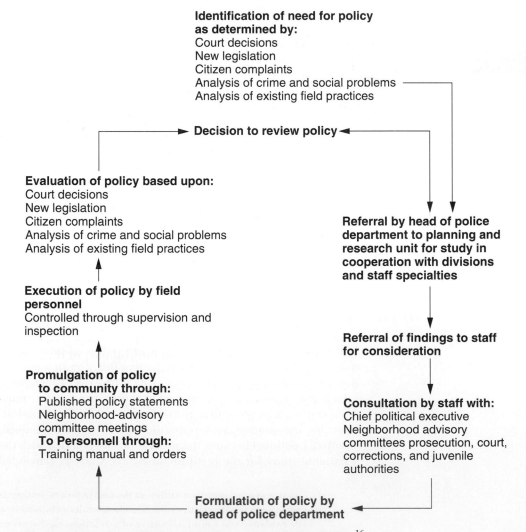

Figure 15-1. Formulation and Execution of Police Policy[16]

police of rules of law which are often necessarily vague or overgeneralized in their language.[15]

Mature participation of police as a responsible administrative agency—along with prosecutors, legislatures, and courts—in the development and execution of enforcement policies is clearly political policing, but it is hardly ill advised, inappropriate, or untimely. In the same vein, the National Advisory Commission on Criminal Justice Standards and Goals recommended:

> All goals and objectives, agencywide and unit, should be directly responsive to community needs. Normally, if problem definition and analysis have been adequate and alternative solutions carefully screened, responsiveness to community needs can be achieved. . . . Obtaining input from within the agency requires an atmosphere that encourages all employees, regardless of rank, to submit ideas.[17]

A common historical assertion on the police administrative-political role is that police professionalization has been impeded by the conferring of appointments as political reward, by the consequent uncertainty of job tenure, by the undermining of personnel standards, by the preservation of the myth that specialized competence is not necessary for law enforcement, and by the erosion of ethics. However, these consequences of partisan politics do not justify the belief that a police agency can ignore the importance of developing and maintaining relationships with the political structure of which it is part:

> As a public administrator, the police executive must be skillful in maintaining relationships within the community power structure whereby the resource needs of his agency are made known to decision-makers, resource allocations obtained, and police problems communicated in a style conducive to obtaining community support. In terms of this responsible version of political skill, the limitation of law enforcement to "real" crime will have little effect toward reducing the difficulties encountered by the executive.[18]

In pragmatic terms, quite plainly, effective police (or public) administration depends on winning support for needed resources and needed changes. It depends on getting votes in legislative bodies. It depends on selling one's program, often in competition for scarce dollars with other agencies of government. There is nothing mysterious or clandestine or reprehensible about this, and there is no reason for police officials to be apologetic or embarrassed about it. To be defensive tends to perpetuate ugly connotations of political policing of a type that cannot and should not be defended. Indeed, one of the strongest arguments that can be mounted for an effective police public relations program, in very practical terms, is exactly what we have been suggesting: the police are an integral part of the community, not a discrete entity. In the political sense, therefore, the police must have the votes in order to accomplish their mission, the very nature of which is a political determination. In a sense, to advocate taking the police out of politics is similar to advocating that civil disobedience should be declared illegal.

The tendency toward defensiveness by some police administrators regarding their political role is understandable, given the long-standing aversion in public opinion toward "political policing." One perspective on this put it this way:

> There has . . . been a traditional political resistance to educating the police. The root of this resistance lies deeply embedded in what seems to me to be a prevailing, but rarely stated, political attitude that if the police are encouraged to become

professional, and thus are made more effective, they will become a much less controllable arm of the executive branch of government and hence less amenable to the interests of political influence that almost always lead to partial rather than impartial enforcement of the law.[19]

Empirically, politics and administration are inseparable, just as politics and power are. Power is a necessary function of society, which can be defined as the actions of some people going about the business of moving other people to act in relation to themselves or in relation to organic or inorganic things. Power centers on decision-making and on seeing to it that necessary things—"power functions" delegated to specific persons—get done.[20]

And now community policing adds yet another dimension to the politics and structure of administration. Traditionally police activities have been dictated by a complete "top-down" approach. That is, police administrators would define programs, the types of crimes that would be addressed, and assorted activities of officers, usually based on a crime analysis that balanced trends with efficiency. Sometimes, this would be even more "top directed" when elected officials asked (or instructed) the police department to focus on specific issues—violent crimes and the illicit drug trade serve as recent examples.

With community policing, officers on the street identify problems, frequently with community input, and thereby determine priorities for problem-solving and major police initiatives. The role of police administrators begins to shift toward the responsibility of facilitating resources in order that officers may (hopefully) accomplish goals and respond to public demands. As officers become increasingly empowered by the community, administrators will increasingly lose influence on departmental policing priorities.

Many contemporary chiefs welcome this change while others, notably those ingrained with reform-style policing in a rigid bureaucratic paramilitary structure, resist it. In many ways, this change may be viewed as "grass roots policing" since the citizens define major priorities. While police administrators will always have the last word on operational issues, the shift toward "bottom-up" priorities will become increasingly prevalent. This change, even at incremental levels, represents a dramatic philosophical shift in the way police organizations are administered. The political dynamic is powerful indeed!

MORE ON THE ADMINISTRATIVE PERSPECTIVE

There are several more ramifications of the administrative perspective in politics and policing that merit further discussion.

One fundamental question, administratively, is how best to organize a police department. The structures of most modern American police organizations are rationalized, hierarchical arrangements that reflect the influence of classical organizational theory as delineated by Max Weber.[21] The salient features of these structure are:

1. Formal structures are defined by a centralized hierarchy of authority.
2. Labor is divided into functional specialties.
3. Activities are conducted according to standardized operating procedures.
4. Career routes are well established and have a common entry point; promotions are based on impersonal evaluations by superiors.
5. Management is conducted through a monocratic system of routinized superior-subordinate relationships.
6. Employee status is directly related to their positions (jobs) and ranks.[22]

These characteristics result in a firmly established, impersonal system in which most of the employees and clients are powerless to initiate changes. One may clearly question the adequacy of this bureaucratic model in the modern police agency. It creates problems in police and community relations, in employee morale, and in communication and control—all documented by the President's Crime Commission as well as the growing body of research in community policing. The concern of police administrators for efficiency and economy (a basic goal of classical organization theory) has caused some lack of concern for side effects detrimental to community relations. Moreover, classical organization concepts do not facilitate adequate flexibility in policy with which, for instance, to meet legitimate needs and values of particular subcultures or groups.

> Classical theory also supports police reformers who insist that police departments be isolated from politics. As police departments become more refined and move nearer their goal, they move further away from another basic goal of democracy— guaranteeing every citizen access to and influence with governmental agencies. Under a highly developed police bureaucracy, nearly all citizens view their police department as essentially beyond their understanding and control. Where the police department is a highly developed, traditional bureaucracy, its structure and its philosophical underpinnings will eventually cause the organization to become socially irrelevant and ineffective. This situation, in turn, will have a profoundly damaging effect upon police and community relations.[23]

Thus, it may be asserted that citizen reluctance to get involved with the police can be traced to the mystique of classical organization structure. Further, such structuring tends to support a perpetual state of low morale among employees of bureaucracies. Weber himself condemned this aspect of bureaucracy. One indicator of this problem can be found in the increased police activism with the police unionization movement. Some research suggests that these are trends that are unlikely to cease.

Another argument against classical bureaucracy is its long-recognized problem of internal communication and control. The chief administrator seldom gets a true picture of what is going on in the department. The assumption that formal authority to command can force compliance from subordinates is everywhere being questioned today. Increasingly, police authority is being invested in subordinates rather than with the supervisor.[24]

One interesting analysis of police administration makes reference to the police literature stressing command as the basis of control. In Weberian terms, the police department "as an order" is legitimated by the principle of command. Commitment to obedience, in this sense, is a sign of membership. The classical status reward is honor.

> In the case of the American municipality, police chiefs . . . are politically accountable officials who ordinarily stand or fall with the fortunes of their civilian superiors. . . . Given the often controversial nature of police work and the often irrational and unpredictable nature of political fortunes in municipal government, the American police chief who is responsible to a politically elected official comes close to the position of a "patrimonial bureaucrat," in Weber's terms. His [or her] tenure as chief, though not necessarily his [or her] tenure in the department, depends on continuing acceptability to the elected official(s). . . .
>   Given strict accountability plus insecurity of tenure, we can expect a kind of obsession with command and a seemingly irrational emphasis on the twinned symbols of the visibility of the commander and the obedience of the force. Some of

the rhetoric of command in the police literature likely arises from an attempt to protect the chief by the compulsive effort to overcontrol subordinates, almost any of whom can get the chief fired. This amounts to saying that as civil superiors increase the formal accountability of the police chief *without changing* the tenure features of the role, the increasing bureaucratization of the police . . . leads to the development of an organization animated by a principle of the commanding person. This "personalized subordination" to the hero-chief can become an operating, if not a formal, principle of organization.[25]

Increased professionalization can be an accommodation to such a situation, aimed not at control of the force but at control of the mayor by changing the grounds of accountability. Perhaps it is difficult to have a professionalized police force without having a professionalized mayor. This latter point pertains to what has been called "the environing system" of the police. The central meaning of police authority itself is its ability to manage relationships.

Directing traffic, investigating complaints, interrogation, arresting suspects, controlling mobs and crowds, urging prosecutors to press or drop charges, testifying in court, participating with (or battling, as the case may be) probation officers in juvenile court, presenting budget requests to the city council, pressing a case with the civil service commission, negotiating with civil rights groups, defense attorneys, reporters, irate citizens, business groups, other city services, and other police systems—even such an incomplete list indicates the probable values of a perspective that emphasizes transactions and external relationships. The list also indicates something else of considerable significance. All of these transactions can be and often are antagonistic ones.[26]

Modern metropolitan police agencies exist not only because communities are legally organized but also because the police are called upon to mediate between the urban community and the legal system. This describes rather starkly the police-government linkage. Some of the questions that we have discussed in earlier chapters have their foundation in this linkage: for example, the position of the police in the legal order, that is, their relation to prosecutors and the courts; police administrative strategies for manipulating the image of crime in the community and measurements of police "success"; and problems of internal relations and morale in police agencies brought about by either or both of the factors just mentioned.

Something should also be said about police officers and their political rights as citizens. The Hatch Act has severely limited the political activities of federal government employees, and it has been copied at the state and local levels and applied to police officers, along with other governmental employees. But in recent years the so-called blue power movement in policing has challenged such restrictions on police political activity.[27] The history of the restrictions goes back many years, embedded in civil service reforms aimed at flagrant abuses arising from political patronage. The Hatch Act was a 1939 chapter in this history. Its coverage was expanded in 1940. Strict rules grew out of major scandals of the past. But by 1966, the appointment by Congress of a Commission on Political Activity of Government Personnel was a tipoff that the pendulum had began to swing. Yet most police departments today still retain many restrictions on political activity by police officers. While some such restrictions are clearly necessary, relaxation of overly rigid rules seems in order, in light of changing social conditions. There is no reason police officers should be less than full citizens.[28]

POLICE UNIONS AND BLUE POWER

Another perspective in policing and politics centers on the line level, although there are supervisory and middle-management labor organizations in some large departments. This is the police unionization movement. The politicization of the police, in this sense, is a phenomenon of increasing importance, generally as legitimate, as inevitable, and probably as desirable in the long run as the administrative politicization discussed previously.

Do police officers have the right to organize for the purpose of collective bargaining? Is this desirable? On the face of it, the answer to these questions today would have to be "yes." Jerome Skolnick wrote twenty-five years ago that the American police officer is overworked, undertrained, underpaid, and undereducated.[29] Looked at today, we would say police are still overworked, but significantly better trained, better paid, and better educated.

In the context of the social circumstances of the late 1960s, many police officers were described as frustrated, alienated, and angry. As a result, they had turned to militancy and political activism: blue power. They had protested via slowdowns and other such actions ("blue flu"), often of questionable legality, directed toward material benefits, changes in governmental policy ("take the handcuffs off the police"), or changes in internal organizational procedures. Direct police challenges to departmental and civic authority followed in the wake of urban disorders, and criticisms of the judiciary had escalated to "court watching" by the police. What were once strictly or largely police fraternal associations had become more and more potent political organizations, more and more in the character of unions, and more and more vociferous toward police management and municipal management on questions of power and control.

In short, the police entered the 1970s as a self-conscious, independent political force. In many cities and states, the police lobby had become quite influential. Yet the police and the courts were still expected somehow to remain politically "neutral," lest public confidence in the legal system be impaired. The upshot was a kind of masquerade, with police unions not overly anxious for the public to know much about their political activities or influence. To this day, police fraternal organizations are a bit reticent about being called unions, and a strike is referred to as a "job action" or "blue flu" because police strikes are generally illegal. In terms of community relations and public attitudes, police unions tend to come across as surreptitious, and the view of them that is often reflected by police administrators, understandably, does little to improve the union image.

It should be added that the politics of police line organizations was not confined to the Fraternal Order of Police, the Policemen's Benevolent Association, and the like. Racial and ethnic police organizations, such as the Guardians Society and other black police officers' groups, were concerned with using the dynamics of power in police agencies to protect the interests of their members. It is hardly news that political and social polarization on racial or ethnic grounds exists *within* big-city police forces. As a matter of fact, there is a view that as the numbers of black and other minority police officers have grown, largely as a result of affirmative action, internal tensions within urban police agencies have increased. Affirmative action has become the focal point of these tensions, and police unions have been heavily involved in the litigations. Organizations such as the Guardians and the National Organization of Black Law Enforcement (NOBLE) have frequently been adversaries of the unions in these legal and political encounters, up to the present time.

Such minority organizations within the police world evidence the same political savoir faire observable in the Black Caucus formed in the House of Representatives during the ninety-second Congress. Years ago, such a development would have been regarded as unthinkable. William Raspberry, the nationally syndicated columnist of the *Washington Post*, commented that this Black Caucus represented something truly special and unprecedented in the realm of national politics. It was, he said, a recognition that black people face some rather special problems, for which they should have special interest representation. At the same time, however, it was also a recognition that to work for the best interests of black people does not necessitate working *against* the best interests of white people.

A further point: years ago, police officers tended to speak with more of a uniform political voice than they do today. While it is undoubtedly still true that police officers are predominantly a conservative political group, there are many officers today who champion a somewhat more liberal position on at least some political issues. Indeed, some research suggests that the conservative view of issues was by no means as consistent or as extreme as some observers were suggesting.

DEALING WITH POLICE UNIONS

Earlier editions of this text provided a brief history of the police union movement in this country. Since this information is available at much greater length in other sources,[30] we are content here simply to direct attention to the contemporary reality of police unions as another significant perspective regarding politics and policing.

A police management philosophy for dealing with unions has been gradually emerging. As early as 1971, then Dayton Police Chief Robert Igleburger and his training director, John Angell, asserted that police administrative opposition to police unions had become pointless. Police executives are faced, they said, with the necessity of dealing with such organizations in good faith. They advocated flexible managerial philosophy and skills with a legitimate interest in the concerns of line officers. This perspective portrays an organization as a cluster of interacting positions and roles, defined by reciprocal behavior expectations. The essential task of the administrator is the intermediary role, to facilitate role consensus among supervisors, middle managers, the employee union, and the city administration.[31]

In such an intermediary role, emphasis is upon the need for flexibility and willingness to modify and redefine positions and to consider alternatives. In short, the administrative role, according to this theory, requires positive political skills and strategies. This principle may also be applied to the specifics of policy development and staff development, and to establishing an information system both inside and outside the department. The process may also be used in establishing effective grievance procedures, in the process of negotiation itself, and in the implementation of the contract after a settlement has been reached.

> In dealing with the union, the administrator must insure his employees and their union fair treatment and due process, but he must also be concerned about protecting the interests of citizens, legislators, his supervisors, and his managers. To adequately fulfill these obligations, the chief must view himself as an intermediary between these various significant groups and individuals who are concerned with the outcome of the collective bargaining process. A prerequisite to the competent fulfillment of this position is a realistic approach to collective negotiations through the use of rational techniques and strategies.[32]

Public administration generally is preoccupied with the need for budget squeezing in every possible way, with stretching funds to provide more and better public services. This is the essence of recent attention to public sector quality performance. Where police services are concerned, the unions clearly must be party to any serious effort of this type. They must be recognized, and their legitimate rights must be recognized. The adversarial element in labor-management relations must be turned to constructive ends. Not only should police unions be "lived with" or tolerated, but the basis for collaboration should be broadened. The matter of performance is an appropriate focus for this collaboration.[33]

Beginning in the late 1980s, police union activity started to increase. While collective bargaining in the private sector began to slow down (even diminish), this was not the case in policing. The presence of police associations began to grow, notably in the South and "right to work" states where levels of unionization were relatively low. This growth was motivated by active national police associations lobbying for growth and the concern about working conditions and benefits among the rank-and-file officers.

Police labor organizations at the state and national levels have become increasingly sophisticated in providing bargaining advice and support to local collective bargaining units. Similarly, they have become influential through political activism and have been able to further their agenda through lobbying for passage of legislation that is beneficial to the labor movement. As evidenced by the erosion of management rights and the increase in concessions earned by labor organizations, police management has not been as successful on matters of political activism. In all likelihood, given changes in the political and economic environment and the maturation of the police labor movement, changes over the next ten years will not be as pronounced as in the past decade.

For labor, the major concerns in any contract negotiation center on benefits and personnel actions. For management, personnel actions and management prerogatives are likely to head the list of important issues. In a national study of labor relations by PERF, a series of issues was presented to police executives, who were asked to rate each issue in terms of its importance to current collective bargaining. Nine of the issues were related directly to benefits: salary, overtime pay, medical insurance, court pay, disability insurance, leave days, retirement eligibility, retirement contributions, and in-service training. The remaining nine issues involved personnel actions and management prerogatives. These included the disciplinary system, shift assignment procedures, transfer priorities and methods, promotion process, participation in decisions, weapons, general equipment, affirmative action, and personnel performance evaluation.[34]

Based on these factors, the issue rated as the most important was salary, followed closely by medical insurance. The third most important issue was the disciplinary system, followed by overtime pay and shift assignment policies. Of the eighteen issues examined, three of the top five were related to benefits. Certainly community support for the police is important if increased taxes are needed to support the department.

Another interesting area examined in the PERF labor survey was related to police job actions and conflict resolution. Job actions that police unions use are diverse. They include work slowdowns, speedups (such as writing large numbers of traffic tickets), picketing, media campaigns, and sick leave ("blue flu").

These job actions are obviously designed to influence the political process. Since police officers are typically prohibited from striking, the job actions are designed to influence the sentiment of citizens through public education and/or inducing fear in the community through the inference that with fewer police officers working, risks of crime increase. While this inference is based on emotional appeal, and not supported by any research, the tactic is successful in many instances. The "bottom line" is that citizens want their police officers working, and their fears translate to political action that contributes to resolution of the labor contract by police management.

As police departments increasingly adopt the community policing philosophy, some interesting labor issues are emerging:

- Will community police officers be given priority assignments based on seniority or their ability to work within a given community environment?
- If officers are permitted to use "flex time" (that is, adjust the times of their shifts based on community needs) are there any restrictions or complications associated with the union contract?
- Should overtime pay be awarded for activities—such as community meetings— officers volunteer to do (rather than being assigned)?
- Can volunteers be allowed to take positions or jobs that would normally be filled by salaried officers?
- Should officers receive salary increases because they are being given additional responsibilities?
- Will officers be less likely to initiate job actions if they feel a greater responsibility to the community?
- Should officers' "out of pocket expenses", which are self-initiated in response to community requests, be reimbursed by the police department?

Based on the limited experiences of labor negotiations on these community policing issues, the future holds some uncharted territory that will need to be addressed cooperatively and professionally.

POLITICS AND COMMUNITY POLICING

When describing politics and the police, many people often assume that there is some type of unprofessional behavior, unethical relationships, or some form of taint on the impartiality of police processes. Political relationships are not inherently "good" or "bad": Rather, they practically reflect processes that are normal in the course of doing business, whether that business is manufacturing, sales, or public service. Political maneuvering and negotiation are as natural as the ebb and flow of the sea. They are activities that, to the experienced navigator, can be used to achieve organizational goals or, to the novice, be a frustrating impediment undermining well-intentioned programming.

Increasingly, police executives are more open about the political nature of their roles. Some have become quite skillful at the process, while others struggle to "learn the ropes." Clearly, managing the politics of police administration is something that comes with experience. That is, one has to explore communication and negotiation strategies that work both within the environment and with the people involved. Similarly, a police leader must be adept at sensing changes on the political terrain that can alter alliances, arguments, and positions. Despite the nebulous nature of these factors, there are some important constants that exist in political relationships, which serve as useful guideposts for effective police management.

Community policing provides a new challenge for police executives in the political arena. The police are exploring redefined organizational configurations and processes—akin to the "reengineering corporations" movement now found in the private sector—which involve a new emphasis on teamwork, leadership, service, organizing work around "processes", job enlargement of patrol officers, empowering the community, and solving problems. Not only does this require radical surgery to traditional police practices (administrative and operational alike), it also places the police in a new dimension of political gamesmanship. This dimension, although ultimately providing more influence, certainly has its pitfalls.

Community Relations and Crime as Political Commodities

Police involvement with the community in a proactive, positive relationship is a key element of the emerging political role. The administrative changes necessary to facilitate this "reengineering" are fundamental to internal political problems, which must be resolved. This is not occurring in a vacuum of policing but is representative of a broader "community movement" signified by recent elections and more vocal "grass roots" concerns voiced by citizens from our communities. These changes are coupled with contemporary movements in the private sector targeted toward quality management, most prominently emerging in the United States during the mid-1980s vis-a-vis Total Quality Management (TQM) followed more recently by the "value-added service" and "benchmark management" concepts found in various contemporary management philosophies. Such philosophical changes in management practices directed toward customers—or a constituency, in political terms—coupled with a new vision of policing that offers hope to effectively deal with crime clearly whets political appetites.

Crime—and the need to prevent it—has consistently received substantial attention from politicians simply because it is of major concern to citizens. Several explicit reasons come to mind when considering why crime is a political factor.

- *Crime is an emotional issue that conjures up feelings of fear and the need for safety and security for oneself and family.* The political process feeds on emotion as evidenced by political advertisements both for and against the "Brady Law" handgun purchase waiting period, news reports about teen violence, or ongoing concerns about drugs. A tug on the heartstrings has far more political clout than the weight of scientific research.
- *Crime will touch most people, either directly or indirectly, at some point in their lifetime.* Nearly every American will be a crime victim or know a victim, consequently crime is something the public can relate to with near unanimity. This comprehensive experience gives the politician a good frame of reference for communicating with his or her constituency—it is a uniform foundation for communication.
- *Crime is one issue on which nearly all people can agree to some extent, regardless of political position, race, ethnicity, age, gender or lifestyle— people do not want crime.* Democrat or Republican, African-American or white, Hispanic or Anglo, young or old, man or woman, gay or straight; all agree that crime and violence must be controlled. Consequently, it is politically safe to oppose crime and offer reasonable initiatives to control it. Anything that offers a relatively high degree of political safety is certainly going to receive attention from politicians.
- *Citizens are willing to make some sacrifices for protection against criminals.* Fear of crime is pervasive, fueled by media reports, gossip, and assumptions. To abate this fear many people are willing to make some sacrifices, including paying more taxes. For example, the citizens of Flint, Michigan voted by a two-

thirds majority to increase their tax mils to support community policing. In Texas, citizens voted to spend over $2 billion to build prisons, even though the state's financial status was lean. In 1994, the most expensive crime bill ever proposed was passed by the U.S. Congress. The point to note is that increased expenditures for crime control are relatively easier to justify than other government initiatives because crime control efforts are not generally seen as a "pork barrel." Spending money on issues of popular concern can be an important way to gain "political chip," as will be discussed later.

- *Crime is visible and piques a morbid curiosity among people.* News reports about murder and mayhem, television programs depicting "real crime", and nonfiction books on "true crime" are all evidence of this. As another illustration, people still go to rural Waco, Texas where the Branch Davidian compound stood, just to see the sight of that calamity (and buy T-shirts). Similarly, the O.J. Simpson double homicide case practically become an industry in itself, spawning numerous books, movies, advertisers for television coverage, expert witnesses, and consultants and selling newspapers and magazines, the inevitable T-shirts, and tacky souvenirs. The Menendez brothers; Susan Smith, the South Carolina mother who drowned her sons; and the Timothy McVeigh and Terry Nichols trials in the Oklahoma City bombing case all reinforce this fascination. These factors clearly illustrate that incidents of crime draw public fascination, particularly when the crime is senseless or an atrocity. As such, crime makes great fodder for politicians to decry, examine, comment, and take action.

In recent years, as crime has become increasingly violent, invading rural communities, the public schools, and touching white, middle-class America, the politics of crime have not only become a readily accessible issue for politicians to safely attack, the public is mandating political action. This emotional firestorm is emerging as yet another reason why crime is an important political factor.

While there is a common ground surrounding the concern for crime and the need to control it, there are also notable disagreements on the proper responses to the problems. For example, opinions vary widely on such issues as:

- Should police authority be increased to deal with crime?
- Should some legal rights be temporarily "suspended" in order to deal more effectively with criminals, notably drug dealers?
- What is the best way to prevent crime—educational programs, physical crime security, more police officers, stiffer prison sentences, youth diversion programs, the death penalty? All of the above? Some of the above? None of the above?
- Will crime be more effectively prevented (and will justice be more effectively served) if convicted criminals are punished or rehabilitated?
- Is punishment versus rehabilitation a legal issue, professional issue, or political issue?
- Should drugs be legalized in order to cut down on drug-related crime?
- Is crime a racial problem? A problem of teens and young adults? An urban problem? A poverty problem? A media problem? A parental problem? A—you fill in the blank—problem?

These questions present a number of issues that stir controversy. Importantly, these questions—and the way they are answered—reflect political perspectives and beliefs far more than substantive knowledge and research. Several examples come to mind. Because violent crime has become a pervasive issue for the public, Congress and state legislatures have attempted to respond with a number of "get tough" measures to deal with the problem.

The label of "get tough" is important from a political perspective. Citizens are both tired and fearful of crime, consequently holding elected officials accountable for doing "something" (particularly as reflected by the November 1993 and 1995 elections). With political sentiment being this explicit, politicians recognize that some action must be taken; and that action cannot be viewed as being "soft" on crime or criminals. Consequently, youth boot camps; providing federal support in the form of COPS hiring incentives for employing up to 100,000 more police officers; increasing the range of offenses for the death penalty; making life sentences mandatory for career criminals; increasing mandatory penalties for offenses where firearms are used; and building more prisons have been among the common responses in recent years. The political dynamic comes into play, not because of actual knowledge about the effectiveness of these measures, but because they lessen the political heat from the public. Just as important as appearing to be "tough on crime" is the prospect that a new crime control strategy has been developed, which holds great hope for preventing crime and making the streets safer. Most recently, the political football of crime is being thrown again, this time in proposals to revise the crime bill to make it "tougher." This is where community policing comes into play and where jeopardy for the concept lies.

Increasingly, community policing is being embraced by many politicians as the means to more effectively deal with crime while at the same time providing better service to the public, with special concern for increasing the quality of life within a community. In reality, there are probably few politicians who truly understand the philosophy. Despite this, they are providing their heartfelt support (in a political sense) for the concept because it addresses crime, links the police and community together in a stronger bond, and provides a demonstrable initiative, which the politician can point to as an effort to show that community concerns are being addressed.

This is not intended to sound cynical; rather, it is realistic. Most politicians realize they have an ethical responsibility to address public concerns. The fact that one's personal future is tied to this responsiveness is not inconsequential. It is, of course, the nature of the beast. Unfortunately, any new initiative—such as community policing—is also politically fragile, because if no "successes" can be demonstrated, support will dwindle.

Political Axioms

To build on these concepts, it is important to understand some fundamental principles of the political process. In this regard, the author has developed several axioms that apply to the political game. Police administrators should recognize the presence of these "truths" and be prepared to deal with them when posturing with elected officials and employees alike. Admittedly, these axioms are offered somewhat "tongue-in-cheek"; however, there is always a foundation of truth in any satirical description.

AXIOM 1: The tendency is to react emotionally rather than act rationally toward a new issue or controversy. It appears to be an artifact of human nature that when we are confronted with an issue, concept, or problem that is inconsistent with our life's experiences we respond immediately with an intuitive conclusion. That conclusion, however, is largely based on what we *feel* rather than what we *think*. This can get us into political hot water if the reaction is publicized or made known to political adversaries. For example, when civil disorder erupted in Los Angeles following the state criminal trial verdicts of the officers charged in the Rodney King excessive force case, former Mayor Tom Bradley, obviously upset and frustrated, stated on television something to the effect that he did not blame rioters for responding to the trial's injustice. This was a politically irresponsible statement, for it essentially gave justification to the rioters. Had Mayor Bradley been more thoughtful about the situation, his statements would likely have been tempered.

In another illustration, often when police officials, regardless of rank, are first introduced to community policing, they respond with something to the effect of "Community policing? It won't work because we can't handle the calls we receive now and we need more officers." Their response is a reaction based upon their experience of traditional policing, not a true understanding of the community-based concept. Moreover, the effects of this axiom are aggravated because it is difficult for one to publicly admit an earlier mistake in judgment. Instead, there is a tendency to cling to one's initial reaction.

AXIOM *2: Superficial suppositions about ideas, programs, and initiatives will have a greater influence than in-depth substantive knowledge.*

Often those in the political limelight will embrace an idea or concept because it sounds good, not because they truly understand the meaning of the concept or what it involves. For example, when the Rahway State Prison (New Jersey) Lifer's Project—also known as "Scared Straight"—was first publicized, it received wide endorsements from politicians. It "made sense" that if incorrigible youth were exposed to a "dose of reality" in prison, listening to the travails of a group of lifers, this experience would "scare" them into a life of lawful behavior; particularly when initial evaluations over the first few months supported these suppositions. Support for similar programs reached the point that legislators began funding projects in other jurisdictions. However, project evaluators at Rahway were not as optimistic: Understanding the precepts of learning theory, along with the need for long-term socialization and reinforcement for behavioral change, it was felt the project's effects would not last. The twelve-month and eighteen-month evaluations showed this to be true. Legislation and program development in replicated projects were based on supposition, not substantive knowledge.

With respect to community policing, suppositions are plentiful. Many politicians hear the concept and want to jump on the bandwagon of popularity. They are surprised, however, when they learn about longer response times and the significant amount of change required of both the police organization and community to implement it. The mandate is to "do it now," not recognizing the organizational and behavioral complexities involved. Nevertheless, it is embraced because it sounds good.

AXIOM *3: When it takes too long to explain an idea and if it requires thought to understand it, then the battle for acceptance will be difficult.*

Political handlers and media consultants have had a wide-ranging influence on politicians, the broadcast media, and the public alike when they began routinely providing the "sound bite" (not to mention the "photo op"). Usually no more than thirty seconds in length, the sound bite is intended to address a specific issue or provide an answer to a problem with memorable language. The sound bite is a neatly packaged presentation that fits well into the rapid-paced format of broadcast news. It has become so prevalent that not only politicians, but public officials, experts, and others who frequently provide commentary for broadcast news tend to encapsulate their ideas so that they virtually appear to speak in sound bites. Both the media and politicians have become so accustomed to this practice, it has become an expectation in interviews.

The problem with sound bites is that only a brief amount of substantive information can be passed on. Trying to deal with complex issues in a sound bite mentality means that the true impact, ideas, and subtleties simply will not get passed along. For example, the author has been asked to explain "in a couple of sentences" why police officers use excessive force. Similarly, the author has been asked to explain community policing in about thirty seconds—reporters cannot understand why a researcher is unable to do this when a politician can. To try and explain complex ideas within such rigid time constraints may be a greater disservice than ignoring the questions completely. Yet, in the real world, a balance must be drawn somewhere. Unfortunately, the sound bite phenomenon has expanded beyond the media and entered into the political realm. Politicians, executives, and the public expect a sound bite response. A method must be found to circumvent this mentality—perhaps through an incremental information exchange—in order for the true concepts of an idea to be presented.

AXIOM 4: A CONCEPTUAL INITIATIVE NEEDS A HOOK OR GIMMICK THAT CAN BE EASILY IDENTIFIED WITH IN ORDER TO GET A POLITICAL FOOTHOLD. Whether it is a product of laziness, shallowness, or simply a modern cultural trait in a fast-paced society, the presence of a readily identifiable icon of a broader, usually more complex, endeavor is a necessity to gain recognition and support. This can be seen in popular music sales, movie previews, and advertising as well as in politics. This explains why things such as "foot patrol," "bike patrol," and "Neighborhood Watch" are so closely identified with community policing even though they are a small part of the initiative. The insightful administrator uses this to his or her advantage, perhaps even creating the "hook" as a means to enlist political support.

AXIOM 5: Timing is everything; to gain maximum political support a new initiative must be proposed at the time it appears to respond to a current, emotional, high-profile public need. We are a generally compulsive "it has to be done now" society. As evidence, look at the popular use and growth of fax machines, e-mail, and overnight package delivery services, not to mention the Nike shoe advertisement that admonishes us to "Just Do It". As a consequence, we tend to not look too far into the future. When problems occur, we play "catch up" and grasp potential solutions, even if they only hold a faint promise to be a successful remedy to the problem. Relying on this political wisdom, an administrator should package a new program or initiative as a response to a current high-profile problem, even though the initiative has broader applications. For example, at this time, community policing is more readily accepted when promoted as a means to fight violence instead of as a means to deal with homelessness. This is not inherently an ethical dilemma as long as the argument is not a pure subterfuge.

AXIOM 6: The probability for greater political support will increase if credit is given where it is not due. This is not fatalistic, but is a realistic strategy to gain political support. If there is a political advocate showing some support for a new activity, maximize that support in any pronouncements by pointing to that individual's leadership and commitment. For example, one may give credit to important, key political decision-makers for developing a new initiative and saying that police department personnel supported the idea, but "simply did the leg work". A similar approach may be used with employees, noting how they have provided leadership. Never underestimate the power of an ego.

AXIOM 7: *If some measures of activity or success cannot be visibly shown in the short term, political support for the initiative will be limited.*   Any new activity that requires reallocated resources and organizational change must realistically be promoted as a means to solve problems and attain goals both efficiently and effectively. Given this fact, an administrator must provide evidence, once the initiative is in place, that progress is being made. Moreover, it is reasonable that politicians and the public hold the department accountable to any promises that have been made. From a political perspective, the maxim to remember is "no demonstrable success, no demonstrable support".

AXIOM 8: *There is a direct relationship between fickleness of the public and political maneuvering; as the public changes its mind, political support for an initiative will change at lightning speed.*   It is the nature of our republic that political support will follow the winds of public concern. Thus, public demands will focus political action. Unfortunately, the public is somewhat fickle in their desire for institutional responses to problems. For example, members of a neighborhood may say they are concerned about traffic accidents and speeding cars, yet be hostile if they are personally stopped for speeding. As another illustration, in response to the public's concern about homelessness, the police develop a cooperative plan with social services, private foundations, and the ministerial alliance to open a large shelter and kitchen. Instead of "taking care of the problem," the food and shelter may attract *more* homeless people to the jurisdiction, thereby, from a political perspective, aggravating the problem in the public's mind, not solving it. In yet another case, if the police department says that it is implementing community policing to respond to quality of life problems in the city, but members of the public do not see a change in that quality (even after a short period of time), then accolades for the police may quickly turn to criticism. In short, if no effects to an initiative can be shown *to the public's satisfaction*, then political support will be dropped like a hot potato.

A Perspective.   The lessons from these axioms are all too evident on the American political landscape. A quick review of elections, program initiatives that have succeeded and failed, and proposals offered to cure the nation's ills, whether they are crime, violence, health care, or free trade, will all show these truths at work to some degree.

As these axioms illustrate, our complex political interactions are based on simple assumptions. For example, the public is concerned about violence, thus simple and fast solutions are sought in the political arena—lock criminals up, create youth boot camps, legalize drugs, increase firearms control, and so forth. Yet, in reality, violence is a complex phenomenon requiring multiple programmatic, educational, and legislative actions over a long term. In order to deal with such long-range, slow change, the prudent administrator will use these axioms as guideposts to help maneuver through the political terrain.

The Political Chip System

Any transaction requires currency. In political transactions the currency is sometimes referred to as "chips." To understand the use of "chips," one must begin by recognizing that a fundamental political *error* is to assume that when a person is "doing the right thing," this action alone will develop political support. Trolling for programmatic (and resource) allies on one's record alone will rarely develop a solid political foundation. Instead, those who work in the political environment must aggressively seek support by showing both the substantive *and* political benefits of the action or issue being pursued. While there is a tendency for this to seem improper, it is a realistic—and legitimate—means of developing and implementing programs or initiatives. If a police leader can show political leaders the benefits the latter may gain—typically public support—from these initiatives, then the police leader will gain "chips" in the relationship.

"Chips" are reciprocal favors and support given in the negotiation of political processes. As a person's effectiveness builds on both goal-directed and political fronts, their power is enhanced. When an individual's influence reaches the level where others seek that person's imprimatur for support of other activities, then chips become golden. That is, a person's political influence becomes stronger when others seek their endorsement. In such cases, those who are politically influential gain more "chips".

This exponential gain of chips by a politically powerful person can be devalued with respect to their use in bartering or gaining favors as one's political strength erodes. Thus, the earning ratio and relative value of "chips" are not constants—a politician who attempts to treat them as such, particularly on a one-to-one ratio (i.e., one favor begets another) will quickly learn how fast chips can be expended.

Chips are used in bartering for resources, developing programmatic support, and influencing the status of current initiatives (i.e., continuing, modifying, or dropping them). In the constant flux of organizational responses to public attitudes and political positioning, chips are among the most valuable of commodities. They can be used to develop alliances, define organizational direction, or secure resources, albeit often with the expenditure of chips.

While police administrators may have to expend some chips when developing a community-based initiative, there are certainly many chips that can be earned in return as the program becomes successful. More importantly, as the police department builds political support in the community, the value of the police executive's chips grows multifold. There is always an investment gamble, however.

If positive effects cannot be demonstrated, if the public is not satisfied with police services, if progress seems to be slow, if the police department does not appear to work as a comprehensive unit, or any number of complications arise, the police chief's chips will be devalued or expended until mid-course corrections can be made. If positive results are seen, then the chief's chips have been successfully reinvested.

The political lesson is that chips are exchanged and differentially valued just as stocks on the market. In much the same way a corporate CEO seeks to direct his or her corporation to maintain its stocks as a highly valued commodity, so must the police chief maintain chips by keeping the organization on track and productive.

"Secret Stuff": Information As a Political Base

The police, politicians, and the community each possess their own "secret stuff," defined as role-specific information or knowledge that is unique to the organization and potentially politically powerful (or *perceived* to be). "Secret police stuff" includes such things as knowledge about actual dangerousness of a community (as opposed to general perceptions of danger), effectiveness of policing techniques, and information about real versus suspected wrongdoing of people (including public officials). "Secret political stuff" may include knowledge held by politicians related to behavioral motives of elected officials, power shifts, parliamentary or legal maneuvers, and budgeting or funding options.

The significance of "secret stuff" is that this knowledge gives information to the holder that can be used for political leveraging or posturing to influence outcomes of political positions or initiatives. Unfortunately, the political environment is one that thrives, first, on empire-building and, second, on coalition building (a facet closely related to both the bureaucratic structure and the typical budgeting processes of government). Therefore, many times in the political world a coalition will likely be built only if it reinforces growth of the empire. "Secret stuff" is the commodity that helps fund the empires and the coalitions.

Obviously, community-based police initiatives seek to forge coalitions between the police and diverse groups—neighborhood associations, other government departments, service organizations, and so forth—in order to solve problems. However, how open will coalition members be if they seek to continue protecting their "stuff"? Moreover, if a breach in the secret occurs, how will it influence the coalition? A common problem is that the influence (or value) of "secret stuff" is exaggerated by the holder. Thus, its value is not as great as it is perceived, yet the paradox is that efforts to protect the "stuff" may be detrimental to the coalition.

When used to build empires—by the police or any other group—actions based on "secret stuff" appear to be conspiratorial or perhaps arrogant. In either case, the leveraging of "secret stuff" and the process of empire building will undermine efforts to build community policing coalitions. Although the process is frequently subtle, its impact will eventually emerge. At the least, these behaviors will be a disincentive to participate in the coalition; at the most, they can cause actual damage to public institutions. The consequence is that efforts to effectively develop a community policing practice will end up in a political dungeon from which escape is improbable unless "secret stuff" is shared by all parties as a means to bridge political differences.

The sharing of these "secrets" goes beyond mere communications. It means opening doors so others can see all aspects of the organization. For example, outsiders may learn that the police department is not a highly efficient crook-catching machine or that elements of the police culture produce conflict about what the police should do and how they should do it. Although it exposes the gritty problems of the police, the sharing of "stuff"—albeit a difficult thing to do—will lead to stronger support in the long term as the police executive remains vigilant in changing the organization, while at the same time pursuing community-based goals. These are lessons we learned from the "spoils system" of politics and they should not be lost.

The Structure of Political Threat

Political threats are factors which may undermine organizational control or impede successful implementation of the community policing philosophy (Figure 15-2). These threats may be characterized in four basic forms. First, threats *external to government* are political influences exerted by the community—the so-called "body politic"—which can place the police in difficult managerial positions. For example, community police officers who develop a strong, substantive rapport with a neighborhood may find community members flexing their political muscles if an officer is to be reassigned. A protest from community members stating that they "don't want to lose their police officer" places unusual demands on the department—particularly if community demands are voiced to political leaders. A community empowered in this manner places limits on administrative flexibility of the department and may even impede the officer's career development. Police organizations must be prepared

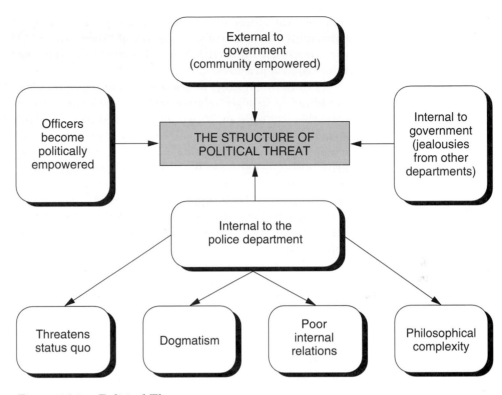

Figure 15-2.   Political Threats

to rationally respond to this pressure in order to maintain organizational control, while at the same time avoiding alienation of the community or political leaders. To buckle to political pressure can open unwanted doors, to not respond can slam needed doors shut. The conundrum is omnipresent.

From an entirely different perspective, external political threats can also be an undermining influence when the community's perceptions of "success" are not met. Given the nature of community-based police activities—crime prevention, resolving quality of life issues, influencing long-term social change, problem-solving—results are difficult to see, or just as importantly, hard to quantify. How do the police demonstrate such things as "prevented crime" or "changed values"? Moreover, the compulsive nature of American society wants to see immediate results from a new initiative; something that does not happen with long-term police programs. When no successes are obvious, political support from the community will begin to erode.

A second type of political threat is when the *officer is politically empowered* by the community as a result of the relationship the officer has established with citizens. As an example, in one Michigan city the residents of a neighborhood were opposed to pending action by the city council to rezone a portion of the area for commercial use. Unsure of what to do, the citizens sought advice from their community police officer on how to fight this proposal. Rather than acting simply as a *resource* for the community, the officer began acting as an *advocate*, taking actions that were essentially a political campaign to oppose the proposal. Acting as both an organizer and catalyst, the officer's actions culminated as he led a protest demonstration (in uniform) at the city hall. (The rezoning proposal was defeated.) When called to task for this action, the officer maintained he was "doing his job" by trying to solve a "quality of life" problem defined by the community he was serving. When the department informed the officer that he may be disciplined (simply a letter of reprimand), the community raised its voice in support of "their officer". Thus, empowering the officer, via citizen support, influenced political decisions and intervened in organizational control practices.

A third threat exists *internal to the government entity*. As the police department establishes a stronger relationship with the community, garnering political support from that constituency, it also gains political leverage within the broader government structure. If the police department finds itself in the position of being the "first among equals" in its relation with other government departments, problems may arise. Other department heads may feel somewhat disenfranchised in the political structure if they feel their departments are being devalued. Rifts and jealousies may occur, leading to poor support and interdepartmental cooperation on activities that are designed to provide better service to the community. Consequently, police executives need to give special attention to team building, noting that any successes that enhance the quality of life in the community are a result of combined efforts, not just those of the police department.

The final political threat exists *within the police department*. This occurs in four basic ways. First, significant organizational change, such as community policing, threatens the *status quo*. People who have invested their energies in a certain career path may find the avenue to professional development has changed. Consequently, they have an incentive to not support, perhaps even to undermine, any new initiative. Second, the natural tendency of dogmatism—the resistance to change—emerges when any new program is proposed—the grander the change, the greater the resistance. Despite the presence of a well-intentioned and well-devised plan for implementing the new initiative, if a political "sales job" is not done to convince all organizational members—sworn and nonsworn alike—of the need and of benefits that can be achieved, then the program will not be successful. In particular, line-level officers are often the linchpin to success and, consequently, hold important political power on which experimentation with new programs rests.

Third, because major programmatic or philosophical changes in law enforcement cannot be explained or demonstrated as easily as a new program—such as Neighborhood Watch, saturation patrol, physical crime prevention, or street sweeps—the concepts are difficult to understand, particularly in the short term. Stereotypes of such new initiatives as community policing are assumed to be the sum and substance of the philosophy; thus, new community-based operational initiatives may be attempted in the traditional philosophical manner.

Poor internal relations, the final element, exists all too frequently and is often more intense in community policing. Such organizational conflict occurs when emphasis is given to new initiatives that replace traditional activities and individuals from the "spotlight" (such as highlighting community policing officers instead of SWAT officers). Aggravating the problem is that typically inadequate attempts are made to incorporate all employees into the new initiative. Those employees who feel disenfranchised by this situation may not participate or support the initiative; in the worst case, the employees may sabotage the effort.

The Politics of "Quality of Life"

An important goal of any community-based police effort is to improve the "quality of life" in a community. Implicitly, this includes a range of factors traditionally related to the police function, including reducing victimization, apprehending criminals, reducing fear of crime, and resolving conflict (such as domestic disturbances). Similarly, regulatory activities, such as traffic control, the towing abandoned cars, and enforcement of laws related to alcohol, health, and safety, have been viewed as a police responsibility but with lesser importance than the crime-related functions. Working with youth has traditionally been viewed as a collateral area in which the police often serve but not so much as an inherent responsibility, although this has slowly changed with programs such as D.A.R.E. and G.R.E.A.T. Dealing with problems of social disorder and neighborhood decay have rarely been viewed as a traditional police responsibility.

The priorities of law enforcement are now beginning to change with the advent of community-based responsibilities that more equally balance traditional foci with those activities historically viewed as being peripheral to law enforcement. As officers begin performing diverse tasks that produce a better quality of life, they build broader expectations in the public's mind with respect to "what the police should do." These broadened—and heightened—expectations have important political ramifications.

The most obvious political issue becomes one of budget. When the public demands broader services, then government is "persuaded" to respond. It is difficult for elected officials, in particular, to deny the mandates of their constituency. Thus, funding support may have to be increased as a means to deal with broadening police activities. It should be noted that many advocates of community policing argue that additional officers and funds are not necessarily needed because police officers are used in different, more efficient, ways. However, in the political environment, public support for popular programming will frequently translate into more funding and growth.

This leads to a problem noted earlier: disenfranchisement of other government departments. At the first level of disenfranchisement, when government leaders decide to increase the police budget, the money typically must come at some expense to other government departments. Thus, even if outright cuts do not occur in other departments, growth and/or sustained levels of staffing or programming may not be maintained. Reduced funding support by one entity in order to build support for another is a sure method to build resentment. Thus, budgeting disenfranchisement not only reduces a department's ability to perform its work, it likely diminishes the quality of the relationship between the police and other departments. This poses an interesting paradox—as other government departments lose their funding and programming ability, they also reduce their ability to effectively work with the police department to solve community problems. Moreover, as resentment builds, other departments may be less inclined to help the police department. The police must respond to their community's quality of life "mandate" in some manner, thus they become more aggressive, hence more politically empowered. Disenfranchisement, therefore, can broaden in a growing spiral.

The movement toward quality of life programming also brings with it new models of government accountability. If the police are providing broader services to the community, what can other government departments do? In essence, as police responsibilities broaden and become more responsive to community demands, citizens may begin to ask how other government departments should change. Should parks and recreation be more aggressive and promote wellness activities? Should the public works department be more aggressive in developing safe and aesthetic roads and rights-of-way rather than focus on maintenance of roadway surfaces? Should the sanitation department aggressively promote a recycling program?

With these changes in accountability, perhaps public administrators should look for interdisciplinary alliances, all of which can help the other develop programming—another example of team building. For example, it may be feasible for fire inspectors to also perform crime prevention "target hardening". Similarly, the public health service may help in programs directed toward reducing violent crime, building inspectors may be given training in "crime prevention through environmental design," and social workers may work more closely with the police in identifying people who are victims or perpetrators of such crimes as domestic violence, sexual assault, drug trafficking, or theft.

Police executives must avoid an inwardly directed myopic view of change to the exclusion of understanding systemic effects posed by community-based initiatives. Enlightened police leaders must develop (and practice) sound political acumen in order to enlist cooperation from other departments, sharing the vision of a broadened "quality of life" toward which all elements of government must contribute.

Broadening the Police Mandate

Unquestionably, as noted in previous discussions, community policing broadens the police mandate, which will eventually either tread on responsibilities of others or be viewed as an inappropriate exercise of police authority. In either case, if police actions are viewed as a political trespass, then conflict will emerge, thereby displacing initiatives and goals. For example, the Portland, Oregon police provide training for landlords in such areas as tenant selection, eviction processes, and other strategies of "tenant management" in order to keep "undesirables" out of rental property (notably public housing). If members of the community or civil libertarians interpret this training as an inappropriate use of police authority, systemic damage could be done to other programs in the community policing initiative.

In another example, you will recall from the previous chapter that the Mission, Texas Police Department's school-based programs have officers assigned to work in all of the schools teaching D.A.R.E., G.R.E.A.T., and serving as Education Resource Officers. Conceivably, initiatives such as this could be viewed by teachers and school officials as a political trespass on their responsibilities, inferring that "anyone can teach" and that "the schools are doing an inadequate job" in their preparation of children to be good citizens. Such a reaction could conceivably undermine the program altogether.

There is little debate that community-based police efforts expand the traditional vision of law enforcement. In many ways this broadened mandate integrates traditional duties with nontraditional tasks as a means to resolve problems (Figure 15-3). Ethically, the police have the obligation to articulate reasoning for this expansion and reach only into those areas that are legitimized by the community and public institutions. Politically, the police must be able to defend their position with logical criteria based on sound reasoning and community needs, not with emotion. Make no mistake, broadening the police mandate is an important decision, which can have a wide-ranging impact on police budgeting, staffing, and operations both now and in the future. It is an endeavor fraught with risk and tenuous support in the political environment. To not recognize and prepare for this political journey is dangerous indeed.

The thorny questions that must be answered in this venue center around the types of programming the police undertake, whose responsibilities they may encroach upon, the extent to which the public wants the police to pursue nontraditional activities, and the intent or reasoning behind the broadened mandate. If the rationale is strong and politically palatable, then expansion will be accepted with the political proviso that some successes will be seen on the horizon. If not, "chips" will be expended and one's political star may begin to fade.

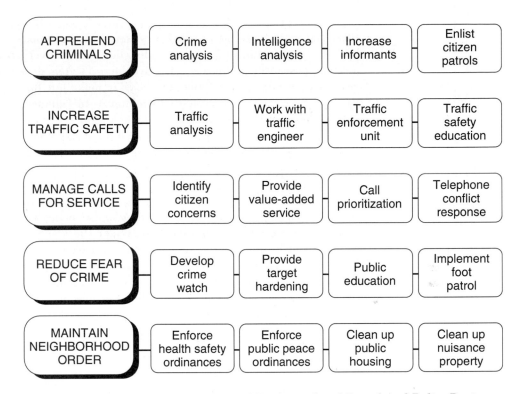

Figure 15-3.   Example of Integration of Traditional and Broadened Police Duties

ISSUES AND PROGRAMS IN CRIME PREVENTION AND CRIME DISPLACEMENT

People have definitive positions that provoke heated debate about the propriety and effectiveness of different crime prevention strategies. Since crime exists within the public eye, the alternatives for prevention certainly come under political scrutiny. The police have learned that, despite these controversial issues, there are certain things that can be done to prevent crime. Perhaps, more accurately, we mean prevent individual victimization. That is, a citizen may take certain precautions that significantly reduce the chance that he or she will be the victim of a crime. This *specific prevention* is the type of prevention on which the police generally focus. The broader issues, *general prevention*, are focused on changing the behavior of criminals so that they will no longer commit crimes. If a criminal decides not to burglarize a home because the resident took crime prevention precautions, the criminal simply goes to another residence that can be more easily burglarized. In this case, the crime was not prevented, but displaced.

Similarly, if the police take aggressive actions, such as using saturation patrol, street sweeps, open surveillance, or any other strategy that is designed to "run the criminals out", this too is displacement. The philosophical issue is whether displacement is a legitimate organizational goal. Most police executives will say yes; most urban sociologists will say no. Of course, the sociologist has the luxury of viewing the issue from the ivory tower, while the chief of police must respond to the public and elected officials.

The phenomenon of displacement was documented in an interesting research project by Paul Cromwell and his associates, who studied burglaries. The research team not only conducted comprehensive interviews with active burglars, they actually went with the burglars when they were "casing" houses for break-ins. In their wide-ranging findings they learned that burglars are very conscious of crime prevention precautions. Alarms, effective locks, watch dogs, and carefully secured premises are among the things the burglar looks out for. Burglars not only want money and property, they want to minimize the chance of being caught. Consequently, they seek to minimize risks. One burglar observed that there were plenty of residences that were not protected. If he did not like the "feel" of one home because of the crime prevention precautions, he simply went to another.[35]

Specific Prevention

Specific crime prevention is characterized by being victim-oriented and implementable in the short term. Operating under the assumption that property crimes occur through opportunity, the approach to specific prevention focuses on *target hardening*.[36] This simply means that an assessment of a person's residence, business, or behavior is done to find ways to minimize the opportunity for a crime to occur and maximize the potential for apprehending any person who attempts to commit a crime. There are several strategies consistently used for this approach.

Block Watch.   Also called a Neighborhood Watch, Vertical Watch (in the case of high rise apartments), or Business Watch, the Block Watch concept brings together people of an identifiable area for a common goal of crime prevention. Initially begun so that neighbors would get to know each other and "keep an eye out" for suspicious persons in the neighborhood, the concept has expanded. Now Block Watches are also involved in identification and problem solving in addition to serving as the facilitating mechanism with which a community police officer may have contact with a neighborhood.

Operation Identification.   Since burglars and thieves steal property to sell (or "fence") rather than convert it to their own use, the idea behind this program is to make property more difficult to sell since it is clearly identifiable. Operation Identification involves engraving property—such as televisions, computers, stereos, appliances, and so forth—with an identification number. Lists of marked property, along with photographs, may be filed personally or with the police department. The home will be given Operation Identification window stickers in order to inform a potential thief that the property is marked and recorded with the hope that this will discourage the crime. In the event that the property is stolen, it will be more difficult to "fence" and more easy to identify for recovery.[37]

Security Surveys.   Relying on principles similar to a risk-assessment in business, this involves a police officer physically examining a residence or business for security weaknesses. Such things as door locks, the types of windows and their locking mechanisms, lighting, shrubbery, and any other physical aspects of the location are reviewed by a trained police officer for their use in minimizing the opportunity for a burglary. Recommendations are then given on how to "harden the target."

Public Education.   Trends in crime, current threats, tips on how to avoid victimization, and other crime-related information are given to the public to help them protect themselves and their families. This is accomplished through Public Service Announcements (PSAs) on radio and television, PSAs in newspapers, presentations to civic or community groups, presentations at schools, and any other venue where there is concern (and interest) in the topic. "McGruff the Crime Dog" and his slogan, "Help take a bite out of crime!," have been a successful mechanism used by the National Crime Prevention Council to educate the public. Importantly, public education must be an ongoing activity over a long period of time to have an influence on behavior.

Crime Stoppers.   Focusing on apprehension, Crime Stoppers has proven to be a successful means of locating criminals. It is established locally as a nonprofit organization and operated by citizens with support from the police and assistance from local radio and/or television stations. When a crime occurs and there is sufficient information obtained to provide some "leads" in the case, Crime Stoppers publicizes the information, via a radio description and/or television reenactment. Anyone having information about the possible perpetrator can report this anonymously to the "Crime Stoppers hotline." If the information leads to the arrest of the criminal, the person calling in the tip will receive a cash reward. Initial assessments indicate that Crime Stoppers has proven quite successful in apprehending criminals. Moreover, some crime will be prevented through this program—at least while the criminal is in jail!

Alarms.   The burglar-alarm industry has grown rapidly throughout the United States in the last ten years. Whereas alarms were traditionally viewed as something that only the rich might have, they are now increasingly commonplace. In many areas of the country, alarms are already installed in new homes being built. Of course the question remains, do they work? One study indicated clearly that they do.[38] Burglars indicated that if a business or residence had a sign announcing an alarm, they were more reluctant to break in. Several said they might go to the house and attempt to see the alarm control panel to ensure that the signs "weren't fake." Nearly all of the burglars agreed that they would not burglarize a residence with an alarm since there were so many more that did not have security systems. Thus, while an alarm may help catch a burglar entering a home, the greatest value of an alarm system appears to be its deterrent effect.

Private Policing.   Largely because of fear of crime, there has also been a significant growth in private policing. Neighborhoods are increasingly hiring their own security police to patrol areas and check homes as a means to both prevent crime and increase the chance of apprehending criminals. Experience with private policing in communities with community policing is relatively rare at this point. However, some indicators are that the private guards are willing—even enthusiastic—to work with the community police officer to help deal with crime problems. Interestingly, it does not appear that citizens who employ private police are dissatisfied with their local police agency; rather they are pragmatists who recognize that there are physical limitations on what the police can do. Consequently, they are willing to pay private companies to help dissuade criminality in the neighborhood.

Beyond target hardening, there are other specific prevention efforts which are directed toward potential victims as a means to help them from becoming victimized. Perhaps most widely known are initiatives directed toward the prevention of sexual assaults. Information on being aware of one's surroundings, how to react if confronted, and how to survive the attack is presented in a wide range of pamphlets and public education forums.

Because of the increased incidents of people being injured by stray bullets in drug trafficking areas (notably in the inner city of our urban areas) some educational efforts have been directed toward avoidance of incidental injury in high crime efforts. Some manufacturers even developed book bags and overcoats for children made of the same bullet-resistant material found in police officers' protective vests.

Most recently, as a result of the increase in "car jackings," crime prevention efforts have been directed toward citizens on how to avoid these crimes as well as what to do in case they are confronted by a "car jacker."

Each of these activities integrates well with police-community relations and community policing activities. They provide the police with a forum to open lines of communication with the community, to disseminate useful (and wanted) information, and provide an avenue for the police and public to work together on other matters of mutual concern related to quality of life in the community.

General Prevention

Unlike specific prevention, general prevention is directed toward the offender (or potential offender). The idea is to prevent crime by influencing the behavior of persons so they will not commit crimes. Behavioral change is a long-term process, so hopes that results will be seen immediately or in the near future are unrealistic. This involves an educational process, which attempts to either reinforce or mold values that hold that committing crimes is wrong. Moreover, committing crimes can have dire consequences, which can affect a person throughout his or her life.

Programs which directly or indirectly are part of general prevention include:

- Drug Abuse Resistance Education (DARE)
- Gang Resistance Education and Training (GREAT)
- Teaching Individuals Positive Solutions (TIPS)
- Substance abuse counseling and treatment
- Nurturing and assistance programs for youth (such as Big Brothers or Big Sisters)
- Offender rehabilitation programs

Because of the long-term nature of these programs, the jury is still out on their effectiveness. There are indicators of success for DARE, for example. Substance abuse treatment has variable success rates and offender rehabilitation appears to depend on the attitude of the person—that is, are they ready to rehabilitate themselves? Community policing activities are important for these programs through direct officer involvement as well as referral and reinforcement. While the true effects may not be known at this point, the programs offer promise and the police should capitalize on these opportunities.

The National Crime Prevention Council (NCPC) has done extensive work in facilitating crime prevention activities of both a specific and general nature. They provide technical support, resources, and expertise to assist in maximizing preventive initiatives. The work done by the NCPC requires local participation from both the police and community in order to have any hope of working. Most of the crime prevention activities are logical and appear to work; however, it is virtually impossible to measure how much crime has been prevented. Thus evaluation is difficult. Dennis Rosenbaum has comprehensively reviewed a wide range of crime prevention initiatives; his work is a valuable guide to further understand the issues.[39]

CRIME PREVENTION AS PROBLEM-SOLVING

Can crime be prevented? There are those pragmatists who are dubious. They hold that very little serious crime can be prevented, that it is more a matter of trying to contain it as best we can, of keeping the loss of life and property as low as possible, and that any goal beyond this is naive idealism. Can crime be eliminated? Clearly not. Is it possible to control it, contain it, and reduce the number and gravity of its occurrences? Clearly it is, given certain conditions. As mentioned previously, when we say "prevention," we mean it in this manageable sense. The reality is that we may displace crime, rather than actually prevent it.

Next question: Would anyone or any group *oppose* the prevention of crime? Obviously, yes—individuals and interests who profit from it. If those who insist that crime does not pay were altogether correct, there would be no crime. Depending upon the particular delinquent or criminal, the payoff for crime may be psychological or political or economic, or a combination of any of these. "Take a chance; you won't get caught!" "What's the matter—chicken?" "What's the difference; nobody cares!" These are typical verbalizations associated with delinquent and criminal behavior. Each expression has a note of cynicism that often is coupled with fear or threat. One effect is a prevailing attitude in society that not much can be done to deal with crime and criminals.

Yet public opinion polls indicate that the community favors crime prevention by a clear margin when asked to rate the importance of the police functions of prevention and criminal apprehension. But until the recent past, many police departments have acted as if they were not listening. They have said, for instance, that they could not give more attention to preventing crime because they are too busy apprehending criminals. Then if brought to task for a lackluster record in apprehensions and clearances, they have explained that they were too busy "doing social work." Once the LEAA grants for crime prevention were exhausted, budget cutting frequently made the crime prevention unit an early casualty. Currently, however, numerous departments have come to recognize this as poor politics, as community pressures for more attention to crime prevention have accelerated. Moreover, crime prevention has become an important element in community policing.

> To interpret the objective of crime prevention in a way that makes sense throughout today's police service is a difficult task because it is not easy to reward [officers] for successful preventive actions . . .[40]

The reinforcement of informal controls on individual behavior is the most vital way to reduce the incidence of crime. "Compliance with most laws does not depend upon the likelihood of their being enforced, but upon an acceptance of informal norms and a concern for the feelings of others."[41] The tendency is to place major responsibility for crime prevention with the police. The crime prevention work of the police can only be meaningfully discussed in the wider context of "criminal policy." This means public policy pertaining to crime and criminals. The formation of such policy, not yet evident in any country, would require the participation of all social institutions with responsibilities toward the public peace—that is, local and national crime prevention councils.

Approached as community problem-solving, crime prevention begins with defining the problem. Immediately we discover that "the crime problem" is not one problem, but many. So-called white-collar crime and street crime are quite different; indeed, each is a general name for a category of crimes with differences. "Fraud" is a category in itself; so is "extortion." Precisely what crime are we trying to prevent? Presumably, the strategy and tactics of prevention vary by the nature of the crime and its causes. Crime prevention sounds easy on automobile bumper stickers, and sometimes even in Neighborhood Watch organizations. But if we are serious in our efforts to cope with crime, the first step is to understand its complexity. Some politicians are impatient with such "academic drivel," but systematic crime preventers are often more realistic than politicians!

In the United States, we have long relied on Uniform Crime Reports (UCR) for statistical impressions of how much crime there is, what types, the characteristics of those arrested, etc. The data for these reports are gathered through a procedure initiated by local police agencies, who report monthly to state police agencies, who in turn have reported, in the past, to the Federal Bureau of Investigation and presently report to the Bureau of Justice Statistics in the U.S. Department of Justice. Quarterly and annual consolidated reports are published. The system has been improved in recent years, but remains the object of considerable criticism because of its shortcomings. Moreover, the system cannot be blamed for the widely recognized estimate that actual crime exceeds reported crime by two to three times. One can conclude that crime prevention programs begin with serious handicaps, represented by the difficulty of grasping accurately the nature and proportions of the problems.

During the 1990s, the UCR is conceptually changing toward an "incident-based" system in an attempt to be more reflective of actual crime. The system, which will take several years to be fully implemented, will be more descriptive of actual crimes, not just the raw number of crimes reported to police in the index categories. To provide even more insight, the U.S. Bureau of Justice Statistics collects victimization data through the National Crime Victimization Survey (discussed in a previous chapter). Collectively, these data provide a better picture of crime than we traditionally have had, but it is still skewed. (We will never have a perfect picture of crime because much of it goes undiscovered or unreported.)

These improved methods of gathering, recording, and reporting crime data have resulted in useful refinements in our understanding of crime. At the same time, crime research is facilitated. Methodological improvements in gathering crime data have somewhat furthered our insight into criminal patterns, but in a larger sense, they force us to realize the limits to the types of questions that can be answered by statistics.

There is little point here in undertaking even a summary highlighting of the statistical profile of crime in the United States. By the time this text is published, such information will already be dated. Suffice it to say that crime in every form and criminal justice processes across the board constitute a major problem, in terms of social cost, public anxiety, and political priority. Whatever the yardstick employed to measure "the problem," there is little doubt about the importance universally attached to it.

Keep in mind that the actual rate of crime in a community—reported or unreported—does not necessarily correspond to citizen attitudes about crime. The public may underestimate or overestimate the scope of the problem, and public opinion about it is easily manipulated by police handling of statistics and by the media.[42] As we have noted, public attitudes and perceptions about crime are an important political reality, even when these attitudes are based more on emotion than on fact. When more than half of the people polled say that they feel more uneasy on the streets than they did a year ago, police administrators had better pay attention. Every year since 1970, almost 70 percent of the respondents in a Louis Harris survey have asserted that "our system of law enforcement does not discourage people from committing crimes." Approximately 30 percent have listed stricter law enforcement and more severe penalties as the best way to prevent crime. More than 50 percent feel that the courts are too lenient. Older residents generally tend to feel more apprehensive about crime. Blacks are much more apt than whites to feel that their vicinities are unsafe.

FOCUS 15.1

NATIONAL INCIDENT-BASED (CRIME) REPORTING SYSTEM—NIBRS

Official crime statistics have been recorded in the Uniform Crime Reporting (UCR) system, which was started in 1930 by the International Association of Chiefs of Police. In response to the increasing amount and complexity of crime in America, and recognizing the need for improved statistics, during the 1980s the police community called for an update of the UCR program. The result was the creation and three-phase implementation of the *National Incident-Based Reporting System* (NIBRS).

The NIBRS was designed as an improvement in the way law enforcement agencies nationwide report information about offenses, victims, and offenders to the FBI. NIBRS requires that offense, offender, and victim records be linked at the "incident level." The system also requires that fifty-two items of information must have incident-based collection for twenty-two offense categories. Data such as this permits detailed crime analysis to understand crime problems as well as factors contributing to (or related to) the criminal incident.

The major difference between the NIBRS and the traditional UCR is in the amount of detail that is reported. The UCR is a "summary reporting system" wherein reporting agencies simply tally the number of reported Part I/Index crimes and Part II offenses and submit the aggregate numbers of offenses through the reporting system. Essentially, all that is known is a generic number of reported crimes in each category.

In incident-based reporting, law enforcement agencies collect detailed data regarding individual crime incidents and arrests. The system then links together, using prescribed data elements and values, the offenses, arrests, and victims. With information about the use of weapons, the presence of alcohol or drugs, ages of victims and perpetrators, times the crimes occurred, and other factors, police agencies have a much stronger foundation on which to base resource decisions and develop strategies for crime-related problem-solving.

The victims of crime have been receiving more attention lately, and no discussion of public attitudes toward crime is complete without the reflection that more crime means more victims of crime. Compensation for crime victims is costly. Perhaps it is not an idle hope that a larger number of crime victims, and cash payments to an ever larger proportion of them at taxpayer expense, will result in less public complacency and increasing pressure to do something about it. A complacent public has often been pointed to as the most significant factor in a worsening crime situation.[43]

The growth of community and problem-oriented policing has redirected our vision of looking at crime more holistically. That is, the police can no longer be content to singularly look at crime. A broader perspective must be adopted to include neighborhood decay, emerging social disorganization in high crime areas, and fear of crime.[44] Increases of violence and growth of unique crime types—computer crime, information crime, and consumer fraud, for example—make the task even more challenging.

CRIME: CAUSES AND REMEDIES

Logically and as next steps in the problem-solving approach to crime prevention, we should move from defining the problem to the diagnostic step (identify causes), and then to the remedial step: what can be done to prevent or cope with crime? But an avalanche of other works deal with these questions. Instead, this discussion will be remedial, to place the issues in context.

Crime is a form of deviant behavior, measured by certain established standards of society. As such, it is caused behavior, and its causes can be identified: physiological, psychological, medical-psychiatric, political, economic, sociological, familial, educational, and so on. Now and then, there is a fresh insight. For instance, it appears likely that criminal justice processes are, to some extent, causes of repeated crime.

It may also be disturbing to observe that constructive efforts to thwart crime— by more effective police activity, or by more effective police-community cooperation in crime-coping programs—will probably produce *more*, rather than less, reported crime in the short run. Again, such a statement draws attention to the yardsticks for measuring crime. For politicians—and for police people who are at the mercy of politicians—simple truths of this nature are anathema. Apparently, it is felt that instructing the public to think sensibly about crime is a task for neither politician nor police official. Both insist that something *must* be done about crime, but leveling with the public about it seems to be seen as "politically risky."

Police practices related to crime control have also come under fire. For example, "sting operations" became a popular method of sophisticated undercover activity to develop cases on criminals where standard methods of investigation were not fruitful. The FBI's ABSCAM investigation of corruption among several Congressmen and the John DeLorean cocaine trial were perhaps among the most noteworthy; however, local and state police agencies have also used this method. A common one is creation of a pawnshop, which is operated by the police, complete with video and audio surveillance of all customers. The police "put the word out" that the pawnshop will buy stolen merchandise. The intent is to identify and gather evidence against thieves who bring their criminal gains in to sell at the pawnshop. A congressional inquiry on this practice found that the pawnshops actually *generated* crime.[45] What this means is that a known outlet to "fence" stolen property with no questions asked provided a temptation for thieves to steal more than they traditionally had. Certainly, the investigatory benefits of these operations do not outweigh the political ramifications when citizens learn of these kinds of results.

Although he recognized that the police are not solely responsible for the political games played with crime and criminal justice, Peter Manning explored what may properly be called the "plight" of the police. He began with the proposition that, to the degree that police agencies lack a legitimate mandate on which there is widespread consensus, they will tend to direct energy either into dramatization of their effectiveness or into repressive actions in attempts to expand their mandate. Most police work is administrative, and therefore not publicly visible. So the police tend to look for what can be dramatized in their activities; for example, they use crime statistics as a symbolic barometer of their effectiveness. This is especially true when the crime rate goes down. It soothes the public into believing that the police protect life and property, and thus are entitled to public trust. This then becomes their mandate to maintain the image of "crook catchers." Manning's analysis unveiled five propositions:

1. To the degree that dramatic aspects of policing become the dominant concern of the police and the public, ceremony replaces instrumentalism and police work becomes redundant: it simply reaffirms other modes and forms of social control. The idea of community leadership goes down the drain.

2. To the degree that instrumentalism replaces the ceremonial features of police work, the degree of sanctity of moral rules that they convey will be reduced. In time, coercion replaces consensus on the police mandate and its legitimation.

3. If the conceptions of policing provided by the police themselves are legitimated by public consensus, then police action frees itself from the community in which it is rooted and may establish its own norms and values.

4. To the degree that formally constituted control agencies are faced with a paradox between what is formally expected of them in the community and what is possible, they will tend to retreat from a collective definition of morality, the law, and social order.

5. The greater the gap between the moral standards of the community and the police culture, the greater the growth of cynicism among the police, and the greater the corruption and the number of internal disciplinary violations.[46]

The police are caught between their rhetoric and the reality that there is very little crime that they can control, solve, or investigate completely. Lest this seem anti-police in orientation, another way to put it is simply to say that police behavior must be understood in its link with police social or environmental context, as we have earlier suggested.

Another example of cause-and-effect difficulties in trying to understand crime and how to control it was provided by a Kansas City study of police patrol patterns, sponsored by the Police Foundation. Recall from earlier discussions that the study indicated sharp reductions or increases in patrol had little effect on crime, arrests, or police response time. The strategy of preventive patrol has not only failed to demonstrate its effectiveness in controlling crime but has also created the worst possible situation: an ineffectiveness that alienates citizens. Studies of police response time show this factor also is ineffective when measured by apprehensions.

Turning now, briefly, to the question of remedies for crime, one instrument of political hoodwinking is the blue ribbon commission, committee, or task force. These bodies, usually inspired by a crisis of some kind, produce reports, financed by tax dollars, and packed with recommendations for revamping the machinery of criminal justice. Knowledgeable people spend countless hours on much public-spirited endeavors, seeking innovative goals and standards to be implemented by executive and legislative officials whose stratagems can be understood only by those who are familiar with political conduct. Thus, reports of blue ribbon bodies are, more often than not, mere relief for political pressure, rather than practical blueprints for solving problems.

Newsletters, press releases, and "white papers" for semipopular reading are often instruments of the political game. A typical story might read:

> The State Criminal Justice Planning agency today announced the award of thirty-five grants totaling $2.6 million mainly to improve anticrime operations—including Operation Identification, neighborhood watch groups, and police agency crime prevention units.

How much of what kind of crime do these programs prevent? What do we learn from them about the nature and causes of crime that might be more generally applied? Increasingly comprehensive evaluations of these programs are being done. In the 1980s the National Institute of Justice (NIJ) began developing a greater focus on how research could be used to direct crime control strategies. In this regard, the NIJ gave more attention to evaluating research projects to learn "what works." At the same time, police administrators were growing more sophisticated, and recognizing the value of program evaluation. Although evaluation is increasingly used to determine the efficiency and effectiveness of our crime control and prevention initiatives, politically inspired programs remain.

For example, Operation Weed and Seed, developed in the last year of the Bush presidency, was designed to be both functional and political. The intent was to control crime and drug trafficking in public housing by weeding out the criminals and "seeding" the residences with law-abiding citizens. Moreover, community policing would be an integral element of keeping control of the housing areas so they would remain safe and relatively crime-free. While there was great hope among the staffs in the Department of Justice, the Department of Housing and Urban Development, and the various cities where the pilot projects were to be implemented, the political process during the election year became overwhelming. One police official in a Weed and Seed city who was responsible for commanding that city's efforts told the author:

> We had national news media and Washington officials here announcing the beginning of the program before I knew we had the grant. We had the evaluation people in here assessing our efforts before we received our grant to fund the project, and I couldn't even get the U.S. Attorney in a meeting with me; even though he's supposed to be in charge of the whole thing. Typical—a good idea implemented in chaos that will probably have the same effect as smoke and mirrors only because of the political posturing to "win the drug war."

One major difficulty with politically inspired programs of crime control, perhaps largely because they *are* political, is their tendency to apply blanket solutions to complex problems. For example, take the current swing away from rehabilitation of offenders toward harsher treatment: mandatory and stiffer sentences, greater reliance on incarceration and less on probation, tougher parole practices, limits on plea bargaining, and the like. These "get tough" prescriptions are merchandised as *the* answer to crime, without regard for the important differences in offense, law, circumstances, and offender that would be revealed in effective presentence investigation. The political approach to crime control frequently treats all alike; there is no patience with individuality. It ducks the hard questions and the delicate and vital distinctions by invoking a single, all-purpose remedy.

The question of how many and what kind of crimes such programs actually prevent can never be answered. What would happen if the program were not operative, nobody can know. But the basic idea of so many people in so many neighborhoods participating in the cause of crime prevention, allied with the police, certainly merits applause and encouragement. The Guardian Angels, based in New York City, on the other hand, have generated some skepticism. The jury, so to speak, is still out. Vigilantism is a danger, although the Angels, through their founder, Curtis Sliwa, deny this charge. If they would work closely with the police in working out ground rules and levels of involvement, the Guardian Angels would avoid much of the suspicion about their motives and, sometimes, their tactics.

PROGRAM EFFECTIVENESS

Increasingly we have evaluated police programs and know more now about policing than we ever have. Yet, a great deal is left unknown. Evaluation actually focuses on two dimensions: *outcome* and *process*. Information on both is needed in order to truly assess the value of a program. Outcome evaluation asks the question, "Are you accomplishing what you want?" It seeks to determine if goals are being met. Process evaluation asks, "Are the methods for accomplishing the outcomes efficient?" That is, we want to ensure that money is not being wasted or spent at an unreasonable rate in comparison to the value we are receiving from the program. Both types of evaluation involve a process that makes comparisons between "conditions." These conditions may range from reported burglary rates to levels of fear of crime to levels of satisfaction with the police. Regardless of the nature of the comparison, we seek to distinguish between what the condition is like with the program as opposed to what it would be like without the program.

Programs of any kind will be assessed from three broad perspectives:

- Organization and development
- Administrative issues
- Operational issues[47]

Within this three-point model, there are a series of questions, in this case related to community policing and community relations, which can be used to guide a determination of program effectiveness.

Organization and Development

- Does the program contribute directly to the department's goals?
- What proportion of the department's total resources is required by the various programs? Does the value of the program justify this expenditure?
- Do the crime patterns and service demands in the jurisdiction warrant personnel or specialization (such as crime prevention or school liaison)? If so, what types?
- Do the anticipated specialized positions have the size, structure, goals, and responsibilities that are consistent with the crime demands, service demands, and other programmatic activities of the department?
- What is the relationship of community policing and community crime-prevention activities to other activities in the department?
- Will there be changes needed in the authority and responsibility for community policing activities?
- How comprehensive will community policing activities be?
- What growth patterns, if any, are expected in community policing activities and what expertise will be needed to respond to growth?
- What are the anticipated equipment needs, depending on changes in size, crimes, service demands, and community policing goals?

Administrative Issues

- Are the criteria and procedures used to target community policing activities and problems throughout the jurisdiction effective?
- What regular activities need to be evaluated and on what schedule?
- Should resources be diverted from other areas in the department to more comprehensively support community policing and crime prevention activities? If so, what areas? What is the criteria for making these resource decisions?
- On what criteria are community policing goals changed or revised?

Operational Issues

- How extensive will community policing activities permeate all departmental activities? Divisional? Shift? Selected officers? Department-wide?
- What will the performance measures be and why?
  1. Obviously difficult to assess—Performance measures are dependent on goals, needs, and unique characteristics of the department and jurisdiction.
  2. Performance measures must be to determine:
     a. Are goals being met?
     b. Are tasks and activities that officers are performing functionally related to goals?
     c. Are tasks cost-effective?
  3. Performance measures, to have a true evaluative impact, must not be designed to weigh individual accountability, but should be designed to see that policy activities are responding to goal needs.
     a. How can ongoing, forward-looking goal preparation be best accomplished?
     b. Based on changing police service needs, are any unique staffing patterns emerging?
     c. Are new training programs needed or anticipated based upon new and emerging responsibilities of officers associated with community policing?
     d. Do changing responsibilities indicate the need for formal links with specialized agencies or groups?
     e. How can community policing activities integrate with non-patrol activities of the department?
- How can community policing activities integrate with other governmental agencies (e.g., fire department, recreation department, street department, health department, and so forth)?

Ideally, program effectiveness will be determined by objective, goal-directed criteria, not purely political decisions. While the political dimension can never be escaped, it will hopefully be balanced with realistic needs in the best interests of the broader community.

QUALITY OF LIFE

Reference is frequently made to issues of "quality of life" in our communities and the responsibility of the police to increase that quality. Perhaps the most well-known reference to this issue was offered by James Q. Wilson and George Kelling in their article "Broken Windows."[48] As a metaphor for neighborhood decay, decreasing quality of life, and fear of crime, "Broken Windows" laid the foundation for the police to rely on a different perspective when viewing needed services in the community.

It was recognized that neighborhood disorder—including drunks, panhandling, gangs, prostitution, and other urban incivilities—creates citizen fear. Just as unrepaired broken windows can signal to people that nobody cares about a building, which will inevitably lead to more vandalism, unattended to disorderly behavior can also signal that nobody cares about the community. In turn, this will lead to more serious disorder and crime. Such signals of social disorganization both create fear among citizens and attract predators to the neighborhood.

If police are to deal with disorder to reduce fear and crime, they must rely on citizens for legitimacy and assistance. The police cannot do this alone, despite traditional assertions to the contrary. They cannot define all of the community concerns nor resolve many problems without input from the citizens. Police have traditionally felt they should deal with serious crime, but were frustrated with a lack of success because of poor citizen assistance and an excess of "calls for service;" which essentially addressed noncriminal matters.

Citizens in decaying neighborhoods concede that crime is a problem, but are more concerned about daily incivilities that disrupt and often destroy neighborhood social, commercial, and political life. In essence, while criminal victimization occurred, it was a relatively rare occurrence even in the most crime-ridden of areas. However, the disruptions, inconveniences, and poor conditions of their daily lives had the greatest impact on citizens and commanded a significant amount of their time and attention.[49] Thus, quality-of-life issues do not place matters of crime at the top of the list of community problems. Rather, factors that make citizens' daily lives feel insecure, unstable and fearful, and generate feelings that the future holds little hope, have far more precedence than crime.

One of the most important factors that influence a person's satisfaction with his or her neighborhood is a feeling of safety. The police must seek to change those neighborhoods that are aesthetically unsightly, where no pride is shown in the care of property, and where disorder is able to continue unchecked. To remedy these problems is the foundation on which effective community relations can be built.

THE COMMUNITY DIMENSION

Because the causes of crime spring from all of a community's social institutions, it follows that crime-coping activities should be just as comprehensive. This simple logic requires constant reenforcement, for too many people are inclined to see crime as a problem solely for the police and the courts. It is similar to the problem of poverty in this respect. Few people think they cause it; therefore, it must be somebody else's job to deal with it. We hire functionaries to do society's "dirty work." But there is no escape from the ultimate responsibility. The attitude that it's not my problem until it affects me, personally, is the real villain in social problems. And politicians exploit this attitude to their advantage, for example, by playing the higher taxes refrain. In the long run, the costs of social bankruptcy accumulate and mount to incalculable proportions.

Yet much has been accomplished in the way of public education. There is no need here to recite the list of dos and don'ts for homeowners, apartment dwellers, automobile owners, vacationers, and the rest. The program generally called Operation Identification is widely known and utilized. Citizens who report tips or suspicious circumstances to the police are paid cash rewards or carry membership cards and lapel buttons for CHEC—Citizens Helping to Eliminate Crime—or a similar organizational title and credential. Neighborhood Watch, Crime Stoppers, Citizens on Patrol, Lady Beware, and Citizens' Alert are familiar tags for programs that are common in the United States and Canada. Block watching, crime prevention vehicles, architecturally secure buildings, new types of alarms systems, watchdogs, Operation Whistlestop— these are among the many trappings of the current community crime prevention emphasis. In some cities, but not enough, groups have formed to attempt to secure jobs and equal rights for released prisoners. Other groups work to remove certain crimes from the criminal code. Some of the programs engage civilians in activities too close to vigilante tactics to be palatable to even the most frustrated police officers, and some raise provocative questions as to whether the police or the citizens should be credited with apparent decreases in crime. But the results of the citizens' movement against crime appear to be substantial in many places.[50] Major cities throughout Canada have extensive programs of this kind, with strong governmental and police agency backing.[51]

Surveillance of neighbor on neighbor ("Nosy Rosy") is, to be sure, a delicate enterprise and can easily create more problems than it solves. Some training for participants is a good idea, and close liaison with the police is essential, provided that the police themselves are properly sensitive to the Bill of Rights. Court watching is another kind of action employed by some citizen groups, sometimes as a method of pressuring judges to toughen sentences. This, too, can be ill-advised. Court monitoring can serve a socially worthwhile purpose, but not when it is based upon a single-theory answer to the crime problem. As a general principle for citizen action, it should be remembered that various measures that may curb crime may also destroy liberty and community.

The National Advisory Commission on Criminal Justice Standards and Goals divided its work into several areas with a task force in each area (as was done by the President's Crime Commission.) One task force focused on community crime prevention. Its report is a treasury of information, recommendations, and suggestions relative to citizen action programs. Nearly all of these recommendations are as applicable three decades later as when they were written. In concluding an appendix to the report, the task force said:

> As someone once remarked, "Law enforcement is not a game of cops and robbers in which the citizens play the trees." Unfortunately, there are still too many trees. If crime reduction is to become anything more than wishful thinking, citizens must care enough to devote energy, money, and—most of all—themselves to the fight for positive results.[52]

In many communities, the results of citizen action have been slow to show up in the statistics, and discouragement has set in. Often it is difficult to secure citizen interest initially. The widespread charge is "public apathy." There are a number of reasons for public apathy, particularly when the subject is crime and involvement with "the law." Fear of retaliation is one reason frequently mentioned. So is the time it takes and the inconvenience, "Just plain dangerous" is another explanation. These and other more or less standard reasons for nonparticipation are familiar, and more or less justified in the particular case.

By way of summary, there are some concerns about community involvement in crime prevention that should be underscored. These include concern regarding:

1. Excesses by vigilante-type citizen patrols bent on self-defense.
2. Citizen groups functioning independently of the police organization.
3. The "Nosy Rosy" syndrome in neighborhood surveillance.
4. Efforts that are deficient in planning, management, and evaluation.
5. The possibility that citizen involvement may not have staying power.
6. Fragmented programs that champion single dimension approaches, as against coordinated, comprehensive impacts.[53]

DIVERSION

The various forms of diversion in criminal justice are rooted in a philosophy of community-based crime prevention. To divert means to turn aside, to deflect in another direction. As applied to crime, there is *primary* diversion, meaning measures taken to prevent initial contact with criminal justice process, and *secondary* diversion, meaning measures taken to prevent further contact following one or more experiences. Obviously, the latter focuses on recidivism, or repeated offenses. The relationship between diversion and crime prevention is intimate, and so is the relationship between diversion and community responsibility.

Diversion is another of the many subjects mentioned in this text that deserve volumes in their own right. The term is used to cover programs with widely diversified functions; for example:

1. Primary diversion can be accomplished by wholesome family, educational, and religious influence—or by any number of other community resources (recreation, sports, neighborhood youth resources centers, PAL, etc.).
2. The exercise of police discretion is diversionary when the decision is not to invoke criminal process, but to refer a youth back to family or community, or simply to drop the case.
3. Pretrial diversion occurs when, rather than proceeding with charges in criminal court, it is decided at the pretrial stage to deal with the case in some other way. This is also called prosecutorial diversion.
4. Alternatives to imprisonment can be diversionary. These include absolute or conditional discharge, restitution, fines, suspended sentence, probation, community service orders, partial detention in a community-based residence (halfway house), and parole release.[54]

To lessen or minimize contact between the offender and the criminal justice system is, thus, one of the chief purposes of secondary diversion. The "absorption of crime by the community" is a phrase that captures the key idea. Restraint in the use of criminal law is another way to put it. Discretion in handling individual situations is a presupposition of any diversionary program.

Diversion raises numerous questions that will have to wait upon future experience for reliable answers. One common attitude is that diversion is simply a new term for "soft" treatment of criminal offenders. This attitude once again reflects the fallacy of trying to conceive of remedies for crime in terms of simplified slogans. A more rational approach is to recognize that diversionary programs will not solve all of the problems that lead people to commit crimes. Yet there is growing disappointment with overreliance on criminal law as a means for dealing with social problems. In this sense, decriminalization is a kind of diversion. There is also acceptance that rehabilitation does not work for every criminal either. Sentencing must increasingly take into account not only the offender, but the community and the victim of crime as well.

There remain important legal and philosophical questions regarding diversion that are not fully resolved.[55] Informal diversion has long been used as a safety valve to curb overflow in justice processes. In recent years, there has been an effort to formalize such practices, under pressure of overcrowding of correctional institutions and a search for less expensive community alternatives.

Diversionary programs such as "shock" probation and offender boot camps are currently popular, although comprehensive evaluation of their effects have not been definitively completed. Perhaps more importantly, we have learned that short diversionary treatments—such as the Rahway, New Jersey State Prison's "Scared Straight" Lifer's Project—have no long-term effects. Rather, young people need to be socialized toward diversion. Educational programming, reinforced each year, offers the greatest hope.

SOME CONCLUDING POINTS

Diversionary programs have the effect of encouraging and facilitating cooperation, collaboration, and mutual assistance among the various components of the criminal justice apparatus and their supportive social agencies. Diversion encourages the system to become more functional, it encourages the community to participate in criminal justice processes, and it encourages the courts to adopt sounder sentencing principles.

Indeed, this matter of working to make the criminal justice "team" function more in the fashion of a team is basic in any consideration of the possibilities of coping more effectively with crime and criminals. Some elements in this perspective should be so obvious as even to bypass the wailing of politicians who have a stake in maintaining a more parochial view, for instance, prudent decriminalization—eliminating from the criminal code some behaviors that ought not to be there. This is crime prevention of a sort, keeping in mind that decriminalizing public drunkenness, for example, does not wipe out community responsibility to deal with it as a problem. Similarly, the call for legalization of drugs would not eliminate the social problems associated with drug usage (other than the criminal justice processes).

Another obvious point is that the multiplication of police agencies in this country makes little sense in today's circumstances. The number of departments with sworn personnel of five or ten or twenty officers is astonishing. In economic as well as in functional effectiveness terms, this situation has little validity. Yet it is maintained, for petty political purposes mainly, with anguished cries for "home rule" and keeping the police closer to the people. Experience with consolidated police organizations in Canada, in the United States, in the United Kingdom, and in other countries demonstrates that there need be no sacrifice of these treasured ideals of democratic government under systems of regional and metropolitan policing.

The National Advisory Commission on Criminal Justice Standards and Goals referred to Criminal Justice Systems 1 and 2. System 1 is the series of agencies: police, prosecution, the courts, and corrections. System 2 includes "many public and private agencies and citizens outside of police, courts, and corrections who are—or ought to be—involved in reducing and preventing crime, the primary goal of criminal justice."[56]

Suppose that crime prevention, then, were *really* to become the primary mission of the police and of other criminal justice agencies. When one stops to think about it and realizes what it would mean in terms of standards for recruitment of personnel, training and education, promotions and incentive systems, and all other organizational and functional aspects—indeed, even for the criteria of productivity and successful performance—one wonders why we delay any longer in adopting such a preventive criminal justice policy.

HER MAJESTY'S INSPECTORATE OF THE CONSTABULARY PROGRAMS OF GOOD PRACTICE IN CRIME PREVENTION AND COMMUNITY RELATIONS

In Britain, Her Majesty's Inspectorate of the Constabulary (HMIC) is responsible for inspecting the forty-two provincial police forces of England and Wales (the London Met is not included) to determine their "value for money" in the operation of police services. During the course of the inspections, one of the elements the Inspectors look for are programs of "good practice." These are exemplary programs in a wide variety of administrative and operational police areas. The following are examples of good practice identified by HMIC in the area of crime prevention (along with the constabulary of the program).

Crime Prevention Surveys (North Yorkshire Police). Domestic security surveys requested by householders are currently carried out by Sub-Divisional personnel, thereby relieving dedicated crime prevention officers for more proactive specialist duties. However, Special Constables (reserves) have now also been trained to undertake this task in support of their colleagues in the regular Force.

Crime Prevention Project Management (Sussex Force). Project management training for Community Relations and Crime Prevention staff has been organized in-force with the help of consultants. It will lead to the future development of all Crime Prevention initiatives according to a standard "project profile," which requires clear identification of problems, objectives, and strategy; activity planned for each unit or agency involved; a program of costings; and measurement and review criteria.

Harbour Guard (North Yorkshire). "Harbour Guard," a collaborative venture involving the police, Harbour Authority, and Her Majesty's Coastguard Service with sponsorship provided by an Insurance Company is proving to be extremely successful in reducing what was a large-scale problem of theft of and from boats in the Whitby and Scarborough areas.

Robbery Seminars (Thames Valley Police). The force has organized seminars for representatives of banks, building societies, garages, sub-post offices, and other interested parties.

Home Security for Pensioners (Thames Valley Police). In one area, a joint Police/Council home-check scheme has been developed under which pensioners may apply for home safety and security surveys and, if eligible, receive grant aid for improvement.

Servicing Neighborhood Watch Schemes (North Yorkshire Police). In an attempt to overcome problems in servicing the rapidly increasing number of Neighborhood Watch schemes, Special Constables in two Divisions of the Force have been appointed as "link coordinators" with responsibility for between four and eight schemes. So successful has this proved to be that the intention is to extend it to the remainder of the Force.

Crime Prevention Playlets (Surrey Police). The Force Crime Prevention Department has joined with a local radio station in the production of a series of role playlets of approximately seven minutes covering crime prevention aspects. They have been sponsored in this venture by an insurance company to the amount of approximately £25,000 [pounds sterling].

Crime Prevention Survey Aide-Memoire (Dorset Police). The force has produced an aide-memoire to assist their community and rural beat officers when carrying out simple domestic crime prevention surveys. It can subsequently be left with the householder for his [or her] information. A basic guide to household security has also been produced as a pocketbook insert for all members of the Force to enable them to answer basic enquiries from the public.

Victim Care Packages (Kent Police). A victim care package has been adopted and has, as a central feature, the generation of informatory letters to victims of crime plus personal contact by investigating officers.

City Help Desk (Leicestershire Police). A central help desk manned by a police officer and located in the switchboard room has been established to deal with all enquiries within the city. This enables any member of the public seeking help or advice and unable to get straight through to the police station of their choice to be immediately referred to a police officer. The system has proved invaluable in identifying problems and offering remedies and is more than repaying the manpower investment.

Advice Unit (Norfolk Police). A small, carefully staffed Advice Unit has been established at the busiest police station to provide general guidance to members of the public and also to record details of crime where no police attendance is necessary at the time of reporting. This has provided an enhanced service to the public and also reduced demand on operational officers and an extremely busy control room.

continued

Racial Incidents Help Line (West Yorkshire Police). To encourage victims to report racially motivated incidents to the police, a "Help Line" facility has been introduced which is connected to an answerphone. Its availability is widely publicized with particular emphasis on Asian Women Support Groups to encourage the reporting of offences against women and children. It provides a positive source of assistance and reassurance for that community.

Report to the Community (Gloucestershire Police). Detailed reports are provided annually to the local communities by each Area Commander. The reports address many of the policing issues frequently of concern to local communities and often raised by representatives of various organizations. Also provided are details of establishment, the demands placed upon police resources, and explanations of current policing strategies and initiatives. The reports are designed to appeal to a wide readership.

Magazine Produced by the Police Authority and Police Force (Merseyside Police). The Police Authority and Police Force jointly produce a magazine for public consumption entitled "Together." The magazine includes items on community issues, crime prevention, policing policies and procedures, articles of particular relevance to the area, information regarding the various watch schemes and other matters of interest.

Police Community Charity (Greater Manchester Police). The Force administers the Greater Manchester Police Community Charity, launched with the aim of helping those less fortunate in the community. Grants are given to worthy causes and serve to offset publicity and promote a high-profile police image.

Young Citizen of the Year Award (Greater Manchester Police). The Force sponsors a "Young Citizen of the Year Award" which seeks to encourage good citizenship and identifies the efforts of young people within the community. Of the total nominations received from schools, ten go forward for final consideration. The winner is awarded £500 (pounds sterling), together with a check for £500 to the recipient's chosen charity.

Domestic Violence Monitoring Unit (South Wales Police). Family support units have been introduced in various parts of the Force area, and within these units a small team is dedicated to the monitoring, investigation if necessary, advising [and] assisting in cases of domestic violence. All incidents are reported to the unit and action taken as appropriate. This positive approach to the increasing problem of domestic violence has enhanced confidence in injured parties, demonstrating the Force's determination to deal effectively with such matters.

Sir John Woodcock, *Directory of Good Practice* (London: Her Majesty's Inspectorate of the Constabulary, 1992).

QUESTIONS FOR DISCUSSION

1. Why is policing inevitably political?
2. Explain the political nature of police-community relations and community policing.
3. Discuss the relationship between police administration and politics.
4. What is "Blue Power?" How should police manager deal with unions?
5. Discuss some of the major labor issues that may have an impact on the implementation of the community policing philosophy.
6. Why is crime so amenable to political gamesmanship?
7. What is the relationship between police-community relations and crime prevention?
8. Distinguish between "specific" and "general" crime prevention.
9. Explain why an increase of community participation in crime-control activities may cause crime rates go up, at least in the short run.
10. What relationship is there between crime and the quality of life in a neighborhood?

NOTES

1. James Q. Wilson, "The Police and Their Problems: A Theory," *Public Policy*, Yearbook of the Harvard University Graduate School of Public Administration (Cambridge, MA, 1963). Reprinted by permission.

2. William Ker Muir, Jr., *Police: Streetcorner Politicians* (Chicago: The University of Chicago Press, 1977).

3. Ibid., pp. 280–282.

4. International City Management Association, *Local Government and Police Management* (Washington, DC: ICMA, 1977), p. 37.

5. See George Kelling and Catherine Coles, *Fixing Broken Windows* (New York: Free Press, 1996).

6. Confidential interview of a Texas police chief on a crime-specific policing project for the *Texas Law Enforcement Management Institute*, 1997.

7. Wilson, *Varieties of Police Behavior*, p. 230. See also James Q. Wilson, *City Politics and Public Policy* (New York: John Wiley & Sons, 1968).

8. Wilson, "The Police and Their Problems," p. 233.

9. Edward C. Banfield and James Q. Wilson, *City Politics* (Cambridge, MA: Harvard University Press, 1963), p. 18.

10. Ibid., Texas Law Enforcement Management Institute, 1997.

11. Norval Morris and Gordon Hawkins, *The Honest Politician's Guide to Crime Control* (Chicago: University of Chicago Press, 1969).

12. George L. Keling, Robert Wassermann, and Hubert Williams, "Police Accountability and Community Policing," *Perspectives on Policing*, (Washington, DC: National Institute of Justice and Kennedy School of Government, Harvard University, 1988).

13. Herman Goldstein, *Problem-Oriented Policing* (New York: McGraw-Hill Publishing Company, 1990).

14. Terry Eisenberg and Sharon Lawrence, *Citizen/Police Relations in Police Policy Setting*. Final Report, October 31, 1980, Los Gatos, Calif., Institute for Social Analysis (Grant No. 79-Ni-AX-0004, National Institute of Justice, U.S. Dept. of Justice).

15. See U.S., President's Commission of Law Enforcement and the Administration of Justice, *Task Force Report: The Police* (Washington, D.C.: U.S. Government Printing Office, 1967), p. 18.

16. Ibid., p.26.

17. U.S. National Advisory Commission on Criminal Justice Standards and Goals, *Report on Police* (Washington, DC: U.S. Government Printing Office, 1973), p. 50.

18. Elmer H. Johnson, "Interrelatedness of Law Enforcement Programs: A Fundamental Dimension," *Journal of Criminal Law, Criminology and Police Science* 60, no. 4 (December 1969): 510–511. Reprinted by special permission of the *Journal of Criminal Law and Criminology*. Copyright © by Northwestern University School of Law, vol. 60, no. 4.

19. Quoted in *Atlantic* (March 1969): 130.

20. Floyd Hunter, *Community Power Structure* (Chapel Hill: University of North Carolina Press, 1933). See also C. Wright Mills, *The Power Elite* (New York: Oxford University Press, 1956).

21. John E. Angell, "Toward an Alternative to the Classical Police Organizational Arrangements: A Democratic Model" (monograph, School of Criminal Justice, Michigan State University, 1970). See Max Weber, *Essays in Sociology*, translated and edited by Hans Gerth and C. Wright Mills (New York: Oxford University Press, 1958); see also Reinhard Bendix, *Max Weber: An Intellectual Portrait* (Garden City, NY: Doubleday, 1962).

22. Angell, "Toward an Alternative."

23. Ibid. See also Alan A. Atshuler, *Community Control* (New York: Western Publishing, 1970); Milton Kotler, *Neighborhood Government* (New York: Bobbs-Merrill, 1969).

24. George Kelling and Catherine Coles, *Fixing Broken Windows* (New York: Free Press, 1996).

25. Albert J. Reiss, Jr., and David J. Bordua, "Environment and Organization: A Perspective on the Police," in Bordua, ed., *The Police: Six Sociological Essays* (New York: John Wiley & Sons, 1967) p. 52. Reprinted by permission.

26. Ibid., p. 26.

27. Roy Roberg and Jack Kuykendall, *Police Management*, 2d ed. (Los Angeles, CA: Roxbury Press, 1997).

28. See Allan D. Hamann and Rebecca Becker, "The Police and Partisan Politics in Middle-sized Communities," *Police* 14, no. 6 (1970): 18–23.

29. U.S. National Commission on the Causes and Prevention of Violence, *The Politics of Protest: Violent Aspects of Protest and Confrontation* (Washington, DC: U.S. Government Printing Office, 1969), pp. 201–217.

30. For example, Hugh O'Neill, "The Growth of Municipal Employee Unions," *Unionization of Municipal Employees: Proceedings of the Academy of Political Science* 30, no. 2 (1970); Jack Stieber, *Public Employee Unionism: Structure, Growth, Policy* (Washington, DC: Brookings Institution, 1973); Tim Bornstein, "Police Unions: Dispelling the Ghost of 1919," *Police Magazine* 1, no. 4 (September 1978): 25–29; C. A. Salerno, *Police at the Bargaining Table* (Springfield, Ill.: Charles C Thomas, 1981); D. Forcese, "Police Unionism—Employee-Management Relations in Canadian Police Forces," *Canadian Police College Journal* 4, no. 2 (1980): 70–129.

31. Robert M. Igleburger and John E. Angell, "Dealing with Police Unions," *Police Chief* 38, no. 5 (May 1971): 50–55; Talcott Parsons and Edward Shils, eds., *Toward a General Theory of Action* (New York: Harper & Brothers, 1962).

32. Igleburger and Angell, "Dealing with Police Unions," p. 55. Reprinted by permission.

33. See John A. Grimes, "The Police, the Union, and the Productivity Imperative," in *Readings on Productivity in Policing* (Washington, DC: Police Foundation, 1975), pp. 47–85.

34. David L. Carter, Allen D. Sapp, and Darrel W. Stephens, *A National Study of Police Labor Relations: Critical Findings* (Washington: Police Executive Research Forum, 1990).

35. Paul Cromwell, James N. Olson, and D'Aunn Wester Avary, *Breaking and Entering: An Ethnographic Analysis of Burglary* (Newbury Park, CA: Sage Publications, 1991).

36. Richard Holden, *Law Enforcement: An Introduction* (New York: Prentice Hall, 1992).

37. For more information see: Bruce L. Berg, *Law Enforcement: An Introduction to Police in Society* (Boston: Allyn and Bacon, 1992) pp. 74–77.

38. *Op. cit.* Cromwell, et al., (1991).

39. Dennis P. Rosenbaum, ed., *Community Crime Prevention: Does It Work?*, (Beverly Hills, CA: Sage Publications, 1986).

40. Michael Banton, "The Definition of the Police Role," *New Community* 3, no. 3 (1974): 164–171. Much of this issue is devoted to articles on police and community relations.

41. Michael Banton, "Crime Prevention in the Context of Criminal Policy," *Police Studies* 1, no. 2 (June 1978): 3. Copyright © 1978.

42. See Terry V. Wilson and Paul Q. Fuqua, *The Police and the Media* (Boston: Little, Brown Educational Associates, 1975).

43. U.S. Bureau of the Census, *Oakland (CA)—Public Attitudes About Crime* and *San Francisco (CA)—Public Attitudes About Crime*, National Criminal Justice Information and Statistics Service, LEAA, 1978.

44. See Robert C. Trojanowicz and Bonnie Bucqueroux, *Community Policing* (Cincinnati, OH: Anderson Publishing Company, 1990).

45. David L. Carter, *Law Enforcement Intelligence Operations* 4th ed. (East Lansing, MI: School of Criminal Justice, Michigan State University, 1997).

46. Peter K. Manning, "Dramatic Aspects of Policing: Selected Propositions," *Sociology and Social Research* 59, no. 1 (October 1974): 22. The list following the quote is paraphrased from the same article. Much of this and related articles by Peter Manning are incorporated in his *Police Work: The Social Organization of Policing* (Cambridge, MA: MIT Press, 1977).

47. David L. Carter and Allen D. Sapp, "Program Evaluation Model for Community Policing" in Larry Hoover, *Program Evaluation* (Washington, DC: Police Executive Research Forum, 1998).

48. James Q. Wilson and George L. Kelling, "Broken Windows: The Police and Neighborhood Safety," *Atlantic*, 256 March (1982) pp. 29–38.

49. George L. Kelling, "Police and Communities: the Quiet Revolution," *Perspectives on Policing* (Washington, DC: National Institute of Justice and Kennedy School of Government, Harvard University, 1988).

50. See Gary T. Marx and Dane Archer, "Citizen Involvement in the Law Enforcement Process," *American Behavioral Scientist* 15, no. 1 (September–October 1971). This article evaluates citizen self-defense groups.

51. Canadian Criminology and Corrections Association, *Crime: A Community Responsibility* (October 1976). See also J. S. Hacker, *Prevention of Youthful Crime—The Great Stumble Forward* (Agincourt, Ontario: Methuen, 1978). The Office of the Solicitor General in Ottawa has additional materials available.

52. U.S. National Advisory Commission on Criminal Justice Standards and Goals, *Report on Community Crime Prevention* (Washington, DC: U.S. Government Printing Office, 1973).

53. Panel Discussion on "Citizen Participation in Crime Reduction" (John C. Klotter, et. al., *The Police Yearbook, 1978*, International Association of Chiefs of Police.

54. See Canada Law Reform Commission, *Working Paper 7, Diversion* (Ottawa: Canada Law Reform Commission, 1975).

55. See William L. Selke, "Diversion and Crime Prevention," *Criminology* 20, no. 2, 3, and 4 (November 1982): 395–406.

56. U.S. National Advisory Commission on Criminal Justice Standards and Goals, *Report on Criminal Justice System* (Washington, DC: U.S. Government Printing Office, 1973), p. 1.

Chapter 16

THE MEDIA

The public and political concern about crime-related issues (as discussed in the last chapter) is a natural focal point for the media. Serial murders, sexual assaults, public corruption, drive-by shootings, conspiracies, armored car robberies, kidnappings and the like, capture public fascination and, consequently, media attention. When fear grips a community about a crime wave, the media report it and then turn to the police to see what they are going to do about it. If it appears that the police are not making progress, the media asks why. If police officials seem less than candid, the media will comment on it. If officers are involved in misconduct, the media will immediately and fully report it. These are not criticisms; it is the obligation, professional and ethical, of journalists to inform the public and hold public officials accountable.

While the reporting of these stories sometimes irritates law enforcement officials, they grudgingly recognize a reporter's responsibilities. Similarly, the police will frequently call on the media to assist in locating persons or to provide public information on specific issues or problems. In these cases, the media is viewed in a different light.

The media has been characterized as the "fourth estate." The other three "estates" are the executive, legislative, and judicial branches of government. The media interacts with all branches of government at all levels—local, state and federal—on a daily basis serving as a surrogate watchdog for the public. Certainly there are unethical reporters and media organizations, just as there are unethical practitioners of any profession. Generally speaking, however, media representatives view their roles professionally and will try to work with the police in a cooperative spirit.

The singular importance of the media as the primary communications vehicle between the police and public is too evident to require elaboration. Suffice it to note at this point, since public opinion about crime and criminals is substantially influenced by media reports, that what the police do and how they do it are subject to constant monitoring.

Indeed, in a broader sense, in democratic societies where the media are not captives of government, relationship problems between governmental bodies and the media are endemic to political processes. Conflict of interest is, to some degree, embedded in their relationship, and this conflict is seen as a vital aspect of the checks and balances so essential in a democracy. If the newspapers and other media did not "police" the police and other government entities, if they did not challenge information and interpret messages between criminal justice agencies and the public, they would be shirking a significant responsibility.

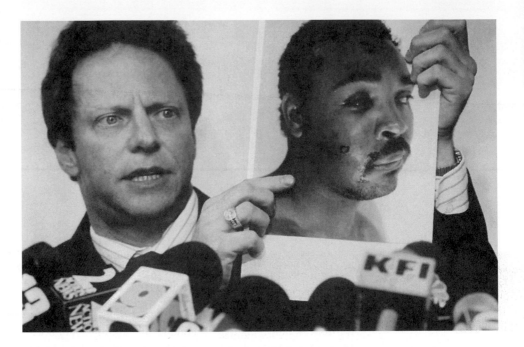

". . . since public opinion about crime and criminals is substantially influenced by media reports, that what the police do and how they do it are subject to constant monitoring."

WHO ARE "THE MEDIA" AND WHAT IS THEIR INFLUENCE?

The police-media relationship consistently generates arguments about the other's behavior. "The police are trying to hide information the public has a right to know," the media argues. "Your endless efforts to get information will jeopardize our investigation and threaten the safety of undercover officers," the police respond. "You are trying to cover-up police wrongdoing," asserts the media. "We are trying to conduct an impartial investigation and protect the rights of all parties involved," retort the police. The relationship is clearly a bittersweet one, which can change dramatically from one of mutual respect to one of reciprocal disdain.

There are some basic facts about the media that should be clear from the outset:

- The police feel they are often the recipient of biased coverage and sensationalism from the media.
- The media feel that the police are unduly closedmouthed on issues about which the public has a right to know.
- The public learns about crime and policing issues—including police misconduct—from the media.
- The police and the media need each other.

The media include sources that are electronic (radio and television) and print (newspapers and magazines). Traditionally, they could be categorized as being oriented toward either news or entertainment. However, this line of distinction has become increasingly blurred in recent years. Television shows such as "Donahue," "Oprah," and "Geraldo" offer a "discussion" format on a wide range of topics—

current events, politics, fashion, or entertainment—which are hoped to be of interest to the public. Other shows, such as "Inside Edition" and "Hard Copy" are presented in the form of news shows, yet have a distinctive sensationalist flavor—a format increasingly referred to as "tabloid TV." And then there is talk radio—"Larry King," "Rush Limbaugh," and many programs at the local level—which also address contemporary issues and allow listeners to call in and offer opinions. This broad genre of media, which is in the blurred area between news and entertainment, is sometimes referred to as "info-tainment."

News Media

Although we hear a great deal about national news organizations—ABC, CBS, CNN, NBC, Fox News, Gannett News Service, Associated Press, United Press International—the police are mostly concerned with their local news organizations. Most areas that are large enough to have a police department are also large enough to have their own newspaper, even if it is a weekly. Similarly, most areas have some type of radio coverage with the mid-size to larger "markets" having their own television stations.

Large or small, electronic or print, the police are a lightning rod for news. The media have a responsibility to inform the public of critical issues and make a profit. Issues of crime and the police are relevant to both of these goals. Competition for stories, aggressive questioning to get as much information as possible in time for a deadline, and cynicism about pronouncements made by public officials all contribute to perceptions that reporters are "arrogant bastards just looking for sensationalistic dirt," as one assistant chief of police told the author. Conversely, the need to balance individual rights with the public's right to know, the need to appear professional and objective, and the desire to not compromise ongoing investigations make comments by the police appear to be "a fanfare of bland pronouncements with absolutely no meaning which are shrouded in 'cop-speak'," as observed by a television reporter to the author.

Both the news media and the police clearly understand the positions of the other, so the quest to use each other effectively becomes a cat-and-mouse game. Virtually every reporter covering a "police beat" has contacts within the police department who will give them "background" information (comments off-the-record) or provide substantive information, which can be reported and attributed to a "highly placed reliable source." Similarly, police officials have contacts in the news media whom they can ask for assistance.

The news media attempt to deal in corroborated fact. Info-tainment programming has a tendency to deal in rumor and facts that may be unsubstantiated. The entertainment media tends to focus on fantasy. This still presents problems for law enforcement.

Entertainment Media

Over the years we have seen many characterizations of the police in the entertainment media. The early cinematic portrayals of the *Keystone Cops* showed ineptitude. Similarly, the 1950s series "Car 54 Where Are You?" portrayed two New York City police officers who were nice, genuine people, but not very bright. Television shows such as "Dragnet" and "Adam-12" changed these perspectives significantly, portraying officers as professional, detached crime fighters (the epitome of reform era policing, which sought to "get the facts, just the facts") who always found their criminal.

FOCUS 16.1

TIPS FOR CREATING EFFECTIVE PUBLIC SERVICE ANNOUNCEMENTS

An important element in working with the electronic media to educate the public is through the use of Public Service Announcements (PSAs). Before deciding to develop a PSA, make sure you know what you hope to accomplish with the announcement that cannot be effectively accomplished through other means. Once the PSA goal is clear, there are some basic tips useful for creating the most effective announcements.

- Use no more than one or two points—keep the ad simple so it is more understandable.
- Show both the problem *and* the solution, with greater emphasis on the latter.
- Consider creating a character (such as "McGruff the Crime Dog") to use regularly in order to identify the theme of the PSA.
- Consider using citizens who speak from experience in order to lend credibility to the message.
- Demonstrate *what* you want people to do or *how* to do it.

This focus changed somewhat with "The Rookies," who became personally involved with citizens' distress and appeared to work in a department that gave them unlimited flexibility. At about the same time, former Los Angeles detective-turned-novelist Joseph Wambaugh's "Police Story" series gave more realism to "TV cops," yet provided a fatalist view of how policing affects the personal life of a police officer.

"Hill Street Blues" introduced another dimension of police work to the public by portraying the more human side of police officers, while also capturing elements of the police subculture. Introducing to the public such terms as "dirt bag" and "sleaze ball," this program illustrated backroom plea negotiations, the diversity of personalities found in law enforcement organizations, and the attitude of "professional irreverence" to life on the streets. "Cagney and Lacey" gave us two women investigators in New York whose characters were both professional and personalized. "Miami Vice" gave the public yet another vision of law enforcement. This time, undercover work that had money, fashion, sex, violence, and crime control, all in an exotic location, was wrapped into a single hour. "NYPD Blue" and "Brooklyn South" built on this popularity, pushing new limits on broadcast television, particularly regarding language and sex.

Because of broadcast restrictions, television shows had limitations on how they portrayed officers; this has not been the case with motion pictures. *Dirty Harry*, the renegade, unaccountable, and lethal San Francisco police inspector who made a practice of having criminals "make his day" set a new standard for violence by police officers. The *Lethal Weapon* series clearly reinforced this. *RoboCop* offered a still different perspective, emphasizing the violence faced by police. *Silence of the Lambs* provided an insight into the more intellectual side of investigative problem-solving, although the concept of an FBI agent in training working on a major case

- Plan a 30-second PSA for prime time—you are more likely to get it.
- Consider the simplest way to deliver the message; typically a credible person talking directly to the viewer.
- Keep phone numbers on a TV screen for at least eight seconds in order that people may write it down; repeat phone numbers on radio.
- Use close-ups for interest and impact.
- Start the PSA with something that arouses curiosity or is startling to get the viewer's or listener's attention.
- Avoid musical announcements unless they are high quality.
- Use superimposed words on the screen to reinforce main points or slogans.
- If the PSA has something that can be shown to illustrate the point, use a "voice-over" announcer; otherwise have the announcer on-camera.
- Limit the number of camera scenes to avoid confusion and simplify the message.
- Effectively use emotion to involve your audience; in the ideal situation, the viewer will not just see and/or hear the message, the viewer will "feel" the emotion of it.

Since commercial radio and television time is at a premium, and considerable effort is devoted to preparing and creating a Public Service Announcement, it is only reasonable to make the PSA as effective as possible.

was surrealistic. The contribution that the series of *Police Academy* movies has given to policing is inexplicable! Regardless of the premise, once can bet that each new movie season will include a "cop movie."

There have been so many movies and television shows about the police it is impossible to discuss them all. Some of the popular portrayals, with their diverse approaches to law enforcement, have illustrated how unrealistic views of the police are created by entertainment media. Consistent themes begin to emerge. After viewing hours of television shows or motion pictures, an unsuspecting citizen may draw some erroneous conclusions about the police:

- Internal affairs investigators are doing a disservice to "real policing" by trying "to get" street cops who are doing a tough job.
- Violence is an accepted and frequent tool of policing; officers may shoot at will and have little accountability.
- The police have an unlimited budget when it comes to crime-fighting.
- A police officer's working hours are spent constantly dealing with major crime.
- Police officers rarely have to write reports about their escapades; when they are required to write a report, they are able to delay it by being insubordinate to a supervisor or manager.
- The police have virtually no contact with law-abiding citizens (who are not victims).
- Police computer systems have virtually unlimited information about citizens and can be accessed from any police computer terminal.
- All police officers have access to an Automated Fingerprint Identification System (AFIS) and can determine identities with a fragment of a fingerprint.

In fact, the media portrayed common usage of AFIS-type systems before the technology was available.

- Patrol officers are not "real cops"; they are the least experienced, least informed, and do less crime fighting of all officers; detectives and undercover officers are "real cops."
- Federal agents are smarter and better investigators who deal with "real crime," compared with local police officers.
- When a crime occurs, it gets immediate and undivided attention by patrol officers and detectives alike.
- There is danger around every corner.
- Motorcycle officers—complete with helmet, leather leggings, bloused trousers, and mirrored sunglasses—are really neo-Nazis.
- Police managers and administrators are purely political animals who only look out for themselves and are operationally inept.
- The most effective police officers are renegades who do not adhere to departmental regulations and are able to follow their own instincts; in fact, rules hamper them from doing "real police work."
- The essence of being a good police officer requires being tough, not intelligent.

It is clear that people learn from the media. We develop attitudes about public issues and controversies—abortion, ecology, the economy, health care, and crime—based largely on media reports. Unfortunately, even fictional portrayals influence beliefs and attitudes. The line of distinction between news, "info-tainment," and entertainment is not clearly drawn in the minds of many people. Consequently, their assumptions about "crime, cops, courts, and cons" may be influenced by the imaginative creativity of a production company rather than fact. The socializing effect of the media is a difficult thing for the police to overcome.[1] When the police do not meet the standards of their fictional counterparts, there emerges a police-community relations problem that must be resolved through both communications and public education.

Any discussion of the media—news or entertainment—must be prefaced with a clear understanding. Whether it seems logical or not, attitudes and beliefs of much of the public are profoundly influenced by news broadcasts, commentary, and entertainment portrayals. To discount this fact is to ignore a major socializing influence in our society.

A COMPLICATED RELATIONSHIP

The relationship between a police agency and media enterprises looks simple but is actually more complicated than first appears. Obviously, police cultivation of good relations with the media is important. It is a logical way to keep the public informed of what is going on in a police department and why. But when a police department hedges on publicity, or a newspaper or other medium violates what the police view as the ethics or ground rules of reporting crime news, problems arise.

Such clashes are most likely to appear when the police deem it necessary to withhold information from the media because the release of certain information would thwart police objectives. It can also happen when the media get on the spoor of what they sense to be misconduct or corruption within a criminal justice agency. For whatever reasons, the impression may be created that somebody is not playing fair with the media, which the media have a habit of translating into the accusation of not playing fair with the public. Yet it may well be that, because of the circumstances, full disclosure of all available information is *not* in the best interests of either the criminal justice agency or of the public.

Thus, the dialogue between a particular police department and particular newspapers or television stations may become quite caustic. Administrative judgments on withholding information are occasionally questioned by the media, and their questions transmitted to the public, to the possible disadvantage of the administrator. Because the administrator cannot explain a decision without disclosing information that he or she believes is best withheld, a terse "no comment" may be interpreted as pugnacity or evasiveness. This dilemma of police-media relations is a typical one in police administration.

There may also be a dilemma on the media side. As noted previously, a newspaper and a radio or television station are ordinarily profit-making enterprises. They also have responsibilities to the public interest. Whatever dilemma arises from these partly conflicting objectives is reconciled by the decisions of media executives, recognized by the public only in somewhat detached notions as to what constitutes a "responsible" newspaper or television station. Public tastes and tolerances in such a matter are as varied and fickle as in their choice of soft drink. Clearly, the public interest is not always best served by the profit-making policies or practices of the media. Among other things, this principle of the public interest might—more often than it does—call into question a newspaper's use of such slogans as "the public's right to know" in a manner suggesting a right as unquestionable as that of life itself. From time to time, one suspects that the media is really using an excuse for doing, in the name of the public interest, what best serves its profit motive. (Sorry about that bit of cynicism, but it is particularly evident in television during the "sweeps weeks.")

So we have a dilemma on the police side of the relationship, and another on the media side. And as Winston Churchill might have put it, we also have a conundrum within the dilemma. For the newspaper, in a highly competitive market, often finds its premium story to be what the police (or the prosecutor, or the court) are most reluctant to disclose. This dual dilemma and the conundrum constitute the essence of the relationship problem of the police and the media—of criminal justice and the media. The ramifications touch on such matters as the fierce competitive dynamics within the media world, the deadline, sensationalism and so-called yellow journalism, the scoop, free press versus fair trial, and disclosure of information sources.

THE DISCLOSURE OF INFORMATION

When, therefore, the discussion turns to issues in police-media relations, there is no escaping the larger context of these issues. The conflicts of interest involved are, at once, as ancient and as current as democratic government. Take the central question of public access to information about governmental operations.

> This conflict often pits the President and the Executive Branch against Congress, regulatory agencies against consumer interests, bureaucrats against environmentalists, Congress against the voter, the courts against the bar and, at times, the news media against all of them.[2]

With respect to what he called "a current cliché from the political lexicon—the people's right to know," John Steele observed:

> The Constitution, as it happens, does not provide for any such right. The courts, moreover, have never interpreted the First Amendment—which prohibits Congress from abridging freedom of speech or the press—as requiring the Government to make unlimited disclosures about its activities.[3]

An uncurbed right to know eventually collides dramatically with what might be called the right *not* to know. Many historians, philosophers, political scientists, and even a few journalists have conceded that there must be some limit to the right of the public to have information about government. By the same token, the right of the government to maintain secrecy must also be restricted. "We can give up a little freedom without surrendering all of it. We can have a little secrecy without having a Government that is altogether secret. Each added measure of secrecy, however, measurably diminishes our freedom."[4]

So the question is: How much secrecy? Under what specific conditions, and by whose judgment, may government officials operate "on and off the record"? Inquisitive news people, as well as inquisitive congressional and private investigators, have turned up some appalling incidents of bare-faced news control by government. No one seems to be willing to admit knowing much about criteria for such control. In fact, sometimes the justification for secrecy seems to be no better than apathy or red tape, or melancholy evidence of the effectiveness of special interest lobbies and pressure groups. Congress has passed little legislation relating to the disclosure of official information in the public interest. The Freedom of Information Act has proved inadequate, because it permits the agency which is the "custodian of the records" to "sanitize" them in order to protect national security or protect individual rights. Despite this limitation, the FOIA has been increasingly used by news organizations, particularly for investigative reporting.

The media, of course, are also subject to criticism. One criticism of the media is that they are, at times, too considerate of the sensibilities of government officials who try to manage the news. The abuse of trust where privileged information has been made available has also occurred. For instance, liberties are sometimes taken with informational release deadlines: "Not to be released prior to 12:01 A.M." on such and such a date. More serious breaches of confidence occur under competitive duress. So it is that we have another two-sided street here, calling for compromise in carefully worked-out ground rules and guidelines, while recognizing that excesses on either side threaten rights best safeguarded by a kind of constructive, creative tension in the relationship. The challenge is again to turn indigenous conflict to constructive ends, to "structure" the relationship by voluntary guidelines, to maximize cooperation and minimize vituperation, in the public interest.

Senator Daniel P. Moynihan contributed a helpful analysis. Writing about the changing relationship between the presidency and the press, he identified five factors:

1. The journalistic tradition of muckraking—the exposure of corruption in government or of the collusion of government with private interests—while still very much alive in the reportorial spirit, is giving way to . . . "the adversary culture" as an element in journalistic practice. Common to both, however, is a mistrust of Government.

2. Journalism has become, if not an elite profession, then at least a profession attractive to elites. The political consequence of the rising social status of journalism is that the press grows more influenced by attitudes genuinely hostile to American society and American government.

3. Washington reporters depend heavily on more or less clandestine information from Federal bureaucracies which are frequently, in some cases routinely, antagonistic to Presidential interests. When the bureaucracies think their interests are threatened, they often turn to the press. Both bureaucrats and journalists "stay in town"; Presidents come and go.

4. Questions of objectivity are often raised in reporting the statements of public figures. While the tradition in journalism is to print "the news," whether or not the reporter

or the editor or the publisher likes it, there is a rub when it comes to a question of whether an event really is news—or simply a happening, staged for the purpose of getting into the papers. The issue, then, is: what is journalistic objectivity, and what is merely an excuse for avoiding judgment? If it becomes clear that someone is lying or "playing games," why print it—or at least, why print it on the front page?

5. Finally, and most important, there is the absence in American journalism of a professional tradition of self-correction—a mark of any developed profession. Honest mistakes ought to be seen as integral to the process of advancing the field. But journalism will never attain to any such condition.[5]

In light of these factors two points should be emphasized. (1) that in the eyes of the media in a democracy, it is hard for government to succeed, even when it has indeed done so; and (2) the conditions are thus set for protracted conflict in which the government "keeps losing." And this is a serious matter of national morale, for which a better balance is needed. He seemed to admit, implicitly, that there was another side to the argument, but he did not spell it out. Perhaps, he said, some sort of national press council would help. But Moynihan backed off and contended that such a council would be the wrong thing to create in this country at this time; there is, he asserted, "a statist quality" to many of the existing press councils abroad. He thought the American press should become much more open about acknowledging mistakes. As for government, he observed that misrepresentations or mistakes of government performance should never be allowed to go unchallenged. The impact of the media on the hearings of Clarence Thomas to serve as Supreme Court Justice serves as one vivid example. So does the disclosure that President Clinton's initial nominee for Attorney General had violated the law by hiring undocumented aliens. Had it not been for the media's vigilance, the public would not have reacted.

BIG GOVERNMENT V. BIG MEDIA

In 1734, John Peter Zenger was accused of libel and jailed for printing in his weekly paper repeated attacks on the colonial governor, William Cosby. A jury finally acquitted him after long deliberation, helping to establish the right of newspapers to criticize the government. Subsequently, this principle was further enshrined by the journalistic activities of Ben Franklin, Thomas Paine, and many others.

This incident may seem to have little to do with police-media relations. Further thought suggests, however, that the larger context of the relationship between a specific police agency and a specific newspaper or TV station is the jousting of Big Government and Big Media.

The gravity of the issues in this drama is beyond question. While government (the police and the criminal justice system are favorite targets, but not, by any means, the sole ones) appears to be increasingly the object of public scrutiny and inquiry, the media also seem to be under more critical examination. One frequent charge is bias. The specifics vary. The poor and the nonwhite accuse the media of unfair treatment. Minorities have long since had their own newspapers, magazines, and radio stations, and alienated groups have had their underground press. These media are especially critical of the police. Recent Asian immigrants are saying that they are not fairly treated by the media. Young radicals proclaim that the popular media distort their image. The police often accuse the media of prejudiced reporting, and sometimes of generalizing to all police based on the actions of a few. (Mark Fuhrman's racist comments during the O.J. Simpson trial is one illustration.) The National Commission on the Causes and Prevention of Violence stated that "a crisis of confidence exists today between the American people and their news media."[6] The

Kerner Commission devoted considerable attention to media reporting, charging that the media had failed to communicate adequately on race relations and ghetto problems, and had failed further to bring more blacks into journalism. Even in Los Angeles in 1992, the live reporting of the Los Angeles civil disturbance was criticized for adding "fuel to the fire."

In short, the so-called credibility gap in the relationship between government and citizens seems to be matched by the credibility gap between the media and "the masses." One explanation for the gap in the late 1960s and early 1970s was the apparently increasing political polarization of the nation. (Indicators from various public opinion surveys suggest that the media is consistently viewed as being "more politically liberal" than the general public.) People "strike out at the messenger who delivers the bad news."[7] Another explanation is distortion of the news by the media, through editorial bias, economic or political pressure, and so on. Still another explanation is the charge that the media have not adapted well to the times, and they have failed to identify for themselves a constructive role in interpreting social change and social conflict. Indeed, there are charges that the media aggravate social conflict by their definition of what constitutes news and by various journalistic tactics that place undue—and sometimes distorted—emphasis on selected aspects of news stories. Newspapers appear, however, to be moving away from the "shotgun" approach, the front-page buildup, with splashy pictures and box scores of the latest crisis. Dramatic but meaningless predictions have also largely disappeared. But serious problems remain. Glaring instances of inaccuracy, exaggeration, distortion, misinterpretation, and bias still occur in all types of news media, as pointed out by the U.S. Commission on Civil Rights.[8] Unprofessional news reporting and unprofessional police behavior represent two sides of what is often unprofessional police-media relations.

Americans, it seems, are viewing or hearing the news more and liking it less. There is obviously enormous power represented by approximately 1,750 daily, 575 Sunday, and 8,000 weekly newspapers; 150 general editorial magazines; more than 6,400 radio stations; and almost 1,000 television outlets, not to mention 24-hour news on CNN, CNBC, and Fox, as well as *USA Today* as "the nation's newspaper." Add to this the vast amount of news and information available on the Internet. The wear-and-tear of competition, increasing publication and circulation costs, the frantic pace of life, and growing public disenchantment with the quality of news reporting are among the factors influencing the media. Politicians, in typical fashion, have moved with what they perceive as a rising tide of criticism directed against the media, and have sought to exploit it for their own political advantage—so emerged the "sound bite" and "photo opportunity."

Some observers who see these signs as threatening the survival of a free press point to various indications of what they interpret as government intimidation of the media. There is concern that distrust of the media apparently increases with education and income level. We have discussed at length the police role predicament in today's society. The media also have a pressing role dilemma. They are expected to stand apart from the society, in a kind of dispassionate, objective, watchdog fashion—despite their other role as members of society, with their own intrinsic pressures and prejudices. To this extent, the similarity in the role predicament of police and press is striking. There are also some differences.

In recent years, the battle of Big Government versus Big Media has been played out spectacularly in such events as the Watergate, the Iran-Contra affair, Whitewater, and improprieties in raising campaign funds. The seamier aspects of government-media relations are often revealed in such situations, where reputations of newsworthy people are at stake and moderation gives way to brawling. But these situations also call attention to the watchdog role of the media. Media coverage of Oliver North's testimony and Supreme Court Justice Clarence Thomas' confirmation hearings were massive examples of the media "riding herd" on government—"doing our job," as media people like to say.

It is not unusual for big-power economic or political confrontations to largely ignore the interests of third parties. Labor-management strife is one illustration. The "G7 countries" making political-economic decisions for the Third World is another. Big Media versus Big Government appears to be another. The third party, generically, is the public, which directs accusations of a credibility gap against both media and government. Where there is power, there is always the question of control. In this confrontation, it is a question of control of the media by the government, or control of the government by the media. Put another way, the ultimate conflicts of interest must be controlled through a negotiated balance of power, lest the conflicts destroy the system or the society.

In a provocative book, John Hohenberg refers to the tendency in public discourse to blame every problem on "a crisis of confidence" in the institutions of democratic society. Under these circumstances, he says, "when it is difficult for either the governors or the governed to find anybody, outside each other, to blame for their troubles, a certain amount of critical fallout is bound to descend on the press."[9] Some of this is the result of the independent newspaper's contention that it is the principal common medium for discourse between the American government and the American people. Therefore, when the communication channels get clogged, the medium must be prepared to take some of the blame.

> What it all comes down to, in reality, is whether the daily newspaper, as presently constituted, is capable of publishing the news at the same time it is trying to get at the truth. The public, as is evidenced by the widespread use of the phrase "newspaper talk," long ago recognized that the two functions were not necessarily identical. . . . Of course the truth is hard to come by in the complicated modern world. But neither the elite of democratic governments nor the paladins of the press can shrug off public dissatisfaction by pleading that the job is difficult and perhaps even impossible to do to everyone's satisfaction. Two thousand years ago, nobody was satisfied, either, with Pontius Pilate's crafty evasion, "What is truth?"[10]

Debate on journalistic ethics is another aspect of the current public debate on the ethics of politicians, lawyers, judges, and other public officials. The ethical questions being asked of the media include these: Is a story true? Is it fair? Is it biased? Is it an unjustified intrusion into someone's privacy? Is the "reliable source" really reliable? The answers are elusive, but every day thousands of reporters, editors, and publishers implicitly answer these questions by writing the news, each guided by his or her own list of dos and don'ts.

Michael T. Malloy, with television particularly in mind, came to this tentative conclusion:

> So our ethical problems . . . seemed often to boil down to the contradictory professional tasks we set ourselves. To televise reporters who are "involved" yet "objective." To report the facts but not neglect the deeper "truth." To explain complex stories but do it in ninety seconds. To make hard subjects easy and dull ones interesting. To give our audience what it wants and what we (arrogantly?) think it needs.[11]

BIAS AND THE MEDIA

What we said about perception in an earlier chapter implies that all of us are biased in the way we see things, simply because we're human. Yet none of us react joyfully to the charge of being biased, content in the illusion that everyone else is biased except ourselves. Academicians, for example, stand on their objectivity as scholars, often rather pompously, while criticizing "biased journalists." An ultimate absurdity is reached when an investigation to determine whether there is bias is conducted by, let us say, a committee or commission of "impeccable credentials," only to have its report branded as "biased."

What are some specifics of the charges of biased reporting directed at the media? We cannot offer an exhaustive listing, nor do we argue the merits or demerits of any of these allegations, but the following are indicative of typical accusations:

- Reporters today are disproportionately "dogmatic liberals" with a strong "leftward bias" and "a set of automatic reactions" that incline them to "oversimplify" the news. As a result, U.S. journalism is out of touch with the American mainstream.
- The media are unduly subservient to the pressures of advertisers.
- The media are unduly subservient to the pressures of politicians.
- Local media depend too much for news coverage and editorial position on hookups with national networks.
- The media all but ignore stories that challenge their basic editorial positions on favored candidates or proposals.
- The media use chauvinistic criteria in judging what is news.
- The media stress spot reporting, usually confined to the unexpected or the unusual. They neglect perspective reporting.
- The media emphasize tragedy, conflict, disorder, the bizarre, and the like in their reporting and tend to neglect joy, cooperation, peace, good works of ordinary people, and so on. The media are more interested in problems than in solutions, in destruction than in construction, in reaction than in action, in fights than in civil dialogue, in irresponsibility than in responsibility, and so on.
- The media distort by telling only part of a story, by promoting a particular viewpoint, or by slanting a story by headlines or by position in the paper.
- Media reporters sometimes side with protesters and demonstrators, thereby embarrassing the police and making the police task more difficult.
- The media sometimes stage news events.
- Interpretive reporting tends to widen the credibility gap, merely revealing the prejudices of the reporter.
- The media are fascinated with glitter and glamor at the expense of significance.
- The media often label people stereotypically.

Such a litany may strike some readers as bias in itself. The subject is sensitive and provocative, more often than not discussed rather irresponsibly, without recourse to evidence substantiating the charges. Critics of the media are usually just as wrong in their complaints about what the papers *do* print as they are about what they think *ought* to be printed.

One study examined prominent dailies across the country, deliberately excluding New York and Washington papers (lest the survey be considered biased!), to determine what, if any, basis in fact there was for some of the main criticisms.[12] The results indicated that the charge that the front pages are filled with crime and violence was without factual basis. So was the charge that the papers feature mostly local news. So was the charge that newspapers do not print good news, or that they are filled with trivialities. So was the charge that the papers offer only the publishers' opinions. It is now common for newspapers to present a broad range of opinion in the editorial section, often spread across two facing pages. It was also discovered that the papers ran many nonviolent stories about nonviolent people occupied with worthwhile, nonviolent activities.

There will be no end to discussions, sometimes heated, of this matter of bias, whether the target is the media, politicians, or sports broadcasters. Only idealists expect more, in their own biases!

CAMERAS IN THE COURTROOM

The issue of cameras in the courtroom has a direct impact on the public perceptions of the police. It goes without saying that the O.J. Simpson trial was a keystone illustration of this. The defense portrayed the Los Angeles Police Department as corrupt and incompetent. Questions about police procedures during the investigation, evidence collection, and evidence analysis all inferred police wrong doing. Capped by Mark Fuhrman's apparent lies under oath about making racist comments, the image of policing took a terrible beating.

This leads to the development of public doubt about police veracity and fairness. In particular, such circumstances reinforce to people—notably minorities—that their suspicions about the police are true. Such negative circumstances are very difficult to overcome. Placing blame on the media or on cameras in the courtroom is not a reasonable reaction for the police, however. Instead, law enforcement agencies must continue on a positive front, performing their responsibilities in a professional manner.

Today, television cameras in the courtroom are by no means routine, but they are more commonplace than in the past. Some states are far more lenient than others, yet the final decision of whether a case will be televised still remains at the discretion of the judge. While a televised case permits citizens to observe the courts in action as well as ensuring that trials are public, a judge must still balance these benefits with the rights of the accused, because the latter take precedent.

An unresolved question is whether a judge could ban television from a courtroom for public safety interests. If a controversial and emotional case were occurring, could the judge ban televising the case, not because of any threat to the accused's rights, but because the judge felt that public discussion of the issues might be a threat to public safety? The jury is still out on this issue (pardon the pun); however it appears that a judge would have the prerogative.

Public fascination with trials appears to be growing. In recent years, for example, a new cable television service, "Court TV," began operation to provide live courtroom "action" of real cases. The 1991 sexual assault trial of William Kennedy Smith in Palm Beach County, Florida is probably one of the most comprehensive illustrations of "Court TV" and public fascination with the trial process. "Court TV" provided live "gavel to gavel" coverage of the trial including the jury selection. (CNN also carried significant portions of the trial live.) Beyond the coverage of the trial per se, noted attorney F. Lee Bailey served as a commentator, along with a "Court TV" announcer, throughout the trial, making observations about legal strategy, effectiveness of witnesses, and even body language of jurors. Mr. Bailey's performance paralleled that of a "color commentator" in a football game. Public opinion polls were done about the trial as well as the "citizen in the street" type interviews. Interestingly, much of the trial was also carried live throughout the world on CNN-International. While in Spain at the time, the author found that many Europeans had been following the trial and had a fairly good grasp of American courtroom processes.

Media coverage of trials is an excellent means of public education as well as assessment of judicial accountability. Perhaps that is what bothers some judges!

THE MEDIA AND PUBLIC CONFIDENCE

This is not the appropriate place to analyze the function of the media in our society. But its role and responsibility in social conflicts and community crises is clearly our concern.

This is a matter that has not had sufficient attention, although we assume it has been discussed by media executives in their professional conferences. Granting this, one wonders to what extent media executives have joined with other public policy decision-makers in such dialogue.

Consider police and criminal justice decision-makers, for example. Conferences of police managers often get some media attention, in a reportorial way. But there has been little evidence of media leaders engaging in round table policy and planning conversations with police and other criminal justice people (and other community leaders), focusing on strategies and tactics to cope effectively with major community crisis and conflict of one kind or another.

Perhaps the media view such an activity as inappropriate to their role and responsibility. Yet the reporting of crime and disorder—the why and the what and the when and the how—is an extremely important part of comprehensive planning and programming to deal with disruptive social crises. If planning and programming in police and community relations are important, why not media-community relations? Why wait for a blue ribbon commission to report retrospectively about what the media might have done or should have done in cases of civil disorder?

Although the media is not viewed in glowing terms, public opinion polls from 1972 through 1996 found that the public had greater confidence in the media than it did in government (at all levels) and major corporations.[13] (The greatest levels of public confidence were given to universities.) Interestingly, television news receives higher confidence ratings than print media—perhaps because the public can actually observe the television journalists and make some judgment based on their observations.

Despite concerns about reporters being "pushy" or not giving people enough respect, the public tends to feel that the media are honest and fairly objective. Exceptions always arise. During the first night of Operation Desert Storm in 1991, several CNN reporters were in Baghdad, Iraq as the United Nations coalition forces began their bombing of that city. The reporters videotaped dramatic action of bombs, anti-aircraft weapons, tracers, and the sirens and chaos associated with a military attack. The reporters were praised for their efforts. During the ensuing months of the Gulf War a few CNN personnel remained, regularly filing reports (and providing unique intelligence for the military). All of the CNN reports were done with Iraqi censors nearby. Similarly, to be able to stay in Iraq, as well as to ensure their personal safety, the news team had to report selected stories at the insistence of Iraqi officials. Some viewers in America began to see this as being "propaganda" and felt that the CNN crew had "sold out" to the Iraqi government. With this perception, many of the accolades turned to criticism. Public confidence in the media can be fickle.

Many people apparently feel that the media are more interested in making a buck than in the public interest. The other side of this is the media impression that Big Government is intent on increasing its control of the flow of information and defining the nature of public debate.[14] Media leaders indicate that it is difficult to be loved—which is not their aim—and at the same time to be the bearer of bad news. But the fundamental question for the public is, can we believe what we hear or see? Reporters have the same question in dealing with governmental leaders. Again, the problem is credibility. Deception and trickery reach a point where editors and publishers wonder if they can trust their own reporters!

This cursory summary of a complicated issue has the single purpose of suggesting the larger context we earlier noted for the police and criminal justice relationship with the media. Recalling Thomas Jefferson's profound commitment to freedom of the press even at its worst, our commentary concludes as follows:

> The crucial role of journalism in a democracy is to provide a common ground of knowledge and analysis, a meeting place for national debate: it is the link between people and institutions. Without the information provided by newspapers and TV, citizens would have little basis for deciding what to believe and whom to support. Just as a pervasive mistrust of police could cause a breakdown of order, a growing hostility to the press could sever the ligaments of a workable society.[15]

VIOLENCE AND THE MEDIA

With a high level of public concern about violent behavior—particularly that exhibited by youth in the form of gang activity and violence in the schools—an increasingly familiar lament is that violence in the media is the cause of violence in society. As in the case of most broad sweeping statements, there may be a grain of truth, but to say that violence is *caused* by the media is far too simplistic. Peer influence, socialization, the effects of substance abuse, fear, and inadequate communications and negotiation skills are among many factors that contribute to violent behavior.

But let us return to the issue at hand: the media. Think about it: starting at the pre-school level with Big Bird or Barney, we use the media to teach. Sesame Street, the Electric Company, and Mr. Rogers' Neighborhood as well as a plethora of other television programming seeks to teach everything from reading and mathematical skills to social skills and human interaction. From the first classroom experience at age five or so through graduate school, we supplement lectures and discussions with videotapes, movies, recordings, and interactive web sites in order to teach. Moreover, we must admit that much of the educational media, while informative, is not always interesting.

Using the same technologies we also have the entertainment media—whether motion pictures, television, computer games, or Web sites. These outlets have typically been produced to be more entertaining, hence not only holding one's attention longer, but frequently being compelling enough that people will want to visit the medium again. Is it not reasonable to assume that we can learn attitudes and behaviors from entertainment media as easily as educational media? Words and phrases from movies and television often appear in the lexicon of daily language. Why can't behaviors? In all likelihood, they do. That is, it is highly probable that violence—as well as other behaviors which are portrayed in the media—blend into the culture. Even if not "causing" violent behavior, the extensive exposure to assaultive acts appears to build a tolerance for violence, particularly among young people.

The effect of the media on violence is the proverbial "chicken-and-egg" proposition: Are some people predisposed to violence by social, psychological, and/or physical variables for which media violence serve as a "triggering mechanism"? Or does exposure to violence in the media develop a predisposition toward violence that is triggered by other environmental factors? While there are no conclusive findings on this issue, there is sufficient anecdotal evidence to conclude that correlations exist to which society should respond.

This much can be said, as we have earlier mentioned: violence has been ingrained in the American ethos from the beginning of our history. The encounters between the early settlers and the Native Americans were hardly a form of nonviolent social protest. The "winning of the West" was not inspired by a philosophy of live and let live. The violent games played by older generations as children could not be blamed on television, for there was no such thing; but the silent and later sound movies most vivid to many older Americans prompted our quarrels about who would be Roy Rogers or Gene Autrey. Then there are Jackie Chan or Steven Seagal movies, football, boxing, hockey, or even occasional moments of the "tame" sports, such as soccer, baseball, or basketball.

Moreover, graphic violence abounds in great literature and the arts. In Shakespeare's plays, in many of the best known operas, in the works of Victor Hugo, Charles Dickens, or Feodor Dostoyevsky, violence abounds. In nature, violence is a part of life and death. In all human affairs, good confronts evil, and evil is often violent.

So the problem may be, not that the media portray violence, but a question of graphic emphasis, of presenting it as a behavioral model in a multitude of ways, of glamorizing it as the only and best way to solve problems, the sole reality.

Eliot Daley, speaking as a parent, zeroed in on television violence with the observation that the *average* child sees 12,000 TV deaths before he or she is fourteen years old. What is real to these children? Daley asks. Far too many programs, he believes, convey the idea that the manipulation of persons through deceit, guilt, pseudohumor, or brute force is legitimized by the eventual getting of one's way. Small wonder that many of today's children are masters of manipulation. Daley thinks that the underlying difficulty for most young viewers is that programming directed at them is really adult fare presented in juvenile dialect. But children have not sampled enough reality in the world at large to be able to put cartoon violence in a context where it can be funny.[16]

Perhaps this is best satirically illustrated on the Fox network program, "The Simpsons." During this animated program, Bart Simpson likes to watch a cartoon called "The Itchy and Scratchy Show." This "cartoon in a cartoon" portrays a cat and mouse who are in constant conflict. The characters do little but fight and use aggressive violence to harm one another while Bart watches and laughs. Of course, "The Simpsons" is an adult cartoon and "Itchy and Scratchy" is a satire of some traditional children's cartoons such as "Tom and Jerry" or the "Roadrunner" (a personal favorite). Unfortunately, there is a great deal of violence, including cartoons, which is directed toward children's programming with the intent of being slapstick humor. The problem lies in the fact that many children cannot distinguish violence from "slapstick." (It should be noted that there does not appear to be a great media conspiracy among animators to increase levels of youth violence. The motivation, of course, is to increase the number of viewers for commercial purposes.) And finally, an entire sociocultural debate could enter on the contributions of the former MTV program, "Beavis and Butthead."

The National Commission on the Causes and Prevention of Violence concluded that television was loaded with violence; that it was teaching American children

FOCUS 16.2

WRITING A PRESS RELEASE

Police departments often need to issue press releases. Among the reasons are: announcing crime rates, new programs, responding to specific inquiries about crime or officer behavior, providing public safety tips, and announcing changing policies that directly affect the public. Too many times, police press releases sound like a memorandum—this is less than inspirational, particularly when you are attempting to increase enthusiasm. Both form and substance are important for a press release to be effective. Some basic tips include:

- Limit the release to two or three pages of double-spaced type. Editors will not take the time to read a lengthy release (unless it is in direct response to a controversial issue).
- Give the most important information in the first sentences.
- Write the press release in third person, using action verbs.
- Specify when the release may be used (date and time or "For Immediate Release") and include the name, title, address, phone, and fax number of a person who may be contacted for more information.
- Check carefully for factual and typographical errors. Sloppiness may raise questions about the importance and/or accuracy of the release.
- Get to know the kinds of stories the local media prefer as well as the interests of some of the reporters. Send the press release to all who may be interested.

It is relatively easy to have a story broadcast or printed on controversial and sensational issues. Public education and public relations, however, present unique problems. Consequently, press releases must be well-planned and executed in order to have the greatest effect.

moral and social values "inconsistent with civilized society." The commission marshalled some frightening statistics to bolster this charge, and contended that the vast majority of experimental studies bearing on the question have found that observed violence stimulates aggressive behavior. The commission was careful to point out that it did not see television as a principal cause of violence in society. But it is, the commission insisted, a contributing factor. Television entertainment based on violence may be effective merchandising, but it is, the commission observed, "an appalling way to serve a civilization—an appalling way to fulfill the requirements of the law that broadcasting serve the public interest, convenience and necessity.[17] The commission approached the question of television violence with great care, at pains not to make television a scapegoat. It recognized that violence is a complex phenomenon, with complex causes.

Since the Kerner Commission issued its report, there have been significant changes in the entertainment media. For example, in the late 1960s when the report was issued, even the largest cities had only three or four television stations. The evening news was frequently only fifteen minutes, and there were virtually no programs that were exclusively prepared for syndication (such as most of the talk shows now). Today, a viewer has a wide selection of channels—perhaps over one hundred with some cable systems and/or satellite dishes. There are usually several hours of news available, specialized news programs (such as "48 Hours" on CBS or "Prime Time Live" on ABC), both the Fox network and CNN, and of course the "info-tainment" programming discussed earlier.

Special effects in motion pictures as well as the attempt to reflect "real crime" in America push the bounds of violence in the media even further. As observed in a National Crime Prevention Council discussion on the subject:

> Television and film have become the prime information sources for most Americans, particularly adolescents. More and more, recorded music contains social and political content; tabloid talk shows can make it seem that high-risk behaviors are the norm; reality-based TV makes the world look like a very dangerous place. The distinctions between entertainment, news, education, and marketing are blurring, as are standards of right and wrong, acceptable and unacceptable.[18]

So the "bottom line" question is, "Does violence in the media cause violent behavior?" No, media portrayals do not "cause" the behavior. If it did, we would see even higher levels of aggressive violent behavior than we do now. There is, however, an apparent relationship between media violence and actual behavior. This appears to exist in three broad categories:

Socialization.   Repeated exposure to violent acts, particularly when they look realistic and are committed "with justification," will socialize youth to consider violence as an appropriate option to deal with conflict. Moreover, repeated viewing of various violent acts establishes a level of tolerance for the behavior. As an illustration, the first time most people saw the videotape of Rodney King being beaten, they were surprised at the aggressive behavior. However, after viewing the tape as few as two or three times, the visual impact of the violence was significantly less. While this socialization does not "cause" violent behavior, it creates a toleration for it.

Unique Circumstances.   Under certain unique circumstance, it appears that violence in the media may precipitate violence, particularly when a person who views the violence can identify with the conditions of the character. A battered woman who violently retaliates, a minority group member who violently reacts to ongoing discrimination, or gang members who go out after a movie to "claim their turf," all illustrate the unique circumstances in which media portrayals may contribute to violence.

Inducement.   It appears from the research that there are some people who have a greater proclivity toward violence than others. The reasons may be wide-ranging and include such things as being a battered child or a substance abuser. For people in this category, viewing violent movies, particularly repeatedly, may induce them to act on this proclivity. This is not to infer that a frustrated woman taken advantage of by an overbearing husband may take off across the country on a crime spree after seeing

Thelma and Louise. Rather, it is suggested that persons who have thought about committing a violent act and perhaps have prepared themselves for it by purchasing a weapon, may be induced to commit the crime by seeing a similar act portrayed in the media. While not conclusive, some strong evidence in support of this has been found by the FBI's Behavioral Sciences Unit in their research on serial rapists.[19]

The Television Ratings Debate.   In 1993, public concern about violence on television came to a head, prompting a Congressional hearing on the issue. Testimony was primarily centered on the socializing effects of television, particularly as it related to children. Witnesses, mostly relying on unique anecdotes or personal experiences, told of horror stories, and concluded that violent behavior was a specific product of violent television programming. Network executives acknowledged that this concern had some merit (stopping short of full agreement, of course) and immediately created a "self-policing" system by providing advisory notices before programs that had violent content. Some criticism faded away, only to resurface again in late 1994, when critics maintained that the advisories gave insufficient information to parents. Moreover, there was a growing concern about sexual themes in television programming. Network executives and professional organizations once again responded by developing a ratings system to be displayed at the beginning of each program, as well as in television listings.

While the television industry's motives were not entirely altruistic—mainly they wanted to avoid government regulation—their commitment satisfied legislators and most critics. A somewhat confusing television ratings system was implemented in 1995. Amid criticism that the system was too convoluted to be useful, a new simplified system was instituted in 1997. Not surprisingly, measuring the effects of the system is nearly impossible. Despite this, the moves have satisfied many critics who felt that television programming contributed to both violent behavior and decaying social values. Superficial responses to complex problems appear to be commonplace in today's society. Unfortunately, this does little to assist us in solving long-term social problems.

Music

While not traditionally included in references to "the media" when discussing law enforcement, music has had a definite role in influencing attitudes. Music can serve as an emotional motivator to stir people to action. The Quincy Jones production of "We Are The World" stirred compassion, and Lee Greenwood's "Proud To Be An American" stirred patriotism. Music has been used to protest, criticize, support, and comment on various public policy issues throughout our history. It has also had a topical influence on behavior.

When Elvis Presley first emerged on the music scene, his songs of love, supported by the strong (and then unusual) rock-and-roll beat, coupled with his pelvic movements in dancing, provoked an ominous warning: *Rock-and-roll will cause juvenile delinquency*. Obviously, it did not. Did Elvis and other early "rockers" contribute to changing perspectives of love, sexual relationships, recreation, and generally "having fun"? Probably so, but the *caveat* to remember is that the music was a characterization, not a cause, of changing values in American culture as the post-World War II "baby boomers" began entering their teenage years. In essence, the music appears to have helped escort a change of values, perhaps even symbolize a change, but not create the change.

The 1960's probably experienced the single greatest growth in music explicitly intended to comment on and change public policy. Generally embodied in folk songs, the music tended to protest the Vietnam War, while also serving as a commentary on society. One classic example is Arlo Guthrie's "Alice's Restaurant," wherein he humorously comments on the police, courts, military, and government behavior in general. Collectively, the "Woodstock experience" was a musically based event, which turned into a broad symbol of change in American society related to values, personal responsibility, and behavior. Although the cry, "Sex, Drugs, and Rock-and-Roll" was heard loudly and frequently, the music did not cause the change, but ushered in change along with many other social forces, and came to symbolize the emergence of a somewhat different generational culture into early adulthood.

In the late 1980s and at the start of the 1990s, two interesting music trends emerged that symbolized changing social processes. Recall in the discussion of violence in an earlier chapter that one of the observations was that there is a growing cultural distinction in American society. This change includes a greater division between the races as well as the "white backlash" against such things as affirmative action, racial quotas, and devaluation of the traditionally held historical contributions of European-Americans (Christopher Columbus serves as an example). It may be argued that simultaneous growth of two distinctly different music styles reflects these social trends. Does it not seem paradoxical that country music and hip-hop/rap could both significantly grow at the same time?

Building on the idea that music represents social trends, one finds that country music significantly reflects Anglo-American culture and concerns. It symbolizes "Middle America" patriotism, "traditional" lifestyles, the Anglo-American experience in this country, and the comfort of generally "simpler times." Conversely, hip-hop/rap music reflects diversity, freedom of expression, frustration with discrimination, a lack of responsiveness by government to minority concerns, and a growth in multicultural values. These divergent musical trends are consistent with the social trends of increased racial distinction. How much more different could Garth Brooks' album "Ropin' the Wind" be from 2 Live Crew's "As Nasty as They Wanna Be"?

Videos add another dimension to the impact of music because they illustrate the songs in a way previously not available. The video significantly increases the "power" of music (and consequently the message or symbolism of the song) by adding a sense of vision to the recording. Although music has long been associated with motion pictures, music videos are more powerful, since the video explicitly concentrates on the message of the song, and does not serve merely to support the theme of a movie.

As a final observation on music and violence, one cannot overlook the highly controversial song entitled "Cop Killer" by black rapper Ice-T. The rap was said to have been written out of frustration with law enforcement treatment of blacks, the Rodney King incident being "the last straw." The lyrics represent hatred toward the police and describe the intent to kill a police officer. As an illustration, some of the lyrics follow:

> I got my twelve gauge sawed off.
> I got my headlights turned off.
> I'm 'bout to bust some shots off.
> I'm 'bout to dust some cops off.
> Chorus
> COP KILLER, it's better you than me.
> COP KILLER, f— police brutality!
> COP KILLER, I know your family's grievin'
> (F— 'EM!)
> COP KILLER, but tonight we get even.[20]

Not surprisingly, police officers reacted strongly to such lyrics. Several police groups called on Time-Warner, the production company, to recall the song. When Time-Warner refused, citing Ice-T's freedom of speech regardless of what the corporate leadership thought about the content of the song, the police groups publicly urged a boycott of the company. The publicity actually increased the album's sales.

The lyrics of "Cop Killer" reflect an important social point that much of the controversy appears to have missed. Given the support of Ice-T in many black communities, it can be concluded that there is something terribly wrong in the police-community relationship. It is a symbol that we need to recognize and explore the underlying problems within our minority communities and not limit ourselves to the ephemeral concerns that arise.

POLICE AND THE MEDIA

To blame the media alone for violence obviously makes no more sense than to blame only the police. Occasionally, under particular circumstances, imprudent or even unethical media (or police) action may trigger mayhem, but usually the causes go much deeper. Hatred and hopelessness are not manufactured by the media nor by the police, though they may play a part. The fact is that violence is entertainment for many in a popular audience, and this is what the media play to, as entertainment vehicles. But the media have other functions and responsibilities that conflict to some extent with their entertainment aims. This is the conflict in so-called "cop shows" on television. Many such shows are criticized by police as unrealistic. They may ask, why not tell it as it is? The media response is that telling it as it is doesn't have much entertainment value. To sell the products of television advertisers requires, first of all, a good Nielsen rating.

For the average police officer, the issue in situations such as the Iran-Contra affair or Watergate seems rather remote to immediate interests. Developing and maintaining good relations with the press and media in the community where that officer works every day: this is something close to home that can be understood easily and is simply a matter of common sense.

Dorothy Guyot observed that crime news is among the easiest to write or broadcast because potential stories are already outlined with all the facts in place and neatly wrapped up in the form of police reports. She goes on to observe that ". . . because the police desk is often the first assignment for fledgling reporters, those covering the police beat change every year or two."[21] Consequently, reporters whom officers must deal with continue to be the least experienced and yet among the "hungriest" because they need to develop a professional reputation. Therefore, stories may tend to be oversensationalized, somewhat short on corroborated fact, and perhaps even less than objective.

Related to this idea, Jerome Skolnick and Candace McCoy found in a study of police-media relations that reporters tend to miss the critical issues because they do not ask the right questions. Rather than examining systemic issues related to the quality of policing or institutional policies related to crime control, reporters tend to consistently focus on isolated and sensational crime *events*.[22] This provides an unbalanced view of all policing activities. Television reporters appear to take the greatest scorn, because of the impression that if they cannot photograph something, it must not be news.

On the other side of the issue, reporters are concerned that they cannot get the information they need and to which they have a right. They cite paranoia, parochialism, and general hard-headedness on behalf of the police with respect to the information they hold. One newspaper reporter commented to the author on his frustration of trying to get information from the police, "You would think that their information is tied to their paychecks—for every word they say to [a reporter], they get docked a dollar. No wonder they are so tight-lipped."

Certainly there are exceptions to these generalizations about both the media and the police. Unfortunately, too many problem areas remain. There are three basic principles which should underlie the police-media relationship:

- A clear policy should be established on the types of information that can be released to the media and the procedures for that release.
- All reporters should be treated objectively, equally, and fairly.
- Be as open as possible to meeting the "public's right to know" and at the same time maintaining appropriate confidentiality of information about victims, witnesses, and suspects.[23]

These suggestions may be a good start in the way of guidelines. With some concerted effort, community by community, much more can be accomplished. There will always be some conflict in the relationship because that's the way the system is supposed to work. But the mutual stake of police (criminal justice) and the media is transcendent: the survival of free society.

QUESTIONS FOR DISCUSSION

1. Who are "the media"?
2. Distinguish between the news media and entertainment media and their impact on the public perception of the police.
3. How can the police overcome erroneous assumptions about law enforcement made by the public as a result of what they have seen in the media?
4. What is the essence of the problem in police-media relations?
5. Indicate some of the ways in which the media are subject to charges of bias.
6. Why are the police sometimes reluctant to disclose information to the media? Do you think this reluctance is justified? Explain your response.
7. Why is the media sometimes referred to as the fifth estate"?
8. Public confidence in the media appears to be diminishing somewhat. What do you feel are some of the reasons for this?
9. Discuss the relationship between the media and violence. What are your views on this issue?
10. Argue both sides of the debate surrounding the lyrics to "Cop Killer."

NOTES

1. For an interesting discussion on myths about policing, see: Victor E. Kappeler, Mark Blumberg, and Gary W. Potter, *The Mythology of Crime and Criminal Justice* (Prospect Heights, OH: Waveland Press, Inc., 1993).
2. John L. Steele, "The People's Right to Know: How Much or How Little?" *Time* (January 11, 1971).
3. Ibid.
4. Quoted by John L. Steele in *Time* (January 11, 1971): 16.
5. Daniel P. Moynihan, "The Presidency and the Press," *National Observer* (March 29, 1971): 22 (first appeared in *Commentary*, March 1971).
6. U.S. National Commission on the Causes and Prevention of Violence, Preface, *Report of Task Force on the Mass Media*, Staff Study Series, vol. 9

(Washington, DC: U.S. Government Printing Office, 1969).
7. Mark R. Arnold, "The News Media—Besieged by Critics," *National Observer* (July 6, 1970).
8. *Civil Rights Digest* 4, no. 1 (Winter 1971).
9. John Hohenberg, *The Best Cause: Free Press—Free People* (New York: Columbia University Press, 1970).
10. John Hohenberg, "The Free Press Is on Trial," *Saturday Review* (April 14, 1970): 109. Reprinted by permission. See also Harry S. Ashmore, "Government by Public Relations," *Center Magazine* 4, no. 5 (1971): 21–28.
11. Michael T. Malloy, "A Rainbow of Gray," *National Observer*, June 26, 1975.

12. John Tebbel, "The Stories the Newspapers *Do* Cover," *Saturday Review* (April 11, 1970): 66.

13. Timothy J. Flanagan and Kathleen Maguire, eds., *Sourcebook of Criminal Justice Statistics* (Washington, DC: Bureau of Justice Statistics, 1996.)

14. As reported in *Time* (December 12, 1983): 77.

15. Ibid., pp. 91–93.

16. Eliot A. Daley, "Is TV Brutalizing Your Child?" *Look* (December 2, 1969): 99–100.

17. As reported in "TV Violence: `Appalling'," *U.S. News & World Report* (October 6, 1969): 55–56. See also University of Chicago Center for Policy Study, *The Media and the Cities*, Charles U. Daly, ed. (Chicago: University of Chicago Press, 1968).

18. Marcy Kelly, "How the Media Handle Violence," *The Catalyst*, National Crime Prevention Council, November (1992) p. 3.

19. Various projects of the FBI's Behavioral Sciences Unit have examined the impact of pornography on serial rapists. Consistently, it was found that serial rapists viewed pornography—both photographs and movies—and began to act out some of the vignettes with their victims. Once again, this was not determined to be a cause and effect relationship, but a strong correlation of behavior, which induced the criminal to commit a crime he was already predisposed to commit.

20. "Cop Killer" sung by Ice-T, Time-Warner Productions (1992).

21. Dorothy Guyot, *Policing as Though People Matter* (Philadelphia, PA: Temple University Press, 1991) p. 151.

22. Jerome Skolnick and Candace McCoy, "Police Accountability and the Media," in *Police Leadership in America*, William Geller, ed. (New York: Praeger Publishers, 1985) pp. 102–135.

23. Kären M. Hess and Henry M. Wrobleski, *Police Operations* (St. Paul, MN: West Publishing Company, 1993) p. 445.

Chapter 17

A LOOK AT THE FUTURE

The importance of looking at the future is to anticipate changing problems and potential avenues for solving those problems. Visions of the future conjure illusions of streamlined, high-technology devices, which help us perform tasks at high speed with great efficacy. We envision problem-solving simplified, job performance increasing, and a higher level of quality of life as a result of these innovations. To some extent this vision is accurate. For example, police communications has evolved through a spectrum of devices and procedures, ranging from signal lights to telephone call boxes, to low-band radios, followed by high-band transceivers with encoding capabilities. Beyond this, police agencies began using mobil laptop networked computers and cellular telephones in cars for communications as well as satellite communications for training, teleconferencing, and global positioning. Similarly, the refinement of computerized fingerprint comparison systems has marked a quantum leap in law enforcement technologies.

The future, however, is not only this immediate vision of technology and equipment. It also represents conceptual and operational changes in the performance of the police function. For example, the use of the police car equipped with the automatic vehicle monitoring (AVM) system and computer-assisted dispatch (CAD) increased the *efficiency* of the police patrol officer. But what about the officer's *effectiveness*. Will such technologies help the officer to *qualitatively* perform the police function better? The answer is not simple. Certainly with the ability to increase efficiency the police are able to respond to more calls, hence, better serve the public. However, this increase in speed may come at a cost—the loss of close relations with the community.

From this lesson we must recognize that the future must embody both "high tech" and "high touch." It is clear that law enforcement is evolving toward a philosophical change that integrates diverse organizations as well as the community in problem-solving strategies. The future of law enforcement must look beyond the technological marvels of "RoboCop." Instead, the future must blend the technology with philosophy—just as it must blend the solutions to the emerging problems.

As observed in the Illinois Criminal Justice Information Authority's publication, *Blueprint for the Future*, a new spirit of community responsiveness and accountability will be found in virtually every aspect of the criminal justice system in the coming generation:

- In new community-based approaches to law enforcement as more police officers (and other criminal justice officials) get out of their squad cars (and offices) and into the community to deal with crime and its underlying causes.

"The importance of looking at the future is to anticipate changing problems and potential avenues for solving those problems."

- In new approaches to fighting drug abuse and drug-related crime—user accountability measures, nuisance abatement efforts, and the integration and coordination of community-based enforcement, education, and treatment programs.
- In new applications of technology—Mobile Digital Terminals, hand-held computers, and other devices that improve police response in the field, as well as crime analysis systems, artificial intelligence applications, and other methods of more closely tying the source of funds with the problems being addressed.
- In new methods of financing the criminal justice system—user fees, public safety taxes and surcharges, forfeiture of offenders' assets and other methods of more closely tying the source of funds with the problems being addressed.
- In new approaches to criminal justice training and education—curricula designed to attract quality people to criminal justice professions and to retain and develop them into tomorrow's leaders.
- In a new focus on young people, on the complex problems they face, and on the justice system's responses to their problems.
- In more comprehensive and sophisticated approaches to the way we deal with victims of crime (and sometimes victims of the criminal justice system).
- In new working relationships with the news media that stress such common goals as improving public safety and educating citizens about crime and justice.
- In new partnerships with community groups and citizens—efforts that go beyond traditional crime prevention programs and move into new areas of activism and volunteerism.[1]

We need to be open, creative, and take a thoughtful look ahead at needs on the horizon. This is not easy, because it requires that we develop a new perspective on our thoughts and responsibilities.

The Need For Perspective

Looking to the future is not easy. It requires a change in thoughts and beliefs for which we frequently have no basis for comparison. It requires accepting factors that appear improbable and developing new perspectives that differ from one's life experiences. It requires critical thinking without the bias of history, the willingness to take intellectual risks, and the forbearance to challenge conventional wisdom.

The Hewlett-Packard Corporation had a series of advertisements based on the phrase, "What if. . . ?" The advertisements suggested the need for creative thought as a means to solve problems. Moreover, it inferred that successful problem solvers (and futurists) need to think geometrically, exploring the different visions of changing variables as they may interact and influence the future.

As I grew up in the small northwest Missouri community of Plattsburg, one of the county courts was under the stewardship of a magistrate judge, Albert R. Alexander. Judge Alexander died in 1966 at the age of 106 years. He was born in 1860 as the Civil War started and Abraham Lincoln was president. He died during the height of the "space race" as NASA developed its plans for the lunar landings. Judge Alexander, who saw space flight on television, was not just born before the first flights at Kitty Hawk, but before the Wright brothers.

Imagine if, in 1870 when young Albert was ten years old, a futurist would have taken him aside and told him of the marvels he would see in his lifetime: hourly commercial jet flights, running water, electricity, phone coverage in virtually every home, microwave ovens, computers, and nuclear weapons. His attitude may have been one of disbelief. In fact, he would have difficulty envisioning the meaning of these words and phrases. Yet, as improbable as these developments may have been to young Albert Alexander in 1870, they are commonplace today. This is just one illustration of how the seemingly improbable can occur.

Noted futurist Alvin Toffler has proven quite successful in his forecasts of social, political, and economic trends. In his book *PowerShift*, Toffler discusses three important factors that will shape the future of our society: *knowledge, wealth, and violence*.[2] In summary, Toffler's argument is that those who possess information and place that information in the context of relationships between social, economic, and political forces will have important power and influence. This knowledge will lead to wealth, which serves as the avenue to influencing change and gaining increased power in one's arena of interest. Those unable to establish a power base in this acceptable manner will resort to alternate methods—typically violence. Power may be at any level from the personal to the global; the essential point to note is that the method of gaining power is dependent upon these "powershifts."

Strong evidence already exists in support of Toffler's arguments. It is important for us to take advantage of this knowledge and use it as we look ahead at issues facing the police.

Throughout this book many "future issues" have already been addressed. Discussions of minority relations, community policing, police use of force, disciplinary systems, community alliance, civilian review, and crime trends, to name a few, have clearly been directed toward future problems and issues. This chapter addresses these factors in summary form as well as other issues the police will likely face as we move toward the twenty-first century. Many of the issues discussed here may initially appear to be nontraditional in the study of police-community relationships. We must remember, however, that virtually everything the police do affects the community. Moreover, we must develop the ability to look at the future *without* linking it to our experiences and assumptions from the past.

Determining the Future

One may reasonably ask how the future is determined. Clairvoyance or premonitions cannot be relied on nor can definitive predictions be made. A prediction is a description of an event or condition in advance of its occurrence. It is typically a specific and frequently nonscientific specification of intuition. In looking to the future of law enforcement—or any other social, political, or behavioral phenomenon— a prediction is simply not functional or reliable. Instead, one must rely on an empirically based approach utilizing various sociocultural indicators of both a qualitative and quantitative nature.[3]

Unlike prediction, *forecasting* describes potential events or conditions that have a high probability of occurrence. The forecast has limited boundaries and is based on some form of empirical assessment. Although different forecasting methods are available, the most reliable use an integration of trend analysis, expert opinion, and extrapolation of known data. What this essentially means is that changes in the police and society, research in law enforcement, emerging social trends, and speculation of experts are all integrated into sophisticated guesses in light of a forecaster's experience. This is the approach used in this chapter. While no guarantees are made about the projections, the conclusions are both logical and probable.

Why are we concerned about the future of policing? It is because we need to plan for changes in service demands, responsibilities, resources, and applications of new technologies. Planning permits us to perform our tasks both efficiently and effectively. That is, we can more fruitfully accomplish our goals without wasting employee expertise and time, equipment, or money. Forecasting gives us a window to the future that permits the opportunity to develop long-range plans and prepare contingencies for smooth and effective changes in direction.[4]

Organizational change—whether in mission, goals, responsibilities, or processes—is a long-term phenomenon that is stressful to the organization and its members. It can invigorate dogmatism, alienate employees, and engender resentment to any form of change. Therefore, anticipation of future events can be an effective means of gradually changing organizational direction, thereby resocializing the organization and its members for greater acceptance of change. Any change that occurs—whether perceived as positive or negative—will occur incrementally. Much like a child growing up, incremental change occurs continually but is often not noticed until comparisons are made over time.

Decisions we make today can have a geometric effect on conditions years from now. We must look at the horizon in order to adequately prepare the police organization for its destiny. The areas discussed in this chapter clearly demand the attention of police leaders in order to prepare for that destiny.

R^3—Refocusing, Refining, Reallocating

With an evolving philosophy of policing, changing demographics in society, greater economic constraints, and diversifying political mandates, the police will find it necessary to explore important—sometimes radical—new directions in police management and operations. Moreover, increased prevalence of multijurisdictional crimes and generally enlarged police officer responsibilities adds more emphasis to the need of looking again at the structure and processes of police organizations. In preparing for the future, the police must engage in a comprehensive self-assessment of their current status—managerially and operationally—and explore the directions that are needed to best face the future.

The self-assessment should take an approach of *refocusing*, *refining*, and *reallocating*—what I will refer to as the R-cubed (R^3) approach. *Refocusing* refers to defining, in written form, what activities and services the police department will handle in the future. It requires a reexamination of the mission, goals, and objectives and a restatement of them as they fit the future of the department. As has been seen throughout this book, police departments seem to be moving more toward a community-based policing model, which increases and broadens services. Moreover, police officers are increasingly urged to use their discretion in solving problems in a proactive manner. These factors need to be articulated in the departments guiding principles. The "Corporate Strategy of the London Metropolitan Police," found in appendix A, provides an illustration of this type of plan with a focus on the future.

Refining refers to fine-tuning the department's infrastructure. Once the direction of the department has been formally refocused, then policies, procedures, job descriptions, personnel evaluations, and training must be adjusted to match the refocused mission. If the infrastructure does not functionally support the mission, goals, and objectives, little forward progress can be made.

The final element of R^3 is *reallocation*. New organizational directions will most likely require a reallocation of resources, i.e., people, budgets, equipment, in order to meet the needs of the refocused direction. For example, community policing is a labor-intensive activity for the patrol force. Thus, officers working in other assignments may have to be transferred back to patrol from, for example, criminal investigation or traffic. Similarly, as problem-solving strategies become the *rigor du jour*, new demands may be placed on the support staff, which will require appropriate resources in order to respond to the changing demands.

The application of R^3 is essential for implementing plans for the next generation of policing. Important areas that must receive particular attention in the R^3 process are:

- Personnel recruitment, evaluation, and development
- Special programs currently in use
- Facilities use and allocation
- Matters of collaboration and cooperation between the police department and other agencies of government
- The nature and operation of support services, and
- Budget planning processes and priorities

Only if a proper foundation is laid, can future problems be addressed and future goals be achieved.

CRIME

Crime remains a focal point of concern between the police and the community. Data on the incidence of criminality are regularly discussed by the media and used as a barometer for community safety and police effectiveness (whether accurate or not). Similarly, police resources are properly directed toward crime deterrence and criminal apprehension. Because of these factors, changes in crime patterns are fundamental to the police-community relationship. Not only must we anticipate changes in crime and emerging criminality, we must also explore how these changes will affect police operations, resource demands, and relations with the community (both individuals and businesses).

Earlier discussions of crime in this book have looked at the issue in a traditional manner as typically related to police-community relations. Since the current chapter focuses on the future, crime will be discussed from a different perspective than one usually found in the police-community relations dialogue.

Information Crime

Based on analysis of a wide range of political-economic indicators, it is becoming clear that the United States is evolving from an industrial society to an "information society." This is further evidenced by the proliferation of computerized information systems used in the stock market, insurance industry, credit cards, research endeavors, multinational business transactions, and "information businesses," such as software companies, research laboratories, and "intellectual property development." Although other countries are rapidly developing their industrial capabilities at costs less than the United States—such as manufacturing plants in Germany and Japan as well as assembly plants in Mexico—American industry is increasingly information-oriented, dealing with the research, planning, financing, and marketing of these products. Information has become big business and has big dollars associated with it.

With our emergence as an information society we may reasonably expect an increase in both the frequency and types of information-related crime. This can include:

- Theft or fraud associated with computerized financial transactions
- Theft of computer software concepts
- Theft of computer architecture plans
- Unlawful access to information or statistical systems
- Industrial espionage, with particular emphasis on research and development work
- "Pirating" of copyrighted audio and video materials, and
- Unauthorized use of radio and satellite channels

We have experienced these crime problems in their infancy and must build on this experience for the future.

These crimes present unique problems for law enforcement. A fundamental problem is that in some circumstances our current laws may not directly address the "new crime." Where laws do exist, they may deal with the information crime in a nontraditional manner, therefore requiring new police procedures to resolve the crime. A second problem is that the investigative techniques, personnel skills and matériel required for detection and evidentiary development may not be refined or even exist for law enforcement use. Information crimes are extremely difficult to investigate with current technologies—prosecution is even more difficult.

Another factor of concern is that the nature of the "information criminal" is significantly different from the "traditional" or predatory criminal. The information criminal is better educated, more sophisticated in committing the crime, often employed, and his or her profile is generally not consistent with the stereotype of the traditional criminal. Further differences include a proportionately higher probability of female offenders and a lower level of social condemnation for information crime than typically exists for predatory crime.

The implications of these factors are that the police need to conduct research on the problem to develop procedures and techniques for effective investigation—sometimes detection—of information crimes. Law enforcement will also need to train personnel in applying these new techniques to actual investigations.

Information crime also poses many issues of law that will need to be addressed through training, policy, and experimentation. Will probable cause be more difficult to determine? How will a reasonable expectation of privacy be applied to information technologies? How can "electronic information" evidence be seized, marked, and stored in custody? While these problems are not insurmountable, they nonetheless require planning in order for the police to be adequately prepared.

As an aside, it is interesting to note that the information criminal may pose unique systemic problems for corrections simply as a result of demography. Will information criminals be more likely to receive probation because of a demographic background and the nonviolent/nonconfrontational nature of the crime? If so, what effect will this have on probation caseloads? If caseloads increase, what effect will this have on the supervision of all probationers? What changes will we see in variables that are examined in presentence investigations? If the information criminal is incarcerated, will the increased number of demographically different information criminals cause more problems for institutions because of a greater degree of sociocultural distinction among the prisoners? Certainly the implications are wide-ranging.

On a dollar-for-dollar basis, information crime will have a significantly greater social impact than robbery, burglary, and theft—perhaps more than these crimes combined. Yet, the information criminal will not pose the same foreboding fear instilled by a street robber or a burglar. The police may receive political pressure to respond to "visible crime" yet need additional resources to deal with information crime. As a result, tough decisions must be made and effective planning must be done to address both the actual crime and the fear of crime.

Environmental Crime

Concern about the quality of the environment has been expressed for three decades but did not emerge as a significant political issue until the late 1980s. Groups such as the Sierra Club, Friends of the Earth, and Greenpeace, as well as consumer advocate Ralph Nader, the late astronomer Carl Sagan, Vice President Al Gore, and a number of leading scientists have all warned about the long-term negative effects that could result with continued abuse of the environment. Concerns include the disintegration of the earth's protective ozone layer, harmful emissions from combustion engines, high-density chemical emissions from industrial plants, litter, the polluting of water, water fraud and theft, toxic chemical and radiation waste, protection of endangered species, and a plethora of associated issues.

As a result of these concerns the U.S. government and virtually every state have created laws (and sometimes agencies) with a wide spectrum of responsibilities for protecting the environment. Oregon passed the first law banning sprays with fluorocarbons; Michigan, New York, and several other states require deposits on beverage bottles and cans to minimize their disposal on the roadways; many states have regulations for emission levels from motor vehicles in excess of federal mandates; Denver has an ordinance restricting days when wood-burning fireplaces may be used; and most states have both civil liabilities and criminal penalties for the unlawful disposal of toxic and medical wastes.

The point to be noted from these illustrations is that environmental protection is an important responsibility and that a significant body of law is already in place to address these concerns. Although most law is currently civil in nature, criminal laws are becoming more prevalent. This is particularly true as research begins to demonstrate the degree of personal injury or illness and environmental damage that is done as a result of careless use or disposal of toxic substances. The problems are aggravated when unlawful disposals or desecration of the environment is done intentionally to increase corporate profits or maliciously by an individual to satisfy some wanton desire.

The trend in environmental law is twofold. First, the number of criminal environmental offenses is increasing. Second, there is an increased tendency for local jurisdictions to pass ordinances on environmental issues. The implication for police agencies is to examine the status of environmental laws in their jurisdiction to determine what responsibility the police have for investigation and enforcement of such law violations. If this responsibility appears to be on the horizon for an agency, then appropriate planning must begin to determine staffing needs, training requirements, organizational adjustments, and new equipment or resources the agency will need to effectively perform this role.

As in the case of information crime, the nontraditional nature of environmental crime does not have the obvious impact of street crime. Yet it is the obsequious nature of this crime that disguises its potential impact. Problem-solving for environmental crimes will require creativity and effective communications between law enforcement and the community. Just as we now see groups such as the Guardian Angels, American Association of Retired Persons (AARP), and countless local volunteer groups serving as community resources in the fight against street crime, similar community action groups may emerge for environmental crime (particularly in rural areas).

Civil Disorder

The nation's foremost police futurist, retired FBI agent William Tafoya, conducted a comprehensive study on the future of policing using the Delphi technique.[5] Although he examined a wide range of factors, one forecast, which received perhaps the most attention, related to the potential for widespread civil unrest and violence, including increases in domestic terrorism by the millennium.[6]

The 1960s riots were primarily focused on institutionalized social change as a result of protests in support of the Civil Rights movement and against the Vietnam War. These were important issues, but they nonetheless involved limited numbers of people in society who had a vested commitment to those changes. In the disorder approaching the twenty-first century, Tafoya forecasts that instead of institutionalized change, the precipitating factors will be economic stress, with greater distinction between the rich and poor, political disenfranchisement, and worsening social conditions for minorities and the poor. These economic, social, and political factors will begin to interact, forming stress that may be somewhat akin to a social earthquake. With an unpredictable triggering movement in any one of the factors, violence and disorder will erupt.

Since making this forecast, there has been violent civil disorder in Shreveport, Louisiana; Tompkins Square Park in New York City, and the Overtown section of

Miami. Each incident contained the elements of Tafoya's model. Perhaps most dramatic, however, was the violence that erupted in Los Angeles after the state court jury failed to convict the four officers charged with assaulting Rodney King. The rhetoric following the riot described the poor economic conditions in south-central Los Angeles, the inability of blacks to influence social conditions within their community, and the renewed acts of discrimination against blacks. Moreover, the disorder found conflict not only between blacks and whites, but Koreans and Hispanics, those at the outer edges of the fray also being drawn into the conflict. Clearly, the social earthquake had erupted. Tafoya's economic, social, and political factors formed the epicenter.

Following the Los Angeles disorder, many people contacted Dr. Tafoya, observing the accuracy of his forecast. His response: The Los Angeles experience was not "the big one"—the worst is yet to come. There are two important implications from this: first, law enforcement needs to plan for the potential of violent civil disorder. This planning must include programming that can enhance community relationships and prevent, or at least minimize, the disorder. Planning must also ensure that the police department has contemporary operational procedures in effect in order to deal with a civil disturbance. Surprisingly, the police departments in Shreveport, New York, Miami, and Los Angeles all found they were ill-prepared.

The second implication is that a forecast of the future is not absolute. That is, the forecast is a probability. If the forecast of the incident or situation does occur, that should not signal the end to continued monitoring of the conditions contributing to the incident. Earthquakes always have aftershocks and they always repeat themselves again after a period of calm.

NARCOTICS AND DRUGS

The "War on Drugs" has been a pervasive issue over the past several years. Concerns have been expressed about the relationship between drugs and violence, the birth of "crack babies," legalization of drugs, use of drugs in the workplace, mandatory life sentences for drug traffickers, and a wide range of other topics which are manifestations of frustrations on how to deal with this problem. Despite the creation of the Office of National Drug Control Policy (ONDCP)[7]—the so-called "Drug Czar"—and broadening the authority of various agencies with respect to drug control, we have not been very successful. Political commentator and humorist P.J. O'Rourke observed why the ONDCP has not been effective: "The drug czar was given the responsibility of curing the entire nation's drug ills and was also given the same approximate civil authority as Ann Landers."[8]

At the outset, we need to look at drug control from a comprehensive perspective. From this broad approach we must then examine the issues that can be addressed in light of the specific or paramount problems in one's jurisdiction. Strategies that address these problems are then planned and resources allocated to implement the strategies. Importantly, law enforcement must develop its future operational plans based on an analysis of *local* problems, not just the priorities of the federal ONDCP.

A Drug Control Strategy for the Future

A comprehensive strategy must have two stages: the first to deal with specific drug control issues and the second focused on drug-related problems. To begin, Figure 17-1

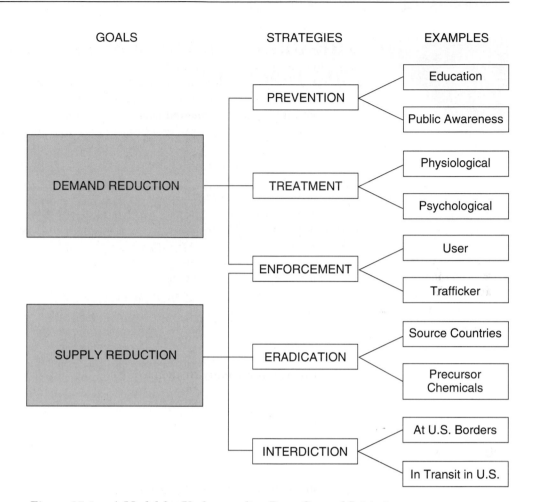

Figure 17-1.   A Model for Understanding Drug Control Initiatives

illustrates my vision of how drug control goals and responsibilities should be viewed. As can be seen, there are two goals of any drug control program:

- *Demand reduction*—Reducing the consumer's desire to purchase and use drugs
- *Supply reduction*—Reducing the quantity and availability of drugs available on the market

In order to achieve these goals, either nationally or within one's own local jurisdiction, there are five basic strategies that can be used:

Prevention.   Keeping people from using drugs in the first place is the best way to reduce demand. Educational programs (such as DARE), public awareness, and ongoing reinforcement programs related to prevention are important goal-directed strategies. More research needs to be conducted to identify and evaluate prevention strategies that truly work.

Treatment.   If persons who are using drugs can have their behavior (or dependency) changed so that they are no longer substance abusers, demand will drop.

FOCUS 17.1

THE DRUG USE FORECASTING (DUF) PROJECT

Drug Use Forecast (DUF) was designed as a tool to measure the presence (and types) of drugs in persons arrested. DUF data are collected in booking facilities throughout the United States. For two consecutive weeks during each quarter of the year urine specimens are gathered from a sample of persons arrested in each of 23 geographically diverse cities. In addition, the arrestees are interviewed about their drug use. In each site, approximately 225 males are sampled. In some sites female arrestees and juveniles are also included in the DUF sample.

Persons who are arrested cannot be forced to participate in the program; however, about 80 percent of those requested usually provide a urine sample with about 90 percent agreeing to be interviewed. To obtain samples with a sufficient distribution of arrest charges, DUF interviewers, where possible, limit the number of male booked arrestees who are charged with the sale or possession of drugs. DUF statistics frequently are minimum estimates of drug use in the arrestee population.

The intent of DUF is to gather information, which can be used for policy development in order to best deal with drugs and drug-related crimes. Information about types of drugs consumed, ages of arrestees with drugs in their system, attitudes toward drugs as it relates to crime, racial, and gender issues, frequency of drug use, and related information can help focus operational responses.

In 1997, a little over 58 percent of all males and some 63 percent of all females had at least one type of drug in their system (excluding alcohol) when tested after arrest. Cocaine use was nearly twice as common as marijuana use and nearly three times more prevalent than heroin use.

National Institute of Justice, *Drug Use Forecasting Report*. (Washington, DC: U.S. Department of Justice, Office of Justice Programs, 1997).

Currently, the effects of treatment programs vary, they are expensive to use, and the access to treatment programs is severely limited, notably for people who are unable to pay for them. These problems must be addressed in order for treatment to be a realistic demand reduction strategy.

Law Enforcement.   The enforcement of criminal drug laws as well as certain civil applications—such as asset seizures and code enforcement—rank among the most visible of all drug control strategies. In theory, law enforcement has applications to both demand reduction and supply reduction goals. On the demand reduction side of the equation, the concept is twofold. First, the threat of criminal sanctions for use of drugs will serve as a deterrent. Second, if users are arrested and punished, they will be deterred from future use. Unfortunately, there is no research to support these assumptions. Moreover, given the breadth of the drug problem and limitations on police resources, sure and swift punishment for users is neither feasible nor functional, thereby reducing the potential impact of law enforcement as a demand reduction strategy.

More success can be claimed on the supply reduction goal, but even this appears to have had a negligible effect on the presence of drugs. The identification and prosecution of drug dealers and traffickers as well as the seizure of their drugs and assets, has the intended effect of reducing drug supplies. While law enforcement has been successful in many of these enforcement efforts, the mammoth breadth of the problem coupled with the extraordinarily high profits involved in the drug trade result in negligible progress in achieving the supply reduction goal.

Interdiction.   This refers to stopping the drug supply before it reaches the actual distribution network (dealers). If drugs in transit—either enroute to the United States or through the U.S. to distribution points—can be seized, the supply can be reduced. In certain projects, such as the Customs Service Operation Blue Thunder and the New Mexico Highway Patrol's Operation Pipeline, interdiction efforts have been quite successful. The size of our country and the vast distances of unprotected U.s. borders, in addition to great expanse, however, serve as significant limitations to a comprehensive interdiction program.

Eradication.   Destroying drugs before they are processed and placed in the distribution network is another means of reducing supply. Whether we are focusing on cocaine production in Columbia, heroin in the "Gold Triangle" of the Far East, or marijuana in Kentucky, the ability to stop drugs at the source is desirable. Once again, our efforts have been limited because of international barriers to comprehensive eradication programs as well as restricted resources to carefully explore drug sources here in the U.S.

Regardless of how it is framed, five strategies are at the heart of the U.S. drug control policy to achieve the goal of demand and supply reduction. Yet, we have failed. Why?

- There has been too much reliance on law enforcement to deal with the problem.
- We seek to have short-term strategies when long-term ones are the only avenue to success.
- There is a tendency to gravitate toward emotionally appealing strategies rather than less popular, but perhaps more effective, ones.
- There has been insufficient research to explore and validate current drug control initiatives.
- Drugs have been stereotypically linked with other issues—such as race or gangs—without looking at deeper issues.
- Despite the rhetoric at the national level, without strong leadership and support at the *local* level, the drug problem will continue.

It goes without saying that the police retain a vital role in the control of drugs. The future, however, must effectively address these issues if any meaningful progress

OPERATION WEED AND SEED

FOCUS 17.2

Many attempts have been made to deal with the prevalence of drugs and their associated violence. A program that formally began in 1993 is Operation Weed and Seed. "This innovation in attacking violent crime and drugs involves 'weeding' out violent criminals and drug traffickers who destroy the peace and security of neighborhoods and 'seeding' [the area] with effective social programs to bring new life to the communities," (Dillingham, 1992:2). The Weed and Seed program complements the Department of Justice law enforcement initiatives under Project Triggerlock, which targets violent offenders for prosecution in federal court in order to take advantage of generally more vigorous firearms laws.

Operation Weed and Seed, with joint funding from the Bureau of Justice Assistance and the Executive Office of the U.S. Attorney, stresses a partnership between federal, state, and local law enforcement officials and prosecutors. According to the Bureau of Justice Statistics, elements of Weed and Seed include:

- Suppression of crime by arresting, convicting, and sending to prison violent street criminals who terrorize neighborhoods and commit a disproportionate percentage of all crimes.
- Increasing police visibility through community policing, with enhanced cooperation between police and residents in targeted areas. Foot patrols, targeted mobile patrols, victim referrals to support services, and other

toward goal attainment is to be realized. In this regard, law enforcement officials must:

- Analyze *local* problems in view of their relationship to the demand reduction and supply reduction goal. The analysis must focus on limiting strategies to local problems. Departments must avoid trying to "do everything."
- Once local problems are analyzed, reasonable drug control strategies and programs must be developed, which are balanced with available resources that can be devoted to drug control.
- A plan must be developed that enlists support of other agencies and groups that can contribute to the development of effective strategies. It must be remembered that drug control is a broad-based, multidisciplinary problem.
- Inherent in any new program development must be an evaluation component that will measure successes—and failures. The department must give itself the "freedom to fail"—not every idea will work. If it doesn't, it should not be continued. As simple as that sounds, it is amazing how difficult it is to eliminate a program or organizational unit from a bureaucracy.

Drug control plans must also be viewed in their total environment. That means collateral problems with drug abuse—violence, gangs, AIDS, burglaries, and so forth—must also be built into the strategic equation. With a reasonable and comprehensive drug control strategy, the community will provide support to the police and, hopefully, experience a better quality of life as a result of effective efforts.

community relations activities will increase positive interaction between the police and community.

- Prevention of crime, intervention where crime is likely, and treatment of causes of crime by promoting youth services, school programs, community and social programs, and support groups to develop positive community attitudes toward combating narcotics use and trafficking.
- Restoration of neighborhoods by improving living conditions and house security; making low-cost physical improvements; developing long-term efforts to renovate and maintain housing; provide educational, social, recreational, and other vital opportunities; and foster self-worth and individual responsibility among community members (Dillingham, 1992:2.)

Inherent in the Weed and Seed plan is the (1) coordination of all available resources, (2) community involvement with both the police and neighborhood rehabilitative activities, and (3) involvement by elements of the private sector to help restore neighborhoods. Community policing is intended to serve as the mechanism that will link these components together and make the program feasible. Thus, even though Operation Weed and Seed involves many non-law enforcement activities, the police serve as the linchpin for the program to achieve its intended goals and community policing provides the avenue for implementation.

Dillingham, Steven D., *Bureau of Justice Statistics*, *National Update* (Washington, DC: Department of Justice, Bureau of Justice Statistics, 1992).

POLICING AN OLDER AMERICA

We are experiencing the "graying of America" as the average age of citizens increases. With healthier lifestyles, growth in medical technology, and World War II "baby boomers" entering middle age, it is evident that by the turn of the twenty-first century the number of retired persons will reach unprecedented levels. What effects will these factors have on the police? What new law enforcement problems will arise? How will service demands change? Planners will need to address these questions to prepare for different dimensions of police service.

The Older Victim and Fear of Crime

There is a stereotype of the elderly crime victim: weak, fearful, and a recurring victim of a strong-arm robbery. What are the actual facts about crime and the elderly? Most research indicates that among the concerns of older Americans in urban and suburban areas, fear of crime ranks as the first or second cause of concern. (Health care is the other predominant issue.) More specifically, some facts about crime and Americans over age sixty are that they:

- . . . are *not* more frequently victimized by crime in general than any other age group.
- . . . appear to be victims of "strong arm" robbery, burglary, vandalism, and consumer fraud—notably con games—more frequently than persons in other age groups.

- • . . . are victimized most severely by "quasi-criminal" offenses, such as harassment and small-scale extortion.
- • . . . appear to have a disproportionately high fear of crime.
- • . . . as a result of social and physical changes inherent in the aging process, they experience behavioral changes focusing on safety and security, which appear to heighten the fear of crime.
- • . . . suffer more severely as a result of their greater economic, psychological, and physical vulnerability.
- • . . . need social and psychological support as much as, perhaps more so, than economic support.
- • . . . are typically strong supporters of the police and the criminal justice process but tend to avoid contact with the police.
- • . . . appear to lack knowledge about the functioning of the criminal justice system, a fact which is aggravated by the high fear of crime.
- • . . . find it difficult to change life-long practices in order to minimize their probability of victimization.

Elder Abuse.   One crime problem uniquely associated with older Americans is *elder abuse*. The U.S. House Committee on Aging estimated that one million older Americans are victims of elder abuse each year. Elder abuse typically includes physical abuse, emotional abuse, and neglect. The problem includes persons of all socioeconomic levels; however, there may be some differentiation based on ethnicity due to a cultural perspective of older persons. As examples, Hispanic and Asian cultures tend to show greater respect and regard for older people than other cultural groups. As result, it appears that elder abuse is significantly less common among these groups. Experiences reported at the annual "Crimes and the Elderly Triad Conference" at the FBI Academy indicated that the rate and frequency of elder abuse occurs only slightly less than child abuse. However, there are fewer laws protecting senior citizens on this matter.

While elder abuse has undoubtedly been occurring for some time, the problem has only visibly surfaced in the past few years. It is an underreported crime that is difficult to investigate because of the older person's embarrassment, fear of losing his or her means of support, and general disenfranchisement because of dependency needs on others. Current efforts related to the problem are identifying the frequency and dynamics of the crime as well as developing social programs to give aid—and in some cases sanctuary—to elder abuse victims. As in the case of most crimes, the police are in the forefront to identify and respond to the initial complaint or suspicion of the crime. Because of the inherent complexities of both identifying elder abuse and dealing with it, the need to look ahead and develop innovative programming becomes essential.

Responding to the Needs of Older Americans

With an aging population, there is a strong statistical likelihood that the number of victimizations among the elderly will increase in all crime categories. With this increase in "real crime," it is reasonable to assume that there will be a concomitant increase in the fear of crime; whether that fear is focused on violent predatory crime or on abuse. The future police role regarding crime and the elderly is to develop programs that will:

- • Reduce fear of crime
- • Increase a sense of security

- Open channels of communication between the police and older citizens
- Develop and inform older persons of means by which they can best protect themselves from crime
- Encourage reporting of all crimes including abuse, and
- Encourage participation in the criminal justice process

These factors are important because of the moral responsibility society has to those persons who have contributed their lives to our social well-being. As stated by Lee Pierson of the AARP at the FBI Triad Conference, "Those persons who built our streets are afraid to walk on those streets."

What does the future hold for the police and the elderly victim? One of the most important beginnings is to develop community-based law enforcement programs focusing on the needs and fears of older persons. The community policing philosophy as well as initiatives such as Neighborhood Watch, Crime Watch and volunteer programs can get the police into the homes of older Americans and open lines of communication. These activities should be informational and provide facts to older persons about:

- Their rights as citizens
- Processes to follow when they are victimized
- Types of crime that may be most threatening to them (particularly fraud and abuse)
- What to do when they see suspicious persons or suspect a crime
- Information about social services that can help them with their quality of life (such as medical and transportation services, counseling assistance, recreational programs, financial assistance), and
- Crime prevention tactics and techniques

Importantly, the goals of these activities are to: (a) reduce the fear of crime, (b) reduce the incidence of crime, (c) increase the probability of arrest of criminal offenders, and (d) increase the overall quality of life for older Americans.

Departments should carefully consider the creation of an *Elder Unit*, or at least explore the feasibility of such a unit. It would serve as a contact point for older victims, act as a clearinghouse of information for senior citizens, and develop special expertise in dealing with both the criminal and social problems faced by the elderly. Establishing new organizational units always requires a commitment of resources by the department. Thus, a police agency must develop plans that assess the need and feasibility of such a unit in order for funding to be secured.

For purposes of training and staffing the Elder Unit (as well as other agency functions), police departments should seriously consider the use of retired persons as volunteers. Older volunteers can be a valuable information resource and an important communications link to the older community. Furthermore, they are highly dependable, help keep down the cost of the department's staffing needs, and instill community support for the police. Operationally, one may also find that older citizens are more comfortable discussing their police-related problems with a peer instead of a young patrol officer.

The Criminal Justice Services Section of the AARP has a series of excellent programs designed to integrate older persons as volunteers in law enforcement agencies. For example, they have a comprehensive training program for crime analysis as well as support material on both how to train volunteers and how to train officers to work with retired persons. The prudent police manager of the future should not only be concerned about the broader responsibilities to be faced with an aging population but also how these same people can be a valuable resource to the police department.

The Older Offender

A final aspect of crime and the elderly, which deserves attention, is diametrically op-posed to the previous discussion: the older person as an offender. Information pre-sented at the FBI's Triad Conference reports that, contrary to popular stereotypes, el-derly offenders today are involved in more crimes against persons, particularly violent crimes with firearms, than was the case in the past. The problems of age—loneliness, loss of role and status, economic restriction, medical problems—often contribute to this criminal activity. Alcohol abuse and psychological frustration with aging may fur-ther contribute to crime by the elderly. Interestingly, some evidence suggests that the need to break the monotony of retirement is also a contributing factor to some elder crime. Finally, some older Americans resort to crime, typically petty thefts, as a means of subsistence to offset the differentiation between a fixed income and inflation.

While the nation is by no means facing a geriatric crime wave, the complexion of the problem is changing. A ten-year examination of arrest data for persons sixty and older indicates that total arrests for all offenses are not increasing for the elderly, al-though index arrests have risen slightly faster for the elderly than the nonelderly. Most of that increase was a result of property crimes, and the rise in violent crimes by the elderly is below the increase for the nonelderly. What is significant to note is that there appears to be a correlation between the increase of elderly offenders and the rising average age of the population. The future implications for law enforcement indicate: (1) a need to sensitize officers that the elderly may be criminal suspects, and (2) older persons should not be discounted as criminals simply because of age. Moreover, departments need to establish procedures for detaining older suspects, taking into account medical, safety, and hygiene factors.

TECHNOLOGY

When exploring the future, we can not avoid the impact of technology. Computers, the Internet, cellular phones, stamped circuitry, processing accelerators, satellite data transmission networks, and other technological derivatives are touching every aspect of our life—law enforcement is no exception. One of the criticisms of technol-ogy in law enforcement is that it takes officers further away from the community rather than supporting community-based efforts such as community policing. As mentioned previously, we need to take advantage of this technology and integrate it with CoP efforts so that the best of "high tech" and "high touch" can be utilized by law enforcement. To this end, an examination of technological applications we may see in the next century is important.

Alvin Toffler, in *The Third Wave*[9], observed that America is well into the third wave of a social-economic-political society. The first wave, which sustained the growth of America, was *agriculture*. The second wave, which truly pushed the United States to world prominence, was *industrial*. The third wave is *technological* in nature. Certainly the police must be part of this wave to both deal with the prob-lems it presents and take advantage of the opportunities it affords.

Word Processing

Traditionally police reports have been written by hand, perhaps typed, and some-times dictated. Once prepared, the officer's report would be reviewed by a sergeant, and perhaps a report review unit, both of which examined it for content, spelling, and grammar. The report would be photocopied and sent to various appropriate units for referral and filing. The information in the report might be used for crime reporting, investigation, crime analysis, and intelligence as well as serve a cumulative foundation for personnel deployment and resource allocation.

Intuitively, we think of word processing as little more than "sophisticated typing." In application, however, it is much more. As more police departments provide officers with easy access to (and training in) computerized word processing, the police report process will be more efficient and effective. Some departments, such as Clearwater and Fort Pierce, Florida, are beginning this trend now through the issuance of laptop computers to all officers.

With word-processed police reporting, we can have the report forms in the computer for the officer to use. The system will prompt the officer on all items that need to be addressed as well as automatically assign the report a case number. After the officer enters the narrative discussion, the report can be checked by "spell check" and "grammar check" programs, both of which can be tailored to meet specific terminology and writing styles for police reports. The report can either be "networked" or transferred via disk to the main computer system.

In the system the sergeant can review the report (without having to use paper) and take appropriate action, such as returning the report to the officer (via electronic mail, for example) or forwarding electronic copies of the report to appropriate units. For example, a burglary report, after being approved by the sergeant, may be automatically "read" by the Uniform Crime Reporting unit and electronic copies forwarded to crime analysis for the burglary investigators who can then glean the information needed from the reports. Investigators can also build their case file in the computer around the original report.

Such a system will be faster and more accurate and save costs through time as well as printing and photocopying. Of course, the first steps must be to develop a plan for a fully computerized crime reporting system, obtain the hardware and software that will make the plan operational, train all personnel on the use of the system, and ensure that everyone has access to the system. This approach will help the police to respond more fully to citizens' needs as well as afford the officers more time to devote to other responsibilities.

CAD—Computer-Assisted Dispatch

Computer-assisted dispatching systems are with us today and have proven to be most useful in setting priorities for calls and defining which patrol units to dispatch to calls. Conceptual development of police CAD systems occurred in the late 1970s when the predominant method of policing was highly reactive, with an emphasis on a quick response. As has been seen throughout this book, both the issues of reactive policing and a fast response have been reduced in importance. Instead, solving problems and dealing with quality of life issues have increased in importance.

The police must always be prepared to respond quickly in life-threatening situations—this aspect of dispatching will remain the same. Change will occur, however, in CAD priorities that support problem-solving and community-based policing activities. This will require careful research and critical decision-making, the most difficult aspect of applying change to this technology.

Two technologies affecting dispatching are global positioning satellites (GPS) and geographic information systems (GIS). Police vehicles—or even foot patrol and bicycle officers—who are equipped with GPS transponders can be monitored for safety and more efficient dispatching. Coupled with three-dimensional mapping software of a community—and in some instances, floor plans of buildings—the police can dispatch officers with greater efficacy while at the same time minimizing officer risk.

These technologies are not without their critics. Officers are concerned that the GPS systems would be used somewhat like "electronic supervision." Rather than being a tool to help officers, they perceive it as a management resource used to ensure officer accountability. Citizens are also concerned about the invasion of privacy and constant monitoring—the "Big Brother Syndrome"—should the police gain these technologies. Both of these concerns are legitimate. Police leaders who use such technologies must be responsible, have rigid control procedures, and have sanctions for abuse in order that these innovations may be used to assist both officers and the community without treading on any legal or ethical standards.

Mobile Computer Terminals

The earliest computers in police cars date back to the early 1970s, when large computer terminals were able to communicate with a mainframe computer over a standard FM radio frequency (the same frequency that was used for police radios.) They were *very* slow and limited alpha-numeric data could be sent in controlled formats. The terminals were used exclusively for checking "wants and warrants" as well as vehicle registration information. Nonetheless, it was a notable beginning for new technologies to be placed in police cars.

As computers and networked systems developed, the next major stride was small Mobile Digital Terminals (MDTs) in police cars. These were also "dumb" terminals—that is, they did not read disks nor have any ability to perform computer functions themselves. Instead, they simply received and transmitted data. Yet, the MDTs used digital technology and were significantly faster. As a result they were used for a wider array of functions, including dispatching and e-mail. The later MDT systems also were able to support graphics.

As one might expect, the next generation of technology put computers in cars. These are essentially laptop computers, which can perform all functions—word processing, data analysis, networking—and have been configured to work "in the field." The advantage is that report forms can be placed in computers as well as resource documents, policies and procedures, and any other information needed to assist the officer in performing work. In addition, the computers can be used to network, send e-mail, and perform any other computer-based function. Trends with these mobile computers include "real time" crime analysis, beat management plans based on crimes and calls for service within a specific geographic area, and computerized problem-solving models.

The future applications of such systems are limitless—essentially any computerized function that can be done in an office or laboratory can now be done in the field. Moreover, expensive special radio frequencies and transceivers are no longer necessary. Laptops are currently on the market that have built-in cellular telephone technology so that officers can transmit data through commercial wireless phone services (which are available nearly everywhere.) This means that even small police agencies can use mobile networked laptop computers for a modest cost.

The development of Internet Websites and e-mail servers by police departments, which citizens can use, adds another dimension to problem-solving and community relations. Citizens and officers will be able to communicate directly via e-mail; right into the officer's patrol car. Moreover, the use of "listserves" and the posting of information on Web pages can be an important tool supporting crime prevention, problem-solving, and public information. In this regard, in the future we are likely to see a citizen access the police department Web page and then, using a directory or search engine, find the Web site for the officer or officers who patrol the area where the citizen lives. The citizen will be able to review crime statistics, problem issues, notices and announcements, and communicate with the local officer directly through hyperlinked e-mail. The technological applications to support community policing are wide ranging—use your imagination!

Micrographics, Holographics, and Laser Technologies

Perhaps we are most familiar with these technologies by observing their use in supermarket checkouts. (Private sector applications of new technologies nearly always outpace public sector uses.) In law enforcement, these technologies will be used for specific identification of evidence, identification of offenders, discovery of evidence, and crime scene reconstruction. In addition, these, along with simulation programs, can be used to experiment with problem-solving alternatives.

New imaging and laser technologies also have important implications for crime prevention and security. Imagine a police officer conducting a security threat survey of a home or business through a portable holographic imaging system. The system, managed by the officer's notebook computer, prepares a threat assessment report for the citizen along with security options. The potential applications of this technology for law enforcement truly beg the question, "What if . . .".

Artificial Intelligence and Modeling

While these are different software applications for computers, they go hand-in-hand for many uses. Artificial intelligence is a software instruction system that compares and evaluates variables based on input data. Relying on parameters of each variable evaluated, the computer will "decide" on a given line of logic. This process can continue for a large number of times, continually refining the variable(s) at issue until a "final decision" is made by the computer.

Modeling is the replication of reality. *Physical* (or iconic) models may be like a model airplane, car, or any other tangible replication of something. *Diagrammatic* models show relationships between elements of reality, such as an organizational chart, blueprint, or flowchart of behavior. *Symbolic* models are mathematical expressions of reality showing relationships as statements between variables. *Isomorphism* refers to the degree of representativeness that is achieved by a model. As isomorphism increases, the model becomes more accurate (and more complex and expensive to create).

Computers can be programmed to test symbolic models and create diagrammatic models. The degree of isomorphism will be predominantly dependent on the complexity of the modeling program as well as the quality and quantity of data used to test the model. The most accurate models will employ artificial intelligence in order to examine the phenomena under different conditions or circumstances.

In law enforcement, this process can be used for staff allocation and deployment, managing attrition, projecting future demands and services, and a wide range of other planning tasks. Similarly, it can also be used in the problem-solving process as a means to help develop alternate solutions. While this is sophisticated technology, it is becoming increasingly "user friendly." Programs such as STELLA™ make model creation comparatively easy (with varying degrees of isomorphism) on a microcomputer for a person with research experience. With the growth of high-speed, high-capacity microcomputers, more compact programming capabilities, and increased compatibility between operating systems, the availability and simplicity of these types of programs will increase, and their use by police personnel at all levels will be more prevalent.

High Technology Monitoring Systems

When proposing any kind of comprehensive, high technology monitoring system by the police, there will inevitably be concerns expressed about "Big Brother." To be sure, this is a concern that the police must take seriously. Law enforcement must have a truly cooperative relationship with the community, not one of oppression.

Keeping this concern balanced, there is a lot of potential for monitoring systems in public places to meet general security needs as well as special threats. For example, in a high crime area, temporary monitoring systems may be employed to identify criminals, increase citizen safety, and decrease fear of crime. As technology increases, the systems provide better images, a broader range of sensors, and are less likely to be vandalized. Similarly, the use of ultraviolet equipment and image transmission by air waves (rather than cable) can provide more flexibility.

Other monitoring systems, using remote sensing, can provide additional assistance to the police. For example, monitoring of individuals, people, or vehicles in conjunction with satellite navigation systems can provide greater accuracy and a broader range, useful for many applications. The technology in this area is well-developed but not widely used. Its application in crime prevention, assistance to citizens, and criminal investigation can be a safe and effective tool, improving the quality of service to the public.

Weaponry

As noted in previous chapters, the use of force—particularly deadly force—is a continuing source of concern for the police. In circumstances where a shooting by the police occurs, there is frequently speculation on whether less than lethal force could have been used to effect control of the individual. One technological avenue currently under research to deal with this issue is the alternative of less than lethal weapons.

Research projects funded by the National Institute of Justice have begun exploring the effects of electronic incapacitating weapons and systems, which deliver tranquilizers to incapacitate violent persons. Research on concentrated tear gas, such as Mace, has already lead to an incapacitation aerosol made from concentrated peppers, such as Capstun. The intent of this is to reduce potential chronic effects, such as serious injury, from use of the weapon.

The point of significance in this research is to note the desire by police officials to seek weapons systems in the future that will protect officers and incapacitate offenders without taking a human life.

WELLNESS IN THE WORKPLACE

Because of the aging American public and implications from both the Americans with Disabilities Act (ADA) and the Age Discrimination in Employment Act (ADEA), there is growing concern about the health and well-being of employees. Moreover, research indicates that healthy and "well" employees are more productive, take fewer "sick days," make fewer claims for health insurance and workman's compensation, and generally appear to have a higher level of job satisfaction. Collectively, these factors will lead more law enforcement agencies to develop plans for "wellness in the workplace."

Physical Fitness

While the overall trend is limited at this point, in the coming decade law enforcement agencies will more aggressively develop mandatory policies for physical fitness of employees. This should not be confused with "physical agility tests," which are frequently used as a screening mechanism for new employees. Rather, policies will address the overall and ongoing health of employees as related to the three cardinal areas of fitness—cardiovascular endurance, strength, and flexibility. A few agencies have explored no-smoking policies and a handful of departments have established policies excluding applicants who smoke (although there are some unresolved legal implications associated with this). This is further evidence of the trend toward wellness. Standards will be established—and adjusted for age—to ensure that employees meet optimum standards on an annual basis.

A *caveat* to the trend toward increased physical fitness is in order. It is easy for the desire toward physical fitness to become zealous—this can lead to dysfunction. The intent of fitness policies should not be to make model physical specimens out of all employees, but to *optimize* health and lifestyle.

Mental Health

Equally important to physical fitness is mental health. Perhaps the most common mental health issue currently addressed in policing is stress. Certainly, however, there are broader mental health issues, including the mental effects of shift work, the effect of the job on the family, the ability to maintain mental equilibrium when constantly dealing with the worst side of humankind, and the overall quality of work life. The future will see police departments focus on preventive and stress reduction programs to "head off" issues before they become mental health problems. Similarly, proactive assistance on a wide variety of issues—such as family counseling, weight loss, financial management, or substance abuse—can help minimize the adverse mental health aspects of these problems. In this regard, Employee Assistance Programs will not only be more commonplace in police departments, but officers will be more likely to take advantage of this resource.

Physical Plant

An important part of wellness in the workplace is having a work environment that is safe, not stressful, clean, and aesthetically pleasing—factors that are *inconsistent* with most current police physical plants. A number of factors can enhance the quality of the physical plant: careful selection of colors, the presence of plants, music, and continual maintenance and custodial services are a few examples. Also, increasing security through subtle means—such as environmental design and discrete monitoring—can enhance the wellness embodied in the physical plant.

Handicapper accessibility is an important aspect of the physical plant, which is being addressed through the Americans with Disabilities Act (ADA). The 1992 ADA regulations require that *all* areas of police facilities be reasonably handicapper accessible, not just the public areas. Exceptions can be made if remodeling costs are "prohibitive"; however, this determination cannot be articulated in precise terms.

Thus, future issues related to the physical plant must include remodeling of old facilities and careful design of future police facilities to ensure that handicapper accessibility requirements are met.

Morale

A final issue of wellness is the maintenance of good morale. Morale involves several things: liking your job, being satisfied with the way the organization treats you, respecting your fellow employees, feeling fully informed and involved in the organization's mission. and generally feeling like a full participant in the "organizational family" rather than an inconvenience to the agency. Good morale can contribute to greater effectiveness, more attentiveness to duty, fewer days of sick leave taken, and lower levels of attrition.

There are several steps that can be taken to enhance morale. To begin, the department should have effective formal communications to all employees. This may be partially accomplished through roll calls and memoranda, but this is too limiting. Newsletters—perhaps on a weekly or biweekly basis—can be effective tools for communications. Stories should address new programs or initiatives, not just as announcements, but in such a manner that all employees feel they are part of the experiment. Personal notes, accomplishments, and recognitions should also be included in the newsletter. Unlike other departmental communications (reports or policies), the newsletter should have a decidedly familiar tone. The Florida Department of Law Enforcement uses an adaptation of the newsletter concept by preparing a videotape called "News and Views for employees.

Other positive morale factors may include commendations, recognition of an employee of the month, merit pay increases, use of "flex time," positive reinforcement of the less visible types of police work, such as referrals and providing positive feedback to officers from supervisors and administrators. Involving officers in the decision-making process—even in only an advisory role—can be a great boost to morale (as long as it is not viewed as "tokenism"). The investment a police executive makes in developing strong morale will repay itself many times.

HUMAN RESOURCES ISSUES

As law enforcement changes toward a more value-based profession employing problem-solving skills, the demands on personnel will also change. Similarly, changes in the economic, social, and political climate of a community will also have an effect on the types of people who are police officers. Thus, the forward thinking police executive will explore these trends and consider what the police officer of the twenty-first century will be like.

One clear factor will be that educational levels will continue to rise. We want police officers who are resourceful and informed decision-makers. A college education significantly contributes to these factors. Similarly, police training will change by providing officers with a greater quantity of subjects, better quality of training, and broader diversity in both the substance and process of training.

Just as we shall see changes in the characteristics and attributes of officers in the coming decade, we shall also see new ways of measuring the performance of those officers. Slowly, quantitative measures of police performance ("bean counting") will give way to qualitative measures. The need to count *how many* reports were written will dissipate as we focus on *how well* the reports were written. Similarly, the need to know how many calls an officer answered during his or her shift will be replaced with descriptions of how the calls were handled in order to solve the citizens' problems. Police performance measures need substance, not "smoke and mirrors," and the future will address this.

The character of personnel in law enforcement agencies will also change, moving toward increased "civilianization." Given the diversity of responsibilities in a contemporary police department, it must be recognized that employing civilian specialists is a more efficient and effective use of human resources. Civilians can perform tasks ranging from a parking enforcement officer to a forensic scientist without the need for law enforcement authority. Related to the "civilianization" movement will be increased use of volunteers in structured programs. The criminal justice service section of the American Association of Retired Persons (AARP) has developed a model for selecting, training, and using volunteers in a structured manner. Such a program is not only efficient management, it helps strengthen the bond between the police and community.

Another change in police personnel issues we are likely to see is a move away from specialists toward greater use of generalist police officers. Particularly during the reform era of policing, we saw a significant increase in specialized policing. However, with the growth of community policing, there is a need to have more officers "on the street." Moreover, those officers need to possess eclectic and creative skills for problem-solving—they need to be the quintessential generalist. As community policing is increasingly adopted across the country, the need for generalist police officers will grow. This has implications for both currently employed officers as well as newly recruited personnel. The current officers will likely be retrained and reassigned from specialized positions to generalist ones, a move likely to meet with a degree of conflict. Thus, police administrators must recognize this and be prepared to face the issue. New recruits will be much easier to indoctrinate into the generalist system because they simply will not know the difference.

When discussing personnel issues, one simply cannot ignore two important facets: *minority recruitment* and *police unions*. Historically, the police have not aggressively recruited minority group members. Prejudice—both conscious and unconscious—has played a role in this, as has culturally biased selection criteria, mistaken assumptions about desires or capabilities of minorities, and a simple lack of recruitment effort directed toward minority communities. Despite these limitations, the nation's larger cities have done a reasonably good job of recruiting blacks and Hispanics in proportions nearly representative of the community.[10] Still, more aggressive recruitment of minorities, including not only blacks and Hispanics but also Japanese, Chinese, Vietnamese, Korean and other émigré populations—must be addressed in the future. Such recruitment is not only proper for nondiscriminatory reasons, but is very functional for community relationships. Similarly, the police must ensure that their recruits of the future have the language skills to communicate with the non–English-speaking minority communities.

With respect to police unions, the evidence suggests that organized labor among the nation's police forces is growing.[11] More "police officer associations" are appearing even in the so-called "right to work" states. The single biggest issue being addressed by police labor groups is health insurance, followed by other benefits such as retirement and vacation leave. All of these factors are expensive personnel items. Police departments have historically been ill-prepared for labor negotiations and have, consequently, frequently agreed to contract provisions that were both expensive and impinged on "management prerogatives" (e.g., personnel assignments). Police labor relations are in a growth stage and administrators must be prepared to fairly and firmly negotiate contracts. If the labor contract becomes too expensive and/or if management prerogatives are lost, then overall police programs and new initiatives will suffer as a result.

A final human resource issue deals with age. Historically, police departments have not hired anyone over the age of thirty-five to be a new officer and typically have a mandatory retirement age somewhere around fifty-seven to sixty-five years. Not only does it appear this will change as a result of the Age Discrimination in Employment Act, but the changing dynamic of an older, yet healthy, American public (described earlier) will also be an important element in the "age equation." The future will likely see police departments hire "rookie" officers who are in their forties and fifties. These people are "proven" employees, who can bring with them experiences that can be helpful for community-based and problem-solving policing.

SOCIOPOLITICAL TRENDS

An entire textbook could easily be written about changing sociopolitical trends in the United States. This discussion cannot possibly address all the issues or discuss factors in depth. Instead, there are certain trends that warrant brief discussion since they will affect the police of the future. The implications of these trends will, of course, vary throughout different regions of the country. Nonetheless, their impact will be omnipresent.

One clear trend emerging out of the 1980s and into the 1990s is a growing conservative ideology among the American public on such issues as crime and the economy. This perspective is illustrated, in part, by the election of Democratic President Clinton in 1992 on a *conservative* criminal justice agenda. In general, political conservatism tends to take an aggressive "law and order" stand on crime issues, emphasizing "tough" tactics to deal with criminals. Unfortunately, community-based policing *appears* to be "soft"—despite its effect on increasing arrests. Nonetheless, *appearances* and *assumptions* tend to have a strong impact on political decision-makers. Consequently, efforts at community policing could be short-circuited through political influences that view community-based initiatives as being "soft on crime."

A paradox that currently exists within our political environment is the coexistence of conservatism, as described above, with the dynamic known as "political correctness." This phenomenon has become a national etiquette on sociopolitical issues, which has had a phobic impact on many public discussions of issues. "Political correctness" refers to the use of terms, phrases, and concepts that are sociopolitically neutral so as not to offend any group—or subgroup—of society. Unfortunately, the impact of this phenomenon has been to stifle public discussions of many issues out of fear of being labeled prejudiced, unjust, or uncaring. When discussion and debate cannot be open for articulation of all views, then creativity is limited and a false status quo emerges. Law enforcement officials of the future must be willing to challenge this dogma by debating issues openly and offering remedies to problems that are based on reason and research rather than political correctness and expediency.

An emerging, albeit limited, sociopolitical trend that offers hope of increasingly efficient and effective law enforcement is *political consolidation*. While this trend is limited, it nonetheless offers innovative opportunities in those areas that do consolidate. Consolidation refers to the integration of services across jurisdictional boundaries. For example, the Las Vegas Metropolitan Police Department is one consolidated force, which provides police service to Las Vegas, several small communities in the area, and Clark County. Rather than have multiple agencies, each with their own command structure, buildings, report systems, personnel systems, and every other aspect of organizational infrastructure, one larger organization covering the same geographic area is much more efficient and effective. Fiscal necessity will most likely influence some growth in consolidation—a move which progressive police leaders should grasp and push forward. Unfortunately, provincialism and the unwillingness to "give up turf" will prevent this movement from becoming widespread.

Sociopolitical trends dictate government actions and represent the collective emotion of the public. Prudent police officials need to actively monitor these trends and develop plans that are consistent with the direction of the trend. This is not only good management, it responds to the public mandate.

OPERATIONAL ISSUES

Operational issues in the future of policing could be examined in many ways: tactical versus strategic issues; issues based on organizational function, such as the future of investigations, patrol, or traffic; or programmatic plans for addressing specific problems within a jurisdiction. The details of these issues go beyond the scope of this book. Instead, I would like to offer some observations on the future of police operations which are directly community-based.

CoP.   As noted previously, community policing (CoP) is a significant philosophical change in policing, which has grown with remarkable speed in a comparatively short amount of time. It is clear from this text that I support CoP and feel it can increase the efficacy of the police service. Having stated that, I must also say that its future is precarious—it has a number of debilitating elements:

- CoP is difficult to test and measure, so its complete effects are unknown.
- It is conceptual, thus difficult to understand.
- It is philosophical, thus difficult to "transplant" between departments.
- It is nontraditional, thus it does not look like "real police work," and requires organizational change.
- It is not "flashy," thus diminishing its political appeal.

Given the wide number of law enforcement agencies in the United States, and the inherent difficulty that exists in implementing any kind of change in institutions (such as policing) these limitations may be too difficult to overcome, at least on a broad scale. Thus, while the operational potential for CoP is strong, its future may be limited unless persistent research, discussion, and debate are continued.

Pragmatic Policing.   The only other aspect of operations I want to mention is the continued *formal acceptance* of "pragmatic policing." For decades, the police maintained they had a limited and exclusive mission: fighting crime and evil in America's streets. The reality was, however, that more time was spent on order maintenance and calls for service rather than crime fighting. Pragmatic policing recognizes the myriad of responsibilities mandated to the police by the public. As a result, policies are implemented to facilitate these responsibilities, officers are increasingly evaluated on the type of "noncrime" work performance they provide, and officers are increasingly urged to solve problems related to noncrime and peripherally related crime issues. Out of necessity, pragmatic policing will be formalized into our nation's law enforcement organization.

MANAGEMENT ISSUES

Just as law enforcement is experiencing philosophical changes about service delivery and relationships with the community, the manner in which police organizations are managed must also be changed. A bureaucratic, paramilitary organization managed in a traditional manner is not necessarily conducive to flexible, innovative community-based policing. There are some fundamental management changes that need to occur in the next generation of policing in order to provide the best service as well as the best value for money invested in law enforcement.

A promising change in management that has been successful in the private sector is *Total Quality Management* (TQM). Also known as the *Deming Method*, named after its founder W. Edwards Deming, TQM seeks to enhance the overall quality of work through employee involvement in decisions and other motivating aspects. Among some of the principles of TQM are:

- The organization must address both internal and external customers (employees and citizens).
- Most individual performance measures are counter-productive because they invite conflict and competition rather than cooperation. Moreover, individual performance measures do not measure *customer needs*; instead they focus on organizational expectations.
- The organization should have a constancy of purpose subscribed to by all employees and the desire to constantly improve service rather than be satisfied with what has been accomplished so far.
- Evaluation should be done on the basis of team accomplishments and comparisons.
- Emphasis should be placed on providing the best possible service the first time and not rely on inspections and reparations.
- All organizational members must be goal-driven and participate in goal-attainment, not personal achievements within the organization.

As can be seen, the emphasis on the customer—i.e., citizen—is an important element of TQM, which is clearly consistent with community-based and problem-solving law enforcement. The Madison, Wisconsin police department has implemented TQM fully within the agency with positive results.[12] While other agencies have explored elements of TQM, it is difficult to break the traditions of decades. While it may not be feasible to fully implement TQM in a police agency, there are certainly many elements of the philosophy that are desirable and would be useful to police organizations.

Research. Beyond TQM there are a number of other management issues that law enforcement must address in the future, which will have a bearing on the ability of the police to effectively provide service as well as fulfill their role in the community. One of these factors is to increasingly rely on research for decision-making, program development, and program evaluation. Historically, police agencies have been reluctant to participate in research. The reason for this reluctance stemmed from a lack of understanding about the process, fear of external inquiry, some paranoid distrust of external researchers, and a fear of what might be learned during the research process.

This attitude has changed over the past several years, with an increasing acceptance that research is useful for decision-making and exploration of alternatives.

Much of this acceptance can be attributed to projects funded by the National Institute of Justice, efforts and activities of the Police Executive Research Forum and the Police Foundation, and broader dissemination of research results in forms that are useful to police administrators. With technological growth, increased educational levels, a new spirit of philosophical exploration, and increasingly creative people emerging as police leaders, the future will see a significant growth in the reliance on research for program development and evaluation.

Political Activism of Chiefs. Particularly since the reform era, police chiefs have attempted to stay politically neutral on virtually all issues. The impression was that political activity would taint the chief's professional responsibilities. The reality is, however, that policing is a political enterprise. Law enforcement agencies are part of political subdivisions, chiefs are political appointees, and crime, violence and disorder are political issues. Budgeting is done through a political process, laws are changed in a political system, and the primary officials to whom a police chief must report are politically elected. Thus, for a police chief to say that he or she is "apolitical" is sheer folly.

Because of the political nature of our system, police chiefs should use the political structure to the fullest extent for the benefit of the organization's purpose. It must first be understood that there is nothing wrong, immoral, or unethical in using the political processes of lobbying, attempting to sway decisions through argument, or issuing statements as part of a political system as long as those activities serve a legitimate purpose. To be sure, this is the way our system works. Thus, police executives must take advantage of the system.

Civilian Accountability. In the chapter on complaints and the police, various types of civilian review mechanisms were discussed. These were generally concerned with reviews of complaints about officer misconduct. Civilian accountability is much broader than complaint review. Accountability is concerned with the quality of policing, whether the police are involved in the types of activities or programming that the public wants, whether the police are providing good "value for money" in the services they provide, and whether the police are holding up their end of the social contract.

Particularly after the 1992 Los Angeles turmoil, questions arose about the Los Angeles Police Department's accountability to the public. What was found (as alluded to in the appended "Christopher Commission" report) was that the LAPD was, in practice, accountable to virtually no one. As a result, in Los Angeles, as well as many other cities, new attention is being given to police accountability.

Accountability can take several forms. It may be a formal Board of Police Commissioners, which has statutory policy authority over police operations. Accountability may be embodied in a standing "Police Committee" of the city council, which oversees police activity on behalf of all elected officials. Another form may be a Police Advisory Board, which serves as a "sounding board" to the police administrator as well as a mechanism for public input on issues. Public Annual Reports published by the police department are an informal means of accountability wherein citizens can review the kinds of activities of the department, budgeting and management concerns, as well as other related operational matters. An increasing number of police departments are conducting regular citizen surveys to solicit information on the kind of services that are needed to gain feedback about the quality of service the department is providing. Not only do the surveys provide input to the department, but publication of the survey results also serves as a means of informal accountability.

Because of tighter budgets, increased frustration with "big government," and the general move toward community-based input in all aspects of government, not just policing, the next decade will see an increased public demand for accountability. Enlightened police leaders will grasp this trend and develop a plan for civilian accountability before a system is forced on them.

Decentralization.   There are two types of decentralization in law enforcement. One is *physical decentralization* wherein police resources are dispersed throughout a jurisdiction in substations and/or special operations facilities. The second is *decentralization of authority* where officers of lower ranks are empowered to make decisions about the use of organizational resources, or to interpret policy. Decentralization goes beyond delegation of authority by giving those in lower ranks greater discretion in their decision making.

Community policing (CoP) requires both kinds of decentralization. In many cases CoP officers will have an office physically located in the areas in which they work. More importantly, however, is that the CoP officer must be empowered to contact various agencies for assistance and services as well as make decisions about policing priorities within the CoP area. Decentralization of authority is particularly antithetical to traditional police management practice. Despite this, and given the trends as they currently exist, police administrators must look to the coming decade and plan the types of resources and policy changes that are necessary for decentralization with respect to the evolution of policing.

Accreditation.   Law enforcement accreditation was conceptualized and developed during the reform era of policing. As such, the standards reflect the practice and management of policing within this philosophical framework. As police management has moved toward CoP, concerns have been expressed by police leaders whether this philosophical change is consistent with the goals of accreditation. In a national study of police chiefs on this issue, the respondents felt that neither management by values nor community-based policing were in conflict with accreditation. Moreover, those that felt as if some conflict existed believed the conflict could be resolved through management practices and/or amendments to the accreditation standards.[13]

With adoption of the principles of quality management and with the traditional orthodoxy of police administration being challenged, accreditation must respond. *If* law enforcement organizations become "flatter," i.e., less bureaucratic, *if* the responsibilities of personnel are enlarged, *if* increased professional discretion is encouraged, and *if* greater decentralization of authority is delegated, then CALEA standards must reflect these changes in the practice of police management.

The research shows that accreditation has a strong foundation and has progressively strengthened over its relatively short history. However, the future of accreditation will likely be influenced by two important variables:

- The general status of the economy and its consequent influence on government—therefore police—budgeting in light of the costs (both direct and indirect) for accreditation and the discernible benefits from accreditation
- The changing administrative environment associated with total quality management and community-based policing

If CALEA does not respond to these concerns through amendment to its standards, then the accreditation movement could wither away.[14]

SUMMARY

It is important to remember that looking to the future requires us to shed our traditionally held notions. Looking to the future along a straight line of trends is misleading. Human behavior, technological growth, political change, social evolution, and economic conditions vary constantly. It is the interactive effects of this variance that are the predicate for the future. Our responsibility as social futurists is to analyze these variances and give meaning to them.

There are few absolutes in forecasting: time will progress, change will occur, and a forecast is little more than an educated guess (albeit a good one)! The greatest disservice that can be done, however, is to discount forecasts because one may not immediately understand it.

The forecasts and observations made in this chapter were specifically selected based on their potential impact on police-community relations in the future—and particularly the changing nature of this relationship. The insightful baseball philosopher, Yogi Berra, once said, "The future ain't what it used to be." I guess we will have to see.

QUESTIONS FOR DISCUSSION

1. Discuss what is meant by the statement that "a new spirit of community responsiveness and accountability will be found in virtually every aspect of the criminal justice system in the coming generation."
2. Why is it difficult for us to think ahead about changes that may face us in the future?
3. What is meant by the concept of R^3 as it relates to planning for the future?
4. Describe why "information crime" poses a serious threat, yet is difficult for most citizens to accept.
5. What is your reaction to the forecast that the United States will experience riots near the turn of the century, which will eclipse the riots of the 1960s in intensity and violence?
6. Do you feel we have been successful in the "war on drugs"? What priorities must we address in the future with respect to drug control?
7. What challenges do we face in the future with respect to an aging population?
8. Discuss some of the technological changes which we can expect in the future of policing.
9. Will the increase of technology take the police even further away from the community or facilitate better relations? Explain your response.
10. What benefits to police performance are provided by a strong "wellness in the workplace" philosophy?

NOTES

1. Illinois Criminal Justice Information Authority, *Blueprint for the Future* (Chicago: ICJIA, 1991).
2. Alvin Toffler, *PowerShift* (New York: Bantam Books, 1990).
3. William Tafoya, *A Delphi Technique of the Future of Law Enforcement*. Ph.D. dissertation (1986). (Criminal Justice and Criminology), University of Maryland.
4. Richard Holden, *Police Management* (New York: Prentice Hall, 1986).
5. William L. Tafoya, Dissertation. University of Maryland. 1986.
6. William L. Tafoya, "Rioting in the Streets: Déjà Vu?", *CJ the Americas* 2;6 (1990) pp. 1, 19–23.
7. Office of National Drug Control Policy, *National Drug Control Strategy* (Washington: U.S. Government Printing Office, 1996).
8. P.J. O'Rourke, *Parliament of Whores* (New York: Vintage Books, 1991), p. 113.
9. Alvin Toffler, *The Third Wave* (New York: Bantam Books, 1980).
10. David L. Carter and Allen D. Sapp, *Higher Education and Minority Recruitment* (Washington: Police Executive Research Forum, 1991).
11. For greater detail on police labor trends, see Allen Sapp and David L. Carter, *A National Study of Police Labor Relations: Critical Findings*. (Washington: Police Executive Research Forum, 1991).

12. See David Couper and Sabine Lobitz, *Quality Policing: The Madison Experience* (Washington: Police Executive Research Forum, 1991).

13. David L. Carter and Allen Sapp, "Issues and Perspectives of Law Enforcement Accreditation," *Journal of Criminal Justice*, 21:5 (1994) pp. 87–108.

14. Gary Cordner and Jerry Williams, "Community Policing and Police Agency Accreditation," in Larry Gaines and Gary Cordner, eds., *Policing Perspectives: An Anthology* (Los Angeles, CA: Roxbury Press, 1998).

Appendix A

LONDON METROPOLITAN POLICE STATEMENT OF COMMON PURPOSE AND VALUES AND CORPORATE STRATEGY*

INTRODUCTION

Since its inception in 1829, the Metropolitan Police has provided a model for policing with the consent of the public not only followed in this country but widely adopted elsewhere in the world; we are proud of that global reputation, hard-earned by our forebears. This, our first Corporate Strategy, now affords us the opportunity to look forward—five years and further—and to so position the organisation that it continues to be relevant and effective to the people we serve, and more influential in the wider debate touching not only the criminal justice system but also social issues and the quality of life in the capital.

PURPOSE OF THE METROPOLITAN POLICE SERVICE

Our purpose and values are already declared and recognised. This clear statement, reproduced below, encapsulates the philosophy which underpins our policing of the capital city.

*The phrasing, spelling, sentence structure, and some words may occasionally seem unusual to the American reader. However, the writing style is that used in Great Britain and has been retained to give the reader the complete "flavour" of the Corporate Strategy. More information about the Corporate Strategy or the Met in general can be obtained by writing: Commissioner's Central Staff, Metropolitan Police Service, Room 815, New Scotland Yard, Broadway, London SW1H OBG, UNITED KINGDOM.

Statement of Our Common Purpose and Values

The purpose of the Metropolitan Police Service is to uphold the law fairly and firmly; to prevent crime; to pursue and bring to justice those who break the law; to keep The Queen's Peace; to protect, help and reassure people in London; and to be seen to do all this with integrity, common sense and sound judgment.

We must be compassionate, courteous and patient, acting without fear or favour or prejudice to the rights of others. We need to be professional, calm and restrained in the face of violence and apply only that force which is necessary to accomplish our lawful duty.

We must strive to reduce the fears of the public and, so far as we can, to reflect their priorities in the action we take. We must respond to well-founded criticism with a willingness to change.

It is no accident that this statement is strikingly similar to the description given by those who charted the establishment of the police service. The continuity of purpose and values is a testament to their strength, durability and constancy in a world that is in so many other ways dramatically different. This touchstone for public and police is not in itself sufficient to guide the development of a dynamic organisation like the Metropolitan Police Service in a constantly changing environment where demand and expectations will ebb and flow. It is also important to formulate a strategic intention for the Service which not only embodies but promotes that statement. This enables priorities to be determined and relevant initiatives to be considered and pursued by the Service. In this way, the creation of our five-year Corporate Strategy is the visible expression of the wisdom and direction embodied in the Statement of our Common Purpose and Values.

STRATEGIC INTENTION

Our strategic intention has seven principal strands. It is our intention:

I. to remain a visible, predominantly unarmed, approachable police service in order to provide a reassuring presence across London. This, our overriding policing style, has its roots deep in the community;

II. to increase consultation with the public and their representatives; to inform and respond to their views, and their particular and changing needs, as far as we can; and to improve our internal communications. We intend to maintain our place as leaders in policing philosophy and practice;

III. to establish a clear view of the relative importance of policing tasks, and improve our performance in those areas of police activity which are identified for priority attention. It may be necessary deliberately to divert manpower away from some areas of work to address these priorities;

IV. to maintain a range of specialist services which, in support of our general policing style, reflect the changing and dynamic needs of those living and working in London. Such specialisms must also encompass those national responsibilities we presently bear;

V. to achieve a sufficiency and disposition of personnel—both police and civilian support staff—to make us more effective in the delivery of our service and to realise the full potential of all individuals within the Service, promoting professionalism together with high standards of personal conduct. All personnel must be well-trained, led, and managed;

VI. to ensure adequate technical and other appropriate support for our workforce. Investment here must be sustained and have as its twin goals the greater effectiveness of staff and the provision of better working conditions for them;

VII. finally, to give a high quality service to all our customers, particularly the public, delivered in a way that represents good value for money. This requires exacting self-scrutiny of our performance, against agreed standards, through inspection and review procedures. We will continue to promote good practice and correct errors; if we are wrong and grievances are justified, we will accept our mistakes.

Our strategic intention cannot be realised in a single step. The rigor of strict prioritisation must be applied in recognition of resource constraints. Equally, if it is to be successful in steering the Metropolitan Police Service along its charted course, the strategic intention must be translated into specific initiatives and activity aligned to the core functions of the organisation.

CORPORATE STRATEGY

The Corporate Strategy is directed towards improving our service delivery. It takes account of development, either predicted or happening, as a result of changes in Europe and the developing role of the Metropolitan Police Service in the national policing arena. Our strategy sets out initiatives to achieve the broad aims of the Service for five years; in this case 1992–1993 to 1996–1997.

The aim of this document is to provide a framework for directing our activities towards high quality of service in areas of work identified as priorities for attention. As flexibility is essential, the Corporate Strategy will be reviewed annually to take account of the unforeseen or change in priorities which so often characterises policing. A strategy cannot reflect all that is being done within by the Metropolitan Police Service. Indeed, it would lose its definition if the focus was too wide and the effort was not concentrated in those areas which were thought critical to securing success for the organisation. Therefore, it is necessary to be selective and, after consultation, to establish priorities which will attract extra effort and resources whilst maintaining other policing services to satisfactory levels of effectiveness. To this end, it is the responsibility of the most senior personnel to give a lead and direction to the Service, having taken account of broad range of opinion and activities both within and outside the organisation.

Measurement remains an elusive feature of policing but is no less important because it is difficult. The more traditional or accepted measures often have flaws but if we build upon them with new data, which is increasingly available as technology eases collection and analysis, properly supplemented by opinion, we will be able to show and debate the results of our efforts. Cost is also an important aspect of any strategy because it is a measure of accountability as much as it must be a constraining factor. From the outset we will endeavour to cost our additional effort to produce improvements. If resources are deployed in pursuit of our goals and success does not follow, then adjustment or even curtailment needs to be considered. In the longer term, activity analysis, the introduction of improved budgetary systems, devolution of the budget itself, and cost-centre accounting will all contribute to improved decision-making.

Whilst this document is primarily for the use of senior and middle management, it also serves as a document of account to our police authority and the public, showing how we are using and intend to use our resources. It is an ambitious strategy and clearly the five-year timescale may have to be expanded for one or two initiatives to secure a significant impact. However, since some programmes of activity are more advanced than others, they will be completed in a shorter timescale. As the support initiatives are ongoing they are not confined to a five-year programme. All initiatives will require regular review; such a review will be a constant feature of the strategy as it rolls forward year on year.

Operational policing has been divided into five main kinds of activity, which are described as *core operational functions*. These are:

- Public security, safety, and reassurance
- Provision of a 24-hour response service
- Management of crime reduction and investigation
- Maintenance of The Queen's Peace
- Traffic management.

All policing activity within Territorial Operations Department and Specialist Operations Department can be brought under these core functions. Under each of these headings, in the pages that follow, are initiatives which are being progressed by improvement programmes. These programmes are at different stages of development. The provision of appropriate support, and value for money from resources, to complement the operational initiatives, is then set out under the following headings:

- Personnel
- The estate
- Communications
- Transport
- Information technology
- Purchasing and provisioning
- Financial management
- Value for money

Underpinning all our activity is the need to improve the service we provide.

TO IMPROVE THE EFFECTIVENESS OF OUR PERFORMANCE IN RESPECT OF CORE OPERATIONAL FUNCTIONS

1) *Public Security, Safety, and Reassurance*

Over the last decade increased workloads, particularly on divisions, relating to crime, public order, and traffic and arising from new legislation, have sometimes diverted our attention away from the important role of contributing to the feeling of confidence and safety amongst people in London. Surveys consistently confirm the concern of the public to see more officers on the streets. In reality, the percentage of our resources devoted to uniformed patrolling has remained fairly constant over the last five years at around 25 percent; this level of uniformed patrols is augmented through the dedicated service provided by the Metropolitan Special Constabulary [*ed. note:* an auxiliary or "reserve" force], whose numbers are increasing. Over that period, however, the level of fear felt by Londoners has increased greatly with the increase in street crime, burglary, and other criminal behaviour. Over the next five years the Metropolitan Police Service will ensure that the cornerstone of policing, the division, will have the benefit of extra manpower redistributed from Areas and headquarters [*ed. note:* an Area is a major divisional breakdown in the Met]. We will confirm our role as a supportive community service by introducing a community-based policing style (sector policing), developing the Partnership Approach, supporting vulnerable groups and contributing positively to creating "safer streets" to improve the quality of life in London. The Metropolitan Police Service will also take positive action to reduce the unwarranted fear of crime, through local consultation, media influence, and other communications with the public.

i) To Introduce Sector Policing throughout the Metropolitan Police Service
The introduction of a community-based policing style (sector policing) is the most significant strategic initiative being undertaken in 1992–1993; it involves moving from a time-based or shift-based policing system to a geographic system. It is a style of policing which, within broad guidelines, can be closely tailored by divisions to meet local needs. In planning and implementing the new structure, each divisional commander will take account of local concerns for a uniformed presence, in particular locations at particular times, balanced against the need for an effective response in emergencies. As the smaller local teams develop, they will pay further attention to the specific needs of their own designated parts of the community and develop relationships with local residents. Management information systems are being explored and developed to provide a better account of local policing activity and its cost implications.

ii) To Make Best Use of Our Resources in Improving the Quality of Life through Partnership with Local Authorities
Both police and local authorities have an important role, through the Partnership Approach, in improving the quality of life within communities in the capital city. This is developing and there have already been examples of the more effective targeting of resources, particularly in projects relating to specific housing estates. The focus is on strategic planning between the Metropolitan Police Service and local authorities, with the setting of joint objectives. The feasibility and implications of moving towards alignment of divisional and borough boundaries will receive particular attention. The implications for community-based policing of closer working relationships with the local authorities will also be considered, and we will examine those areas where an overlapping responsibility exists between police and local authorities considering joint strategies and discreet areas of responsibility within those strategies.

iii) To Increase the Support Given to Vulnerable Groups
Domestic violence units and child protection teams are now well established. Our treatment of rape victims has been improved through training and the provision of special accommodation. Increased satisfaction with our service in this area has been confirmed through a survey of such victims. We recognize that young people are responsible for a disproportionate amount of crime, and that they are particularly vulnerable as victims of criminal activity and abuse. We will continue to cooperate with schools, local communities, and other agencies, working together to resolve the problem of juvenile offending and to promote the concept of good citizenship. We will join with local authorities, agencies, and community groups to tackle policing issues arising from our multicultural society. We will support initiatives to tackle attacks upon and harassment of all minority groups.

iv) To Introduce Initiatives to Reduce the Unwarranted Fear of Crime   The fear of crime is sometimes out of proportion to the actual threat. However, it is a real and worrying perception within the community. We will try to establish the reasons for this, and then work with others to reach effective solutions. Attention to local concerns and criminal behaviour on the streets will enhance the feeling of safety. The Director of Public Affairs and Internal Communication intends to take a proactive role in the projection of crime strategies and statistics to reduce the unwarranted fear of crime.

2) Provision of a 24-Hour Response Service

The public has a right to expect an effective 24-hour response service from the police as one of the recognised emergency services. The provision of a high quality response depends not only on promptness, but also on the availability of appropriate skills. These aspects will be relevant in setting standards for policing.

i) To Improve the Quality of Response to Emergency Calls   The Operational Policing Review revealed this as a major priority for both the public and police. Internal studies and inspections have already been undertaken to identify methods of measuring and managing the promptness and quality of the response to calls from the public. The implementation of recent proposals would provide an improved response to emergency calls. The quality of responses will now be the focus of our attention.

3) Management of Crime Reduction and Investigation

The reduction of crime is one of our highest priorities. It includes crime prevention measures taken by individuals and organisations and the whole range of educational programmes that stimulate those measures. It also includes initiatives to improve our performance in solving crimes and bringing criminals to justice. Against a background of ever-rising crime levels, several aspects of our performance have been identified as requiring improvement, and some action is well advanced.

i) To Seek a Reduction in Crime through Partnership with Other Agencies   Public participation in problem identification and solution is becoming well established through our working closely with Consultative Groups, Crime Prevention Panels, and more recently, Youth Crime Prevention Panels. This multiagency involvement, complementing the Partnership Approach with local authorities, will be developed in order to examine and review all aspects of crime prevention. The roles of sector officers, crime prevention officers, schools involvement officers, community liaison officers, and senior police officers will be refocused to improve the Metropolitan Police Service contribution to crime reduction; the concept of "designing out" crime will also be further promoted. In addition, we will consider the implications of the National Audit Office report on crime reduction taking into account the progress we have made since their survey was conducted.

ii) To Improve the Collection and Presentation of Police Evidence
The public's perception of police competence and integrity has recently been adversely affected by a number of well publicised cases in both the criminal and the civil courts. The quality and integrity of our input to the criminal justice system is

crucial and must be seen to be by all personnel. The Priority Project on Police Evidence recommendations will lead to redesigned training for officers at all levels beginning in 1992–1993. Scientific, forensic, technical, and expert aids will be further developed.

iii) To Improve Our Investigative Processes and Deployments   A need for improvement in this area was identified several years ago. This resulted in an internal study, the Crime Investigation Priority Project (CIPP), which produced a final report in April 1989. The recommendations, which include definition of the investigative role of the first officer at the scene, the role of CID officers, and the appropriate treatment of victims, have already been implemented. If the crime rate continues to rise, there may be a need for further increases in divisional officers. We will also be examining the policy in relation to the cautioning and charging of suspects.

iv) To Improve Our Performance in Respect of Specific Crimes
Terrorism, where the initiative always rests with the terrorist, remains at the top of the priority list. Considerable progress has already been made in respect of armed robberies and sexual offences. However, the high levels of burglary, street robbery, and motor vehicle offences contribute to the public's fear of crime and, together with the growing concern about drugs, directly affect peoples' lives. In response to public concern about these specific crimes, we are examining good practice and will establish systems for its dissemination. Strategies will be aimed at prevention, detection, and accurate presentation of police performance. The Partnership Approach with local authorities and other agencies, together with improved local communication, will be key elements in this process. More specifically, the strategy towards improving our performance in dealing with sexual offences, including those involving male victims, is well advanced. The Central Drugs Squad has now been integrated into the Regional Crime Squad structure. Preventive measures for drug offences and offenders and the education of drug abusers, as well as detection and seizure, will remain priorities.

4) Maintenance of the Queen's Peace

Maintenance of the Queen's Peace involves policing planned events in public places, including ceremonial and other high risk occasions, and preparing contingency plans to respond to spontaneous disorder and major civil emergencies. The requirement in respect to public order is to a large extent unpredictable, apart from planned events (some of which are undertaken on a fairly short notice) and contingency arrangements to deal with the unexpected.

i) To Improve the Policing of Marches, Demonstrations, Ceremonial Events, Safety at Sporting Events, Spontaneous Public Disorder, and Major Civil Emergencies   A series of recent internal reviews has produced recommendations aimed at improving training, event planning and management, communications, equipment, and post-event investigation. These recommendations have been progressed through detailed planning to a stage of substantial organisational activity. Full implementation will require the reequipping of Area control rooms, additional specialist vehicles, additional training for senior officers, and improved radio facilities. In respect of spontaneous disorder, our overall plans and response schemes will be reassessed and developed to meet any foreseeable

challenge; these plans will be developed against the background of improvements achieved in our overall public order capability. Ceremonial and other events will also be subject to enhanced security arrangements. This will include improved search training and search awareness. Concern has also centered on aspects of safety at sporting events and the role of local authorities. The police contribution will be part of broader advances designed to achieve both greater safety and public perception of safety. We also intend to review our arrangements for major civil emergencies and propose update training, briefing and coordination when necessary, and further develop our contingency planning.

5) Traffic Management

Within the capital, several diverse agencies have overlapping responsibilities for traffic matters. The Metropolitan Police Service will establish its precise role within a multi-agency approach to a London-wide traffic strategy. In seeking with others to improve road safety and traffic flow, we will need to examine the balance of our enforcement and service activities. The Road Traffic Act will require close liaison over parking enforcement with local authorities setting up special parking areas. A Metropolitan Police Traffic Strategy has been prepared in the light of our present role in respect to traffic in London. We will concentrate on improving our performance through the following initiative.

i) To Increase Police Input into Traffic Flow and Road Safety   There is a rapidly increasing public and political awareness of the social, commercial, and environmental costs of traffic congestion. Traffic problems in London will continue to increase unless radical measures are taken. Consequently, the Service will have to cope with even greater congestion. Policing of the full Red Routes scheme will require additional manpower. Our traffic strategy review has made some recommendations aimed at reducing traffic congestion and improving road safety. Our role within a multi-agency approach must be examined, but will focus on existing channels such as School Improvement Programmes, publicity campaigns, and police input into the development of traffic management schemes.

6) Personnel

i) To Plan and Provide for the Future Manpower Needs of the Metropolitan Police Service in the Most Effective and Efficient Way
The police manpower priorities for 1992–1993 onwards are to restore divisional manning levels of uniformed constables to the 1989 level, and to enhance crime investigation on division to meet the demands of rising crime. Bids for additional manpower are being made to the Home Office through the Public Expenditure Survey (PES) process. We shall keep under review the balance between different types of manpower (police and civil staff; operational support and support). Our objective will be to increase operational police manpower and reduce support police manpower, mainly through an accelerated programme of civilianisation. We are working with the Home Office to develop a more flexible approach to manpower controls for both police and civil staff. Profiles showing the experience and skills of others on Areas and divisions will be developed in line with the move towards a community-based policing style (sector policing) and, during 1992–1993 and 1993–1994, management information systems will be refined to enable us to deploy officers more efficiently.

In considering the best use of manpower we shall continue to review the balance between police manpower and the allocation of resources to support that manpower. The main challenge will be to meet the demands from Areas, divisions, and other operational departments and branches for human resources, including technical and managerial skills, which will enable them to fulfill their operational objectives. We shall seek to respond to this challenge through the development of systematic human resource planning. We shall establish a long-term strategy to improve the recruitment, retention, development, selection, and motivation of our staff, in order to provide a better trained and more flexible workforce. A personnel information data base covering all our staff will be developed for use by all parts of the Metropolitan Police Service.

ii) To Provide the Means for Developing and Training all Metropolitan Police Service Personnel

During 1992–1993, we shall develop and publish a corporate training strategy for all Metropolitan Police Service personnel. This will reflect and be consistent with the national police training strategy, and will fit with our broader human resource development strategy. A management development strategy will be formulated to take account of the special requirements of managers operating in the Metropolitan Police Service. A system will be introduced to advise all members of the Service of the opportunities that exist for lateral career development. On a broader front extra emphasis will be given to a wide range of personal development opportunities. More sophisticated police promotion systems will be introduced, which focus upon the practical skills of candidates. The introduction of assessment centres will ensure that each candidate has the competencies required in the next rank. Training will be designed and developed in such a way as to minimise abstraction from operational duty and will be conducted at or as near to the workplace as is practicable. Standards will be maintained through systematic training, evaluation, and updating of instructors, and the monitoring of trainee performance. An integrated system to match the provision of training against identified operational needs will be developed with the aid of information technology. Training courses will be tailored so as to fit the requirements and resources of internal customers, who will be more closely involved in major training initiatives. Budgets for external training will continue to be devolved.

iii) To Develop and Publish Personnel Policies which Fulfill the Responsibilities of and Improve the Attractiveness of the Metropolitan Police Service as an Employer

All major personnel policies will be published and recorded in ways that make them more readily accessible to our workforce. New grievance procedures will be introduced to deal with complaints about managerial behaviour and unfair treatment. We shall promulgate a corporate Equal Opportunities Policy and Strategy for the Metropolitan Police Service and establish systems to monitor their effectiveness. Flexible working patterns will be further developed and the feasibility of part-time work by police officers is being explored. The number of job-sharers, part-time staff, and staff on short-term contract will be increased. The scope for homeworking and part-year appointments will be reviewed. The Occupational Health Service will formulate and publish a strategy to improve all aspects of health, fitness, and welfare, and safety at work for all staff. We shall introduce new methods for the management and monitoring of sickness absence and other abstractions from duty. All aspects of new employee legislation emanating from central Government and the European commission will be monitored and implemented as necessary.

7) *The Estate*

i) To Implement the Programme for the Rationalisation, Replacement, and Refurbishment of the Estate

We are committed to a comprehensive programme for the rationalisation, replacement, and refurbishment of the estate, so as to improve its quality for the benefit of those who work in or visit police premises. The Estate Strategy, reviewed and published annually, provides an integrated and long-term strategy for the whole of the estate, and is supported by supplementary strategies for particular parts of the estate. The Operational Building Strategy aims to reduce, within the next thirty years, the average age of police stations to thirty years. Programmes for the rationalisation of the residential, warehouse, and headquarters office estates are under way. 1992–1993 is the second year of a four-year programme to improve access and facilities for disabled people at police stations. The building maintenance backlog is being eliminated with the help of a rolling programme of condition surveys. The energy conservation programme will continue to be vigorously pursued. A new comprehensive property and estate management computer system (PREMISYS) is being progressively implemented. The first phase will be introduced in January 1992, and it is planned to complete the later phases by the end of 1994–1995.

8) *Communications*

i) To Provide Improved Communications Systems

The third phase of the re-designing and re-equipping of the Metropolitan Police radio system, which derives from decisions taken at or consequent on the 1979 World Administrative Radio Conference (WARC), will be progressed Area by Area for completion in 1995. It involves the change from VHF to UHF of the divisional, public order, and certain other personal radio systems, and will provide improvements in the quality of service to operational officers and in flexibility of use. Trials are being made of the personal issue of radios to establish whether the benefits of their increased availability to operational officers and reduced maintenance costs offset the cost of the additional radios required. The need to support traffic wardens with suitable and cost-effective communications is recognised, and it is hoped to initiate provisioning in 1992–1993. A new, properly structured, all-digital, service-wide telephone network ("Metphone") is being installed Area by Area and will be completed in 1994. It will bring many benefits to the user and provide good value for money. A rationalisation of line networks for telephones, radios, and data will be carried out in conjunction with the Metphone project, to improve the resilience of all three networks and to give improved value for money.

9) *Transport*

i) To Provide Effectively and Efficiently for the Transport Needs of the Metropolitan Police Service

The Transport Strategy is reviewed and published annually. A main thrust of policy is to set up a system under which the user can, within budget, choose the vehicles to meet the local needs of operational officers; it is proposed to extend this system to all Areas in 1992–1993, and to post a vehicle fleet manager to each area by August 1992. Another primary aim is to improve the efficiency of the maintenance operation through a number of initiatives, including the introduction of an integrated training package and a revised bonus incentive scheme. The number of vehicles under repair and being serviced at any one time is being reduced, and thus the number of spare vehicles needed is also being reduced. Service level agreements will be developed as part of this programme. In order to release money for the Crime Report Information System (CRIS), the replacement parameters for Metropolitan Police vehicles, which number just over 4000, have for a number of years had to be extended beyond desirable limits; but they are gradually being reduced, particularly for high profile operational vehicles, and it is planned to return to optimum parameters in 1994–1995.

10) Information Technology

i) To Implement the Information Strategy and the Information Technology Strategy

The demand for wider availability of information technology (IT) is growing and becoming more insistent. Under the Information Strategy agreed in 1988 and currently under review, the following major systems are in the process of being implemented: The Crime Report Information System (CRIS), due for completion in 1995–1996; a Corporate Names Database (NAMES Project), due for completion in 1993–1994; the property and estate management information system (PREMISYS), due for completion in 1994–1995; and the corporate financial and management accounting system (FINESSE), due for completion in 1994–1995. These major projects will be followed by an integrated personnel system (MIPS), a comprehensive system for divisional administrative support (Processing), and Event and Resource Management, which will be closely linked with the Command and Control system and record all events and the allocation of staff to them. The Metropolitan Police Service is firmly committed to an open systems IT architecture into which new databases, applications, hardware and users can easily be plugged and within which existing services can easily be upgraded or extended. The architecture, which will provide an infrastructure of integrated communications and computing hardware and software, extending from the centre to divisional level, is crucial to the successful implementation of most of the planned major systems. Continued improvements will be made in the Command and Control system. Metnet, the Service-wide data network, was completed in 1989. A five year strategic plan, to enable the network to support changing patterns to traffic and workload, was approved in 1990 and is now being implemented. Plans have been made for local area networks, which provide for data entry and access for a variety of applications at many points within a building, to be installed progressively in selected divisional, Area, and headquarters buildings from 1992–1993. The fingerprint system (Videofile) will be replaced in 1992–1993, and the automated fingerprint recognition system (FOCUS) will then be upgraded.

11) Purchasing and Provisioning

i) To Conduct Purchasing and Provisioning in the Most Effective, Efficient and Economical Way, with Due Regard to Environmental Considerations

Under a process known as the Provisioning Review the activities of the provisioning departments have been divided into those which have to be carried out in-house and those which do not. This division is reviewed annually, and a programme of efficiency initiatives is prepared each year, designed to produce target savings in targeted areas of expenditure. The Purchasing Unit provides a service to help heads of department to meet their targets. The potential for contracting out is considered as part of the process. Among other things, a contract for the repair of 2000 divisional personal radios has been let, and the maintenance of some 230 vehicles has been contracted out. The catering operation on one of the Areas has been contracted out in a pilot scheme. Performance under these contracts will be closely monitored. The in-house printing operation is being purchased out. The Purchasing Unit will ensure that all aspects of contract action and purchasing affected by developments in Europe are fully taken into account. The optimum arrangements for the purchasing function with the Metropolitan Police Service are being worked out, and a purchasing training strategy will be implemented. A coordinated environmental strategy in purchasing and provisioning will be developed.

12) Financial Management

i) To Improve Financial Systems and Devolve Financial Control Financial management, responsibility and accountability will be devolved to the users of resources to the maximum extent and to the lowest levels that are consistent with good management practice and with obtaining value for money. The scope for including additional items within the local budgets will be extended to headquarters departments (there will be a pilot scheme in 1992–1993). Cost-centre accounting will in due course be extended throughout the Service. Its extension to Areas and divisions will begin in 1992–1993. The FINESSE system now being developed will revolutionise financial procedures and be the core of all financial information processing within the Service. It will commence live running in September 1992 for the estimating system and in April 1993 for the accounting system. It will be extended to the provisioning departments in 1993–1994, and will provide improved information for cost-centre accounting in 1994–1995. The extension of terminal facilities to Areas and divisions will then be considered.

13) Value for Money

i) To Give Optimum Value for Money from Metropolitan Police Service Resources The achievement of value for money is a primary aim in all our activities. Individual managers are directly responsible for the cost-effective use of the resources under their control and are assisted by internal bodies, such as the Inspectorate and internal audit, which pay close attention to this matter. The Deputy Commissioner is responsible for the overall coordination of effort to achieve value for money within the Service; he chairs a newly-formed senior level group, which aims to promote good practice in this area and to establish a Service-wide system of measuring and reporting performance in terms of value for money. This group will be particularly concerned to ensure that optimum value is achieved in the development of police and civil staff manpower. It will also seek to increase the range and quality of indicators available for measuring the progress achieved. In the case of expenditure on supplies and services, the provisioning departments fix specific value for money targets and actual performance is monitored on a quarterly basis.

TO IMPROVE STRUCTURES, PERFORMANCE, AND STANDARDS

Further programmes of activity to improve structures, performance, and standards at all levels and thus to improve our delivery of service to the public. Management information systems are being developed to facilitate performance monitoring and to support decision-making processes. Many systems are already in existence; none is yet fully developed. Personnel, manpower deployment and overtime monitoring systems, the accounting and costing systems described above, an abundance of operational performance statistics, and the growing bank of quality service information have important contributions to make. The most effective use of these systems in support of Service management will depend on the development of a corporate management information database, including a Performance Information Bureau. This will be greatly facilitated by the implementation of open systems information technology. Coordination of these systems, together with inspection and review strategies and procedures, will contribute to the evaluation of individual and organisational performance and provide the opportunity for innovation and change to be managed more effectively.

14) Structure of Organisation

i) To Implement the Recommendation of PLUS in Respect of a New Headquarters Structure The aim is to clarify individual responsibility and to complement the changes to the policy-making process by restructuring the headquarters organisation. This embraces the clarification of responsibilities between the operations departments, adjustments in the arrangements at the centre for strategic coordination, consultancy, inspection and review, and the rationalisation of support departments. This restructuring will consolidate and strengthen the Service. It will improve coordination between the operational user and the support provider, focusing resources and efforts on the quality of service provided at the point of delivery of that service. Implementation will be mainly during 1992–1993, following the detailed planning stage.

ii) To Review the Structure and Role of Area in the Light of Headquarters Restructuring As a result of the headquarters restructuring, there will be a need to examine the roles of Area and division, and indeed of individual posts. This important review will follow and complement the headquarters restructuring.

iii) To Review the Role and Structure of the Metropolitan Police Service (Particularly Specialist Operations) in the Light of Regional and National Developments Possible changes to the regional or national structure of policing would have a direct effect on a range of tasks currently undertaken by the Metropolitan Police Service, especially in relation to intelligence gathering and combating organised crime.

15) Performance

i) To Enhance the Quality of Leadership Throughout the Metropolitan Police Service Good morale and motivation, and in turn good service delivery, are dependent on good leadership. PLUS has produced guidance that clarifies the roles and responsibilities of leaders. The implementation of this and other initiatives arising from the Personnel and Training Priority Project is now being coordinated by a Steering Group, chaired by an Area DAC [Deputy Assistant Commissioner]. The restructuring of the headquarters organisation will prepare the way for enhanced accountability, supported by a programme of education and training in respect of leadership. This will continue during 1992–1993.

ii) To Improve Performance on Service Delivery throughout the Metropolitan Police Service The appearance of Station Reception Offices will be further improved during 1992–1993 to complement the way in which service is delivered to the public. Civilianisation will be extended and training programmes further developed. Research has revealed the need to improve our response to all our customers, especially in our dealings with members of the public whether it be by way of telephone call or letter. We will review our response, refining and developing systems to ensure that recommended best practice is carried out and on-the-job training is provided for all staff. Additionally, various studies of divisional administrative support systems have identified a range of problems that hamper the performance of individuals, such as the excessive duplication and lack of information. The whole range of such systems and their interrelationships will be examined to assess where improvements are necessary.

iii) To Refine Those Newly Grouped Functions, within Headquarters, Responsible for Assessing Performance Across the Service The role of the Performance Information Bureau will be to promote the establishment of standards, following consultation with our customers, and Areas and departments. It is our intention to inspect the Service and review performance against common standards agreed with all managers in the Metropolitan Police. Performance measures will be developed and worked up in conjunction with our customers as well as the officers who will be governed by them and charged with the task of delivering service to the public.

16) Service Ethos and Ethical Standards

The statement of our Common Purpose and Values is our philosophical touchstone. It establishes our "service ethos" and promotes ethical standards.

i) To Promote the "Service" Ethos Quality of Service is an important product of PLUS. The programme has addressed organisational and personal values and now looks to management to ensure that these ideals are transplanted into practical action that embraces the range and quality of service we deliver to the people of London. Integrity, commitment, and resilience are all qualities we will continue to promote across our workforce.

ii) To Respond Positively to the Expectations of the Individual in Society and to Promote the Integrity of Individuals within the Metropolitan Police Service The proposed Citizens' Charter intends to empower the individual within society and is directly related to the quality of service provided by public agencies, including ourselves. As a result of positive action flowing from PLUS, we are confident that we will not only match but often exceed the agreed standards. An exploratory study is currently being conducted within the Service. The Statement of our Common Purpose and Values identifies our own code of ethics. We are looking to all our personnel, and in particular our managers, to continue the work of addressing the organisational and personal values embodied within it. This will involve a positive commitment to respecting and encouraging integrity, openness and the application of moral values to decision-making at all levels within the Service. This will enable us to deliver a high quality service to our customers.

Appendix B

REPORT OF THE INDEPENDENT COMMISSION OF THE LOS ANGELES POLICE DEPARTMENT* ("THE CHRISTOPHER COMMISSION")

SUMMARY OF THE REPORT

The videotaped beating of Rodney C. King by three uniformed officers of the Los Angeles Police Department (LAPD), in the presence of a sergeant and with a large group of other officers standing by, galvanized public demand for evaluation and reform of police procedures involving the use of force. In the wake of the incident and widespread outcry, the Independent Commission on the Los Angeles Police Department was created. The Commission sought to examine all aspects of the law enforcement structure in Los Angeles that might cause or contribute to the problem of excessive force. The Report is unanimous.

The King beating raised fundamental questions about the LAPD, including:

*Christopher, William, et al. "Summary Report." *Report of the Independent Commission on the Los Angeles Police Department*. Los Angeles, CA: City of Los Angeles, 1991.

- The apparent failure to control or discipline officers who had repeated complaints of excessive force on their records
- Concerns about the LAPD's "culture" and officers' attitudes toward racial and other minorities
- The difficulties the public encounters in attempting to make complaints against LAPD officers
- The role of the LAPD leadership and civilian oversight authorities in addressing or contributing to these problems

These and related questions and concerns form the basis for the Commission's work.

Los Angeles and Its Police Force

The LAPD is headed by Police Chief Daryl Gates with an executive staff currently consisting of two assistant chiefs, five deputy chiefs, and seventeen commanders. The City Charter provides that the Department is ultimately under the control and oversight of the five-member civilian Board of Police Commissioners. The Office of Operations, headed by Assistant Chief Robert Vernon, accounts for approximately 84 percent of the Department's personnel, including most patrol officers and detectives. The Office of Operations has 18 separate geographic areas within the City, divided among four bureaus (Central, South, West and Valley). There are currently about 8,450 sworn police officers augmented by more than 2,000 civilian LAPD employees.

While the overall rate of violent crime in the United States increased by three and one-half times between 1960 and 1989, the rate in Los Angeles during the same period was more than twice the national average. According to 1986 data recently published by the Police Foundation, the Los Angeles police were among the busiest among the officers in the nation's six largest cities. As crime rates soar, police officers must contend with more and more potential and actual violence each day. One moment officers must confront a life-threatening situation; the next they must deal with citizen problems requiring understanding and kindness. The difficulties of policing in Los Angeles are compounded by its vast geographic area and the ethnic diversity of its population. The 1990 census data reflect how enormous that diversity is: Latinos constitute 40 percent of the total population; whites, 37 percent; African-Americans, 13 percent; and Asian/Pacific Islanders and others, 10 percent. Of the police departments of the six largest United States cities, the LAPD has the fewest officers per resident and the fewest officers per square mile. Yet, the LAPD boasts more arrests per officer than other forces. Moreover, by all accounts, the LAPD is generally efficient, sophisticated, and free of corruption.

THE PROBLEM OF EXCESSIVE FORCE

LAPD officers exercising physical force must comply with the Department's Use of Force Policy and guidelines, as well as California law. Both the LAPD Policy and the Penal Code require that force be reasonable: the Policy also requires that force be necessary. An officer may resort to force only where he or she faces a credible threat, and then may use only the minimum amount necessary to control the suspect.

The Commission has found that there is a significant number of LAPD officers who repetitively misuse force and persistently ignore the written policies and guidelines of the Department regarding force. The evidence obtained by the Commission shows that this group has received inadequate supervisory and management attention.

Former Assistant Chief Jesse Brewer testified that this lack of management attention and accountability is the "essence of the excessive force problem . . . We know who the bad guys are. Reputations become well known, especially to the sergeants and then of course to lieutenants and the captains in the areas . . . But I don't see anyone bring these people up. . . ." Assistant Chief David Dotson testified that "we have failed miserably" to hold supervisors accountable for excessive force by officers under their command. Interviews with a large number of present and former LAPD officers yield similar conclusions. Senior rank-and-file officers generally stated that a significant number of officers tended to use force excessively, that these problem officers were well known in their divisions, that the Department's efforts to control or discipline those officers were inadequate, and that their supervisors were not held accountable for excessive use of force by officers in their command.

The Commission's extensive computerized analysis of the data provided by the Department (personnel complaints, use of force reports, and reports of officer-involved shootings) shows that a significant group of problem officers pose a much higher risk of excessive force than other officers:

- Of approximately 1,800 officers against whom an allegation of excessive force or improper tactics was made from 1986 to 1990, more than 1,400 had only one or two allegations. But 183 officers had four or more allegations, 44 had six or more, 16 had eight or more, and one had sixteen such allegations.
- Of nearly 6,000 officers identified as involved in use of force reports from January 1987 to March 1991, more than 4,000 had fewer than five reports each. But 63 officers had twenty or more reports each. The top 5 percent of the officers (ranked by number of reports) accounted for more than 20 percent of all reports.

Blending the data disclosed even more troubling patterns. For example, in the years covered, one officer had thirteen allegations of excessive force and improper tactics, five other complaint allegations, twenty-eight use of force reports, and one shooting. Another had six excessive force/improper tactic allegations, nineteen other complaint allegations, ten use of force reports, and three shootings. A third officer had seven excessive force/improper tactic allegations, seven other complaint allegations, seven use of force reports, and one shooting.

A review of personnel files of the forty-four officers identified from the LAPD database who had six or more allegations of excessive force or improper tactics for the period of 1986 through 1990 disclosed that the picture conveyed was often incomplete and at odds with contemporaneous comments appearing in complaint files. As a general matter, the performance evaluation reports for those problem officers was very positive, documenting every complimentary comment received and expressing optimism about the officer's progress in the Department. The performance evaluations generally did not give an accurate picture of the officers' disciplinary history, failing to record "sustained" complaints or to discuss their significance, and failing to assess the officer's judgment and contacts with the public in light of disturbing patterns of complaints.

The existence of a significant number of officers with unacceptable and improper attitude regarding the use of force is supported by the Commission's extensive review of computer messages sent to and from patrol cars throughout the city over the units' Mobile Digital terminals (MDTs). The Commission's staff examined 182 days of MDT transmissions selected from the period from November 1989 to March 1991. Although the vast majority of messages reviewed consisted of routine police communications, there were hundreds of improper messages, including scores in which officers talked about beating suspects: "Capture him, beat him and treat him like dirt. . . ." Officers also used the communications system to express their eagerness to be involved in shooting incidents. The transmissions also make clear that some officers enjoy the excitement of a pursuit and view it as an opportunity for violence against a fleeing suspect.

The patrol car transmissions can be monitored by a field supervisor and are stored in a database where they could be (but were not) audited. That many officers would feel free to type messages about force under such circumstances suggests a serious problem with respect to excessive force. That supervisors made no effort to monitor or control those messages evidences a significant breakdown in the Department's management responsibility.

The Commission also reviewed the LAPD's investigation and discipline of the officers involved in all 83 civil lawsuits alleging excessive or improper force by LAPD officers for the period 1986 through 1990 that resulted in a settlement or judgment of more than $15,000. A majority of these cases involved a clear and often egregious officer misconduct resulting in serious injury or death to the victim. The LAPD's investigation of these 83 cases was deficient in many respects, and discipline against the officers involved was frequently light and often nonexistent.

While the precise size and identity of the problem group of officers cannot be specified without significant further investigation, its existence must be recognized and addressed. The LAPD has a number of tools to promote and enforce its policy that only reasonable and necessary force be used by officers. There are rewards and incentives such as promotions and pay upgrades. The discipline system exists to impose sanctions for misconduct. Officers can be reassigned. Supervisors can monitor and counsel officers under their command. Officers can be trained at the Police Academy and, more importantly, in the field, in the proper use of force.

The Commission believes that the Department has not made sufficient efforts to use those tools effectively to address the significant number of officers who appear to be using force excessively and improperly. The leadership of the LAPD must send a much clearer and more effective message that excessive force will not be tolerated and that officers and their supervisors will be evaluated to an important extent by how well they abide by and advance the Department's policy regarding use of force.

Racism and Bias

The problem of excessive force is aggravated by racism and bias within the LAPD. That nexus is sharply illustrated by the results of a survey recently taken by the LAPD of the attitudes of its sworn officers. The survey of 900 officers found that approximately one-quarter (24.5 percent) of 650 officers responding agreed that "racial bias (prejudice) on the part of officers toward minority citizens currently exists and contributes to a negative interaction between police and community." More than one quarter (27.6 percent) agreed that "an officers's prejudice towards the suspect's race may lead to the use of excessive force."

The Commission's review of MDT transmissions revealed an appreciable number of disturbing and recurrent racial remarks. Some of the remarks describe minorities through animal analogies ("sounds like monkey slapping time"). Often made in the context of discussing pursuits or beating suspects, the offensive remarks cover the spectrum of racial and ethnic minorities in the City ("I would love to drive down Slauson with a flame thrower . . . we would have a barbecue"; "I almost got me a Mexican last night but he dropped the damn gun too quick, lots of wit"). The officers typing the MDT messages apparently had little concern that they would be disciplined for making such remarks. Supervisors failed to monitor the messages or to impose discipline for improper remarks and were themselves frequently the source of offensive comments when in the field.

These attitudes of prejudice and intolerance are translated into unacceptable behavior in the field. Testimony from a variety of witnesses depict the LAPD as an organization with practices and procedures that are conducive to discriminatory treatment and officer misconduct directed to members of minority groups. Witnesses repeatedly told of LAPD officers verbally harassing minorities, detaining African-American and Latino men who fit certain generalized descriptions of suspects, employing unnecessarily invasive or humiliating tactics in minority neighborhoods, and using excessive force. While the Commission does not purport to adjudicate the validity of any one of these numerous complaints, the intensity and frequency of them reveal a serious problem.

Bias within the LAPD is not confined to officers' treatment of the public, but is also reflected in conduct directed to fellow officers who are members of racial or ethnic minority groups. The MDT messages and other evidence suggest that minority officers are still too frequently subjected to racist slurs and comments and to discriminatory treatment within the Department. While the relative number of officers who openly make racially derogatory comments or treat minority officers in a demeaning manner is small, their attitudes and behavior have a large impact because of the failure of supervisors to enforce vigorously and consistently the Department's policies against racism. That failure conveys to minority and nonminority officers alike the message that such conduct is in practice condoned by the Department.

The LAPD has made substantial progress in hiring minorities and women since the 1981 consent decree settling discrimination lawsuits against the Department. That effort should continue, including efforts to recruit Asians and other minorities who are not covered by the consent decree. The Department's statistics show, however, that the vast majority of minority officers are concentrated in the entry-level police officer ranks in the Department. More than 80 percent of African-American, Latino, and Asian officers hold the rank of Police Officer I-III. Many minority officers cite white dominance of managerial positions within the LAPD as one reason for the Department's continued tolerance of racially motivated language and behavior.

Bias within the LAPD is not limited to racist and ethnic prejudices but includes strongly felt bias on gender and sexual orientation. Current LAPD policy prohibits all discrimination, including that based on sexual orientation. A tension remains, however, between the LAPD's official policy and actual practice. The Commission believes that the LAPD must act to implement fully its formal policy of nondiscrimination in the recruitment and promotion of gay and lesbian officers.

A 1987 LAPD study concluded that female officers were subjected to a double standard and subtle harassment and were not accepted as part of the working culture. As revealed in interviews of many of the officers charged with training new recruits, the problem has not abated in the last four years. Although female LAPD officers are in fact performing effectively, they are having a difficult time being accepted on a full and equal basis.

The Commission heard substantial evidence that female officers utilize a style of policing that minimizes the use of excessive force. Data examined by the Commission indicate that LAPD female officers are involved in use of excessive force at rates substantially below those of male officers. Those statistics, as confirmed by both academic studies and anecdotal evidence, also indicate that women officers perform at least as well as their male counterparts when measured by traditional standards.

The Commission believes that the Chief of Police must seek tangible ways, for example, through the use of the discipline system, to establish the principle that racism and bias based on ethnicity, gender, or sexual orientation will not be tolerated within the Department. Racism and bias cannot be eliminated without active leadership from the top. Minority and female officers must be given full and equal opportunity to assume leadership positions in the LAPD. They must be assigned on a fully nondiscriminatory basis to the more desirable, "coveted" positions and promoted on the same nondiscriminatory basis to supervisory and management positions.

Community Policing

The LAPD has an organizational culture that emphasizes crime control over crime prevention and that isolates the police from the communities and the people they serve. With the full support of many, the LAPD insists on aggressive detection of major crimes and a rapid, seven-minute response time to calls for service. Patrol officers are evaluated by statistical measures (for example, the number of calls handled and arrests made) and are rewarded for being "hardnosed." This style of policing produces results, but it does so at the risk of creating a siege mentality that alienates the officer from the community.

Witness after witness testified to unnecessarily aggressive confrontations between LAPD officers and citizens, particularly members of minority communities. From the statements of these citizens, as well as many present and former LAPD officers, it is apparent that too many LAPD patrol officers view citizens with resentment and hostility; too many treat the public with rudeness and disrespect. LAPD officers themselves seem to recognize the extent of the problem, nearly two-thirds (62.9 percent) of the 650 officers who responded to the recent LAPD survey expressed the opinion that "increased interaction with the community would improve the Department's relations with citizens."

A model of community policing has gained increased acceptance in other parts of the country during the past ten years. The community policing model places service to the public and prevention of crime as the primary role of the police in society and emphasizes problem-solving, with active citizen involvement in defining those matters that are important to the community, rather than arrest statistics. Officers at the patrol level are required to spend less time in their cars communicating with other officers and more time on the street communicating with citizens. Proponents of this style of policing insist that addressing the causes of crime makes police officers more effective crime-fighters, and at the same time enhances the quality of life in the neighborhood.

The LAPD made early efforts to incorporate community policing principles and has continued to experiment with those concepts. For example, the LAPD's nationally recognized DARE program has been viewed by officers and the public alike as a major achievement. The LAPD remains committed, however, to its traditional style of law enforcement with an emphasis on crime control and arrests. LAPD officers are encouraged to command and confront, not to communicate. Community policing concepts, if successfully implemented, offer the prospect of effective crime prevention and substantially improved community relations. Although community-based policing is not a panacea for the problem of crime in society, the LAPD should carefully implement this model on a city-wide basis. This will require a fundamental change in values. The department must recognize the merits of community involvement in matters that affect local neighborhoods, develop programs to gain an adequate understanding of what is important to particular communities, and learn to manage departmental affairs in ways that are consistent with the community views expressed. Above all, the department must understand that it is accountable to all segments of the community.

Recruitment

Although 40 percent of the candidates for admission to the Police Academy are disqualified as a result of psychological testing and background investigation, the commission's review indicated that the initial psychological evaluation is an ineffective predictor of an applicant's tendencies toward violent behavior and that the background investigation pays too little attention to a candidate's history of violence. Experts agree that the best predictor of future behavior is previous behavior. Thus, the background investigation offers the best hope of screening out violence-prone applicants. Unfortunately, the background investigators are overworked and inadequately trained.

Improved screening of applicants is not enough. Police work modifies behavior. Many emotional and psychological problems may develop during an officer's tenure on the force. Officers may enter the force well-suited psychologically for the job, but may suffer from burnout, alcohol-related problems, cynicism, or disenchantment, all of which can result in poor control over their behavior. A person's susceptibility to the behavior-modifying experiences of police work may not be revealed during even the most skilled and sophisticated psychological evaluation process. Accordingly, officers should be retested periodically to determine both psychological and physical problems. In addition, supervisors must understand their role to include training and counseling officers to cope with the problems policing can often entail, so that they may be dealt with before an officer loses control or requires disciplinary action.

Training

LAPD officer training has three phases. Each recruit spends approximately six months at the Police Academy. The new officer then spends one year on probation working with more experienced patrol officers who serve as Field Training Officers (FTOs). Thereafter, all officers receive continuing training, which includes mandatory field training and daily training at roll call. The commission believes that in each phase of the training additional emphasis is needed on the use of verbal skills rather than physical force to control potentially volatile situations and on the development of human relationship skills.

The quality of instruction at the Police Academy is generally impressive. However, at present the curriculum provides only eight hours in cultural awareness training. No more than one and one-half hours is devoted to any ethnic group. Substantially more training on this important topic is essential. In addition, the Academy's current Spanish language program needs to be reviewed and current deficiencies corrected. Officers with an interest in developing broader language skills should be encouraged to do so.

Upon graduation the new officer works as a "probationary officer" assigned to various field training officers. The FTOs guide new officers' first contacts with citizens and have primary responsibility for introducing the probationers to the culture and traditions of the Department. The Commission's interviews of FTOs in four representative divisions revealed that many FTOs openly perpetuate the siege mentality that alienates the patrol officers from the community and pass on to their trainees confrontational attitudes of hostility and disrespect for the public. The problem is in part the result of flaws in how the FTOs are selected and trained. The hiring of a very large number of new officers in 1989, which required the use of less experienced FTOs, greatly exacerbated the problem.

Any officer promoted to Police Officer III by passing a written examination covering Department policies and procedures is eligible to serve as an FTO. At present there are no formal eligibility or disqualification criteria for the FTO position based on an applicant's disciplinary records. Fourteen of the FTOs in the four divisions the Commission studied had been promoted to FTO despite having been disciplined for use of excessive force or use of improper tactics. There also appears to be little emphasis on selecting FTOs who have an interest in training junior officers, and an FTO's training ability is given little weight in his or her evaluation.

The most influential training received by a probationer comes from the example set by his or her FTO. Virtually all of the FTOs interviewed stated that their primary objective in training probationers is to instill good "officer safety skills." While the Commission recognizes the importance of such skills in police work, the probationers' world is quickly divided into "we/they" categories, which is exacerbated by the failure to integrate any cultural awareness or sensitivity training into field training.

The Commission believes that, to become FTOs, officers should be required to pass written and oral tests designed to measure communications skills, teaching aptitude, and knowledge of Departmental policies regarding appropriate use of force, cultural sensitivity, community relations, and nondiscrimination. Officers with an aptitude for and interest in training junior officers should be encouraged by effective incentives to apply for FTO positions. In addition, the training program for FTOs should be modified to place greater emphasis on communication skills and the appropriate use of force. Successful completion of FTO School should be required before an FTO begins teaching probationers.

PROMOTION, ASSIGNMENT, AND OTHER PERSONNEL ISSUES

In the civil service process for promotion of officers in the LAPD, the information considered includes performance evaluations, educational and training background, and all sustained complaints. The number and nature of any "unsustained" complaints, however, are not considered. The Commission recommends that a summary of unsustained complaints be considered in promotion decisions, as well as in pay-grade advancements and assignments to desirable positions that are discretionary within the LAPD and outside of the civil service system.

This is not to say that a past complaint history, even including a sustained complaint for excessive force, should automatically bar an officer from promotion. But there should be a careful consideration of the officer's complaint history including a summary of unsustained complaints, and particularly multiple complaints with similar fact patterns.

Complaint histories should also be considered in assignment of problem officers who may be using force improperly. For example, a problem officer can be paired with an officer with excellent communications skills that may lessen the need for use of force, as opposed to a partner involved in prior incidents of force with that problem officer. Another example is assignments to the jail facilities where potential for abuse by officers with a propensity to use excessive force is high. As several incidents examined by the Commission made clear, transfer of an officer to another geographical area is not likely to address a problem of excessive force without other remedial measures, such as increased supervising, training, and counseling.

Since 1980 the Department has permitted police officers working in patrol to select the geographic area or division for their patrol assignment subsequent to their initial assignment after completion of probation. As a result sergeants and patrol officers tend to remain in one division for extended periods. The Commission believes that assignment procedures should be modified to require rotation through various divisions to ensure that officers work in a wide range of police functions and varied patrol locations during their careers. Such a rotation program will increase officers' experience and also will enable the Department to deploy police patrols with greater diversity throughout the City.

Under the current promotion system officers generally must leave patrol to advance within the Department. Notwithstanding the importance of the patrol function, therefore, the better officers are encouraged to abandon patrol. To give patrol increased emphasis and to retain good, experienced officers, the LAPD should increase rewards and incentives for patrol officers.

PERSONNEL COMPLAINTS AND OFFICER DISCIPLINE

No area of police operations received more adverse comment during the Commission's public hearings than the Department's handling of complaints against LAPD officers, particularly allegations involving the use of excessive force. Statistics make the public's frustration understandable. Of the 2,152 citizen allegations of excessive force from 1986 through 1990, only 42 were sustained.

All personnel complaints are reviewed by a captain in the LAPD's Internal Affairs Division (IAD) to determine whether the complaint will be investigated by IAD or the charged officer's division. Generally, IAD investigates only a few cases because of limited resources. Wherever investigated, the matter is initially adjudicated by the charged officer's division commanding officer, with a review by the area and bureau commanders.

The Commission has found that the complaint system is skewed against complainants. People who wish to file complaints face significant hurdles. Some intake officers actively discourage filing by being uncooperative or requiring long waits before completing a complaint form. In many heavily Latino divisions, there is often no Spanish speaking officer available to take complaints.

Division investigators are frequently inadequate. Based on a review of more than seven hundred complaint investigation files, the Commission found many deficiencies. For example, in a number of complaint files the Commission reviewed, there was no indication that the investigators had attempted to identify or locate independent witnesses or, if identified, to interview them. IAD investigations, on the whole, were of a higher quality than the division investigations. Although the LAPD has a special "officer involved shooting team," the Commission also found serious flaws in the investigation of shooting cases. Officers are frequently interviewed as a group, and statements are often not recorded until the completion of a "pre-interview."

The process of complaint adjudication is also flawed. First, there is no uniform basis for categorizing witnesses as "independent" or "noninvolved" as opposed to "involved," although that distinction can determine whether a complaint is "unsustained" or "sustained." Some commanding officers also evaluate witnesses' credibility in inconsistent and biased ways that improperly favor the officer. Moreover, even when excessive force complaints are sustained, the punishment is more lenient than it should be. As explained by one deputy chief, there is greater punishment for conduct that embarrasses the Department (such as theft or drug use) than for conduct that reflects improper treatment of citizens. Statistical data also support the inference that the Department treats excessive force violations more leniently than it treats other types of officer misconduct.

Perhaps the greatest single barrier to the effective investigation and adjudication of complaints is the officers' unwritten code of silence: an officer does not provide adverse information against a fellow officer. While loyalty and support are necessary qualities, they cannot justify the violation of an officer's public responsibilities to ensure compliance with the law, including LAPD regulations.

A major overhaul of the disciplinary system is necessary to correct these problems. The Commission recommends creation of the Office of the Inspector General within the Police Commission with responsibility to oversee the disciplinary process and to participate in the adjudication and punishment of the most serious cases. The Police Commission should be responsible for overseeing the complaint intake process. Citizens must believe they can lodge complaints that will be investigated and determined fairly. All complaints relating to excessive force (including improper tactics) should be investigated by IAD, rather than at the involved officer's division, and should be subject to periodic audits by the Inspector General. While the Chief of Police should remain the one primarily responsible for imposing discipline in individual cases, the Police Commission should set guidelines as a matter of policy and hold the Chief accountable for following them.

STRUCTURAL ISSUES

Although the City Charter assigns the Police Commission ultimate control over Department policies, its authority over the Department and the Chief of Police is illusory. Structural and operational constraints greatly weaken the Police Commission's power to hold the Chief accountable and therefore its ability to perform its management responsibilities, including effective oversight. Real power and authority reside in the Chief.

The Chief of Police is the general manager and chief administrative officer of the Police Department. The Police Commission selects the Chief from among top competitors in a civil service examination administered by the Personnel Department. Candidates from outside the Department are disadvantaged by the city charter provisions and seniority rules.

The Chief's civil service status largely protects him or her from disciplinary action or discharge by giving him a "substantial property right" in his job and declaring that he cannot be suspended or removed except for "good and sufficient cause" based upon an act or omission occurring within the prior year. In addition, recently enacted Charter Amendment Five empowers the City Council to review and override the actions of the City's commissioners, including the Police Commission.

The Police Commission's staff is headed by the Commanding Officer, Commission Operations, a sworn LAPD officer chosen by the Police Commission, who normally serves in that post for two to three years. Because the Police Commission depends heavily on the Commanding Officer to review information received from the Department and to identify issues, it must also rely on his willingness to criticize his superior officers. However, he lacks the requisite independence because his future transfer and promotion are at the discretion of the Chief of Police, and he is part of the Chief's command structure as well as being answerable to the Police Commission.

The Police Commission receives summaries, prepared by the Department, of disciplinary actions against sworn officers, but cannot itself impose discipline. The summaries are brief and often late, making it impossible for the Police Commission to monitor systematically the discipline imposed by the Chief in use of force and other cases.

The Commission believes that the Department should continue to be under the general oversight and control of a five-member, part-time citizen Police Commission. Commissioners' compensation should be increased substantially. They should serve a maximum of five years with staggered terms. The Police Commission's independent staff should be increased by adding civilian employees, including management auditors, computer systems data analysts, and investigators with law enforcement experience. It is vital that the Police Commission's staff be placed under the control of an independent civilian Chief of Staff, a general manager level employee.

The Chief of Police must be more responsive to the Police Commission and the City's elected leadership, but also must be protected against improper political influences. To achieve this balance, the Chief should serve a five-year term, renewable at the discretion of the Police Commission for one additional five-year term. The selection, tenure, discipline, and removal of the Chief should be exempted from existing civil service provisions. The Chief should be appointed by the Mayor, with advice from the Police Commission and the consent of the City Council after an open competition. The Police Commission should have the authority to terminate the Chief prior to the expiration of the first or second five-year term, but the final decision to terminate should require the concurrence of the Mayor and be subject to a reversal by vote of two-thirds of the City Council.

Implementation

Full implementation of this Report will require action by the Mayor, the City Council, the Police Commission, the Police Department, and ultimately the voters. To monitor the progress of reform, the City Council should require reports on implementation at six month intervals from the Mayor, the Council's own Human Resources and Labor Relations Committee, the Police Commission, and the Police Department. The Commission should reconvene in six months to assess the implementation of its recommendations and to report to the public.

Chief Gates has served the LAPD and the City for forty-two years, the last thirteen years as Chief of Police. He has achieved a noteworthy record of public service in a stressful and demanding profession. For the reasons set forth in support of the recommendation that the Chief of Police be limited to two five-year terms, the Commission believes the commencement of a transition in that office is now appropriate. The Commission also believes that the interests of harmony and healing would be served if the Police Commission is now reconstituted with members not identified with the recent controversy involving the Chief.

More than any other factor, the attitude and actions of the leaders of the Police Department and other City agencies will determine whether the recommendations of this Report are adopted. To make genuine progress on issues relating to excessive force, racism, and bias, leadership must avoid sending mixed signals. We urge those leaders to give priority to stopping the use of excessive force and curbing racism and bias and, thereby, to bring the LAPD to a new level of excellence and esteem throughout Los Angeles.

Appendix C

SUMMARY OF SELECTED FEDERAL RESEARCH INITIATIVES

The U.S. Department of Justice, through the National Institute of Justice and Bureau of Justice Statistics, explores a wide range of issues related to all aspects of criminal justice. Conducting experimental research, program evaluation, and survey research and collecting justice "census" data, these agencies produce an array of publications to assist policy makers and researchers.

To provide the reader with additional resources, some selected studies have been summarized on the following pages. These studies were selected because they specifically relate to topics covered in this text as well as for the insight and usefulness they provide to policymakers and students of the police-community relationship. Complete reports are available from the noted agencies, should more information be desired.

NATIONAL INSTITUTE OF JUSTICE UNDERSTANDING AND PREVENTING VIOLENCE (1994)

Discussed: The findings of the National Academy of Sciences Panel on the Understanding and Control of Violent Behavior, established to review the current status of research.

Key Issues: The extent and nature of violence in the U.S.; promising opportunities for prevention; and areas in which further research and better measures are needed, particularly to identify causes and prevention opportunities.

Key Findings:

- The level of violent crime in the U.S. has reached high, though not unprecedented, levels.
- Between 1975 and 1989, harsher prison sentencing prevented some violent crimes through incapacitation and deterrence, but crimes committed by persons still "on the street" offset those preventive efforts.

- The strategy for violence reduction should include a criminal justice response and preventive interventions directed at multiple violence risk factors.
- Long-term prevention should include strategies directed toward children and their caregivers; interventions undertaken at the social and community level; and biomedical strategies in such areas as substance abuse by pregnant women. More immediate effects may be obtained by intervening in situations where violent events cluster, such as illegal drug markets, certain places where alcohol and firearms are readily available, and physical locations are that conducive to crime.
- Violence control policy should proceed through a problem-solving strategy in which many tactics are tested, evaluated, and refined. This effort requires sustained integrated work by criminal justice, social service, and community-based organizations.
- The knowledge base needs to be increased by developing better systems to measure violence, expanding research support in certain neglected areas, and through long-term study of the factors that give rise to violent behavior.

NATIONAL INSTITUTE OF JUSTICE CASE STUDIES OF COMMUNITY ANTI-DRUG EFFORTS (1994)

Discussed: Case studies of thirteen grassroots community responses to illegal drugs their neighborhoods.

Key Issues: The wide variety of citizen initiatives revealed by the case studies showed how the groups assumed different levels of responsibility, functioned within social networks, and were influenced by various leaders. Assessing success of their efforts involves determining improvement in the quality of life in the neighborhood with respect to the drug trade.

Key Findings:

- Effective community anti-drug efforts show wide variations in institutional robustness and in the breadth of approach to drug problems. In general, researchers recommend that citizens be encouraged and helped to address drug problems from a perspective broader than that of drug abuse alone. In addition, community efforts that provide a comprehensive approach to drugs and crime are more likely to be sustained.
- Policymakers need to appreciate and support community efforts focused primarily on drugs. Although some of these efforts were found to be fragile and tenuous, such informal associations can be an effective and viable entity in combating drug problems.
- Useful forms of citizen anti-drug efforts have emerged in a variety of neighborhoods, including those seriously afflicted by crime and violence that were previously not considered likely to engage in this form of community action.
- Citizen drug fighters emerge from a variety of backgrounds and experiences. They need and appropriately use both conventional and unconventional resources to meet their objectives.
- Policymakers should consider carefully the broad scope of help they can provide citizens, which ranges from financial help to granting access to decision makers, from providing a meeting room to offering technical assistance on organizing and implementing program activities.

- Police play a particularly pivotal role in citizens' assault on drugs. Many citizens initially regard the drug problem as one of obtaining adequate police protection but, in general, partnerships involving citizens, police, and other agencies provide useful strategies to combat drugs.
- To forge productive relationships between police and citizens, police executives should actively support local patrol officers in working with citizen groups. Police officers should be encouraged to respond to all interested citizens, even those who may initially be rancorous and complain, since these individuals often evolve into hardworking partners with the police.
- No single community response to drugs can be considered the best, so research should be conducted to identify the approaches that work best under specific conditions and in various neighborhood settings.

NATIONAL INSTITUTE OF JUSTICE FIREARMS AND VIOLENCE (1994)

Discussed: The current status of research and evaluations concerning firearms and violent crime, as reviewed by the National Academy of Sciences Panel on the Understanding and Control of Violent Behavior.

Key Issues: Most murders involve firearms, and young minority men are at especially high risk of being murdered with a gun. Innovations in laws, law enforcement, public education, and technology all show promise of reducing gun murders by selectively making firearms less available to persons likely to use them in violence, less accessible in situations where violence is likely to occur, or less lethal. Evaluations are needed to test the effectiveness of these innovations.

Key Findings:

- Firearms are used in about 60 percent of the murders committed in the U.S. and attacks with firearms injure thousands of others. The risk of being murdered with a firearm falls disproportionately on young people, particularly young black men.
- Greater gun availability increases the rates of murder and felony gun use, but does not appear to affect general violence levels.
- Self-defense is the most commonly cited reason for acquiring a gun, but it is unclear how often these guns are used for self-protection against unprovoked attacks.
- According to the latest available data, those who use guns in violent crimes rarely purchase them directly from licensed dealers; most guns used in crime have been stolen or transferred between individuals after the original purchase.
- In robberies and assaults, victims are far more likely to die when the perpetrator is armed with a gun than when he or she has another weapon or is unarmed.
- Several strategies may succeed in reducing gun murders, but rigorous evaluations are needed to ascertain their effectiveness. Among these strategies are: reducing firearm lethality (e.g., by banning certain types of ammunition), reducing unauthorized use (e.g., through combination locks on triggers, or sentence enhancements for burglary and fencing violations that involve guns), and educating the public about safe use and storage.
- Evaluation findings indicate that the following kinds of laws can reduce gun murder rates when they are enforced: prohibitions on carrying concealed

weapons, extending sentences for robbery and assault when a gun is used, and restrictive licensing requirements for handgun ownership.

- Where there is local support, priority should be given to three enforcement objectives: disrupting illegal gun markets; reducing juveniles' access to guns; and close cooperation between the police and the community to set priorities and enforce laws, in order to reduce the fears that lead to gun ownership for self-defense.

NATIONAL INSTITUTE OF JUSTICE NATIONAL ASSESSMENT PROGRAM (1995)

Discussed: Findings of the NIJ National Assessment Program, which is conducted every three years to identify the most pressing problems faced by the various components of the criminal justice system at state and local levels.

Key Issues: More than 2,500 criminal justice officials were asked whether various problems contributed to their workload, what they were doing to solve them, whether their approaches needed improvement, and what their priorities were for future research and evaluation.

Key Findings:

- Respondents were most concerned with violence, drugs, and firearms—particularly as they affected young people, both as victims and offenders.
- More than 65 percent of respondents indicated that cases involving violence caused problems in workload management. Police chiefs and sheriffs indicated domestic violence as the primary concern and prosecutors highly ranked child abuse and domestic violence.
- Drug-related crime caused workload difficulties to an even greater extent than violent crime.
- More than 80 percent of police chiefs and sheriffs said crimes committed with a firearm contributed to their workload problems, and they were concerned particularly about the availability of firearms to juveniles.
- Police chiefs and sheriffs cited community policing most frequently as their approach to deter crime.
- Almost three-fourths of the police chiefs had programs for at-risk youths, and most other chiefs expressed that they would like to see such programs established.
- The response to gang-related crime, a problem in the vast majority of large jurisdictions and a growing concern in less-populated areas, has involved enforcement and prevention. Among correctional facilities, gangs were a more serious problem in prisons than jails.
- The vast majority of police and sheriffs' offices have strategies in recruitment and training for working with culturally diverse communities.
- The greatest need revealed in the study was the need for adequate information systems, although specific needs varied by category of respondent.

BUREAU OF JUSTICE STATISTICS FIREARM INJURY FROM CRIME (1996)

- Of the victims of nonfatal violent crime who faced an assailant armed with a firearm, 3 percent suffered gunshot wounds.

- Over half of all nonfatal firearm injuries treated in emergency departments were known to have resulted from an assault.
- An estimated 57,500 nonfatal gunshot wounds from assaults were treated in hospital emergency departments from June 1992 through May 1993.
- Of those victims who received nonfatal gunshot wounds from crime and were treated in an emergency room, 65 percent arrived by emergency medical service, rescue squad, or ambulance.
- Almost half of the victims of nonfatal gunshot wounds from crime were shot in the arm, hand, leg, or foot.
- About 60 percent of the victims of nonfatal firearm injury from crime who went to an emergency room were subsequently hospitalized.
- Over half of the victims of nonfatal gunshot wounds from crime who were treated in emergency departments were black males; a quarter were black males aged fifteen to twenty-four.
- While the majority of victims of intentional gunshot wounds were black, most victims of unintentional firearm injury and suicide attempts with firearms were white.
- For 12 percent of the victims of nonfatal gunshot wounds from crime, the term "drive-by" was used to describe the assault.
- The firearm injury rate for police officers declined in early 1980 and began climbing again after 1987, but has not exceeded the peak reached in 1980 to 1981.

BUREAU OF JUSTICE STATISTICS GUNS USED IN CRIME (1996)

- Although most crime is not committed with guns, most gun-related crime is committed with handguns.
- Although most available guns are not used in crime, information about the 223 million guns available to the general public provides a context for evaluating criminal preferences for guns.
- By definition, stolen guns are available to criminals. The FBI's National Crime Information Center (NCIC) stolen gun file contains over two million reports; 60 percent are reports of stolen handguns.
- In 1994, the Bureau of Alcohol, Tobacco, and Firearms (ATF) received over 85,132 requests from law enforcement agencies for traces of guns used in crime. Over three-quarters of the guns traced by the ATF in 1994 were handguns and almost a third were less than three years old.
- Surveys of inmates show that they prefer concealable, large-caliber guns. Juvenile offenders appear to be more likely to possess guns than adults.
- Studies of the guns used in homicides show that large-caliber revolvers are the most frequent type of gun used in homicides, but the number of large-caliber semi-automatic guns used in murders is increasing.
- Little information exists about the use of so-called "assault weapons" in crime. The information that does exist uses varying definitions of assault weapons that were developed before the federal assault weapons ban was enacted.

BUREAU OF JUSTICE STATISTICS WEAPONS OFFENSES AND OFFENDERS (1995)

- Weapons arrestees are predominantly male, age 18 or over, and white. However, weapons arrest rates per 100,000 population are highest for teens and for blacks.

- Arrests of juveniles comprise an increasing proportion of weapons arrests.
- The number of federal weapons offenses investigated and prosecuted has increased at least at least fourfold since 1980.
- Average prison sentence lengths for federal weapons offenders have increased, while those for state offenders have decreased.
- Of the defendants in felony weapons cases in the seventy-five largest counties in 1992, two-fifths were on probation, parole, or pretrial release at the time of the offense, and one-third had previously been convicted of a felony.
- Weapons offenses are making up an increasing proportion of admissions to state and federal prisons.
- Although many more offenders are admitted to federal prison for drug offenses than for weapons offenses, from 1985 to 1992 the rate of increase in admissions of weapons offenders was four times greater than the rate of increase of drug offenders.
- Weapons charges as an addition to other charges are more common at the federal level than the state level.

NATIONAL INSTITUTE OF JUSTICE IMPLEMENTATION CHALLENGES IN COMMUNITY POLICING (1996)

Discussed: This was an NIJ-sponsored evaluation of Innovative Neighborhood-Oriented Policing (INOP) programs, which were established with Bureau of Justice Assistance support in eight urban sites. Distinguished by their focus on neighborhood drug problems, the programs used community policing techniques, particularly police-community partnerships, to attempt to lower the demand for illegal drugs.

Key Issues: Implementation issues received special emphasis in the study, including the extent to which police officers understood and supported the projects and the degree to which other public agencies and the community were involved. The study also examined police and residents' perceptions of INOP's impact. Because the evaluation was conducted relatively soon after the programs were adopted, it could not assess long-term effects. the cities involved in the evaluation were: Hayward, CA; Houston, TX; Louisville, KY; New York, NY; Norfolk, VA; Portland, OR; Prince George's County, MD; and Tempe, AZ.

Key Findings: Evaluation of INOP programs revealed . . .

- The major implementation challenges were resistance by police officers to community policing and the difficulty involving other public agencies and of organizing the community.
- With the exception of one site, the involvement of other public agencies was limited.
- Police officers generally did not understand community policing; saw INOP assignments as conferring an elite status; perceived INOP as less productive, more time-consuming, and more resource-intensive than traditional policing; and felt their powers, particularly to enforce the law, were restrained.
- Average citizens had less knowledge than community leaders about INOP and were reluctant to participate; their reasons included fear of drug dealers' retaliation and cynicism about the perceived short duration of the project.

- The perceived effects of INOP on drug trafficking were mixed; they resulted in geographic and temporal displacement of markets. In the sites where people thought INOP had reduced crime, fear of crime declined.
- Most site residents believed their relationship with the police had improved, even where the effect on drugs, crime, and fear was believed to be minimal.
- INOP's limited success in reducing drug crime and fear may be related to the obstacles generally encountered in transforming program ideas into action—especially within the short timeframe of this evaluation.

NATIONAL INSTITUTE OF JUSTICE STREET GANGS AND DRUG SALES IN TWO SUBURBAN CITIES (1995)

Discussed: The results of a study to determine the level of street gang involvement in drug sales arrests in two Los Angeles suburban cities (Pomona and Pasadena). Results are compared with those from an earlier study of gang involvement in cocaine sales based on arrest incidents in south-central Los Angeles.

Key Issues: The connection among street gangs, drug sales, and violence has been debated in police and academic circles as well as the media. The study assessed the magnitude of gang involvement in cocaine and other drug sales; compared the characteristics of drug sales incidents involving gangs with the characteristics of drug sales incidents not involving gangs; assessed the generalizability of cocaine-related findings to other drugs, and from urban to more suburban settings; and identified the implications of the research findings for development of law enforcement strategies.

Key Findings: The statistical connection between street gangs, drug sales, and violence was smaller than anticipated. Specific findings included:

- Gang members were arrested in 27 percent of 1,563 cocaine sale arrest incidents in Pasadena and Pomona.
- Rock or crack forms of cocaine were more often present in gang cases, but most aspects of cocaine sales incidents (e.g., location, firearm presence, and amount of cash) did not vary with gang involvement. Cases with gang members were more likely to include males, younger ages (by about five years), and blacks.
- Rates of gang involvement and gang/nongang differences were very similar to those reported in the 1985 south-central Los Angeles study. Thus, there was consistency over the ensuing decade.
- The presence of identified gang members in arrest incidents for sales other than cocaine was far lower (less than 12 percent of 471 cases). No differences were noted in the incident characteristics of the two types of cases. Higher percentages of Hispanics were arrested in other drug cases compared with cocaine sale incidents, but black suspects and younger people were more common in gang cases.
- Lower than expected rates of gang involvement in drug sales coupled with a lack of evidence of special impacts associated with gang involvement suggest a reconsideration of gang specialization in narcotics enforcement. The exception may be in the unusual case of the extremely involved drug-selling street gang. Investigation of homicides and other violent incidents may benefit more directly from the expertise of law enforcement gang specialists.

NATIONAL INSTITUTE OF JUSTICE THE USE OF COMPUTERIZED MAPPING IN CRIME CONTROL AND PREVENTION PROGRAMS (1995)

Computerized mapping has many crime prevention and control applications. Mapping software's unique ability to overlay disparate data sets makes it an excellent tool for identifying factors related to multidimensional, multifaceted crime problems. On the basis of a literature review and telephone interviews, various organizations were identified that use mapping technologies in crime control and prevention programs. These programs were assessed for the overall utility of these technologies, and the study identifies some obstacles to increased use of mapping. Highlights include:

- For crime control and prevention, mapping software has two primary goals: to further an understanding of the nature and extent of criminal and social problems in a community, particularly the relationship between criminal activity and possible contributing factors, and to improve the allocation of resources to combat these problems.
- Mapping efforts for crime prevention and control rely on police department data, particularly call for service and incident data. Community groups and multiagency task forces also use geographic and demographic data from the Census Bureau, other state and local government agencies, or commercial vendors.
- Mapping software is most widely used for crime analysis in medium and large police departments where computerized, "geocoded" data are a byproduct of routine, day-to-day work.
- Examples of mapping software applications in police departments include Chicago patrol officers' ability to produce their own maps (based on incident type or data range) and dispatchers' ability to locate calls for service and the nearest patrol cars and other response units.
- Examples of applications of mapping software by community organizations include mapping data on street-specific problems (Hartford) and abandoned houses and bars (Chicago).
- Multiagency task force applications include Denver's Pulling America's Communities Together (PACT) program's goals to map crime and delinquency risk factors as well as efforts in Savannah, Georgia, to map factors contributing to the city's crime problem.
- The main obstacles to mapping software use in crime control and prevention relate to hardware and software costs, user expertise, data acquisition costs, and data quality. Lower costs, increased data availability, improved data quality, and growing user sophistication are expected to lower these obstacles.

NATIONAL INSTITUTE OF JUSTICE "BOOT CAMP" DRUG TREATMENT AND AFTERCARE INTERVENTIONS: AN EVALUATION REVIEW (1995)

Discussed: An NIJ-sponsored assessment of adult boot camp programming, particularly those components dealing with substance abuse treatment and aftercare, based on empirical data from survey responses, site visits, and interviews.

Key Issues: There are few descriptive or evaluative studies on the nature of boot camp substance abuse programs, their impact on offenders, or the effectiveness of specific treatment strategies. However, the limited information available suggests that extant programming available in correctional boot camps is not likely to result in reduced recidivism or drug dependence among "graduates" who have been returned to the community. This Research in Brief examines the integrity of substance abuse treatment programs in correctional boot camps and whether such programming adheres to the general principles of effective drug treatment.

Key Findings: The state and federal officials, administrators, and program staff who participated in this study generally agreed on the importance of offender rehabilitation as an organizational goal, but for reasons of politics, structure, or statutory constraint, the study found that the substance abuse education/treatment programs actually implemented in boot camp facilities are not likely to result in the rehabilitation of boot camp participants. Specific findings suggest that a maximally effective boot camp treatment regime would:

- Include substance abuse education and treatment programs involving psychotherapeutic-based interventions, such as individual and small group therapies, with a focus on multimodal approaches that are relevant to the offender population.
- Arise from comprehensive planning processes that are sensitive to the unique environment and offender population of the facility and include input from substance abuse treatment professionals.
- Use standardized assessment processes to place inmates in individualized treatment programs.
- Employ or contract with well-trained, qualified substance abuse treatment providers to run facility programs and ensure that the ratio of inmates assigned to each of these professionals is sufficiently low to permit individualized approaches.
- Adopt the therapeutic community model, involving frequent staff/inmate interaction, the use of peer pressure to reinforce positive behavior and eliminate negative behavior, and a de-emphasis on the punitive aspects of boot camp experience.
- Include pre-release and post-release programming to ensure continuity of care throughout the institutional and aftercare phases of the program.

NATIONAL INSTITUTE OF JUSTICE THE DRUG USE FORECASTING PROGRAM: HOW FINDINGS ARE USED (1993)

Discussed: Examples of how some jurisdictions have used findings from NIJ's Drug Use Forecasting (DUF) program, which measures drug use levels within samples of the arrestee population in twenty-four cities.

Key Issues: DUF information is specific to the twenty-four sites and to the populations tested. However, on a local level, the information provides officials with an up-to-date picture of drug use and drug trends in the arrestee population and thus offers a means of allocating scarce prevention, enforcement, and treatment resources more effectively. On state and national levels, DUF findings supplement the data gathered by other measures of drug use that do not cover the arrestee population.

Key Findings:

- Specifically, DUF data have been used by localities to:
  —Inform law enforcement agencies about drugs of choice so they can develop anti-drug strategies.
  —Give drug treatment providers the specifics they need to design programs appropriate to the target population.
  —Raise public support for anti-drug legislation and programs.
- On the state level, DUF information has been used to:
  —Supplement other information gathered by networks of researchers, such as Community Epidemiology Work Groups, to develop statewide profiles of drug use.
  —Support appropriations for statewide drug prevention and treatment programs.
- In addition, the DUF voluntary self-report questionnaire has been amplified in specific cities to obtain more subjective information on how particular drugs are obtained and used as well as the precautions being taken (or not taken) by individual users to protect themselves from HIV infection.
- Since DUF findings are time-sensitive, the key to their maximum utility lies in their reaching the appropriate officials quickly and in brief, readable form.

BIBLIOGRAPHY

Aaronson, David E., et al. *Public Policy and Police Discretion: Processes of Decriminalization*. New York, NY: Clark Boardman, (1984).

Adams, R. "Criminal Justice: An Emerging Academic Profession and Discipline." *Journal of Criminal Justice*. Vol. 4 (1976).

Alex, Nicholas. *Black in Blue: A Study of the Negro Policeman*. New York, NY: Appleton-Century-Crofts, (1969).

American Bar Association Project on Standards for Criminal Justice. *Standards Relating to the Urban Police Function*. Chicago, IL: American Bar Association, (1975).

Attorney General's Task Force on Family Violence. *Final Report*. Washington, DC: U.S. Government Printing Office, (1984).

Avery, M. and D. Rudovsky. *Police Misconduct: Law and Litigation*. New York, NY: Clark Boardman, (1987).

Baehr, M. E., et al. *Psychological Assessment of Patrolmen Qualifications in Relation to Field Performance*. Washington, DC: U.S. Government Printing Office, (1968).

Baines, John M., et al. *Mutual Aid Planning*. Washington, DC: National Sheriffs' Association, (1973).

Baltimore County Police, Field Operations Bureau. *Community Foot Patrol Officer Guidelines and Procedures*. Towson, MD: Baltimore County Police Department, (1988).

Banton, Michael. *The Police in The Community*. New York, NY: Basic Books, (1964).

Barker, Thomas and David L. Carter (eds.). *Police Deviance*. 3d ed. Cincinnati, OH: Anderson Publishing Co., (1994).

Barker, Thomas and David L. Carter. "'Fluffing Up The Evidence and Covering Your Ass:' Some Conceptual Notes on Police Lying." In Larry Gaines and Gary Cordner. *Policing Perspectives: An Anthology*. Los Angeles: Roxbury Press, 1998.

Barry, D. M. "A Survey of Student and Agency Views on Higher Education in Criminal Justice." *Journal of Police Science and Administration*. Vol. 6; No.3:345–354 (1978).

Bastian, Lisa D. and Bruce M. Taylor. *School Crime: A National Crime Victimization Survey Report*, Washington, DC: Bureau of Justice Statistics (1991).

Bayley, David H. *Police and Society*. Beverly Hills, CA: Sage Publications, (1977).

Bayley, David H. and Harold Mendelson. *Minorities and the Police: Confrontation in America*. New York, NY: Free Press, (1969).

Beckman, Eric. "Police Education and Training—Where are We? Where Are We Going?" *Journal of Criminal Justice*. Vol. 4 (1976).

Belcher, John R. "Are jails replacing the mental health system for the homeless mentally ill?" *Community Mental Health Journal*, 24:3, pp. 185–195 (1988).

Bell, Daniel J. "The Police Role and Higher Education." *Journal of Police Science and Administration*. 7:467–75 (1979).

Benda, Brent B. "Crime, drug abuse, mental illness, and homelessness." *Deviant Behavior*. 8:4, p. 371 (1987).

Bennett, Richard R. and I. H. Marshall. "Criminal Justice Education in the United States: A Profile." *Journal of Criminal Justice*. Vol. 7 (1979).

Bent, Allen E. and Ralph A. Possum. *Police, Criminal Justice and Community*. New York: Harper & Row, (1976).

Berg, Bruce L. *Law Enforcement: An Introduction to Police in Society*, Boston: Allyn and Bacon, (1992).

Beto, George and Marsh, R. "Problems in Development of an Undergraduate Criminal Justice Curriculum." *Federal Probation*. 38:38–40 (1974).

Beyer, L. R. *Community Policing: Lessons Learned From Victoria*. Canberra, Australia: Australian Institute of Criminology, (1993).

Binder, Arnold, et al. *Use of Deadly Force by Police Officers*. Washington, DC: National Institute of Justice (1982).

Black, Algernon D. *The People and the Police*. New York, NY: McGraw-Hill, (1968).

Blake, G. F., et al. *Program Histories: Seven Consortium Universities*. Volume 1. Washington, DC: National Criminal Justice Educational Consortium (1976).

Block, Peter B. and D. Specht. *Neighborhood Team Policing*. Washington, DC: U.S. Government Printing Office, (1973).

Block, Peter B. and Deborah Anderson. *Policewomen on Patrol: Final Report*. Washington, DC: Police Foundation, (1974).

Blumberg, A. and E. Niederhoffer (1985). *The Ambivalent Force*. 4th ed. New York, NY: Holt, Rinehart & Winston.

Bordua, David J. (ed.) *The Police: Six Sociological Essays*. New York, NY: John Wiley and Sons, (1967).

Boydston, John E., et al. *Patrol Staffing in San Diego*. Washington, DC: Police Foundation, (1977.)

Brandstatter, Arthur F. and Larry T. Hoover. "Systematic Criminal Justice Education." *Journal of Criminal Justice*. Vol. 4 (1976).

Brantingham, Paul and Patricia Brantingham. *Patterns in Crime*. New York: Macmillan (1984).

Braswell, Mickey C. and Stephen E. Brown. "Teaching Behavioral Arts and Science to Law Enforcement Students: A Discussion of Some Issues." *Journal of Police Science and Administration*. Vol. 9 No. 1:19–23 (1981).

Broderick, John J. *Police in Time of Change*. Morristown, NJ: General Learning Press (1977).

Brown, Lee P. "The Police and Higher Education: The Challenge of the Times." *Criminology*. Vol. 12; No. 3:114–124 (1974).

Brown, Lee P. and H. Locke. "The Police and the Community." In R. A. Staufenberger (ed.), *Progress in Policing: Essays in Change*. Washington, DC: The Police Foundation (1980).

Brown, Michael K. *Working the Street: Police Discretion and the Dilemma of Reform*. New York, NY: Russell Sage Foundation (1981).

Bruns, Gilbert E. and C. O'Hearn. *An Analysis of the Consortium Endeavor.* Volume II. Washington, DC: National Criminal Justice Educational Consortium Reports (1976).

Bryant, Dan. *Community-wide Responses Crucial for Dealing with Youth Gangs.* Washington, DC: Office of Juvenile Justice and Delinquency Prevention, (1989).

Buck, George A., et al. *Police Crime Analysis Unit Handbook.* Washington, DC: National Institute of Law Enforcement and Criminal Justice (1973).

Bureau of Justice Statistics. *Report to the Nation on Crime and Justice.* 2d ed. Washington, DC: U.S. Department of Justice (1988).

Bureau of Justice Statistics. *Survey of Youth in Custody 1987.* Washington, DC: U.S. Government Printing Office (1988).

Bureau of Justice Statistics. *Criminal Justice Information Policy: Research Access to Criminal Justice Data.* Washington, DC: U.S. Department of Justice (Undated).

Bureau of the Census. *Statistical Abstract of the United States 1992.* Washington, DC: U.S. Government Printing Office, (1992).

Bursik, Robert J. and Harold Gramsick. *Neighborhoods and Crime: The Dimensions of Effective Community Control.* New York, NY: Lexington Books, (1993).

Burt, Martha R. and Barbara E. Cohen. "Differences among homeless single women, women with children, and single men." *Social Problems.* 36:5, pp. 521, (1989).

Cahn, Michael and James M. Tien. *An Evaluation Report of an Alternative Approach in Police Response: The Wilmington Management of Demand Program.* Cambridge, MA: Public Systems Evaluation, Inc. (1980).

Campbell, John. "Computer Support for Community Oriented Policing." *FBI Law Enforcement Bulletin.* (February, 1994), pp. 16–18.

Caplan, Gerald M. (ed.) *ABSCAM Ethics: Moral Issues and Deception in Law Enforcement.* Washington, DC: Police Foundation, (1983).

Carter, David L. "A Forecast of Growth of Organized Crime in Europe: New Challenges for Law Enforcement." *Police Studies.* Fall, (1992).

Carter, David L. "An Overview of Drug-Related Misconduct of Police Officers: Drug Abuse and Narcotic Corruption." Chapter in R. Weisheit. *Drugs and the Criminal Justice System.* Cincinnati, OH: Anderson Publishing Company (1990).

Carter, David L. "Community Alliance." In Larry T. Hoover, (ed.) *Police Management: Issues and Practices.* Washington, DC: Police Executive Research Forum (1992).

Carter, David L. *Community Policing and DARE.* Washington, DC: Bureau of Justice Assistance, (1995).

Carter, David L. "Drug Related Corruption of Police Officers: A Contemporary Typology." *Journal of Criminal Justice.* Vol. 18, No. 2 (1990).

Carter, David L. "Hispanic Interaction With the Criminal Justice System." *Journal of Criminal Justice*, Vol. 11, pp. 213–227 (1983).

Carter, David L. "Hispanic Perception of Police Performance: A Empirical Assessment." *Journal of Criminal Justice*, Vol. 13, pp. 487–500, (1985).

Carter, David L. "Issues and Trends in Police Education." *Criminal Justice Monograph.* Huntsville, TX: College of Criminal Justice, Sam Houston State University (1974).

Carter, David L. *Law Enforcement Intelligence Operations.* 5th ed. East Lansing, MI: School of Criminal Justice, Michigan State University, (1998).

Carter, David L. "Methods and Measures." In R. Trojanowicz and B. Bucqueroux, *Community Policing*. Cincinnati, OH: Anderson, (1989).

Carter, David L. "Police Brutality: A Model for Definition, Perspective, and Control." In A. Blumberg and E. Niederhoffer, (eds.). *The Ambivalent Force*. 3d ed. New York: Holt, Rinehart, and Winston, (1985).

Carter, David L. "Police Disciplinary Procedures: A Review of Selected Police Departments." In T. Barker and D. L. Carter, *Police Deviance*. 2d ed. Cincinnati: Anderson Publishing Company (1991).

Carter, David L. "Police Drug Corruption." In Larry Gaines and Gary Cordner, *Policing Perspectives: An Anthology*. Los Angeles: Roxbury Press, 1998.

Carter, David L. "Theoretical Dimensions in the Abuse of Authority by Police Officers." *Police Studies*. Vol. 7, No. 4 (Winter), pp. 224–236 (1984).

Carter, David L., Allen D. Sapp, and Darrel W. Stephens. *The State of Police Education: Policy Direction for the 21st Century*. Washington, DC: Police Executive Research Forum (1988).

Carter, David L. and Allen D. Sapp. *Police Chief Perspectives of Accreditation: Findings of a National Study*. Paper presented at the annual meeting of the Academy of Criminal Justice Sciences, Pittsburgh, Pennsylvania, 1992.

Carter, David L. and Allen D. Sapp. "Police Education and Minority Recruitment: The Impact of a College Requirement." *A PERF Discussion Paper*. Washington, DC: Police Executive Research Forum (1991).

Carter, David L. and Allen D. Sapp. *Program Evaluation Model for Community Policing*, Huntsville, TX: Texas Law Enforcement Management Institute (1991).

Carter, David L. and Allen D. Sapp. *Violence in America's Public Schools: Critical Findings*. Washington, DC: Police Executive Research Forum (1993).

Carter, David L. and Allen D. Sapp. "Police Experiences and Responses Related to the Homeless." *Journal of Crime and Justice*. (1993).

Carter, David L. and Allen D. Sapp. "The Effect of Higher Education on Police Liability: Implications for Police Personnel Policy." *American Journal of Police*. 8(1):153–66 (Spring 1989).

Carter, David L. and Allen Sapp. "The Evolution of Higher Education in Law Enforcement Organizations: Preliminary Findings from a National Study." *Journal of Criminal Justice Education*. Vol. 1, No. 1. (Spring 1990).

Carter, David L. and Darrel W. Stephens. *Drug Abuse By Police Officers: An Analysis of Policy Issues*, Springfield, IL: Charles C. Thomas, Publisher (1988).

Carter, David L., Allen D. Sapp, and Darrel W. Stephens. *Toy Guns: Involvement in Crime and Encounters With the Police*, Washington, DC: Police Executive Research Forum (1989).

Carter, David L., Allen D. Sapp, and Darrel W. Stephens. "Higher Education as a Bona Fide Occupational Qualification (BFOQ) for Police: A Blueprint." *American Journal of Police*. 7(2):1–27 (1988).

Carter, David L., Allen D. Sapp, and Darrel W. Stephens. *A National Study of Police Labor Relations: Critical Findings*, Washington, DC: Police Executive Research Forum (1990).

Carter, David L., Allen D. Sapp, and Darrel W. Stephens. *Survey of Contemporary Police Issues: Critical Findings*. Washington, DC: Police Executive Research Forum (1991).

Cascio, W. F. "Formal Education and Police Officer Performance." *Journal of Police Science and Administration*. 5:89–96 (1977).

Cascio, W. F. and L. J. Real. "Educational Standards for Police Officer Personnel." *The Police Chief*. Vol. 43, No. 8:89–96 (1976).

Caught in the Crossfire: A Report on Gun Violence in the Nation's Schools. Washington, DC: Center to Prevent Handgun Violence, (1991).

Cohen, B. and J. Chaiken. *Police Background Characteristics and Performance*. New York, NY: Rand Institute (1972).

Cohn, Alvin W. (ed.) *The Future of Policing*. Beverly Hills, CA: Sage Publications, (1978).

Cohn, Alvin and Emilio Viano (eds.) *Police-Community Relations: Images, Roles and Realities*. Philadelphia: Lippincott, (1976).

Commission on Accreditation of Law Enforcement Agencies. *Standards for Law Enforcement*. Alexandria, VA: CALEA, (1987).

Commission on Narcotic Drugs. *Situation and Trends in Drug Abuse and Illicit Traffic*. Vienna, Austria: United Nations (1991).

Committee on Government Operations. *A Citizen's Guide on Using the Freedom of Information Act and the Privacy Act of 1974 to Request Government Records*. Washington, DC: U.S. House of Representatives (1987).

Community Policing Consortium. *Understanding Community Policing: A Framework for Action*. Washington, DC: Bureau of Justice Assistance, (1994).

Conrad, John P. and Richard A. Myren. *Two Views of Criminology and Criminal Justice: Definitions, Trends, and the Future*. Joint Commission on Criminology and Criminal Justice Education and Standards (1979).

Constantine, T. "Higher Education for Police." *The Police Chief*. Vol. 39 No. 6 (1972).

Cordner, Gary and Gerald Williams. "Community Policing and Police Agency Accreditation." In Larry Gaines and Gary Cordner. *Policing Perspectives: An Anthology*. Los Angeles: Roxbury Press, 1998.

Couper, David C. *How to Rate Your Local Police*. Washington, DC: Police Executive Research Forum (1983).

Couper, David C. "Quality Leadership: The First Step Toward Quality Policing." *The Police Chief*. Vol. 55 No. 4:79–85 (1988).

Couper, David C. and Sabine Lobitz. *Quality Policing: The Madison Experience*. Washington, DC: Police Executive Research Forum, (1991).

Cox, John F. "Small Departments and Community Policing." *FBI Law Enforcement Bulletin*. (August, 1994), pp. 1–5.

Criminal Justice Accreditation Council. *Accreditation Guidelines for Post-Secondary Criminal Justice Programs*. Highland Heights, KY: Academy of Criminal Justice Sciences (1976).

Criminal Victimization in the United States. Washington, DC: U.S. Bureau of Justice Statistics, (1992.)

Cromwell, Paul F. and George Keefer (eds.) *Police Community Relations: Selected Readings*. St. Paul, MN: West Publishing Co., (1978).

Cromwell, Paul F. *Police-Community Relations: A Guide to Strengthening Relations with the Public*. Santa Cruz, CA: Davis, (1978).

Cromwell, Paul, James N. Olson, and D'Aunn Wester Avary, *Breaking and Entering: An Ethnographic Analysis of Burglary*. Newbury Park, CA: Sage Publications (1991).

Cronin, R. C. *Innovative Community Partnerships: Working Together for Change (Program Summary)*. Washington, DC: Office of Juvenile Justice and Delinquency Programs, (1994).

Culbertson, Robert G. and A. F. Carr. *Syllabus Design and Construction in Criminal Justice*. Washington, DC: Joint Commission on Criminology and Criminal Justice Education and Standards, (1981).

Dalley, A. F. "University and Non-University Graduated Policemen: A Study of Police Attitudes." *Journal of Police Science and Administration*. 3:458–68 (1975).

Davis, Kenneth Culp. *Police Discretion*. St. Paul, MN: West Publishing Co., (1975).

del Carmen, Rolando V. "Civil and Criminal Liabilities of Police Officers." In T. Barker and D. L. Carter (eds.). *Police Deviance*. 2d ed. Cincinnati: Anderson Publishing, (1991).

DeZee, M. R. *The Productivity of Criminology and Criminal Justice Faculty*. Joint Commission on Criminology and Criminal Justice Education and Standards (1980).

Dolbeare, Kenneth M. (ed.). *Public Policy Evaluation*. Beverly Hills, CA: Sage Publications, (1975).

Dombrink, John. "The Touchables: Vice and Police Corruption in the 1980s." In Thomas Barker and David L. Carter (eds.). *Police Deviance*. 2d ed. Cincinnati, OH: Anderson Publishing Co, (1991).

Donahue, M. E. and A. A. Felts. "Police Ethics: A Critical Perspective." *Journal of Criminal Justice*. Vol. 21, No. 4 (1993), pp. 339–352.

Dowling, Jerry. *Criminal Investigation*. New York, NY: Harcourt, Brace, Jovanovich, (1979).

Dunham, Roger G. and Geoffrey Alpert. *Critical Issues in Policing*. 2d. ed. Prospect Heights, IL: Waveland Press, 1993.

Durkheim, Emile. *Professional Ethics and Civic Morals*. Translated by C. Brookfield. Glencoe, IL: The Free Press, (1958).

Eck, John E. *Managing Case Assignments: The Burglary Investigation Decision Model Replication*. Washington, DC: Police Executive Research Forum (1979).

Eisenberg, Terry, et al. *Police Community Action: A Program for Change in Police-Community Behavior*. New York, NY: Praeger, (1973).

Elliston, Frederick and Michael Feldberg (eds.) *Moral Issues in Police Work*. Totowa, NJ: Rowman & Alleanheld Publishers, (1984).

Erickson, J. M. and M. J. Neary. "Criminal Justice Education—Is It Criminal?" *The Police Chief*. Vol. 43 No. 8 (1976).

Eskridge, Chris W. "Problems in the Use of Educational Standards—Another Side of the Controversy." *The Police Chief*. Vol. 44 No. 8 (1977).

Farmer, Michael. *Differential Police Response Strategies*. Washington, DC: Police Executive Research Forum, (1981.)

Felkenes, George T. "The Criminal Justice Component in an Educational Institution." *Journal of Criminal Justice*. Vol. 7 (1975).

Finckenauer, James O. "Higher Education and Police Discretion." *Journal of Police Science and Administration*. Vol. 3 No. 4:450–457 (1975).

Finnegan, J. C. "A Study of Relationships Between College Education and Police Performance in Baltimore, Maryland." *The Police Chief*. Vol. 43 No. 8 (1976).

Fischer, Pamela J. "Criminal activity among the homeless: a study of arrests in Baltimore." *Hospital and Community Psychiatry*. 39:1, p. 46 (1988).

Fischer, R. J. "Is Education Really an Alternative? The End of a Long Controversy." *Journal of Police Science and Administration*. Vol. 9 No. 3:313–316 (1981).

Fischer, R. J., et al. "Issues in Higher Education for Law Enforcement Officers: An Illinois Study." *Journal of Criminal Justice*. Vol. 13 (1985).

Flanagan, Timothy, et al. *Sourcebook of Criminal Justice Statistics*, Washington, DC: U.S. Government Printing Office, (1992.)

Fleissner, D., et al. *Community Policing in Seattle: A Model Partnership be Citizens and Police*. Washington, DC: National Institute of Justice, (1992).

Florida Chamber of Commerce. *Business Alliance: Planning for Business and Community Partnerships*. Washington, DC: Bureau of Justice Assistance, (1994).

Fogelson, Robert M. *Big City Police*. Cambridge, MA: Harvard University Press, (1977).

Fosdick, Raymond. *American Police Systems*. New York, NY: Century, (1920).

Fox, J. W. and R. W. Ullman. *Criminal Justice Education Manpower Survey*. Volume III. Washington, DC: National Criminal Justice Educational Consortium Reports (1976).

Franklin, Jack L. and Jean Thrasher. *An Introduction to Program Evaluation*. New York, NY: John Wiley and Sons (1976).

Friedman, Robert R. *Community Policing: Comparative Perspectives and Prospects*. New York, NY: St. Martin's Press, (1992).

Fyfe, James. *Good Policing*. Paper presented at the Annual Meeting of the Academy of Criminal Justice Sciences, (1993).

Fyfe, James J. "Police Use of Deadly Force: Research and Reform." *Justice Quarterly*. Vol. 5 No. 2:165–205 (1988).

Fyfe, James J. (ed.) *Readings on Police Use of Deadly Force*. Washington, DC: Police Foundation, (1982).

Gaines, Larry. "Community Oriented Policing: Management Issues, Concerns, and Problems." *Journal of Contemporary Criminal Justice* (March, 1994), 17–35.

Gaines, Larry K. "Criminal Justice Education Marches On." In R. Muraskin. *The Future of Criminal Justice Education*. Criminal Justice Institute. Brookeville, NY: Long Island University (1987).

Gaines, Larry and Gary Cordner. *Policing Perspectives: An Anthology*. Los Angeles, Roxbury Press, 1998.

Gaines, Larry, Mittie Southerland, and John Angell. *Police Administration*, New York: McGraw-Hill (1991).

Gambino, F. J. "Higher Education for Police—Pros and Cons." *Law and Order*. Vol. 21 No. 2 (1973).

Gardiner, John A. *The Politics of Corruption: Organized Crime in An American City*. New York, NY: Russell Sage Foundation (1970).

Geary, D. P. "College-Educated Cops—Three Years Later." *The Police Chief*. Vol. 37 (1970).

Geller, William G. *Police Leadership in America*. New York, NY: Pergamon Press (1986).

Geller, William G. and Michael Scott. *Deadly Force: What We Know*. Washington, DC: Police Executive Research Forum, (1992.)

Georges-Abezie, Daniel (ed.) *The Criminal Justice System and Blacks*. New York, NY: Clark Boardman, (1984).

Gibbons, Don C. and G. F. Blake. "Perspectives in Criminology and Criminal Justice: The Implications for Higher Education." *Criminal Justice Review*. Vol. 2 No. 2:23–40 (1977).

Girand, D. "What is Right for Education in Law Enforcement?" *The Police Chief*. Vol. 44 No. 8 (1977).

Goldstein, Herman. *Police Corruption: A Perspective on its Nature and Control*. Washington, DC: Police Foundation, (1975).

Goldstein, Herman. *Policing a Free Society*. Cambridge, MA: Ballinger (1977).

Goldstein, Herman. *Problem-Oriented Policing*. New York, NY: McGraw-Hill, (1990.)

Goldstein, Herman. "The New Policing: Confronting Complexity." *Research In Brief*. Washington, DC: National Institute of Justice, (1993).

Greene, Helen Taylor. "Community Oriented Policing in Florida." *American Journal of Police*. Vol. 12, No. 3 (1993), pp. 141–156.

Greene, Jack. "Personnel Policy Reform in American Law Enforcement: A Preliminary Inquiry." *American Journal of Police*. Fall:45–65 (1986).

Greene, Jack, et al. "Patterns of Entry, Professional Identity, and Attitudes Toward Crime-related Education: A Study of Criminal Justice and Criminology Faculty." *Journal of Criminal Justice*. Vol. 12:pp. 39–60 (1984).

Greene, Jack, et al. "Values and Culture in Two American Police Departments: Lessons from King Arthur." *Journal of Contemporary Criminal Justice*. Vol. 8, No. 3. (1992), pp. 182–207.

Greene, Jack and Ralph Taylor. "Community Based Policing and Foot Patrol: Issues of Theory and Evaluation." In J. Greene and S. Mastrofski (eds.,) *Community Policing: Rhetoric or Reality?* New York: Praeger Press (1988.)

Griffin, G. R. *A Study of Relationships between Level of College Education and Police Patrolmen's Performance*. Saratoga, CA: R & E Publishing (1980).

Gross, S. "Higher Education and Police: Is There a Need for a Closer Look?" *Journal of Police Science and Administration*. Vol. 1 No. 4 (1973).

Guller, I. B. "Higher Education and Policemen: Attitudinal Differences between Freshmen and Senior Police College Students." *Journal of Criminal Law, Criminology, and Police Science*. Vol. 63 No. 3 (1972).

Guyot, Dorothy. *Policing as Though People Matter*. Philadelphia, PA: Temple University Press, (1991).

Hale, Donna and Stacey Wyland. "Dragons and Dinosaurs: The Plight of Patrol Women." In Larry Gaines and Gary Cordner. *Policing Perspectives: An Anthology*. Los Angeles, Roxbury Press, 1998.

Hartmann, Francis X., Lee P. Brown, and Darrel W. Stephens. *Community Policing: Would You Know It If You Saw It?* East Lansing, MI: National Center for Community Policing, (1989).

Hatry, Harry P., et al. *Practical Program Evaluation for State and Local Governments*. Washington, DC: Urban Institute Press (1981).

Hess, Kären M. and Linda Miller. *Community Policing: Theory and Practice*. St. Paul, MN: West Publishing Company, (1994).

Hess, Kären M. and Henry M. Wrobleski. *Police Operations*. St. Paul, MN: West Publishing, Company (1993).

Hicks, John W. "DNA Profiling: A Tool for Law Enforcement." *FBI Law Enforcement Bulletin*. (August), pp. 1–5 (1988).

Hillgren, J. S., et al. "Primary Stressors in Police Administration and Law Enforcement." *Journal of Police Science and Administration*. Vol. 4 No. 4:445–449 (1976).

Holden, Richard. *Law Enforcement: An Introduction*. New York, NY: Prentice Hall, (1992).

Holden, Richard. *Police Management*. New York, NY: Prentice Hall (1986).

Hoover, Larry (ed.). *Police Management: Issue and Perspectives*. Washington, DC: Police Executive Research Forum, (1993).

Hoover, Larry T. *Evaluating the Impact of Education on Police Performance*. Paper presented at the annual meeting of the Academy of Criminal Justice Sciences, San Mateo, CA, (1976).

Hoover, Larry T. *Police Educational Characteristics and Curricula*. Washington, DC: National Institute of Law Enforcement and Criminal Justice (1975).

Hoover, Larry T. *Program Evaluation*. Washington: Police Executive Research Forum, 1998.

Hudzik, John K. "College Education for Police: Problems in Measuring Component and Extraneous Variables." *Journal of Criminal Justice*. Vol. 6 (1978).

Illinois Criminal Justice Information Authority, *Blueprint for the Future*. Chicago: ICJIA, (1991).

Institute for Law and Justice. "Community Policing for Safe Neighborhoods 2000: Partnerships for the 21st Century." *Conference Proceedings*. Washington, DC: National Institute of Justice, (1993).

International Association of Chiefs of Police. *Building Integrity and Reducing Drug Corruption in Police Departments*, Washington, DC: U.S. Department of Justice, Office of Justice Programs (1989).

International Association of Chiefs of Police. *Police Community Relations, Policies, and Practices*. Washington, DC: IACP and U.S. Conference of Mayors, (1964).

International City Management Association. *Community Oriented Policing: An Alternative Strategy*. Washington, DC: ICMA. (1992).

Jacobs, J. B. and S. B. Magdovitz. "At LEEP's End? A Review of the Law Enforcement Education Program." *Journal of Police Science and Administration*. Vol. 5 No. 1:1–18(1977).

Jeffery, C. Ray. *Crime Prevention Through Environmental Design*. Beverly Hills, CA: Sage Publications, (1977).

Johnson, Robert P. "Implementing Community Policing in a University Environment." *Campus Law Enforcement Journal*. (May/June, 1994), pp. 20–21, 34–35.

Kaminer, Wendy. "Crime and the Community." *Atlantic Monthly*. (May, 1994), pp. 111–120.

Kansas City, Missouri Police Department. *Response Time Analysis: Executive Summary*. Kansas City, MO: Board of Police Commissioners (1977).

Kappeler, Victor E. and Rolando V. del Carmen. "Police Civil Liability for Failure to Arrest Drunk Drivers." *The Police Chief*. Vol. 55, No. 10 (1988).

Kappeler, Victor, Allen Sapp, and David L. Carter. "Police Officer Higher Education, Citizens Complaints, and Department Rule Violations," *American Journal of Police*, Vol. XI, No. 2, pp. 37–54 (1992).

Kappeler, Victor E., Mark Blumberg, and Gary W. Potter. *The Mythology of Crime and Criminal Justice*. Prospect Heights, OH: Waveland Press, Inc. (1993).

Katzer, Jeffrey, et al. *Evaluating Information: A Guide for Users of Social Science Research.* Menlo Park, CA: Addison-Wesley Publishing Company (1978).

Kelley, Clarence M. *Kelley: The Story of An FBI Director.* Kansas City, MO: Andrews, McMeel, and Parker (1987).

Kelling, George L. "Police and Communities: The Quiet Revolution," *Perspectives on Policing,* Washington, DC: National Institute of Justice and Kennedy School of Government, Harvard University, (1988).

Kelling, George. *The Newark Foot Patrol Experiment.* Washington, DC: Police Foundation (1981.)

Kelling, George and William Bratton. "Implementing Community Policing: The Administrative Model." *Perspectives on Policing.* Washington, DC: National Institute of Justice, (1993).

Kelling, George L. and Catherine M. Coles. *Fixing Broken Windows.* New York: Free Press, 1996.

Kelling, George L. and Mark H. Moore. (1988). "The Evolving Strategy of Policing." *National Institute of Justice/Harvard University Perspectives on Policing.* Washington, DC: National Institute of Justice.

Kelling, George L., et al. *The Kansas City Preventive Patrol Experiment: Technical Report.* Washington, DC: Police Foundation, (1974.).

Kelling, George L., Robert Wasserman, and Hubert Williams. "Police Accountability and Community Policing." *Perspectives on Policing.* Washington, DC: National Institute of Justice and Kennedy School of Government, Harvard University, (1988).

Kelling, George, et al. (1974). *The Kansas City Preventive Patrol Experiment: Technical Report.* Washington, DC: Police Foundation.

Kelly Charles, Chief Constable. *Annual Report of the Staffordshire Constabulary.* Stafford, United Kingdom: Staffordshire Police, (1992).

Kelly, Marcy. "How the Media Handle Violence." *The Catalyst.* National Crime Prevention Council, November, p. 3 (1992).

Kennedy, Daniel M. "The Strategic Management of Police Resources." *Perspectives on Policing.* Washington, DC: National Institute of Justice, (1993).

Kleiman, Mark, et al. *Street-Level Drug Enforcement: Examining the Issues.* Washington, DC: National Institute of Justice (1988).

Klockars, Carl B. and Stephen D. Mastrofski (eds). *Thinking About Police: Contemporary Readings.* 2d. ed. New York, NY: McGraw-Hill (1991).

Kraska, Peter and Victor Kappeler. "Police On-Duty Drug Use: A Theoretical and Descriptive Examination." *American Journal of Police,* 7:1, pp. 1–28 (1988).

Kuykendall, Jack L. "Criminal Justice Programs in Higher Education: Courses and Curriculum Orientations." *Journal of Criminal Justice.* Vol. 5 (1977).

Kuykendall, Jack L. *Community Police Administration.* Chicago, IL: Nelson-Hall, (1975).

Langworthy, R. and E. Latessa. *Criminal Justice Education: A National Assessment.* Paper presented at the annual meeting of the Midwestern Criminal Justice Association, Chicago, IL, (1988).

Larson Richard C. and Michael Cahn. *Synthesizing and Extending the Results of Police Patrol Studies.* Washington, DC: National Institute of Justice, (1985).

LeDoux, John and Edward Tully. "A Study of Factors Influencing the Continuing Education of Police Officers." *FBI Law Enforcement Bulletin.* Vol. 51 No. 7 (1982).

Leonard, Vernon A. *Police Organization and Management*. Brooklyn, NY: Foundation Press, (1951).

Levenbach, Hans and James P. Cleary. *The Modern Forecaster: The Forecasting Process Through Data Analysis*. Belmont, CA: Lifetime Learning Publications (1984).

Levine, Michael and J. Thomas McEwen. *Patrol Deployment*. Washington, DC: National Institute of Justice (1985).

Lurigio, A. and R. C. Davis (eds.). *Victims of Crime: Problems, Policies and Programs*. Newbury Park, CA: Sage, (1994).

Lurigio, A. and Wesley Skogan. "Winning the Hearts and Minds of Police Officers: An Assessment of Staff Perceptions of Community Policing in Chicago." *Crime and Delinquency*. Vol. 40, No. 3 (1994), pp. 315–330.

Lynch, Gerald W. "The Contributions of Higher Education to Ethical Behavior in Law Enforcement." *Journal of Criminal Justice*. Vol. 4, 285–290 (1976).

Lynch, Gerald W. (1987). "A Police Command College." In R. Muraskin. *The Future of Criminal Justice Education*. Criminal Justice Institute, Brookeville, NY: Long Island University.

Lynden, Patricia. "Why I'm a Cop: Interviews From a Reporter's Notebook," *Atlantic*, 223, No. 3 (March) pp. 104–108 (1969).

Madison, Wisconsin Police Department. *Planning Report for the Experimental Policing District*. Madison, WI: Police Department (1988.)

Mann, Stephanie. *Safe Homes, Safe Neighborhoods: Stopping Crime Where You Live*. Berkeley, CA: Nolo Press, (1993).

Manning, Peter K. "The Police: Mandate, Strategies, and Appearance." In Peter K. Manning and John Van Maanen (eds.). *Policing: A View From The Street*. Santa Monica, CA: Goodyear Publishing Co., (1978).

Manning, Peter K. and John Van Maanen. *Policing: A View From the Street*. Santa Monica, CA: Goodyear Publishing, (1978).

Manning, Peter K. *The Narc's Game: Organizational and Informational Limits on Drug Law Enforcement*. Cambridge, MA: MIT Press, (1980).

Manning, Peter K. *Police Work: The Social Organization of Policing*. Cambridge, MA: MIT Press, (1977).

Marx, Gary T. "The Interweaving of Public and Private Police in Undercover Work." In Clifford Shearing and Philip Stenning, *Private Policing*. New York, NY: Sage Publications, (1987).

Marx, Gary T. *Undercover: Police Surveillance in America*. Berkeley, CA: University of California Press, (1988).

Marx, Gary T. "Commentary: Some Trends and Issues in Citizen Involvement in the Law Enforcement Process." *Crime & Delinquency*. 35:3(July):500–519 (1989).

Massey, D. "Why Us and Why? Some Reflections on Teaching Ethics to Police." *Police Studies*. Vol. 16, No. 3, (1993), pp. 77–83.

Mastrofski, Stephen D. "Eyeing the Donut: Community Policing and Progressive Reform." *American Journal of Police*. Vol. 12, No. 4 (1993), pp. 65–77.

Mastrofski, Stephen D. "Varieties of Community Policing." *American Journal of Police* " Vol. 12, No. 3 (1993).

McConville, Michael and Dan Shepherd. *Watching Police, Watching Communities*. New York, NY: Routledge, (1992).

McElroy, Jerome E., et al. *Community Policing in New York: The CPOP Research*. Newbury Park, CA: Sage Publications, 1993.

McEwen, Thomas. *Dedicated Computer Crime Units*. Washington: National Institute of Justice, (1989).

McEwen Thomas, et al. *Evaluation of the Differential Police Response Field Test*. Washington: National Institute of Justice, (1969.)

McLeod, Maureen. "Women Against Men: A Examination of Domestic Violence Based on an Analysis of Official Data and National Victimization Data," *Justice Quarterly*, Vol. 1, No. 2 (1984).

Meagher, M. S. *Perception of the Police Patrol Function: Does Officer Education Make a Difference?* Paper presented at the annual meeting of the Academy of Criminal Justice Sciences, San Antonio, TX, (1983).

Meese, Edward. "Community Policing and the Police Officer." *Perspectives on Policing*.Washington, DC: National Institute of Justice, (1993).

Meese, Edwin, et al. "Community Policing and the Investigator." *Journal of Contemporary Criminal Justice*. (December, 1993), pp. 289–302.

Miller, J. and L. Fry. "Reexamining Assumptions About Education and Professionalism in Law Enforcement." *Journal of Police Science and Administration*. Vol. 4 No. 2:187–196 (1976).

Milton, Catherine. *Police Use of Deadly Force*. Washington, DC: Police Foundation, (1977).

Milton, Catherine. *Women in Policing*. Washington, DC: Police Foundation, (1972).

Misner, Gordon E. *Criminal Justice Education: A National Profile*. Omaha, NE: The Academy of Criminal Justice Sciences, (1978).

Misner, Gordon E. *Criminal Justice Studies: Their Transdisciplinary Nature*. St. Louis, MO: Mosby Publishing (1981).

Morash, Merry and A. Anderson. "Impact Assessment: A Technique for Evaluating Criminal Justice Programs." *Criminal Justice Review*. Vol. 2 No. 2:23–33 (1977).

Morn, Frank T. *Academic Disciplines and Debates: An Essay on Criminology and Criminal Justice as Professions in Higher Education*. Joint Commission on Criminology and Criminal Justice Education and Standards (1980).

Muir, William Ker, Jr. *Police: Streetcorner Politicians*. Chicago, IL: University of Chicago Press, (1977).

Muraskin, Roslyn. *The Future of Criminal Justice Education*. Criminal Justice Institute. Brookeville, NY: Long Island University (1987).

Murphy, Patrick V. and Thomas Plate. *Commissioner: A View From the Top of American Law Enforcement*. New York, NY: Simon and Schuster, (1977).

Myren, Richard A. "Higher Education For Criminal Justice Careers." In R. J. McLean (ed.), *Education for Crime Prevention and Control*. Springfield, IL: Charles C. Thomas, (1975).

Myren, Richard A. *The Role of the Police*. Washington, DC: U.S. Government Printing Office, (1967).

National Advisory Committee on Criminal Justice Standards and Goals. *Disorders and Terrorism: Report of the Task Force*. Washington, DC: U.S. Government Printing Office, (1976).

National Advisory Council on Criminal Justice. *The Inequality of Justice: A Report on Crime and the Administration of Justice in the Minority Community*. Washington, DC: U.S. Government Printing Office, (1980).

National Advisory Commission on Civil Disorders. *Commission Report*. Washington, DC: U.S. Government Printing Office, (1968).

National Advisory Commission on Criminal Justice Standards and Goals. *A National Strategy to Reduce Crime*. Washington, DC: U.S. Government Printing Office, (1973).

National Advisory Commission on Criminal Justice Standards and Goals. *Police*. Washington, DC: U.S. Government Printing Office, (1973).

National Advisory Commission on Criminal Justice Standards and Goals. *Report on Community Crime Prevention*. Washington, DC: U.S. Government Printing Office, (1973).

National Advisory Commission on Criminal Justice Standards and Goals. *Report on the Criminal Justice System* Washington, DC: U.S. Government Printing Office, (1973).

National Commission on Higher Education for Police Officers. *Proceedings of the National Symposium on Higher Education for Police Officers*. Washington, DC: The Police Foundation (1979).

National Commission on Law Observance and Enforcement (Wickersham Commission). *Report on Police*. Washington, DC: U.S. Government Printing Office, (1931).

National Commission on the Causes and Prevention of Violence. *Crimes of Violence*. Washington: U.S. Government Printing Office (1969).

National Commission on the Causes and Prevention of Violence. *Law and Order Reconsidered*. Washington, DC: U.S. Government Printing Office, (1969).

National Commission on the Causes and Prevention of Violence. *Report of the Task Force on the Mass Media*. Washington, DC: U.S. Government Printing Office, (1969).

National Commission on the Causes and Prevention of Violence. *The Politics of Protest*. Washington, DC: U.S. Government Printing Office, (1969).

National Commission on the Causes and Prevention of Violence. *To Establish Justice, To Insure Domestic Tranquillity*. Washington, DC: U.S. Government Printing Office, (1969).

National Crime Prevention Council. *National Service and Public Safety: Partnerships for Safer Communities*. Washington, DC: Bureau of Justice Assistance, (1994).

National Crime Prevention Council. *Working as Partners with Community Groups*. Washington, DC: Bureau of Justice Assistance, (1994).

National Institute of Law Enforcement and Criminal Justice. *The National Manpower Survey of the Criminal Justice System: Law Enforcement. Vol. 2*. Washington, DC: U.S. Government Printing Office (1978).

Neary, M. *Higher Education for Police*. New York, NY: American Academy for Professional Law Enforcement (1977).

Nelligan, Peter J. and Robert W. Taylor. "Ethical Issues in Community Policing." *Journal of Contemporary Criminal Justice*. (March, 1994), pp. 59–66.

Niederhoffer, Arthur. *Behind the Shield*. Garden City, NY: Doubleday & Co., Inc., (1969).

Niederhoffer, Arthur and Alexander Smith. *New Directions in Police Community Relations*. San Francisco, CA: Holt, Rinehart and Winston, (1974).

Niederhoffer, Arthur and Elaine Niederhoffer. *The Police Family*. Lexington, MA: Lexington Books, (1975).

Normandeau, Andre. "Community Policing in Canada: A Review of Some Recent Studies." *American Journal of Police*. Vol. 12, No. 1 (1994), pp. 57–73.

North Carolina Criminal Justice Education and Training Standards Commission. *Certification Guidelines Manual for Post Secondary Criminal Justice Education Programs.* State of North Carolina (1988).

Nugent, M. Elaine. "Why Johnny Carries a Gun to School," *NCTAP News*, Alexandria, VA: Institute of Law and Justice (1992).

Oakley, R. "A Specialist Support Unit for Community and Race Relations Training for the British Police." *Police Studies.* Vol. 16, No. 4, (1993), pp. 129–137.

O'Rourke, W. J. "Should All Policemen Be College Trained?" *The Police Chief.* Vol. 38 No. 12 (1971).

O'Rourke, P. J. *Parliament of Whores.* New York, NY: Vintage Books, p. 113 (1991).

Office of National Drug Control Policy. *National Drug Control Strategy.* Volume 1. Washington, DC: U.S. Government Printing Office (1989).

Office of National Drug Control Policy. *National Drug Control Strategy.* Volume 2. Washington, DC: U.S. Government Printing Office (1990).

Office of National Drug Control Policy. *National Drug Control Strategy.* Volume 3. Washington, DC: U.S. Government Printing Office (1991).

Office of Technology Assessment. *The Border War on Drugs.* Washington, DC: Congress of the United States (1987).

Ostrom, Elinor, et al. *Patterns of Metropolitan Policing.* Cambridge, MA: Ballinger, (1978).

Ostrom, Elinor. *Police Department Policies Toward Education.* Washington, DC: The Police Foundation, (1978).

Ostrom, Elinor and William Baugh. *Community Organization and the Provision of Police Services.* Beverly Hills, CA: Sage Publications, (1973).

Parker, L. C., et al. "Higher Education: Its Impact on Police Attitudes." *The Police Chief.* Vol. 43 No. 7 (1976).

Peak, Kenneth J. *Policing America: Methods, Issues, Challenges.* Englewood Cliffs, NJ: Prentice Hall, (1993).

Pearson, R., et al. *Criminal Justice Education: The End of the Beginning.* New York, NY: John Jay Press (1980).

Peirson, G. *Higher Educational Requirements and Minority Recruitment for the Police: Conflicting Goals?* Washington, DC: The Police Foundation (1978).

"Police Efforts to Win and Solve Crime Win the Approval of Majority in Survey." *Law Enforcement News*, (pp. 1, 7) November 15, (1992).

Police Executive Research Forum and National Crime Prevention Council. *Neighborhood Oriented Policing in Rural Communities.* Washington, DC: Bureau of Justice Assistance, (1994).

Powell, D. D. "An Assessment of Attitudes Toward Police Education Needs." *Journal of Police and Criminal Psychology.* Vol. 2 No. 1 (1986).

President's Commission on Law Enforcement and Administration of Justice. *Challenge of Crime in a Free Society.* Washington, DC: U.S. Government Printing Office, (1967).

President's Commission on Law Enforcement and Administration of Justice. *Field Survey V: A National Survey on Police and Community Relations.* Washington, DC: U.S. Government Printing Office, (1967).

President's Commission on Law Enforcement and Administration of Justice. *Task Force Report: Police.* Washington, DC: U.S. Government Printing Office (1967).

President's Commission on Organized Crime. *America's Habit: Drug Abuse, Drug Trafficking, and Organized Crime*. Washington, DC: U.S. Government Printing Office (1986).

President's Commission on Campus Unrest. *Report: Campus Unrest*. Washington, DC: U.S. Government Printing Office, (1970).

President's Task Force on Victims of Crime. *Final Report*. Washington, DC: U.S. Government Printing Office, (1982).

Project Star. *The Impact of Social Trends on Crime and Criminal Justice*. Cincinnati, OH: Anderson-Davis Publishing Companies, (1976).

"Public Solidly Favors Mixed Police/Civilian Review Boards," *Law Enforcement News*, (pp. 1, 6) October 31, (1992).

Reardon, J. "Toward Paperless Police Department: the Use of Laptop Computers." *Research in Brief*. Washington, DC: National Institute of Justice, (1993).

Redlinger, Lawrence J. "Community Policing and Changes in the Organizational Structure." *Journal of Contemporary Criminal Justice*. (March, 1994), pp. 36–58.

Regoli, Robert M. "The Effects of College Education on the Maintenance of Police Cynicism." *Journal of Police Science and Administration*. Vol. 4 No. 3:340–345 (1976).

Regoli, Robert M. and A. W. Miracle *Professionalism Among Criminal Justice Educators*. Washington, DC: Joint Commission on Criminology and Criminal Justice Education and Standards (1980).

Reiss, Albert J. *The Police and the Public*. New Haven, CT: Yale University Press, (1971).

Reppetto, T. J. "Higher Education for Police Officers." *FBI Law Enforcement Bulletin*. Vol. 49 No. 1 (1980).

Riddle, Don H. *Liberal Arts and Vocationalism in Higher Education for Police Officers*. Washington, DC: The Police Foundation (1978).

Riksheim, L. R. and S. Chermak. "Causes of Police Behavior Revisited." *Journal of Criminal Justice*. Vol. 21, No. 4, (1993), pp. 353–382.

Roberg, Roy R. "An Analysis of the Relationships Among Higher Education, Belief Systems, and Job Performance of Patrol Officers." *Journal of Police Science and Administration*. Vol. 6 No. 3:336–344, (1978).

Roberg, Roy and Jack Kuykendall. *Police and Society*. Belmont, CA: Wadsworth Publishing Co., 1993.

Roberg, Roy and Jack Kuykendall. *Police Management*. 2d ed. Los Angeles: Roxbury Press, 1997.

Roberts, Albert R. *Critical Issues in Crime and Justice*. Thousand Oaks, CA: Sage, (1994).

Roberts, M. D. "Job Stress in Law Enforcement: A Treatment and Prevention Program." In W. H. Kroes and J. J. Hurell, Jr. (eds.), *Job Stress and the Police Officer*. U.S. Department of Health, Education and Welfare, Public Health Services. Washington, DC: U.S. Government Printing Office (1975).

Rosenbaum, Dennis P. (ed.). *Community Crime Prevention: Does It Work?* Beverly Hills, CA: Sage Publications, (1986).

Rosenbaum, Dennis and A. J. Lurigio. "An Inside Look at Community Policing Reform: Definitions, Organizational Changes, and Evaluation Findings." *Crime and Delinquency*. Vol. 40, No. 3, (1994), pp. 299–314.

Rosenbaum, Dennis P. (ed.). *The Challenge of Community Policing: Testing the Promises.* Thousand Oaks, CA: Sage, (1994).

Rosenbaum, Dennis, et al. "Impact of Community Policing on Police Personnel: A Quasi-Experimental Test." *Crime and Delinquency.* Vol. 40, No. 3, (1994), pp. 331–353.

Rosenbaum, Dennis, et al. *Aurora-Joliet Neighborhood-Oriented Policing and Problem-Solving Demonstration Project.* Project report submitted to the Illinois, Criminal Justice Information Authority, Chicago, Illinois, (1994).

Sapp, Allen D. "Issues and Trends in Police Professionalism." *Criminal Justice Monograph.* College of Criminal Justice, Huntsville, TX: Sam Houston State University, (1978).

Sapp, Allen D. "A National Survey of Police Education and Training Requirements." *The Police Chief.* Vol. 53 No. 11 (1986).

Sapp, Allen and David L. Carter. *A National Study of Police Labor Relations: Critical Findings.* Washington, DC: Police Executive Research Forum (1991).

Saunders, C. B. *Upgrading the American Police.* Washington, DC: The Brookings Institution (1970).

Scharf, Peter and Arnold Binder. *The Badge and the Bullet: Police Use of Deadly Force.* New York, NY: Praeger Press, (1983).

Scheetz, L. P. *Recruiting Trends.* East Lansing, MI: Collegiate Employment Research Institute, Michigan State University, (1990.)

Schick, R. P. *Structural and Attitudinal Barriers to High Educational Requirements for Police Officers.* Washington, DC: The Police Foundation (1978).

Scott, W. R. "College Education Requirements for Police Entry Level and Promotion: A Study." *Journal of Police and Criminal Psychology.* Vol. 2 No. 1 (1986).

SEARCH Group, Inc. *Public Access to Criminal History and Record Information.* Washington, DC: Bureau of Justice Statistics (1988).

Senna, J. J. "Criminal Justice Higher Education—Its Growth and Direction." *Crime and Delinquency.* Vol. 20 October:389–397, (1974).

Sheehy, Patrick, et al. *Inquiry into Police Responsibilities and Rewards: Executive Summary.* London, England: Her Majesty's Stationery Office, (1994).

Sherman, Lawrence W. and Mark Blumberg. "Higher Education and Police Use of Deadly Force," *Journal of Criminal Justice.* Vol. 9 317–331, (1981).

Sherman, Lawrence W. and the National Advisory Commission on Higher Education of Police Officers. *The Quality of Police Education.* Washington, DC: Josey-Bass, (1978).

Sherman, Lawrence W. "Learning Police Ethics." *Criminal Justice Ethics.* Winter/Spring, (1982).

Sherman, Lawrence W. "Execution Without Trial: Police Homicide and the Constitution," in Thomas Barker and David L. Carter, *Police Deviance*, 2d edition, Cincinnati, OH: Anderson Publishing Company, (1991.)

Sherman, Lawrence W. and Ellen G. Cohn. *Citizens Killed by Big-City Police, 1970–1984*, Washington, DC: Crime Control Institute (1986).

Sherman, Lawrence W. and Richard A. Berk. "The Specific Deterrent Effects of Arrests on Domestic Assault," *American Sociological Review*, Vol. 9, April, pp. 261–272, (1984).

Sherman, Lawrence W. and Richard A. Berk. *The Minneapolis Domestic Violence Experiment*, Washington, DC: Police Foundation (1984).

Sherman, Lawrence W. *Police Corruption: A Sociological Perspective*. Garden City, NY: Anchor Books, (1974).

Sherman, Lawrence W. *Scandal and Reform: Controlling Police Corruption*. Berkeley, CA: University of California Press, (1978).

Sherman, Lawrence W., et al., *Team Policing*. Washington, DC: Police Foundation, (1973).

Simpson, A. E. *Accreditation and Its Significance for Programs of Higher Education in Criminology and Criminal Justice: A Review of the Literature*. Joint Commission on Criminology and Criminal Justice Education and Standards (1979).

Skolnick, Jerome and Candace McCoy, "Police Accountability and the Media," in William Geller (ed.) *Police Leadership in America*, New York, NY: Praeger Publishers, (1985).

Skolnick, Jerome and David Bailey. *The New Blue Line*. New York, NY: The Free Press (1986.)

Skolnick, Jerome H. (ed.) *Police in America*. Boston, MA: Little, Brown Educational Association, (1975).

Skolnick, Jerome H. *Justice Without Trial: Law Enforcement in Democratic Society*. New York, NY: John Wiley & Sons, (1966).

Skolnick, Jerome H. *Professional Police in a Free Society*. New York, NY: National Conference of Christian and Jews, (1967).

Smith, A. B., et al. "Authoritarianism in Policemen: Who are College Graduates and Non-college Police." *Journal of Criminal Law, Criminology, and Police Science*. Vol. 61 No. 2:313–315 (1970).

Smith, D. C. "Dangers of Police Professionalization: An Empirical Analysis." *Journal of Criminal Justice*. Vol. 6 199–216 (1978).

Smith, D. C. *Empirical Studies of Higher Education and Police Performance*. Washington, DC: The Police Foundation (1978).

Smith, D. C. and Elinor Ostrom. "The Effects of Training and Education on Police Attitudes and Performance: A Preliminary Analysis." In H. Jacob (ed.), *The Potential for Reforms in Criminal Justice*. Beverly Hills, CA: Sage Publications (1974).

Snow, David A. Susan G. Baker and Leon Anderson. "Criminality and homeless men: an empirical assessment." *Social Problems*. 36:5 p. 532 (1989).

Solarz, Andrea. *An Examination of Criminal Behavior Among the Homeless*. A paper presented to the annual meeting of the American Society of Criminology, San Diego, CA, (1985).

Southerland, Mittie. *The Active Valuing of Education by Police Organizations*. Unpublished doctoral dissertation, University of Kentucky, Lexington, KY, (1984).

Southerland, Mittie. "Organizational Communication." In Larry Hoover (ed.), *Police Management: Issues and Perspectives*. Washington, DC: Police Executive Research Forum, (1992).

Sparrow, Malcolm K. "Information Systems and the Development of Policing." *Perspectives on Policing*. Washington, DC: National Institute of Justice, (1993).

Sparrow, Malcolm, K., et al. *Beyond 911: A New Era for Policing*. New York, NY: Basic Books, (1992).

Spelman, W. and J. E. Eck *Research in Brief: Problem-Oriented Policing*. Washington, DC: National Institute of Justice (1987).

Spelman, William and Dale Brown. *Calling the Police: Citizen Reporting of Serious Crime*. Washington, DC: National Institute of Justice (1984).

Spelman, William and John Eck. *Problem-Oriented Policing: The Newport News Experiment*. Washington, DC: Police Executive Research Forum (1987).

Staufenberger, Richard A. (ed.) *Progress in Policing: Essays on Change*. Washington, DC: Police Foundation, (1980).

Sterling, James W. *Changes in Role Concepts of Police Officers during Recruit Training*. Washington, DC: International Association of Chiefs of Police, (1972).

Sterling. James W. "The College Level Entry Requirement." *The Police Chief*. Vol. 41 No. 8 (1974).

Stratton, John. *Police Passages*. Manhattan Beach, CA: Glennon Publishing, (1984).

Strecher, Victor G. "Stimuli of Police Education: Wickersham and LBJ's Commission." *The Justice Professional*. Vol. 3 No. 2 (1988).

Strecher, Victor G. *The Environment of Law Enforcement: A Community Relations Guide*. Englewood Cliffs, NJ: Prentice-Hall, (1971).

Surgeon General's Scientific Advisory Committee on Television and Social Behavior. *Television and Growing Up: the Impact of Televised Violence*. Washington, DC: U.S. Government Printing Office, (1972).

Swanson, Charles R. "An Uneasy Look at College Education and the Police Organization." *Journal of Criminal Justice*. Vol. 5 311–320 (1977).

Sykes, Gary W. "Accreditation and Community Policing: Passing Fads or Basic Reforms?" *Journal of Contemporary Criminal Justice*. (March, 1994), pp. 1–16.

Tafoya, William L. *A Delphi Forecast of the Future of Law Enforcement*. Unpublished doctoral dissertation, University of Maryland, College Park, MD, (1986).

Tafoya, William L. "Rioting in the Streets: Déjà Vu?" *CJ the Americas*, 2:6, pp. 1, 19–23 (1990).

Toch, Hans J., et al. *Agents of Change: A Study in Police Reform*. New York, NY: John Wiley & Sons, (1975).

Toffler, Alvin. *PowerShift: Knowledge, Wealth and Violence in the 21st Century*. New York, NY: Bantam Books (1990).

Toffler, Alvin. *The Third Wave*, New York, NY: Bantam Books (1980).

Trojanowicz, Robert. "Building Support for Community Policing: An Effective Strategy." *FBI Law Enforcement Bulletin*. (May, 1992), pp. 7–12.

Trojanowicz, Robert C. and T. Nicholson. "A Comparison of Behavioral Styles of College Graduate Police Officers v. Non-College-Going Police Officers." *The Police Chief*. Vol. 43 No. 8 (1976).

Trojanowicz, Robert and Bonnie Bucqueroux, *Community Policing*, Cincinnati, OH: Anderson Publishing company, (1990.)

Trojanowicz, Robert and Bonnie Bucqueroux. *Community Policing: How to Get Started*. Cincinnati, OH: Anderson Publishing Company, (1994).

Trojanowicz, Robert and David L. Carter. *The Philosophy and Role of Community Policing*. East Lansing, MI: National Center for Community Policing (1988).

Trojanowicz, Robert C. "Community Policing is Not Police Community Relations." *FBI Law Enforcement Bulletin*. (October: pp 6–11) (1990).

Trojanowicz, Robert C. and Bonnie Bucqueroux. *Toward Development of Meaningful and Effective Performance Evaluations*. East Lansing, MI: National Center for Community Policing (1992.)

Trojanowicz, Robert C. and David L. Carter. "The Changing Face of America," *FBI Law Enforcement Bulletin*, January, pp. 6–12, (1990).

Trojanowicz, Robert. *The Neighborhood Foot Patrol Program in Flint, Michigan*. East Lansing, MI: National Neighborhood Foot Patrol Center (Undated).

U.S. Commission on Civil Rights. *Mexican-Americans and the Administration of Justice in the Southwest*. Washington, DC: U.S. Government Printing Office, (1970).

U.S. Commission on Civil Rights. *Police Practices and the Preservation of Civil Rights*. Washington, DC: U.S. Government Printing Office, (1978).

U.S. Commission on Civil Rights. *Social Indicators of Equality for Minorities and Women* Washington, DC: U.S. Government Printing Office, (1978).

U.S. Commission on Civil Rights. *The Federal Response to Domestic Violence*. Washington, DC: U.S. Government Printing Office, (1982).

U.S. Commission on Civil Rights. *Who Is Guarding the Guardians?*. Washington, DC: U.S. Government Printing Office, (1981).

U.S. House of Representatives. *FBI Undercover Operations*. Report of the Subcommittee on Civil and Constitutional Rights, House Committee on the Judiciary, (1987).

Van Maanen, J. "Observations on the Making of Policemen." In A. Blumberg and E. Niederhoffer (eds.), *The Ambivalent Force*. New York: Holt, Rinehart & Winston (1985).

Van Maanen, John. "The Asshole," in Peter K. Manning and John Van Maanen (eds.), *Policing: A View From the Street*, Santa Monica, CA: Goodyear Publishing Company, (1978).

Vollmer, August. *The Police and Modern Society*. Berkeley, CA: University of California Press., (1936).

Wachtel, David. "University Criminal Justice Education." *The Police Chief*. Vol. 47, No. 12:62–65, (1980).

Wadman, Robert C. and Sir Stanley E. Bailey. *Community Policing and Crime Prevention in America and England*. Chicago, IL: Office of International Criminal Justice, University of Illinois, (1993).

Walker, Samuel. "Does Anyone Remember Team Policing? Lessons of the Team Policing Experience for Community Policing." *American Journal of Police*. Vol. 12, No. 1. (1993), pp. 33–35.

Walker, Samuel. *The Police in America: An Introduction*, 2d ed., New York, NY: McGraw-Hill, Inc., pp. 116–117, (1992).

Ward, Richard H. and Vince J. Webb. *Quest for Quality: Report of the Joint Commission on Criminology and Criminal Justice Education and Standards*. New York, NY: University Publications and the Joint Commission on Criminology and Criminal Justice Education and Standards (1981).

Wasserman, Robert and Mark Moore. "Values in Policing." *Perspectives in Policing*. Washington, DC: National Institute of Justice, (1988).

Wasserman, Robert, et al. *Improving Police Community Relations*. Washington, DC: U.S. Government Printing Office, (1967).

Watt, Ian. *Police Higher Education and Training in the United Kingdom*. Office of International Criminal Justice, Chicago, IL: University of Illinois at Chicago (1988).

Webb, Vince J. "Criminal Justice Education in the Twenty-First Century: Whatever Happened to Justicology." In R. Muraskin, *The Future of Criminal Justice Education*. Criminal Justice Institute. Brookeville, NY: Long Island University, (1987).

Weber, J. K. "It Can Work for You—Multinomah County Has No Difficulty Recruiting and Retaining College Graduates." *The Police Chief*. Vol. 40 (1973).

Weirman, C. and W. Archambeault. "Assessing the Effects of LEAA on Criminal Justice Higher Education." *Journal of Criminal Justice*. Vol. 11, (1983).

Weisburd, D., et al. *Police Innovation and Control of the Police*. New York, NY: Springer-Verlag, (1993).

Weisheit, Ralph, et al. "Community Policing in Small Town and Rural America." *Crime and Delinquency*. Vol. 40, No. 4, (1994), pp. 549–566.

Weitz, J. *KIDS COUNT*. Washington, DC: The Center for the Study of Social Policy, (1991).

Welty, G. "Bureaucracies and Professions: The Future of the Police." *Southern Journal of Criminal Justice*. Vol. 3 (1978).

West, Paul. "Investigation and Review of Complaints Against Police Officers." In Thomas Barker and David L. Carter (eds.). *Police Deviance*. 2d ed. Cincinnati, OH: Anderson Publishing Co., (1991).

Westley, William A. *Violence and the Police: A Sociological Study of Law, Custom, and Morality*. Cambridge, MA: MIT Press, (1972).

Whitaker, Gerald, et al. *Basic Issues in Police Performance*. Washington, DC: National Institute of Justice, (1992.)

White House Conference for a Drug Free America. *Final Report*. Washington, DC: U.S. Government Printing Office, (1988).

White, S. O. "A Perspective on Police Professionalization." *Law and Society Review*. Vol. 7 Fall: 61–85, (1972).

Whitmire, Kathryn and Lee P. Brown. City of *Houston Command Station/Neighborhood Oriented Policing Overview*. Houston, TX: Houston Police Department (undated).

Whitmire, Kathryn and Lee P. Brown. *City of Houston Command Station/Neighborhood Oriented Policing Overview*. Houston, TX: Houston Police Department (undated.)

Wilson James Q. and George L. Kelling, "Broken Windows: The Police and Neighborhood Safety," *Atlantic*, 256 March, pp 29–38, (1982).

Wilson, James Q. (ed.) *Crime and Public Policy*. San Francisco, CA: ICS Press, (1983).

Wilson, James Q. *Varieties of Police Behavior*. Cambridge, MA: Harvard University Press, (1968).

Wilson, O. W. and Roy C. McLaren. *Police Administration*. 4th ed. New York, NY: McGraw-Hill Publishing, (1977).

Winfree, L. T. and R. C. Evans. "Educational Saliency and Careers in Criminal Justice: The Case of Louisiana." *Journal of Criminal Justice*. Vol. 12 (1984).

Worden, Rob. "A Badge and a Baccalaureate: The Effect of College Education on Police Officers' Attitudes and Behaviors." Paper presented at the annual meeting of the Midwest Criminal Justice Association, Chicago, IL, (1988).

Wycoff, Mary Ann and C. E. Susmilch. "The Relevance of College Education for Policing: Continuing the Dialogue." In D. M. Peterson (ed.), *Police Work: Strategies and Outcomes in Law Enforcement*. Beverly Hills, CA: Sage Publications (1979).

Wycoff, Mary Ann and George L. Kelling. *The Dallas Experience: Human Resource Development*. Vol. 1. Washington, DC: Police Foundation, (1978).

Wycoff, Mary Ann and Timothy Ottmeier. *Evaluating Patrol Officer Performance Under Community Policing: The Houston Experience*. Washington, DC: National Institute of Justice, (1994).

Wycoff, Mary Ann and Wesley Skogan. "The Effect of Community Policing Management Style on Officers' Attitudes." *Crime and Delinquency*. Vol. 40, No. 3, (1994), pp. 371–383.

Zalman, Marvin. *A Heuristic Model of Criminology and Criminal Justice*. Joint Commission on Criminology and Criminal Justice Education and Standards, (1981).

INDEX